Why Vergil?

A Collection of Interpretations

ALAN COHEN
from the series <u>NOW</u> (Dachau) 26-2, 1992

Stephanie Quinn

Why Vergil?

A Collection of Interpretations

With a Foreword
by **Michael C. J. Putnam**

Bolchazy-Carducci Publishers, Inc.
Wauconda, Illinois

General Editor
Laurie K. Haight

Contributing Editors
Georgia Irby-Massie
Allan Kershaw

Cover Design and Typesetting
Charlene M. Hernandez

Golden Bough Graphic
Charlene Hernandez

Printed in the United States of America
2000
by Bang Printing

Bolchazy-Carducci Publishers, Inc.

1000 Brown Street
Wauconda, Illinois 60084 USA

http://www.bolchazy.com

Paperback: ISBN 0-86516-418-5
Hardbound: ISBN 0-86516-435-5

Library of Congress Cataloging-in-Publication Data

Why Vergil? : a collection of interpretations / [compiled by] Stephanie Quinn
    p. cm.
  Includes bibliographical references (p.).
  ISBN 0-86516-435-5 (alk. paper) — ISBN 0-86516-418-5 (pbk.: alk. paper)
    1. Vergil—Criticism and interpretation. 2. Epic poetry, Latin—History and criticism. 3.
Pastoral poetry, Latin—History and criticism. 4. Didactic poetry, Latin—History and
criticism. 5. Aeneas (Legendary character) in literature. 6. Country life in literature. 7.
Agriculture in literature. 8. Rome—in literature. I. Quinn, Stephanie, 1947–
PA6825.W46 1999
871'.01--dc21   99-051845
                                                                                 CIP

Contents

Part II: The Uses of Tradition and the Making of Meaning

Michael C. J. Putnam

FOREWORD

W hy Vergil? Why, in fact, the author of any classical masterpiece, at this moment in history and, in particular, in the history of interpretation? We no longer read the literature of the ancient world in the search for idealizing models for emulation or even as source of analogies between a distant time and our own era, however valuable and sobering such comparisons might be as we contemplate a major source of our intellectual heritage. The great texts of the Greco-Roman past still speak tellingly to us but with voices that now take the measure of diversity, of ambiguity, of unresolved and unresolvable complexity, of horror as well as exaltation at human doings, of passion and violence in action as well as of philosophy evolved in contemplation.

The collection of essays that follows, together with Stephanie Quinn's "Introduction" and "Conclusion," both as individual statements and as a total exercise, offers a positive answer to the question posed by the book's title, an answer so compelling, in the case of Vergil, as to dispel any sentiments to the contrary. His is an unquiet vision that elicits a response of familiarity. We are drawn to Vergil now not so much because of his celebrated melancholy, the inner "tears" which he seems readily to shed at the sufferings that fall to our lot, but rather from the very unease that such pervasive dichotomies as ideal and real, public and private, political order and individual freedom, arouse in us from their treatment in his texts.

In the *Aeneid* we have an epic story, presented objectively in third-person narrative. It nevertheless often breaks the inexorability of its goal-ridden pattern with lyric pauses that halt the onrush of events and demand a personal response to the spiritual pressures the story line brings. We plunge into a linear tale with its inevitable forward thrust based on developing power, but we soon find that very momentum disrupted by the constancy of loss and death and by the poem's emotional histories, the repeated inner struggles of both its human and divine characters.

On three salient occasions, in books 1, 6 and 8, Vergil's vision has the epic's protagonists imagine a radiant future, which is the present for the poet and his contemporaries, when the emperor Augustus will bring civil war to an end and restore a Saturnian age of peace and plenty. This, according to Aeneas' father Anchises in book 6, is the ambition of Rome's renewer which in the future parallels Aeneas' immediate purpose in bringing Troy to Rome. But the circularity of the epic's foreground action, which begins with the vehement wrath of Juno towards the Trojans and ends with Aeneas, "terrible in his anger," as he slays Turnus, his suppliant foe, offers a carefully posed provocation to the linearity that anticipates for Rome a brilliant time to come.

How we read this conclusion and interpret its relation to the poem as a whole, for all the importance an answer might offer for our comprehension of the epic, is but one instance of the problematics of interpretation which Vergil poses for us and with which the essays composing this collection grapple. All are acts of under-standing which, from a variety of angles, allow us better to appreciate Vergil's genius. There is no richer way to realize this goal, which is to say, to find a cogent response to the question *Why Vergil?*, than to evaluate the intellectual enigmas his text poses. In the pages that follow I will examine briefly some of the paradoxes that the reader of the *Aeneid* must confront, for it is our need to accept such challenges and to wrestle with their meaning that is perhaps the greatest single accolade that we can give to Vergil's writing. In pursuing this task we must strive to do full justice to our poet's words and, in the act of criticism, aspire to the humor of self-distance.

Let me for a moment engage more closely with just one of these challenges, namely the poem's tension between public and private, and expand upon the in-sights of Adam Parry in one of the most influential of the essays that follow. Parry illustrates with great sensitivity how the saga of Aeneas, especially as it anticipates Augustan magnificence, is ever counterbalanced, in Vergil's telling, by the hurt, sorrow and death of those who are forced for a time to share the hero's destiny. But it is instructive also to press beyond Parry's distinctions and to ponder those mo-ments in the epic when public and private inextricably merge. Again the poem's ending offers a particularly remarkable example. Vergil has us watch the watchers at a highly theatrical event: the Rutulians groan at the sight of Turnus' wounding by Aeneas, the mountains and woods echo their sad cry, and Turnus, the humbled hero, calls to his conqueror's attention that the Ausonii, his fellow Italians in their aboriginal guise, are witnesses to his gesture of supplication. When Aeneas pro-ceeds to kill him, we share with the Trojans and the Latins, first, in Aeneas' words that speak of vengeance for the loss of his protégé Pallas, earlier slain by Turnus, then, in the formidable wrath under whose influence he dispatches his enemy.

Here in a deeply ethical sense public and private come into collision. Anchises, at the conclusion of their interview in the Underworld, addresses his son as *Romanus*, that is, as prototype of future Romans, and burdens him with the poem's most portentous moral dictum: to spare the humbled and war down the proud. It is a plausible reading of the poem's conclusion, therefore, that by killing his prostrate foe in grandly public fashion, out of grieving memory of personal loss and a resultant desire for revenge, Aeneas allies himself not with his father but with Achilles, the dominant hero of Homer's *Iliad*, which served as one of Vergil's primary models for his epic. We expect the son, in recognition of his father's command for the restrained use of force against the subjected, to suppress his own singular feelings in recognition of a larger communal good, to set a pattern, individually, for all Romans who in the future might subsume their selfhood in the state's general good. By killing in the heat of emotion, Aeneas, instead, becomes his Homeric prototype, who tracks Hector, his chief antagonist, not even out of desire to better the Greek chances of victory, but to assuage his own inner suffering at the death of his close comrade Patroclus.

The fact that Augustus himself might not have agreed with this interpretation of the poem's ending raises a significant irony for all students of the *Aeneid*. The emperor, in two of his major public monuments, the Temple to Apollo on the Palatine and the Forum Augustum, memorializes the idea of revenge. On the doors of the temple to Apollo dedicated in October, 28 BCE, a year when Vergil had already be-gun the composition of his epic, were two acts of vendetta on the god's part, one against boastful Niobe and her offspring, the other against Brennus for his incursion into the god's sacred precinct at Delphi. Adjacent to the temple was a portico con-taining statues of the newly-wedded Danaids in the act of killing their husbands, executing their own stealthy revenge and furthering the vendetta of their father against his brother. Likewise the centerpiece of Augustus' forum, dedicated in 2 BCE, was the temple of Mars Ultor, the Avenger, vowed forty years earlier on the battlefield of Philippi should he, then still Octavian, succeed in avenging the murder of his adoptive father, Julius Caesar, which had occurred two years previously.

In the light of the way Vergil's emperor grandly commemorated personal acts of revenge, in permanent and open fashion, over a length of his career, we should ponder the deeply ambiguous friction between individual feelings and civic duty that the *Aeneid's* ending suggests. But, as a task more àpropos for our purposes as readers of the *Aeneid,* we must reflect on how this friction operates from within the poem itself. Here I would like to concentrate specifically on the last word the wounded Turnus utters to Aeneas in his final prayer, a speech that causes Aeneas to hesitate and "repress his hand." The word is *odium,* which Vergil has Turnus employ in the plural as if the vanquished hero experienced his conqueror's recent and present deeds as a cumulative series of manifestations of deep anger: "Do not stretch further in your hatred" (*ulterius ne tende odiis*), he begs. *Odium* is also the vice that is most regularly associated throughout the epic with Juno, Aeneas' Olympian opponent, who from the beginning of the epic, and for reasons of her own grief, anger, and desire for revenge, has thwarted his progress as best she can. It is no accident that the language Vergil gives to Aeneas at the end, once he becomes enthralled to his own anger and readies himself for his final sword-thrust, he has already associated with Juno throughout the poem. The passive hero, tracked at the epic's start by the vengeful goddess, has by its conclusion become the active stalker of his own prey (Vergil earlier in the final book compares him to a hunter hound), an incorporation of Juno's negative potency.

Turnus' reference to "hatred" asks of the reader to ponder, in particular, the interrelationship Vergil establishes between public action and private passion. Such a meditation is further encouraged by Martha Nussbaum's recent probing essay on "social hatred," to which Stephanie Quinn refers in the Conclusion to *Why Vergil.* For a modern student of the *Aeneid,* and with considerable support from Vergil's text, Turnus seems to suggest to Aeneas the latter's inability to comprehend Turnus' point of view, to appreciate what it means not only to suffer the mortification of public defeat but also to lose one's beloved as well as one's complete basis of power. It would be Aeneas' great moment both to display a penetrating understanding of his opponent and to implement his father's endorsement of clemency. Vergil in fact has been at pains, since Turnus began sharing in the epic's action, to show parallels as well as dissimilarities between the two protagonists.

But do we have the right or, more to the point, does Vergil grant us the authority, to place so much weight on the feelings of Turnus, not only to sympathize with his plight but, based on our own judgment as well as his, to join him in imputing hatred to Aeneas? Is his emotional plea meant to be one we share with him? The answer, at least as far as empathy is concerned, remains a full affirmative. The famous Vergilian compassion is widespread. It manifests itself for figures as diverse as Aeneas' helmsman, Palinurus, or Umbro, one of Aeneas' Italian opponents (who figures prominently in Parry's essay), both victims of Aeneas' progress who are drawn close to the reader because the narrator apostrophizes them. But it is also palpable for characters whose disrepute or innocence is presented to us as a matter for debate. Dido is a forceful example. Both she and the narrator consider her failure to maintain fidelity to her first husband as blameworthy (the noun Vergil uses is *culpa*). One source, therefore, of her unfolding tragedy is a self-generated fault. Yet at a crucial point, when Dido could, but does not, pursue the departing Trojans and their (to her mind) faithless leader, who are essentially without defense, Vergil, by twice addressing her in the second person as "you," places himself and us close to the suffering queen and thus allows us more intimately to share her sensations of bitterness and grief.

But Turnus, in the lines that precede the final confrontation, receives from the poet an even more special rhetorical honor that notably distinguishes his poetic treatment from that of his opponent. Vergil uses third-person narrative and a brief speech to tell us the reasons for Aeneas' action as he kills, namely the remembrance of past grief provoking present anger, and we debate the pros and cons of his concluding deed as our interpretation of the epic's evidence dictates. (Aeneas as he kills is no more clear of reasons for censure than Turnus. Vergil has carefully set up the latter as an emblem of pride, but his conqueror's rampage at the death of Pallas in book 10 is without equal in the epic for the extent and depth of its brutality.) But we actually become Turnus. For, in the poem's last simile, as Turnus in his debilitude before facing Aeneas is compared to someone who in sleep attempts to function but cannot, he is treated as "we" ("we seem," "we collapse"), and that very "we" embraces, in one magic gesture, Vergil, the singing "I" of the poem's opening, his contemporaries and us ourselves, readers of these essays, and whoever studies the poem, in whatever present to come, for its richness of meaning.

Vergil's universality thus has us observe closely both victims and victimizers, those who are subject to the power and emotionality of their stronger opponents and those who exert that strength. For, on one level at least, the epic is an exploration into what it means to consolidate and employ power. When we first see Aeneas, he is the passive sufferer of someone else's vendetta, and that same passivity takes emblematic form in his act of carrying his father on his shoulders out of Troy's devastation. Receiving this literal burden connotes for Aeneas the acceptance of *pietas,* of responsibility toward Anchises and Iulus, his son, toward future fatherland, and to the gods who preside over his manifest destiny. The last six books, however, find the hero taking active control of his destiny to the point that, at the epic's conclusion, he does away with an arch-enemy who is completely at his mercy. I mentioned earlier the ambiguities of this ending in relation to Anchises' plea to his son to spare the now humbled and set a pattern for restraint in victory, that is, for the civilized use of power. Aeneas the individual is to stand for all future Romans, for Rome as a communal entity as it goes about the task of establishing and governing its empire.

In this same speech Anchises also speaks of Rome's public necessity "to impose a custom for peace" (*paci...imponere morem*). Vergil's readers are without doubt meant to view this as a laudable endeavor, but the word "impose" has ambivalent implications. It intimates, first, that force must be used to gain this end and second that there are indeed people to whom the *pax Romana,* "Roman peace," must be prescribed. The historian may document the nations and territories that are gradually absorbed into the Roman order as her world domination advances. The reader of the *Aeneid* sees in the tale of its hero's securing of hegemony in Latium at least a partial metonymy for Rome's march toward empire, and as a consequence he or she may ask how the morality of Aeneas' rise to power and of the conduct that assures its continuity is echoed in the career of Octavian, who became Augustus while Vergil was writing his poem, and, in at least some readings of those moments in the *Aeneid* that look to the Augustan future, whose gaining of full political control seems capable of renewing a "golden" age for Rome and its people.

But who are the "others" within the *Aeneid* and how does the "imposition" of embryonic Rome affect their private existences? Do they include Dido, forced to suicide because Roman destiny takes precedence over individual feelings? Are they the mothers who burn the ships because they prefer a settled existence in the here and now to Rome's anticipated but still vague good fortune? Do we number among them Palinurus, and the many other scapegoats throughout the poem, in his case offered as sacrifice to Neptune because he is no longer needed for Aeneas' advancement? Are they Turnus and his Latin allies who must be crushed in order to be assimilated, or are they any opposers of the Roman order? Do we so categorize external nature that regularly stands in threatening counterpoint to the logic of ideal government? We find it exemplified in the storm that embroils the Trojan ships at the start of the poem or in the "indignation" of the river Araxes, as portrayed on Vulcan's miraculous shield, which must be tamed by a bridge emblematic of the dominion which Augustus, like any culture hero, needs to exert to effect his golden time and, above all, to make peace customary rather than occasional. Or does the "other" claim for itself the realm of inner nature, of the emotional demons that possess us all as we live out our lives and that, in the *Aeneid,* are evident in the furies of eroticism, in the resentments, angers and hatreds that lead especially to the violence of revenge?

All these and many further "others" are present throughout the poem. From time to time, as we have seen, we are made through the poet's genius to share in their anguish and, in the climactic scene of Turnus' suffering, actually to become the "other." But if inner nature, in particular, is a prime enemy of the principle of order that, for Vergil, Rome should incorporate, and I believe that it is, then we must face perhaps the most stimulating paradox that the master-poet offers his readers. For Aeneas himself, "blazing" and "terrible in his wrath" as he thrusts his sword through the chest of his suppliant opponent in the epic's final moment, is also, now, the "other." We have witnessed earlier in the poem what anger and the need for vengeance cause him to contemplate (the killing of Helen in book 2) or actually accomplish (the initiating of human sacrifice, among other horrors, at the death of Pallas in book 10). And it is this anger, parallel to the initial rage of Juno, the prime "other" among the immortals, that Vergil would have us take away as our final remembrance of his hero in action.

In so doing Vergil leaves to us any gesture of balance among, or reconciliation to, the poem's polarities, some of which we have mentioned before — of the circularity and linearity of history, of present and future, of private and public, of iron age and golden age, of Saturn and Jupiter, poetry and power among others — as we contemplate the saga of Aeneas and attentively project it, as Vergil would expect us to do, onto the world of Augustan Rome and onto our own. For this is Vergil's great gesture as teacher, to ask that we cope with these polarities and find our own rationale for their pervasive presence. To do so and in a way that brings satisfaction is to provide yet again a positive reply to this book's demanding title.

Finally, let us attend for a moment to those objects which, as Stephanie Quinn reminds us, it is our primary concern to interpret, the poet's words and the imagination with which they are deployed. I am thinking here not so much of their allure as of their power. They can elevate the mind and bring delight but they can also shock, they can tell falsehoods along with truths, and, in the hands of the Orphic bard, they can civilize and educate but also deceive. In its multi-leveled patterning Vergil's poem offers us models for nobility, for refinement, for the orderly uses of power but it also documents evil and the irrational at work. Great poetry endures because it speaks in many voices. Vergil himself was certain of his immortality and therefore of his ability to immortalize. He announces this potency prominently, for instance, at one poignant moment in the *Aeneid's* ninth book after he has told the story of the nocturnal adventure of Nisus and Euryalus: "Blessed by fortune, both of you," exclaims the poet. "If my songs have any power, no day will ever banish you from time's memory, as long as the house of Aeneas will dwell by the immovable rock of the Capitol and the father of Rome will hold sway."

It is interesting to ask why Vergil chose this particular moment, out of the many his mind had created, for such singular praise which at the same time reminds us that the Latin word he uses for song, *carmen,* means charm, that is, in this case, words carrying an enchantment capable of actuating and securing their purpose. The story tells of two young warriors who, with the backing of the Trojan elders, set out to alert to his people's danger Aeneas, who is with the Arcadian king, Evander, on the site of Rome. As they make their way through and, in the case of one of the heroes, beyond the intervening Rutulian encampment, they are killed. In other words, the story recounts the history of the search for Aeneas, which is to say the quest for any principle combining rationality and strength, moderation and mastery, which is subverted by emotionality. In this instance the downfall of the ambitious pair is brought about by a "dread yearning" (*dira cupido*) for hazard and glory that leads to a destructive lust for slaughter after which the profferers of violence receive violence in return. We might see in this tale, should we choose, an encapsulation of the total poem of which it is a prominent episode. The incident is one of many that immortalize, and extend enormous sympathy to, youths who die as Aeneas, Rome's agent, carries his mission forward. Through these moments Vergil epitomizes the tensions between real and ideal, between individual passions and the larger goals of informed, judicious statesmanship, that are a great part of the poem's intellectual schema.

That schema is projected through the brilliant deployment of words, and it is the words of the poet that, from a rich variety of perspectives, are the objects of study of each of the essays in the splendid collection that follows. And it is this very diversity — of the questions posed and of the answers suggested, of ideas whether challenged or affirmed, or of approaches to the observation of the sheer beauty and grandeur of Vergil's language — that abundantly illustrates the claim that the present generation of readers asserts on Vergil as especially its own.

Stephanie Quinn

PREFACE

Why Vergil? Though people have been asking the question for a long time, it is an especially crucial one now, in the world the way it is, in the late 1990s in the United States. This book offers both an answer to the question and a way to think about it, especially in reference to the *Aeneid*, Vergil's epic poem. Since the *Aeneid* was written 2,000 years ago, at the end of the Roman Republic and beginning of the Roman Empire, in the time of Caesar Augustus, I am in fact also inquiring about the durability and reliability of art.

The "world the way it is" or "the way things are,"[1] translates part of what may be the *Aeneid's* most famous phrase — *lacrimae rerum*, the tears of things, of the world, of reality (*Aeneid* 1.462). The duty to learn what one should cry for — what deserves our tears — is the subject of Aeneas' heroic lesson, the mission of his epic journey. This collection of scholarly essays on Vergil's ancient poetry and on the twentieth-century literature influenced by it situates Vergil's works and influence within academic and public issues that concern us today, in the world the way it is.

I offer my response to the question, why Vergil, in the Introduction and Conclusion to this volume. In the Introduction, I describe a cumulative answer to the question of the book's title as it is progressively developed by the contents of the collection. In the Conclusion, I explain why I, a university administrator and teacher, read Vergil's works and urge others to do so as well.

This Preface to the collection maps its individual contents and explains how they can be used by teachers, students, and general readers. My hope for the anthology is that it will serve several audiences. One audience is teachers and students who are reading Vergil's *Aeneid* in Latin and presumably by choice, but who are also reading it most probably in small snippets and slowly, perhaps arduously at first, and for whom therefore the pleasure and meaning of the whole may be elusive. One of the contributors to this volume recalls falling in love with Vergil on first reading parts of the *Aeneid* in a high school Latin class.[2] So did I. I hope this volume will help those who are teaching Vergil now to inspire in today's high school and college Latin students an attachment to Vergil's words similar to the one my first Latin teacher, Mr. Irving Kizner, to whom this book is dedicated, inspired in me. The book aims to teach and to help teachers and learners. Although it is not a traditional teachers' guide for the Advanced Placement examination in Vergil, the contents frequently reflect the AP syllabus.

Another audience is teachers and students of the *Aeneid* in translation. These students may be undergraduates who find themselves reading Vergil perhaps unexpectedly or perhaps reluctantly (for example in my literature courses to fulfill graduation requirements in science or business). For these students, answers to the "Why Vergil" question such as "Because we at this university have decided you should" or "I, the professor in this class, say so," no longer suffice, if they ever did.

For these readers, my hope is for their pleasure in Vergil's poem, in world-class mastery of a craft and in the workings of a great mind and profound heart.

I hope for yet another audience for this book and ultimately of course for Vergil's poetry, an audience of general readers and of those with interests in the humanities and the liberal arts. The question in the title, or variations of it, is asked by people in many different spheres and for different reasons. It is asked, for example, by faculty members throughout the humanities, not only in ancient Latin or Greek literature, who must explain, even to the best students, the value of any academic task that does not seem to yield immediate, practical results. It is asked by university administrators who must make decisions about which academic programs will survive and in what form.[3] Many adult, general readers, who in their early years thought the answer to the question was easy (there was no good reason), are now asking again, as parents, voters, and thinkers about life. And in general form, the question is being discussed earnestly and often by opinion makers and legislators who influence or make decisions on issues of policy and funding for education and culture. I hope this volume will help them formulate their questions and explore responses in useful terms that avoid simplistic polarization, and thus do its part to help the academy respond thoughtfully and respectfully to this expanded audience.

The most important agenda for this book is to enhance readers' ease and pleasure in the art of words. The *Aeneid* is not an easy text; the analysis of Vergil's poetry and its meaning is not a lightweight exercise. Some of the contents intentionally are easier to work with and some more difficult. On the other hand, words belong to everyone; we all use them every day. They are not an esoteric preserve, and poetry and literature, the arts in general, need not be reserved for only certain people with special backgrounds.

That a task or a text demands effort from us need not make it wholly inaccessible, if only we wish to make the effort. To create and nurture that wish, the desire to stretch toward learning that takes some work from us, is itself a goal of teaching, perhaps the first and most important goal if the arts and humanities are to find their fitting place in a democratic society. Then follows the responsibility to provide the means to fulfill the wish, through methods and tools which can be learned and practiced, just as we engage together in baseball practice or choir practice.

The "texts" of the arts and humanities come to us often with centuries—in Vergil's case—millennia of history and attitudes attached to them, history of and attitudes about high culture, elitism, snobbery, privilege. In this collection, Vergil's words are not treated as if they are someone else's fine china that we may touch only on special occasions and good behavior. They are a source of pleasure and deep satisfaction to people who have been reading them for 2,000 years, including those whose work is included here. This collection is an effort to share that experience of pleasure and meaning. It is the experience, the engagement both intellectual and affective in reading Vergil's works that I hope to evoke in this volume, as I try to do in my classes. This book is both a collection and a pedagogy.

Among many others, I have two particular debts for my pedagogical approach, in this book and in class. One is the book *Western Wind: An Introduction to Poetry*, by the poet John Frederick Nims, which is a textbook on learning to read poetry. The other debt is a series of conversations several colleagues and I had with faculty members who teach the creative and performing arts.[4]

Nims and my colleagues all use a similar technique. They teach the artistic experience, which is a large, complex and tightly woven enterprise, as the artistic craft, which is composed of many discrete elements. By doing roughly the same thing here, I am trying to capture for the readers of a work of art, the *Aeneid* of Vergil, the particularity of its making and thus of its meaning, since for the creator, unlike the reader, those experiences are simultaneous. The goal is to help us understand better what Vergil did, the high level of skill he achieved in his craft of poetry-making, and how that skill coalesces into meaning.

I have organized this book into two parts, each dealing with one of the two main tools — words and literary tradition — Vergil and other poets use to make meaning. The first part focuses on Vergil's words themselves and how he worked with them. In the second part, the focus is on literary traditions, the tradition Vergil received and the tradition of which he became a part. Through this approach, I would encourage teachers and learners to attend to those skills of reading essential for the enjoyment of heightened literature (a phrase used by theater educators of works appropriate for advanced students).

Readers, like poets, use the tools of language. This collection takes as its starting point lessons on the way words work. This is not grammar and vocabulary for its own sake, but as means of understanding how, word by word, we make meaning. Part One, The Power of Words and the Meaning of Form, contains essays that examine through close reading and analysis of Vergil's language how he used words in their precise combinations to produce his particular meaning. These articles, presented roughly in the order of the twelve books of the *Aeneid*, generally focus on small selections of text that most high school or undergraduate students of the *Aeneid* in Latin would read. At the same time, the authors derive interpretations based on their close readings that bear on themes important for understanding the epic as a whole, whether in Latin or in translation. A couple of selections deal also with matters of structure in the poem.

Readers with some Latin will benefit from the close textual analyses both to understand the passages and also to place the passages in an interpretive context. Readers with little or no Latin will follow the arguments about Vergil's language. They can then use the passages in translation, of which they will now have a deeper understanding, to pose questions, begin discussions, and inform their understanding of the poem's meaning and value.

In Part Two, The Use of Tradition and the Making of Meaning, the selections explore Vergil's use of the literary traditions he inherited and the subsequent use by other artists of Vergil's works as their literary inheritance. Thus we span in an eye blink almost 3,000 years of Western literature and Vergil's place in it. There are selections on Vergil and Homer, Vergil and his near contemporary, the poet Catullus. Vergil's early works, the *Eclogues* and *Georgics*, deserve their own volume, but here they are treated as complex examples of Vergilian poetic technique and as part of the tradition of European literature.

The afterlife of the *Aeneid*, that is, the repeated and very different uses made of it in the centuries after it was written, indicate ways it can be useful and valuable for us still. And so this volume contains selections on Vergil in the Middle Ages, and in relation to Dante, Shakespeare, and Milton, with him icons of Western letters. Vergil as a maker of origins — the founding of Rome by Aeneas, is addressed not only with respect to Roman but also to early American foundings. And Vergil in the twentieth century is treated here through the voices of both scholars and artists, in a long line of cultural descent. Some of them radically modify their inheritance from him, as Vergil modified his, responding to new times that require new ways of knowing the world.

An overarching topic of these selections, which reflects an important aspect of the *Aeneid*, is the work of poetry-making itself. How does the *Aeneid* tell us Vergil understood his role as artist, and what does his understanding teach us about the role of art? If Vergil's work addresses these issues usefully for us today, when they are so heatedly debated, we have an answer to our title's question.

The selections can be used separately, as aids to reading parts of the *Aeneid* or as ways of understanding Vergil's influence. They can also be read consecutively, as an extended argument in answer to the book's title, Why Vergil. The brief summary of the contents below, my reading of them in the introductory essay "Why Words," and the short paragraphs that introduce each selection provide further information about each item in order to guide readers in its use.

The scholarly selections rest on a body of intellectual work that partakes of a centuries-old tradition and are currently among the best in the field. I have edited most of the scholarly pieces to help them speak directly, concisely, and intelligibly to my audience, which is, more often than not, a readership different from the author's originally intended one. Editing has reduced the number of examples illustrating the same point, a feature which, though indispensable to rigorous scholarship, is superfluous to students and general readers. I have eliminated most references to scholarly disagreements, which, again, are crucial to advancing the understanding of the poem over time but which will not readily help new readers. And sometimes I have untwined a complex argument to present a single thread that is directly relevant to the topic. A small omission in the original article is indicated by an elipsis (three dots), longer ones by the symbols ✧ ✧ ✧ in the text and notes. Readers should refer to the original sources of the selections for the full texts, arguments, evidence, and citations. All the works of literature except for the very long ones are reproduced in their entirety.

In order that the volume be inviting and accessible, passages in Latin and other languages are translated into English, by either the authors or me. (If by me, the translations are in brackets and aim to make the original language comprehensible for readers without Latin or even without an intuition of the relationships among languages.)[5]

For the sake of readability, formatting and punctuation have been standardized throughout, and minor errors within articles corrected, although I have not altered British spellings. Indeed, readers will discover that the spelling of Vergil's name varies from entry to entry, as either Vergil or Virgil. Vergil's name in Latin is *Publius Vergilius Maro*, and the closer English spelling is Vergil. Centuries of custom from the early Middle Ages on have changed the "e" to an "i," and I have left to each author his or her chosen form. Nor have I amended locutions that some readers may find gender specific, for example, "men" for "people"; "the reader…he" instead of "readers…they"; and the like. The editorial role here is to point selections toward the collection's purposes but not to alter the content of the originals.

The chronology will help readers situate a few important events in the history of ancient Greece and Rome, especially as they relate to the *Aeneid*. The bibliography is a starting point for those who would like to read further; it emphasizes fairly recent books as well as essay collections, in English. The list of electronic resources is likewise a starting point for continued investigation.

Part I. The Power of Words and the Meaning of Form

Of the articles and books excerpts included in Part I, most discuss important passages in nine of the 12 books of the *Aeneid*: Books 1, 2, 4, 6, 7, 8, 9, 10, and 12. (The first excerpt in Part II discusses a section of Book 5.) Two selections consider aspects of form and structure in the epic. The passages of the *Aeneid* that are the main subjects of the collected essays are indicated below in bold letters.

The collection begins at the heart of what motivated me to assemble it, Vergil's words, and Part I holds that focus through most its selections. The first 11 lines of the epic are given in Latin, **Aeneid 1.1–11**, along with five examples of excellent English translations of them, by John Dryden, Allen Mandelbaum, Frank O. Copley, Robert Fitzgerald and Edward B. McCrorie, and an extended, book by book, synopsis of the poem. The pages from Daniel Garrison's book, *The Language of Virgil: An Introduction to the Poetry of the Aeneid*, provide some help in reading the Latin. Edgar Reinke's article on "Onomatopoetic Alliteration in Vergil's *Aeneid*," introduces readers to poetic techniques that enable the sounds of words to create meaning.

Most of the rest of the articles in Part I explore Vergil's language in passages that are important for the development of the *Aeneid's* major themes. Gregory Staley's article on **Aeneid 1.180–94** discusses Aeneas' first act in the poem, the killing of stags. The now famous reading of **Book 2** by Bernard M. W. Knox in his article, "The Serpent and the Flame," analyzes Vergil's intricate weave of symbols and imagery in that book. The similes that relate to the Carthaginian queen Dido in **Book 4** are Roger A. Hornsby's subject, while Charles Segal considers Dido and all of that book through his reading of one line and a half, **Aeneid 4.133–34**. Marilyn Skinner continues the study of the Dido and Aeneas story through her analysis of their meeting in the Underworld in Book 6, at **Aeneid 6.450–76**. D. C. Feeney reviews Vergil's selection and treatment of his historical examples in the "parade of heroes," **Aeneid 6.710–886**, Anchises' predictions for Rome's future up to the death of Augustus' protégé, Marcellus. Helen H. Bacon reads **Book 6** and other parts of the poem, especially the central third in **Books 5–8**, to locate the meaning of the hero's spiritual journey.

At the midpoint of the poem's 12 books, after close reading of several individual passages in the first half of the epic, we pause to consider the structure of the work as a whole. John Frederick Nims reminds us that precision and art complement each other. The pages included from his book show us how a mathematical sequence known as the Fibonacci series, which structures patterns of elements in the natural world, might also, it would seem, be an organizing principle for passages of the *Aeneid*, regarding specifically **Aeneid 4.416–36**. George E. Duckworth's article summarizes several ways to view the structure of the epic—in halves, thirds, as sets of alternating books, and through a pattern of internal correspondences. The minutely careful writing of small sections of text plus the creation of large structural patterns for the poem as a whole are tools our poet uses to craft his epic.

In "The Two Voices in Virgil's *Aeneid*," another famous essay, Adam Parry introduces us to the second half of the poem and to an idea that has occupied Vergilian studies for over thirty years: that Vergil creates more than one perspective on many situations and requires his readers or listeners to keep both in mind simultaneously. Parry develops this idea through his explication of **Aeneid 7.759–60**, from which he expands his reading to the work as a whole. Robert Gurval's chapter, from *Actium and Augustus: The Politics and Emotions of the Civil War,"* takes us to

Book 8 through his analysis of the stories depicted on the shield Vulcan crafts for Aeneas, at *Aeneid* **8.626–731**. The selection from Susan Ford Wiltshire's book, *Public and Private in Vergil's Aeneid*, focuses on the Nisus and Euryalus episode in **Book 9**, with references to Book 5. Herbert W. Benario provides a reading of **Book 10** as a whole, helping us to understand the story of Pallas in context. Two selections help us read Book 12. M. Owen Lee focuses on *Aeneid* **12.384–429** as it recapitulates themes from throughout the poem. Gerald Petter offers a way to understand the **last scene of the Aeneid**, as it has been prepared throughout the work. Part I ends by looking back on the whole poem, as the *Aeneid* prompts us to do, in this case through Michael C. J. Putnam's article on a section of Book 6, *Aeneid* **6.14–37**. In the Daedalus story, Putnam reads Vergil as discoursing on the role art plays in his own work, especially as we are to understand that role from the point of view of the end of the poem.

Part II. The Uses of Tradition and the Making of Meaning

Part II addresses issues of influence, especially as great artists engage with the traditions they inherit and rework. Brooks Otis, in an excerpt from *Virgil: A Study in Civilized Poetry*, analyzes a section in Book 5, *Aeneid* **5.315–42**, the Nisus and Euryalus episode that anticipates the boys' story in Book 9, as Vergil reworks it from his Homeric model in the *Iliad*. Michael Putnam considers the influence on the *Aeneid* of the first-century B.C.E. Roman poet Catullus. He notes echoes of Catullus 11 diffused throughout the *Aeneid* and observes that one passage in the epic, *Aeneid* **6.687–94**, shows the influence of a number of Catullus' poems.

We then step back briefly to Vergil's early works, the *Eclogues and Georgics* as Annabel Patterson and William W. Batstone analyze philologically and theoretically the first lines of those two works, which established the themes and methods of the *Aeneid* and have also been significant influences on subsequent European literature. Next, Charles Fantazzi in "Homage to Virgil" gives us an overview of Vergil's influence from the early Christian period to the twentieth century. The selections that follow enlarge on that influence: Rachel Jacoff and Jeffrey T. Schnapp on Vergil and Dante; John E. Rexine regarding Vergil and Shakespeare; and Barbara Kiefer Lewalski on Vergil and Milton. Vergil's influence on earlier inhabitants of the United States is reviewed by Meyer Reinhold, and a poem by Phillis Wheatley supplies an example of this influence. W. R. Johnson, in an excerpt from *Darkness Visible: A Study of Vergil's Aeneid*, analyzes the reception of the *Aeneid* in the nineteenth and twentieth centuries, particularly as it manifests itself in important essays by Matthew Arnold and T. S. Eliot.

A selection of twentieth-century literature demonstrates the nature and strength of Vergil's continuing influence. Three poems by Robert Frost, "Build Soil — A Political Pastoral," "Two Tramps in Mud Time," and "For John F. Kennedy His Inauguration," reveal the presence in that artist's work, as in Vergil's, of pastoral, georgic, and epic sensibilities. Joseph Brodsky's "Eclogue IV" reflects on the meaning of pastoral for Russia, a country so unlike Vergil's Italy. Dana L. Burgess' article on Spike Lee's movie, "Do the Right Thing," reminds us that the pastoral mode can still be effective today in a wide array of venues and media. Allen Tate's poem reflects on the complex affinities between the story of the fall of Troy and United States history. "The Shield of Achilles," by W. H. Auden, updates for the modern world the famous description of the shield in Homer's *Iliad*, Book 18, on which Vergil had modeled his story of the shield of Aeneas. Rosanna Warren's poem on the *Aeneid's* final scene, "Turnus (*Aeneid* XII)," describes the effect on one poet of another's words.

Excerpts from two long works of twentieth-century literature conclude the survey. Derek Walcott's *Omeros* is a 325-page epic poem in English, published in 1990. Its debts to Homer and Vergil are evident, as is Walcott's recrafting of their works. And the 1945 novel, *The Death of Virgil*, by Hermann Broch, offers us Broch's imagination of Vergil's extended fever-ridden contemplation of his life's work.

Part II of the anthology ends as did Part I, with a scholarly essay on Vergil's self-reflections in the *Aeneid* on his role as artist. "Art and the Hero: Participation, Detachment and Narrative Point of View in *Aeneid* 1," by Charles Segal, calls on us to return from the end to the beginning, both the end of the *Aeneid* and of this collection, to the beginning of the poem in **Book 1** and its first questions, about the role of art and the artist in society and history. In this context, the collection is served eloquently by its frontispiece, a photograph by Alan Cohen of the extant traces of our century's grim history.

My immediate goal in this anthology is to let the fine work of the scholars and artists whose writings are included here serve as guide for Vergil's readers, helping to develop the skill to experience meaning in a text judged over two millennia to be of enduring value. My ultimate goal is to help give these readers the tools to judge that 2000-year judgment for themselves so that they may answer for themselves and for today the question with which we began: Why Vergil.

Notes

[1]Charles Segal, "Art and the Hero: Narrative Point of View in *Aeneid* 1," *Arethusa* 14 (1981) 1, 67–83, 77), and herein, translates *sunt lacrimae rerum* as "There are tears for the way things are."

[2]"When I was sixteen, I had my first love affair—with a book. It was Vergil's *Aeneid*—and I haven't been the same since." Meyer Reinhold, "The Americanzation of Vergil, From Colonial Times to 1882, *Augustan Age* 6 (1987) 207–18, 207, herein.

[3]"When a harassed university president wakes up in euphoric mood, with a delicious but unaccountable impression that he has cut half a million off next year's budget, he has been dreaming about *us*." Bernard M. W. Knox, "On Two Fronts," *Backing Into the Future: Classical Tradition and its Renewal*, W. W. Norton, New York, 1994, 306.

[4]New York, Random House (1973; 2ᵈ ed., 1984). A chapter of Nims' book is excerpted herein. The conversations were part of an "ethnography" project on teaching practices in the arts programs at DePaul University, and the "enthnographers" on the project were Susanna Fajardo, Stephanie Quinn, co-chair, Charles Suchar, co-chair, and Donna Younger, of DePaul University. The project was part of DePaul's efforts to understand the assessment of student learning in its creative and performing arts programs.

[5]To save space, I have not translated the notes, which I assume are of use to specialists with specialists' training in languages.

Stephanie Quinn

ACKNOWLEDGEMENTS

I have more people to thank for their help with this book than many authors and editors do. The book's very nature, size, and scope suggest that it has a strong collaborative component, and I have sought and received the help and counsel of many friends and colleagues. Further, since I am a full-time university administrator, I have relied in various ways on my administrative associates in my "day job" in order to work on this Vergil job. Altogether, scholars, colleagues, friends, and family have offered abundant encouragement and solid help. To recognize everyone, I will reflect on the two years' work on *Why Vergil?* and tell the book's readers about those who have helped me produce it. Much scholarship is lonely business; this project was not.

The project had an apparently casual origin, in a conversation with the publisher, Lou Bolchazy of Bolchazy-Carducci Publishers, Inc., at the spring 1997 luncheon/lecture of the Chicago Classical Club. In one of those fortunate coincidences, I had just been encouraged a few weeks earlier, by Professor Sandi Jackson, of the DePaul University School of Education, to be receptive to the notion of editing as a fruitful labor, as we discussed an administrator's difficulty in sustaining any scholarship. Lou's offer resonated with Sandi's advice, and *Why Vergil?* was launched.

The policy of open access to visiting researchers at the Loyola University Cudahy Library afforded me serene hours of reading, concentrated especially in the summer of 1997, with Lake Michigan as my companion. Loyola's hospitality has been essential to the production of this book, as has DePaul University's expeditious interlibrary loan process.

In order to create an anthology that would be responsive to the needs of its potential audiences, I requested and received suggestions about contents from many teachers and scholars of Vergil's works, starting in the fall of 1997. That initial request yielded responses for which I am grateful to the following people: John Ambrose, Steve Ciraolo, Carrie Cowherd, Gregory Neil Daugherty, Sally Davis, Edward Gaffney, Roger Hornsby, W. R. Johnson, Richard A. Lafleur, M. Owen Lee, Mark Morford, Joseph O'Connor, and Harry Rutledge. By winter 1998 I had a working draft of the table of contents, on which several people offered additional comments and suggestions: Gary Cestaro, Christine Kalke, Helen Marlborough, Michael C. J. Putnam, and Susan Ford Wiltshire.

Authors of the selections were encouraging as I informed them about the project, and many also pitched in to confirm and frequently improve my editorial changes to their work. I appreciate their flexibility in allowing me to adapt their articles to the needs of the collection: Helen H. Bacon, William Batstone, Herbert W. Benario, Charles Fantazzi, Denis C. Feeney, Daniel H. Garrison, Erich S. Gruen, Robert Alan Gurval, W. R. Johnson, Bernard M. W. Knox, M. Owen Lee, Barbara Kiefer Lewalski, Annabel Patterson, Gerald Petter, Michael Putnam, Charles Segal, Gregory Staley, and Susan Ford Wiltshire. For advice on translations from German and Italian, I am grateful to Gary Cestaro, Clara Orban, and Inca Rumold of DePaul University.

The book's readers will discover that it is not only a collection; it is also an argument, a case, for the reading of Vergil's poetry. The argument is developed through the choices of the individual selections. I also make the case more directly, in the Introduction and the Conclusion. A number of friends and colleagues read the introductory and concluding essays in various forms from spring 1998 to winter 1999, always with a sympathetically critical and analytical eye. It has been a pleasure to participate in this community dedicated to the world of letters, including among others, Miriam Ben Yoseph, Sally Kitt Chappell, Walter Kitt, Helmut Epp, Elaine Harrington, Kevin Harrington, Richard Jones, Helen Marlborough, Dan Nichols, Susanna Pagliaro, Barbara Sizemore, and Ashley Wiltshire.

Michael C. J. Putnam, the essays' first reader, provided all important early encouragement and timely advice thereafter. His generosity is manifest in this volume's Foreword. Two early readers, Ralph Johnson and Susan Wiltshire, made influential observations and suggestions about strategy that helped shape my essays. I am happy to pay additional thanks to Richard Lanham and Charles Segal, who read the penultimate version of the Conclusion and offered important suggestions. The encouragement of all these readers has been confirming about the direction of the project and energizing for its labors.

In addition to the scholarly and creative efforts involved in preparing a book such as this, there is indeed labor. Much of the second year of the book's production was occupied in securing copyrights, making scores of editorial decisions large and small, refining language, and in manifold details. Not all of this labor is the most fun, of course, but all of it for *Why Vergil?* has been finely collegial (and some fun too).

The holders of copyrights are formally acknowledged with the selections. Besides the formalities, I wish to record the consistent responsiveness of copyright holders with respect to the "properties" with high commercial value. In addition, Ruth Scodel and Marilyn Skinner for *TAPA*, Catherine Parry Marcial, Michael Rexine, and Helen Tate were helpful in unusual copyright situations. And I am grateful to the several authors who hold the rights to their works.

I hope the book repays the dedicated labor of Bolchazy-Carducci's editor, Laurie Haight, whose good judgment and good cheer have been consistently supportive and sensible. It is a pleasure to acknowledge as well Charlene Hernandez' cover design. I was also fortunate in the services of Jean Gottlieb, who saved months of time in cleaning up my prose with skill and sensitivity, and Allan Kershaw, for his thorough proofreading. Luz Agosto advised me frequently on word processing issues beyond my capacity.

I am grateful for Matthew Pacholec's research assistance, especially regarding interlibrary loans and some circuitous copyright searches, and to Kaz Saghafi for help with a previous project that contributed to this one, both of whom are Ph.D. candidates in Philosophy at DePaul University. The University Research Council at DePaul supported a portion of the copyright permission fees for the anthology's most costly items.

For their support throughout the past two years, I am indebted to Ms. Agosto, Julie Casey and Susanna Pagliaro, my colleagues in the Office of Academic Affairs. Their professionalism in carrying out their responsibilities freed me completely from worry about my own, leaving only the pleasure of our good work together. I am also grateful to Richard Meister, Executive Vice President for Academic Affairs, for the working environment he fosters, which supports creativity both in accomplishing DePaul's academic mission and in accommodating a scholarly project such as this within the parameters of senior administrative responsibilities.

I am fortunate in having friends and family members who seemed not to mind hearing about the stages of the *Why Vergil?* saga and who even, unbidden, asked for updates and longer recitals of the book's progress.

Complementing my many hours of pleasure reading Vergilian scholarship, planning this volume, and writing my own contributions, this large company continually contributed doses of useful advice and meaningful assistance. Remaining faults of commission or omission are solely mine, of course. I hope that the completed book repays the thoughtfulness and effort of those who encouraged me while I was preparing it. And I hope the book is worthy of Vergil's poetry — its legacy and its future.

CHICAGO, 1999

A Few Important Dates*

Trojan War .... 1200 B.C.E., traditional date

Founding of Rome .... 753 B.C.E., traditional date

Homer, creation of the .... ca. 725 B.C.E.
    Iliad and *Odyssey*

Founding of the Roman Republic .... 509 B.C.E., traditional date

Classical Athens .... 490–338 B.C.E., Battle of Marathon to Battle of
    Chaeronea

Punic Wars (the wars between Rome and Carthage)
    First .... 264–241 B.C.E.
    Second .... 218–201 B.C.E.
    Third .... 149–146 B.C.E.

The Late Republic .... 133–52 B.C.E., Tiberius Gracchus, Gaius Gracchus,
    Marius, Sulla, Spartacus, Pompey, Cicero,
    Catiline, Julius Caesar; Lucretius, Catullus

Birth of Vergil .... 70 B.C.E.

The Roman Civil Wars .... 48–27 B.C.E., Battle of Pharsalus, Assassination
    of Julius Caesar, Battle of Philippi, Battle of
    Actium, designation of Octavian as Augustus

Augustan Poets .... Horace (65–8 B.C.E), Tibullus (ca. 55–19 B.C.E),
    Propertius (ca. 54–2 B.C.E)

Eclogues .... 42–37 B.C.E.

Georgics .... 37–30 B.C.E.

Aeneid .... 30–19 B.C.E.

Death of Vergil .... 19 B.C.E.

*Derived primarily from D. Brendan Nagle, *The Ancient World: A Social and Cultural History* (Englewood Cliffs, NJ: Prentice Hall, 1989) and R. D. Williams, ed., *The Aeneid of Virgil, Books 7–12* (Basingstoke and London: St Martin's Press, 1973).

The Power of Words
and Meaning of Form

Stephanie Quinn

INTRODUCTION—WHY WORDS?

Words are the focus of this volume; I take them very seriously. They are also a source of pleasure and delight. And in the hands of a master like Vergil, words have power. At some level, the way words exercise their power remains a mystery, but at another, it is knowable. The more thoroughly we learn the way words work, the closer we can come to what is ineffable, unsayable, which only poetry, art, can speak.[1]

All the entries in this anthology were chosen because they serve two purposes. Each individually helps readers understand Vergil's poetry, his words. In addition, they serve a collective purpose, for taken together they present an argument for the reading of Vergil and an answer to the book's title, *Why Vergil*?

In this essay, I describe the contribution of each selection in the volume. In addition, the selections are organized to make a case for the value of the play of words and for their power, about ideas and history, and art. The selections accumulate into an argument for a way to learn to read Vergil's poetry and offer an approach for interpreting its meaning and understanding its value.

The Play of Words

I love words, have always loved them.

Sometimes we feel like jumping a fence for the fun of jumping, or we burst into song for the fun of singing, or we string words together just for the fun of saying them....Fun is an expression of the exuberance we feel at being alive, an overflow of the spirit of play that characterizes so much human activity.[2]

This playfulness gets lost in much of our pedagogy in the liberal arts, in literature, in classical studies. The opposite of play is not work, but drudgery. An object of this book on Vergil is to translate the precise use and understanding of language, which could seem the work of the drudge, into the play of words.[3]

I played with words like toys from an early age, spent hours in my parents' home with an old poetry anthology.[4] One of my favorite poems as a child was Edgar Allan Poe's, "The Bells," which is a little case study in rhythm, rhyme, and the music of sounds through repetitions of vowels and consonants (poetic tools called assonance and alliteration).

> Hear the sledges with the bells—
> Silver bells!
> What a world of merriment their melody foretells!

How they tinkle, tinkle, tinkle
    In the icy air of night!
While the stars that oversprinkle
All the heavens, seem to twinkle
    With a crystalline delight;
Keeping time, time, time
    In a sort of Runic rhyme,
To the tintinnabulation that so musically wells
    From the bells, bells, bells, bells,
      Bells, bells, bell —
    From the jingling and the tinkling of the bells.[5]

I remember being surprised as a child, and I am still, that the repetition seven times of a simple word like "bells" could be pleasing, and that words I did not understand at the time, like "crystalline" and "Runic" could be enjoyable. ("Runic" is the adjective for "rune," which is a very old Germanic or Anglo-Saxon incantation or charm.) Later, in high school, when I met the infamous line of the early Roman poet Ennius, his use of alliteration was familiar territory.

O Tite tute Tati tibi tanta tyranne tulisti[6]

O Titus, you, Titus Tatius the tyrant, you took upon yourself such great matters.

How much more effective is the following phrase, at *Aeneid* 1.55, where the repeated *m* sounds imitate the sound they are describing, which was my first lesson in high school on a poetic device called onomatopoeia:

…magno cum murmure montis[7]

with a mighty moaning of the mountain

Better still, Edgar Reinke reminds us in his article included herein, is the following, at *Aeneid* 8.596, with its "metrically harmonious onomatopoetic effect of the galloping horse's hoof-beats trampling upon the crumbling plain":

quadripedante putrem sonitu quatit ungula campum.

With four-footed sound the horse-hoof shakes the crumbling plain.

Poe's poem is charming, but Vergil's use of the poetic tricks of the trade is far more subtle and effective, in ways we associate with music.
    I fell hard in love with words in the seventh grade when I first met Latin. These word-toys I had been playing with as a little child lived, I discovered (although I could not have said it this way then), in a universe of orderliness that was graspable in a single breath but also possessed precision and power that existed on an ever receding horizon of mastery.

Poetry is the horizon line,
the marriage of sea and sky.[8]

Then in the eleventh grade, on reading from Vergil's *Aeneid* for the first time, my fellow students and I met a master of words who lived exactly at that elusive horizon. We learned how exactingly artists work with the tools of their craft and that their skill at doing so, not just for effect, as in the line of Ennius, but to enhance sense, as in Poe's poem, is a measure of their talent. Vergil's skill at this work was great, one of the greatest talents in almost three thousand years of Western poetry.[9] I have felt partnered with Vergil ever since those high school days and remain moved by his words as by those of no other writer of my acquaintance. There may be no more important justification for this volume than my wish to share with others that experience and pleasure.

PART I:
THE POWER OF WORDS AND THE MEANING OF FORM

The agenda for Part I of this book is to explicate, to unfold, Vergil's artistic mastery as we begin to answer its guiding question, why Vergil. The selections help us penetrate Vergil's mastery of the shaping and placement of words and the way he marshals them to create his story and its layers of meaning.

Language and Play — Language and Power

The first selections in this volume invite us to be playful with the first eleven lines of the *Aeneid*. Readers will find included the Latin lines themselves and several translations of the lines. There follow a full synopsis of the *Aeneid* by book, as a reference while reading the selections; Daniel Garrison's helpful pages on reading the Latin and Vergil's meter; and Edgar Reinke's article on Vergil's use of sounds and meaning. Read the Latin words, even if you do not know what they mean exactly, sense their sounds and rhythm. Read the several translations of these few lines, noting how they differ. Use Garrison's transliteration, where every word in Latin occurs with a word in English, to note the way poets and professional translators have turned Vergil's Latin art into English, as artfully as they can. Take your time, play with Vergil's words.

> But words, like crystals, have facets and axes of rotation with different properties, and light is refracted differently according to how these word crystals are placed, and how the polarizing surfaces are cut and superimposed.[10]

Watch how all these words work, what these word-workers, these poets do with them, and the varied effects their labors have on us. (The words "poet" and "poem" are from the ancient Greek word to do or make, *poiêo*; a *poíema* is something made or done, created.)

For example, Vergil's first word of the nearly 10,000 in his poem is *arma*, "arms" as in armament; the second is *virumque*, "and a man" and the third *cano*, "I sing." A simple beginning, which reminds me of the first notes of Beethoven's famous Fifth Symphony. How do the translators handle just those three words, *arma virumque cano*?

What difference does it make that one translator captures Vergil's first words in his order, "Arms, and the man I sing," and others use "I" or "my" as the first word, "I sing of arms and of a man,"or "My song is arms and a man?" What shift in emphasis results for the meaning of the poem—which of the main subjects, the hero or the singing poet, are we being told is primary and which secondary? What difference does it make that some translators use the word "arms" and others the words "war" or "warfare," "I sing of warfare and a man at war," arms being something an individual carries and warfare a collective enterprise? How does the very beginning of the work prepare us to anticipate the story? Will we be surprised at the ending, twelve books away, where in the poem's final moment the hero's last act involves a weapon? How differently do we think and feel about arms and a man in the beginning of the epic from the way we will react to them at the end?

To be sure, such questions as these are impossible to ask with the same precision when using a translation. It is possible, however, for Latinless readers to follow the analysis of others. I also believe that readers in Latin can find this comparative exercise especially useful. Although orthodoxy may discourage language students from reading in translation, I find the exercise when well crafted to be pedagogically useful. The lesson here is to respect the plasticity, flexibility, and ambiguity of language and avoid the trap of confusing grammatical accuracy, important as that is, with poetic truth. [11]

Having engaged with the *Aeneid*'s first eleven lines, readers are next invited to consider a fifteen-line passage that occurs shortly after, starting at line 180 of book 1, in which Vergil presents the first act in the poem of its hero, Aeneas. Aeneas and his followers, refugees from the defeated city of Troy (on the coast of Asia Minor, in modern Turkey), have just escaped a mighty storm, caused by the unleashing of winds that caused the mountain's mighty moan (*magno cum murmure montis*, 1.55) and from which only some of them survive. Finally reaching land with seven ships intact, Aeneas explores the territory as his people rest and make a meal. He comes upon seven stags, which the hero shoots with arrows and kills, one for each ship. The hero's first action reflects the poem's first words: *arma virumque cano*.

Gregory A. Staley analyzes Aeneas' first act in its ambiguity—Aeneas as leader and Aeneas as killer, a question that resonates throughout the poem and especially in Aeneas' very last act in the poem, when he also kills. How do we interpret this opening action? What literary sources did Vergil use and how? How does Vergil handle the image of the hunt? How do these lines prepare us for the work as a whole and relate to our overall interpretation of it? Staley's article relies on detailed readings of individual words and symbols to evoke fine points of feeling and meaning as he also situates us within current scholarly thinking on the *Aeneid*.

In this study of language and image, Staley's analysis rests on excellent precedent. Now almost fifty years old, "The Serpent and the Flame," by Bernard M. W. Knox, traces the interweaving images and themes of book 2 that Vergil uses to portray the night when Troy fell, as Aeneas relates the story to the Carthaginians and their queen Dido. In book 1 she had rescued the Trojans when they landed in northern Africa after the terrible storm. Knox's analysis teaches us how, line by line and word by word, Vergil's language cumulates through the whole of book 2, building its story around sets of images, metaphors, themes, and questions (fire, serpents, the wooden horse), with spiraling virtuosity of technique and deepening circulation of meaning.[12]

The storytelling continues in book 3, about the wanderings of the Trojans and their adventures, evoking similar parts of Homer's *Odyssey*.[13] Aeneas finishes his story at the end of *Aeneid* 3, in recounting the death of his father, Anchises.

In book 4, we enter upon perhaps the most famous part of the epic. A queen and a hero — the queen a widow sworn to be faithful to her dead husband, the hero bound to a vague but compelling destiny to found a new home for his refugee Trojans — become enmeshed in a love affair that ends with the hero's departure for his destiny and the heroine's departure in death. The pair meet again briefly and for the last time in book 6, during Aeneas' journey to the Underworld where he encounters Dido's unforgiving shade.

In his 1944 essay, "What is a Classic?" T. S. Eliot finds the meeting of Dido and Aeneas in book 6 "one of the most civilized passages in poetry," an "instance of civilized manners" and testimony to "civilized consciousness and conscience."[14] Few readers today would use this language or would consider these statements sufficient as an analysis of the episode, even though some parts of Eliot's reading of this passage remain sympathetic.

Less than forty years after Eliot's essay, in 1982, Carol Gilligan uses the Dido and Aeneas story of book 4 in her analysis of modern psychological theories of maturity. In those theories, Gilligan says, development becomes equated with separation, "where progress can readily be charted by measuring the distance between mother and child," which results in turn "in the absence of women from accounts of adult development." Gilligan goes on to explain that in one such theory, development towards maturity consists in having a dream, a vision to attain. The maturing male becomes attached to a female figure as he seeks to achieve his vision, but he must necessarily leave the female behind when she becomes an impediment to the dream. Gilligan cites the Dido and Aeneas story as typical of this theoretical process. Her critique of the theory and, by implication, of Vergil's story challenges the fundamental assumptions of maturity as defined by male detachment from and denigration of the female.[15]

According to Eliot and Gilligan, the story of Dido and Aeneas conveys, on the one hand, a set of civilized manners and on the other a set of sexist assumptions, both of which epitomize the culture of Europe. It is curious that Eliot and Gilligan might actually have agreed on the exemplary nature of Vergil's story. In the value they place on the example, however, they would be worlds apart. After several decades of sophisticated feminist thinking, such questions can be addressed with the seriousness worthy of the *Aeneid* and of women.[16]

The three essays on the Dido and Aeneas story included here do not deal directly with the gulf between Eliot and Gilligan, but they can be read in light of it. Roger Hornsby offers a compelling psychological portrait of Dido, drawn from close reading of Vergil's language, that insists on Dido's culpability for her abandonment and suicide and the rightness of Aeneas' departure from Carthage and her. One could say that Hornsby's reading was consistent with the theories Gilligan criticizes: woman as an obstacle to male heroic destiny. One could also claim that in giving Dido responsibility for her fate instead of portraying her as a victim, Vergil, in Hornsby's view, has afforded her the only possible route to heroism. In the epic convention, heroism is the highest good and is usually reserved for the male world of warfare, since in the ancient Greek and Roman worlds, mere victimhood was not heroic. In that view, Vergil is making male heroism available to a female, although the definition of heroism remains male.

Charles Segal's analysis of Dido's story focuses on half a line, at *Aeneid* 4.133, as Dido hesitates in leaving her chamber to join Aeneas on the hunt during which they will consummate their passion. Using as exacting an analysis of Vergil's language as

Hornsby, Segal finds more emotional sympathy in Vergil's story of the queen, which he readily looks upon as a tragedy as Hornsby in 1964 did not. From the vantage point of a generation's thinking about portrayals of women in literature, Segal asked in 1990, "Could Vergil have meant us to see Dido's tragedy as a failure of his culture to transcend the inherited patterns of a woman's story" which could be told either in the "language of reason and responsibility" or that of "madness, magic, and tragedy?" That question itself is new to the study of the poem. Do we pose it in order to save Vergil from complicity in the sexist sins of Europe? Does the question signal our ever greater recognition of the wide embrace of Vergil's poetic art, anticipating, even if fleetingly, a sensibility the modern world is only now acquiring—and slowly at that?

I mentioned above Eliot's reading of the encounter of Dido and Aeneas in book 6, and we leave the discussion of the story through Marilyn B. Skinner's reading of the same episode. Skinner's analysis reveals something we will come to expect in Vergil's poetry—an inextricable duality of perspectives, intentionally woven into the narrative through the operation of the language itself at minute levels of detail. We see two viewpoints on the Dido and Aeneas story in the two episodes in books 4 and 6, in which the roles of weeping need and silent refusal are paradoxically reversed between the man and the woman. Most important, we learn from Skinner that the conjoining of the two stories is itself the single story that Vergil composes for our attention.

It is difficult both intellectually and emotionally for us to sustain the pull of oppositions within two evocations of the same incident. But the capacity to grasp paradox is one of the most powerful tools of human understanding, and Vergil is its great teacher. We will use this skill of holding on simultaneously to opposite ideas and feelings, as we continue our progress through the books of the *Aeneid*, with its increasingly intricate accumulations of internal references to prior images, scenes, and stories, even specific phrases and words. We will study the way Vergil invokes the power of words, crafting words on power, and words on the power of words. And we will expand the arena of our learning, from delight and play, however serious, in the power of words, to the undeniably serious work of words as they make not only poetry but history.

Language and Form—Ideas and History

Over the centuries, attempts to understand the way Vergil's language operates have been accompanied by similar efforts to understand his ideas, even to decipher his precise philosophy. Is he Epicurean, Stoic, proto-Christian? Most recent studies of the *Aeneid*'s philosophical content no longer mine it for a systematic philosophy. Rather, they see at work an eclectic blending of diverse elements that achieve poetic although not philosophic unity.[17] Such efforts focus particularly on book 6, Aeneas' trip to the Underworld, where regions of good and evil have been designed, a theory of transmigration of souls adumbrated, and, within that context, the future of Rome revealed.

Book 5 recounts the diversion of the Trojans' course from Italy to return instead to Sicily, where Aeneas' father Anchises had died and Aeneas establishes elaborate funeral games in honor of his father. Near the end of book 5, Anchises appears to his son and advises him to visit the Underworld before he arrives in Italy. Book 6 is the story of that mystical journey, facilitated by the Sibyl of Cumae and the golden bough, during which Anchises recounts for Aeneas the future of the people Aeneas will establish, the story of Romulus, Julius Caesar, and Caesar Augustus.

> Hic vir, hic est, tibi quem promitti saepius audis,
> Augustus Caesar, divi genus, aurea condet
> saecula qui rursus Latio regnata per arva
> Saturno quondam, super et Garamantas et Indos
> proferet imperium;

> This is the man, this is he, whom you so often hear promised to you, Caesar Augustus, descended of a god, who will found the golden age again in Latium throughout fields once ruled by Saturn, and who will extend Roman sway beyond even the Garamantes [in northern Africa] and the Indi.

> (*Aeneid* 6.791–5)

Aeneas also hears from his father the role Anchises foresees for the great empire of the Romans.

> Tu regere imperio populos, Romane, memento
> (hae tibi erunt artes), pacisque imponere morem,
> parcere subiectis et debellare superbos.

> You, Roman, remember to rule peoples with your power (these will be your arts) and impose the custom for peace, to spare the humbled and fight to the finish the proud.

> (*Aeneid* 6.851–3)

The meaning of the *Aeneid* as a whole rests in large measure in the way a reader understands these two parts of Anchises' prophecy, the meaning of world empire and of the injunction to spare the subjected and bring down the proud.

The two approaches to book 6 presented in this volume investigate less Vergil's philosophic sources than two other elements, his treatment of history and of spirit. D. C. Feeney studies Anchises' recitation of events in what for him and Aeneas within the poem is Rome's future, but which for Vergil and his contemporaries is their past and present. He analyzes Vergil's arrangement of known history to produce new insights, in what he calls the parade of heroes, roughly from line 710 nearly to the end of the book. His analysis rests on precise knowledge of Roman history, which Vergil's audience of course had, and on Vergil's precise choices of what historical elements to present and how.

Feeney observes a fundamental paradox in book 6, especially in relation to Vergil's models in the work of Plato, the fourth-century B.C.E. Greek philosopher, and Cicero, Vergil's near contemporary, perhaps Rome's greatest master of prose, and a translator of Greek philosophy to Roman language and needs. Vergil paradoxically casts the exploration of the afterlife in terms of the real life of Roman history: the "paradox is not inert, however, but operative; it is not one which the poet glosses over, or leaves tactfully unstressed, but one to which he regularly directs our attention." Feeney demonstrates that Vergil qualifies the Roman examples ostensibly offered in panegyric and praise, unsettling us, destabilizing his narrative, creating ambivalence. The greatest ambivalence may be, according to Feeney, in the initial contrast, between a Platonic, ideal vision and the realities of history, in which such a vision is simultaneously offered and called into question by the very way Vergil composes the story.

Whereas for Feeney Vergil in book 6 denies us "the beauty and the consolation of the myths of philosophy, immortality and redemption," Helen H. Bacon takes another view, seeing Aeneas as a "hero destined for immortality." In linking Aeschylus' *Oresteia*, Sophocles' *Oedipus at Colonus*, the *Aeneid*, and Milton's *Paradise Lost*, all as *commedia* — neither tragedy nor romance but stories about an ultimate reconciliation between human and divine — Bacon claims, along with Feeney, that Vergil's is a clouded portrayal of Roman history. She concludes however that Vergil disregards the consolation of history but not the consolation of spirit. She extends her analysis to the books of the middle third of the *Aeneid*, books 5–8, as the central structural whole that effects Aeneas' "gradual reorientation" from the mortal to the immortal, although he never comprehends his ultimate destiny.

Bacon further explores the *Aeneid*'s spirituality, an aspect of the poem that has been neglected as centuries of over-interpretation have sought to Christianize Vergil, seeing in his works predictions of the coming of Jesus Christ. That neglect is understandable, but it diminishes our understanding of the book and the epic. We need not make of Vergil a nascent medieval Christian to recognize him as an artist with serious spiritual interests: "Though Vergil, like Plato, makes it clear that his myths of the afterlife are not to be taken literally, must we assume that in this moment of high poetry at the climax of the central element of his poem, Vergil did not mean them to be taken *seriously?*"

We are invited by Feeney and Bacon to consider Vergil in several ways, as a maker of a people's historical self-understanding and also as a man of spirit, however differently he may have understood such a phrase from the way we do. With those two perspectives, the *Aeneid* raises the idea of spirit moving in history, of the fate, not only of individuals, but of peoples and nations. At the same time, Vergil writes the story of an individual actor operating within historical constraints and responsible for the actual as well as moral founding of what Vergil may have surmised, along with Augustus, would be the greatest power in the world as he knew it.

For a task no less than to write the history of the spirit of his age, Vergil used artistic tools of greater scope even than the masterly, miniaturist[18] combination of small sets of words. An epic poem is an empire of words, through which the poet who rules the artistic universe of his culture's past and present may influence its future. The immense reach of Vergil's epic imagination calls into play the arrangement of word and symbol on the broad scale of form and structure, perhaps on a mathematical basis or regarding the poetic arrangement of the large shapes of the poem, aptly described by George Duckworth as an architecture. Just as Vergil is a master wordsmith, so he is also a master architect.

A fascinating exploration of one mystery in Vergil's poetry is offered to us by John Frederick Nims in his chapter, "Golden Numbers: On Nature and Form," excerpted herein. What for us may be an odd juxtaposition of science, poetry, and a phenomenon at first so strange as to seem almost magical — the golden numbers of the Fibonacci sequence and the mathematical ratio of the golden mean — may help us make a leap of historical imagination, to a way of understanding the world through compartments of related knowledge different from our own.

Number was inherent in Greek philosophy, and our philosopher-poet would find it not only natural but I believe necessary to incorporate into his encyclopedic universe of the *Aeneid* principles that order the natural, mathematical, and philosophical worlds.[19] These elements of order and structure can make meaning by using techniques similar to those discussed above, which allow a poet to manipulate words and lines through sound and rhythm. In the pages of Nims's chapter included here, he diagrams the Fibonacci series in a section of book 4, in a translation that matches the numbering of Vergil's lines.

As we know from Bacon's essay, structural issues affect the interpretation of the *Aeneid*. Duckworth was particularly interested in Vergilian form and structure. His essay included here emphasizes the structural and thematic importance of the second half of the poem. He reminds us that Vergil's earlier works, the *Eclogues* and *Georgics*, also respond to analysis of structure. The essay surveys several structural interpretations, noting that the emphasis on different designs among various scholars "merely gives added testimony of the structural richness of the epic." Duckworth's essay also charts for readers a set of detailed correspondences across books, especially between the two halves of the poem, books 1–6 and books 7–12.

Impressive as Vergil's control over such a large scale may be, the value and meaning of that skill lie in more than his virtuosity. The epic's structural patterns signal interpretive issues. Analysis of the poem in its two halves supports a generally positive view of the whole, with the first half describing the assignment of Aeneas' mission and the second telling the story of its achievement. From this perspective, one is tempted to identify poetic form with the idea of moral order. Analysis of the poem by three thirds, books 1–4, 5–8, 9–12, suggests different questions. Dido's death at the end of the first third of the poem comes into perspective in balance with the death we know occurs at the end of the third part of the tripartite structure. From that structural perspective, the optimistic prophesies of the middle four books seem to be qualified by the suffering that precedes and follows them. In this view, poetic form complicates and qualifies its own securing creation of orderliness.

In regard to another book of poetry, Horace's Fourth Book of *Odes*, Michael C. J. Putnam reminds us that, whatever a work's structural designs, we experience them in the linear progression of the work as the poet created it for our experience: "…structure is the covert servant of a linear reading, raising or modifying expectations, confirming or reshaping patterns of order, and pushing the reader, in ways he or she may only dimly sense on first study, inexorably toward the book's conclusion…."[20] Just as we attune ourselves to observe Vergil the miniaturist create meaning through the smallest details, so too we can expand our perception of meaning to operate on a large canvas, on the scale, for example, of a symphony or an opera. Further, as our ear becomes more and more skilled, we read simultaneously both dimensions, small and large, of Vergil's art.

As we turn from the first six books of the *Aeneid* to the poem's second half in books 7–12, which is both the middle of the poem and the transition from the Underworld to the new world in Italy, we have a vantage point that is like a promontory, as Aeneas had in book 1 when he observed the seven stags. We have learned now that we can read such moments as having been designed with poetic intention and we realize that they carry a weight of meaning. From here, the turning point between the poem's two halves, we can see that reminders of Homer's *Odyssey* have been sketched just behind us, in books 1–6. From that perspective, we may intuit that in books 7–12 an experience like that of Homer's *Iliad*, of the Trojan War, awaits us.

Vergil marks the transition from one half of the poem to the other by calling upon a new guiding Muse. Paradoxically, the poet invokes Erato, the patron Muse of the poetry of love, to help him tell the story of the terrible wars to come. At the literal level, the task for hero and poet is to describe the Iliadic experience of the war in Italy. Another and perhaps still greater project is to conjoin the epic arts of war and the lyric arts of love, in effect to tell this one story from two perspectives, as Vergil did with Dido's story in books 4 and 6. Now Vergil tells us explicitly that he will be drawing on two literary styles, two voices, and two ways of experiencing reality — to conquer artistically the story of hellish warfare and also embrace it with loving empathy and empathic passion, accomplishing each paradoxically by means of the other.

On the Trojans' arrival in Italy, at the pastoral site of the river Tiber, *fluvio Tiberinus amoeno* ("the Tiber with pleasing stream," 7.30), the place promised since the beginning of the poem and most recently by Anchises in book 6, we hear immediately from the poet himself that telling this half of the story will be his greater task.

> Dicam horrida bella,
> dicam acies actosque animis in funera reges,
> Tyrrhenamque manum totamque sub arma coactam
> Hesperiam. Maior rerum mihi nascitur ordo,
> maius opus moveo.

> I will tell of horrible wars, I will tell of battle lines, and kings driven by their passions to death, the Tyrrhenian band and all Hesperia assembled in arms. The greater course of events arises for me, greater the work I begin.

> (*Aeneid* 7.41–45)

After all that the Trojans have experienced up to this point, it may be hard for us to believe Vergil, but what he says is true. A difficult path awaits hero and audience, but perhaps poet most of all.

Aeneas' hopes for peace and home are thwarted early in book 7, when through Juno's intervention, war flares among the native Latins, led by the warrior Turnus, and madness invades their pastoral landscape. The arrival of the Trojans in Italy, the new home they have sought for ten years, soon precipitates war, recapitulating in the second half of the poem the wars at Troy from which the first lines remind us they had fled. But this time, Aeneas, introduced to us in the very first lines of the poem as fate's exile (*fato profugus*), will arrive in the new land, no longer its victim but fate's agent. Once again, Vergil obliges us to understand a situation from two points of view. The arrival of the Trojans is joyous for them as the end to their travels and fulfillment of their destiny. For the Latins the same event is disastrous.

This dual vision or voicing in the *Aeneid* — especially regarding the effect on individual lives — was perceived and discussed by Adam Parry over thirty years ago. We saw above how Charles Segal drew rich interpretation from a mere half-line in book 4. In the line and a half at Aeneid 7.759–60, Parry found another microcosm of meaning, a pastoral moment of empathic landscape that resonates with epic consequences. Parry was among the first critics to examine two sets of feelings we experience in Vergil's poetry, naming one public and the other personal or private, "a public voice of triumph, and a private voice of regret." The public voice recounts in joyful tones Rome's glories and those of its leaders, Aeneas in myth and by implication Augustus in history, the one the founder of Rome, the second the refounder of the Republic become Empire. The private voice counts the bodies and the tears that paid for the glory.

Parry's perception has influenced scholarly efforts to understand many issues central to the work: Vergil's relation to and opinion about Augustus, emperor and patron; the *Aeneid* as a work of propaganda and the poem's message about the potentialities and pitfalls of historical action; and even the role and value of art itself. Interpreters since Parry have debated the merits of these two voices within the poem, some of them finding greater weight in the optimistic voice and others in the pessimistic. When not a simplistic reduction of Vergil's subtlety and complexity, the polarities and ramifications of these interpretations have fruitfully occupied Vergilian scholarship for several decades.[21]

Our century's experience with totalitarian regimes that developed policies to control art and thought, and our current, enormous power to manipulate mass communication — from consumer advertising to the management of the news — make us skeptical of an artistic enterprise like the *Aeneid*. How are we to regard a work of art that relates so closely to real historical events and a sitting leader, especially a leader who was patron to a circle of distinguished artists, Vergil among them? The *Aeneid* contains several prophesies of Rome's fated and glorious history as the Mediterranean world's greatest empire. In the middle third of the poem, books 5–8, Anchises' inspiring predictions for Rome's future in book 6 anticipate the scenes of Roman destiny depicted on the shield Aeneas receives at the end of book 8. Combined, these two extended prophesies, projecting into Aeneas' future events Vergil's audience knew to be historically true, create an impression of historical hope and possibility. How are we today to understand such hopes?

In book 8, Aeneas leaves the fighting to seek help from a remote group of Greek settlers, as Vergil injects another paradox into the narrative, confounding the meaning of friend and foe: defeated by Greeks in Troy, the Trojans ally themselves with Greeks in Italy against the Italians with whom they will eventually unite. The Greek leader Evander gives arms and aid, and entrusts to Aeneas his young son Pallas for his first war. During their meeting, Evander relates the story of how the hero Hercules saved his people from the ravages of a monster, Cacus, perhaps a model for Aeneas' role. At the end of book 8, as Aeneas prepares to return to the battle between Trojans and Latins, his mother Venus, the goddess of love, gives him a mighty shield made for him by her husband, the god Vulcan, maker of the tools of battle, as Vergil joins in their union and its fruit, the arts of love and war. On the shield, in a technique called ekphrasis, Vergil describes the work of art that Vulcan has embossed on it, scenes from Roman history.

A prominent scene on the shield depicts the Battle of Actium, at which, in 31 B.C.E., Augustus, still known as Octavian, defeated the forces of Antony and Cleopatra, solidified his hold on the Roman empire and ended what had been a century of Roman civil war. Robert Gurval has written a study of the Battle of Actium and its meaning for Rome, and one chapter of his book is devoted to the shield of Aeneas in *Aeneid* 8, excerpted below. Using a method we will recognize from Feeney's and Bacon's essays, Gurval studies the scenes on the shield, exploring what episodes from Rome's history Vergil chose to depict, what elements of the stories he included, how he combined the elements, and how the total effect of the shield is constructed. Finding continuing value in the analysis of public and private voices in the poem, Gurval explains that in telling the stories on the shield Vergil "complicates his reader's emotions," leaving us to wonder whether its final meaning is hopeful or elegaic. In doing so, Gurval adds nuance to W. H. Auden's interpretation of the *Aeneid*. Parts of Auden's poem "Secondary Epic" introduce and end Gurval's chapter. In that poem, Auden chastises Vergil for what he reads as Vergil's historical optimism, a kind of "nineteenth-century nationalism." We learn from Gurval that the *Aeneid* is not so simple as that.

The issue of the *Aeneid* as propaganda for the new Augustan regime has occupied readers of the poem. Recently, critics detect a complex relationship between Vergil and Augustus, an affinity more subtle than the promptings of day-to-day politics. For the circle of poets around him, Augustus held a fascination, according to Peter White: "Although the regime [Augustus] founded outlasted him and even grew stronger after his death, no later emperor remotely equaled his hold over the imagination of poets. And if we are to understand what fascinated them, we have no choice but to try to surrender our imagination to him in the way they did. To the extent that we succeed, it can be a disconcerting exercise."[22] A poet whose subject was history and the future may understand that his own ambition in art was as great as Augustus' ambition in history, with equally profound and disconcerting risks. He may have known that to write Aeneas' (and Augustus') story, he had to tap his own creative force in its full passion and fury.[23]

But if statecraft is a highly ambiguous art, in which one can claim, for example, to "wage peace," does the art of words have similar moral potential for both good and ill? Can the art of words deceive the artist himself, so deluding him by his power to make beauty that he may falsify history, the way a *princeps* ("the first one," which became a title for Augustus) might confuse stability with justice or peace with freedom?[24] Vergil contends with that problem, I believe, in the second half of the *Aeneid*. He asks that we, poet and audience alike, surrender our imaginations to the story, than which there is hardly a greater task.

In order to tell with truth and empathy the story of Aeneas and his horrible wars, to imagine Aeneas from within his hero's being, our tender-hearted poet would have to imagine himself as a man in arms. Books 9 through 12 tell the story of the hero's and the poet's acceptance of that trial, in lyric, loving surrender to the epic arts of war. In the meantime, at the end of book 8, Aeneas, and we with him, lift up the mighty shield, *ignarus imagine gaudet* (8.730), happy in its predictions, ignorant of their meaning.

Language, Empire, and Art

In the final third of the *Aeneid*, the Trojans' new-found home in Italy is embroiled in war. In a paradoxical reversal, the Trojans are now allied with their conquerors, a colony of Greeks, and they do battle against the Italians, the people who are destined to be the Trojans' kin. Books 9–12 tell stories of death — of beautiful young warriors and of hateful outlaws, of fathers and sons, daughters and mothers, of humans as sacrifice in mournful retribution, and of fallen heroes. Commentators question the meaning of these deaths — what dies with all these people? What of the dreams and promises made earlier in the poem, especially in its centerpiece, books 5–8? Do they survive? And if they do, in what form, how are they changed? The essays in this part of the anthology work with the same philological techniques we have seen throughout. Several help us further understand Vergil's cumulative internal references, analyzing his allusive technique across the whole reach of the poem as Bernard Knox's article did regarding book 2. Through such an approach, Vergil will guide us to read the poem's ending in light of every word that precedes it.

Books 9 through 12 tell the story of the new *Iliad* in Italy, of battles, treaties made and broken, slaughters of men and women, warriors maddened for bloodshed or revenge. Throughout, Aeneas and Turnus, the Trojan and Italian leaders, approach each other gradually, book by book, until finally, at the end of the twelfth and last book, they meet in combat. In the final lines of the book and the epic, Aeneas defeats Turnus. In supplication before Aeneas, Turnus invokes the memories of their fathers and in their memory begs mercy. About to relent, Aeneas sees on Turnus' shoulder part of the arms he had ripped from Evander's son Pallas, the young man who, while under Aeneas' protection, was killed by Turnus in swaggering victory. Infuriated by the sight of the trophy and the set of long, painful memories it evokes, Aeneas, instead of sparing, kills. All the meaning of the poem is captured in that action; what that meaning is has been the source of controversy. Is Aeneas' killing of Turnus morally and historically justified or is it a mark of moral and historical failure? Starting with an analysis of portions of book 9, the final essays in this part of the collection help us comprehend that question.

I mentioned above some of the heated interpretive issues over the *Aeneid* and ancient Greek and Roman studies in general, particularly with respect to feminist criticism. Feminist scholarship contributes more than controversy to our reading, however; it helps us hear parts of the song to which we might otherwise have been deaf.[25] In the chapter of her book, "Grieving Mothers and the Costs of Attachment," excerpted here, Susan Ford Wiltshire blends two lines of criticism, one from feminism and one from Adam Parry, to analyze several images of mothers, animal and human, developed, as Wiltshire notes, "beyond the necessity of the context." Wiltshire reveals the way Vergil has injected the private world of mothers into the public world of war, and examines the effect of those voices on how we hear the poem as a whole. Vergil first introduced the pair of young heroes Wiltshire discusses, Nisus and Euryalus, at the funeral games in book 5. This second appearance of the pair in book 9 can be read in relation to their earlier story of rivalry in sport, where winning and losing were the only consequences. Heroic valor rests on the same attitudes and skills as games, but with different results. Boys' games become a mother's tears.

Book 10 is a pivotal part of the *Aeneid*'s story, which Herbert W. Benario recounts through his article's close reading of Vergil's text. The book also sets the stage for the ending of the epic, through the story of Pallas, entrusted into Aeneas' care by his father Evander. In the course of the book, Pallas is killed at the hands of Turnus. One's reading of the conclusion and the meaning of the *Aeneid* are informed by the actions and emotions portrayed in book 10.

After the truces, calls for revenge, and continued preparation for battle in book 11, and yet another singular death, that of the warrior-maiden Camilla, we enter upon the conclusion of the epic in book 12. Amidst the vast, excellent and often polemical studies of this book, I have chosen two that continue our exploration of the *Aeneid*'s meaning through close reading of the text.

M. Owen Lee has studied several aspects of the *Aeneid*, including the relationships it creates between fathers and sons and also the traits the poem shares with music. The article of Lee's included here discusses in terms of the development and recapitulation of themes one short passage in the final book of the *Aeneid*, in which Aeneas is wounded and healed. In his approach, Lee enlarges our understanding of how a small detail of the work adds to the meaning of the whole. He also demonstrates the way such a detail is built into a larger framework or structure, as happens in great works of music and as Nims and Duckworth point out in the *Aeneid*.[26]

As we approach the final scenes of the *Aeneid*, Lee refers us to crucial moments particularly at the end of the first half, the hesitation of the golden bough and especially of Anchises' injunction to Aeneas: *parcere subiectis et debellare superbos* ("spare the subjected and fight to the finish the proud"). Lee focuses our attention on the *Aeneid*'s "shocking and abrupt conclusion" — Aeneas' enraged killing of his enemy Turnus, whose breaking of treaties prolonged the war that Aeneas had never wanted to fight. As Turnus pleads for mercy in the name of the bonds of fatherhood so dear to Aeneas' heart, is Aeneas respecting the standard to "fight to the finish the proud" or he is violating the imperative to "spare the humbled?"

It is not surprising that the meaning of anger and rage is crucial to the controversy. Those emotions play a dominant role from the very beginning of the poem, when we are introduced to Juno's rage against the Trojans at line 11 of the first book (*tantaene animis caelestibus irae*, "is the rage in celestial spirits so great?"). But what do they mean for us, for our reading of the work? Do we interpret those feelings by trying to understand what the Romans would have thought and felt, or do we interpret them according to the way the poem operates on us reading it today, or, somehow, both?[27] How should and do those two ways of knowing the poem, of experiencing it, interact? Is an ancient work of art valuable as an artifact that we know or as an experience that we feel? How in general do knowledge and feeling, past and present, interact in the study of and response to art? Vergil exercises great skill in negotiating that question, for in writing the *Aeneid*, he was working with the archaic Homeric epics and applying to them what were for him modern sensibilities, just as we do now, reading his epic two thousand years later.

Gerald Petter addresses the dichotomy in the interpretation of Aeneas' final act of rage, offering insight into ideas relevant to the *Aeneid* and contemporary with its creation. He analyzes the concluding passage and Vergil's moral stance as a whole from the point of view of a "body of unwritten law," "recognized universally in the Greco-Roman world." In that context, Petter reviews instances in the *Aeneid* when the moral order is violated — which he calls desecrations — and responses to those violations that seek in some way to rectify them, which he calls expiations. Petter traces this theme throughout the *Aeneid* with special attention to the wooden horse in book 2 and the story in book 8 of Hercules saving Evander and the Greeks from the monster Cacus. The final example, of course, is the saga of Turnus and Aeneas. Petter claims that, in killing Turnus, Aeneas expiates a series of wrongs, and the poem ends in a way that had been prepared by the poet from the time of the fall of Troy and had been building throughout the second half of the poem. Petter's analysis is helpful in sorting many elements of the story as they relate to the final action, an effort similar to Lee's.

These articles have helped us read the *Aeneid* by focusing on small sections of the poem that carry major interpretive significance. To conclude the first half of this anthology, we end as Vergil does, by returning to other endings and other beginnings within the poem. Michael C. J. Putnam in his article included here has analyzed an early scene in book 6, the last book of the first half of the epic — the description of the sculptures of Daedalus on the doors of Apollo's temple at Cumae, where Aeneas goes in search of the Sibyl who will guide him through the Underworld.

In this ekphrasis, the artist Vergil uses his art, the poetry of *Aeneid*, to tell the story of another artist, Daedalus, and how he used his art, sculpture, to tell the story of himself as creator of an artifice. Daedalus made the wings that carried him to the sky and that later bore his son on a fatal flight too near the sun. Putnam calls this the "triply fictive world of poet imagining artist crafting himself in art." Starting with the Daedalus lines, Putnam returns to many of the themes and issues raised so far. He redirects our attention to the early books and stories, the wooden horse, the Dido story, Anchises' lines on the Roman arts of governance in war and peace, the story of Nisus and Euryalus, and others, in an accumulation of internal allusions and of compact and manifold meaning. He reminds us of the interpretive significance of the epic's structure, both in its halves and thirds.

Putnam also uses the Daedalus story to ask another set of questions of our poem, questions about the work of the artist and about the role, power, and meaning of art itself. He points out that the artist Vergil uses the Daedalus story to investigate the way art may mislead, lie, or fail. Daedalus fails to finish the sculpture of his story, the story of his own son's death as he attempted the artificial technique of flying that his father had imperfectly taught him. Through the telling of this story, Putnam contends, Vergil calls into question his own artistic enterprise, the creation of the *Aeneid* itself, making of the Daedalus story a "metaphor for the progress of any artist, for his imaginative diary." Thus Vergil introduces the descent to the Underworld in book 6 as historical and prophetic but also artistic. To what paradise will the artist aspire, to what hell submit? What failure will he risk, with what result, for his art, his soul, his dying wish? If the biographical tradition is true and Vergil on his deathbed wished that the *Aeneid* be destroyed, was it his own failure, like that of Daedalus, that he wished to obliterate? And was he right finally to relent?

With Putnam, we leave this reading of the *Aeneid* on a question central to it—the power of art to tell truths or lies, about heroes and heroism, about progress, hope, and history, even about itself. This artistic question is also clearly a philosophic one, Platonic in fact.[28] Putnam helps us understand that by linking the poetic and political enterprises, Vergil injected into the *Aeneid* a deeply problematical question of art's complicity in sweetening too much by its magic the destructive power of history.

As we will see in Part II, Vergil mastered a sophisticated skill, the technique of artistic distancing and layering, specifically in order to embed within his poetry a discourse on poetry. Vergil uses this conceptual and aesthetic method throughout his work. It is the intricate scaffolding that underlies the manifold paradoxes we have been tracing throughout the *Aeneid*, all held together by a supporting architecture of meaning-bearing form. Using philological and interpretive skills examined by the contributors to this volume and taught by Vergil himself, readers can reflect both in detail and in sum on the meaning of the entire poem, as in the final lines Vergil, master lover of words, takes his leave of us, leaving us alone with his ending.

PART II:
THE USES OF TRADITION AND THE MAKING OF MEANING

In the second part of the investigation of this book's title, *Why Vergil?*, we turn from the intrinsic quality of Vergil's poetry and the benefits and pleasures of understanding a master's craft to questions of poetic, cultural, and historical context, meaning, and use. Why did Vergil use the traditions he inherited as he did, especially those from Homer? Why was it that so many figures of Western letters since Vergil have engaged him in a centuries-long conversation, especially about the power of words to construct meaning? This conversation, still vibrant among some of the best poets and artists of the twentieth century, is one whose terms some critics say Vergil has set. What empire of cultural discourse did our poet found?

And if we ask the question that way, we must ask another — what is the value of that cultural empire? Could Vergil have been right to wish his masterpiece destroyed, perhaps anticipating our era's cultural critics? Or does his mastery make possible the creative destruction of the very empire he founded, in order for us to re-create, as he did for Rome in the first-century B.C.E., a new sensibility for a new world?

How do we understand the fact that we are still reading today a poem that is over two thousand years old? What has happened during those two millennia to keep our text alive? How has Vergil been understood during all that time, and how does that history affect the way we understand him today? These are the kinds of questions implied in this book's title. Just as the selections in Part I are assembled in answer to questions about why we should read Vergil's epic as poetry and story, so I have selected essays and poetry in Part II that help us consider why and how we read Vergil's work within the European literary tradition and in the United States in 1999, and beyond.

Vergil as Modern Poet

As chance would have it, the first work of Vergilian criticism I ever read was Brooks Otis' book, *Virgil: A Study in Civilized Poetry*, first published in 1964, now challenged on important and, I think, valid grounds.[29] The questions that Otis posed advanced my interest in Vergil early in my career from one of philological pleasure to intellectual weight, for Otis identified Vergil as *modern*: "What did [Vergil] do that Homer did not do, so that in the doing an obvious 'imitation' of Homer could become the true epic of a metropolis that has vastly more in common with contemporary New York than with [the Homeric cities of] Mycenae or Tiryns?" In his Introduction, Otis studied a phenomenon similar to the one Adam Parry had referred to as Vergil's two voices. Thirty-five years later, the nature of Vergil's modernity and of his voice remain the core concern of Vergilian scholarship.

Otis asked what poetic tools and techniques Vergil used to create that modernity. His chapter, "The Mystery of the *Aeneid*," claims that the work was "unprecedented in both its aim and its execution." From the point of view of a strong and important strand of Vergilian studies this is a striking statement, because much study of the *Aeneid* and Vergil's other works involves searches for his poetic sources, a method called *Quellenforschung*. Vergil's major source is the Homeric epics, the *Iliad* and the *Odyssey*, and in this discussion I have suggested how powerful the imprint of those works is within the *Aeneid*. Readers of the essays in this collection will notice how frequently authors cite Homer and other Greek and Roman writers in discussing Vergilian passages. And we will also see that some of the nineteenth century's negative critical opinion about Vergil's work stemmed from the assumption that Vergil was merely an imitator of his sources, especially Homer, and not an original, authentic voice. All the more important then was Otis' thesis about Vergil's originality.

To explain the nature of Vergil's originality, Otis analyzes Vergil's "imitation" of a Homeric episode, the accidental falls of Ajax and Nisus in their respective foot races in *Iliad* 23 and *Aeneid* 5. In the section included here of his chapter on what he calls Vergil's "subjectivity," Otis exposes Vergil's construction of his subjective voice, a radical revision of his Homeric inheritance. In his analysis of occasionally minute points of grammar, meter, word order, and narrative sequence, Otis reveals Vergil at work making of Homer's straightforward story what Otis calls a "psycho-drama." It is especially significant that in the drama the poet himself becomes one of the dramatis personae, one of the voices in the narrative through a "tell-tale phrase or word which either describes the character's feelings or Virgil's own feeling for him or — what is nearest to the fact — a subtle blend of both." It is the introduction or blending of the author's presence among the feelings of the characters that Otis terms Vergil's "subjective style," a style and voice absent from his Homeric models.

Michael Putnam advances this investigation by examining one of Vergil's "voices" in the *Aeneid*, the lyric voice, through Vergil's integration of Catullan influence in his epic. The poetry of Catullus, Vergil's near contemporary and a practitioner of the Neoteric style, is highly personal and emotional, often about love or hate, sometimes about both.

> Odi et amo. Quare id faciam, fortasse requiris.
>   nescio, sed fieri sentio et excrucior.

> I love and I hate. How could that be, perhaps you ask.
>   I don't know, but I feel it happening and I am in agony.

> (Catullus 85)[30]

It is all the more enlightening to understand through Putnam's article, "The Lyric Genius of the *Aeneid*," excerpted here, how Vergil "lyricizes" his epic, as he notified us he would do in his invocation to Erato in book 7. Thus we have another analysis of the multiplicity of voices that Vergil wove into his poem. Specifically, Putnam analyzes the many ways throughout the *Aeneid* that Vergil recalls one fairly short poem, Catullus 11,[31] and then he analyzes a variety of Catullan influences in one Vergilian passage, when Aeneas meets his father Anchises in the Underworld. Putnam thus enables us to consider book 6 from yet another perspective. His article ends by turning our attention again to the end of the *Aeneid*, and the meaning of Vergil's lyric voice for that ending.

In the analysis of Vergil's poem, with Otis and Putnam as our guides, we learn to observe Vergil remaking an old form and its attendant worldview through confrontation and amalgamation of a new literary sensibility and thus of different types of human experience. That agenda — to remake the old through confrontation with the new — may be at the core of the vitality of Western literature and culture.[32] It is also a prototype of the terrain on which today's cultural confrontations are taking place.

Vergil's artistic biography reveals a consistent practice of formal revision and reconstruction, starting with his early works, the book of ten short pastoral poems called the *Eclogues* or *Bucolics*. The *Eclogues* takes as its model not Homer but Theocritus, a Greek poet of the third century B.C.E. Theocritus wrote poems, called *Idylls*, about shepherds in summer song and repose from their rustic labors, singing often about love and loss. With many clear imitations of his Theocritean models,

Vergil's *Eclogues* have long been acknowledged as foundational for European poetry, indeed in the words of Richard Jenkyns, "probably the most influential group of short poems ever written."[33]

These apparently light, even frivolous little poems are in fact endlessly complex, and worlds of scholarly and critical prose have been written about them. From the point of view of our study of the *Aeneid*, it is important to include a brief look at these marvelous poems, for Vergil's poetic method and agenda are largely set in them: to inject his contemporary Roman content into ancient and venerable Greek cultural conventions and to revise a traditional form so that it can carry meaning that is fundamentally different from that of its antecedent.

The excerpt by Annabel Patterson, taken from the introduction to her book, *Pastoral and Ideology: Virgil to Valéry*, is an example of the vast and superb literature on the *Eclogues*. Patterson's book helps place the *Eclogues* in the European tradition, in which, she notes, the cultural reception of these poems often reflects the cultural assumptions of the readers and their times, a phenomenon that surrounds the *Aeneid* as well.

Patterson's Introduction starts — as did our discussion of the *Aeneid* — with the first lines of the first poem:

> Tityre, tu patulae recubans sub tegmine fagi
> Silvestrem tenui Musam meditaris avena;
> Nos patria finis et dulcia linquimus arva.
> Nos patriam fugimus; tu, Tityre, lentus in umbra
> Formosam resonare doces Amaryllida silvas.

> Tityrus, you, reclining under the covering of the spreading beech, meditate a silvan Muse on a slender pipe. I leave my fatherland's boundaries and sweet fields; I depart my fatherland in exile. You, Tityrus, at ease in the shade, are teaching the forests to echo shapely Amaryllis.

> (*Eclogue* 1.1–5)

Among many issues important to our study of the *Aeneid*, Patterson considers the complexity in the *Eclogues* of the author's role within his poems in terms of twentieth-century theories of authorship and the role of the author within the work. In particular, she examines the pronouns "*tu…nos…nos…tu*" in lines 1, 3, and 4, "you…we…we…you," and thereby the relationship of the characters to each other within the poem, to events and ideas outside the poem, and to the poet.

Patterson's discussion is difficult, as are the *Eclogues*. She alerts us to Vergil's complexity, especially regarding comparisons among apparently simple elements. When we meet language in the *Aeneid* that recalls the pastoral sensibility of the *Eclogues* — for example, the Trojans' arrival in Italy in book 7 and Aeneas' meeting with Evander in book 8 — we can hear also a signal that a complex poetic technique is operating in these apparently simple moments.

Our interest in opening lines continues, as William W. Batstone introduces us to the first lines of Vergil's middle work, the *Georgics*. After working with a snippet of Shakespeare so that we can observe his technique in English before practicing it in Latin, Batstone uses another modern approach to reading, called reader-response criticism, to take us carefully through two passages, *Georgics* 1.1–5 and 43–46. As a result, he reveals the effects on the reader or listener of the precise choices of word order and grammatical form that Vergil used. The technique also reminds us that a reader's, even a beginning student's, first reactions to the poetry can be a starting place for valuable understanding.

Batstone also considers, as we have done in Part I of this essay, why all this technique matters. His answer corresponds to a characteristic of the *Aeneid* as well.

> The *Georgics* are a rich poem. They continually say that everything they consider is not one thing but always many things. And they not only say this; they make their reader participate in an experience of mutability and shifting perspectives. The poem's surface speaks of and imitates *varietas* ["diversity"] which is not merely aesthetic, but epistemological and ethical....[I]t is the number of thoughts we can and do think about things, the number of ways we feel, that tell us both who we are and what the world we live in is like.[34]

The subjectivity of the *Aeneid*, its multiple voices, are ways to describe the phenomenon that Batstone is also describing. Vergil makes us participate in his poem, not just read it. The poem's shifting stances provide ethical exercise through aesthetic and intellectual pleasure. If we read well, the result, as Batstone tells, is that Vergil can "make his audience large" and help us individually to "contain multitudes," as he did, multitudes of meaning, knowledge, and empathy.

Both Patterson and Batstone engage current theories of literary criticism to understand and appreciate Vergil's art and contributions, with good result in my view. Their investigations of Vergil's two early works that precede the *Aeneid* help us grasp yet more deeply the richness of his achievement and why it is that his works have had such long and important influence on subsequent artists.[35]

Vergil and European Letters

For an overview of the influence of Vergil's works, the early *Nachleben* or after-life of Vergil's works, Charles Fantazzi's article, included here, provides guidance. He takes us through the reception of the works in the Roman Empire and especially their early Christian use, notably in regard to *Eclogue* 4, in which a prophetic vision of a utopian future begins with the birth of a child. Vergil's works were consulted up to the Renaissance as a source of prophecy, the *sortes Vergilianae*, and Vergil himself, though a pagan, was seen as one who was "unwittingly inspired by the Christian god." The reaction to Christian allegorization of Vergil's works during the Enlightenment and modern period may account for the paucity of contemporary attention given to their genuine spiritual content; Bacon's article, included here, is an exception. Fantazzi also discusses Vergil's role in Dante's *Divine Comedy*. Dante's work was written in Italian not Latin, then the 'official language' of Europe. In using Italian, Dante opened the "way for national literatures in the vernacular languages," thus breaking through the convention of the dominant culture in Dante's time, which was Roman.

Fantazzi goes on to remind us of Matthew Arnold's opinion of Vergil's poetry in the nineteenth century, and of T. S. Eliot's in the twentieth. Fantazzi ends his review of Vergil's European reception with the 1945 novel of Hermann Broch, *The*

Death of Virgil, also discussed by Annabel Patterson, and of which a few passages are reprinted here. Broch was a refugee from the Nazis, and his novel, a Joycean tour de force, recounts the final day of Vergil's life through the internal conversation Broch creates for him about the meaning of his life and his art.

With Fantazzi's overview, we are prepared for more analysis of Vergil's influence on his European successors, starting with Dante (1265-1321). Rachel Jacoff and Jeffrey T. Schnapp have assembled a collection of essays on the influence of both Vergil and Ovid on Dante's works through a study of the manifold allusions from the Latin authors in the Italian, especially in the ways Dante rewrites his sources. Sections from the introduction to their book are included here.

Jacoff and Schnapp see Dante performing on his sources a process of revision similar to the one Vergil performed on his, a process of "continual subversion and revisionary rewriting": "Virgil's authority is simultaneously affirmed and denied, built up and undermined." Thus the study of Dante's allusions places "the narrowly literary issue of imitation within a broader historical frame: that of the overlap and opposition between Christian and classical culture." In this kind of ambivalence about his model we see Dante at his most Vergilian.

Another contribution in this brief survey of Vergil's progeny is John Rexine's review of a book by Donna B. Hamilton about Vergil's influence on Shakespeare, specifically in *The Tempest*. Rexine reminds us of the play's contemporary political context in the time of King James I (1566-1625, king from 1603), citing Hamilton's argument that *The Tempest* contains both apology for and an indirect, constitutionalist rhetoric of opposition to the king's absolutist policies. Hamilton contends that Shakespeare used the first six books of the *Aeneid* as a referent, which he remodeled to serve contemporary needs: "[c]ontemporary culture is seen reworked in the Shakespearean reworking of Vergilian structures." Rexine notes that once again we have evidence of two great poets in "profound relationship" with each other and in "creative use" of inherited cultural tradition.

Finally, Barbara Kiefer Lewalski studies John Milton's use of genre in the seventeenth century as a way to convey meaning, an approach reminiscent of Vergil's, discussed by Otis and Putnam. In *Paradise Lost and the Rhetoric of Literary Forms*, Lewalski reviews the way Milton embedded a variety of literary forms within his epic, itself, of course, deeply indebted to Vergil's work. Like Dante, Milton reworked his source, redefining classical heroism in terms of Christian understandings. Renaissance literary theory also influenced Milton's understanding of the meanings and messages that individual genres carried, as Roman ideas about poetry influenced Vergil. Just as we learned above from Putnam that Vergil incorporated elements of lyric poetry into his epic in order to add to the epic's emotional repertoire parts of human experience it did not normally carry, so too Lewalski studies the way Milton wove meaning throughout his great epic by using a variety of literary genres.

From these brief examples of scholarly analysis, we can see the nature of Vergil's guidance in works of Western letters: Dante's project to make from pagan epic the story of Christian salvation in the *Divine Comedy*; Shakespeare's work in *The Tempest* to negotiate the polarities of contemporary political controversy; and Milton's encyclopedic taxonomy of genre as interpretive signals for a Christian worldview built from pagan Roman material in *Paradise Lost*. These poets, now monuments of tradition, each made a revolution in the tradition he inherited. Vergil showed them how.

Vergil and Modern History

Several readers of the *Aeneid* have noted a parallel between the temper of the times and the times' reception of the *Aeneid*, and between readers' personal politics and their interpretations of the poem.[36] The *Aeneid* invites this historical pendulum of interpretation and popularity because it is a historical poem, referring both explicitly and allusively to the history of Vergil's time. From his early works through to the *Aeneid*, Vergil, like Dante, Shakespeare and Milton, engaged the world in which he lived through his art. Each in turn affected, was in part responsible for, the cultural consciousness of his time. Such consciousness is a fragile, amorphous, and elusive entity, of which art is both reflection and creator.

It is startling and unsettling to discover, in the course of becoming educated, the degree to which aspects of life that we take for granted within our cultures and histories are in fact products of time, place, and circumstance.[37] Among the most disturbing discoveries is the idea that even our understanding of our collective past, our history, taught early in our schooling as a set of fixed facts within a single reality, is rather a cumulative product about which cultural choices have been made, often unconsciously though sometimes not.

Erich Gruen's 1992 Presidential address to the American Philological Association recounts the process that shaped Roman consciousness of historical origins prior to the creation of the *Aeneid*. It was a collective sorting of possibilities about Aeneas and other candidates for the founder of Rome, so as to situate the Roman world in a creative and subtle relationship to its predecessor and perceived cultural superior, Greece. Gruen places Rome's creation of cultural identity in the context of our contemporary questions about the value and status of cultural traditions and perspectives newly asserting their worth in relation to long-accepted understandings of European and American history.[38]

Just as the Romans sifted diverse traditions to create their founding myths, so too the founders of the United States mined classical and especially Roman Republican traditions in search of cultural elements to adopt. They chose aspects of the Greek and Roman past that graced and legitimated their revolutionary venture and new world, as Meyer Reinhold tells us, in his article included in the collection. More comfortable with Cato than Aeneas[39] and finding greater community with Vergil's pastoral and georgic works as being more suited to our country's early interests and realities, our ancestors in the United States, with a few exceptions such as John Adams, rarely prized Vergil's *Aeneid*.

How much we have still to learn about the early making of our freedom, and its withholding, is glimpsed in the fact that John Adams' positive view of the *Aeneid* was shared, not by his civic peers, but by a female slave, Phillis Wheatley, roughly his contemporary, Bostonians both (John Adams 1735–1826; Wheatley arrived in Boston in 1761). This young black woman, excluded from formal education and thus European culture by the laws and customs of her time, nonetheless knew Latin. She loved and imitated the literature that was being used in the early years of our country to help define the society that excluded her. Wheatley's poem, "To Maecenas," appeals to Maecenas for the kind of literary support for her work that he afforded the poets of his day. (Maecenas was the great literary patron in Augustan Rome for the circle of poets to which Vergil, Horace, and others belonged; he was also a close comrade of the emperor Augustus.) Her poem refers throughout to ancient Greek and Roman literature, including the Muses and of course Homer and Vergil. The only other poet she names in this poem is the African-born ancient Latin play-wright Terence, her fellow countryman.[40]

Despite exceptions such as Adams and Wheatley, Atlantic disinterest in the *Aeneid* nonetheless continued into the nineteeth century. Percy Bysshe Shelley con-ferred on the works of Homer, Dante, and Milton the mantle of epic but suggested that "the title of epic in its highest sense be refused to the *Aeneid*," for "Virgil, with a modesty which ill became his genius, had affected the fame of an imitator, even whilst he created anew all that he copied."[41] The nineteen-hundred-year anniversaries of Vergil's birth and death went uncelebrated in Europe and the United States, a situation markedly different from this century's experience.

In *Darkness Visible: A Study of Vergil's Aeneid*, the introduction of which is antholo-gized here, W. R. Johnson reviews the history of Vergil's reputation from roughly 1825 to 1975, especially as it was influenced by Matthew Arnold in the nineteenth century and T. S. Eliot in the twentieth: Arnold, unsympathetic to Vergil although perhaps for the right reasons; Eliot a fan, but much, in Johnson's view, for the wrong reasons.

Johnson locates scholarly criticism of the *Aeneid* on an interpretive divide between optimists and pessimists, two "political allegories." On the one hand are those whose sensibility aligns them with Eliot and for whom the *Aeneid* offers optimistic hope in history and for humankind. On the other hand are those who read with Arnold and for whom the *Aeneid*, in its subjective multiplicity of voices, forever qualifies such hopes in the name of history's victims.

Johnson demonstrates how closely critical thought about the *Aeneid* parallels contemporary thoughts and attitudes about history and politics, a thesis Patterson develops regarding the *Eclogues*. Such parallels within the perilous universe where poetry and power co-exist do not diminish the value of Vergil's art. On the con-trary, they indicate its relevance to issues that have mattered compellingly to Vergil's readers over millennial distances of time.

Vergil and Twentieth-Century Letters

We have seen how some of Vergil's early descendants modeled his ability to invest form with new content. What of his current heirs? How have twentieth-century artists used their inheritance from Vergil to graft our new realities onto his ancient art?

Some of the modern works included here refer explicitly to their Vergilian ante-cedent, as in Joseph Brodsky's "Eclogue IV"; sometimes the reference is only generic, as in Robert Frost's poem of georgic labor, "Two Tramps in Mud Time." And some-times the debt is so large that it permeates the whole in debts manifold, as in Derek Walcott's *Omeros*, Homeric to be sure in title and characters, Vergilian in its trans-formation of cultural code. I have devoted considerable space in this volume to contemporary artists not only because of my desire to share my pleasure in their new words. I wish also to make an argument for the vitality of Vergil's work across huge gaps of historical and cultural experience, of its flexibility across time and hegemony, and of the continuing utility of its lessons on the marriage of poetry and power.

I have chosen for this collection only a few of the twentieth-century works that bear the mark of Vergil's influence; it is by no means an exhaustive survey.[42] It is, however, designed to demonstrate the continuing concern of world-class artists with issues of historical and cultural significance and to let us hear their conversation with each other across centuries and cultures.[43] The works are presented roughly in the order of Vergil's own works from pastoral through georgic to epic verse.

Three poems by Robert Frost are included to demonstrate the presence in one poet's work, as in Vergil's, of poetry in the pastoral, georgic, and epic modes. The first of his poems here is "Build Soil—A Political Pastoral," which explicitly evokes Vergil's *Eclogue* 1 through the characters in the two poems, Tityrus and Meliboeus. It also unites a poetic and a political agenda, in its poet-farmer's platform criticizing New Deal agricultural policy.[44] Joseph Brodsky's "Eclogue IV" is another pastoral poem, in which Brodsky rewrites Vergilian pastoral, as Vergil rewrote Theocritean. Brodsky accomplishes this revision not by making forests worthy of consuls as Vergil did in his *Eclogue* 4, but by making snowbound Russian forests worthy of the pastoral tradition of perpetual Italian spring. He injects into the tradition of Western European letters a culture for centuries in contested relation to it, which changes the tropes of both. Dana Burgess imaginatively reads Spike Lee's movie, *Do The Right Thing*, set in ghetto Brooklyn, as a pastoral exercise in which the audience is wrenched out of predictable meanings to see in the Brooklyn neighborhood of Bedford-Stuyvesant, not a ghettoized hell on earth, but an urban garden of social harmony, whose fragile peace is imperiled by the forces of hate outside it.

In the dedication of his translation of Vergil's *Georgics*, "Dedicatory Stanzas: To Stephen Spender," C. Day Lewis reminds us, as Vergil did in his *Georgics*, of the harsh reassurance of the land especially in times that know the starker realities of war, of georgic labor and the labor of the word in times of epic destruction, in this case, World War II. In "Two Tramps in Mud Time," Frost's New England farmer contemplates the morality of labor, pleasure, need, and love—in the country, in the woods, in art.

Allen Tate's poem, "Aeneas at Washington," transports Aeneas from his old home in Troy not to his new world in Italy, but to ours, in our own kindred war of refounding. And Rosanna Warren recalls Turnus' last moment in "Turnus (*Aeneid* XII)," in concise summary of the pastoral hope and epic bloodshed of the *Aeneid*'s last moment of love and rage, capturing the taut instant of poetic and moral suspension at the end of the poem when all meaning is simultaneous and as essential to life as blood. Auden's poem, "The Shield of Achilles," enables us to compare three settings of the same image: Homer's in *Iliad* 18 in the eighth century B.C.E.; Vergil's revision of it in the first century B.C.E. in *Aeneid* 8; and Auden's own twentieth-century version. On Vergil's model of critical imitation, Auden contrasts epic splendor to the twin madnesses of modern times—war and poverty. The third Frost work is the poem he wrote and recited for the inauguration of John F. Kennedy in 1960. It has given us the phrase, the "marriage of poetry and power," and its hopefulness seemed far less complicated then than it does now.

All these artists refashion the Vergilian tradition, but perhaps none so thoroughly as Derek Walcott in his long epic poem, *Omeros*. That new monument, published in 1990, is Homeric in appearance and Vergilian in method, for Walcott, like Vergil, redefines our idea of heroism, making of a kidnapped African's forced voyage into slavery an epic journey, of the recreation of one world from the destruction of another.[45] In this poem of 325 pages, only a few of which are included here of course, we can see fully at work Vergil's method in his reworking of Homer, as Walcott reworks them both. It is difficult for me to imagine a more radical reformulation of the world through poetry's agency than the tearing away of the meaning of heroism from its original epic vision of martial, agonistic strength to mean instead the strength of a people in their valorous survival of the most profound victimization. That revolution in meaning is comparable to the new questions Vergil posed through his hero's final enraged act in the *Aeneid*, a question unthought of in the Homeric code. In Homer's name, Walcott continues Vergil's artistic reformation of the Homeric world that is the inheritance of us all.[46]

Broad questions about the power, role, and responsibility of art are Hermann Broch's subject in his novel, *The Death of Virgil*, published in 1945. Both Patterson and Fantazzi in this collection have prepared us to meet Broch's complex novel, in which he asks as surely as any scholar if, how, and why Vergil speaks to us across millennia.

If the pedagogical agenda of this collection of essays has been a success, readers will have less trepidation at its end than they may have had at the start about tackling difficult texts such as *Omeros* and *The Death of Virgil*. With confidence gained from the practice of play with the *Aeneid*'s first Latin words, they will meet Walcott's poetry and Broch's prose also with the spirit of play and adventure in a task that will repay the effort.

Here are a few of the words Broch gives Vergil in his last, fever-ridden day. The first passage is pastoral in description, still resonating from the *Eclogues*. The second concerns the intention, drive, and will of the artist, which could also describe the hero's journey. In the third selection, Broch's Vergil meditates on the relation between art and transcendent truth, art and spirit, moving from the literal allegorization of Vergil as a pre-Christian visionary to a Vergil of profound but more general spiritual insight. The fourth excerpt records Broch's warning about the deceptiveness of artistic beauty, reminding us again of Plato's worry about art's lies, a subject that we know occupies the *Aeneid* as well.

> ...and it was as if all brooks and ponds of yore poured themselves into this stream of memory, drizzling between the fragrant willows, drizzling between banks verdant with trembling reeds, lovely images without end, themselves a cluster picked by the hands of a child, a cluster of lilies, gilly-flowers, poppies, narcissus and buttercups...

> ...but the great line of his life was not of his choosing nor in accord with his free will, it had been a compulsion, a compulsion on a level with the redemption and the evil of existence, a fate-enjoined yet fate-surpassing compulsion, commanding him to search for his own shape in that of death and thus to win the freedom of his soul...

> ...and he knew also that the duty of all art lay in this sort of truth, lay in the self-perceptive finding and proclaiming of truth, the duty which has been laid on the artist, so that the soul, realizing the great equilibrium between the ego and the universe, might recover herself in the universe, perceiving in this self-recognition that the deepening of the ego was an increase of substance in the universe, in the world...it was precisely by this means that it was enabled to widen the inner and outer boundaries of existence to new reality...

> ...but he knew also that the beauty of the symbol, were it ever so precise in its reality, was never its own excuse for being, that whenever such was the

case, whenever beauty existed for its own sake, there art was attacked at its very roots, because the created deed then came to be its own opposite, because the thing created was then suddenly substituted for that which creates...

As we have seen, Broch's investigation of Vergil's misgivings about his work in the *Aeneid* are justified by the ancient traditions about his life, which say that in dying he wished the *Aeneid* destroyed. Broch's own experience of world war and of art is a modern analogue of the artist's need to understand the value of his work in a world falling apart.

Yet another justification for Broch's approach lies within the poem itself. Michael C. J. Putnam, as we saw, reads in Vergil's introduction to *Aeneid* 7 and his *maius opus* ["great work"] an essay on the role of the artist. Charles Segal finds a similar message in the *Aeneid*'s very beginning. Segal reminds us that, through Vergil's repetition in the next-to-the-last line of the epic, *Aeneid* 12.951, of the line used to describe Aeneas in his first appearance in book 1, *Aeneid* 1.92 (*solvuntur frigore membra*, "his limbs weaken with chill"), Vergil returns us at the very end to the very beginning, with ritualistic satisfaction. On that pattern, we turn last in this collection to Segal's article on the *Aeneid*'s first book, returning to the practice of close reading of Vergil's language, to build interpretive meaning with philological care.

Segal's discussion echoes many topics and themes in the contents of this collection. He is also concerned with Vergil as artist, recounting the several moments in the *Aeneid* when art becomes the subject of itself. Thus notably in introducing each half of his poem, Vergil puts prominently before his audience opportunities to reflect on their experience of his poetry as they are experiencing it. This is a pastoral trope, of artist creating a work of art whose subject is the creation of a work of art. It evokes an artist's consciousness at work as surely as does Broch's modern psychological stream.

In ending his essay with the end of the epic, Segal wonders about the connection between hero, poet, and emperor, about the violence of creativity regardless of its object, the tragic knowledge of the intimacy between violence and creation, and a poet's responsibility to withhold or reveal it, no matter the cost in tears. We return at the very end of the *Aeneid* to the very first questions of the *Eclogues*, to the exercise of poetic self-scrutiny on the value of the poetic enterprise, especially in the context of the history it records and shapes.

Why Words?

Simple toys, intricately woven sets of symbols, perennial questions of value and meaning—all this is the work of words and of Vergil, one of the West's great masters of the craft of constructing words into poetry. Disassembling Vergil's construction to understand it better is the reading skill exercised through this collection, as one takes apart a clock to see how it works. The discovery of the machinery seems only to increase the questions about the mechanism: not only how time works, but why time.

The essays and literature collected here for readers of Vergil's *Aeneid* similarly scrutinize the machinery to understand the creation. The various analyses of the poetry of the *Aeneid* take us progressively through a poetry workroom so that we can see the edifice from the inside, be familiar with its elements and feel at home among them. The story of the epic's own past and future, before and after its creation, lengthens our perspective on it, contextualizing its achievement. At the end of our reading, we can know the *Aeneid* both from deeply within and with extended vision. We can understand the first book in its opening lines of turmoil and uncertainty through to their establishment of a foundation that will turn out to support ages of human and historical struggle, hope, and tragedy. We will do so armed with virtues inspired by the gods and taught, in suffering and in joy, through our own experience and each other's words.

Notes

[1]"... — only singing itself into the structure of the verses — opening up between the very words a swooning, breathless, momentary abyss so that life could be comprehended and death be apprehended in these silent depths, which have become silent to disclose the completeness of the whole, the simultaneous stream of creation in which the eternal rests;...," Hermann Broch, *The Death of Virgil*, Jean Starr Untermeyer, trans. (New York: Grosset & Dunlap. The Universal Library) 1945, 84, and herein.

[2]John Frederick Nims, *Western Wind. An Introduction to Poetry*, 2nd ed. (New York: Random House, 1983). An excerpt from Nims' book is included herein. Also consider the following by Larry Gelbart: "'I love to play with language; make it do tricks, turn a word inside out to see if it's got a hidden meaning tucked away somewhere, or perhaps find that it's capable of an extra entendre or two.'" *Laughing Matters: On Writing 'M*A*S*H,' 'Tootsie,' 'Oh, God!' and a Few Other Funny Things.* Quoted by Christopher Lehmann-Haupt in his review of Gelbart's book, *New York Times*, March 12, 1998, E8. See also John Hollander, *The Work of Poetry* (New York: Columbia University Press, 1997): "Art in general grows out of a development of — rather than maturation *out of* — certain aspects of childhood. Just so with poetry and the language games children play....It is not in an early love for truth, nor for persuasion, nor even for order, that poets emerge, but in a love of language. That, ultimately, language can be coaxed into strange sorts of truth-telling is never the point at the beginning," 8; and Thomas N. Habinek, *The Politics of Latin Literature: Writing, Identity, and Empire in Ancient Rome* (Princeton, NJ: Princeton University Press, 1998): "The ludic experience of literature has an educative function potentially more meaningful and more progressive than does indoctrination in any canon, regardless of who constructs it," 5.

[3]Josiah Ober suggests that it is possible to popularize, and I would add to teach, "in ways that are at once accessible and serious, to be responsible without losing [the] sense of fun." "Responsible Popularization: An Introduction," *CB* 72.2 (1996) 85–91, 85.

[4]I include a few references to my own experience, including the early years, as an invitation to young readers of Vergil and of poetry in general, and in gratitude to all their teachers. I also include them to indicate my interest in the modes of scholarship that are questioning the rigid separation of the personal and the professional, of subjectivity and objectivity, which is an issue important in Vergil's works. Note for example the session on "Autobiographical Criticism and Medieval Studies" at the Illinois Medieval Association conference, February 21, 1998, Eastern Illinois University, Charleston IL, and the paper by Anne Clark Bartlett, "Linking Lives: Autobiographical Criticism and Medieval Studies," forthcoming in *Essays in Medieval Studies* 15 (1998). For a set of essays on autobiography and scholarly careers in Classics, see Judith P. Hallett and Thomas Van Nortwick, *Compromising Traditions: The Personal Voice in Classical Scholarship* (London and New York: Routledge, 1997).

[5]Edgar Allan Poe, "The Bells," *The Complete Poetry of Edgar Allan Poe*, ed. Jay Parini (New York: Signet Classics, 1996) 118–121.

[6]Ennius, *Ann.* 109, Otto Skutsch, ed. (Oxford: Clarendon Press, 1985).

[7]Quotations from the works of Vergil are taken from the R. A. B. Mynors ed., *P. Vergili Maronis Opera* (Oxford: Oxford University Press, 1969). See also Edgar C. Reinke, "Onomatopoetic Alliteration in Vergil's *Aeneid*, Books 1–6," *CB* 62.3 (1986) 37–42 and herein, and compare the following line of Ennius with Vergil's adaptation of it: *At tuba*

terribili sonitu taratantara dixit, Ann. 451 (Skutsch); *At tuba terribilem sonitu procul aere canoro, Aen.* 9.503.

[8]Richard Jones, from "Have you written much prose?" *48 Questions* (Los Angeles: Bombshelter Press, a Tebot Bach Book,1998) 31.

[9]"...Virgil may not be, surely is not, the greatest poet who ever lived; but…in this mastery of the disposition of words within a formal pattern, he has no rivals," Adam Parry, "The Two Voices of Virgil's *Aeneid*," *Arion* 2.4 (1963) 66–80, 67, and herein.

[10]Italo Calvino, "Philosophy and Literature," in *The Uses of Literature: Essays*, trans. Patrick Creagh (San Diego: Harcourt Brace, Harvest Book, 1986) 39–49, 40.

[11]See Barbara Johnson, "Philology: What is at Stake?" in *On Philology*, Jan Ziolkowski, ed. (University Park, PA: Pennsylvania State University Press, 1990) 26–30.

[12]"We are trapped in meanings that circulate like blood." Rosanna Warren, "Turnus (*Aeneid XII*)," *Arion* 3rd ser., 3.2 & 3 (Fall 1995/Winter 1996) 174, and herein.

[13]For a good discussion of Book 3, see David Quint, *Epic and Empire. Politics and Generic Form from Virgil to Milton* (Princeton, NJ: Princeton University Press, 1993) 55–61.

[14]T. S. Eliot, "What Is a Classic?," *On Poetry and Poets* (New York: Farrar, Straus & Giroux, Noonday Press, 1961) 52–74, 63–64.

[15]"Visions of Maturity," *In a Different Voice* (Cambridge, MA: Harvard University Press, 1982) 151–74, esp. 151–53.

[16]For a collection of essays on women in the ancient Greek and Roman worlds and literature, see Helene P. Foley, ed., *Reflections of Women in Antiquity* (New York: Gordon and Breach Science Publishers, 1981), esp. Christine G. Perkell, "On Creusa, Dido, and the Quality of Victory in Virgil's *Aeneid*," 355–77. More recently, see Nancy Sorkin Rabinowitz and Amy Richlin, eds., *Feminist Theory and the Classics* (New York: Routledge, 1993). On Roman women writers, see the bibliographical note in Thomas N. Habinek, *The Politics of Latin Literature: Writing, Identity, and Empire in Ancient Rome* (Princeton, NJ: Princeton University Press, 1998) 209–10.

[17]"In that secluded vale (*in valle reducta*) where Aeneas finds his father, he receives from him something of an answer to the mysteries of life and death. The answer — part Plato, part Pythagoras, part Orphic, part Stoic, and, in its language, part Epicurean…." M. Owen Lee, *The Olive-Tree Bed and Other Quests* (Toronto: University of Toronto Press, 1997). Similarly R. J. Tarrant, "Aeneas and the Gates of Sleep," *CP* 77 (1982) 51–55: "It would be wrong to suggest that the outlook of the *Aeneid* is consistently Platonic, any more than it is consistently Stoic or Epicurean…," 54. See also Helen Bacon's article in this collection, "The *Aeneid* as a Drama of Election," *TAPA* 116 (1986) 305–34, 321, and herein.

[18]The term "miniaturist" occurs regularly regarding Vergil's style, but I came upon it in David West, "Multiple-Correspondence Similes in the *Aeneid*," *JRS* 59 (1969) 40–49, 49. See also Lee, *Olive-Tree Bed*, 61.

[19]That philosophy and poetry fruitfully co-exist is certainly not to be taken for granted. Quite the opposite; from Plato on, Western letters have been occupied instead with something of a war between the two, or at least a quarrel. See Thomas Gould, *The Ancient Quarrel Between Poetry and Philosophy* (Princeton: Princeton University Press, 1990); note page 209 for a glimpse of the connection between mathematics and philosophy; Stanley Rosen, *The Quarrel Between Philosophy and Poetry: Studies in Ancient Thought* (New York: Routledge, 1988). I believe Vergil, however, was creating at the intersection of this quarreling pair. See George Santayana: "In philosophy itself investigation and reasoning are only preparatory and servile parts, means to an end. They terminate in insight.…Such contemplation is imaginative. No one can reach it who has not enlarged his mind and tamed his heart. A philosopher who attains it is, for the moment, a poet; and a poet who turns his practiced and passionate imagination on the order of all things, or on anything in the light of the whole, is for that moment a philosopher," *Three Philosophical Poets: Lucretius, Dante and Goethe* (Cambridge, MA: Harvard University Press, 1910) 10–11. See also Calvino, "Philosophy and Literature." In the Conclusion, I consider the importance of the quarrel between poetry and philosophy for understanding Vergil's works.

[20]*Artifices of Eternity: Horace's Fourth Book of Odes* (Ithaca, NY: Cornell University Press, 1986) 320–321.

[21]See Matthew S. Santirocco for a discussion on the tendency in scholarship on the Augustan poets to describe "the poets' representation of Augustus and of themselves in relation to him in terms of simple pro and con positions which fail to do justice either to the complexity

of the textual strategies or to the personal and political experiences out of which those strategies arose," "Horace and Augustan Ideology," *Arethusa* 28.1 (Winter 1995) 225–43, 226–27. Similarly, Gordon Williams, "Ideas and the Epic Poet," in the H. Bloom collection, *Virgil* (New York: Chelsea House Publishers, 1986) 181–91, 185; also, William S. Anderson, responding to Farrell, "Which *Aeneid* in Whose Nineties?," *Vergilius* 36 (1990) 81. For a critique of Parry's article, see Charles Martindale, "Rereading Virgil: divertimento," *Redeeming the text: Latin poetry and the hermeneutics of reception* (Cambridge: Cambridge University Press, 1993) 35–54.

[22]Peter White, *Promised Verse: Poets in the Society of Augustan Rome* (Cambridge, MA: Harvard University Press, 1993) 208. See also Tony Woodman and David West, *Poetry and Politics in the Age of Augustus* (Cambridge: Cambridge University Press, 1984); Anton Powell, ed., *Roman Poetry and Propaganda in the Age of Augustus* (London: London Classical Society, 1992); Barbara K. Gold, *Literary Patronage in Greece and Rome* (Chapel Hill, NC: University of North Carolina Press, 1987).

[23]Unlike Augustus, it would seem, both Aeneas and our poet accepted their destinies only with reluctance; see *Eclogue* 6.2–8 and *Georgics* 3.40–48.

[24]Richard Jenkyns ("Pathos, Tragedy and Hope in the *Aeneid*, *JRS* 77 [1985] 60–77) reminds us that, although the *Aeneid* deals explicitly with certain political issues, such as peace and authority, Vergil remains silent on others in the epic. His first *Eclogue*, for example, is concerned with liberty, a theme dropped in the *Aeneid*. Jenkyns concludes that Vergil "was not deceived," 62.

[25]On the silence of women's voices in the *Aeneid*, see S. Georgia Nugent, "Vergil's 'Voice of the Women' in *Aeneid* V," *Arethusa* 25.2 (Spring 1992) 255–289.

[26]See Lee's *Fathers and Sons in Virgil's Aeneid, Tum Genitor Natum* (Albany, NY: State University of New York Press, 1979). Lee, who hosted the intermission talks for the Saturday broadcasts of the Metropolitan Opera for several years, regularly combines music commentary with his readings of Vergil's works. See Lee's *"Per Nubila Lunam*: The Moon in Virgil's *Aeneid,"* *Vergilius* 34 (1988) 9–14 and "The Holy Grail," in *Olive-Tree Bed*.

[27]For a discussion of anger in Republican Rome and in the *Aeneid*, see Karl Galinsky, "The Anger of Aeneas," *AJP* 109 (Fall 1988) 321–48: anger can be a sign of "emotional security — as distinguished from hate and hostility" 312; "…Aeneas' anger is a fitting closure which, like the entire epic, is far from being one-dimensional and has several registers of significance," 326; "It is poetically fitting, then, that the end of the *Aeneid* should recapitulate the central theme on which the *Iliad* begins and by which it is permeated, that of mênis ["wrath"]. There is an unbroken line from the first book of the *Iliad* to the last book of the *Aeneid*," 345. Christine Perkell responds to Galinsky (and others), not primarily in regard to this article but more generally about approaches to reading texts, in "Ambiguity and Irony: The Last Resort?" *Helios*, 21.1 (1994) 63–74. On anger see also Roger A. Hornsby: "Rage is a given....It drives us through life, as the actions of the poem show, and it dies only at death as the suicide of Dido dramatically portrays. Without rage there can be no life, for rage is the will struggling to express itself. As a result it can be either destructive or constructive for the individual and for others. It follows then that the individual's rage must be organized so that it harms neither the person nor another." According to Hornsby, Aeneas learns that "to educate the will, is to educate the rage" *"Maior Nascitur Ordo,"* in *Mnemai, Classical Studies in Memory of Karl K. Hulley,* Harold D. Evjen, ed., (Chico, CA: Scholars Press, 1984) 103–120, 116–117.

[28]As Plato knew, an artist risks creating a "true lie," a lie that prevents one "from distinguishing between reality and unreality…whereby [one] is continually deceived and irrevocably ignorant." *The Republic*, Richard W. Sterling and William C. Scott, trans. (New York: Norton 1985), 2.382a–b.

[29]The grounds for my departure from Otis, from whom I have learned much, are related to his very title, "Civilized Poetry." In 1998, thirty-five years after Otis' book appeared, many people question the automatic equation of modernity with civilization.

[30]*Catulli Veronensis Liber*, Werner Eisenhut, ed. (Leipzig: Teubner, 1983).

[31]The image of the cut flower that appears in Catullus 11 occurs in Homer's *Iliad* at 8.306–308, and Fr. Lee discusses its appearance in the *Aeneid* in his article herein. It is rewarding to read the three versions of the image especially in light of the discussions of Otis, Putnam, and Lee.

[32]This conflictedness, along many parameters, may characterize Western cultural tradition as a whole. Francis Oakley, for example, criticizes proponents of the Western tradition for

failing "to recognize how conflicted in its intellectual commitments and educational ideas that tradition has been. In that very conflictedness, indeed, may be found the wellsprings of that cultural singularity which the proponents of the great books approach rightly think students should be helped to recognize and understand," *Community of Learning: The American College and the Liberal Arts Tradition* (Oxford: Oxford University Press, 1992) 125. Many such proponents, however, seem to advocate the great books not on these grounds but rather on the grounds, in my view, of an imagined stability they are presumed to embody.

[33]"Virgil and Arcadia," *JRS* 79 (1989) 26–39, 26.

[34] William W. Batstone, "On the Surface of the *Georgics,* " *Arethusa* 21 (1988) 227–45, 242, and herein.

[35]For the importance of relating Vergilian scholarship to twentieth-century critical theory, see Joseph Farrell, *op. cit.*, esp. 77–78.

[36]See Farrell, *ibid.*, 75, n. 33.

[37]See for example Oakley, *Community of Learning*, regarding the pervasiveness, largely invisible and thus taken for granted, of Western modes of thinking in the typical undergraduate curriculum: "So multiple, indeed, is the exposure of our students to things Western, that having examined or bumped up against so many Western 'trees' in the course of their studies, they may fail to grasp the dimension and distinguishing characteristics of the cultural wood of which those trees are a part, or, worse, fail to perceive that there *is* indeed such a wood, or, even, that they themselves are in it," 146–47. For an alternative view, regarding philology specifically, see Jan Ziolkowski, "Introduction," in *On Philology*, 10: "Nowhere in the descriptions of these courses [the 'Literature and Arts A' division of the Core Curriculum at Harvard] does one's eye meet the word *philology*, whereas anthropological and psychoanalytic approachs are mentioned explicitly....Philologists could make a strong case that lately they have been the victims, not the perpetrators, of exclusion." Ziolkowski's observation may not so much refute Oakley's contention as confirm it.

[38]Several scholars have been discussing what we have long thought of as the ancient Greek and Roman world in different terms recently, as the ancient Mediterranean world. That world was highly diverse, in race, ethnicity, and cultural tradition. Our image of a monolithic, Greco-Roman past is as false as the image of pristine white marble columns, instead of the bright, shiny, even gaudy displays they were. See Thomas N. Habinek, "Culture Wars: First Century B.C.E.," *The Politics of Latin Literature: Writing, Identity, and Empire in Ancient Rome* (Princeton, NJ: Princeton University Press, 1998); Molly Levine, "Multiculturalism and the Classics," *Arethusa*, 25.1 (Winter 1992) 215–20; Martha C. Nussbaum, *Cultivating Humanity: A Classical Defense of Reform in Liberal Education* (Cambridge, MA: Harvard Univeresity Press, 1997) 53ff.; James J. O'Donnell, "The Ancient and the Moderns," *Avatars of the Word. From Papyrus to Cyberspace* (Cambridge, MA: Harvard University Press, 1998).

More generally, see Wendy Steiner quoting Salman Rushdie: "*The Satanic Verses* celebrates hybridity, impurity, intermingling, the transformation that comes of new and unexpected combinations of human beings, cultures, ideas, politics, movies, songs. It rejoices in mongrelisation and fears the absolutism of the Pure. Melange, hotch-potch, a bit of this and a bit of that is how *newness enters the world*," (Chicago: University of Chicago Press, 1995) 114. Also Margaret Alexiou, "Greek Philology: Diversity and Difference," in *On Philology*, 53–56: "As the Nobel-prize-winning Greek poet, Odysseas Elytis, once said, every culture, especially as it gets older, needs 'intravenous infusions of civilisation serum' from younger and stronger ones," 60.

[39]See John D. Bernard, "Vergil: Prince of Song," in John D. Bernard, ed., *Vergil at 2000: Commemorative Essays on the Poet and his Influence* (New York, AMS Press, 1986) 1–12, 2:

> "Few of our greatest minds are—nor, if Reinhold is right, have ever been—informed by Vergil's complex vision or troubled by his song. We have heard Philomela infrequently, have only rarely seen into the tears of things.

> "This aspect of our cultural history is surprising. On the face of it, few great poetic *oeuvres* have been more suited to the American experience than Vergil's. The very pattern of his itinerary, from pastoral to georgic to epic, would seem to mirror that of our national dream: the search for Eden, the pioneering ordeal by labor, the imperial expansion finding its limits at last in the very nature of man."

[40]"The desire to tell the epic tale of Africa in the New World and to assert interconnections with the philologus of Europe is a fundamental aspect of Afro-American literature but is virtually unacknowledged and unaccepted. There appears to be nothing more startling to classicists and Afro-Americanists alike than a presentation of the facts of classical connections in Afro-American literature and culture. While radical breakers of traditional literary canons insist upon their rights to study the periphery of literature—the exclusions of the third-world literatures, women, irregular genres such as slave narratives—for Afro-American literature the most radical statement we can make is that Phillis Wheatley loved to read Latin poetry...." Carolivia Herron, "Philology as Subversion: The Case of Afro-America," in *On Philology*, 62–65, 63. The history of the education of African-Americans is in one sense a far remove from the study of Vergil's *Aeneid*. On the other hand, the topic is closely connected to the question, Why Vergil?, the question of the uses and misuses of culture and learning. See James D. Anderson, *The Education of Blacks in the South, 1960–1935* (Chapel Hill, NC: The University of North Carolina Press, 1988), especially regarding the controversy over the proper education for African-Americans as either "industrial" or classical and professional.

[41]Percy Bysshe Shelley, "A Defence of Poetry," in *Essays and Letters*, Ernest Rhys, ed. (Freeport, NY: Books for Libraries Press, 1971) 1–41, 28. For a brief discussion of Vergil's reception in nineteenth-century Europe, see Antonie Wlosok's "Preface" to the new translation and edition of *Virgil's Epic Technique* [*Virgils epische Technik*], by Richard Heinze, Hazel and David Harvey, and Fred Robertson, trans., (Berkeley: University of California Press, 1993) x–xiv; and also Philip Hardie's "Review Article,Virgil's Epic Technique: Heinze Ninety years On," *CP* 90 (1995) 267–76, esp. 267–68.

[42]For additional examples, see the survey of Vergil's English translators and poetry in English influenced by Vergil, from Chaucer on, in *Virgil in English*, K. W. Gransden, ed. (London, Penguin Books, 1996). See also Theodore Ziolkowski, *Virgil and the Moderns* (Princeton, NJ: Princeton University Press, 1993).

[43]That conversation is palpable among the artists and scholars represented in this collection. Brodsky's "Eclogue IV: Winter" is dedicated to Derek Walcott; Warren's poem, "Turnus (*Aeneid* XII)," is dedicated to Michael Putnam. C. Day Lewis's poem is itself a dedication of Lewis's translation of the *Georgics* to another poet, Stephen Spender. Gurval introduces the chapter from his book excerpted here with a quotation from W. H. Auden. Hermann Broch's novel, *The Death of Virgil*, opens with quotations from Vergil and Dante.

[44]See Annabel Patterson for a discussion of this poem, "Post-Romanticism: Wordsworth to Valéry," 263–69, esp. 263–66, in *Pastoral and Ideology. Virgil to Valéry* (Berkeley: University of California Press, 1987). The Introduction to this book is excerpted herein.

[45]I am reminded of Bernard Knox's discussion, in his article herein, on the serpent as a symbol of both destruction and rebirth.

[46]I benefitted from the panel session at the December 1997 American Philological Association annual meeting devoted to this work: "From Homer to Omeros: Approaches to Derek Walcott's *Omeros* and the *Odyssey*: A Stage Version," organized by Gregson Davis and Timothy Hofmeister, including on the program papers by John Van Sickle, Norman Austin, Gregson Davis, Timothy Hofmeister, and Peter Burian. The proceedings are expected to appear in *Classical World*. See also Oliver Taplin, "Derek Walcott's *Omeros* and Derek Walcott's Homer," *Arion*, 3rd ser. 1.2 (Spring 1991) 213–26; also Sander M. Goldberg, *Epic in Republican Rome* (Oxford: Oxford University Press 1995), "Envoi," 158–71.

AENEID 1.1–11 IN LATIN AND FIVE TRANSLATIONS; SYNOPSIS OF THE *AENEID*

Since this volume focuses on the poetry of Vergil, it opens with the beginning of the *Aeneid*, book 1, lines 1–11. The first lines introduce the story of a man, of war and fate, of suffering and history, and of Rome. In addition to the Latin text, five translations demonstrate various ways to render Vergil's poetry in English. The five translations are, of course, similar. The fun is reading them for their differences. A full synopsis of the *Aeneid* follows. Born in 70 B.C.E. in Mantua, a town in northern Italy, Vergil lived through the Roman civil wars and the end of the Roman Republic. His life spanned the tumultuous era of Cicero, Pompey, Julius Caesar, Antony and Cleopatra, and Octavian, later known as Augustus. He was a contemporary or near contemporary of the poets Lucretius, Catullus, Horace, Tibullus, Propertius, and Ovid, who collectively comprise the golden age of Latin poetry. Vergil began composing the *Aeneid* in about 29 B.C.E. and continued working on it until his death in 19 B.C.E., near the beginning of what was to become the Roman Empire. (Ed.)

AENEID, BOOK 1, LINES 1–11[1]

*A*rma virumque cano, Troiae qui primus ab oris
Italiam fato profugus Laviniaque venit
litora, multum ille et terris iactatus et alto
vi superum, saevae memorem Iunonis ob iram,
multa quoque et bello passus, dum conderet urbem
inferretque deos Latio: genus unde Latinum
Albanique patres atque altae moenia Romae.
Musa, mihi causas memora, quo numine laeso
quidve dolens regina deum tot volvere casus
insignem pietate virum, tot adire labores
impulerit. Tantaene animis caelestibus irae?

AENEID, BOOK 1, LINES 1–11 — FIVE VERSE TRANSLATIONS[2]

Arms, and the man I sing, who, forc'd by fate,
And haughty Juno's unrelenting hate,
Expell'd and exil'd, left the Trojan shore.
Long labors, both by sea and land, he bore,
And in the doubtful war, before he won
The Latian realm, and built the destin'd town;
His banish'd gods restor'd to rites divine,
And settled sure summon in his line,
From whence the race of Alban fathers come,
And the long glories of majestic Rome.
O Muse! the causes and the crimes relate;
What goddess was provok'd, and whence her hate;
For what offense the Queen of Heav'n began
To persecute so brave, so just a man;
Involv'd his anxious life in endless cares,
Expos'd to wants, and hurried into wars!
Can heav'nly minds such high resentment show,
Or exercise their spite in human woe?

John Dryden, 1697

I sing of arms and of a man: his fate
had made him fugitive; he was the first
to journey from the coasts of Troy as far
as Italy and the Lavinian shores.
Across the lands and waters he was battered
beneath the violence of High Ones, for
the savage Juno's unforgetting anger;
and many sufferings were his in war —
until he brought a city into being
and carried in his gods to Latium;
from this have come the Latin race, the lords
of Alba, and the ramparts of high Rome.

Tell me the reason, Muse: what was the wound
to her divinity, so hurting her
that she, the queen of gods, compelled a man
remarkable for goodness to endure
so many crises, meet so many trials?
Can such resentment hold the minds of gods?

Allen Mandelbaum, 1964

My song is arms and a man, the first of Troy
to come to Italy and Lavinian shores,
a fated fugitive, harried on land and sea
by heaven's huge might and Juno's endless hate,
pommeled by wars, till he could found the City
and bring his gods to Latium, whence the race
of Latins, our Alban sires, and towering Rome.

Muse, tell me the causes: how was godhead wronged,
how injured the queen of heaven that she must force
through many a fall of fate and many a toil
that great, good man: can heaven hold such ill will?

Frank O. Copley, 1965

I sing of warfare and a man at war
From the sea-coast of Troy in early days
He came to Italy by destiny,
To our Lavinian western shore,
A fugitive, this captain, buffeted
Cruelly on land as on the sea
By blows from powers of the air — behind them
Baleful Juno in her sleepless rage.
And cruel losses were his lot in war,
Till he could found a city and bring home
His gods to Latium, land of the Latin race,
The Alban lords, and the high walls of Rome.
Tell me the causes now, O Muse, how galled
In her divine pride, and how sore at heart
From her old wound, the queen of gods compelled him —
A man apart, devoted to his mission —
To undergo so many perilous days
And enter on so many trials. Can anger
Black as this prey on the minds of heaven?

Robert Fitzgerald, 1983

My song is of war and the first man from a Trojan
coast to arrive in Italy, forced by Fates to Lavinian
shore: the power of Gods repeatedly tossed him
on land and sea, Juno's fierce and remembering anger
caused him to suffer greatly in war while founding a city,
bringing his Gods to Latium, leading to Latin
and Alban fathers, to high walls of the Romans.

Muse, tell me the reasons: what slight to her power,
what grief drove the Queen of the Gods to involve him,
a man so known for reverence, in struggle and hardship
over and over? Can so much spite reside in a Goddess?

Edward B. McCrorie, 1991

SYNOPSIS OF THE *AENEID* [3]

Book 1

After the invocation, ending with the question about Juno's wrath that will persist throughout the epic, we come upon Aeneas and the Trojans in the midst of their journeys following the fall of Troy. A great storm, arranged by Juno with Aeolus the lord of the winds, drives them off course. Neptune calms the storm and is compared with a leader who calms a mob. Part of Aeneas' fleet was separated from him; Aeneas and his seven remaining ships find a harbor, and Aeneas climbs a rock to view the surroundings. He shoots seven deer, shares them, and encourages his people, hiding his own anguish. Meanwhile on Mt. Olympus, Venus, worried for her son, addresses Jupiter, seeking assurance, which he gives. He foretells that Aeneas will reach Latium and found a people whose empire will last forever and will bring peace.

Aeneas explores the surrounding countryside and is met by his mother Venus in disguise. She explains that they are in Carthage and tells him the story of its queen, Dido. Aeneas, made invisible by his mother, enters Carthage, observes its activity, and gazes in wonder at the carvings on the temple to Juno, carvings that depict his own story and that of Troy. He watches as his comrade Ilioneus, whom he had thought lost in the storm, petitions Queen Dido for aid, which she grants. Aeneas and his comrade Achates reveal themselves to the company, and they are welcomed with feasting, to which Aeneas summons his son Ascanius. But Venus, fearing that Juno might turn Dido against Aeneas, disguises her son Cupid as Aeneas' son Ascanius, causing Dido to forget her vow of fidelity to her dead husband and instead feel attraction for Aeneas. At the end of the feast, Dido asks Aeneas to tell them his story, and reluctantly, he begins.

Book 2

Aeneas recounts his story in a first-person narrative, renewing his sorrows. The Greeks, stalemated in the Trojan War, devised a stratagem, the great Trojan horse. They spread a rumor that the wooden horse was an offering to Minerva, so that the Trojans would accept it. In truth, the horse concealed many Greek warriors in its belly. When the Trojans found it, they debated what to do, and Laocoon warned them against it. Sinon, a Greek posing as a deserter, induced the Trojans to accept the horse. Meanwhile Laocoon and his two young boys were attacked by two huge snakes, which the Trojans interpreted as a divine punishment for his advice to reject the horse. Rejoicing, the Trojans brought the horse within their walls and fell peacefully asleep. As they slept, the concealed Greeks descended from the horse and they and their comrades poured into the doomed city of Troy.

Hector's ghost appeared to Aeneas in a dream and ordered him to leave Troy with the city's gods. Aeneas disobeyed and instead seized his arms and ran through the city. Fighting and confronting death and ruin everywhere, he exchanged armor with some fallen Greeks after which he was mistakenly attacked by his fellow-Trojans. Aeneas escaped and found himself at king Priam's palace, where there was fierce fighting. Aeneas watched Priam's slaughter in front of his family at the altars and at the hands of Achilles' son Neoptolemus. Aeneas then remembered his own family, his father Anchises, his wife Creusa, and son Ascanius. Returning for them, he came upon Helen, cause of the war, and debated killing her but did not. His goddess mother Venus revealed to him the scene of all the gods taking sides in the war, and the doom of Troy. At home Anchises refused to leave until a magical flame played about Ascanius' head, an omen that they should depart. Aeneas lifted his father onto his shoulders and took Ascanius by the hand, with Creusa following. As they proceeded through the city, Creusa was lost. Aeneas, beside himself, returned to find her. What he found instead was her shade, which he tried and failed to embrace three times. Creusa told him to search for a far land and better fate. He returned to his comrades to find their number had swelled, and the band headed for the mountains.

Book 3

Aeneas continues his story. The Trojans built a fleet and fled Troy. Their wanderings took them to Thrace and then to Delos, where they heard a prophecy that they should seek their ancient mother and build a lasting empire. Mistaking the prophecy, they headed for Crete, but there a plague beset them, so they returned to Delos to consult the oracle again. The Trojan household gods appeared to Aeneas in his sleep, bidding him to seek the western land named Italy. A storm drove them to the land of the Harpies, whence they made other travels, finding Andromache, Hector's widow, and other Trojans, including Helenus, who offered another prophecy. The Trojans would know they had found far away Italy when they saw a white sow with thirty white young, and hunger would drive them to "eat their tables." They were to beware of the straits of Scylla and the whirlpools of Charybdis, and were to pray to Juno for protection. When they reached Italy, Aeneas was to consult the Sibyl at Cumae. The Trojan survivors headed for Italy and upon sighting it, their destination, they offered sacrifices. Then they passed by Scylla, Charybdis, volcanic Aetna, the one-eyed Cyclops, Polyphemus, and were driven off course again by heavy winds and passed by many towns, including Drepanum, where Aeneas' father Anchises died, a loss neither oracle nor prophecy had foretold. Then they landed at Carthage. Ending his tale, Aeneas grows quiet.

Book 4

Queen Dido, moved by his stories, cannot rest, and in the morning tells her sister Anna of the impression Aeneas had made on her, despite her vow, which she prays she can keep, not to betray her dead husband. Anna urges her to yield to her attraction. Smitten, Dido tours her city with Aeneas, forgets her duties, and the city's work stops. Juno and Venus conspire to unite Dido and Aeneas. A hunting party is assembled, at which Dido and Aeneas both appear, resplendent. During the hunt, a great storm arises, and Dido and Aeneas take shelter alone together in a cave amid thunder and lightning. Rumor of their union spreads, even to a suitor whom Dido had rejected and who complains to Jupiter. In response, Jupiter bids Mercury to remind Aeneas of his mission in Italy. Mercury finds Aeneas overseeing the building of Carthage.

Aeneas begins preparations to leave. When Dido learns what is happening, she confronts Aeneas bitterly. Aeneas responds by reminding her of his duty, ignoring Dido's tears and concealing his own. Dido curses him. She asks her sister to intercede and persuade Aeneas to stay at least until the weather improves, but he refuses. Dido broods about death and dreams about loneliness and madness. She convinces Anna that she has consulted a sorceress but actually she is deceiving Anna in order to plan her suicide. She says she is going to burn her mementos of Aeneas on a pyre. As Dido prays and doubts, Mercury visits Aeneas again, warning him about Dido's threats, and Aeneas sets sail immediately. At dawn, as she sees the Trojan ships departing, Dido rages at Aeneas, again cursing him and his descendents, swearing that her people and his will be enemies. She mounts the pyre and surrounded by Aeneas' belongings, kills herself with his sword. Juno pities her and releases her from her body.

Book 5

As the Trojans sail away from Carthage, they see a fire but do not know that it comes from Dido's pyre. A violent storm arises, and Palinurus advises Aeneas to seek harbor. They land near the tomb of Anchises, Aeneas' father. It is the anniversary of his death, and Aeneas arranges a festival and rowing, running, boxing, and archery games. At Anchises' tomb, a great snake appears, eats the funeral offerings and slides away, a good omen. The boat race is the first contest. In the next contest, the footrace, Nisus and his friend Euryalus along with Helymus, Diores, and Salius are running, Nisus in the lead and Salius next. When Nisus slips and falls, he trips Salius so that Euryalus wins. Salius objects, but Aeneas resolves the dispute. In the boxing match, similar drama occurs among the contestants. The games end with archery. Throughout, the contestants all vie strenuously, and Aeneas distributes prizes of victory and consolation. Then Ascanius and his band of young horsemen give a performance of elaborately choreographed horsemanship.

Juno has been observing, and she sends Iris down to the Trojan women as her messenger. The women are mourning Anchises and their own lot, and Iris, disguised as one of them, Beroe, encourages them to set fire to the fleet so that they will no longer be obliged to wander but will stay in Sicily. When Aeneas and the Trojans discover the fires, Aeneas prays to Jupiter to send rain, and a great storm extinguishes the flames. Aeneas wonders if he too should stay in Sicily, but the seer Nautes encourages him to move on, leaving behind those who are weary of the quest for Italy. Anchises appears to Aeneas in a dream, confirming that advice. He adds that in Italy Aeneas should seek out the Sibyl and with her visit Anchises in the Underworld to learn about the future of his people. The Trojans agree to leave some comrades behind and to advance with the remaining party. After they have set sail, the god of Sleep causes Palinurus, who is steering Aeneas' ship, to fall overboard. Aeneas, stunned by the loss, takes the helm.

Book 6

The Trojans arrive in Italy, and Aeneas seeks the Sibyl. On the temple of Apollo near the Sibyl's cave, Aeneas sees the carvings of the story of Daedalus. Daedalus had crafted wings to escape the Minotaur; when his son Icarus used them, he flew too near the sun, and their wax fastenings melted, causing Icarus to fall into the sea and drown. The Sibyl, inspired by Apollo, foretells a long future in Italy but only after arduous wars. The Sibyl instructs Aeneas how to gain access to the Underworld. First, he must find the golden bough. He must also bury an unburied comrade. As the Sibyl and Aeneas cross the River Styx, they meet the shades of the unburied who may not cross the river. Palinurus, who had died at the end of Book 5, is the first, and he begs them to bury him. Charon the boatmaster then conducts Aeneas and the Sibyl across the Styx, having drugged Cerberus, the monster who guards the Underworld. They meet the shades of those who died before their time. Then come the ghosts of those who died because of unhappy love, among them Queen Dido, who is with her husband. In tears, Aeneas tries vainly to comfort her; she remains silent and turns away from him. Next they meet those who died in battle, including the Trojan and Greek warriors of the Trojan War. They pass by Tartarus, the region where the shades of the guilty receive their punishment. They proceed to Elysium, where they meet Anchises.

Anchises tells Aeneas about the transmigration of souls, which allows some souls to return to earth from the Underworld. Anchises points out those shades who will become Romans, names that are known to Vergil's readers as historical figures but that are only predictions to Aeneas. Anchises foretells Rome's future greatness and the terms on which that greatness will rest—not the arts of sculpture or oratory but of governance. Aeneas notices Marcellus, a young man on whom the future hopes of Augustan Rome had rested, but who had died prematurely. Then Anchises sends Aeneas back to the upper air, through the gate of ivory and of false dreams.

Book 7
Book 7 opens with the death of Aeneas' nurse, Caieta. The Trojans pass the isle of Circe and reach the mouth of the Italian river, the Tiber. At this point, the poet offers a second invocation, to Erato, the Muse of lyric poetry, announcing the second half of his poem as his greater task. We then learn that the local king, Latinus, has a daughter, Lavinia, who is betrothed to Turnus, an Italian noble, although the oracles say she will marry a stranger. When the Trojans land, they wind up eating the bread on which their food is placed, and Ascanius remarks that they are "eating their tables," thus confirming the prophecy told in Book 3. The Trojans send an embassy to King Latinus. He welcomes them, and they tell him that fate has ordered them to Italy. Latinus understands that Aeneas is the husband foretold for Lavinia, and he makes alliance with the Trojans.

Juno, who has been observing all the while, is enraged, and sends to earth the powers of Hell in the form of Allecto, her agent. She induces Latinus' wife, Amata, to oppose the marriage of Lavinia to Aeneas. When Latinus will not be persuaded to her view, Amata becomes frenzied, and the women of Latium join her. Allecto then incites Turnus to fight for his right to Lavinia, and he craves war. Allecto creates the situation in which Ascanius kills a sacred stag, and the Latins seek revenge. She sounds the war trumpet and the killing starts. Latinus, incapable of stopping the war, withdraws. Then follows a catalogue of Latin heroes. First there is Mezentius and his son Lausus, and many others, including Turnus, and finally the female warrior, Camilla.

Book 8
The Latins prepare for war. Meanwhile, the river god of the Tiber appears to Aeneas and advises him to seek help from Evander. As he rows peacefully up the Tiber, Aeneas sees the white sow that had been prophesied. When Aeneas reaches Evander's settlement on the future site of Rome, the people, who are descended from Greeks, are celebrating a feast to honor Hercules. Evander's son Pallas meets Aeneas and welcomes him. Aeneas asks for Evander's aid. Evander tells Aeneas the story of the monster Cacus, who had terrorized the countryside until he was

killed by Hercules, the event being celebrated in the annual festival. Evander recounts the history of Latium and shows Aeneas places that are destined to become
famous in Roman history.

Meanwhile, Venus visits her husband, Vulcan, blacksmith to the gods, and persuades
him, through her arts of love, to use his skills to craft for Aeneas a set of arms,
implements of war. Evander continues his account of Latium's history, telling Aeneas
about Mezentius, who is much hated by the neighboring Etruscans. Evander and
Aeneas enter into an alliance, and Evander entrusts his son Pallas to Aeneas. Venus
delivers Vulcan's arms. On the shield are embossed scenes that describe events
which for Aeneas lie in the future and for Vergil's audience are part of Roman history.
In the center is depicted the Battle of Actium of 31 B.C.E. and Augustus, victorious
over Antony and Cleopatra. Aeneas, not knowing what all this means, lifts to his
shoulder the future of Rome.

Book 9
Juno tells Turnus that Aeneas is away and that the time is right to attack. The Trojans, following their absent chieftain's orders, remain within their camp, while
Turnus, compared to a bloodthirsty wolf at a sheepfold, rages for war. Frustrated,
he prepares to burn the Trojan fleet, but the ships, made from sacred pines, are
transformed into nymphs. Nisus and Euryalus, who first appeared in the foot race
in Book 5, plan to make their way through the Rutulians, commanded by Turnus,
to alert Aeneas that he is needed. The pair ask only that Ascanius care for Euryalus'
mother, the only mother not to have remained on Sicily, should they not return. At
first they evade the Rutulians, but their own lust for blood and plunder betrays
them, through the glint on a stolen helmet, and both die. The Rutulians launch a
full attack on the Trojans and the slaughter begins. Turnus manages to get inside
the Trojan camp, kills many, but finally is forced to flee.

Book 10
At a council of gods on Olympus, Jupiter urges the gods to stop interfering in this
war, since the time for battle will come later, between Carthage and Rome (the
Punic Wars). Venus and Juno exchange angry speeches, but Jupiter remains neutral.
Meanwhile the Rutulian attack on the Trojans continues, while Aeneas is returning
with young Pallas and the Etruscan forces. He encounters the ship-nymphs, who
warn him about the attack. The Trojans rejoice at Aeneas' return. The battle begins
anew, but neither side prevails. Turnus and Evander's son Pallas meet in single
combat. Turnus kills him and, gloating, strips off Pallas' swordbelt, which we are
told he will regret. When Aeneas hears the news of Pallas' death and understands
that his promise to Evander is broken, he is enraged and seeks revenge, killing
wildly. Juno obtains permission from Jupiter to save Turnus temporarily. Mezentius
battles heavily until he meets Aeneas, who wounds him. Mezentius' son Lausus
tries to help his father but is killed by Aeneas, who restores his body to his people.
Mezentius learns of his son's death and fights Aeneas, dying at his hands.

Book 11
Aeneas dedicates Mezentius' spoils and in great grief arranges to bring Pallas' body
back to his father. The Latins request a truce to bury their dead, which Aeneas
readily grants. At the funeral of Pallas, Evander asks Aeneas to seek revenge on

Turnus for his son's death. Latinus proposes peace, and the Latin spokesman Drances supports him, opposing Turnus. Turnus accuses Drances of cowardice and then suggests that he and Aeneas meet in single combat. Turnus learns that Aeneas is preparing to attack, and both sides prepare for war. The warrior-maiden Camilla offers to help Turnus, and he accepts, but the goddess Diana laments Camilla's impending death. The tide of battle shifts from one side to the other. Camilla, though valorous, is killed as night falls.

Book 12

Turnus repeats his desire to fight Aeneas in single combat, even though Latinus and his wife Amata try to dissuade him. Both sides prepare to watch the two heroes, and Juno tells Juturna, Turnus' sister, that she may try to help her brother but that Juno herself can do nothing more. Juturna urges the Rutulians to break the truce established for the single combat. Aeneas tries to prevent the Trojans from doing this, but he is wounded, and the fighting resumes. Aeneas, healed through Venus' intervention, arms himself, and again pursues Turnus alone. Juturna in disguise diverts Turnus from Aeneas, and Aeneas attacks the Latins instead. General fighting breaks out yet again, and the Trojans attack the Latin capital. When Amata sees this, she kills herself. Turnus learns of her death and asks his fellows to let him fight Aeneas alone.

The single combat begins. Aeneas and Turnus attack each other, with interventions from the gods. Jupiter orders the gods to leave the scene. Juno demands that in defeat the Latins keep their name and dress, remaining Latins in Rome's future greatness; Jupiter agrees. The combat continues. When Turnus tries to throw a huge rock at Aeneas, he feels like a person in a dream who cannot speak or move. Aeneas wounds Turnus in the thigh. Humbled, Turnus begs Aeneas for his life in the name of their fathers. As he is about to relent, Aeneas sees the swordbelt Turnus had stripped from Pallas after he had killed him, and in Pallas' name, Aeneas kills Turnus in anger and rage, and Turnus' soul flees to the shades. (Ed.)

Notes

[1] R. A. B. Mynors, ed., *P. Vergili Maronis Opera* (Oxford: Oxford University Press, 1969).

[2] *Virgil's Aeneid*, trans. John Dryden (New York: Airmont Publishing, 1968); *The Aeneid of Virgil*, by Allen Mandelbaum (New York: Bantam Books, 1971); Vergil, *The Aeneid: A Verse Translation by Frank O. Copley* (Indianapolis, IN: Bobbs-Merrill,1965); *The Aeneid. Virgil*, trans. Robert Fitzgerald (New York: Random House, Vintage Books, 1984); *The Aeneid of Virgil*, trans. Edward McCrorie, (Hampton Falls, NH: Donald M. Grant, 1991).

[3] The starting point for the synopsis was both the Page and Williams editions of the *Aeneid*: T. E. Page, ed. *The Aeneid of Virgil* (London: MacMillan, 1962); R. D. Williams, ed., *The Aeneid of Virgil* (London: St Martin's Press, 1973).

THE LANGUAGE OF VIRGIL

In these few pages Garrison assists those whose Latin may be rusty to read the *Aeneid*'s first eleven lines. Even for readers with no Latin, the vocabulary notes and linear translation will help reveal how the Latin language works. For example, the most literal, word-for-word translation of the first line would be the following: "arms the man and I sing of Troy who the first from the shores." Obviously Latin has a way to establish meaning regardless of word order. That characteristic gives writers in Latin enormous flexibility. It is important therefore to notice how precise Vergil was in exploiting this flexibility, how carefully he designed the occurrence of his words in their various forms. Readers can begin to make these observations with the help Garrison provides. (Garrison's book also provides an introduction to Vergil's Latin grammar, which is essential for an understanding of Vergil's idiom.) In addition, he has indicated scansion, marking the role of each word in the meter or rhythm of the poetry, long and short syllables that, taken together, make up the six units, or feet, in each line. Within a rather fixed set of metrical rules, a talented poet can vary the rhythm, speed, and emphases within each line to enhance the meaning of the words. Allow yourself to take some minutes to sit quietly with Vergil's first lines. It does not matter for this purpose that your reading may not be professional. Any greater acquaintance with the words will be a gain in the experience and pleasure of Vergil's poetry. (Ed.)

❖ ❖ ❖

This [excerpt] gives you a little bit of the real thing. It cannot replace a regular, systematic introduction to the Latin language, but it contains enough of the language of Virgil to make Classical Studies less remote and intimidating. It should satisfy some of your curiosity, and it may stimulate you to try more.

Like any profitable enterprise, the task you assume in working through these pages is demanding. This is a work book, not bedside reading, and you must give it your best attention if it is to be worth your while at all.

❖ ❖ ❖

[Y]ou are provided with an interlinear translation of the text [*Aeneid* 1.1–11], with scansion. Like all crutches, the translations are stiff and wooden, their only purpose being to give you the general drift of what is being said and to help you over any difficulty you may have in seeing how Virgil's Latin is fitting together.

Daniel H. Garrison, *The Language of Virgil: An Introduction to the Poetry of the Aeneid* (New York: Peter Lang Publisher, 1984) 60–61. Reprinted by permission of Peter Lang Publisher.

The scansion marks will help you read the Latin out loud without being delayed by the mechanics of scansion. Facing [the] page is an alphabetical list giving the vocabulary form of every word that occurs in that passage to save you the trouble of thumbing through an entire Latin dictionary. Above the vocabulary are a few notes on the text. On the facing page are listed alphabetically all the words used in that passage, with their English meaning. Above that word list you will find a few notes about difficult points of grammar, necessary background information, and items of essential interest....

Robert Frost said that poetry is what is lost in translation. This [excerpt] will help you discover why he was right. The objectives of the [exercise] are as simple as they are ambitious:

❧ To give you a sense of what Latin is like.
❧ To give you a new way to discover what poetry is.
❧ To give you the experience of Virgil's *Aeneid* — or a first taste of it.

❧ ❧ ❧

[T]he *Aeneid* should be approached not as a story with a message, but an actual experience with a meaning. Its chief impact is affective, not simply logical or propositional. It can be compared to a gothic cathedral. You can read piles of art history books telling you about the development of the gothic style, you can pore over floor plans, elevations, and models, you can study color prints of interiors and façades, or contemplate the flying buttress. But none of this can prepare you for what happens when you first walk into an actual gothic cathedral. Suddenly you feel a presence, an aura. No matter if you are an atheist: the presence of that interior, its echoing vaults and towering spaces, enchant you in spite of yourself. The meaning of a gothic cathedral is what you feel when you are inside it. Likewise, the meaning of the *Aeneid* is what happens to you when you read it out loud in Latin and understand the words. You have gone beyond mere translations, professors, grammars, and footnotes. The purpose of [these pages] is to lead you toward that experience. The rest is up to you.

I: PROEM

I sing of arms and the man who first from the shores of Troy
Ārmă vĭrūmquĕ cănō, Trōĭāē quī prīmŭs ăb ōrĭs

came to Italy and the Lavinian shores, by fate an exile —
Ītălĭăm fātō prŏfŭgūs Lāvīnĭăquĕ vēnĭt

he much tossed about both on the lands and on the deep
lītŏră — mūltum ĭllĕ ĕt tērrīs iāctātŭs ĕt āltō

by the force of the gods, because of the remembering wrath of savage Juno,
vī sŭpĕrūm, saēvāē mĕmŏrēm Iūnōnĭs ŏb īrăm,

and having suffered many things also in war, until he should build a city
mūltă quŏquĕ ĕt bēllō pāssūs, dūm cōndĕrĕt ūrbĕm

3

and bring (his) gods into Latium — whence the Latin race
īnferrētque̮ de̅ōs Lătiō — gĕnŭs ūndĕ Lătīnŭm.   6

and the Alban fathers and the walls of high Rome.
Ālbānīque̮ pătrēs ātque̮ a̮ltae̅ mōēnĭa̮ Rōmae̮.

Muse, tell me the causes, for what divinity wounded
Mūsă, mĭhī cāusās mĕmŏrā, quō nūmĭnĕ lae̅sŏ

or grieving for what did the queen of the gods compel
quĭdvĕ dŏlēns rēgīnă dĕūm tŏt vŏlvĕrĕ cāsŭs   9

a man distinguished for pietas to circle through so many misfortunes,
īnsīgnēm pĭe̮tātĕ vĭrūm, tŏt ădīrĕ lăbōrĕs

to enter so many labors. Are there such rages in celestial hearts?
īmpŭlĕrīt. Tāntae̅ne̮ a̮nĭmīs cae̅lēstĭbŭs īrae̮?

1. **Arma virumque**: Virgil announces his dual Homeric theme by alluding to Iliadic "arms" and the study of a "man" — the first word of the Odyssey. **Troiae**: Virgil follows the tradition that Rome was founded by refugees from Troy.

3. **iactatus**: the first of several words presenting the theme of the suffering hero. Cf. *profugus* (2), *passus* (5), *casus* (9), and *labores* (10).

5–6. ...**dum** [takes] the subjunctives *conderet* and *inferret*....

8. **Musa**: the traditional epic prayer to the Muse for inspiration.

9. **regina**: Juno is traditionally a vengeful goddess, here playing the epic role of the hero's divine antagonist, as Poseidon persecutes Odysseus in Homer's Odyssey. **deum**: shortened from *deorum*; cf. *superum*, line 4.

10. **pietate**: thematic for Aeneas, whose cardinal virtue is *pietas*. In Latin, this is more than religious zeal; it includes duty to gods, ancestors, family, nation, posterity — for Virgil, even civilization itself. It is sometimes translated "goodness" or "duty," but there is no corresponding English word, and it is left untranslated here. *labores*: like the "labors" of Hercules, a favorite hero of the time; and the word also implies pain.

11. **irae**: one of many "poetic plurals"....Virgil's question in line 11 underlines a religious problem that troubled people in his time: why are the traditional Olympian gods so ungodlike in their passions and vendettas? How can they be just gods and fickle personalities at the same time?

ā, ab: from
adeō, -īre,- ivī, -itus: enter, approach
Albānus, -a, -um: Alban, from Alba
   Longa, a few miles s. of Rome
altus, -a, -um: high
animus, -ī, m.: soul, spirit, mind
arma, -ōrum, n.: arms
atque: and
bellum, -ī, n.: war
caelestis, -e: heavenly
canō, -ere, cecinī, cantus: sing
cāsus, -ūs, m.: chance, misfortune
causa, -ae, f.: cause
condō, -ere, -didi, -ditus: found
deus, -ī, m., gen. pl. *deum*: god
doleō, -ēre, -uī, -itus: grieve
dum + subjunctive: until
fātum, -ī, n.: fate
genus, -eris, n.: race, family
iactō (1): throw around, toss, buffet
ille, illa, illud: that; he, she, it
impellō, -pellere, -pulī, -pulsus: compel
inferō, -ferre, -tulī, -lātus: bring into
insignis, -e: distinguished, marked
īra, -ae, f.: anger, ire, wrath
Italia, -ae, f.: Italy
Iūnō, -ōnis, f.: Juno, wife of Jove
labor, -ōris, m.: hardship; task
laedō, -ere, -si, -sus: wound, offend
Latīnus, -a, -um: Latin; of Latium
Latium, -ī, n.: area around Rome
Lāvīnus, -a, -um: of Lavinium
lītus, -oris, n.: shore
memor, -oris: mindful, remembering

memorō (1): recall, recount
mihi: (dative) to me
moenia, -ium, n.: walls
multa, -ōrum, n.: many things
multum: much
Mūsa, -ae, f.: the Muse
nūmen, -inis, n.: divinity, divine power
ob: on account of
ōra, -ae, f.: shore, coast, region
pater, -tris, m.: father
patior, patī, passus: suffer, endure
pietās, -ātis, f.: loyalty, duty
prīmus, -a, -um: first
profugus, -a, -um: fugitive; refugee
-que (enclitic): and
quī, quae, quod: who, which
quid (interrog. pron.): what?
quoque: also
rēgīna, -ae, f.: queen
Rōma, -ae, f.: Rome
saevus, -a, -um: cruel, fierce, savage
superī, -erum, m.: those above, the gods
tantus, -a, -um: so great
tot (indeclinable): so many
terra, -ae, f.: land
Troia, -ae, f.: Troy, Ilium
unde: whence, from which
urbs, urbis, f.: city
-ve (enclitic): or
veniō, -īre, vēnī, ventus: come; go
vir, -ī, m.: man
vīs, vis, f.: force
volvō, -ere, -uī, volūtus: roll through

Arma virumque cano, Troiae qui primus ab oris
Italiam fato profugus Laviniaque venit
litora — multum ille et terris iactatus et alto
vi superum, saevae memorem Iunonis ob iram,
multa quoque et bello passus, dum conderet urbem
inferret deos Latio — genus unde Latinum
Albanique patres atque altae moenia Romae.
Musa, mihi causas memora, quo numine laeso
quidve dolens regina deum tot volvere casus
insignem pietate virum, tot adire labores
impulerit. Tantaene animis caelestibus irae?

Edgar C. Reinke

ONOMATOPOETIC ALLITERATION IN VERGIL'S *AENEID*, BOOKS 1-6

The flexibility of Latin word order gives a poet abundant opportunities to arrange words in order to produce effects that support meaning. Among the most useful poetic tools are words' actual sounds. The use of the sounds of words to mimic their meaning is known as onomatopoeia (from the Greek words for making names, *poiêin* and *ónoma*). That effect can be achieved by the repetition of consonants (called alliteration) or of vowels (called assonance). Reinke offers us several examples of onomatopoeia in books 1 through 6 in the *Aeneid*, especially through alliteration, a technique in which Vergil is a master. (Ed.)

Nothing in organized form seems to have appeared in print on onomatopoetic alliteration in the poetry of Vergil. William M. Clarke has in recent years published an exhaustive, amply documented paper on alliteration in Vergil and Ovid, a study of metrical sound patterns and techniques employed by these two poets.[1]

❖ ❖ ❖

The purpose of this study is quite similar: to marshal before the reader a selection of instances of Vergilian alliterative effects that may be felt in the linear repetition of one or more of several initial consonants.[2] The lines and passages cited, moreover, will be restricted to the first six books of the *Aeneid*. The Latin is based on the Loeb text.

Since poetry is an art, the citation of any instance of alliteration as onomatopoetic must, to some degree, be regarded as subjective. However, R. D. Williams is supportive of a subjective interpretation provided that it is judged to be compatible with the rhythm and thought of the line in which the alliteration occurs.[3] This criterion has been adopted in the present paper. Furthermore, the terms onomatopoetic alliteration and alliterative effect are here employed interchangeably.

Following are several examples of alliteration involving the letter *m*, where the alliterative effect may range from reverberation on land or sea or in the sky to quiet musing on some arresting sight: *Aen.* 1.55, *magno cum murmure montis*, "with mighty rumbling of the mountain," said of the winds of King Aeolus struggling to escape from their cavernous barrier; *Aen.* 1.124, *magno misceri murmure*, of the storm-tossed sea espied by King Neptune, its billows mingling with mighty moaning;[4] *Aen.* 4.160,

Edgar C. Reinke, "Onomatopoetic Alliteration in Vergil's *Aeneid*, Books 1-6," *The Classical Bulletin* 62.3 (1986) 37–42. © copyright 1986, *The Classical Bulletin*. Reprinted by permission.

Magno misceri murmure caelum, with reference to the rumbling of thunder preceding the deluge that forced Queen Dido and her hunting party to scatter and seek shelter from the elements;...*Aen.* 1.421f., *miratur molem Aeneas, magalia quondam / miratur...*["Aeneas marvels at the massive structures, once huts / he marvels..."], the repetition of *miratur* in the second line and the alliteration in the hexameter with its five spondees picturing Aeneas musing in silent admiration for the Queen's rising city, as if he were murmuring to himself, "Marvelous, marvelous indeed!"

❖ ❖ ❖

We now proceed to citations in which the consonant *s*, sometimes in conjunction with liquid *l*, produces a lulling or somnolent effect. At *Aen.* 2.8f., with nightfall approaching, Aeneas tells Dido that he will content himself with a mere summary of the fall of Troy: *et iam nox humida caelo / praecipitat suadentque cadentia sidera somnos* ["and now dewy night advances and the stars falling induce sleep"], the alliteration of the sibilant thus encouraging the eyelids to close in slumber. Similarly, at *Aen.* 2.265: *invadunt urbem somno vinoque sepultam,* of invaded Troy buried in sleep and wine, as the Greeks storm the city. *Aen.* 4.527: *somno positae sub nocte silenti,* "all the world (except the distraught Dido) settled in sleep beneath the silent night." *Aen.* 2.794: *par levibus ventis volucrique simillima somno* ["like light breezes and most similar to a winged dream"]; here the image of sleep, intensified by the alliteration of *s*, is supported by the initial consonant *l* (and double occurrence of initial *v*) in the vivid comparison of Creusa's disappearing faint image to a light breeze or winged dream. *Aen.* 1.680: *hunc ego sopitum somno super alta Cythera / aut super Idalium sacra sede recondam;* in her plan to remove the boy Iulus from Dido's banquet for Aeneas, Venus says to Cupid, "him, when steeped in slumber, I shall hide above high Cythera or Idalium in my sacred seat" (note the sixfold presence of initial *s* in the two verses).

❖ ❖ ❖

In addition to somnolence, the alliteration of the consonant *s* may yield a whizzing or grating sound, as at...*Aen.* 6.573f.: *Tum demum horrisono stridentes cardine sacrae / panduntur portae,* of the entrance gates to Tartarus grating on their harsh-sounding hinges. (Observe, too, the slow opening of the gates due to their heaviness, felt in the spondees of the initial words in the second verse.)

But the alliteration of this sibilant can also echo the sound of churning or foaming. Thus, when the Aeneadae were cheerfully setting sail from Sicily before encountering the storm, we read, in *Aen.* 1.35: *vela dabant laeti et spumas salis aere ruebant,* the bronze plow plowing the foam of the salty sea....At *Aen.* 4.664f., *ensemque cruore / spumantem sparsasque manus,* the allusion is to pathetic Dido's self-inflicted lethal stab, her sword reeking with gore and hands bespattered. Equally gruesome are these verses from the Laocoon scene, *Aen.* 2.206–11:

pectora quorum inter fluctus arrecta iubaeque
sanguineae superant undas; pars cetera pontum
pone legit sinuatque immensa volumine terga.
fit sonitus spumante salo; iamque arva tenebant
ardentisque oculos suffecti sanguine et igni
sibila lambebant linguis vibrantibus ora.

["(The serpents') chests rise high through the waters and their bloody crests top the waves; the other part of them from behind skirts the sea, and their immense backs slither in a coil. A sound comes from the spuming salt sea; and now they were making for the fields, and suffused in their eyes blazing with blood and fire, they were licking their hissing mouths with flickering tongues."]

To be appreciated in this passage are the repeated occurrences of the words with initial sibilant that effectively evoke the sound of churning and hissing and also the striking sight of the vibrating tongues vivified by the alliteration of liquid *l* in the last cited line.

Note also the effective alliteration of *l* and *s* at *Aen.* 6.202f.: *liquidumque per aera lapsae / sedibus optatis gemina super arbore sidunt*, describing the twin doves gliding through the limpid air and then settling on the two-fold tree above, whence the golden bough sought by Aeneas was happily gleaming. (Here the double liquid suggests an easy gliding; the alliteration of the sibilant, however, a settling with wings rustling.)

✧ ✧ ✧

At *Aen.* 6.673ff., *lucis habitamus opacis / riparumque toros et prata recentia rivis / incolimus,* the bard Musaeus, speaking to the Sibyl in the precincts of Elysium, is describing the luxurious leisure enjoyed by its happy residents resting "on cushioned river-banks and in meadows fresh with streams" (Loeb tr.); here the onomatopoetic effect is felt in the triple linear occurrence of *r,* companion liquid of *l.*

Not to be omitted are…highly emotional, climactic lines,…in which the sound effect can be derived from the alliteration of the explosive consonantal stops *p* or *t* or fricative *f.*

✧ ✧ ✧

Consider…the reaction of the aged King Priam to the slaying of his son Polites by Pelides, scion of Achilles, at *Aen.* 2.535–39:

'at tibi pro scelere,' exclamat, 'pro talibus ausis
di, si qua est caelo pietas, quae talia curet,
persolvant grates dignas et praemia reddant
debita, qui nati coram me cernere letum
fecisti et patrios foedasti funere voltus.'

["'And for your crime,' he exclaims, 'for such acts as you have dared, if there is any piety in heaven, which cares about such things, may the gods unloose worthy thanks and repay the reward you deserve, you who made me see my son's destruction in front of me and who befouled a father's face with death.'"]

In these impressive verses note the ample alliteration, which serves to heighten the great agitation of the lamentable king; and in the last line the onomatopoetic enunciation of the three words commencing with *f* and of the *p* in *patrios* echoes his uncontrollable indignation for the murderer who befouled a father's countenance in a crime committed at the very altar.

✧ ✧ ✧

The alliterative effect in the last verse of the…passage, where Aeneas relates the fall of Troy to Dido, is most astonishing in the refinement of its composition. Here the captive Sinon, following a psychologically superb pause in his reply to his interrogator King Priam, is ostensibly induced by his captors to continue his seemingly plausible tale: *Aen.* 2.105–107, "Then in truth we burn to know and to ask the causes, unaware of so great crimes and Pelasgian guile. He continues, trembling, and professes with false heart": *Tum vero ardemus scitari et quaerere causas, / ignari scelerum tantorum artisque Pelasgae. / prosequitur pavitans et ficto pectore fatur.* Note in the last verse the three-fold occurrence of initial *p* and double presence of initial *f*, as well as the five internal syllables beginning with *t*, all this remarkable artistry displayed in all but one of the hexameter's six words. Here the perceptive Vergilian may behold an explosive, frothing Aeneas in retrospect despising the wily Greek prevaricator with utter disdain.

Clarke's definitive paper dealt with the question of intentional alliteration in Vergil's *Aeneid*. Repeated attempts have in fact been made to distinguish alliteration in Latin poetry as a natural phenomenon from its employment as an intentional device.[5] We recall that according to tradition, Vergil devoted ten full years to the composition of the *Aeneid*, averaging merely a few verses per day.[6] In pointing out the careful craftsmanship of the poet, his biographer Aelius Donatus asserts that Vergil licked the verses of his narrative epic into shape like a bear her cubs.[7] Although there is the view that results are what count, and that alliteration, whether intentional or accidental, is there to be appreciated, it is naive to suppose that the poet of the *Aeneid*, though blessed with the *afflatus divinus* ["divine inspiration"], did not consciously grace the large majority of its verses with the repetition of sounds congenial to the ear.[8]

At the same time, it is freely admitted that alliteration in itself is not necessarily an attractive figure of poetry. This is jarringly demonstrated in the staccato repetitions of the notoriously grotesque Ennian line: *O Tite tute Tati tibi tanta tyranne tulisti* ["O Titus, you, Titus Tatius the tyrant, you took upon yourself such great matters"] (*Ann.* 109, Loeb ed.). The harshness of these repeated sounds may be compared to this oft-cited Vergilian line: *quadrupedante putrem sonitu quatit ungula campum (Aen.* 8.596), where the metrically harmonious onomatopoetic effect of the galloping horse's hoof-beats trampling upon the crumbling plain is quite agreeable.[9] Similarly, compare these two lines: Ennius, *Ann.* 143, *At tuba terribili sonitu taratantara dixit* ["But the trumpet spoke the ta-ra-tan-ta-ra with a terrible sound"], and Vergil, *Aen.* 9.503, *At tuba terribilem sonitum procul aere canoro / increpuit* ["But the trumpet blasted its terrible sound from afar with a brazen song"]; observe that Vergil's refined line avoids Ennius' unpoetic jingle…. And one may wonder what Vergil's reaction was to literal tmesis, found in Ennius, *Varia* 13: *Saxo cere comminuit brum,* "with a stone he his crani split um" (Loeb tr.).[10]

Surely Vergil's sensitive ear must have been attuned to the negative and positive effects produced by these verses. Added support for this view may be derived from striking examples of onomatopoeia present in certain monosyllabic verse-endings of the *Aeneid*, e.g., in *Aen.* 1.105: … *insequitur cumulo praeruptus aquae mons* ["...it falls in a heap, the mountain of water broken through"], in *Aen.* 5.481: *sternitur examinisque tremens procumbit humi bos* ["the ox lies strewn, lifeless and trembling it falls to the ground"]. Here the sharp monosyllabic ending of the hexameter in itself graphically pictures, in the one instance, the sudden fall of the mountain of water; in the second, the fall of the ox collapsing in death. Also note the monosyllabic ending in *Aen.* 6.346: *fides est?* [*en haec promissa fides est?*, "is this the faithfulness that was promised?"] (bitter emphasis); and in *Aen.* 10.864: *viam vis* [*aperit si nulla viam vis*, "if no force opens a path"] (violent desire for vengeance).[11]

To Vergil's acute aural perception, alliteration in all likelihood had the appeal of an arrestingly beautiful figure. We know that, in his day and later, poetry was to be recited, whether by the amanuensis or in the public recitation hall. Tradition has it that Vergil himself recited portions of his unfinished *Aeneid* to the Emperor Augustus and his sister Octavia at the emperor's court.[12] The edifying sounds of the letters recurring in the abundant alliteration of this grand epic serve to enliven the imagination and enhance the aesthetic sensibilities. To derive pleasure and satisfaction from the flowing cadences of alliteration, its music must be recognized and felt.[13]

To attain this objective, students would be well advised not to stop with a mere mechanical scansion of lines from the *Aeneid*. Let them acquire practice in reciting entire passages until they can declaim with proper intonation and expression. This writer would welcome the inclusion of declamation in the competitive programs of our Latin fora, state and national. Talented, ambitious Latin students would be sure to greet this dramatic competition with lively enthusiasm.

But are we at present neglecting our appreciation of Vergil's inspired music? Shakespeare has declared that

> The man that hath no music in himself,
> Nor is not moved with concord of sweet sounds,
> Is fit for treasons, stratagems and spoils;
> The motions of his spirit are dull as night
> And his affections dark as Erebus:
> Let no such man be trusted. Mark the music.[14]

It is finally because of the music of Vergil's poetry and its grandeur that Tennyson saluted Mantovano as "Wielder of the stateliest measure ever moulded by the lips of man."[15]

Notes

[1]William M. Clarke, "Intentional Alliteration in Vergil and Ovid," *Latomus* 35 (1976): 276–300.

❖ ❖ ❖

[2]The writer's independent scrutiny of each verse of the *Aeneid*, Books 1–6, has yielded hundreds of alliterative lines. The citations offered in this paper he has judged to be representative.

[3]R. D. Williams (ed.) *P. Vergili Maronis Aeneidos: Liber Quintus* (Oxford, 1960) 85, n. on verse 198.

[4]Ronald G. Austin (ed.), *P. Vergili Maronis Aeneidos: Liber Primus* (Oxford, 1971) 59, n. on verse 124: "The alliteration suggests the mass of noise." Austin then cites *Aen.* 4.160, as producing a similar alliterative effect. See also n. 9 below.

❖ ❖ ❖

[5]For commentators who readily accept the view of intentional alliteration in Latin poetry, Clarke (above, n. 1) 277 cites J. Morouzeau, *Traité de stylistique latine* (Paris, 1946); for those who hesitate, N. T. Herescu, *La Poésie Latine* (Paris, 1960).

[6]W. F. Jackson Knight, *Roman Vergil* (New York, 1966; repr. 1971) 107, citing C. G. Hardie (ed.), *Vitae Vergilianae antiquae, Vita Donati*...(Oxford, 1954) 66.

[7]Knight (above, n. 6).

[8]For an edifying statement on Vergil's acute descriptive sensibilities, see W. Y. Seller, *The Roman Poets of the Augustan Age, Vergil*, 3rd ed. (Oxford, 1908), 419.

[9]By way of contrast with the Ennian line, Clarke (above, n. 1) 299f. cites also Aen. 11.47: *mitteret in magnum imperium metuensque moneret*, asserting that the *m*-sounds give the verse "the unity of a rolling grandeur."

[10]For Vergil's imitation of Ennius, see Kenneth Quinn, *Vergil's Aeneid* (Ann Arbor, Mich., 1968) 357–70. Vergil regarded Ennius with affection; many of his imitations of the Father of Latin Poetry are ornamental verse-tags.

[11]As cited by Williams (above, n. 3) 135, n. on *Aen.* 5.481.

[12]According to Aelius Donatus, Vergil read "with amazingly attractive appeal," Knight (above, n. 6) 337. On Vergil's reading at the emperor's court, see Knight (above, n. 6) 362.

[13]"He gave the language a new music," J. W. Mackail, *Virgil and His Meaning to the World of Today* (Boston, 1922) 146.

[14]*Merchant of Venice*, act 5, sc. 1, lines 83–88.

[15]"To Virgil," *The Poetic and Dramatic Works of Alfred Lord Tennyson*, Horace E. Scudder (ed.) (Boston, 1898) 511.

Gregory A. Staley

AENEAS' FIRST ACT: 1.180–194

The *Aeneid* is about what it means to take action, especially on a historical level. Staley's article on the hero's first action in the epic, the killing of stags, introduces us to important interpretive questions, especially regarding the triumph of cosmic and historical order, or its opposite. With Staley, readers can practice a fundamental method for interpreting the *Aeneid*, which is a comparison of Vergil's rendering of a scene with its literary ancestors, particularly in Homer's *Iliad* or *Odyssey*, or in Greek tragedy. Further, we learn to evaluate Aeneas' actions as they reflect the influence of both Jupiter and Juno, the divine guarantor and the divine opponent of the Trojans' fate. Finally, Staley views the ambiguous image of the hunt as a function of both primitive and civilized human experience, and as a recurrent image in the *Aeneid*, books 4, 7, and 12. Staley concludes with observations on the importance of this image for the meaning of the poem: "It can be no accident that Vergil chooses to present Aeneas' hunt, his first act in Book One, as an act of war and his act of war in Book Twelve, his last act in the epic, as a hunt." (Ed.)

Aeneas scopulum interea conscendit, et omnem
prospectum late pelago petit, Anthea si quem
iactatum vento videat Phrygiasque biremis
aut Capyn aut celsis in puppibus arma Caici.
navem in conspectu nullam, tris litore cervos
prospicit errantis; hos tota armenta sequuntur
a tergo et longum per vallis pascitur agmen.
constitit hic arcumque manu celerisque sagittas
corripuit fidus quae tela gerebat Achates,
ductoresque ipsos primum capita alta ferentis
cornibus arboreis sternit, tum vulgus et omnem
miscet agens telis nemora inter frondea turbam;
nec prius absistit quam septem ingentia victor
corpora fundat humi et numerum cum navibus aequet.
hinc portum petit et socios partitur in omnis.[1]

["Aeneas in the meantime climbs the rocky lookout and seeks a full prospect wide over the sea, if he might see Antheus who had been tossed by the wind and the Phrygian/Trojan bireme ships, or Capys or on high decks

Gregory A. Staley, "Aeneas' First Act, 1.180–194," *Classical World* 84.1 (1990) 25–29. Reprinted by permission of *Classical World*.

the arms of Caicus. A ship in sight there is none, three stags he catches sight of wandering along the shore; the entire herd follows behind them and the long formation feeds throughout the valley. He stopped short here, and he snatched up his bow in his hand and the swift arrows, the weapons which faithful Achates was carrying, and the leaders themselves he lays low first, as they bear their heads high with tree-like antlers, then also the whole crowd he disturbs, driving the mob with his weapons throughout the leafy groves; nor does he back away until he, the victor, strews on the ground seven great bodies and equals the number with his ships. From here he seeks the port and makes division among all his comrades."]

I.

Victor Pöschl has taught us to read very carefully the opening scenes of the *Aeneid* because "they contain in essence all the forces which constitute the whole."[2] It is surprising, in light of this now widely-accepted point of view, that Aeneas' first act in the *Aeneid*, his shooting of seven stags, has not been closely analyzed.[3] It is an act which, in various forms, recurs later to punctuate events at important turning points, in Aeneas' "wounding" of Dido, in Ascanius' hunt which precipitates war, and in Aeneas' final confrontation with Turnus. Surely Vergil did not choose lightly to give Aeneas' stag hunt such a prominent place at the opening of the epic.

Coming as it does between Aeneas' first words in the epic, his wish to have died at Troy (*O terque quaterque beati* ["O three and four times blessed"], 1.94), and his speech of encouragement to his men (*O socii...*, ["O comrades"] 1.198f.), the stag scene has generally been interpreted as a sign of Aeneas' leadership and resistance to despair.[4] Although Pöschl does not focus on Aeneas' hunt, it is clear how he would interpret it. The opening scenes of the epic (1.8–296) present, in Pöschl's view, a struggle between the forces of order and the forces of chaos, culminating in the victory of order. As such, they foreshadow the movement and message of the *Aeneid* as a whole. This "idea of regulation" is portrayed in Neptune's calming of the storm, in "Aeneas' reaction to fortune's blow," of which the hunt is a part, and in Jupiter's reassurance to the troubled Venus that the fates of the Trojans *manent immota* ["remain unmoved"] (1.257).

I intend to show that such an understanding of Aeneas' hunt presents a one-sided reading of a complex event. The "optimistic" and "pessimistic" traditions of Vergilian criticism each emphasize but one component of what is in reality an ambiguous blend. Through a comparative analysis of Vergil's transformation of his Homeric sources, a New Critical reading of Vergil's language, and a structuralist interpretation of the symbolic uses of hunting, I would argue that Aeneas the hunter is both a Jupiter and a Juno, both a force for order and a force for chaos. As an agent of civilization, he must combine both of these roles; for all creation involves destruction, an insight implicit in Rome's birth from the ashes of Troy.[5]

II.

Any detailed assessment of Aeneas' hunt must begin with a backward glance to Homer. Pöschl has noted how closely Vergil models *Aeneid* 1 in general on the

Odyssey.[6] Aeneas' first act in particular is based on *Odyssey* 10.142–70, where Odysseus, newly landed on Circe's island, sets out to scout the territory and turns to hunting when a stag fortuitously crosses his path. W. R. Johnson has shown how the detailed realism of the Homeric scene has been condensed and abstracted in Vergil's account.[7] Homer carefully describes how Odysseus manages to carry his one stag back to the ship; but Vergil, even though Aeneas has seven with which to contend, simply reports: *hinc portum petit*…["From here he seeks the port"] (1.194).

It is surprising, given his fidelity to (yet condensation of) his Homeric model, that Vergil has nonetheless transformed Odysseus' hunt in telling ways. First of all, Vergil has conflated two of Odysseus' hunts, both the stag hunt on Circe's island and a goat hunt at *Odyssey* 9.152–60. From the goat hunt Vergil borrows the idea that the object of the hunt is not a solitary animal but a herd and that its results are shared equally among the ships. Why, in the face of the obvious "logistical" problems it creates, does Vergil have Aeneas confront not a single stag but a herd?

In part the answer is that Vergil wishes to present Aeneas as the just provider who kills a stag for each of his surviving ships; but this, I believe, is not all of the answer. Like Odysseus, Aeneas does not consciously set off to hunt for food.[8] He is concerned about his comrades lost at sea; the verb used to describe his ascent to a rocky lookout, *conscendit* ["climbs"], reinforces that motive, since *conscendere* is often used to mean "to board ship."[9] It is as if Aeneas were still at sea climbing high in his ship to look for the remainder of his fleet. His heart, in other words, is not on land with his men who are dining but at sea with those who may be dying. Vergil emphasizes the thoroughness of his search (*omnem/prospectum late*…["full prospect wide"]) and his desire to spy even one of his comrades (*Anthea…aut Capyn…aut…arma Caici* ["Antheus…or Capys…or…the arms of Caicus"]).[10]

Aeneas can see none of these three; but, as his attention shifts abruptly, he catches sight of three stags on the shore. In every sense these deer are presented as a contrasting parallel to the Trojans themselves. The three stags are "leaders" who have behind them their "entire herd." The three commanders for whom Aeneas has been searching are apparently lost, and their men along with them. The deer "feed throughout the valley," while those Trojans who have survived the storm are eating only salvaged grain. The three stags are "wandering" along the shore; *errare* ["to wander"] is Vergil's and Aeneas' own verb to describe the Trojans in Book One.[11] In a passage which is otherwise a pared-down version of Homer's precise description, those details which are Vergil's own must have special significance. Here, it seems to me, Vergil has modified the Homeric episode in a way clearly intended to present the deer as a counterpart to the Trojans themselves.[12]

Vergil has made Homer's stag not just a herd, but also an army, for the language of the scene is clearly not that of the hunt but of the battlefield. The herd of deer follow the three stags (*hos tota armenta sequuntur* ["the entire herd follows them"]) just as elsewhere in the poem soldiers are said to follow their commanders (10.799: *socii magno clamore sequuntur* ["his comrades follow with a great cry"]; 9.54: *socii fremituque sequuntur* ["and his comrades follow with a roar"]; and 9.162:…*ast illos centeni quemque sequuntur/purpurei cristis iuvenes*… ["but a hundred follow each of them, youth of purple crests"]). *Armentum* ["herd of cattle"], as Servius perceived, is a surprising word to use of deer: *Armenta videtur nove de cervis dixisse, cum proprie boum sint vel equorum vel ceterorum quibus in armis utimur* ["he seems newly to have said 'armenta' of stags, since they are properly 'armenta' of cattle, or of horses or other animals which we use in war"]. Vergil's choice of it here may in fact have something to do with its link to *arma* ["arms"] and the military connotations of that word.[13] Deer, which are proverbially timid animals, have here been presented as if they were prepared for war.[14] This interpretation is reinforced by Vergil's use of *agmen* ["formation"] to characterize the line of stags in 1.186. Although in its root sense this word simply means "something that is driven," it is most generally used to mean "an army on the march" and this latter sense is the one most prevalent by far in Vergil. Even when the word is applied to insects and animals, it is usually because they are acting like armies.[15] This *agmen* has its *ductores* ["leaders"], whom Aeneas "lays low" (*sternit*).[16] The military language in which this entire event is described is crowned by an Homeric formula always used on the battlefield:[17]

nec prius absistit quam septem ingentia victor
corpora fundat humi...   1.192–3

["nor does he back away until he, the victor, strews bodies on the ground"]

alla kai empês
ou lêxô prin Trôas hadên elasai polemoio.
Iliad 19.422–3

["But even so I will not stop until I have driven the Trojans to their fill of war."]

Trôas d' ou prin lêxô hyperphialous enarizôn
prin elsai kata astu...   Iliad 21.224–5

["But I will not stop killing the arrogant Trojans until I have penned them in their city."]

At the end of the hunt Aeneas is characterized as a *victor*, an epithet applied to him on six other occasions, all but one of them martial.[18]

Some would argue that language of this sort is appropriate for a hunt. After all, hunting was regularly seen in the ancient world as training for war.[19] The more relevant issue, however, is whether epic poets shared that assumption and reflected it in their diction. As Edward Schmoll has recently pointed out, the equivalent episode in the *Odyssey* likewise has a martial tone.[20] Since Odysseus is himself the narrator of his hunt, he is, Schmoll argues, using martial terms in order to convey to the peaceful Phaeacians a sense of what war is like. But the hunt also meets his own need to play the warrior in a world where there are now few opportunities to do so. Clearly Vergil found the starting point for his diction in Homer, but his purposes can not be entirely the same as Homer's. For it is not Aeneas who describes his hunt in this way but the poet himself; moreover, the audience is not Dido and her Carthaginians but we the readers of the poem. Is Vergil trying to impress us with Aeneas' prowess as a warrior just as Odysseus was trying to impress the Phaeacians? In a poem which begins with the hendiadys *arma virumque* ["arms and the man"], such a purpose would seem only natural.[21]

Before we conclude too readily, however, that Vergil is glorifying both Aeneas and war, we need to consider yet another feature of Vergil's language: the parallel it suggests between what Aeneas does to the deer and what Juno has, through the storm, already done to Aeneas himself. Juno, angry that she has been unable to impede Aeneas' progress toward Italy, calls upon Aeolus and his winds to attack Aeneas' fleet. Juno models her action on that of Minerva, who had snatched up *corripuit* (1.45) Ajax and impaled him on a rock. It is this same verb of swift and emotional action which Vergil uses to describe Aeneas' snatching up *corripuit* (1.188) of his weapons to attack the stags. Juno's orders to Aeolus are to scatter Aeneas' fleet and to cast out his men into the sea: *age diversos et dissice corpora ponto* ["drive them apart and scatter bodies over the sea"] (1.70). Aeneas' attack on the stags has a similar disruptive effect: *miscet agens telis nemora inter frondea turbam* ["he disturbs the crowd driving them with his weapons throughout the leafy groves"] (1.191). *Miscere* ["to mix up, disturb"] is used on two occasions to describe the effect of Aeolus' winds *magno misceri murmure pontum* ["to disturb the sea with mighty rumbling"] (1.124); *miscere et tantas audetis tollere moles?* ["do you dare to mix up and raise such great trouble?"] (1.134); Aeneas' attack, *miscet agens telis* ["he disturbs driving with weapons"], is matched by that of the wind-stirred wave which *torquet agens circum* ["twists driving round"] (1.117). Juno's command, *dissice corpora ponto* ["scatter bodies over the sea"], is paralleled in the outcome of Aeneas' hunt: *corpora fundat humo* ["strew bodies on the ground"] (1.193). Just as Aeneas' attack on the *agmen* ["formation"] of stags is presented as an act of war, so too the winds' attack on the Trojans is likened to an army besieging a city: *ac venti velut agmine facto,/ qua data porta, ruunt....*["and the winds, just like a company in formation, where gateway is given, rush"] (1.82–3).[22]

As if these verbal parallels were not enough, Vergil confirms the link between Juno's and Aeneas' actions through an omen which Venus interprets for us later in Book One. Venus, disguised as a huntress, seeks to assure Aeneas that the remainder of his fleet is safe (1.393–6):

> aspice bis senos laetantis agmine cycnos,
> aetheria quos lapsa plaga Iovis ales aperto
> turbabat caelo; nunc terras ordine longo
> aut capere aut captas iam despectare videntur.

> ["Look at the twice six swans rejoicing in their formation, which the bird of Jove, gliding from airy space, was throwing into disarray in the open sky; now in a long line, regrouped, they seem either to take the ground or look down on ground already taken."]

Aeneas' men are like the *agmen* of swans who have been thrown into disarray (*turbabat*) by the bird of Jove, which here represents the anger of Juno.[23] Now they have regrouped (*ordine longo*) and are safely reaching land again. The parallel which the omen suggests between the Trojans and an *agmen* of birds was already at work in Vergil's mind, I submit, in the stag hunt as well. There the *longum...agmen* ["long...formation"] (1.186) of stags is a parallel to the situation of the Trojans before Juno's storm has struck and ultimately after it as well, a situation which the omen compares to that of *laetantis agmine cycnos* ["swans rejoicing in their formation"].[24] Aeneas' effect on the stags (*et omnem/ miscet...turbam* ["also the whole crowd...he disturbs"], 1.190–1) is likewise that which Juno, through the storm, has had on his fleet, an effect which the omen compares to that of Jupiter's bird on the swans: *"quos...turbabat caelo"* ["which...it was throwing into disarray in the sky"]. Aeneas' first act in the poem, then, however beneficent its results may be for the Trojans, presents him as a victim of Juno who acts in the ways of Juno herself.

III.

✧   ✧   ✧

Traditionally Aeneas' hunt has been interpreted as the civilized creation of order out of chaos. The very fact that what Aeneas does here, on the most literal level, is not to create order out of chaos, but chaos out of the previously ordered herd of deer, should make us cautious about this symbolic equation between hunting and civilized order.

✧   ✧   ✧

As hunter, Aeneas is a Junonian figure. From the very beginning of the *Aeneid*,...Juno is characterized as a huntress with the Trojans as her prey. But Juno does more than just hunt Aeneas; she also indirectly makes Aeneas turn hunter himself. Aeneas hunts in Book One because Juno's storm has driven him to an unknown shore. In Book Four Juno uses Aeneas' hunt with Dido to serve her own purposes. It is Allecto, working at Juno's behest, who drives Ascanius' hounds in Book Seven to attack Sylvia's pet deer; and it is because of Allecto's influence as well that Turnus is brought into conflict with Aeneas, only to be, in Vergil's simile (12.749–51), "hunted down" in the end.

Aeneas does not, however, play the role of Juno consciously in Book One.

✧   ✧   ✧

Aeneas' thoughts are on his lost comrades when he turns toward the stags, who appear to have what he has now seemingly lost: a community which is together, with the people following behind its leaders. Both the vigor of his attack and the violence which it does to the previously pastoral scene suggest that the hunt grows out of the pain and suffering which the storm and, through it, Juno have inflicted on Aeneas. Having been so long a victim, at last Aeneas has—through the hunt—obtained the chance to be a *victor*. During both the collapse of Troy and the storm at sea, Aeneas had wanted to pick up his arms, to fight back. The hunt represents his first chance to do that, as its language of war makes clear.[25] Hunted by Juno, Aeneas emerges "victorious" by turning hunter himself. In the process, just as his first hunt destroys the orderly and pastoral community of deer, so his later hunts will bring destruction to Carthage and Latium.[26] Hunting, then, is here not just the symbolic equivalent of civilization, of order, of Neptune calming the waves; it also parallels...the storm and all it represents: violence and destruction.[27]

This ambiguity in the symbolism of Aeneas' first hunt is reinforced by the parallels between that hunt and the first simile in the poem, which comes but a few lines earlier. Neptune, in stilling the waves, is likened there to a leader who seeks to calm a crowd: *ille regit dictis animos et pectora mulcet* ["he orders their minds with words and calms their hearts"] (1.153). Critics have rightly suggested that this simile announces the role which Aeneas himself, like Augustus, is intended to perform:

that of the political leader who restores order in a strife-torn world. Vergil emphasizes that Aeneas has assumed this role by using almost the same words (*dictis
maerentia pectora mulcet* ["he calms with words their grieving hearts"], 1.197) to
characterize Aeneas' famous speech to his men as he had used in the earlier simile
to describe the effect of a political leader upon the angry masses. In the hunt itself,
however, the hunt which immediately precedes the calming speech, Aeneas does
not play the same role which is assigned to the political leader in the simile. For in
the simile it is the masses which are violent (*saevitque animis ignobile vulgus* ["and
the masses rage, ignoble in spirit"], 1.149) and the leader who restores order. But in
the hunt, the masses, the "*vulgus*" of deer, are peaceful and Aeneas is the one who
attacks and confuses them: *tum vulgus.../ miscet agens telis...* ["then he disturbs...the
crowd, driving with weapons"] (1.190–1).[28] If Vergil intends us to use his first simile
as the point of reference by which to measure his hero, then Aeneas in his first act
only partially succeeds: he restores order for the Trojans *but* he also creates chaos
for his victims.

IV.

In arguing that Aeneas as hunter is "an image of civilized man," J. Roger Dunkle
seems to suggest that Vergil derived this equation from the Greek tragedians.[29] It is
certainly true that Aeschylus portrayed Prometheus as a hunter in his quest to give
men the use of fire; hunting was regularly included in lists of man's civilizing
achievements such as Sophocles' "Ode to Man" (*Antigone* 332–75).[30] Recent studies
of hunting in Greek literature, however, have shown the inherent ambiguity of hunting vis-a-vis civilization:

> Hunters and shepherds...are also felt as ambiguous throughout classical
> Greek literature, from Homer to Theocritus. Literally and metaphorically,
> they inhabit the borderland between savage and civilized realms: they jour-
> ney between mountain and plain, country and city, and live in intimate
> contact with the wild.[31]

Such a conception of the hunter and his role fits well the circumstances of Aeneas
as hunter in *Aeneid* 1, where Aeneas is the borderland between savage and civilized
and on a journey between country and city. If we examine Aeneas' hunting through
the eyes of the structuralist, we can, I believe, better understand the complex and
ambiguous process by which humankind seeks to move from Nature to Culture, a
process which Aeneas undertakes in his first act in the guise of the hunter and
which, in a broader sense, is the subject of the *Aeneid* as a whole.[32]

When Aeneas and his men are finally blown to shore after the storm, they enter
a harbor whose primitive rockiness is emphasized (*hinc atque hinc vastae rupes
geminique minantur/ in caelum scopuli* ["on this side and that, the vast rocks and twin
cliffs menace to the sky"], 1.162–3; *fronte sub adversa scopulis pendentibus antrum* ["under
the opposite face the cave from hanging cliffs"], 1.166). As Eugene Vance has nicely
argued, the storm has driven Aeneas back to a primitive stage of human existence,
where he must again use flint to make fire.[33] Aeneas' hunting is another mark of his
status now as primitive man. But even in this natural setting, Aeneas emphasizes
the civilized goal of the city (*tendimus in Latium* ["we are making for Latium"],

1.205) toward which he journeys. In a narrative sense, Aeneas' hunt leads from the rocky harbor to the city of Carthage (Venus' guise as a hunter as she steers Aeneas there reinforces this function). Paradigmatically, the hunt partakes both of the primitive wildness and the civilized city. By its very nature, hunting is a primitive activity, one which takes place spatially outside of the city and chronologically before the city, since the city arises only when humankind, having discovered the art of growing grain, abandons the nomadic life of the hunter. But Aeneas' hunt also reflects, in its systematic process (as Vance has suggested) and in its civilized values (Aeneas shares the meat equally with all the ships and comrades), the arts which make the city possible.[34] Aeneas' speech to his men reiterates this contrast between wilderness and city, and re-enacts through words what the hunt has accomplished in deeds: the movement from Nature to Culture. In recalling the hardships which the Trojans have endured in the past, Aeneas lays emphasis upon rockiness: *vos et Scyllaeam rabiem penitusque sonantis/ accestis scopulos, vos et Cyclopia saxa/ experti* ["you have come near even the fury of Scylla and the cliffs sounding deep within and you have experienced the Cyclopean rocks"] (1.200-2). But there is still reason to be encouraged, because *per tot discrimina rerum/ tendimus in Latium, sedes ubi fata quietas/ ostendunt* ["through so many crises of events we are making for Latium, where the fates hold out tranquil sites"] (1.204-6). In Aeneas' first act, hunting facilitates this passage from the rocks of nature to the city of culture.

The ambiguities of that passage are most notable in the way in which hunting mirrors the actions both of Jupiter and of Juno. Like Jupiter, Aeneas looks out over the storm-tossed sea (Aeneas 1.181: *prospectum...petit* ["seeks...the prospect"], [cf. 1.185]; Jupiter, 1.223-4: *Juppiter...despiciens mare...*["Jupiter...looking down on the sea..."]; likewise Neptune, 1.126-7: *et alto/ prospiciens...*["and looking out on the deep"] [cf. 1.155]) and stops abruptly at what he sees (*constitit* ["stopped short"] Aeneas, 1.187, Jupiter, 1.226). Aeneas then proceeds to soothe his troubled men with words just as Neptune had calmed the waves and as Jupiter will console Venus.[35] Yet in the hunt Aeneas, like Juno and the winds she summons, uses violence and war to create chaos where there had been a natural sense of order and community. Hunting here, then, is like a storm and a war; but it also serves to restore peace and calm.

Since the hunt serves to provide food, it clearly is linked to the culinary code. When the Trojans are washed ashore, their only food is *Cererem corruptam* ["the spoiled grain of Ceres"] (1.177). Grain is paradigmatically linked with civilization, but here, driven back into a primitive setting, the Trojans have only "ruined" or "spoiled grain." It is a sign of their movement back toward civilization that the Trojans set out to transform this "spoiled" food through cooking. The language which describes this process, however, has savage overtones which are reflected in the hunt as well. The utensils by which the cooking is done are *Cerealiaque arma* ["grain's armaments"] (1.177).[36] Cooking, then, is an act of "war" and equally destructive: *frugesque receptas/ et torrere parant flammis et frangere saxo* ["they prepare to roast the rescued grains with fire and to crush them with rock"] (1.178-9).[37] To be nourished, the language suggests, we must destroy. This is precisely the message and function of the hunt as well. Burning and breaking transforms grain into food just as scattering and shooting transforms animals into food. The primitiveness of the process is highlighted in the description of the cooking of the venison: *tergora diripiunt costis et viscera nudant;/ pars in frusta secant veribusque trementia figunt* ["they rip the hides from the ribs and lay bare the innards; one group cuts up pieces and they pierce the trembling pieces with spits"] (1.211-12). Cooking, hunting, and warfare are here parallel processes. All three seek to transform nature into culture, but they do so in ways which are violent and destructive.

In presenting Aeneas' first act as a hunt, Vergil has shown the terrible duality of human existence: in order to live, we must kill. In order for Rome to be born, for the city and civilization to be made possible, other peoples and cities must fall as victims. Readings of the poem which are optimistic or pessimistic may well miss the inherently ambiguous nature of human and societal development. In the very act of creating the "civilized" city, Aeneas must act in ways which link him with the "natural," with violence, storm and animal.

V.

❖ ❖ ❖

A unity...links Aeneas' first act with all the hunts which follow. We should remember that Aeneas' stag hunt is his first act in North Africa; the disruptive effect which the hunt visits upon the leaders of the stags and their "peaceful" community foreshadows the equally disruptive effect which Aeneas will have on Dido and Carthage. Ascanius' hunt in Book Seven (7.475f.) has much the same effect as well. The martial imagery of Aeneas' first hunt foreshadows the war which Ascanius' hunt will initiate, a war which will culminate in Aeneas' "hunt" of Turnus (12.749–51). It can be no accident that Vergil chooses to present Aeneas' hunt, his first act in Book One, as an act of war and his act of war in Book Twelve, his last act in the epic, as a hunt. The death of Turnus, like Aeneas' killing of the stags, grows out of a concern for and loyalty to Aeneas' comrades. But the implicitly Junonian violence of Aeneas' first hunt is explicit and far more vivid in his last. If hunting is an act of civilization, we are left to wonder whether the journey from Nature to Culture, from *arma virumque* ["arms and the man"] to the *altae moenia Romae* ["the high walls of Rome"], really takes us very far.[38]

Notes

[1]Citations of Vergil are from the OCT edition, ed. by R. A. B. Mynors (Oxford 1969). Citations of Homer are from the OCT editions, ed. by D. B. Monro and T. W. Allen: *Iliad* (Oxford 1920[3]), *Odyssey* (Oxford 1917–19[2]).

[2]*The Art of the Aeneid*, trans. by Gerda Seligson (Ann Arbor 1962) 24.

[3]John Arthur Hanson first led me to think about the passage which is the focus of this paper in a seminar on Vergil at Princeton. I dedicate this article to his memory, as a small token of appreciation for a prodding but gentle teacher and a loyal and constant friend. I have chosen the title "first act" to characterize Aeneas' hunt because up to this point in Book One he has only spoken and reacted; the hunt is the first major action which he initiates in the epic. It was only after choosing this title that I read Art Hanson's chapter on Vergil in *Ancient Writers: Greece and Rome* (New York 1982) 2:669–701. It seems appropriate, somehow, that there I found my title echoed in Art's own words: "Aeneas' first act in the poem...is to shoot down seven tall stags..." (699).

At different stages of its development, this paper was presented orally to the Classical Association of the Midwest and South (Minneapolis, April 11, 1985) and in substantially revised form to the Classical Association of the Atlantic States (Princeton, September 25, 1987).

[4]For example, William S. Anderson, *The Art of the Aeneid* (Englewood Cliffs 1969) 25 ("Still refusing to yield to weariness or discouragement, he locates a herd of deer, kills seven

and brings back rich meat to his men."), and Roger A. Hornsby, *Patterns of Action in the Aeneid* (Iowa City 1970) 2 ("He finds and slays seven deer with which he feeds and refreshes his men after their harrowing escape from the storm. His intention is clearly beneficent and so is the result."). The very fact that Aeneas is not expressing his real emotions in this speech, as Vergil immediately tells us (*spem vultu simulat*, 1.209), should make us cautious about using the speech as our explanation of the acts which precede it. Moreover, the hunt and the speech may not be as intimately linked as they have been seen to be. Aeneas does not mention food during his speech; perhaps this would not be surprising except for the fact that Odysseus, in his much shorter speech (*Od.* 10.174–77), says, in essence: "We are not dead yet, so let us eat and drink." The successful hunt is explicit cause for encouragement in the *Odyssey*; it is not so in the *Aeneid*.

⁵For a summary of the "optimistic" and "pessimistic" approaches to Vergil, see W. R. Johnson, *Darkness Visible* (Berkeley 1976) 11 and footnote 10. If it seems in what follows that I favor one-sidedly the pessimistic school, the reason is my desire to correct the overly optimistic readings of this episode which have prevailed.

⁶p. 25; cf. also R. D. Williams, "Vergil and the *Odyssey*," *Phoenix* 17 (1963) 271.

⁷Note 5, above, 36.

⁸Both R. G. Austin, *P. Vergili Maronis Aeneidos Liber Primus* (Oxford 1971) and the TLL VII.1.2183, 67f. interpret *interea* in 1.180 to mean that the narrative is turning to a new subject. In other words, Aeneas' departure from his men does not suggest that he has missed his meal nor that his expedition grows out of the desire to find food to augment the meal then in progress. In the passage from the *Odyssey* which is Vergil's immediate model, there is no meal preceding Odysseus' hunt. Vergil perhaps derived the idea for the meal from an earlier scene in the *Odyssey* (10.56–60) where Odysseus, driven back by the winds to Aiolia, has a midday meal before setting off to meet Aiolos.

⁹Vergil uses the verb with this specific meaning at *Aeneid* 1.381 and 10.155, the equivalent verb in the *Odyssey* (10.146), "*anêion*," lacks this connotation.

¹⁰Vergil heightens the pathos of Aeneas' search, in contrast with Odysseus', by substituting the particular for the general. Odysseus was searching only "for sight or sound of human labor," whereas Aeneas is searching for comrades whom he knows by name and whose situation he can visualize in detail because he has experienced it himself as well. He imagines Antheus as being *iactatum vento*, a phrase which recalls the description of Aeneas himself in the opening lines of the epic, *et terris iactatus et alto* (1.3). He pictures to himself the arms of Caicus as *celsis in puppibus*, a phrase used of Aeneas at 4.554 and 10.261. Cf. Theodore M. Andersson, *Early Epic Scenery: Homer, Virgil and the Medieval Legacy* (Ithaca 1976) 60: "Another significant feature of the psychological portrait is Aeneas' seaward gaze....The psychological model is not so much the exploratory gaze of Odysseus among the Laestrygonians or on Aeaea as his forlorn gaze into the empty sea from Calypso's island (5.158)."

¹¹Cf. 1.32 (*multosque per annos/ errabant acti fatis maria omnia circum*) and 1.333 (*erramus vento huc vastis et fluctibus acti*).

¹²Homer's stag is described as coming down from his pasture (*ek nomou hulês*, 10.159) to the river to get a drink; Vergil has expanded this description by placing the leaders of the herd on the shore (presumably they, too, have come down to drink) and by adding a herd behind them which is feeding in the valley.

¹³As the TLL II.611.7–8 suggests, *armentum* and *arma* may perhaps be linked through a common ancestry with the Greek verb *arariskô*, "to fit on." Servius' use of the phrase *in armis* to explain the correct usage of *armenta* is but another suggestion of the possible link between these two words. Vergil himself shows his awareness of the link when he makes a pun in *Aeneid* 3.540: *bello armantur equi, bellum haec armenta minantur*. Another possible etymology, the one favored by Varro (*LL* 5.96), links *armentum* with *arare*, "to plow."

¹⁴In *Georgics* 3.265 Vergil speaks of *cervi* as *imbelles* and in *Aeneid* 4.158 deer are, in Ascanius' eyes, *pecora...inertia*. In Seneca's *Phaedra* 341-2, deer only fight when their marriages are threatened: *si coniugio timuere, poscunt timidi proelia cervi*.

¹⁵E.g., in 1.393 Vergil speaks of an *agmen* of swans, but, as we shall see shortly, the swans are an omen representing Aeneas' fleet. In 4.404 and 406 the departure of Aeneas' men from Carthage is compared to an *agmen* of ants as they plunder a heap of grain and bear it away to store it up for the winter; the action of these ants is appropriately compared with that of an

army carrying away booty (*praeda*) from a captured city. In the famous bee simile at 1.430f., an *agmen* of bees protects the hive, but again their defensive function makes the military language appropriate.

[16]Vergil uses *ductores* in *Georgics* 4.88 to characterize two bees fighting for supremacy in the hive; otherwise he always uses the word to describe men. Even in the *Georgics*, the word is applied to bees because they are venturing out into the battlefield, in human fashion, to fight a duel. *Sternere*, in the sense "to lay low," is used most frequently by Vergil to describe the killing of a warrior on the battlefield.

[17]Cf. *Iliad* 5.287f., 8.473f., 21.294f., 21.340f.; the formula is found once in the *Odyssey* (22.63–64), where Odysseus says, *oude ken hôs eti cheiras emas lêxaimi phonoio/prin pasan mnêstêras huperbasiên apotisai.*

[18]*Victor* is used to characterize Aeneas as a victor by prayer over Juno in 3.439. Elsewhere it is used to characterize him as a victor in battle in 5.261, 8.50, 8.61, 10.569 and 11.4.

[19]See J. K. Anderson, *Hunting in the Ancient World* (Berkeley 1985), chapters one and five.

[20]"Odysseus and the Stag: The Parander," *Helios* 14.1 (Spring 1987) 22–28. Schmoll's article, which only came to my attention after this article was completed, looks at Odysseus' hunt in much the same way in which I look at Aeneas'.

[21]The closest parallel I can find to the military imagery of Aeneas' hunt comes in the opening of Seneca's *Phaedra*, where Hippolytus issues orders for a hunt, orders which characterize the hunt as a military expedition. Of this Senecan passage A. J. Boyle ("In Nature's Bonds: A Study of Seneca's 'Phaedra'," *ANRW* 32.2 [1985] 1293) has commented: "The military imagery of the monody is telling in this regard—the *victor* (52), the spoils (*praeda*, 77), the triumph (*triumpho*, 80)—imagery which, drawing an analogy between Hippolytus' confident aggression, his worship of destructive power, and that of Rome's military, underscores the former and intimates its contemporary relevance." In a similar way, the military language of Aeneas' hunt might well suggest the tools by which Rome will ultimately be built. But I doubt that Aeneas' hunt has quite the contemporary relevance which D. L. Drew, *The Allegory of the Aeneid* (Oxford 1927) 67 wishes to give it: "I would urge that Vergil is alluding to the series of disasters, some of them due to bad weather, suffered by Augustus in the protracted naval war waged against Sextus Pompeius, 38–36 B.C, in general and to the great storm of the first year's operations, in particular...."

[22]The parallel here is not symmetrical, because the winds, the attacking force, are the *agmen* in the storm, but the stags, the victims in Aeneas' attack, are the *agmen* in the hunt.

[23]See Michael C. J. Putnam, *The Poetry of the Aeneid* (Cambridge, MA 1965) 166.

[24]The omen's specific reference is to the Trojans after the storm, when they will be reunited again. But implicitly such a link would also have been appropriate before the storm had done its damage as well. During the hunt itself, however, the fact that the stags are an *agmen* all together seems not a parallel to the situation of the Trojans but a contrast to it, as emphasized by Aeneas' failure to find his comrades at sea.

❖ ❖ ❖

[25]Schmoll (note 20, above) 25 argues for a similar motive in Odysseus' hunt: "So this combat, proffered by the god, serves to bolster the waning self-worth of the hero in terms of the archaic standards to which he still clings, a temporary but necessary fillip for a hero beleaguered by the press of anonymity and oblivion."

[26]C. Grier Davis, "The Motif of the Hunt in Vergil's *Aeneid*," in *Landmarks in Western Culture*, ed. by Donald N. Baker and George W. Fasel (Englewood Cliffs 1968) suggests (205) that the victory of order in history is coupled with a tension or chaos on the level of personal relationships. But it is not only on the individual level that such disorder exists. Rome's victory in history requires national, not just individual victims. Davis might well have seen this when he argued that there is a parallelism between the fall of Troy and Dido's death at Carthage. Dido's personal tragedy, in its links with Troy's, takes on a broader scope, foreshadowing the national tragedy which Rome will bring to Carthage.

[27]In fact, of the three later hunts in the epic, two are accompanied, either literally or figuratively by a storm. A storm, again sent by Juno, strikes during Dido's and Aeneas' hunt: 4.160–61: *Interea magno misceri murmure caelum/ incipit.* This line is a clear echo of the storm in book 1.124–5: *Interea magno misceri murmure pontum/ emissamque hiemem sensit Neptunus...* When in book 12.746–55 Aeneas is compared to a hunting dog who has cornered his prey, the

description of the battle likens it to a storm: 12.756-7: *tum vero exoritur clamor ripaeque lacusque/ responsant circa et caelum tonat omne tumultu.*

[28]Vergil uses *vulgus* on two other occasions to describe a group composed of other than men: In *Georgics* 3.469 of sheep, in *Georgics* 4.69 of bees. In the latter case, the word is clearly used because the bees are acting like a human crowd about to watch a duel.

[29]J. Roger Dunkle, "The Hunter and Hunting in the *Aeneid*," *Ramus* 2 (1973) note 4.

[30]On hunting as a part of man's progress toward civilization, see Eric Havelock, *The Liberal Temper in Greek Politics* (London 1957). It is worth noting that the examples cited by Dunkle mostly show how man as hunter is a failure at civilization (Creon in the *Antigone*, Pentheus in the *Bacchae:* "But as in Sophocles' *Antigone* man's effort to conquer nature as represented in the *Bacchae* by Dionysus ends in complete failure and in even more terrible destruction" [p. 141]). The one positive example cited by Dunkle is the Prometheus of Aeschylus' *Prometheus Bound,* who is presented as hunter in his search for civilizing fire. But as Walter Moskalew, *Formular Language and Poetic Design in the Aeneid* (Leiden 1982) 166, note 69 points out, a more likely source for Vergil's use of the image of hunting "is not Aeschylus' *Prometheus Bound*…but rather the *Oresteia,* where hunting expresses the chaotic cycle of blood vengeance." I agree with Moskalew and wonder, in fact, whether Vergil, in choosing a stag hunt as Aeneas' first act, was not recalling Agamemnon's stag hunt and its painful consequences. Sophocles' account (*Electra* 558f.) of that hunt parallels Vergil's in several ways: Agamemnon was not intending to hunt but surprised a full-antlered stag and was triumphant over his success.

[31]Charles Segal, *Tragedy and Civilization* (Cambridge, MA 1981) 31.

[32]Schmoll (above, note 20) 24 finds a similar dichotomy in Odysseus' hunt: "While endeavoring to be heroic, Odysseus brings forth in his tale elements which indicate that his archaic heroism is being tempered with civilized values." The function of the episode is thus to show the transition which Odysseus must undergo in order to return from the warrior culture of the *Iliad* to the domestic world of Ithaka.

In suggesting a structuralist approach to hunting in the *Aeneid,* I am aware that the procedure is not, strictly speaking, applicable. The structuralist seeks to find similarities between patterns of thought in a text and those in the structure of the society which produced that text. With regard to hunting and its ambiguity, such a correlation exists for the Greeks but not so clearly for the Romans. Following the example of the Hellenistic Greeks, aristocratic Romans came to see hunting as a sport compatible with civilized life. The hunts which Julius Caesar staged for the people of Rome enhanced his career, and Augustus encouraged athletic activities like hunting for their moral value. Consequently, I would not argue that Vergil's treatment of hunting is a reflection of its meaning in his own culture but rather part of the tradition which he derives from the Greeks. If one were to approach the issue from the perspective of audience response, it seems likely that Vergil's Roman audience would have seen Aeneas' hunting in an heroic light.

[33]"Sylvia's Pet Stag: Wildness and Domesticity in Virgil's *Aeneid*," *Arethusa* 14.1 (Spring 1981) 127-138.

[34]In the story which Protagoras tells in Plato's dialogue of that same name, the ability to make war on animals is a sign that man has mastered the art of politics: "Thus provided for, they lived at first in scattered groups; there were not cities. Consequently they were devoured by wild beasts, since they were in every respect the weaker, and their technical skill, though a sufficient aid to their nurture, did not extend to making war on the beasts, for they had not the art of politics of which the art of war is a part" (322a-b, trans. by W. K. C. Guthrie). When Hermes, at Zeus' instruction, bestows on men the civic arts, men acquire "qualities of respect for others and a sense of Justice, so as to bring order into our cities and create a bond of friendship and union" (322c). Both Aeneas' ability to make war on the animals and his sense of justice in sharing the meat suggest that this hunt illustrates the political arts. Vance (above, note 33) sees a contrast between Aeneas' rational and organized hunt and the sort which primitive men conduct, as described in *Georgics* 3.371-75.

[35]Charles Segal, "Art and the Hero: Narrative Point of View in *Aeneid* 1," *Arethusa* 14.1 (Spring 1981) 71, notes this link between Aeneas and Jupiter and further compares it with Lucretius, *De Rerum Natura* 2.1-10: "We are reminded of the philosopher's godlike removal and distanced prospect in the introductory lines to Lucretius' second book." My reading of Aeneas' first act, however, suggests that Aeneas is quite different from Lucretius' god:

Suave, mari magno turbantibus aequora ventis,
e terra magnum alterius spectare laborem;
non quia vexari quemquamst iucunda voluptas,
sed quibus ipse malis careas quia cernere suave est.
suave etiam belli certamina magna tueri
per campos instructa tua sine parte pericli.
sed nil dulcius est, bene quam munita tenere
edita doctrina sapientum templa serena,
despicere unde queas alios passimque videre
errare atque viam palantis quaerere vitae...

(1) We first should see that Aeneas, unlike the god, is not withdrawn from the stormy strife of the sea. That is what is foremost in his mind as he stands on the rocky overlook: he is worried about his comrades lost in the storm. Thus it is certainly not *suave* for him to look at the troubles of another, because he sees those troubles as his own. (2) Aeneas does not look down on *certamina magna* and rejoice that he is not part of them (*sine parte pericli, De Rerum Natura* 2.6). Rather, as the imagery of the hunt makes clear, he is eager to join in strife and battle. (3) In looking down on the wandering (*errantis, Aeneid* 1.185) herd of deer, Aeneas does not, as does Lucretius' god, see people wandering (*errare, De Rerum Natura* 2.10) in search of a way of life, but animals whose condition is secure, in contrast with his own uncertain one. These contrasts with Lucretius' god are one measure of Aeneas' likeness, not just with Jupiter, but with Juno as well.

[36]Robert Seymour Conway, *P. Vergili Maronis Aeneidos I* (Cambridge 1935) 50 suggests that *arma* is used here in an archaic sense meaning "fittings, tools" and is possibly derived from an older poet. To see any military connotation in the word, he seems to suggest, is to overlook the original etymology of the word and to read into it connotations associated with its English derivatives. But Brooks Otis, *Virgil: A Study in Civilized Poetry* (Oxford 1963) 158, in discussing Vergil's use of *arma* in the *Georgics* (1.160) to describe the farmer's implements, concludes that Vergil consciously plays on the military associations of the word: "But even in [*Georgics,* book 1], Virgil's attitude toward civilization is anything but optimistic... His [i.e., the farmer's] implements (the plough, waggon, winnowing fan, etc.) are but his *weapons* in a hard fight."

[37]Servius explains this procedure as due to the fact that the Romans lacked a grain mill.

❖ ❖ ❖

[38]This article was first drafted while I held a fellowship at the American Academy in Rome. I wish to thank the Academy and the National Endowment for the Humanities, which funded the fellowship, for their support. At the Academy I benefited from the critical but helpful advice of Katherine Geffcken and Charles Henderson, Jr., and I wish to express to them my appreciation.

Bernard M. W. Knox

THE SERPENT AND THE FLAME.
THE IMAGERY OF THE SECOND BOOK
OF THE *AENEID*

Knox's essay on book 2 of the *Aeneid* is one of the perduring works of Vergilian scholarship. Now nearly fifty years old, it remains a model of philological study, elegant argument, and enlightening literary analysis. Knox traces the occurrences, manifest and covert, of serpent images throughout the book that link the "principal instruments of Troy's downfall": the horse, the serpents, the ships, the Greek agent Sinon. He further reveals the serpent image's ambivalence and evolution, as an emblem of both destruction and eventually also rebirth, of concealment and of light. Through Knox's analysis, we study not only this particular image but also Vergil's practice of sustaining imagery as a means to weave themes across long stretches of narrative, to fashion in readers a cumulative poetic memory that deepens book by book. (Ed.)

The Second Book of the *Aeneid* displays the full magnificence of Virgil's imagery. In this account of Troy's last night images of raging fire and flood, ravening wolves, storms at sea, the fall of an ancient tree, lend to the events with which they are combined the proportions of a universal cataclysm.[1] Among these tremendous images of destruction there is one which by its emphatic recurrence comes to dominate all the rest. This is the image of the serpent.

Infandum regina iubes renovare dolorem ["Unspeakable, queen, the grief you order me to renew"]. Aeneas tells Dido the story of the violence of Troy's fall, engineered by concealment and completed by flames. The ferocity of the attackers, their deceit, and the flames which crown their work are time after time compared, sometimes explicitly but more often by combinations of subdued metaphor, verbal echo, and parallel situation, to the action of the serpent.

For these connotations of the serpent, violence, concealment and flames, Virgil had good precedent in the Latin tradition. It is a commonplace of Latin writing (as it is of English) to compare the serpent and the flame; in English both hiss, creep, and have flickering tongues....The serpent traditionally strikes from concealment, as the Greeks did from the horse. Finally, violence as a characteristic of the serpent...is forced on the reader's attention in the second book of the *Aeneid* by the description of the fate of Laocoon and his sons.

The serpent is thus an apt comparison for the essential nature of the Greek attackers, ferocity, their typical method, concealment, and their principal weapon, fire. But it is an ambivalent image. Besides suggesting the forces of destruction, it

Bernard M. W. Knox, "The Serpent and the Flame," *American Journal of Philology* 70.1 (1950) 379–400. Reprinted by permission of The Johns Hopkins University Press.

may also stand for rebirth, the renewal which the Latin poetic tradition associated with the casting-off of the serpent's old skin in the spring.[2] And this connotation of the serpent is of the utmost importance for the second book of the *Aeneid*, which tells of the promise of renewal given in the throes of destruction; the death agonies of Troy are the birth-pangs of Rome.

Only three passages in the book deal explicitly with serpents. In addition to the elaborate description of the death of Laocoon and his sons, there are two serpent similes; Androgeos is compared to a man who comes unaware upon a snake,[3] and Pyrrhus is compared to the snake which has cast away its old skin in the spring. These three passages are the base which supports a complex structure of references to the dominant image; elsewhere in the book the figure of the serpent is evoked by phrase after phrase which reminds us of its presence where it lies half-concealed in the language — *latet anguis in herba* ["a snake hiding in the grass"]. This dominant metaphor creeps into many contexts where its presence is surprising, and the result is in some cases a mixture of imagery which borders on the grotesque — a mixture which is typical of Shakespeare too, and which has recently been explained, in the case of *Macbeth*, as a result of the same process which can be seen in the second book of the *Aeneid*, the working of a dominant, obsessive metaphor.[4]

The manifestations of the serpent are widely distributed; the suggestions which they make form a pattern full of meaning for the book as a whole. The pattern of the metaphor runs parallel to the pattern of events, the plot; but it does more than enforce the impression made by the events, it interprets them. At the emotional climax of the book, the death of Priam, it is in the image of the serpent that the complete meaning of the event is to be seen. And as the pattern of the metaphor unfolds, an independent process of development is revealed; the imagery has, as it were, a plot of its own. In the course of its many appearances in the book the metaphor undergoes a transformation like that of the serpent which it evokes, it casts its old skin. At first suggestive of Greek violence and Trojan doom, it finally announces triumphantly the certainty of Troy's rebirth.

The first overt appearance of the serpent is the description of the fate of Laocoon and his sons (199–227). This is one of the events of the narrative, an incident in the fall of the city; there is, on the surface, nothing metaphorical about these serpents; they exist, and destroy. Their action is an essential part of the plot; the death of Laocoon removes an influential figure who might have barred the wooden horse's way. But they are something more, as both Servius and Donatus realized. The incident is a symbolic prophecy of the fall of Troy as a whole.

The serpents come from Tenedos, where the Greeks, characteristically, are in hiding. (*Huc se provecti deserto in litore condunt* ["To here they advanced and conceal themselves on the deserted shore"].)...Henry elaborates this *signum*, the prophetic significance of the serpents, in the following terms.[5] "The twin serpents prefigure the Grecian armament, which, like them, comes from Tenedos, ...like them crosses the tranquil deep, ...lands, ...slaughters the surprised and unsuspecting Trojans (prefigured by Laocoon's sons) and overturns the religion and drives out the gods (prefigured by Laocoon)." Henry supports his parallel by reference to "minute particulars," some of them verbal echoes, and points out finally that "when their work is done they take possession of the citadel under the protection of Pallas," a fact which he connects with Venus' announcement of the consummation of the city's fall — *Iam summas arces Tritonia respice Pallas insedit* ["Now on the highest citadels, look, Tritonian Pallas is seated"] (615).

✧ ✧ ✧

In fact,…the echoes of the Laocoon passage in the lines describing the fleet's arrival are only the beginning of a long series of echoes which culminates in the unmistakable parallel between the sea-serpents and Pyrrhus, son of Achilles.

This description of the death of Laocoon and his sons is the principal basis of the subsequent serpent imagery. It is one of Virgil's most impressive descriptive passages, and any echo of it which occurs later in the book brings these terrible serpents back to mind at once. There are many such echoes, and they awaken metaphors which without the connection provided by the echo might have lain dormant or dead.

The description begins (201) with Laocoon sacrificing at the altars, *ad aras. Ecce autem gemini a Tenedo* ["Look now twins from Tenedos"] – they are twin serpents, and this word is repeated later in line 225, *at gemini* ["but twins"]. The Atridae are twice described with this word later in the book, *gemini Atridae* (415) and *geminos Atridas* (500) ["twin Atridae, twin sons of Atreus"]….The twin Atridae are compared to the twin serpents; both couples are forces of merciless destruction.

The serpents proceed side by side to the shore, *pariterque ad litora tendunt.* Their bloody crests tower over the waves, *iubaeque sanguineae superant undas*; their length behind wreathes their huge backs in voluminous folds, *pars cetera…sinuatque immensa volumine terga.* Their eyes blaze, *ardentisque oculos,* and they lick their hissing mouths with flickering tongues, *sibila lambebant linguis vibrantibus ora.* They make for Laocoon, but first attack his sons. Embracing the childrens' bodies, they twist around them, *corpora natorum serpens amplexus uterque implicat,* and biting deep feed on their wretched limbs, *miseros morsu depascitur artus.* Next Laocoon himself, as he tries to intervene, *auxilio subeuntem ac tela ferentem,* is seized and enfolded; the serpents tower head and neck above him, *superant capite et cervicibus altis.* Their task fulfilled, they glide off to shelter, *at gemini lapsu…effugiunt,* and hide beneath the feet of the statue of Pallas, *sub pedibusque deae…teguntur.*

This terrifying picture, as verbal echo and parallel event and situation recall it to the memory throughout the rest of the book, is seen in retrospect to contain all the violence of the sack of Troy. These lines foreshadow not only the arrival of the Greek fleet, but the attack, the Trojan resistance, the deaths of Polites and Priam, and the flames which tower over the burning city. They present the fall of Troy as the action of the serpent.[6]

The next forty lines (228-68) apply the metaphor to the particular agents and events of the city's fall. The process begins at once. The two lines which follow immediately (228-9) describe the reaction of the Trojan bystanders to Laocoon's death:

Tum vero tremefacta novus per pectora cunctis
insinuat pavor.

["Then truly through our trembling hearts a new fear creeps into everyone."]

"A new fear winds into our breast" (Mackail). *Insinuat pavor* ["fear creeps in"] is a reminiscence of Lucretius' *Divom metus insinuarit pectora* ["Fear of the gods crept into our hearts"] (V, 73), but in Virgil's line the word *insinuat* ["creeps into"] stands out sharply, for though it is one of Lucretius' favorite words[7] Virgil uses it only here. *Sinuare* ["to creep"], which it brings to mind, is one of the stock words used of the serpent,[8] and *insinuat* ["creeps into"] is a striking echo of *sinuat* ["creeps"], which has been used only twenty lines previously — *sinuatque immensa volumine terga* ["their length behind wreathes their huge backs in voluminous folds"] (208). This terror, which causes the Trojans to accept Laocoon's fate and disregard his advice, helps to prepare for the fall of Troy; it is one of the agents of the disaster, and it is here suggested, lightly but none the less impressively, that it is itself a serpent.

The narrative proceeds to the description of the entry of the horse into the city (234 ff.), and here the same suggestion is made, this time more emphatically. The Trojans attach wheels[9] to the horse's feet, and Virgil describes this action in the words *pedibusque rotarum subiciunt lapsus* ["they place the gliding of the wheels under the feet"] (235-6). *Rotarum lapsus*, "the gliding of the wheels," is an arresting phrase, a Grecism, as Mackail points out, and probably a specific imitation of τρόχων βάσεις ["strides of wheels"] in Sophocles' *Electra* 718, as Conington suggests. In that case it is a typically Virgilian imitation, for the phrase has undergone a transformation, the metaphor has changed. βάσεις (βαίνω) ["strides, I walk"] suggests the "strides" made by the chariots overtaking one another in the race, but *lapsus* ["the gliding"], though it can be used to convey the same impression of speed, suggests methods of moving which have nothing to do with strides. Virgil uses forms of *labi* ["to glide"] together with *rotae* ["wheels"] in two other places, and in both passages the combination is used to describe the speed of a chariot; a racing chariot in *Georgics*, III, 180, *aut Alphaea rotis praelabi flumina Pisae* ["to glide on wheels along the Alphaean streams of Pisa"], and a divine (and amphibious) chariot in *Aeneid*, I, 147, *atque rotis summas levibus perlabitur undas* ["and it glides over the tops of the waves on light wheels"]. But this impression of speed, in the case of Neptune's chariot of effortless, frictionless speed, is violently incongruous in a description of the movement of the wooden horse. The other phrases of Virgil's description suggest, not speed, but the laborious effort involved in moving the horse into the city. *Dividimus muros* ["we divide the walls apart"], says Aeneas, the horse, as Conington says, was "heaved over broken walls." *Accingunt operi, scandit fatalis machina muros* ["they apply themselves to the task, the fateful machine scales the walls"]. Far from gliding swiftly, the horse sticks four times at the entry, *substitit* ["sticks"]; the word recreates the sudden friction-bound halt of the vast mass. The incongruous suggestion of speed is emphasized by a repetition of the disturbing word, *inlabitur urbi* ["glides into the city"]. The emphatic repetition increases the strain to which this word is being subjected, and an unusually elaborate echo makes it clear that this word, like *insinuat* ["creeps into"] in line 229, recalls the figure of the serpent. The closing lines of the description of the serpents, only ten lines back, are recalled by three verbal echoes, and the reappearance of *lapsus* ["gliding"], the emphatic word, in the same position in the line. The serpents (225-7) — at gemini *lapsu*…*effugiunt*…*sub pedibusque* deae…*teguntur* ["but the twins *with gliding*…*flee*…*under the feet* of the goddess…hide themselves"]. The horse (235-6) — *pedibusque rotarum subiciunt lapsus* ["they place *the gliding of the wheels under the feet*"]. The echo suggests the likeness of the horse to the serpents; *lapsus* ["gliding"] and *inlabitur* ["it glides into"] intensify the suggestion, for *labi* ["to glide"] and its compounds are words that occur sooner or later in almost any passage which describes the movement of the serpent;[10] indeed, were it not that *serpere* ["to creep"] claims the honor, *labi* ["to glide"] might be described as the *vox propria* ["characteristic word"] of the serpent.…

The metaphor is surprising, if not grotesque; a horse is not much like a serpent, and a wooden horse less so than a live one. But that this image, the Trojan horse moving like a serpent upon its prey (*inlabitur urbi* ["glides into the city"]), was possible for a Latin poet, is indicated by Propertius' description of the same event (III, 13, 63-4). "Cassandra alone," he says, "proclaimed the horse a trick, as it crept upon her fatherland":

> sola
> fallacem patriae serpere dixit equum.

In the Virgilian *lapsus* and *inlabitur* ["gliding, it glides into"] the metaphor is latent; but Propertius' *serpere* ["to creep"] can hardly suggest anything else but the horse as a serpent....

Virgil emphasizes his comparison of the horse to a serpent later in Book II, by another significant echo. The line which describes the snake to which Pyrrhus is compared (475) *arduus ad solem et linguis micat ore trisulcis* ["towering toward the sun and flickers from its mouth with three-forked tongue"], repeats the salient word of Panthus' description of the wooden horse (328[-9]) *arduus armatos mediis in moenibus adstans [fundit]* ["towering, standing amidst the walls, it pours forth armed men"]. This repetition of *arduus* ["towering"] (not used elsewhere in Book II) would be negligible were it not for the fact that Virgil often associated this word with both horses and serpents; he applies it elsewhere four times to horses,[11] and three times to serpents.[12]

The lines which follow the account of the triumphal entry of the horse (250 ff.) contain a description of the night approach and arrival of the Greek fleet. The verbal parallels between these lines and those which describe the approach and arrival of the serpents from Tenedos have already been mentioned.... The most striking correspondences are: *gemini a Tenedo* ["twins from Tenedos"], of the serpents, *a Tenedo* ["from Tenedos"], of the fleet (203 and 255); *tranquilla per alta* ["through the tranquil deep"], of the serpents, *tacitae per amica silentia lunae* ["through the friendly silences of the quiet moon"], of the fleet (203 and 255); *pariter* ["side by side"], of the serpents, *instructis navibus* ["with ships arrayed"], of the fleet (205 and 254); *ad litora tendunt* ["they head for the shore"], of the serpents, *litora nota petens* ["seeking the familiar shore"], of the fleet (205 and 256)....

One of the essential factors in the fall of Troy is the deep sleep of the Trojans on that fatal night. *Invadunt urbem somno vinoque sepultam* ["They invade the city entombed with sleep and wine"]. This sleep is mentioned in line 253, in the passage which describes the approach of the Greek fleet. *Sopor fessos complectitur artus* ["Sleep enfolds their weary limbs"]. The image of the serpent appears again, for this phrase is a complex echo of the words which described the death of Laocoon's children, thirty-five lines before (214-15):

> serpens amplexus uterque
> implicat et miseros morsu depascitur artus.

> ["creeping each entwines its embraces and feeds deeply with bites on their wretched limbs."]

The metaphor *sopor complectitur artus* ["sleep enfolds limbs"], which Virgil uses nowhere else,[13] is revealed as another manifestation of the dominant image by the elaboration of

the echo. The verbal echo *amplexus...artus, complectitur artus* ["embraces...limbs, enfolds limbs"] is strengthened by the metrical repetition, *depascitur artus, complectitur
artus* ["feeds deeply on limbs, enfolds limbs"]; even the onomatopoeic sibilance of *miseros
morsu depascitur artus* reappears in *sopor fessos complectitur artus*.

The word *complectitur* ["enfolds"] is full of a tension which is typical of Virgil's
language. Its associations of friendly or loving embrace are appropriate for the Trojans'
feeling as they yield to the sleep that ends their first day of peace, and by its evocation
of the serpent the word represents Aeneas' horror at the recollection of that sleep as he
tells his tale some seven years later. This tension is even more striking in the passage
which follows immediately, Aeneas' preface to his account of his dream (268–9):

> Tempus erat quo prima quies mortalibus aegris
> incipit et dono divum gratissima serpit.

> ["It was the time when rest first begins for afflicted mortals and, as a gift of
> the gods, most pleasing, creeps."]

In the melody of the first line we feel again the Trojans' welcome acceptance of
sleep, but there is a touch of foreboding in the sadness of *mortalibus aegris* ["for
afflicted mortals"]. The second line is filled with foreboding. *Dono divum* ["gift of
the gods"] is a hint of discord, for *donum* ["gift"], which has been used five times
already in Book II, has always appeared in a menacing context, it has referred each
time to the horse.[14] Aeneas' statement is couched in general terms — rest is a gift of
the gods — but the associations of *donum* remind us that his general statement has a
precise and terrible application. This rest is indeed a gift from the gods; it is part of
the divine plan for Troy's overthrow. *Inimicaque Troiae numina magna deum* ["Hostile to Troy are the great spirits of the gods"]. And the last word of the line brings
back the familiar metaphor; *serpit* ["creeps"], this rest creeps like a serpent....The
metaphor *quies...serpit* ["rest...creeps"] is a violent one, and I have not been able to
find any parallel to it in the Latin poets.[15]

❖ ❖ ❖

Aeneas awakes from his dream to see all Troy in flames. The spectacle is compared to a crop-fire and a flood (304–7). Deiphobus' house collapses in flames, and
the fire towers over it, *Volcano superante.* This phrase recalls the serpents again, the
serpents whose crests tower over the waves, *superant undas,* and who tower over
Laocoon, *superant capite et cervicibus altis* ["they tower over with head and tall necks"].
The reminiscence is repeated much later, when Aeneas sees his own house in flames,
exsuperant flammae ["flames tower above"] (759).[16]

The principal instruments of the Trojan downfall, the Trojan fear, the horse, the
Greek fleet, the deep sleep, the fire, have all now been linked with the image of the
serpent. All except one, Sinon, the personification of Greek treachery. The actions of
Sinon are described before the arrival of the serpents from Tenedos, so that in his
case there can be no question of verbal reminiscence; yet the same metaphor is
implied, in at least one place strongly, in the language which Virgil puts into his
mouth.[17] His name itself, with its resemblance to *sinus, sinuo* ["hiding place, to wind,
creep"], etc.[18] helps to bring out the suggestion; it is contained in his lying story of
his escape from sacrifice at the hands of the Greeks (134–6):

> ...vincula rupi,
> limosoque lacu per noctem obscurus in ulva
> delitui...

["...I broke the fetters, and in a muddy lake and swamp grass all night
long concealed I lurked..."]

Delitescere ["to lurk, hide away"] is an uncommon word, and one which is used
with peculiar appropriateness of the serpent; "iam ista serpens " says Cicero, "quae
tum hic delitescit..." ["now that thing is a serpent which lurks here..."] (*De
Haruspicum Responsis,* 25), and Virgil, in the only other place where he uses this
word, applies it to the viper *(Georgics,* III, 416–17):

> Saepe sub immotis praesepibus aut mala tactu
> vipera delituit...

["Or frequently under undisturbed huts dangerous to touch the viper
lurks..."]

Sinon's *delitui* ["I lurked"] is no more than a suggestion, but seen in the context of
the imagery of Book II as a whole, it is a significant one.

When Aeneas sees Troy in flames, and hears the explanation given him by
Panthus, he loses his head, and forgets his duty. His duty is to run away; he is ordered
to do so three times, in almost identical words: by Hector, Venus, and Anchises.[19]
Hector's command, the first, is ignored. Aeneas turns instead to violence. It is mad
violence, and he admits it, *arma amens capio* ["arms out of my mind I seize"] (314).

Aeneas' first victim is the Greek Androgeos, who appears in a line which almost
exactly reproduces the line which introduced the first Trojan victim, Laocoon (40
and 370):

> Primus ibi ante omnis magna comitante caterva
> Laocoon...
> Primus se Danaum magna comitante caterva
> Androgeos...

["First there, ahead of everyone, a great crowd accompanying,/ Laocoon..."]
["First, with a great crowd of Greeks accompanying him,/ Androgeos..."]

Virgil does not use the Homeric formulaic line, and this close correspondence is
unique.[20] Its significance is clear. Laocoon and Androgeos are somehow alike; the
likeness is revealed by the simile which follows. The first Trojan victim was destroyed by serpents, and so is the first Greek victim. Androgeos is killed by Aeneas
and his companions, and it is at this point that Androgeos is compared to a man
who has come unaware upon a snake (378–81):

> Obstipuit, retroque pedem cum voce repressit.
> improvisum aspris veluti qui sentibus anguem
> pressit humi nitens, trepidusque repente refugit
> attolentem iras et caerula colla tumentem.

["He stood still, and held back his step along with his voice. Just like one who, treading the ground hard, steps on a snake unforeseen in rough underbrush, and trembling shrinks back suddenly at it rising in wrath and swelling its shiny neck."]

Improvisum, unforeseen, because concealed; the word reminds us of Sinon's ironical prophecy *improvisi aderunt* ["unforeseen they will be at hand"] (182). But now the rôles are reversed. Aeneas and his Trojans now deal in the violence of the serpent to which they are compared, and they proceed at once to assume another characteristic of the serpent, concealment. At the suggestion of Coroebus, they disguise themselves in the armor and insignia of the Greeks they have killed. *Dolus an virtus, quis in hoste requirat?* ["Guile or courage, who inquires in war?"] says Coroebus (390). The Trojans adopt the Greek weapon, *dolus* ["guile"],[21] as their own; it is the mark of the serpent, they fight now from concealment, *haud numine nostro* ["not with our own god"], as Aeneas says (396).

This appearance of the serpent, for the moment identified with Aeneas and his Trojans, interprets the events. Aeneas himself admits that his action is madness; this is emphasized by the melodramatic despair of his speech to his men (348 ff.)[22] and his comparison of his Trojans to a band of ravening wolves (355-8). But the suggestion, implicit in the simile and its immediate sequel, that Aeneas has usurped the attributes of the serpent that has so far stood for violence and deceit deepens immeasurably the sense of his wrongness and folly, and reminds us how far Aeneas has strayed from his duty, which is not to fight, but to yield to a greater purpose, as he does yield in the end. *Cessi* ["I yielded"], runs his concluding line, *et sublato montis genitore petivi* ["and, having lifted up my father, I sought the mountains"].

By the time the violence of Book II reaches its climax in the assault on Priam's palace, Aeneas' impulsive counter-attack has failed. He is betrayed by his own deceit; the Greek crests on the borrowed helmets draw fire from the Trojans. This fatal confusion is expressed in the phrase *Graiarum errore iubarum* ["by the confusion of the Greek crests"] (412), a reminiscence of the crests, *sanguineae iubae* ["blood-red crests"] (206), of the serpents that killed Laocoon and his sons. At this moment the Greeks too attack him; his men are cut down, and he escapes from the slaughter with only two companions, one an old, the other a wounded, man. Aeneas' violence has ended in failure, and his brief assumption of the characteristics of the serpent is revealed, in the succeeding lines, as a pathetic masquerade; the real serpent is at the gates of Priam's palace.

This is Pyrrhus, son of Achilles. The verbs alone of lines 480 ff. are enough to make it clear that he is violence personified – *perrumpit vellit cavavit instat insequitur premit* ["he breaks through, tears, made a gap in, presses close, pursues, presses"]. This is the man who, as Aeneas says later, "cuts down the son before the face of his father, the father at the altar," *natum ante ora patris, patrem qui obtruncat ad aras* (663). The time for concealment is past; Pyrrhus' violence is open, like that of the serpents which killed Laocoon and his sons; like them he kills the son first, and then the father who attempts to intervene;[23] like them, he kills his victim at the altars. When Pyrrhus twists his left hand in Priam's hair to hold the king's body firm for the final stroke, *implicuitque comam laeva* ["and he twists the hair with his left hand"] (552), the words recall the serpents that twisted their coils round Laocoon's sons, *corpora natorum serpens amplexus uterque implicat* ["creeping, embracing, each enfolds the children's bodies"] (214-15).

This parallel is emphasized by the simile which, at the very beginning of this magnificent passage, compares Pyrrhus to a snake (471–5):

Qualis ubi in lucem coluber mala gramina pastus
frigida sub terra tumidum quem bruma tegebat
nunc positis novus exuviis nitidusque iuventa
lubrica convolvit sublato pectore terga
arduus ad solem et linguis micat ore trisulcis.

["Just as when into the light there's a snake, fed on poison grasses, which cold winter has been hiding swollen underground, now having cast off its old hide, a fresh and shining youth, it coils up its slithering skin with its front raised, towering toward the sun and flickers from its mouth with three-forked tongue."]

This simile illustrates the general transition, now complete, from concealment to open violence; from the lies of Sinon and the subterfuge of the horse to the ferocity of the assault on the palace; for Pyrrhus in particular, the transition from concealment in the dark belly of the horse to violence in the glare of the burning city. The caverns of the horse's belly are twice (38 and 55) called *latebrae* ["hiding place"], a word suggestive of the serpent's hiding-place; Pyrrhus is the serpent that has emerged.

This is the third overt appearance of the serpent in Book II, and it is different from those that precede it. The simile presents the serpent as the symbol of rebirth and this new connotation of the serpent is appropriate for the immediate object of the comparison, Pyrrhus. The snake, in contrast to the darkness from which it came (*sub terra...quem bruma tegebat* ["which winter was hiding...under the earth"]), is bright and shiny, *nitidus,* and this corresponds with the real Pyrrhus, *luce coruscus aena* ["shimmering with bronzy light"], and with his name, Pyrrhus, Πυρρός ["flame-colored"].[24] The snake is new, *positis novus exuviis* ["fresh, having cast off its hide"], and this reminds us of Pyrrhus' other name, Neoptolemus, new war, new warrior.[25] He is the renewal of the old war, the rebirth of the old warrior; Pyrrhus is Achilles reborn in his son. Just as Achilles killed and mutilated Hector before the eyes of Hecuba and Priam,[26] Neoptolemus now kills Polites before the same unhappy pair who witnessed his father's cruelty. *Instat vi patria* ["he presses on with his father's strength"], says Virgil (491), and Neoptolemus is followed by his father's constant companion, *equorum agitator Achillis armiger Automedon* ["the driver of Achilles' horses, arms bearer Automedon"].

The terms of the simile at the same time subtly qualify the identification of father and son which they suggest. If on the one hand they make a comparison between Achilles and his son, they none the less suggest a contrast between them. The serpent in this book of the *Aeneid* has come to stand for the merciless and unthinking violence which was typical of Achilles at his worst; but we remember, even before Priam reminds us of it, that he had a better side. Achilles killed the son, but revered, in the person of Priam, old age; Neoptolemus kills father and son alike. This Achilles reborn is not the true Achilles; the comparison of Neoptolemus to a serpent (his father was a lion)[27] anticipates Priam's taunt *satum quo te mentiris Achilles* ["you lie that it is Achilles from whom you are sired"] (540). Only the worst of the father is reborn in the son; his sarcastic words to Priam, *degeneremque Neoptolemum* ["degenerate Neoptolemus"] (549), are the truth.

The simile is complex in application and rich in meaning, for it is loaded with the cumulative significance of the dominant image. There is more to it still. For this new association of the serpent, the cycle of winter hibernation and spring renewal, death and rebirth, though applied specifically to the re-appearance of Achilles in his son, is not so limited in the reader's imagination. It is a familiar and universal symbol, suggesting the process which is common to all nature, the process of life, death, and rebirth. Troy too is to be reborn; that is the implication of Hector's ne-glected command to Aeneas, *his moenia quaere magna* ["for these seek high walls"] (294–5). At the climax of Troy's destruction, just before the most terrible incident of the city's last night, the image of the serpent appears again, not only to portray the invincible ferocity of the attackers, but also to suggest the promise of salvation for the defeated. In this image is a hint that the fate of Priam is more than the cruel murder of an old man; this death is part of a birth.

This simile is the turning-point in the development of the dominant metaphor; it prepares for the final appearance of the serpent, which is unequivocal, an unmis-takable portent of Troy's eventual rebirth. But meanwhile there is a last glimpse of the old serpent, with its connotations of concealment and destruction unmodified. It is contained in the famous lines that describe Helen (567–74). Aeneas comes upon her in hiding:

> limina Vestae
> servantem et tacitam secreta in sede latentem.

["keeping to the thresholds of Vesta and quiet, hiding in the secreted place"]

Secreta in sede latentem ["hiding in a secreted place"] is a familiar suggestion, and it is repeated a few lines later, *abdiderat sese* ["had hidden herself away"] (574).[28] *Limina servantem* ["keeping to the thresholds"] sounds like a reminiscence of Virgil's descrip-tion of the serpent that killed Eurydice, *servantem ripas* ["keeping to the banks"] (*Georg.*, IV, 459); there are other reminiscences of the Eurydice passage in this book of the *Aeneid.*[29]

The final appearance of the dominant metaphor is a celebrated passage. Aeneas, now intent on his duty, prepares to leave Troy with all his family, but his plans are hindered by old Anchises' refusal to leave. Aeneas returns to counsels of despair, *rursus in arma feror* ["again into arms I am borne"] (655), but Anchises' mind is changed by a portent, the flame which appears on the head of Iulus (682–7):

> ecce levis summo de vertice visus Iuli
> fundere lumen apex, tactuque innoxia mollis
> lambere flamma comas et circum tempora pasci.
> nos pavidi trepidare metu crinemque flagrantem
> excutere et sanctos restinguere fontibus ignis.

["Look, from the tip of Iulus' head, the top seems to pour forth a gentle light, and with harmless touch a soft flame licks his hair and feeds around his temples. Quaking, we tremble with fear and beat out the flaming hair and extinguish the holy fire with water."]

These words are full of reminiscences and suggestions of the serpent. *Lambere* ["to lick"] brings to mind the serpents which attacked Laocoon, *sibila lambebant linguis vibrantibus ora* ["they lick their hissing mouths with flickering tongues"], and *pasci* ["feeds"] recalls the snake, *mala gramina pastus* ["fed on poison grasses"], to which Pyrrhus was compared and the serpents that fed on Laocoon's children, *miseros morsu depascitur artus* ["feeds deep with bites on their wretched limbs"]. *Tactuque innoxia* ["with harmless touch"][30] refers by contrast to the proverbial untouchableness of serpents, *mala tactu* ["dangerous to touch"] Virgil calls the viper in *Georgics*, III, 416; and *innoxia* ["harmless"], in the only other place where Virgil uses it, *Aen.*, V, 92 (a passage which echoes and clearly refers to the one under consideration),[31] describes the serpent which came out of Anchises' tomb:

> libavitque dapes, rursusque *innoxius* imo
> successit tumulo, et depasta altaria liquit.

> ["It tasted the feast, and harmless retreated again into the deep burial mound, and left the altars on which it had fed."]

❖ ❖ ❖

In this flame the pattern of the dominant metaphor is complete. The development of the image, the increasing complication of meaning which constitutes its plot, comes to an end. The serpent has cast its old skin. All previous significances of the serpent are here by implication summed up and rejected in favor of the new. In the shape of Sinon, Helen, and the wooden horse, the serpent stood for concealment; here all is light, and abundance of it, *fundere lumen* ["poured forth light"]. In the form of Pyrrhus, the serpents from Tenedos, and even Aeneas himself in his madness, it stood for violence; here it is *tactu innoxia*, harmless to the touch, and *mollis* ["soft"], though grammatically it may qualify *comas* ["hair"], adds to the contrast. The serpent stood also for the destructive flames of Troy's fall; here it is still a flame, but a sacred one, *sanctos ignis*, a harmless one, *innoxia*, more, a beneficent flame. The fourth connotation of the serpent image, rebirth, a significance held in reserve in the earlier part of the book and first faintly suggested at the climax of the violence, the lowest depth of Troy's fortunes, is here its proclaimed and only meaning. The flame, which Virgil's allusive language presents as the final manifestation of the serpent metaphor,[32] is a portent of Troy's rebirth. Anchises does not realize its full significance, but he is joyful (*laetus* 687), and prays that the omen be confirmed (691). The confirmation comes in the form of thunder on the left, a falling star, and finally Creusa's prophecy to Aeneas of a new kingdom in the West.[33]

This analysis is an attempt to examine some of the rich complexities of one of Virgil's many sustained images. To support it by an appeal to Virgil's intentions would be barren and irrelevant. But in this particular case there is some ground, apart from the analysis itself, for suggesting that Virgil, as he composed the second book of his *Aeneid*, did have serpents in mind throughout, for the book is full of echoes of some earlier lines of his which constitute a short "catalogue of serpents."[34] The short passage in the third *Georgic* (414–39) which describes the snakes the horse-breeder must beware of contains the phrase *mala tactu vipera delituit* ["the viper lurked harmful to touch"] (416–17) which is echoed in Sinon's *delitui* ["I lurked"] (II, 136) and in *tactuque innoxia* ["harmless to touch"] (II, 683), the description of the flame; the same passage contains also the line (421) *tollentemque minas et sibila colla tumentem* ["rising in threats and swelling its hissing neck"], which is the basis of a line in the Androgeos simile, *attolentem iras et caerula colla tumentem* ["rising in wrath and swelling its shiny neck"] (381); finally it contains three separate lines *(Georg.,* III, 426, 437, and 439),

> Squamea convolvens sublato pectore terga
> cum positis novus exuviis nitidusque iuventa
> arduus ad solem et linguis micat ore trisulcis

> ["Twisting its scaly back, its front raised up, when having cast off its old hide, a fresh and shining youth, towering to the sun and flickers from its mouth with three-forked tongue."]

which all reappear, with little or no change, in the Pyrrhus simile *(Aen.,* II, 473–5). Further, this early passage contains an account of a savage serpent, the terror of the country-side in the dry season,

> exsilit in siccum, et flammantia lumina torquens
> saevit agris

> ["it springs out into the dry land, and twisting its flaming eyes rages in the fields"]

(Georg., III, 433–4), which sounds like the basis of the description of the serpents that came from Tenedos.

    This is clearly a passage which was often present in Virgil's mind as he wrote the second book of the *Aeneid;* its presence there may be connected with the dominance which the image of the serpent assumed. More than this can hardly be suggested, for in the complexity of a great poet's imagery we must recognize a mystery which lies beyond the frontiers of conscious art. Οὐκ ἐκ τέχνης ["not from skill"], says Plato ἀλλ᾽ ἔνθεοι ὄντες καὶ κατεχόμενοι ["but being inspired by the gods and possessed"],[35] and although here, as always, he is grinding his anti-poetic axe, he is more right than wrong. To probe Virgil's mind at work is beyond any powers of analysis,[36] though analysis may occasionally reveal fresh treasures in the poetry which his mind produced. There is no fear, in Virgil's case, that the process may dissipate the poetry; its riches are inexhaustible. In his use of the sustained metaphor, a power which he shares with Aeschylus and Shakespeare, Virgil defies any final analysis; a glimpse such as this into the "chambers of his imagery"[37] reveals only further chambers beyond: *Apparet domus intus et atria longa patescunt* ["The inner house appears and the long halls are revealed"].

Notes

[1] For a discussion of the imagery of the book as a whole, and its relation to the *Georgics,* see J. Masson, "Les comparaisons dans le deuxième livre de l'Enéide," *Les Études Classiques,* 1935, pp. 635–43.

◇ ◇ ◇

[2] Cf. Ovid, *Met.,* IX, 266: *Utque novus serpens posita cum pelle senecta luxuriare solet, squamaque virere recenti; idem, A. A.,* III, 77; Lucretius, III, 614; Tibullus, I, 4, 35; Lucan, IX, 718; Pliny, *Hist. Nat.,* VIII, 41 (99).

[3] *Serpens* and *anguis* are confidently distinguished by Servius on II, 204. *Angues aquarum sunt, serpentes terrarum, dracones templorum.* His definitions appear to be based on Virgil's

usage in this particular passage; for the snakes are called *angues* in line 204 (the snakes are still on the sea), *serpens* in line 214 (they are now on land), and *dracones* in line 225 (they are on their way to the temple). Servius admits that his distinction is not always observed — *sed haec significatio plerumque confunditur*. It was apparently unknown to Virgil, who uses the terms indiscriminately in other passages where there is no change of locale. Cf. *Aen.*, VII, 346 ff.: Allecto throws a snake (*anguem*) into Amata's bosom (346); a few lines later the same snake is described as *serpens*: *serpentis furiale malum* (375). Cf. also Ovid, *Met.*, IV, 575 ff.: Cadmus prays to be changed into a serpent — *ipse precor serpens in longam porrigar alvum*, and ten lines later, as the metamorphosis is taking place he says *accipe dum manus est, dum non totum occupat anguis* (585).

⁴Cf. Cleanth Brooks, *The Well-wrought Urn* (N.Y., 1947), pp. 27–36.

⁵Henry, *Aeneidea*, II, pp. 115–16.

⁶The twin serpents appear three more times in the *Aeneid*. (On their dramatic function for the poem as a whole see G. E. Duckworth, *Foreshadowing and Suspense in the Epics of Homer, Apollonius and Vergil* [Princeton, 1933], p. 57, and references there.) They are in all three cases portents of destruction. Allecto (VII, 450) rouses the hesitating Turnus by rearing two snakes from her tresses, *geminos erexit crinibus angues*, Hercules (VIII, 289) strangles the twin serpents sent by Juno, *geminosque premens eliserit anguis*, and on the shield of Aeneas Cleopatra calls on her army and does not see the twin snakes behind her (VIII, 697), *necdum etiam geminos a tergo respicit anguis*.

⁷Lucretius uses the word thirty times.

⁸Cf. Ovid, *Met.*, III, 42, IX, 64; *Aetna*, 47.

⁹Mackail notes, "Here, however, *rotae* strictly means rollers." The other two passages in which Virgil uses *labi* and *rotae* together suggest otherwise, and in any case this technical meaning is inappropriate, for it adds a concrete detail to a picture which seems to be deliberately vague. Virgil's reference to the horse in VI, 515, *cum fatalis equus saltu super ardua venit Pergama*, indicates a vision of the wooden horse as something with a will of its own, almost alive, something magical; the same impression is produced by the words *scandit...subit...inlabitur...* and *monstrum* in our passage. (Cf. G. E. Duckworth, *C. J.*, 1944, pp. 99 ff.) To insist on the connotations of *rota* as a technical engineering term destroys this fine effect.

¹⁰Cf. Virgil, *Georg.*, I, 244, *Aen.*, VII, 349; Ovid, *Met.*, IX, 63, XV, 721, *Amores*, II, 13, 13; Silius Italicus, II, 589; Statius, *Theb.*, V, 514; Propertius, III, 22, 27; Livy, XXV, 16, 2, XXVIII, 11, 2; Lucan, IX, 712.

❖ ❖ ❖

¹¹*Georg.*, II, 145, III, 79, *Aen.*, V, 567, XI, 638.

¹²*Georg.*, III, 439, *Aen.*, V, 278, XI, 755.

❖ ❖ ❖

¹³The whole phrase is one of a series of variations on an epic formula, but the combination *sopor...complectitur* is unique. Cf. *Georg.*, IV, 190: *fessosque sopor suus occupat artus*, *Aen.*, III, 511: *fessos sopor irrigat artus*, *Aen.*, VIII, 26–7: *animalia fessa...sopor altus habebat*, *Aen.*, IV, 522, etc.

¹⁴*Aen.*, II, 31: *donum exitiale Minervae*, 36: *suspectaque dona*, 44: *dona carere dolis Danaum*, 49: *Danaos et dona ferentis*, 189: *dona Minervae*.

¹⁵The only parallel, as far as I know, is Pliny, *Hist. Nat.*, VII, 24 (90): *somno serpente*. In this context, too, the approach of sleep is viewed as hostile: *somno quoque serpente (memoria) amputator*.

❖ ❖ ❖

¹⁶There are traces of a MS tradition which emphasizes the echo more firmly. P, for example, reads VOLCANOESUPERANTE at 311; Ribbeck (1894) adopts *exsuperante* in this line, and Mackail remarks that the reading of P indicates a "variant reading *exsuperante* which might be thought preferable if it were better supported." One late MS (so Conington describes it) has *exsuperant* at 207; this reading was adopted by most of the old editions.

¹⁷Cf. also *seu versare dolos* (62). *Versare* is often used of the serpent moving his coils; cf. for example *Aen.*, XI, 753: *serpens sinuosa volumina versat*.

¹⁸For Virgil's use of the suggestions (etymologically justified or not) inherent in proper names, see below on *Pyrrhus* and *Neoptolemus*.

¹⁹*Heu fuge nate dea* (289), *eripe nate fugam* (619), *fuge nate* (733).

[20]Virgil uses a phrase containing *caterva* and occupying the final position in the line seven times in the *Aeneid*. The two discussed here are the only two which are identical; all the rest show some variation. Cf. I, 497, IV, 136, V, 76, XI, 478, 564.

[21]For *dolus* and the Greeks see II, 44, 62, 152, 196, 252, 264.

[22]For some stimulating remarks on this whole passage see D. L. Drew, *The Allegory of the Aeneid* (Blackwell, 1927), pp. 62-3.

[23]Cf. *auxilio subeuntem ac tela ferentem* (216, Laocoon) and *Telumque imbelle sine ictu coniecit* (644, Priam).

❖ ❖ ❖

[24]This is the point of the emphatic position of *in lucem;* these two words convey the immediate significance of the simile. Virgil puts them first and lets the syntax take care of itself. As Conington says, *in lucem* "does the duty of a verb."

[25]Cf. Conington, *ad loc.* G. Wijdeveld (*Mnemosyne*, X, 3rd Series [1941-2], p. 238) discusses the significance of the name Pyrrhus. He equates the Greek word πυρρός with the Latin *aenus,* and sees in *exsultat telis* (470) a reference to the πυρρίχη which he suggests was originally a spring ritual. He rejects Conington's comment that *positis novus exuviis* points to the name Neoptolemus on the ground that Virgil has not yet mentioned Pyrrhus' other name: "v. demum 500 Neoptolemus vocatur. Num credi potest Vergilium in legentibus tantam expectasse sagacitatem ut meminissent nominis de quo mentionem poeta nondum fecisset?" This is an oversight, for the name Neoptolemus has already occurred in the list of the warriors whom Sinon released from the horse, *Pelidesque Neoptolemus* (263).

[26]Cf. *Iliad*, XXII, 405 ff.

[27]Cf. *Iliad* XX, 164, XXIV, 40-3. *Mala gramina pastus* is a reminiscence of *Iliad*, XXII, 94, where Hector awaiting Achilles' attack is compared to a serpent. Aristotle's choice of an example to illustrate the difference between simile and metaphor *(Rhet.*, III, 4, 1) indicates that the comparison to a lion was the standard one for Achilles.

[28]Cf. *Georg.*, III, 422: *(coluber) timidum caput abdidit alte.*

[29]Cf. *Aen.*, II, 790-1 and *Georg.*, IV, 501-2; *Aen.*, II, 725 and *Georg.*, IV, 487.

[30]The variant reading *tractu* (see Conington, *ad loc.*) is an interesting one, for it may refer either to flames (as in Virgil, *Georg.*, I, 367; Lucretius II, 207), or to serpents (as in Virgil, *Georg.*, II, 154; Ovid, *Met.*, XV 725; Statius, *Theb.*, V, 506; *Culex*, 163, 181).

[31]Both portents are connected with Anchises. The passage in Book V echoes *pasci* in *depasta* as well as *innoxia* in *innoxius.*

❖ ❖ ❖

[32]On the shield of Aeneas, where the twin serpents appear behind Cleopatra as a sign of her eventual destruction (VIII, 697), the opposing figure of Augustus is seen with twin flames at his temples, *geminas cui tempora flammas laeta vomunt* (680-1). The serpent and the flame, which at the end of *Aeneid* II are united as a double symbol of Troy's rebirth, are on the shield separated and opposed.

[33]The similar omen described in VII, 71 ff., where Lavinia's hair is seen to burst into flame, is interpreted by those who saw it in a very different fashion:

namque fore inlustrem fame fatisque canebant
ipsam, sed populo magnum portendere bellum.

It has been pointed out to me that this same interpretation might be applied to the flame omen in Book II. "Ascanius will also become famous (like Lavinia), and be the cause of war to his people (he starts the actual warfare between Trojans and Latins by killing the stag of Tyrrheus)." The parallel is striking, but against it may be urged the fact that Virgil makes no attempt to connect the two flames, they are contrasted rather than compared. Iulus' flame is *mirabile monstrum*, a neutral phrase implying neither good nor bad (cf. V, 523, where *monstrum* is used of Acestes' arrow, his reaction is joyful, *laetum* [531]; VIII, 81, of the sow; IX, 120, of the transformation of the ships of Aeneas); Lavinia's flame is described as *horrendum ac visu mirabile ferri* (VII, 78), and the description begins with the words *visa nefas...*(VII, 73). The reaction of Latinus is anxiety, *sollicitus monstris* (VII, 81), that of Anchises joy, *laetus* (II, 687). There is not one important verbal echo in the Lavinia passage of the description of the flame in

Book II; each passage has a vocabulary of its own, a striking phenomenon when the similarity of the subject-matter is considered. It is striking too that in the Lavinia description the words used to describe the flame have none of the serpentine connotations of the key words of the Iulus passage; their absence in the one throws into clearer relief their presence in the other.

[34]The *Culex* contains (163–197) an elaborate description of an immense serpent. It is curious, if it is Virgil's work, that Book II of the *Aeneid* contains hardly any echoes of it; the only two are *Culex*, 166: *vibranti lingua*, *Aen.*, II, 211: *linguis vibrantibus* and (perhaps) *Culex*, 168: *tollebant irae...visus*, *Aen.*, II, 381: *attollentem iras.* The "serpent catalogue" in *Georg.*, III, 414–39 is the quarry from which most of the serpentine phraseology of *Aeneid*, II is drawn.

[35]Plato, *Ion*, 533E.

[36]For an interesting but unconvincing attempt see R. W. Cruttwell, *Virgil's Mind at Work* (Blackwell, 1947).

[37]Ezekiel, VIII, 12.

THE VERGILIAN SIMILE
AS MEANS OF JUDGMENT

A simile, usually signalled by the words "as" or "like," is an explicit comparison between two elements. Vergil uses similes extensively, many of them modeled on Homer, and interpreters find in them keys to the meaning of Vergil's poetry. Hornsby analyzes the similes related to the Carthaginian queen Dido, in books 1, 4 and 6, to understand and make a judgment on her character and actions. We again meet the image of the hunt, which Staley discussed regarding book 1, and again there are connections with Greek tragedy. We also observe the way Vergil's poetic technique creates "reverberating significance." Through his analysis of similes, Hornsby reads Dido as unable to distinguish appearance from reality. For Hornsby, Dido's story is a chapter in Aeneas' development as a hero and a discourse on the meaning of both love and tragedy. The genuine pity we feel for Dido, Hornsby maintains, does not preclude our judging her to be responsible for her fate. (Ed.)

Modern literary criticism, especially in discussions of English poetry, has made us aware of the importance of metaphor as a means whereby the poet interprets the matter he presents.[1] Classicists recognize the same phenomenon in ancient poetry, and this recognition has slowly begun to affect our understanding of the great works of Greece and Rome. Connected to metaphor, as species is to genus, are similes, those formal equations which deliberately compare two things. By similes no less than by metaphors, the poet indicates his attitudes and his judgments which he wishes the reader to observe. Vergil's use of similes, particularly those known as Homeric, is in no way exceptional to these general remarks about metaphorical language. It is to them that I want to direct attention, for by means of a careful scrutiny of the similes in the *Aeneid* we can perhaps correct, or at least modify, some of the current interpretations of the *Aeneid*.

As a result of Pöschl's and Guillemin's work, we are far more conscious of how complex a poem the *Aeneid* is; we have become aware that the *Aeneid* is an organic unity whose parts—plot, verse, characters, themes—interact with one another. Nothing happens in the poem without affecting not only the immediate situation but also all other parts of the poem. For example, what happens in the first six books intimately concerns the events in the last six; the converse is also true: what happens in the last six books conditions our understanding of what went on in the first six. The Vergilian simile plays a role in the *Aeneid* no less complex than do the other elements which make up the work. To cite a specific example of this point, illustrating

---

Roger A. Hornsby, "The Vergilian Simile as Means of Judgment," *Classical Journal* 60 (1964) 337–44. Reprinted by permission of *Classical Journal* and Roger A. Hornsby.

the 'reverberating quality' of the poem and of the similes in particular, let us consider those used to describe the battles in the latter half of the *Aeneid*. They draw their power from what happened in the first half: the sea which had been so hostile an element to Aeneas' search for Hesperia, for Italy, in the first half of the poem becomes in the second half the source of the potent similes used to describe warfare whose battles are like storms at sea. Conversely, in the light of the similes in Books 7–12 we see how almost human in its capriciousness the sea had been.

If we bear these general considerations in mind, we can see something of how Vergil by his manipulation of similes informs the affair between Dido and Aeneas in order to illuminate the characters of both and to permit a judgment on both. Specifically I want to examine how the similes that describe Dido interpret and judge her character and behavior. To this end I intend to examine the similes in the light of the context in which they appear and in the light of subsequent events in the history of the affair.

When Dido first appears in her own right in the *Aeneid*, surrounded by a great throng of youth, Vergil immediately uses a simile describing, characterizing, and illuminating her (1.496–503):

> regina ad templum, forma pulcherrima Dido,
> incessit magna iuvenum stipante caterva.
> qualis in Eurotae ripis aut per iuga Cynthi
> exercet Diana choros, quam mille secutae
> hinc atque hinc glomerantur Oreades; illa pharetram
> fert umero gradiensque deas supereminet omnis
> (Latonae tacitum pertemptant gaudia pectus):
> talis erat Dido, talem se laeta ferebat....

["The queen, Dido, most beautiful in form, approached the temple, with a large throng of youth crowding about her. Just as Diana on Eurotas' banks or the ridges of Cynthus trains her band, she whom a thousand mountain nymphs follow clustering from this side and that; she carries a quiver on her shoulder and, as she progresses, stands out above all the goddesses (joys incite Latona's quiet heart): like this was Dido, like this, happy, did she bear herself."]

Within the terms of the simile, she is like Diana who trains her band clustered about their queen on the banks of the Eurotas or along the ridges of Cynthus. Diana stands out above all the rest as Dido excels her companions. The emphasis is chiefly on Dido as being in appearance like the goddess of hunting. So she appears to Aeneas, whose viewpoint we share. She is a beautiful and compelling woman. The simile recalls the appearance of Venus in this same book, who was described in terms of a young Spartan or Thracian maiden who also hunts (1.314–17). The encounter with Venus anticipates Aeneas' first sight of Dido. The similes are parallel in that both stress the beauty of the person compared and the virginal appearance of each, which has at the same time an undertone of sexuality. But there is also the notion of the huntress in both: Venus appears as a huntress and Dido is likened to the goddess of the hunt. The emphasis on hunting is to be crucial for the love affair of Dido and Aeneas, for it is, after all, on the hunt in Book 4 that Aeneas succumbs to Dido the huntress and joins her in what she terms a *coniugium* ["union"]. The allusion to

Diana the huntress finds its realization in that scene. But from the very beginning in Book 1 we are not allowed to forget that Dido is somehow hunting, and most obviously she is hunting a man, a marriage. Yet neither the goddess of love nor the widowed queen is a virgin. Vergil is at great pains to make the point clear, for Venus in departing from Aeneas reveals that she is his goddess mother and she has also told him of Dido's first marriage. The point, then, of the simile describing Dido in terms of Diana is a deliberate emphasis both on Dido as huntress and on a discrepancy between appearance and reality in that, unlike Diana, Dido is neither a goddess nor a virgin. Both notions operate together and need to be observed in concord. Further, it is worth observing that the two similes and their contexts reveal much about the two kinds of love Aeneas is to enjoy from the goddess and from the queen. In one, he is given a beneficent, fostering love which is able to reveal itself, even as Venus reveals herself to Aeneas; in the other, the love will turn to deadly hatred because of the disparity between appearance and reality.

That we should bear in mind all these facets of the Diana simile is further confirmed when we recall, as commentators both ancient and modern observe, that Vergil has borrowed his simile from Homer, who uses it to describe Nausicaa.[2] In the *Odyssey* the simile is especially fitting, for the nubile daughter of Alcinous is still the untouched young maiden. Furthermore, when we remember the modesty of Nausicaa and her chasteness with regard to Odysseus, as Vergil's use of the simile clearly means us to do, we can appreciate the ironic contrast Vergil is making between Dido and Nausicaa by comparing his heroine to Diana. The purpose of the irony lies in letting us, the readers or listeners, know that Dido in some way or other is in a false position: her appearance does not mirror the actuality. This discrepancy between appearance and reality is, as we shall see in Book 4, the essential clue to the behavior of Dido and to an understanding of her character.

The second simile used of Dido occurs in 4.68–73:

uritur infelix Dido totaque vagatur
urbe furens, qualis coniecta cerva sagitta,
quam procul incautam nemora inter Cresia fixit
pastor agens telis liquitque volatile ferrum
nescius: illa fuga silvas saltusque peragrat
Dictaeos; haeret lateri letalis harundo.

["She burns, unfortunate Dido, and in the whole city she wanders, frenzied, like a doe, when the arrow has been shot, whom incautious and far off, the shepherd pierces, driving her through the Cretan woods with his weapons, and leaves behind his flying iron, unaware: thus she in flight wanders through forests and Dictaean glens; a fatal shaft clings to her side."]

The simile continues some of the ideas seen in the first one. Dido, inflamed with passion for Aeneas, wanders madly through the city just as a doe, struck by the arrow of a shepherd who is unaware of what he has accomplished, wanders wounded through forests and glen. Dido who had been the hunter now becomes the hunted, and the wound is the wound of her passion for Aeneas. The wound for both the deer and for Dido is to prove fatal (*haeret lateri letalis harundo* ["a fatal shaft clings to her side"]). Several things should be observed about this simile and its position in the narrative. First, Aeneas, like the *pastor* ["shepherd"], has been unaware of the passion he has elicited: he does not know that his sufferings and his bearing have aroused so fervent a feeling in Dido. In a sense he is an innocent. But so also is the doe in the simile, which would prefer obviously enough not to be wounded. Yet the doe is described as *incautam* ["incautious"]. This adjective really becomes Dido more than the doe. The simile suggests that Dido is in some way responsible for her own plight. Again we can see a discrepancy between the vehicle and the tenor of the simile; Dido is not quite the same as the innocent doe. The wound may have been inflicted in appearance by Aeneas, but it is really her own passion, her own desires, which have caused her to suffer.[3] This point the narrative of Book 4 has made abundantly clear before the appearance of the simile. Dido in her conversation with Anna has paid scrupulous attention to the letter of her vow to remain faithful to Sychaeus, but not to the spirit which prompted that vow. Her mind, as lines 60–66 indicate, has been wilfully ignorant of her spirit. But the simile also functions in another way, too, for it emphasizes Dido's reduction to the level of an animal. Her passion has made her respond as a wounded animal would, not as a thinking, sentient, human being. Indeed the animal similes in the *Aeneid* tend always to reduce the person so compared to the level of a beast, and these animal images are always ominous for the person involved, for they portend some sort of disaster. The simile of hungry wolves, used to describe Aeneas and his band of Trojans (2.355–60), operated in just this way. The band, you will recall, became marauding beasts in their own city, and eventually the would-be despoilers became despoiled by their own men. Aeneas, by giving way to untutored impulse and by defying the clear injunctions of Hector and the gods, behaves no differently from an animal. His own unreasoning passion, his own madness, like Dido's in Book 4, reduced him to something less than a man. In the doe simile this point is there, but the tone is not so savage as in the wolf simile of Book 2. Vergil has softened the impact by appealing to his readers' sympathies for any wounded creature. Our pity is aroused for Dido for what she is doing to herself. It is a tribute to Vergil's artistry that in arousing that pity he makes us also aware of Dido's own responsibility in her act.

Within this simile we have seen how Dido, who had been likened to the huntress-goddess in the earlier simile, becomes the hunted victim. This change anticipates the hunt which Dido will soon organize for Aeneas' enjoyment and amusement, and in which Dido herself will be caught by the snares of her own devising. But the doe simile also anticipates the simile used to describe Aeneas as he sets forth on the hunt. The simile, interesting in its own right, shows Vergil's technique of combining and changing previous similes and metaphors and thereby adding reverberating significance to his material (4.141–50):

> ipse ante alios pulcherrimus omnis
> infert se socium Aeneas atque agmina iungit.
> qualis ubi hibernam Lyciam Xanthique fluenta
> deserit ac Delum maternam invisit Apollo
> instauratque choros, mixtique altaria circum
> Cretesque Dryopesque fremunt pictique Agathyrsi:
> ipse iugis Cynthi graditur mollique fluentem
> fronde premit crinem fingens atque implicat auro,
> tela sonant umeris: haud illo segnior ibat
> Aeneas, tantum egregio decus enitet ore.

["Aeneas, most handsome beyond all others, adds himself as ally and combines their bands. Just as when Apollo leaves wintery Lycia and the streams of Xanthus and visits his mother's Delos, and he takes up the chorus, and joined around the altars Cretans and Dryopians and painted Agathyrsians shout: he walks the ridges of Cynthus, twisting his flowing hair with soft boughs and braiding it with gold, and his weapons sound on his shoulders: no less graceful was Aeneas going about, such the beauty shining from his noble face."]

The simile is a companion piece to that used to describe Dido in Book 1. Aeneas is likened to Apollo leading the chorus at Delos and to Apollo the hunter. Aeneas shares some of the characteristics of Dido, as the simile suggests. Both appeared amid a throng of others and both stood out for their handsomeness. In fact, in brief compass the simile describes Aeneas' life until he reaches North Africa and Dido's Carthage, and his life has been similar to Dido's own. The appropriateness of similes drawing on the gods who were the twin children of Latona becomes apparent. Indeed, the use of the two similes suggests that there should be a continuing similarity between the lives of Aeneas and Dido. But we know there will not be. For the simile also recalls the one used to describe Aeneas when he first appeared to Dido in Book 1, where his beauty, enhanced by his mother's skill, was compared to a chryselephantine statue (1.589–93). There he was compared to a statue of a god; here he is compared to a god. The change is significant for the role Aeneas is to play vis-à-vis Dido. Her passion at this point in the affair has invested him with godlike qualities (cf. 4.12–13), and so he appears. But it is crucial that the god should be Apollo, for the simile emphasizes the god as the singer and hunter, just as Aeneas has been the singer to Dido of the fall of Troy and his wanderings and is the hunter, not only of beasts as at the moment, but also of a secure haven for himself and his companions. Furthermore, as the phrase *tela sonant umeris* ["his weapons sound on his shoulders"] hints there is an ominous tone to this hunting, ominous specifically for Dido. Apollo is the god of doom (cf. the Homeric 'far-darter'), and Aeneas will be the man of doom by being the one who precipitates Dido's own destruction. Vergil in this simile catches all these allusions and hints which have so far appeared in the *Aeneid*. But in the very comparison with Apollo, Aeneas becomes almost transcendent. Such a point emphasizes the way he appears to Dido. He will be for her an impossible goal which she can never attain, no matter how ardently she desires it. Aeneas becomes for Dido a godlike creature indeed whom she might enjoy (as she will) but never possess. Her failure to observe this distinction will contribute to her own destruction. Thus Vergil not only involves in his simile what has already happened in the *Aeneid,* but anticipates what will happen, and thereby indicates to the reader how the action is to be observed.

To return to the similes of Dido. Rumor has made Dido aware that Aeneas is preparing to depart, and Vergil compares her to a bacchante (4.300–303):

saevit inops animi totamque incensa per urbem
bacchatur, qualis commotis excita sacris
Thyias, ubi audito stimulant trieterica Baccho
orgia nocturnusque vocat clamore Cithaeron.

["She rages, bereft of mind, inflamed she raves like a Bacchic reveler through the whole city, just as a Thyiad roused by the shaken sacred objects, when the Bacchic sound is heard, the orgies of Bacchus excite her and the evening-time Mt. Cithaeron calls her with shouting."]

This short simile notes that Dido's lack of reason has made her into the mindless inflamed thing that is the bacchante inspired by the god. There still exists, however, that crucial disparity between Dido and the terms of the simile, the disparity we have observed before in the similes connected with Dido. The bacchante is inspired *commotis sacris* ["the shaken sacred objects"], and the bacchic rites are religious in origin, whereby the participant becomes joined with the god. But Dido's passion is not religious in origin. Her madness comes about from her self-induced passion, not from a frenzy produced by an enthusiasm for the god Bacchus. The simile advances our understanding of Dido by forcing to our attention the fact that her reason is in abeyance, that, as is traditionally true of the bacchante, she is no longer able to distinguish between appearance and reality. Her ensuing scene with Aeneas makes this very point clear enough. She asserts wilfully that he is betraying their *coniugium* ["union"], and when Aeneas denies that he had ever agreed to such terms, she cannot face the reality of the situation. From now on what had been latent in Dido's character becomes manifest.

Connected with the previous simile is the next, in which Dido in her mad passion is compared to Pentheus and Orestes (4.465–73):

> agit ipse furentem
> in somnis ferus Aeneas, semperque relinqui
> sola sibi, semper longam incomitata videtur
> ire viam et Tyrios deserta quaerere terra,
> Eumenidum veluti demens videt agmina Pentheus
> et solem geminum et duplices se ostendere Thebas,
> aut Agamemnonius scaenis agitatus Orestes.
> armatam facibus matrem et serpentibus atris
> cum fugit ultricesque sedent in limine Dirae.

["Wild Aeneas in her dreams drives her raging, she seems to be left alone by herself, to travel unaccompanied on a long road and to seek the Tyrians in her deserted land, just as Pentheus out of his mind sees the throng of Furies, and the twin suns and double Thebes show themselves, or like Orestes son of Agamemnon driven on the stage, when he flees his mother armed with funeral torches and dread serpents, and avenging goddesses take their seat on the threshold."]

In the introduction to the simile, Vergil indicates that to Dido Aeneas has become *ferus* ["wild"]. She dreams of herself as hunted by a wild beast who drives her mad. The lines pick up the hunting metaphor already employed in earlier similes, and she who once would be the hunter now sees herself as the hunted, and the beast she would hunt has become the creature which hunts her. She has transferred to Aeneas the attitude she herself has for him. In her dreams she further sees herself abandoned, forced to travel alone (no longer the chief member of a throng), and to seek the 'Tyrians,' leaving her own land deserted. The use of *Tyrios* is ambiguous, and so is indicative of Dido's state, for it means either the Thebans (and thus Aeneas) or the Tyrians (and thus the Phoenicians or Carthaginians). In the one instance she is forced to seek what she regards as the cause of her present illness, Aeneas; in the other she is forced to seek again the homeland which once she was forced to flee. The emphasis on Aeneas as beast makes clear the likeness to the madness of Pentheus, who in his refusal to acknowledge the power of Bacchus was driven mad so that he saw two suns and two Thebes as well as the Eumenides. Dido, like Pentheus, cannot see the actual world; the double visions signify the inability on the part of Pentheus (and Dido) to distinguish appearance from reality. Dido in her dreams is also like Orestes, forced to flee the source of danger to herself. But Dido's danger, unlike Orestes', comes from herself, not from an armed mother nor from the Dirae. Vergil indicates in the simile that he is drawing from earlier literature, probably from the plays of Pacuvius, Euripides, and Aeschylus,[4] to align Dido's madness with that of previous victims. Contained in the simile as well is the clear implication that death is the final outlet from the madness, as the phrase *longam...ire viam* ["to travel a long road"] suggests; thus it anticipates the resolve Dido herself undertakes in the immediately ensuing scene. Aeneas in the light of the simile has become for Dido a figure of vengeance and of punishment. But when we recall that such an idea operates only within Dido's own mind and that she is not really the victim of external agents as were Pentheus and Orestes, we see how she has constructed in fantasy her own guilt and suffering, and we see also that she has done so by her repeated failure to perceive the reality of her situation, i.e., that she is the cause of her own attitudes. The reference to Pentheus makes the point clear. Her passion has led her to a wholly deluded way of perceiving herself and her plight, as the simile indicates.

The similes of Books 1 and 4 relating specifically to Dido illuminate not only her passion and its relationships with previous passions in literature, but also her character and how we are to judge it. They suggest that her inability to distinguish between appearance and reality lies at the root of her character and causes her own destruction. If we examine Dido's behavior, we find confirmation of the evidence of the similes.

Dido first appears in Book 1 as a worthy ruler whom circumstances have forced to assume the role of a man, a king. She has successfully led her people from a dangerous situation to a safe one; she has skillfully avoided the various pitfalls along the way and when she first appears she is at the peak of her powers. Upon seeing Aeneas for the first time, she is attracted to him and longs to hear of his adventures. But in listening to those tales, which she wants retold often, she fails to understand their full import. Book 2 makes clear that the fall of Troy came about through a variety of causes, but chief among them was the Trojans' own wilful blindness. Dido in Book 4 never gives evidence of understanding the reasons for the fall of Troy nor subsequently of understanding her own responsibility for her plight. Vergil's use of metaphors derived from the beleaguered city to describe Dido in Book 4 suggests that Dido herself is like Troy not only in being destroyed, but in contributing to that destruction. By such metaphorical language, Vergil reinforces the similarity between Dido and Troy.[5] Dido's behavior throughout Book 4 progressively reveals her own self-delusion. Her first conversation with Anna at the opening of the book reveals a queen who behaves as an adolescent. Her unwillingness to admit to herself or to Anna what she wants from Aeneas forces Anna to state Dido's most obvious longings. In the confrontation scene with Aeneas, she refuses to admit that he could love her and at the same time leave her. She repeatedly refuses to acknowledge the validity of his claim that he must go to Italy. Even after that scene when she sends Anna to plead for a little time, she is acting in a foolish, self-infatuated manner. Her final resolve to kill herself is the culmination of her own desire to force the world to her will. The death she plans for herself and which she finally accomplishes is in accord with her romantic and sentimental notions of love. She has never learned the very thing Aeneas learns in the course of Book 4, namely that love goes outward towards others and that in so doing it returns to the lover many times over. Aeneas' concern for Iulus and for his men is the turning point in his decision to leave Dido, when he himself is clearly enough satisfied to remain. Dido, on the other hand, is incapable of extending that same generous impulse to Aeneas. Her refusal to recognize his destiny and his responsibility to others and so to himself are symptomatic of her narcissistic love. The love she once felt for Aeneas turns at the end of Book 4 to bitter hatred, and in invoking the great curse upon Aeneas and his family, Dido becomes the emasculating witch who would destroy what she cannot have. This point is most dramatically presented in the description of the funeral pyre she erects, in her placing an effigy of the hero upon it, and in her using his sword to stab herself. Her narcissism, which can admit only her view of reality, turns not against Aeneas and Iulus, whom she would destroy if she could, but upon herself. Only when she sees Aeneas sail away does the full venom of her self-love spew forth to her own hurt. So long as he remained, no matter how aloof he might be, she could in her own eyes find justification for her actions and attitudes. By arranging her death agony in the fashion he does, Vergil shows us how Dido's delusion is a baneful thing, and so how the narcissistic behavior of the queen can lead only to her destruction. For confirmation of this point we need only turn to the actual death. Dido has plunged the sword into herself but yet does not die. She raises herself three times and falls back three times and with wandering eyes she searches for the light of the sun and, having seen it, she groans (4.690–92). She groans not only at leaving the world of light, but also from the realization of what she has done. Light has flooded in on her clouded mind and at last she sees the full enormity of her actions. It is for this reason that she cannot die immediately on stabbing herself, and it is only when the light does appear that she is able to be released from her death agony.

The discrepancy between appearance and reality which lies at the heart of Dido's character comes out in Vergil's handling of the similes used to describe the queen. At each crucial stage in the dramatic narrative, he employs a simile which indicates both the similarity between Dido and something else and the disparity between Dido and the thing compared. Thus the similes admit the possibility of illumination and judgment.

But we are not done with Dido and the similes surrounding her. In Book 6 two more occur, when Aeneas sees Dido in the underworld and when he leaves her. The two similes frame the appearance of the dead queen (6.450–55):

> inter quas Phoenissa recens a vulnere Dido
> errabat silva in magna; quam Troius heros
> ut primum iuxta stetit agnovitque per umbras
> obscuram, qualem primo qui surgere mense
> aut videt aut vidisse putat per nubila lunam,
> demisit lacrimas dulcique adfatus amore est…

["Among them Phoenician Dido fresh from her wound was wandering in the great wood; the Trojan hero stopped near her and recognized her, dim

through shadows, just as at the start of the month, one sees or thinks one
has seen the moon rise through the clouds, he let go his tears and spoke
with tender love…"]

The point of view is again that of Aeneas, as in the simile in Book 1, but unlike those
used in Book 4. Dido is again amidst a crowd, but she stands out this time only for
Aeneas. No longer is she a great, commanding queen, but only one shade among
the dead. To Aeneas she seems like the moon fitfully seen on cloudy nights. She has
become only a pale reflection of what she once was. The simile reveals the consequences of Dido's character and actions and her effect on Aeneas. In so doing it
summarizes the significance of Dido for Aeneas. She was like the moon in being a
creature of deceptive appearance, a reflection of light rather than a source of light.
The light Aeneas thought he found turned out to be a false light or at best a shifting
one; the harbor of safety he thought he had entered when he reached the court of
Dido proved treacherous in the extreme. The simile makes clear how illusory was
Dido's love for Aeneas and thus how baneful. The fact too that it is the moon to
which Dido is compared recalls that Diana was the goddess of the moon and that in
another of her aspects Diana is Hecate, who functions in moonlight and to whom
Dido offered the sacrifice of her death. Dido has become completely identified with
all aspects of Diana. Aeneas' own sacrifice to Hecate, before he entered Avernus,
becomes a parallel action to Dido's sacrifice and suggests also, in view of his encounter with Dido and this simile, that he was unknowingly then sacrificing to
Dido in order to appease her as well as Hecate. The simile is a marvelous example of
how rich in significance Vergilian similes are: it recalls Aeneas' actions, Dido's first
appearance in the poem, her subsequent behavior, and her last appearance in Book 4.

The second simile, which occurs at the end of the encounter, describes Dido as
unyielding to Aeneas' final plea to her for understanding. In effect she rejects his
'sacrifice' (6.469-71):

illa solo fixos oculos aversa tenebat
nec magis incepto vultum sermone movetur
quam si dura silex aut stet Marpesia cautes.

["She, turning away, held her eyes fixed on the ground, nor was she more
moved in expression by the speech he began than if she stood as hard
flintstone or sharp-pointed Marpesian rock."]

She is compared to a *silex* and to a *cautes,* a flintstone and a sharp-pointed rock. The
point of the comparison is of course to emphasize her hardheartedness, her intran-
sigence, and her unforgiving hatred which if it could would still cause him injury
or death. But in addition the simile conveys how terrestrial Dido has been, how like
an elemental rock, indifferent, finally, to Aeneas. In this final simile of Dido Vergil
conveys to us how inhuman Dido's character actually was. The love she once thought
she felt or was supposed to feel for Aeneas turns out to have been only a hard
indifference for him the man. Her self-love was the rock on which he could well
have foundered.

The importance of Dido to the *Aeneid* lies in her relationship to Aeneas' developing
character. She is a test of his character, one he must undergo if he is ever to become
the rightful bearer of civilization. In her own turning away from love, she serves for

Aeneas as a moral lesson in what love is and is not. Through experience of Dido, Aeneas discovers what it signifies to love and how love can be the liberating force it should be for the individual. The passage of Aeneas with Dido tests him in offering to him the great temptation to rest content in a childlike security where he will be forever loved but will never be forced to achieve his own destiny. Aeneas' arrival in North Africa is descriptive of this security, for Vergil makes it quite clear that the harbor is like the return to the womb, to that elemental security where one need only be and never do. Aeneas' reluctance to leave Dido in Book 4, his reluctance to leave his own peace and contentment at Carthage, reinforce the point. But were he to remain with Dido, he would have denied forever his growth and his assumption of the role of manhood. The love Dido offers him is a deluding love, one that arises from her own delusions and that also involves him in delusion, and it is also one that eventually becomes, or could become, an emasculating one. Yet it is also a sweet one, one any man willing to settle only for his own enjoyment would readily welcome. Were he to do so he would fall victim to a delusive love and ultimately become the partial cause of his own destruction. Dido's love is so deluding because it cannot face reality, specifically the reality or the existence of another human being: for her the other person can exist only on her terms.

If we regard Dido's story from only her point of view, it can easily be looked upon as a tragedy. Recent criticism seems to consider Dido a tragic victim.[6] In doing so critics tend to simplify the complexity of Vergil's creation and to distort its significance by a false emphasis. Dido is culpable, pathetically so. We can feel pity and sympathy for her blindness, as Vergil wants us to: but he also wants us to be aware of her blindness as a moral blindness as well, one which will not heed the clear evidence presented to it or hearken to the reality it confronts. We are expected to judge Dido as well as to feel pity for her. If we do not do so, we fail to understand the crucial importance her role plays in Aeneas' life and in the structure of the *Aeneid*. Vergil indicates in his similes how we are to perceive and judge Dido and her relationship to Aeneas.

Vergil's use of similes in conjunction with the Dido-Aeneas love affair reveals how complex the similes are and how they function on several levels of significance. The repeated use of motifs from simile to simile reinforces the meanings and significance which the similes convey, so that they enhance and reflect on one another and on the material compared. We can see how reverberating the similes are and how Vergil adapted and reorganized for his own purposes similes which he borrowed from earlier writers. An attentive scrutiny of the similes reveals anew how densely organized is Vergilian poetry.

Notes

[1] I wish to thank Professor Earling Holtsmark for his careful criticism of this paper when it was in ms.

[2] *Odyssey* 6.102–9.

[3] The question of the influence of the gods on the characters of the poem need not detain us, for the gods always function in accord with the desires of men.

[4] Servius, *Commentarii* (ed. G. Thilo, Leipzig 1881), *ad loc.*

[5] Francis L. Newton has ably discussed this point in "Recurrent imagery in *Aeneid IV*," *TAPA* 88 (1957) 31–43.

[6] This, it seems to me, is Pöschl's point in his work, and also that of K. Quinn in *Latin Explorations*, and of Madeline C. Covi, "Dido in Vergil's *Aeneid*," *CJ* 60 (1964), 57–60.

DIDO'S HESITATION IN *AENEID* 4

Beginning with Dido's fleeting moment of hesitation at *Aeneid* 4.133, before she joins Aeneas for the great hunt, Segal creates a context for understanding what he views as the queen's tragedy, a moment of "blindness and insight in tense coincidence." With a look back to the woman-warrior Penthesilea in book 1 and ahead to the Egyptian queen Cleopatra, we see Dido caught in archetypical women's stories—self-sufficient queen and doomed lover. Her hesitation also connects her to similar moments in the epic: the hesitation of the Trojan horse in book 2, of the golden bough in book 6, and Aeneas' final hesitation at the end of book 12. Through his analysis of this one small detail, Segal reveals the way Vergil "illustrates in microcosm" his creation of "a subjective reality behind the objective events." (Ed.)

The fourth book of the *Aeneid* remains one of great portrayals of a woman's tragedy in Western literature. A small detail, however, seems to have been neglected or misinterpreted by the critics, namely the moment of the queen's hesitation at the threshold of her palace in *Aeneid* 4.133: *reginam thalamo cunctantem ad limina primi / Poenorum exspectant* ("The first lords of the Carthagians await the queen at the threshold as she hesitates in her chamber"). Given the slowness and the care with which Virgil composed (cf. *Vita Donati* 22), it may not be presumptuous to devote a few pages to the scrutiny of half a line, particularly when, as is often the case in this poem, Virgil can condense many meanings into a small compass.

Early in Book 4 Dido confesses to Anna her love for Aeneas, is encouraged, and exhibits all the symptoms of passion: wandering over the city, sleepless nights, neglect of her public responsibilities (1–89). Virgil then breaks off from the more or less naturalistic psychology of the queen's falling in love and suddenly introduces a dialogue between Juno and Venus (4.90–128).[1] For different reasons the two goddesses agree to collaborate in fostering this passion. Each divinity speaks in a characteristic fashion. Juno angrily attacks her opponent for bringing her and Cupid's forces to bear on a mere mortal woman. Venus replies with a flattering speech on Juno's greater influence with Jupiter and her uncertainties about what his *fata* ["fate"] may hold for the future union, if any, of the two peoples.

After this speech Juno declares her intention to unite the king and queen in the cave, as if in legitimate marriage: *conubio iungam stabili propriamque dicabo* (4.126, "I will join her in firm wedlock and dedicate her as his very own").[2] Venus says nothing more, but in a verse of famous ambiguity "smiles" or "laughs" (4.128): *adnuit atque*

Charles Segal, "Dido's Hesitation in *Aeneid* 4," *Classical World* 84.1 (1990) 1–12. Reprinted by permission of *Classical World*.

dolis risit Cytherea repertis ["Cytherea nods in assent and smiles at the discovered wiles"]. Venus may be smiling "at the wiles that Juno has invented," or she may be smiling because she has "found out or detected the wiles" with which her rival thought to deceive her, or she may be "smiling at her own wiles that she has (thus) invented." Commentators are divided about which of these meanings is the "correct" one.[3] Venus, of course, is just being herself: the love-goddess works by guile, deviousness, and treachery and acts out her characteristic mode of behavior within the human heart. Juno is imperious, remote, and complicated. As with Aeolus in Book 1, Iris in Book 5, and Allecto in Book 7, she works through the influence of another divinity.[4] She is also willing to sacrifice the human pawns in her game.

No divine intervention was required to depict Dido's falling in love with Aeneas. But through the gods' presence we understand that we are not engaged in an unmediated perception of reality but are experiencing a work of art whose creator has absolute control over his characters. The gods' intervention, in other words, may reflect authorial as well as divine control. Venus' plotting in a privileged, inaccessible space above the earth — and therefore also above the area of naturalistic human emotions — sensitizes us to Virgil's conscious structuring of emotions in his own plotting, the literary construct as an artificial creation of his own mind.

As readers, we enjoy the privilege of knowing the divine plots practiced from above. While the poet can use the gods to remind us of his authorial omnipotence, the two areas of guidance from above, the gods' and the poet's, are not entirely symmetrical. Virgil often exploits the discrepancy or disharmony between the gods as controlling forces and the human sensibilities that they replace or overrun. Venus' smile reminds us of the poet's control of narrative perspective and point of view, distance and involvement. But as the story unfolds, this smile is also the measure of our more serious, compassionate response, not as distanced, godlike spectators but as human fellow-sufferers.

Dido's entrance brings us back to this human perspective. Virgil gives a resplendent description of her hunting party, with its elaborate dress, fine trappings on prancing steeds, and abundant gold and purple (130–50). Even the sunrise is recounted twice, with mythical fullness: "Aurora leaves Ocean and rises up" and "the sun's ray comes forth" *(Oceanum interea surgens Aurora reliquit./...iubare exorto,* 129f.).[5]

This luxury, movement, and color of Dido's setting forth seems to set a happy mood. But Dido's brief moment of quiet in 4.133–35 sounds a more solemn note. *Cunctantem* ["hesitating"] in particular stands out against the active, impatient verbs that describe the waiting Carthaginians and the elaborate details of clothing and hunting gear (4.129–35):

Oceanum interea surgens Aurora reliquit.
it portis iubare exorto delecta iuventus,
retia rara, plagae, lato venabula ferro,
Massylique ruunt equites et odora canum vis.
reginam thalamo cunctantem ad limina primi
Poenorum exspectant ostroque insignis et auro
stat sonipes ac frena ferox spumantia mandit.

Meanwhile Dawn, rising, left the Ocean. When the sun had risen the chosen youth set forth from the gates; the close-woven nets, toils, hunting spears with broad iron points, and the Massylian knights come rushing forth and the keen-scented hounds. The first lords of the Carthaginians await the queen at the threshold as she hesitates in her chamber; and the steed of resounding hoofs, brilliant in purple and gold, full-spirited, champs at the foaming bit.

As Dido steps forth from her momentary safety of inaction— *cunctantem* — in the interior chamber, she is herself absorbed into this visual exuberance (4.136–41):

> tandem progreditur magna stipante caterva
> Sidoniam picto chlamydem circumdata limbo;
> cui pharetra ex auro, crines nodantur in aurum,
> aurea purpuream subnectit fibula vestem.
> nec non et Phrygii comites et laetus Iulus
> incedunt.

Finally she comes forth, her large escort crowding around her, enveloped in a Sidonian cloak with a figured border. Of gold is her quiver, into gold is her hair braided, golden the brooch that fastens her purple dress. So too advance her Trojan companions and the joyful Iulus.

Ascanius may be "joyful" (*laetus*, 140; cf. *gaudet* ["rejoices"], 157), but Virgil does not tell us that Dido is. While everything around her, from the horses to her escort, is impelled forward in a whirl of movement, carefree enthusiasm, sumptuous apparel, and glittering equipment, she is shown as alone and "hesitant" (131–42). Soon after, the whole of the natural world is swept up into the same energetic motion of "following," "rushing," "shouting" (cf. 151–55, 160–64, 166–68). This rapid accumulation of divinities, followers, and animals around her, along with the massive luxury of golden and purple accoutrements, contributes to the heavy pressure of decision and destiny of this all too brief moment of "delay."

There is another warning note amid all this gold: Dido's luxurious dress echoes the situation of another doomed female leader, Penthesilea in Book 1. We may compare 4.139, *aurea purpuream subnectit fibula vestem* ["golden the broach that fastens her purple dress"], with 1.490–93, the last scene that Aeneas observes in Dido's temple, immediately before his first meeting with the queen:

> ducit Amazonidum lunatis agmina peltis
> Penthesilea furens mediisque in milibus ardet,
> *aurea subnectens* exsertae cingula mammae
> bellatrix, audetque viris concurrere virgo.

Penthesilea, raging, leads her bands of Amazons with their half-moon shields, and is ablaze among the thousands of soldiers, binding the golden strap beneath her exposed breast, a woman-warrior. A maiden, she has the boldness to clash with men.

Though not a *virgo* ["maiden"], Dido, like Penthesilea, is a woman who attempts masculine achievements, is subject to *furor* ["rage"], and (a point particularly relevant to the echo of this passage in Book 4) is killed by a natural enemy who has fallen in love with her. The connection between the two passages is all the more likely because 4.136, just before, *tandem progreditur magna stipante caterva* ["finally she comes forth, her large escort crowding around her"], recalls 1.497, Dido's first appearance as an actor in the poem.

The word *tandem* ["finally"] in 4.136 may convey a lingering attachment to the privacy of the *thalamus* ["chamber"], perhaps even a reluctance to step outside its shelter. It underlines the momentousness of this "stepping forth" (*progreditur*) to the throng of her eager, joyful followers. (The *limen* ["threshold"] where Dido's attendants wait for her in 133 is obviously not directly outside her *thalamus*, but this does not change Virgil's dramatic effect.) When Dido returns to the *thalamus*, both it and she are radically changed. Instead of being the protected inner sanctum of a ruler's privacy or the bower of a happy bride-to-be, the *thalamus* has become the place of her final trial and her ultimate agony (cf. 391f., 494–98).

In presenting Dido at this crucial moment in so subtle, understated a way, Virgil uses two almost antithetical techniques: the vagueness of the divine action on the one hand and the richness of the physical details on the other. This pull between fullness and austerity of description is appropriate to the unobtrusive non-action of "delaying." Read as part of the stylistic elaboration of the event, the queen's hesitation forms part of the rhetorical build-up toward the fateful union in the cave. It adds still another element of suspense to the power of this decisive moment. It deepens the erotic atmosphere and adds to the sexual tension that will explode climactically in the thunder and lightning over the cave when the royal pair make love.

Virgil does not tell us why Dido delays. To some critics that is the end of the matter. Yet other moments of hesitation in the poem, particularly the hesitation of the Golden Bough in Book 6 (211) and the fatal hesitation of Turnus and then of Aeneas in the closing scene (12.916, 919, 940), have received considerable atten-tion.[6] Brooks Otis notes the "excitement before the hunt begins," but he finds all the characters of the scene opaque, "encased in an armour of guilt that, for the moment, forbids the penetration of other minds and hearts."[7] Heinze is enthusiastic about the masterly visualization of the hunt, the storm, and the supernatural fireworks, but says nothing of Dido at the threshold.[8]

Other commentators, both ancient and modern, have eagerly filled in Dido's motives. Servius suggests that Dido is taking the time to make herself pleasing to a prospective lover (*studio placendi* ["out of eagerness to please"]).[9] This psychologi-cal approach combines mimetic realism with a certain tone of male superiority to female emotionality and so has naturally endeared itself to nineteenth-century (male) commentators, most of whom repeat Servius' remark without much qualification.[10] Writing in the 1920's Cartault added to this approach a touch of Gallic understanding of the female heart: the queen is, after all, a woman who wants to show herself in the full splendor of her beauty.[11] Buscaroli, soon after, heartily endorsed Cartault's inter-pretation.[12] Paratore took a similar line: "The queen is more than ever a woman in this situation that she has artfully contrived for the more successful seduction of Aeneas."[13]

It was not hard to improve on this, and R. G. Austin did so in his Oxford com-mentary, combining the psychological analysis of motivation with a recognition of the typology of the action, i.e., allusive reference to the rituals of marriage: "Her hesitation is not due to a desire to be impressive, nor...because she was taking so long to dress; she hesitates as a bride might, even though she did not know what was to be the outcome of the day."[14] This allusion to the nuptial moment has the merit of placing Dido's hesitation in the central zone of her tragedy, with its con-flicts between passion and duty, love and rule, private life and public achievement.

Austin, however, seems unduly confident that this passage has but one meaning which necessarily excludes all others. It is more likely for Virgil that there are coincident and overlapping meanings. Dido may be delaying over her toilette because she is deeply in love and wants to appear at her best on a public occasion where she will be in her beloved's company. But may not her hesitation mark the complexity and contradictoriness of her motives: critical self-consciousness and surrender to feeling, reluctance and desire, knowledge and self-deception?

In any case, the hesitation ushers in a new point of crisis. Dido is at a point of no return, and there are heavy consequences to taking that step outside. The necessary limitation of her human perspective creates the mood of tragedy. Her hesitation and then decision join her with the tragic figures of Greek drama, who, like Aeschylus' Agamemnon or Sophocles' Oedipus, combine blindness and insight in tense coincidence.[15]

Viewed both psychologically and typologically, Dido's hesitation is a last saving instinct, a natural pull back to the safety of her home and her goals before she enters upon her hard *fata* ["fates"]. We may recall the saving power of strategic delay for another leader, but one on the "right" side: *unus qui nobis cunctando restituis rem* ["you are he alone who restores the state to us by delaying"] (6.846). Dido's *fata*, however, define her, ultimately, as an element in someone else's story and another people's history, the doomed instrument of the historical process. Seen in this light, Dido's hesitation retrospectively illuminates in still another way the ambiguities of Venus' smile and its object, the "uncovered" or "invented guiles" (4.128). For the human sufferer it does not much matter to which divinity the guiles belong. In either case Virgil presents Dido as the victim (in part) of higher powers and non-human forces pushing her life into a path over which she can only "hesitate" for a brightly lit, weighty moment. The amorous intrigue that can bring a smile to the love-goddess's lips spells the bitterness of betrayal, shame, and death for Dido. "This lone occurrence of the verb for laughing in the *Aeneid,* apart from the playful setting of the Sicilian games in Book 5," as Anderson observes, "reflects chillingly on the divine humor."[16]

The crowd thronging around Dido as she sets forth in 4.136, *tandem progreditur magna stipante caterva,* echoes her first appearance in the poem, *incessit magna iuvenum stipante caterva* ["she approached, with a large escort of youth crowding round"] (1.497).[17] There she combines womanly beauty (1.496–502) with regal authority, and she experiences the active joy of founding a city and administering justice (1.503–8). The Penthesilea echo noted above, however, suggests that she is doomed to suffering and death in this role of leader. In moving from queen to bride, she sacrifices the male role of kingship with which she began (*dux femina facti* ["the leader of the work a woman"], 1.364) and surrenders to the traditional female concerns of erotic emotion and domestic life (cf. her wish for a *parvulus Aeneas* ["a tiny Aeneas"] later in 4.327–30).[18]

In this respect, Dido has affinities with another doomed female leader, also from Africa, Cleopatra, who, like her, will "grow pale with future death" (4.644 = 8.709). Virgil calls the latter's union a criminal horror: *sequitur (nefas) Aegyptia coniunx* ["the Egyptian wife (horror) follows"] (8.688). United with this Egyptian queen, Antony is a warning example, fulfilled in historical time, of what might have been Aeneas' condition had he remained with Dido. Viewed from this later perspective, Dido seems to stand between two opposite but equally dangerous extremes: the Amazonian leader, Penthesilea (1.490–93), like her a *dux* (*ducit,* 1.490; cf. *dux femina,*

1.364), and an Eastern seductress. In both cases, her sexuality is deeply implicated in the "future doom."

In this early part of Book 4 the first lords of the people await Dido as their queen: *reginam...primi Poenorum exspectant* ["the first lords of the Carthaginians await their queen"] (4.133f., cf. 1.496); but she is soon to betray their hopes by abandoning her task as founder and ruler of their city for love. She has already been marked out by the gods as a bride (cf. 4.126f.). As a new bride, however, herself awaiting transition to her new status, she stands under the sign of misfortune: the evil omen of hesitation at the threshold, a passage from one form of *thalamus* to another.

As the divine plan is realized through (and above) the hunt, the earth moves, the sky flashes, and the Nymphs cry on the mountaintop (160–68). This is the point for which Virgil reserves the supernatural signs (*dant signum* ["they give the sign"]) from Earth and Juno as *pronuba* ["bride's attendant"] and the suggestive detail of the Nymph's strange cry on the top of the mountain (*summoque ulularunt vertice Nymphae*, 166–68). Here too he adds the Homeric comment on the "beginning of evils": *ille dies primus leti primusque malorum / causa fuit* ["that day was the first of death and the first cause of evils"] (169f.).[19] Yet even after the storm spreads its dark flashes of chiaroscuro passion over the scene, Virgil keeps the action poised subtly between realistic psychology and obscure divine forces. Not a word is said of actual physical union. Instead, the heavy moment of "delay" or "hesitation" in 133 is reversed as the queen "no longer contemplates a secret love." The return to the subjective mode, *nec iam furtivum Dido meditator amorem* ("Nor does Dido any longer contemplate a secret love," 172), fills out the pattern of recognition, choice, and self-conscious foreboding in her "hesitation" earlier. Virgil here uses the utmost tact in blending the divine and the human. Like the conductor of a symphony, now he allows the voice of the purely human emotions to be heard; now he quiets them and lets the supernatural become more strongly audible.

Virgil's gods are many things: marks of authorial control (see p. 91, above) and symbols for the invisible movements within Dido's heart.[20] They also embody the objective necessities of the situation, the fated plan of history, of which Dido is only a small, expendable part. Their plotting constitutes the design or shape of events that is gradually stamping Dido's life with its tragic form. As the book progresses, Dido's doom becomes overdetermined by a triple play of divine action as revealed in three dialogues involving gods: those between Venus and Juno, Iarbas and Jupiter, and Jupiter and Mercury.

Although both Juno and Venus, directly or indirectly, have alluded to Jupiter and the "fates" which he is directing for the future of the two peoples (e.g., 110ff.), Jupiter is himself strangely inattentive to what might be thought an important juncture. It takes the prayers of the minor character, Iarbas, motivated not by a concern for destiny or empire but by a rejected suitor's jealousy, to cause "the omnipotent Jupiter" (206, 220) to "turn his eyes to the royal walls (of Carthage) and to the lovers who have forgotten their better fame" (220f.). Jupiter has turned his eyes elsewhere;[21] Venus smiles ambiguously; Juno, who will later intervene as "omnipotent" to end Dido's agony (4.693), is unaccountably taken in by a lesser divinity.

Unlike mortals, gods can afford to be distracted or deceived. They can be playful, or they can be outwitted at their own games. For Dido, error, self-deception, inattention prove fatal. She may "hesitate," but she cannot stop. No vacuum of divine idleness surrounds her; she has no other space toward which she can look away. Her entire future is channeled to this one point of waiting; she leaves her chamber and is swept up into the excited throng of the hunters and into the ambiguously defined plan of the goddesses.

Dido's hesitation in her *thalamus* ["chamber"], as I noted earlier, belongs to a pattern of bridal ritual that is carefully manipulated by the gods (and therefore by the poet) who introduce the episode.[22] The *thalamus* of 133 is, of course, only a bedroom; and Dido is not yet a bride (but cf. 4.126f.). Yet we are sensitized to the word's marital significance in Dido's first speech of the book. Here she takes the crucial step of separating herself emotionally from the revered *thalamus* of her former husband: *si non pertaesum thalami taedaeque fuisset, / huic uni forsan potui succumbere culpae* ("If I had not been thoroughly weary of the marriage-chamber and the wedding-torch, to this one fault, perhaps, I could have yielded," 4.18f.). She harks back to this sentiment after she recognizes her betrayal (4.550f.): *non licuit thalami expertem sine crimine vitam / degere more ferae* ("It was not permitted me to pass my life free of the marriage-chamber, without crime, in the manner of a wild beast").[23] Shortly before, her vast pyre in the interior space of the palace has become a monstrous perversion of the marriage torch (504f.); and we recall her allusion to the marriage torch in line 18, her first speech in the book. The marriage-bed is then grotesquely metamorphosed into her bier-to-be, decorated by flowers and wreaths and holding the lifeless statue and the deadly sword instead of the loving husband (504–8):

> at regina pyra penetrali in sede sub auras
> erecta ingenti taedis atque ilice secta,
> intenditque locum sertis et fronde coronat
> funerea; super exuvias ensemque relictum
> effigiemque toro locat haud ignara futuri.

> But the queen, when the pyre in the interior chamber was raised up toward the winds, huge with its torches and its split oak, covers the place with garlands and crowns it with foliage appropriate to death; above the bed she places the spoils that remain, the abandoned sword and the image, not unknowing of what is to come.[24]

Thus the small hint of trouble in the hesitation at the threshold in 133 expands into a gigantic nightmare of perverted marriage.

This pattern of perverted bridal ritual is foreshadowed in Book 2 when the wooden horse stumbles at the threshold amid the solemn chants of the boys and girls of Troy (2.238–45); cf. *cunctantem ad limina primi*, 4.133 and *in limine portae / substitit* ["it stopped on the threshold of the gate"], 2.242f. In both cases joy, birth, and creation are replaced by pain, violence, and death. But the differences are as interesting as the similarities. Instead of the figuratively and murderously "pregnant" female machine (2.243), there is the human decision by a flesh-and-blood solitary woman, a non-bride who pleads in vain for a child (4.327–30). In the one case a warrior-band of purposive solidarity executes a carefully wrought plan to win a great victory. In the other a woman, alone, victim of a divine love-plot, leaves her last place of shelter. Dido's crossing of the threshold is an entirely private act; and this movement from public to private is already foreshadowed in the shift from Venus's "joining of peoples and treaties" to Juno's "joining" Dido to Aeneas in the (ironically) proprietary bond of single marriage (*propriam*): *populos aut foedera iungi* ["to join peoples or treaties"] (112); *conubio iungam stabili propriamque dicabo* ["I will join her in firm wedlock and dedicate her as his very own"] (126).[25]

When Dido sees the honor of her previous *thalamus* ["chamber"] and the hope for the future *thalamus* both betrayed, she invokes the forest world (550f.): *non licuit thalami expertem sine crimine vitam / degere more ferae....* ["It was not permitted me to pass my life free of the marriage-chamber, without crime, in the manner of a wild beast...."]. The *thalamus* swings from connotations of happy marriage to connotations of loneliness, savagery, and even the realm of the dead. This movement is reinforced by the often discussed motif of the hunt. Dido, a Diana-like huntress in her beauty, is nevertheless secure in her city and civic role (cf. 1.498–503), until the wound of love makes her an injured doe roaming the woods and doomed by the hunter's arrow to die there (4.68–73).[26] In negating the marriage-chamber by the forest, Dido reverses the book's dominant movement from the outside toward the interior recesses of her palace (cf. *tecto interiore...thalamo* ["in the inner house...chamber"], 494f.; *penetrali in sede* ["in the interior chamber"], 504; *interiora domus inrumpit limina* ["she rushes into the inner thresholds of the house"], 645). These have now become, both literally and symbolically, the abode of suffering, despair, and total loss.

The contrasting but complementary images of savage forest and corrupted marriage-chamber provide a spatial analogue for the destruction of Dido's emotional world. Betrayed in her most cherished values, she has, in effect, no place on this earth. She is trapped and exiled at the same time. True freedom, release from the funereal *thalamus* to the winds of the upper air, will come only when Iris mercifully severs the thread of life and sends her shade to the Underworld (693–705).

After Jupiter orders Aeneas to sail from Carthage, Dido leaves him "hesitating over many things in fear and preparing to say many" *(multa metu cunctantem et multa parantem / dicere,* 4.390f.) Now it is Aeneas who "hesitates" as he did at his last moments with Creusa in Book 2 (790f.). Whereas Dido merely "hesitated" in 133, Aeneas here "hesitates in fear" (390). Yet divine destiny protects Aeneas from the consequences of "hesitating"; for Dido, as for Turnus in his last encounter with Aeneas, the hesitation is fatal (12.916, 919).

When Dido crosses the threshold, she not only leaves behind one future for another; she is also leaving behind one story-pattern for another: she abandons the role of the self-sufficient queen of Book 1 (like Herodotus' Tomyris or Artemisia) for that of the abandoned woman in love (Medea, Ariadne, even Calypso). Could Virgil have meant us to see Dido's tragedy as a failure of his culture to transcend the inherited patterns of a woman's story? There is perhaps some justification for such a view in Dido's very last words (657f.): *felix, heu nimium felix, si litora tantum / numquam Dardaniae tetigissent nostra carinae* ("Alas happy, only too happy, had the Trojan ships never touched our shores"). But Dido remains a woman who, when blocked in the passional and erotic dimensions of her life, turns to death, indeed to a Liebestod ["death for love"] with the sword of her beloved. She does not exercise the option of returning to the public, political life that she had already successfully launched before Aeneas' arrival.[27] Her woman's story cannot avoid being pulled into the orbit of an all-absorbing passion. Although she and Aeneas begin almost as doublets of one another,[28] they soon move to opposite modes of discourse, he speaking the language of responsibility and reason, she that of madness, magic, and tragedy.

All narratives contain gaps in the story that the reader or hearer has to fill in. In the great masters of literature these indeterminacies are a fundamental part of the work and a source of ever-renewed interpretability.[29] They constitute, in part, the work's resistance to schematization. More positively, they reveal the author's insistence on the complexity of the human and divine worlds that he is trying to represent.

Why does Venus smile in 128? Whose "guiles" are in question? Why is Jupiter so inattentive to what seems to have been one of his main preoccupations in the first book? And, finally, why does Dido hesitate? There are, perforce, no final answers to these questions; perhaps the important thing is that they remain questions. To the last question our analysis suggests at least one answer. This small, seemingly gratuitous detail illustrates in microcosm Virgil's technique of creating a tragic tone by suggesting a subjective reality behind the objective events. In all of Virgil's treatment of character, from Tityrus and Meliboeus in *Eclogue* 1 to Aeneas and Turnus in the last line of the *Aeneid*, every conquest carries with it a vanquished human being whose suffering we are made to feel as keenly as we do the triumph of the victor.[30]

Notes

[1]On the use of the gods and the literary background see Gordon Williams, *Tradition and Originality in Roman Poetry* (Oxford 1968) 476ff.

[2]On the meaning of 4.126 and the problem of its repetition of 1.73 see R. G. Austin, *P. Vergili Maronis Aeneidos Liber Quartus* (Oxford 1955) ad loc.

[3]For recent discussion and bibliography see David Sider, "Vergil's *Aeneid* and Hesiod's *Theogony*," *Vergilius* 34 (1988) 22–24; David Konstan, "Venus's Enigmatic Smile," *Vergilius* 32 (1986) 18–25; W. S. Anderson, "Servius and the 'Comic Style' of *Aeneid* 4," *Arethusa* 14 (1981) 116f., who takes Venus' laughter as directed at her uncovering of Juno's attempted guile. Commentators call attention to the parallels with Hera and Athena's enlisting of Aphrodite's aid in the opening scene of Apollonius' *Argonautica*, Book 3, especially the *dolos* and smiling at 3.11–15 and 51. But the situation and the role of Aphrodite are quite different. See Matilde Bandini, "Dido, Enea, gli dei e il motivo dell' inganno in Virgilio, *Eneide* IV," *Euphrosyne*, n. s. 15 (1987) 90f.

[4]With Venus, the reader perhaps detects Juno's characteristic use of marriage as an instrument of power and vengeance, for 4.126, *conubio iungam stabili propriamque dicabo*, repeats 1.73, Juno's matrimonial bribe to persuade Aeolus to let loose his winds against Aeneas' ships.

[5]As Austin (note 2, above) observes ad loc., 4.130 is the only time in the *Aeneid* that Virgil used the Ennian *iubare*. The passage thus combines the archaic Roman epic with the Homeric Aurora/Eos.

[6]On the hesitation of the Golden Bough see Charles Segal, "The Hesitation of the Golden Bough. A Re-examination," *Hermes* 96 (1968) 74–79. On the ambiguity, pathos, and tragedy in the other moments of hesitation see A. J. Boyle, "The Meaning of the *Aeneid*. A Critical Inquiry," Part II, *Ramus* 1 (1972) 138f.; M. C. J. Putnam, "The Hesitation of Aeneas," *Atti del Convegno mondiale scientifico di studi su Virgilio* (Accademia Nazionale Virgiliana, Mantova, Rome, Naples 1981) 233–52, especially 237f.; W. R. Johnson, *Darkness Visible* (Berkeley and Los Angeles 1976) 131f. Turnus' hesitation in 7.449 also has a tragic cast: despite the resistance to Allecto's madness implied in *cunctantem*, his gesture is unavailing against the end awaiting him. Similarly his initial resistance to the *furor* that Allecto inspires differentiates him from Amata but is in the last analysis inconsequential: 7.435ff. The motif of tragic hesitation constitutes another link between Dido and Turnus, on which see, among others, J. W. Hunt, *Forms of Glory* (Carbondale, IL 1973) 83–96.

[7]Brooks Otis, *Virgil. A Study in Civilized Poetry* (Oxford 1963) 80f.

[8]Richard Heinze, *Vergils Epische Technik* ed. 3 (Berlin 1915) 131: "Seine Erzählung ist meisterhaft in der natürlichen Motivierung des nach göttlichem Willen Geschehenden, anschaulich in der Beschreibung der glänzenden Jagd wie des Unwetters, vortrefflich in jeder Beziehung die knappen Verse, die der verhängnisvollen Hochzeitsfeier gewidmet sind, wobei Blitze als Hochzeitsfackeln leuchten, das Jauchzen der Nymphen von der Höhe der Waldberge den Hymenaeus vertritt."

[9]A. S. Pease, *P. Vergili Maronis Aeneidos Liber Quartus* (Cambridge, Mass. 1935) ad loc., gives numerous examples of such female delays in amorous contexts from Roman comedy and also adds Ovid, *A. A.* 3.752.

[10]So, e. g., John Conington and Henry Nettleship, *The Works of Virgil*, vol. 2, 4th ed. (London 1884) ad 4.133.

[11]A. Cartault, *L'art de Virgile dans l'Énéide* (Paris 1926) 309.

[12]C. Buscaroli, *Il libro di Didone* (Rome and Milan 1932) ad loc.

[13]E. Paratore, *Virgilio, Eneide, Libro IV* (Rome 1947) ad loc.: "La regina è più che mai donna in questa circonstanza da lei ad arte provocata per sedurre più efficacemente Enea...."

[14]Austin (note 2, above), ad loc., cites Catullus 61.79. The marital associations are also noted by Paratore, ad loc. The fact that Dido is leaving rather than entering the *thalamus*, as a bride would, does not change the nuptial allusion. On the ritual of carrying the bride over the threshold see M. B. Ogle, "The House-Door in Greek and Roman Religion and Folklore," *AJP* 32 (1911) 251–71, especially 253. Cf. Catullus 61.166.

[15]The tragic element in Dido's story has been much discussed: see, e.g., Pease (note 9, above) 38f.; Viktor Pöschl, *The Art of Virgil,* trans. G. Seligson (Ann Arbor 1962) 70–91, especially 90f.; Heinze 133ff.; Kenneth Quinn, "Virgil's Tragic Queen," in *Latin Explorations* (London 1963) 29–58, especially 35ff.; Antonie Wlosok, "Vergils Didotragödie. Ein Beitrag zum Problem des Tragischen in der Aeneis," *Studien zum antiken Epos,* eds. H. Görgemanns and E. A. Schmidt (Meisenheim am Glan 1976) 228–250, with ample bibliography; Christine G. Perkell, "On Creusa, Dido, and the Quality of Victory in Virgil's *Aeneid,*" in Helene Foley, ed., *Reflections of Women in Antiquity* (London 1981) 355–77, especially 362ff.; and most recently, Bandini (note 3, above) 104f., and Wendell Clausen, *The Aeneid and the Tradition of Hellenistic Poetry,* Sather Classical Lectures 51 (Berkeley and Los Angeles 1987) 53–60.

[16]Anderson (note 3, above), 117.

[17] On the echo see A. Forbiger, *P. Vergili Maronis Opera,* ed. 4 (Lepizig 1873) ad loc.

[18]On gender reversals in the story of Dido and their tragic dimension see Grace Starry West, "Caeneus and Dido," *TAPA* 110 (1980) 315–24, especially 318–22. On the tragedy of Dido's abandonment of her public role see Susan Ford Wiltshire, *Public and Private in Vergil's "Aeneid"* (Amherst, MA 1989) 63, 90–92. For an interesting typology of female roles and their fusions and interactions in the *Aeneid* see Paul Allen Miller, "*Sive Deae Seu Sint Dirae Obscenaeque Volucres,*" *Arethusa* 22 (1989) 50–61, especially 52f. on associations between Dido, Penthesilea, and Camilla.

[19]See the good remarks on "divine, cosmic forces" in this passage by F. Klingner, *Virgil* (Zurich and Stuttgart 1967) 444.

[20]For Virgil's use of the gods as tropes of human emotion see most recently Gordon Williams, *Technique and Ideas in the Aeneid* (New Haven 1983) 20–35.

[21]Contrast, for example, Jupiter's watchful eyes in 11.725f.

[22]For the underlying motifs of Roman wedding ceremonies and expectations about marriage see Williams, *Tradition and Originality* (note 1, above) 378–84.

[23]I agree with Pease (note 9, above) ad loc., as against Austin, that the much discussed *more ferae* means the savage life of beasts, without civilized marriage, rather than "something like 'in simple innocence'" (Austin [above, note 2] ad loc., p. 164). Not only is Quintilian (9.2.64) emphatically in favor of this view (pace Austin); we should also observe that *ferus* throughout the *Aeneid* usually connotes savagery and bestiality and nowhere refers to "simple innocence." Wiltshire (above, note 18) 92, who follows Austin's approach, would translate *thalami expertem* as "as a widow," but this is unnecessarily narrow. On the echo between 4.18 and 550 and the importance of the *thalamus* motif in the book generally see Quinn (above, note 15) 55f.

[24]One may wonder whether *exuviae* here in 507, which here has the primary meaning of "memento," may not also carry, ironically, its common meaning of "spoils of war," especially in juxtaposition with *ensem*. It would thus reenforce Dido's tragic reversal from ruler to betrayed lover. Her *exuviae* are a sign not of victory but of defeat in love, again on the model of Penthesilea.

[25]On the motif of dynastic marriage in Venus' remarks of 110–12 see Richard C. Monti, *The Dido Episode and the Aeneid, Mnemosyne Supplement* 66 (Leiden 1981) 30.

[26]The Diana simile of Dido's first appearance is obviously answered by the Apollo simile of Aeneas in 4.141–50, where the association of male beauty is made ominous by the recollection of the plague-sending Apollo of *Iliad* 1 in *tela sonant umeris* (4.149). Cf. also the love-wound of Dido in 4.1–5 and the "savage Aeneas" who "drives" her in her dreams (*agit ipse furentem / in somnis ferus Aeneas,* 4.465f.). On the motif of hunting generally see, inter alios, J. Roger Dunkle, "The Hunter and Hunting in the Aeneid," *Ramus* 2 (1973) 127–42, especially 130–34;

Eugene Vance, "Sylvia's Pet Stag: Wildness and Domesticity in Virgil's *Aeneid*," *Arethusa* 14 (1981) 127–38. On the Diana simile and its ramifications see Pöschl (above, note 15) 60ff.

[27]This refusal to regain her public, regal role is all the more striking and tragic because, as Monti has argued, Dido never does lose touch completely with the political and social dimension of her union with Aeneas: Monti (note 25, above) 37–69 especially 39f. and 57–65.

[28]Dido is "Aeneas' *alter ego*," remarks Otis (note 7, above) 236, apropos of her story in Book 1.

[29]On indeterminacy as a principle of narrative structure see Frank Kermode, The *Genesis of Secrecy: On the Interpretation of Narrative* (Cambridge, Mass. 1979) passim, especially 44ff., 64ff., 116ff., 130ff.

[30]For an elegant statement of the price of victory as essential to the spirit of the *Aeneid* see Adam Parry, "The Two Voices of Virgil's *Aeneid*" (1963), in Steele Commager, ed., *Virgil: A Collection of Critical Essays* (Englewood Cliffs, N.J. 1966) 120–23. I wish to thank the anonymous referees of *CW* for helpful criticism and suggestions. This paper was presented, in a somewhat different form, at a meeting of the Classical Association of the Atlantic States, held at Princeton on September 25, 1987.

Marilyn B. Skinner

THE LAST ENCOUNTER OF DIDO AND AENEAS: AEN. 6.450–476

Though Skinner, like Hornsby and Segal, reflects on the meaning of the Dido and Aeneas story as tragedy, she views it from the perspective of the pair's final meeting, in the Underworld in book 6. That meeting, by reversing the emotional roles of the hero and queen, teaches Aeneas a painful lesson in empathy. Vergil's readers learn lessons too. We learn to read his narrative not only in a linear fashion but as a commentary that continually reflects back on itself. From that perspective, the temptation to blame or praise either Dido or Aeneas becomes complicated, for "the text permits these two irreconcilable attitudes to be entertained simultaneously." Skinner comments on the similes in the Underworld scene, especially the ambiguity of their meaning for interpretations of character. (Ed.)

F ew scenes in poetry are so charged with unresolved tension as that remarkable episode in *Aeneid* 6 wherein Aeneas, making his way through a dim underworld region populated by the ghosts of the untimely dead, suddenly confronts the shade of Dido. With concentrated power, the narrative summons back all the emotional strife of the fourth book, all the conflicting desires and the hopelessly misunderstood intentions. Beneath the acknowledged tonal complexity of these lines, sensitive readers often intuit a deeper dimension of moral uncertainty and an exquisite but ultimately futile balancing of rights and wrongs.[1] Nevertheless, much classical scholarship has lately devoted itself to ignoring complexity and turning the incident into a simple moralistic pronouncement upon the affair at Carthage. Two versions are available: one fastens upon Dido's culpability, the other stresses the guilt of Aeneas. Observers who condemn the Tyrian queen as the wrongheaded victim of her own passions see nothing but petty bitchiness in her cold rejection of her former lover.[2] At the opposite extreme, several commentators find grim satisfaction in Aeneas' tardy recognition of responsibility for bringing about Dido's emotional breakdown and suicide.[3] Both readings can be defended: as I hope to demonstrate later, each is called into play through an intricate network of ironic allusions to what has gone before. But neither is given preference; the text permits these two irreconcilable attitudes to be entertained simultaneously. Thus critics oversimplify at their peril. The compelling poignancy of the final confrontation is achieved by the juxtaposition of radically opposed assessments of what is, in any case, irrevocably done and over.

Marilyn B. Skinner, "The Last Encounter of Dido and Aeneas: *Aen.* 6.450–476," *Vergilius* 29 (1983) 12–18. Reprint here by permission of the author.

A haunting sense of *déjà vu* permeates the dense atmosphere of the Mourning Fields. Nostalgia and vain regret are actually woven into the poetic fabric of the encounter-scene, for upon analysis it proves to be a web of reminiscences of earlier episodes — reminiscences that comment, often disturbingly, upon the past and present behavior of the two principal figures. Scholars have noted a number of mechanical correspondences and remarked upon the striking effects produced by individual parallels. No one, however, has studied the combined force of all these similarities as a device to recall prior tragedy and examine it from an altered perspective. In this paper I intend to document Vergil's use of situational reversals and verbal echoes as a means of passing judgment upon the late events in Carthage.

In an important study, Michael von Albrecht has shown that the pattern of action in this episode reverses the roles that Dido and Aeneas had assumed in the quarrel-scene of Book 4.[4] Here it is Aeneas' turn to plead tearfully, Dido's turn to stand hard and silent; her turn, at length, to run away, his to make hopeless efforts to prevent her. This interchange of roles brings home to Aeneas the part he has played in Dido's tragedy. Forsaken by her, he experiences the same grief that had impelled her to take her own life. Two similes applied to Dido at the beginning and near the end of the scene underscore the role-reversal: each comparison evokes the memory of a past set of circumstances, only to invert them. At 451–454 the ghost of the queen appears as a new moon vaguely glimpsed through clouds; this image looks back to her first interview with Aeneas, when the cloud concealing the Trojan hero had parted to reveal him in godlike glory (1.586–589). Later, as Dido listens unmoved to his appeal, she is compared to rock or Marpesian marble, an ironic transposition of that rhetorical trope with which she had begun her memorable tirade: *nec tibi diva parens generis nec Dardanus auctor, / perfide, sed duris genuit te cautibus horrens / Caucasus* ["you had no divine parent nor was Dardanus ancestor of your clan, you faithless one, but the bristling Caucasus with its harsh crags bore you"] (4.365–367). Both similes function as objective expressions of a psychological conversion that now permits Aeneas to realize what Dido has suffered. This cluster of inversions, then, forms the dominant structural pattern of the encounter-scene, and von Albrecht correctly defines its most immediate purpose: to mirror the change in Aeneas' own personal understanding of prior events brought about by his new empathy with Dido's unhappiness.

But here, as elsewhere in the *Aeneid*, the structural and verbal patterning may contain thematic implications reaching beyond the direct perceptions of the protagonist to touch upon a central tragic paradox, the radical conflict between private values and public concerns. Examined in this light, Vergil's poetic statement becomes more equivocal. Surface pathos is undercut by ironic verbal echoes that discourage a simple, predictable response, forcing the reader into detached intellectual consideration of an intricate problem in contesting loyalties. The simile of the new moon seen through clouds can be read as a programmatic warning of subsequent ambiguity. Von Albrecht is of course right to note a passing allusion to the first meeting of the lovers, hinting, perhaps, at old memories momentarily stirred in Aeneas' consciousness. Yet the language of lines 451–454 also resembles the famous description of the Trojan hero and the Sibyl at the start of their underworld journey (6.268–272). Dido in the Mourning Fields, an obscure shape wandering *silva in magna...per umbras* ["in the great wood...through the shadows"], recalls Aeneas himself, equally *obscurus* in the eerie gloom: *quale per incertam lunam sub luce maligna / est iter in silvis* ["just as by an unsure moon under grudging light lies a path through the woods"] (270–271). In that simile the menacing shadows and the fitful darkness had externalized an inner state of apprehension, suggesting the cloud of unknowing in the wayfarer's own mind. Now the physical image of the new moon uncertainly glimpsed again foreshadows error and confusion. *Aut videt aut vidisse putat* ["either he sees or thinks he has seen"] casts doubt upon Aeneas' ability to interpret the present experience correctly: fact and opinion are not easily distinguished in this realm of the dead past.[5] The moon simile thus raises a problem of human fallibility crucial to evaluating the conduct of both actors in the drama. The ensuing scene is a replay of the violent clash of wills at Carthage, viewed through the eyes of Aeneas from a perspective altered by time and circumstance.[6] For him, Dido's rancor strengthens his own subjective misgivings about the decision taken so long ago. But the image of the clouded moon warns us that his vision of the past may be distorted, and that blame and responsibility are not so readily determined, nor so concrete.

While his former mistress stands dry-eyed, unyielding as stone, Aeneas himself weeps profusely. Here is a fundamental role-reversal, as ambiguous as the moon simile and charged with a terrible irony. Throughout the *Aeneid*, tears are the symbol of that comprehensive pity informing Vergil's tragic awareness.[7] *Sunt lacrimae rerum* ["these are the tears of the world"] epitomizes the poet's compassion for human folly and misfortune. In Aeneas he has created a hero keenly sensitive to the demands of a common mortality, a hero who embodies his own pensive hope that suffering can be alleviated through recognition of the universal grief inherent in man's condition. Yet in the pursuit of his divinely ordained goal, Vergil's hero is more than once compelled to disregard his natural sympathy for victims of fate. When he struggles to take his leave of Dido, he ignores her pain and his own, and conceals his feelings behind a mask of Stoic detachment. What for him is a desperate attempt at self-control appears to her as brutal indifference and proof that he had never loved her: *num fletu ingemuit nostro? num lumina flexit? / num lacrimas victus dedit aut miseratus amantem est?* ["Did he groan at my weeping? Did he turn his gaze? Was he overcome to shed tears or did he take pity on her who loved him?"] (4.369–370). Anna makes a last distraught appeal on her sister's behalf, but Aeneas still will not yield: *mens immota manet, lacrimae volvuntur inanes* ["his mind remains unmoved, tears fall in vain"] (4.449). By a calculated ambiguity, the final phrase allows the inference that he has been moved to tears at last.[8] But Dido is not there to see them; and they are, in any case, *inanes* ["in vain"], neither altering his resolution nor bringing her any comfort. Only after all tears fail her does she turn to suicide. In her distracted state, she experiences horrifying dreams in which *ferus Aeneas* ["wild Aeneas"] hunts her down, or in which she blindly wanders along a deserted road (4.465–468). Those nightmares mirror her conviction that Aeneas has abandoned her not only physically but emotionally: she betrayed her vow, only to be used and lightly tossed aside. Desolate, she chooses death as her one remaining release from pain and guilt. Aeneas' impassivity thus contributes in no small way to her final end.

In the fourth book, the Trojan leader's ruthless treatment of the woman he loved had seemed a harsh but necessary step. Divine mandates were sufficient justification for what must be done; given the pressing circumstances, the human cost had to be disregarded. Two books later, he is made to calculate the price of his heroically inhuman austerity in terms of its impact upon the life of another.[9] When he recognizes Dido among the shadowy ghosts and perceives the consequences of his well-meant sin of omission, the tears that now spring to his eyes are an eloquent enough confession of his true feelings: *demisit lacrimas dulcique adfatus amore est* ["he let go his tears and spoke with tender love"]. But the collocation of *lacrimas* and *adfatus amore est,* with its relatively uncommon sixth-foot elision, may remind us disturbingly of Dido's bewildered *num lacrimas victus dedit aut miseratus amantem est?* (4.370). In the speech that follows, Aeneas seeks not only to appease her anger but to elicit some indication of a corresponding sympathy, which would be manifested by her own tears: *talibus Aeneas ardentem et torva tuentem / lenibat dictis animum lacrimasque ciebat* ["with such words Aeneas was soothing (Dido's) burning spirit, gazing fierceness, and attempting to stir her tears"]. [10] This frank display of emotional need contrasts sharply with his behavior during the quarrel, when he had struggled to keep his face composed *(ille Iovis monitis immota tenebat / lumina et obnixus curam sub corde premebat* ["at Jove's warnings he held his eyes unmoved and struggling suppressed his care within his heart"], 4.331–332); repulsed Dido's efforts to arouse his compassion *(desine meque tuis incendere teque querelis* ["stop enflaming me and yourself with your complaints"] 4.360); and even refrained from consoling her, in the belief that duty did not permit it *(at pius Aeneas, quamquam lenire dolentem / solando cupit et dictis avertere curas /...iussa tamen divum exsequitur* ["but pious Aeneas, although he yearns to lighten her grieving with consolation and turn away her cares with his words / ...nonetheless follows the orders of the gods"], 4.393–396). Impassivity had then served as the negative counterpart of the *lacrimae rerum,* the tears of pity. Together with the haunting verbal echo in line 455, the transfer of that motif from Aeneas to Dido underscores the futility of his belated expressions of sorrow.

We can have no doubt that the silence of Dido is meant to call into question Aeneas' stern self-restraint. But it also diminishes the pathetic effect of her previous reproaches. We have recognized the justice of her earlier plea for a sincere statement of regret, an admission that the break was as agonizing for her departing lover as it was for her. Now she shows Aeneas the same pitiless inflexibility — not out of any mistaken concept of *pietas* ["piety"], but because she seems dead to all emotion save hatred. Still, there are indications that she is not in fact unaffected by his words. Her *ardentem...animum* ["ardent spirit"] recalls the onset of infatuation at 1.713, *ardescitque tuendo* ["she grows enflamed with gazing"], as well as the flare-up of full passion in 4.54, *[Anna] incensum animum flammavit amore* ["(Anna) enflames her spirit burning with love"]. And the *curae* ["cares"] that Sychaeus eventually requites surely hint at a renewal of her grief and distress. But of that inner turmoil she gives no sign: to do so would indicate that some feeling for Aeneas still remains, and she will not allow him that bare comfort. The rock simile therefore becomes a bitter reminder of her frantic attack upon his apparent indifference to her, while the verbal reminiscence *dura silex aut...Marpesia cautes* ["hard flint...or Marpesian crag"] condemns her present hardness even more than his.

The focal incident of the encounter-scene is Aeneas' poignant speech of self-justification at 456–466. Not surprisingly, the greatest concentration of allusions to earlier passages occurs here: no less than seven reminiscences of Book 4 are contained in these ten lines. The associations of all those remembered phrases are curiously disquieting.[11] *Infelix Dido* ["unhappy Dido"] repeats the narrator's description of the distracted queen at 1.749 and 4.68 and her own melancholy self-address at 4.596; here the epithet reveals Aeneas' sudden perception of the depth of her suffering. With the phrase *ferroque extrema secutam* ["seeking the end with the sword"], the reader is sharply reminded of 4.361, *Italiam non sponte sequor* ["Italy I seek not of my own will"] and Dido's caustic borrowing of the verb *i, sequere Italiam ventis...sequar atris ignibus absens* ["go, seek Italy on the winds...I though distant will seek you with gloomy fires"] (4.381 and 4.384). To witness that his intentions were good, her former lover calls upon remote and numinous powers: *per sidera iuro, / per superos et si qua fides tellure sub ima est* ["by the stars I swear, / by the gods above and by whatever faith there is in the earth below"]. Dido, we recollect, had appealed to more immediate, personal realities:

> per ego has lacrimas dextramque tuam te...
> per conubia nostra, per inceptos hymenaeos,
> si bene quid de te merui, fuit aut tibi quicquam
> dulce meum...
>
> (4.314–318)

> ["Through these tears and your right hand (I pray) you...through our union, the marriage rites begun, if I deserved any good from you, or if anything of mine was sweet to you..."]

Once more Aeneas cites *iussa deum* ["orders of the gods"] as a justification for his actions, even though that familiar argument has in the meantime lost much of its power, and even though she had sarcastically dismissed those divine orders as *horrida iussa* ["horrible orders"] (4.378). His reaction to his fearsome surroundings is graphically expressed: *has ire per umbras, / per loca senta situ...noctemque profundam* ["to pass through these shadows, / through places thick with decay and through deep night"]. But these lines ironically echo Dido's prayer at 4.24–27:

> sed mihi vel tellus optem prius ima dehiscat
> vel pater omnipotens adigat me fulmine ad umbras,
> pallentis umbras Erebo noctemque profundam,
> ante, pudor, quam te violo...

> ["But I would prefer that the earth gape open for me in its depth or that the all-powerful father send me to the shades with his thunderbolt, to the pallid shades in Erebus and the deep night, before, oh shame, I violate you..."]

She did indeed violate her ideal of chastity, and this is the result. But what for her is an enduring condition is only a temporary ordeal for her partner in the transgression: while Aeneas shrinks from the horror of her situation, we are made to recognize the disparity in the consequences of an action mutually committed. In a similar manner, his awkward euphemism for her death *hunc tantum...dolorem* ["this sorrow...so great"] recalls her use of the same phrase to describe her agony — and her false resolution to endure it: *hunc ego si potui tantum sperare dolorem, / et perferre, soror, potero* ["If I was able to expect so great a sorrow, / I would be able, sister, to bear it"] (4.419–420). Last of all, *quem fugis?* ["whom are you fleeing?"] is a heartbreaking reminder of Dido's *mene fugis?* ["from me are you fleeing?"] (4.314). By using such verbal echoes to qualify surface sentiments, Vergil is able to convey the doubt and self-reproach in the mind of his speaker. At the same time, all these allusions to the past draw attention to the ethical dilemma now perceived in what formerly had been thought of as a right and proper, albeit painful, course of action.[12]

The dreadful finality of Aeneas and Dido's last meeting is heightened by these newly emphasized moral ambiguities. As he reverses the roles taken by the lovers during their stormy argument at Carthage, as he allows Aeneas the opportunity to restate his case and to realize, in the process of restating it, that he may have no case, Vergil deliberately calls into question that general view of events he was at pains to establish earlier in the epic. Aeneas' stern Stoic deportment loses its heroic quality, becoming in retrospect pathetically defensive. Dido is no longer seen as the helpless victim of *furor* ["rage"]; the depth of cold hatred in her unforgiving silence is shockingly at odds with the generous, ardent temper she had displayed in life. Her death appears less tragically necessary; it seems, instead, a wretched preventable accident. The memory of past happiness is poisoned by animosity and remorse, and a sense of waste and loss is all-pervasive. Yet Dido's barren hatred does not repel us, but moves us to greater pity for the woman she once was. And we forgive Aeneas more readily than he will ever forgive himself. For the poet will not affix blame. In the murky domain of Pluto, that labyrinth of the dead past, there are no true villains. Rather, the capacity for injury to self or another is seen to be inherent in the kinds of choices a human being must make. The ultimate tragedy may consist in being forced to choose.[13]

Notes

[1]See, for example, W. R. Johnson's remarks upon the physical and moral "blurred clarities" of this passage (*Darkness Visible: A Study of Vergil's Aeneid* [Berkeley and Los Angeles 1976] 82–84). The impression of a scrupulous, almost Jamesian, ethical consciousness at work seems to lie behind T. S. Eliot's celebrated identification of the episode as "one of the most civilized passages in poetry" (in his 1944 Presidential Address to the Virgil Society, "What is a Classic?," reprinted in *On Poetry and Poets* [1956: New York 1961] 63).

[2]William S. Anderson, *The Art of the Aeneid* (Englewood Cliffs, N. J. 1969) 59 believes that her rejection of Aeneas is "Vergil's final comment on Dido's irresponsible, self-destructive passion." Roger A. Hornsby, *Patterns of Action in the Aeneid* (Iowa City 1970) 97–100 argues that the moon simile points to Dido's deceptive and unreliable nature, while the rock simile suggests an element of callousness. Similar attitudes are voiced by R. D. Williams, "Dido's Reply to Aeneas (*Aen.* 4.362–387) " in *Vergiliana: Recherches sur Virgile*, ed. Henri Bardon and Raoul Verdière (Leiden 1971) 422–428 and by T. R. Bryce, "The Dido-Aeneas Relationship: A Re-examination," *CW* 67 (1974) 257–269.

[3]Franz de Ruyt, "Infelix Dido!," *LES* 11 (1942) 320–324; Madeline C. Covi, "Dido in Vergil's Aeneid," *CJ* 60 (1964) 57–60; Viktor Pöschl, "Dido und Aeneas," in *Festschrift Karl Vretska*, ed. Doris Ableitinger and Helmut Gugel (Heidelberg 1970) 148–173; most recently, Steven Farron, "The Aeneas-Dido Episode as an Attack on Aeneas' Mission and Rome," *G&R* n.s. 27 (1980) 34–47. R. D. Williams, *The Aeneid of Virgil, Books 1–6* (Basingstoke and London 1972) 485 sums up the stern judgment upon Aeneas pronounced by many readers: "He has to learn the hard lesson that he has caused Dido's death, that her ghost is implacably hostile to him, and that there is nothing he can now do about what has happened except to leave the past behind."

[4]"Die Kunst der Spiegelung in Vergils Aeneis," *Hermes* 93 (1965) 54–64.

[5]That the first part of Aeneas' journey through Hades represents a conscious exploration of his own past experiences is a suggestion of Brooks Otis (*Virgil: A Study in Civilized Poetry* [Oxford 1963] 289–297) accepted by numerous recent commentators. For *aut videt aut vidisse putat* as a reflection of his present confusion, see further Johnson (above, note 1) 83–84.

[6]Eliot (above, note 1) 63–64 notes that Dido's treatment of Aeneas is presented almost as though it were a projection of Aeneas' own conscience.

[7]My discussion of the *topos* of weeping in this passage is greatly indebted to Otto Seel, "Um einen Vergilvers (*Aeneis*, VI 468)," in *Hommages à Marcel Renard* I, ed. Jacqueline Bibauw, Collection Latomus 101 (Brussels 1969) 677–688.

[8]A. Hudson-Williams, *"Lacrimae Illae Inanes," G&R* n.s. 25 (1978) 16–23 emphatically denies that Aeneas weeps at this point; his submerged feelings are only revealed for the first time in Book 6. This reading seems unnecessarily restrictive. If the *lacrimae...inanes* of 4.449 may be thought of as Aeneas', his equally vain tears at 6.455 gain particular poignancy. An instructive parallel occurs at 10.465, where Hercules sheds *lacrimas...inanis* but cannot prevent Pallas' imminent death. In addition to Servius and Augustine, *CD* 9.4, several modern commentators firmly ascribe the *lacrimae* at 4.449 to Aeneas: Viktor Pöschl, *Die Dichtkunst Virgils* (Wiesbaden 1950), translated by Gerda Seligson as *The Art of Vergil* (Ann Arbor 1962) 45–47; Kenneth Quinn, *Latin Explorations* (London 1963) 41 n. 1; Otis (above, note 5) 84 and 269. For the intentional character of the ambiguity, see R. G. Austin, *P. Vergili Maronis Aeneidos Liber Quartus* (Oxford 1955) 135 and Williams (above, note 3) 373.

[9]For the negative aspects of Aeneas' decision to pursue his mission at the price of Dido's happiness, see now Christine G. Perkell, "On Creusa, Dido, and the Quality of Victory in Virgil's *Aeneid," Women's Studies* 8 (1981) 201–223.

[10]In spite of the arguments of R. G. Austin (*P. Vergili Maronis Aeneidos Liber Sextus* [Oxford 1977] 166) I am not convinced that these particular tears must be Aeneas'. The structure of the line demands that we take *ciebat* as coordinate with *lenibat*, a conative imperfect denoting effort aimed at Dido. That *ciere* is normally used of the emotions of the subject is not reason enough to think otherwise: Vergil is poet enough to employ a verb in a novel manner. To tell us, at the conclusion of the speech, that Aeneas is still weeping adds nothing new; but there is special point in his trying in vain to make Dido weep. See Seel (above, note 7) 682–684.

[11]Many of the following parallels were long ago pointed out by Eduard Norden, *P. Vergilius Maro Aeneis Buch VI* (Leipzig 1903) 246. R. G. Austin, "Virgil, *Aeneid* vi. 384–476," *PVS* 8 (1968–1969) 51–60 and Gilbert Highet, *The Speeches in Vergil's Aeneid* (Princeton 1972) 138–139 comment on some of these reminiscences, but without considering their implications for the moral quality of Aeneas' earlier conduct.

[12]Although line 460 is not, strictly speaking, a reminiscence of an earlier passage in the *Aeneid*, I do not think it inappropriate to examine the overtones of this much-debated allusion to Catullus 66.39. I have no doubt that it is deliberate, and made with conscious awareness of the disturbing incongruity between the model and the derived text. To suppose otherwise is to impute to Vergil an impossible degree of poetic coarseness and insensitivity to nuance. Attempts to explain away the difficulty by tracing strained parallels between Aeneas himself and the recently catasterized Lock of Berenice (e.g., Agathe H. F. Thornton, "A Catullan Quotation in Virgil's Aeneid Book VI," *AUMLA* 17 [1962] 77–79) substitute intellectual ingenuity for aesthetic response. The dissonance between Catullus' high-spirited frivolity and the pathos of the Vergilian context is meant to undercut the speaker's protest of unwilling departure, forcing us to consider how little time he did spend in regretting his imminent leavetaking. Like all the other reminiscences in Aeneas' speech, it elicits from the reader reactions independent of, and to some degree in conflict with, the feelings expressed — praiseworthy though they may be.

[13]My thanks to Professors Michael Haslam, William R. Nethercut, John Van Sickle, and the anonymous referee of *Vergilius*, whose probing comments helped improve this paper. The responsibility for errors remains my own.

D. C. Feeney

HISTORY AND REVELATION
IN VERGIL'S UNDERWORLD*

Book 6 is the most difficult in the *Aeneid*, because here Vergil makes it clear that his poem is concerned with much more than a heroic story. This is philosophical poetry about a grand vista of history. Although the two articles in this collection devoted to book 6 are also difficult, they will repay the effort of studying them. Feeney focuses on Anchises' speech on the future of Rome, *Aeneid* 6.710–886. He notes a tension within the book: it is an eschatology or study of the mystery of life after death, but also a worldly, historical, nationalistic prediction for the living. Further, Feeney discovers a conflict between the apparent purpose of Anchises' speech, a panegyric or song of praise, and the actual telling of the stories, which is often ambiguous, even a threnody, or song of lamentation. Observing that the stories in Anchises' speech are organized by the great Roman families, Feeney analyzes the way Vergil sometimes confuses readers as to which family member's story he means to recall, evoking episodes both glorious and troubling from Rome's past. In that way, Vergil disrupts our expectation that Anchises' stories will be instruction, or protreptic. Feeney places the book within the context of Plato's work and Cicero's transmission of it to Rome. (Ed.)

Vergil's parade of heroes, a panegyric that becomes a threnody, is an odd blend. It is framed by an elaborate quasi-philosophical eschatology, whose relation to the parade is problematical. Much of the passage puts itself forward as high panegyric, yet certain sections are at variance with that tendency. The lament for Marcellus (868–86) is most commonly remarked upon; other passages are equally, or more, anomalous.[1] Still, the massive self-assurance of the picture of the underworld has its own imposing conviction, so that although the disparateness of the contributing elements has been documented often enough,[2] few have felt the need to dispute the question of whether the blend coheres as a single statement.

❖ ❖ ❖

In formal terms, Anchises' eulogistic speech is genealogical protreptic, using historical *exempla* ["examples, models"] and the promise of glory to steer Aeneas towards virtuous rule.[3] The opportunity for the speech is provided by a substantial and complex eschatology, made up mainly from Plato (especially *Republic* 10), and from Cicero's *Somnium Scipionis* ["Dream of Scipio"] (itself the last book of a *Republic*, and intimately linked with the myth of Er).[4] The eschatology relates the toils of the soul in its progress between this life and the next (724–51). Too few readers are

D. C. Feeney, "History and Revelation in Vergil's Underworld," *PCPS* 212 (New Series, No. 32) (1986) 1–24. Reprinted by permission of the Cambridge Philological Society.

puzzled by this blend of mysticism and worldly motivation; the stark oddity of nationalistic, glorifying protreptic in such a setting and tradition is perhaps not sufficiently appreciated.[5]

No one systematic picture emerges from Plato's account of the soul's fate after death,[6] but certain basic themes and patterns do emerge. The entire tendency is to encourage the reader to cultivate the life of philosophic virtue. Plato's contempt for the carnal unrealities of actual life, which are irreconcilably inimical to the interests of the soul, leads him to urge us to live in such a way that we may emancipate ourselves totally from earthly concerns, and escape one day from the tomb that is our body into the upper regions.[7] Within the terms of reincarnation, this means that when we come to select our next lot in life, we must choose according to the priorities of the soul, not of the body. The main temptation in our path here is the life of politics, public affairs, tyranny (Rep. 619a, Phaedo 82c–d). Plato allows that there are a very few decent characters amongst the public men (Gorg. 526a–b, Phaedrus 248d), but asserts that such a life almost necessarily involves one in the inflicting and the suffering of great evil and pain, since scarcely any can resist the corruption of power (Laws 691c–d, Rep. 494b–c).[8] Thus, in the myth of Er, the soul with the first lot chooses straightaway the life of the greatest tyrant and does not see until too late the destiny that awaits him — παίδων αὐτοῦ βρώσεις καὶ ἄλλα κακά ["the eating of his own children and other evils"] (619c). The last named soul of Plato's catalogue is that of Odysseus, who has learnt through suffering, and abandoned φιλοτιμία ["love of renown"]. He hunts out the inconspicuous life of a private citizen who minds his own business (620c).[9]

Such a perspective does not commend itself to Roman sentiment. It is in fact remarkable how much Platonic matter Cicero retains for his adaptations in the Tusculan Disputations and the Somnium Scipionis. As regards the slighting of renown and achievement, the consul, proconsul and augur has some scruples. A brief section of the Disputations attempts, not altogether happily, to reconcile a philosopher's disdain for the matters of this life with the patriot and statesman's partiality for the goods of fame (1.109–11). The problem had engaged Cicero more extensively in the Somnium Scipionis. There he follows Plato in teaching the inferiority of the body's interests (19), the pettiness of earthly glory (esp. 20–25), and the immortal reward of the virtuous soul (14–16), while at the same time trying to assert that it is the rulers and preservers of states who have the surest title to that immortal reward.[10] Again, the success of the blending is not complete, and the uncertainties of Cicero's presentation highlight the striking incongruities of the amalgam of Platonic and imperial thought. Yet the attempt alone was bold, and a strong impulse on Vergil's imagination.

Vergil's debt to Plato and Cicero is clear, and well-documented.[11] Anchises' description of the cycle of purification and rebirth (724–51) has Platonic matter mixed with Stoic, and owes much in expression to the Somnium Scipionis.[12] Especially Platonic is the presentation of corporeal existence as entrapment in a sinful prison.[13] If the speech itself puts us in mind of Plato's doctrines, the personal setting recalls the situation of the Somnium Scipionis, where a son meets a deceased father and is given a discourse on the role of the statesman.[14]

The reader who has his expectations primed by such reminiscences is going to be considerably puzzled at a number of points where Vergil's drift runs directly counter to his models. It is not the mere fact of inconsistency which should arrest us, for Vergil's eclecticism is by no means always synthetic.[15] At issue here is a fundamental paradox, an eschatology which is expressed and presented within a recognised philosophical tradition, but which appears to champion mundane values disparaged by that tradition, turning our eyes insistently towards this corporeal world, away from the concerns of the soul. Various writers have commented on the difficulties of the link between the 'philosophical' exposition and the subsequent praise of Rome, but for the most part they accept the independence of the two sections.[16] The paradox is not inert, however, but operative; it is not one which the poet glosses over, or leaves tactfully unstressed, but one to which he regularly directs our attention.

When Aeneas sees the shades gathered at the river of Lethe, he shudders at the sight, and asks what is the reason for what he sees: *causasque requirit/inscius Aeneas* ["he asks the reasons, unknowing Aeneas"] (710-11). He is being cast as the ignorant disciple, who wishes to be told *causae* by his mentor. Anchises explains that the souls are ready to return to earth once they drink of the river (713-5). He continues:

> has equidem memorare tibi atque ostendere coram
> iampridem, hanc prolem cupio enumerare meorum,
> quo magis Italia mecum laetere reperta.
>
> (716-8)

["These indeed I have been wanting to recall for you for a long time, and to show you face to face, to enumerate my descendants, so that you may rejoice all the more with me now that Italy has been found."]

These almost jaunty words might stand in themselves as sufficient introduction to the parade of heroes, but we are interrupted by a shocked question from the enduring hero:

> o pater, anne aliquas ad caelum hinc ire putandum est
> sublimis animas iterumque ad tarda reuerti
> corpora? quae lucis miseris tam dira cupido?
>
> (719-21)

["O father, must one think that any of these sublime souls goes from here to the sky and reverts again to sluggish bodies? What is the wish, so dire, among these wretches for the light?"]

That, as Servius saw, is *the* pertinent philosophical question at this point.[17] Possibly, it may also be that Vergil puts us in mind of the characteristic Platonic mode of composition here, for this is the only occasion in the poem where Vergil uses *dialogue* in this way—Anchises, Aeneas, and again Anchises—without any intervening narrative to introduce the speaker.[18]

The expectations that Aeneas' questions set up are reinforced by Anchises' 'Platonic' account of reincarnation, in which life on earth is represented as something in its essence antipathetic to the soul. Yet the parade of heroes, when it comes, is a catalogue of earthly achievement, of kings and statesmen, the very category against which Plato warns so strenuously. No Odysseus here, seeking the ordinary life— rather, to go no further, two men whose public position caused them to put their children to death (Brutus, 817-23, and Torquatus, 825). The question of Aeneas is there precisely to point the contrast between this 'earthly' eschatology and the otherworldly direction of the models.

✧ ✧ ✧

The effects of Vergil's deliberate, even blatant, reversals remain to be assessed. First, we must examine in more detail, as well as the setting, the contents — Anchises' speech itself, the parade of heroes. At the beginning I observed that various elements of the speech were at odds with its ostensible role as high panegyric. A consideration of the conventions behind the oration will establish the perspective for the discussion.

The speech becomes something of a history of Rome, by way of providing Aeneas with a series of *exempla* which will incite him to greatness.[19] The *exempla* are given a notional co-ordination in that the persons figuring in them are taken to be descendants of the speaker and the addressee (756-8). The presumed continuity of the *gens Iulia* ["Julian clan"] underpins the whole, but in the second half of the speech the great republican *gentes* ["clans"] come into their own — Marcii, Bruti, Decii, Drusi, and so on (815-86). The emphasis on the *gens* and the continuity of the *gens* is felt throughout:[20] it is one of the features which most markedly links Anchises' speech with the *laudatio funebris* ["funeral oration of praise, eulogy"] (and a *laudatio funebris* it becomes overtly, with the lament for Marcellus, 868-86).[21] The funereal associations have been well discussed by Skard and Burke.[22] We have a procession of men whose faces Anchises recognises as one would the ancestral *imagines* ["por-traits"] in the funeral parade of a noble (*omnis longo ordine posset/aduersos legere et uenientum discere uultus* ["he might view those opposite him in long procession and learn the faces of those coming by"], (754-5); Aeneas has the individuals pointed out and explained to him by his father, as would any son in a Roman street, watching the procession go by. We have the praise of the family line. Especially, we receive the impression that representatives of the *gens* from many, many generations are rubbing shoulders together on the same spot, as would the actors wearing the masks at an actual funeral. At various places in the speech there is a rough chronological schema in the groupings, but behind it all is the notion that the members of each *gens* stand together. Thus, when Aeneas sees the Marcellus of the first century B.C. standing beside the Marcellus of the third, he can tell the family resemblance, but he does not know whether this is a son, or a more remote descendant (*filius, anne aliquis magna de stirpe nepotum?* ["a son, or someone from the great line of descendants?"], 864); and Anchises sees all the Fabii before him, so that he cannot speak of all of them (*quo fessum rapitis, Fabii?* ["where do you speed me — tired, O Fabii?"], 845).

This theme of the continuity of the *gens* is most important. One of its effects is to set up what Ahl has called 'a number of riddles for the reader,'[23] for Vergil is often studiedly vague about which members of a family we are meant to see behind the name. Which Drusi does he mean in 824? Which Gracchi, which Scipiones in 842-3? Here we may be helped by the exemplary character of the speech, for by looking at the associations of such names in other exemplary contexts, it is often possible to divine what Vergil is driving at. A proficient exploiter of the exemplary tradition is Lucan; consistently he sheds light on problematic Vergilian passages. Cicero and Seneca are likewise valuable. Another effect of the focus on the continuity of the *gens* is to put us in mind of a man's descendants when an individual is named, since to a Roman a noble was, in one side of his persona at least, the temporary incarnation of the essence of his family.[24]

It is this frame of mind which produces and explains the riddles. If Vergil mentions, for example, the *first* Brutus, his audience is readily suggestible to associations with the assassin of Caesar; while mention of Gracchi or Drusi is potentially provoking, as the audience is invited to reflect upon the diverse fates and worth of successive bearers of the same name.

✧ ✧ ✧

[I]n the hands of Vergil these confusions become vehicles for a sophisticated and profound conception. The riddles will emerge as being part of a process whereby the entire panegyric receives extensive qualification. Whole sections of the speech treat openly of dark and painful matters—the civil wars of Pompey and Caesar (826–35), Brutus' execution of his children (820–3), and Marcellus' funeral (868–86). These larger passages have attracted much comment. We will need to recognise that the glorifying impetus of the speech as a whole is checked and intermittently retarded by countervailing tendencies of dubiety, mourning, even disparagement.

✧ ✧ ✧

The first problem we encounter is at 773–6, with the listed towns of the *prisci Latini* ["ancient Latins"]:

> hi tibi Nomentum et Gabios urbemque Fidenam,
> hi Collatinas imponent montibus arces,
> Pometios Castrumque Inui Bolamque Coramque;
> haec tum nomina erunt, nunc sunt sine nomine terrae.

> ["These are the ones, I tell you, who will found Nomentum and Gabii and the city Fidena, who will put Collatina's citadels on the hills, and Pometii, and the Camp of Inuus, and Bola and Cora. These will be the names then, that now are lands without a name."]

tum erunt, nunc sunt...["then they will be, now they are..."]; the words invite us to ask what the towns were in Vergil's day. Look at these places:

Nomentum   A byword for an out-of-the-way backwater in Seneca and Martial.[25]

Gabii   In Horace, a yardstick of depopulation, together with Fidenae, the next town in Vergil's list.[26] To Cicero and Juvenal it is emblematic of insignificance, while Propertius and Dionysius of Halicarnassus draw a contrast between its former and present condition.[27]

Fidenae   Strabo has the town in a list of places, τότε μὲν πολίχνια, νῦν δὲ κῶμαι, ἢ κτήσεις ἰδιωτῶν ["at one time very small towns, now villages, or pieces of land of private individuals"] (5.3.2). Note that Vergil pointedly calls it an *urbs* ["city"]. The place also figures in a similar list of vanished towns in Pliny (*Nat.* 3.68–70).

Collatia   In Strabo's and Pliny's lists.

Pometia   Likewise in Pliny's list.

Castrum Inui   Vanished very early in the Republic, a victim to fever.[28]

Bola   Likewise in Pliny's list.

Cora   Florus treats the erstwhile power of Cora almost as a joke: *Cora—quis credat?—et Alsium terrori fuerunt* ["Cora—who would believe it?—and Alsium were a source of terror"] (1.11.6).[29]

haec tum nomina erunt, nunc sunt sine nomine terrae....["these will be the names then, that now are lands without names"]. The tenses are intriguingly two-sided, depending on whether one's perspective in time is that of Aeneas, or of Vergil's audience. To Aeneas, the words say that these will be famous names after his time, whereas now, in his lifetime, they are areas of land without any title (or else, places that exist but have no fame). To the contemporary audience, the words are saying that the places will be what they are in fact — *mere names;* now, for 'us,' they are only *pieces of land,* without the *reputation* they once had....The shifts in tense and reference are unsettling. What is proferred as praise becomes disparagement, or condolence, as it is uttered. The glorious future of the independent states is taken away from them before it has even happened, as the poet nudges his audience into remembering their contemporary eclipse, swallowed into obscurity by the dominance of the metropolis. The fate of these places is embodied, indeed, in the name of the first town in the list: *Nomen-tum* ["Name-then"].[30] In such a context of instability, one is perhaps prompted to ask (as I was by Professor West) whether Vergil can conceive of a time when even Rome will be only a name. It has not happened yet.

✧ ✧ ✧

Romulus comes next. He is introduced as making himself the 'comrade or associate of his grandfather' (*quin et auo comitem sese Mauortius addet/Romulus* ["But indeed, the son of Mars, Romulus, will make himself his grandfather's companion"], 777–8). Vergil refers to the story we see in Livy (1.3.10–6.2). The grandfather of Romulus and Remus was one Numitor (his name occurs earlier at 768, preparing us for this story). He was disinherited and exiled by his younger brother Amulius. Amulius was responsible for the exposure of the twins, but, when grown, Romulus collaborated with his grandfather Numitor to kill the usurper by stealth (1.5.6). He and Remus then restored Numitor to the throne of Alba Longa.

The man who began adult life by killing his great-uncle went on to kill his brother. Vergil does not mention the deed here, nor even the brother, but there is a hint, in *huius...auspiciis* ["under his auspices"] (781). The taking of the auspices at the foundation of Rome, Vergil obliquely reminds us, was a *competition,* which Remus lost (Ennius, *Ann.* 72–91 Skutsch). If an earlier argument of mine is correct, then 780 also refers to this competition, and to the prize of divinity which Romulus won at the expense of his brother.[31]

The founder of the city was a genuinely ambiguous figure, never more so than in the years when Vergil was at work on the *Aeneid.* He had an important role in Caesarian and Augustan cult, and in the literature of the time.[32] Dio reports that Octavian wanted the name for himself (53.16.7). In the end, a less controversial title won the day, though one which itself had associations with the *conditor urbis* ["founder of the city"] (Suet. Aug. 7.2) — less controversial, because much in the Romulus myth was disquieting (and not only the fratricide).[33] When Anchises speaks of Romulus, his words have a strong and primary panegyrical direction, which I do not mean to shut out — and yet Vergil does not allow us to block Remus from our memory. A very similar operation is to be seen in Jupiter's prophetic speech in Book 1. Jupiter describes the birth of the *twins: geminam partu dabit Ilia prolem* ["Ilia will give twin offspring in birth"] (274). The first five feet of the next line allude to the wolf who nursed the twins (*inde lupae fuluo nutricis tegmine*) ["then in the tawny hide of the wolf-nurse"], and it is with considerable shock that we reach the final word and discover that it is *singular* (*laetus*) ["happy"].[34] We carry on to find Romulus as the subject: *Romulus excipiet gentem* ["Romulus will carry on the clan"] (276).

Remo scilicet interempto ["Remus of course having been killed"], comments Servius. Just so. We continue: *Mauortia condet/moenia Romanosque suo de nomine dicet* ["the walls of Mars he will found and call the people Romans from his own name"] (276–7). It was when Remus jumped over Romulus' *moenia* that he was killed,[35] while the naming of the people after Romulus rather than after Remus was a result of Romulus' victory in the contest of auspices: *certabant urbem Romam Remoramne uocarent* ["they vied whether to call the city Roma or Remora"] (Ennius, *Ann.* 77 Skutsch). And yet Vergil does not leave us here, for at the end of the speech, in the vision of hoped-for peace after the civil wars, the brothers are shown as reconciled: *cana Fides et Vesta, Remo cum fratre Quirinus/iura dabunt* ["Hoary Fidelity and Vesta, Quirinus (Romulus) with his brother Remus/ will give laws"] (292–3). It was possible simply to suppress mention of Remus (as does Cicero, for example, in the *Republic,* 2.4–12); what is striking in Vergil is the way in which we are reminded of Remus even as we hear the praise of Romulus the founder.

✧ ✧ ✧

Once Vergil has dealt with Romulus, there follows a panegyric on Rome (781–7), which develops into the praise of Augustus (791–805). Rome's other kings follow (808–17; note that Augustus, by this arrangement, is one of the *reges* ["kings"]); as the establishment of the Republic approaches, equivocation returns.[36]

✧ ✧ ✧

The tension becomes acute as we turn to the Tarquins, linked with Brutus, who introduce a passage of notorious ambivalence, compounded of awed pride and shock:

> uis et Tarquinios reges animamque superbam
> ultoris Bruti, fascisque uidere receptos?
> consulis imperium hic primus saeuasque securis
> accipiet, natosque pater noua bella mouentis
> ad poenam pulchra pro libertate uocabit,
> infelix, utcumque ferent ea facta minores:
> uincet amor patriae laudumque immensa cupido.

> (817–23)

["Do you wish to see also the Tarquin kings and the arrogant spirit of avenging Brutus, and the fasces regained? He will be the first to receive the consul's power and savage axes, and, a father, he will call to punishment his sons agitating a new war, for the sake of beautiful liberty, he unfortunate, even though descendants will celebrate these deeds: love of fatherland will prevail and immense desire for praise."]

Here the theme of the continuity of the *gens* is at its most powerful. Also at its most evident, for the associations made by Vergil's contemporaries between the assassin of Julius Caesar and his supposed ancestor, the first consul, are well-established facts.[37] With a number of touches Vergil draws our attention to the similarities linking the two deeds, at the beginning and the end of the *res publica* ["republic"]. The essential truth was stated by Fletcher, in his note on *superbam* ["arrogant"] (817): 'Here as applied to the spirit of Brutus it is a reminder that arrogance is not a monopoly of "tyrants" (*reges*). None of Virgil's readers could fail to think of the descendant, another *ultor Brutus* ["avenging Brutus"],[38] whose intellectual arrogance they had known. He had also violated natural ties in the belief that he was serving his country: the killing of Julius Caesar, like the execution of his own sons by the elder Brutus, was an act praised by some and blamed by others, and Virgil's comment in 822–3 may be applied equally to either action.'[39]

Certainly the tyrannicide was the object of a considerable industry of hagiography, which began soon after his death, and which is exemplified for us in Plutarch's *Life*.[40] Not all approved, however: Brutus was far less popular than Cato as an *exemplum*, and controversy concentrated on the clash between two types of *pietas* ["piety"], between patriotism and humanity.[41]

✧ ✧ ✧

Vergil's language enmeshes us in [a] dilemma of judgement: *uincet amor patriae laudumque immensa cupido* ["love of fatherland will prevail and immense desire for praise"] (823). The phrasing invites the reader's decision: do we accord or withhold the *laudes* ["praise"] which Brutus wishes to have?...

Two lines, in which the pressure does not altogether relent, separate us from Caesar and Pompey, and the civil wars:

quin Decios Drusosque procul saeuumque securi
aspice Torquatum et referentem signa Camillum.

(824–5)

["But look far off at the Decii and the Drusi, and Torquatus savage with his ax, and Camillus bringing back the standards."]

'These names,' observes Horsfall, 'and not Brutus' alone, sandwiched between the great monumental blocks of the Kings and Caesar and Pompey must be of particular importance.'[42]

✧ ✧ ✧

In the case of the Drusi, Servius saw the link with Augustus' wife Livia, who was one of the Livii Drusi. Such an association may well be felt, while Horsfall's identification of a 'Gallic' connection in the vicinity is also very appealing.[43] But our context...is one of names listed as *exempla*, and we must look to other similar contexts in order to establish the full tone of the allusion.

As Horsfall remarks, 'the alliteration of *Decios Drusosque* is striking. Vergil highlights the strength of the *gens*.'[44] The juxtaposition is very important....The Decii were father and son,[45] with the son following exactly in the footsteps of the father....The Drusi of this exemplary tradition were also father and son. Here, however, the son did not live up to the standard of the father, but fell off disastrously, and became a byword for degeneration.

✧ ✧ ✧

The name Drusus does not occur in a laudatory context in lists of *exempla*. The reference is always to the younger Drusus, and it is always condemnatory, linking him with other notorious demagogues, such as the Gracchi, Saturninus, Sulpicius, Cinna (*Herenn.* 4.31, Cic. *Vat.* 23)....This theme of sons falling short of their father's standards is one which Vergil will pick up later in the parade, in speaking of the Gracchi (842); it is the theme with which he had first experimented in *Georgics* 2.

There were many things to say about the great Torquatus. Vergil chooses his execution of his son, so that we see Torquatus alone, in the singular, after Decii, father and son, and Drusi, father and son. The language takes us back to Brutus' like deed (*saeuumque securi*, 824; *saeuasque securis*, 819 ["savage with his ax; savage axes"]). When Camillus follows Torquatus, we may feel that Vergil's dubieties are on the ebb; but immediately Anchises shows us the shades of Caesar and Pompey (826–35). Their calamitous wars are too painful to be described directly. Anchises beseeches both of them to abstain (832–3). He prays then to Caesar to relent first:

> tuque prior, tu parce, genus qui ducis Olympo,
> proice tela manu, sanguis meus!

(834–5)

> ["And you, first, you be sparing, you who descend the clan from Olympus,
> throw the weapon from your hand, you, my own blood!"]

This plea is sometimes seen as a reference to Caesar's famous *clementia* ["mercy"].[46] Certainly Caesar was *clemens* ["merciful"], but only once he had begun the war; here Anchises is begging his descendant to lay down his arms first, before Pompey does.

If Augustus is the central peak of the first half of the speech, the glimpse of the civil wars is the peak of the second.[47] In a manner by now familiar, Vergil then veers away from these horrors into a celebratory passage (836–46); but it is possible that even here there are traces of civil strife to be recognised.

The victories over Greece come next, with a couple of easy riddles of identity for the reader to answer (*ille* ["he"] is L. Mummius at 836, L. Aemilius Paullus at 838). At 841 a riddle of more moment may be presented:

> quis te, magne Cato, tacitum aut te, Cosse, relinquat?

> ["who will leave you silent, great Cato, or you, Cossus?"]

The commentators tell us that Cato the Censor is meant here. In Vergil's time he could be called *Cato maior*, 'Cato the elder.'[48] When Anchises addresses someone as '*great* Cato,' then the positive form of the adjective, if it prompts thoughts of the comparative, is perhaps disconcerting. Was Cato Censorius then *greater* than Cato Uticensis? Which Cato *was* the greater?[49] When seen from this angle, the question form becomes energised: the question of whether to leave Cato the younger unmentioned was, after all, not untopical.[50]

Following Cato and Cossus comes *Gracchi genus* ["clan of Gracchus"] (842). The phrase has caused difficulty,[51] but once again the *gens* is the focus,[52] and once more, as in the case of the Drusi, the exemplary tradition directs our attention to the degeneration of demagogic sons from optimate fathers. Ti. Sempronius Gracchus (cos. 177), father of the tribunes, was a model for later generations.[53] It is noteworthy that although Cicero speaks of him with warm praise, he never includes the name of Gracchus in his frequent lists of exemplary names — except once, and then specifically, in the singular, in strict chronological sequence, so that this representative of the family alone could be understood (*Nat. deor.* 2.165). The name was simply too loaded, tied in men's minds to the sons. Thus Cicero, in the *De provinciis consularibus* ["On consular provinces"], mentions Ti. Gracchus, and hastily assures his audience that he did not mean the tribune: *an Ti. Gracchus (patrem dico, cuius utinam filii ne degenerassent a grauitate patria!)...*["or Tiberius Gracchus (I mean the father, would that his sons had not fallen away from the weighty seriousness of their father)"] (18). These words illustrate the fixed attitude of the exemplary tradition.[54]

✧ ✧ ✧

The mother of the tribunes was the daughter of Scipio Africanus Maior, and the family of the Scipiones is the next to appear:

> geminos, duo fulmina belli,
> Scipiadas, cladem Libyae.

(842–3)

["twin Scipios, two thunderbolts of war, the ruin of Libya."]

Who are these Scipiones? As we move through the lines, a number of different suggestions present themselves in sequence, so that the extension of the *gens* is once more brought home to us.

When a Roman listener had heard as far as *geminos, duo fulmina belli,/Scipiadas* ["twins, two thunderbolts of war,/Scipios"], he would have thought he knew who was meant: the two brothers Gn. Cornelius Scipio Calvus (cos. 222), and P. Cornelius Scipio (cos. 218), respectively uncle and father of Africanus Maior (*geminos* ["twins"] would reinforce the expectation that *brothers* are being spoken of). This is how Servius takes it, and it is plain from the language of Cicero and Silius that Servius' interpretation has some sanction.[55] Generally, when Cicero speaks *tout court* ["simply"] of *duo Scipiones* ["two Scipios"], he means these two, as is seen most clearly at *Tusc.* 1.110, where in an exemplary list he has *duos Scipiones, duos Africanos* ["the two Scipios, two Africani"].[56]

It was Ennius who devised the pun in *fulmina* ["thunderbolts"], and he applied it to Africanus Maior as well as to the two brothers.[57] Vergil picks up this reference to Africanus with *cladem Libyae* ["ruin of Libya"], a phrase that cannot apply to the two brothers, who did not campaign in Africa. All at once the reader is forced into some readjustment. It must then be Africanus — no, not just he, but *both* Africani (*duo fulmina*). The second of these, Africanus Minor, the captor of Carthage, was of course not in Ennius: the historical perspective suddenly opens up, as Vergil squeezes another two generations from the Ennian phrase, extending the reference down to 146, with Africanus Minor's sack of Carthage. In seven words we see the family of the Scipiones over four generations.

And for more than four generations. *cladem Libyae* applies to the disasters which the two Africani *inflicted* upon Libya. Exactly a hundred years after Scipio Aemilianus annihilated Carthage, another Scipio, Q. Caecilius Metellus Pius Scipio, *suffered* a disaster in Libya, as commander of the Republican forces against Caesar in the Thapsus campaign of 46. The African fate of the Scipiones was taken seriously by both sides in the Thapsus campaign,[58] and the varying fortune of bearers of the name became something of a topic.

✧ ✧ ✧

If the mention of the Scipiones in Africa does contain ambivalence, then it is the last such citation in the speech. Fabricius, Regulus and the Cunctator round off the *exempla* in noble fashion. Before Anchises closes, he enunciates his celebrated doctrine of empire, fixing for the Romans the nature and the limits of their achievement:

> excudent alii spirantia mollius aera
> (credo equidem), uiuos ducent de marmore uultus,
> orabunt causas melius, caelique meatus
> describent radio et surgentia sidera dicent;
> tu regere imperio populos, Romane, memento
> (hae tibi erunt artes), pacique imponere morem,
> parcere subiectis et debellare superbos
>
> (847–53)

["Others will beat out more gently the breathing bronzes (indeed I do believe), will draw out living faces from marble, will speak cases better, describe with a rod the paths of the sky and tell of the rising stars. You, Roman, remember to rule peoples with your power (these will be your arts) and impose the way of peace, spare those brought low, and war down the proud."]

Griffin has best clarified the way in which these words hold back as much as they offer, deny as much as they assert.[59] Many admirable forms of artistic and intellectual endeavour must be spurned in the cause of political and military preeminence. Yet, of course, the irony is not inert, as we hear Anchises proclaim that the Romans must abjure a faith in ideals of artistic attainment, when the very existence of the poem in which he is a character is witness to the power of that faith.[60]

We think we have come to the end, but Anchises resumes, showing us the great Marcellus of the Hannibalic war, leading us into the lament for the young Marcellus who had recently died. There is no question of seeing this lament as a late addition to an existing parade. The melancholy coda was part of the basic conception from the very beginning.[61] Augustus' designated heir receives high praise, but waste and futility are the ruling tones. The formal cast of Anchises' speech throughout has been that of a prophecy, and here at the end that prophesying form becomes activated, as the perspective makes itself, for the poet and his readers, genuinely forward-looking. Marcellus had embodied the future,[62] a future which is painted gloriously (872–81), and then taken away from us, unrealised. As Anchises closes, scattering flowers in his descendant's honour (883–6), the contemporary of Vergil is left suspended, his attention all forward, all expectant: what, then, will follow Marcellus? Will the divine Augustus, as promised, be able to carry us through?

When, shortly afterwards, Aeneas comes to leave the underworld (893–8), his departure is described in terms which recall the philosophical myths introducing the parade. Here we are much indebted to R. J. Tarrant, who has clarified the longstanding difficulties of the gates of horn and ivory, by setting their imagery in the context of the Platonic doctrines of the soul.[63] Aeneas leaves by the gate of the *falsa insomnia* ["false dreams"] because he is still alive, still a prisoner of the body and of the illusions of the 'real' world which the body is doomed to inhabit.[64] Tarrant is completely convincing when he goes on (p. 54) to draw more general conclusions on the effect of such a setting for the view of mortal achievements in the historical vision: 'Virgil seems to have found Plato's view of the physical world as a mere shadow of a purer world a useful structure of thought by which to express his own sense of the evanescence of mortal aspirations.'

We have been led by this framing device back to the unresolved questions which occupied us at the beginning, concerning the paradox presented by Vergil's use of the otherworldly myths of philosophy to introduce a show of mundane achievement, and a celebration of *gloria* ["glory"].

The parade of heroes exhibits mighty national and individual accomplishments. It also covers civil war, *populares* ["popular leaders"] and demagogues, fathers executing sons, the disappearance of once-great cities, the falling-off of families, the stifling of promise, the shunning of art, the hunger for personal glory: in short, the political life's intolerable demands on human nature, together with the 'evanescence' (to use Tarrant's fine phrase) 'of mortal aspirations.' The insistent stress on *gloria* is not only remarkable in this 'philosophical' context; it is altogether striking in a poem that is so preoccupied with the great contemporary ethical shift in attitudes to *gloria,* away from the ruinous competition and egoism that was the essence of traditional *gloria.*[65]

The 'Platonic' setting creates two principal effects (if we may be so blunt in fixing the passage's diffused force). The personal aims and sufferings of the politicians on view are put into a disconcerting perspective once we have been invited to see them as characters in a Platonic myth, once we have been reminded of the moral exhortations for which Plato's myths were a vehicle, turning us away from the vanity of this world, and especially from the vain, hollow harshness of public life. Further, the setting presents the Roman state as the τέλος ["end-point, fulfillment"] of the way in which the world is ordered, while making it difficult or impossible for us to decide on a clear response. Rome *is* celebrated by the device, but the reader has been given the perspective of a Platonist, and it is bewildering to be promised an elaborate revelation which ultimately declares that there is in fact nothing more than the mixed uncertainties of actual history. From the standpoint of a moral philosopher, the achievements of the Roman state do not have a self-evident importance. When Vergil leads us to expect a Platonic vision, and deceives our expectation, a complex rearrangement of priorities ensues. He gives us instead something powerful and something of one kind of beauty; but when he denies his poem and his audience the beauty and the consolation of the myths of philosophy, immortality and redemption, this formal and aesthetic exclusion mirrors and recreates the exclusion which is the lot of the chief character in the poem, and of the poem's audience in the world.[66]

This world is indeed what concerns Vergil here. The very elaboration of the picture of the underworld had led many to speculate on the religious sentiment or message to be found there, but as far as the elements of religion or philosophy are concerned, I take the truth to be more or less as Servius stated it: *sectis philosophorum poetae pro qualitate negotiorum semper utuntur* ["poets always use the methods of philosophers for the essential nature of the matters at hand"].[67] In the meeting of Aeneas and Anchises, the 'essential nature of the matter in hand' is not a religious revelation,

but an image of the nature of Rome and of the political process, an image of the life
of the Roman statesman, or of any such statesman.

❖ ❖ ❖

Notes

*A version of this paper was read to a meeting of the Cambridge Philological Society on
October 10, 1985. I thank those present for a valuable discussion. For their help and criticism
I am also grateful to N. M. Horsfall, Professor R. G. M. Nisbet, Professor David West, Philip
Hardie, R. O. A. M. Lyne, Stephen Hinds, and J. M. Masters.
I use author's name only in referring to the editions of *Aeneid* 6 by E. Norden, ed. 3
(1935), F. Fletcher (1941), and R. G. Austin (1977). All ancient dates are B.C.
[1]Cf. K. Büchner, *RE* 8A 1391. Important discussions by W. V. Clausen, 'An interpretation
of the *Aeneid*,' *HSCPh* 68 (1964) 139–47; R. D. Williams in J. R. C. Martyn (ed.), *Cicero and
Virgil* (1972) 207–17; J. Griffin, 'The Fourth Georgic, Virgil, and Rome,' *G&R* n.s. 26 (1979) 61–
80; R. J. Tarrant, 'Aeneas and the gates of sleep,' *CPh* 77 (1982) 51–5; above all, W. R. Johnson,
Darkness visible. A study of Vergil's Aeneid (1976) 105–11.
[2]Bibliography on this disparateness in F. Solmsen, *CPh* 67 (1972) 31–3; cf. N. M. Horsfall,
Antichthon 15 (1981) 145.
[3]Bibliography in N. M. Horsfall, *Prudentia* 8 (1976) 84 n. 102; note especially M. von
Albrecht, *WS* n.f. 1 (1967) 156–82.
[4]Norden's discussion is still indispensable (47–8). See further n. 11 below.
[5]It is recognised by Johnson, *Darkness visible* 105–11.
[6]As is stressed by Julia Annas, 'Plato's myths of judgement,' *Phronesis* 27 (1982) 119–43 (a
reference I owe to M. M. Mackenzie, whom I thank for help on these Platonic matters). The
main Platonic passages are *Gorg.* 523a–27e; *Phaedo*, 112e–14c; *Rep.* 614b–21d; *Phaedrus* 245c–50c.
[7]Although hope of this escape is not actually held out in the myth of Er.
[8]The philosopher-king may be free from this corruption, but Plato seems to have become
increasingly pessimistic on this score; see Julia Annas, *An introduction to Plato's* Republic (1981) 106.
[9]For praise of the inconspicuous life in such contexts, cf. *Phaedo* 82c–d, *Gorg.* 526c.
[10]This is, as it were, a base version of the Platonic problem involved in why the Guard-
ian should go back into the cave after attaining his own enlightenment (Annas, *Introduction*
262–70). On these links between Cicero and Plato, see P. Boyancé, *Études sur le songe de Scipion*
(1936) 147–60. Many writings on Cicero's Platonic debts are discussed by P. L. Schmidt in
ANRW I 4.309–10.
[11]On the Platonic element, see the works cited by Solmsen (n. 2). On the Ciceronian, see
Norden 47; F. Klingner, *Virgil* (1967) 485–92; W. A. Camps, *An introduction to Virgil's Aeneid*
(1969) 89–90; R. Lamacchia, *RhM* 107 (1964) 261–78.
[12]cf. Austin 221.
[13]Note 731–4 in particular, and the language of malaise and imprisonment to describe
earthly life in 734 (*clausae...corpore caeco*), 736 (*malum*), 737 (*corporeae pestes*), 739 (*malorum*),
742 (*infectum scelus*). Very Ciceronian language here: cf. esp. *Somn.* 29.
[14]Cf. (besides works in n. 11) Boyancé, *Études* 39–40; L. Alfonsi, *Aevum* 29 (1955) 375–6.
[15]As we have recently been well reminded by Horsfall (n. 2).
[16]Thus B. Otis, *Virgil. A study in civilized poetry* (1963) 300–1; Solmsen (n. 2); R. J. Clark,
Catabasis: Vergil and the wisdom-tradition (1979) 182–3.
[17]Note, especially, these words: *miscet philosophiae figmenta poetica et ostendit tam quod est
uulgare, quam quod continet ueritas et ratio naturalis.*
[18]Cf. H. C. Lipscomb, *CW* 2 (1908–9) 116.

❖ ❖ ❖

[19]On *exempla*, see H. W. Litchfield, *HSCPh* 25 (1914) 1–71; Pease on Cic. *Nat. deor.* 2.165.
[20]Cf. von Albrecht (n. 3) 176–7; N. M. Horsfall, 'Virgil, Varro's *Imagines* and the Forum of
Augustus,' *Anc. Soc.* (Macquarie) 10 (1980) 20–3; id., 'The structure and purpose of Vergil's
Parade of Heroes,' *Anc. Soc.* (Macquarie) 12 (1982) 12–18.

[21]Horsfall points out to me that there must be links with the *laudatio funebris* which Augustus spoke over Marcellus (fragments in H. Malcovati, *Caesaris Augusti Imperatoris Operum Fragmenta²* [1928] 53–4).

[22]O. Skard, 'Die Heldenschau in Vergils Aeneis,' *SO* 40 (1965) 53–65: P. F. Burke, 'Roman rites for the dead and *Aeneid* 6,' *CJ* 74 (1979) 220–8.

[23]*Lucan. An Introduction* (1976) 143.

[24]Cf. R. MacMullen, *Enemies of the Roman order* (1966) 7–8; J. Griffin in B. K. Gold (ed.), *Literary and artistic patronage in ancient Rome* (1982) 124.

✧ ✧ ✧

[25]Sen. *Epist.* 104.1; Mart. 6.43, 10.44.3 f., 12.57.1 f.

[26]*Epist.* 1.11.7–8.

[27]Cic. *Planc.* 23; Juv. 6.56–7, 10.100; Prop. 4.1.34 *qui nunc nulli maxima turba Gabi;* Dion. Hal. *Ant. Rom.* 4.53. On this theme of contrast between cities' former and present condition, see A. J. Gossage, *G&R* n.s. 2 (1955) 72–4.

[28]H. Nissen, *Italische Landeskunde* (1883) 2.579.

[29]On Cora's obscurity see Nissen 2.644. The disappearance of the towns of the Campagna was a general phenomenon: cf. T. Ashby, *The Roman campagna in classical times* (1927) 18–19.

[30]As pointed out to me by Simon Goldhill. Norden and Austin (on 730) are, then, only half right to draw a distinction between the pride of Vergil and the realism of Horace *(Epist.* 1.11.7–8).

✧ ✧ ✧

[31]*CQ* n.s. 34 (1984) 185–91.

[32]Cf. R. Syme, *The Roman revolution* (1939) 305–6; S. Weinstock, *Divus Julius* (1971) 176–85.

[33]Cf. Syme (n. 40) 313–4; H. Wagenvoort, 'The crime of fratricide,' in *Studies in Roman literature, culture* and *religion* (1956) 169–83; H. Fuchs, *Der geistige Widerstand gegen Rom* (1964) 85–7.

[34]'The position of *laetus* gives the adjective marked emphasis,' remarks Austin, making a different point.

[35]Enn. *Ann.* 92–4 Skutsch; Ov. *Fast.* 4.841–4.

[36]Cf. Büchner, *RE* 8A 1391: 'Der 2. Teil, der weitere Gestalten mustert, Könige nach Romulus und Helden der Republik, zeigt neben dem Stolz auch alles bedenkliche der römischen Geschichte.'

✧ ✧ ✧

[37]Cf. MacMullen, 8–10.

[38]Cf. Luc. 5.207, *ultores...Brutos;* 9.17 f.

[39]Similarly Austin ad loc.; W. F. Jackson Knight, *Roman Vergil* (1966) 368; Williams (n. l) 212–3.

[40]cf. MacMullen, *Enemies* 18.

[41]cf. Litchfield (n. 19) 41–2; E. Wistrand, *The policy of Brutus the tyrannicide* (1981) 5–6.

✧ ✧ ✧

[42]'Structure and purpose' (n. 23) 12.

[43]13.

[44]12.

[45]A grandson is occasionally mentioned as having also sacrificed himself in *deuotio* (Cic. *Fin.* 2.61).

✧ ✧ ✧

[46]Thus Austin ad loc.

[47]cf. Williams (n. l) 208–9.

[48]At least, such was the title Cicero gave his essay on old age (*Att.* 14.21.3; *Amic.* 4, *Off.* 1.151) and there seems to be an allusion to the usage in a punning passage of Lucan (6.789–90). How regular this nomenclature was remains uncertain; Cicero may only have used the title *Cato Maior* to avoid confusion with his *Cato* (on Uticensis). I am grateful to Jonathan Powell for help on this point.

[49]Ahl first pointed out the problem (*Lucan* 140).

[50]It is typical of Vergil's manner in this section that the unproblematic Cossus should be mentioned in the same breath; cf. esp. 824–5.

[51]See Ahl, *Lucan* 140–1.

[52]Cf. von Albrecht (n. 3) 168.

[53]See Norden on 842; *RE* 2A.1409.

[54]Cf. Cic. *Off.* 2.43, *Fin.* 4.65, *Har.* 41; [Sen.] *Oct.* 882–9 (this last passage links the Gracchi brothers and the younger Drusus as examples of demagogic degeneration within a family).

[55]*Gn. et P. Scipiones, duo fulmina nostri imperii,* Cic. *Parad.* 12; *Balb.* 34; Sil. 7.106–7; *geminos…Scipiadas,* 13.382–4; 15.3–4, 16.87.

[56]See Pease on Cic. *Nat. deor.* 3.80; cf. *Planc.* 25, *quis Gn. et P. Scipionibus, quis Africano?*

[57]See O. Skutsch, *Studia Enniana* (1968) 145–50. Austin's note expounds the pun, which depends on the similarity between the Greek words for *scipio,* 'staff' (σκῆπτρον) and *fulmen,* 'thunderbolt' (σκηπτός).

[58]Cf. Suet. *Jul.* 59; Plut. *Caes.* 52.2; Dio 42.58.

✧ ✧ ✧

[59]'The Fourth *Georgic*' (n. 1) 65–6.

[60]Cf. Johnson, *Darkness visible* 108.

[61]Convincingly argued by Otis, *Virgil* 303–4, and Horsfall, 'Structure and purpose' (n. 20) 15–16.

[62]Cf. von Albrecht (n. 3) 178–9; S. V. Tracey, *CJ* 70 (1975) 38.

[63]n. 1.

[64]Cf. Cic. *Somn.* 14. *immo uero…hi uiuunt, qui e corporum uinculis tamquam e carcere euolauerunt, uestra uero quae dicitur uita mors est.*

[65]On this see D. Earl, *The moral and political tradition of Rome* (1967) 59–79 (a reference I owe to I. M. LeM. DuQuesnay). Note too (as Professor Reeve pointed out in discussion) how the next book opens with the *fama, honos,* and *nomen* of Aeneas' nurse Caieta — *si qua est ea gloria* (7.4).

[66]Cf. especially Griffin (n. 1) 68; and Johnson, *Darkness visible* 105–11, for an excellent discussion of Vergil's use of perspective here.

[67]*Aen.* 10.467; cf. *Aen.* 1.227, Donatus I 6.1ff. (Georgii).

✧ ✧ ✧

THE *AENEID* AS A DRAMA OF ELECTION*

Bacon's article delves into another difficult subject in the *Aeneid*, the role and meaning of spirituality, of the divine. Written within a generation before the birth of Jesus, the *Aeneid*, along with Vergil's *Fourth Eclogue*, has been interpreted as a prophecy of Christianity in Europe. Bacon asks, however, about the spiritual content of the *Aeneid* on its own terms, not in relation to later developments. Her approach respects the instincts of Christian readers that spiritual content may be present without imposing later meaning back onto the work. Specifically, Bacon studies Aeneas' role as a hero on a divine mission, destined for divinity without knowing it. Just as the *Aeneid* mixes past, present, and future, so too it crosses the boundaries between mortal and immortal. To support her thesis, Bacon analyzes portions of book 6, but also the structural middle of the epic, books 5–8, and thus provides an overview of those books. (Ed.)

In the *Iliad* and the *Odyssey* the ultimate demonstration of heroism by which the heroes win personal renown in life and after death is their acceptance of death, of their own humanity and mortality. In the *Aeneid*, in contrast, the hero, as is often observed, is the bearer of a divine and specifically national mission, first resisted, ultimately accepted, in which personal glory and fulfillment have no part.[1] In a series of visions and ordeals he gradually comes to terms with the fact that he has been elected to initiate a process that is to culminate in a new golden age of peace and brotherhood and that this entails relinquishing all personal bonds, all mortal hopes and ambitions. His heroic acceptance of this mission will lead to gradual loss of humanity, culminating in godhood. Achilles and Odysseus are, in Seth Schein's phrase, "mortal heroes." Aeneas is a hero destined for immortality.[2]

✧ ✧ ✧

Divinity, godhood, in the *Aeneid* is sometimes described in traditional mythological terms as acceptance into the ranks of the immortals and recognition in cult (e.g., 1.259-60, 289-90). But it is also presented in less traditional terms as renunciation of the material world in the form of earthly pleasure, pomp, and splendor. Evander proposes a distinctly otherworldly view of what qualifies a mortal for godhood when he welcomes Aeneas into his thatched hut on the Palatine, where he had previously entertained Hercules, also destined to become a god:

Helen Bacon, "The *Aeneid* as a Drama of Election," was originally published in *Transactions of the American Philological Association* 116 (1986) 305–34 and is reprinted here by permission of the American Philological Association.

"haec" inquit "limina victor
Alcides subiit, haec illum regia cepit.
aude, hospes, contemnere opes et te quoque dignum
finge deo, rebusque veni non asper egenis."

(8.362–65)

"This threshold," he said,
"victorius Alcides crossed, this is the regal dwelling that received him.
Dare, oh guest, to despise wealth and power. Do you too make yourself
    deserving
Of godhood, and graciously deign to visit a poor household."

❖ ❖ ❖

In contrast to the *Iliad* and the *Odyssey*, whose outcome is the affirmation of humanity and mortality, the outcome of the *Aeneid* is the achievement of immortality and otherworldly spirituality. The *Aeneid* is a drama of election, of a series of *labores* ["labors"] which entail the gradual shedding of humanity, the anguishing transition from matter to spirit, from mortal to immortal, from human to divine.[3]

Unlike Homer's heroes, however, Aeneas remains to the end *ignarus* ["ignorant"] of the full implications of his choice (see below, 129). Almost nothing in the poem suggests that he realizes that his acceptance of the mission to which he has been elected by the gods sets him apart as destined to become one of them. The visions of the soul's destiny and the Roman future in Books 6 and 8 do not include foreknowledge of his own deification. His self-dedication is an act of blind faith, a surrender to a divine summons whose ultimate goal he does not fully grasp. Further, he lacks the certainty of being destined for heaven which gives confidence and authority to the words and deeds of Milton's Jesus in *Paradise Regained*. For he is not, like Jesus, an incarnate god. As long as his soul, "on its way to the stars," is imprisoned in the flesh, he is subject to the passions and limited vision of the body.[4]

Seen in the context of this overarching, but relatively unnoticed, element of the action of the poem, both Vergil's apparent ambivalence about Rome and its achievements and his oblique and evocative way of telling his story acquire special significance, and some of the difficulties of interpretation that these occasion are resolved. In contrast to the timeless war and quest of Homer's heroes, Aeneas' war and quest, his specifically Roman mission, is to initiate a process which is to culminate in a new golden age of peace and brotherhood, in which *furor* ["fury"] will yield to *pietas* ["piety"]. Vergil presents this process in incidents so laden with overtones and other kinds of ambiguity that it is difficult to determine whether he thought Augustus could or would bring it to fruition, or whether the poet meant to present it as a beautiful but unattainable dream. If, as I have been suggesting, the goal of the hero's *labores* is not in this world but in the world of the spirit, Vergil's paradoxical ambivalence about Rome is less difficult to understand. If spirit is the ultimate reality even historical Rome must take second place and be understood as a symbol, an emblem, not the realization of the new spirit, but the place where it is born and tested. The story of Rome's founding is not a survey of human existence as we know it — as the Homeric poems are — but the record of a spiritual achievement, of the creation of a vision of a new way of life, repeatedly sought but never realized in this world. It is affirmed by the recurrent struggle to realize it of a series of heroes destined for godhood, Hercules, Aeneas, Romulus, Julius Caesar, Augustus. In Sara Mack's words the story though "rooted in time becomes itself timeless."[5]

Pöschl is right, I believe, in his intuition that the descriptions of the Roman order as *imperium sine fine* (1.279), "rule without end," extending *extra sidera...anni solisque vias* (6.795–97), "beyond the stars...and the track of the sun," where Romulus and Remus give laws together (1.292–93), and of the Romans themselves as excelling men and even gods in *pietas* ["piety"] (12.839), are not mere encomiastic hyperbole.[6] Where he sees these phrases as referring to a cosmic order which Rome reflects, I see them rather as locating the realization of the Roman ideal of universal brotherhood outside this world in the regions inhabited by the gods, in the realm of divinity, which Aeneas and all the other "founders" of Rome are destined to attain. As we learn in Book 6 (730–38), matter obstructs the full realization of the order of spirit. The attempt to found Rome in this world can succeed only partially.

Commentators, beginning with Servius, have had difficulty with the idea of the feuding brothers giving laws together in a new golden age that is to come into existence on earth under Augustus. Various figurative explanations have been proposed.[7] But within the framework of the story the era in which Fides and Vesta will join Romulus and Remus in giving laws is no figure of speech. With its own future indicative verb, *dabunt* ["they will give"] (293), this event is part of the climax of the series of events to come all presented by Jupiter in the future indicative. This fated series progresses from the deification of Aeneas to the birth, triumphs, and deification of Augustus, to the coming of the new golden age in which the brothers will be reconciled and *furor impius* ["impious rage"] will be imprisoned (1.253–96). There is no difficulty about understanding the brothers' participation as "real" for story purposes if, with the other millennial events of the prophecy — the deification of Aeneas and Augustus and the golden age of which the reconciliation of Romulus and Remus is a manifestation — it is understood to occur not in this world but in the world of the spirit. It is not in this world that Romulus and his murdered brother will give laws together. Aeneas will kill Turnus as Romulus killed Remus, Caesar killed Pompey, and, Vergil obliquely reminds us, Augustus caused the deaths of many outstanding citizens including Cicero.[8] But in the attempt to found Rome, the hero, the leader, undergoes a spiritual transformation which entitles him at his death to take his place among the gods.

Vergil's oblique and evocative narrative technique is a function of the fact that the *Aeneid* is a visionary epic, an epic of transcendence, neither tragedy nor romance. The best term for it comes from another epic, of a much later time, that drew a great deal of its inspiration from Vergil, *commedia* ["comedy"].[9] In the Greek tradition the story type that incorporates a vision, not necessarily a vision of transcendence, is at least as old as the fifth century B.C. Who can tell how much older? As far as I know John Herington was the first to point out that *Oresteia* is such a story.[10] In *Oresteia*, and also in *Oedipus at Colonus*, as in the *Aeneid*, tragic action and its consequences for individuals and communities are subordinated to a vision of a new way of life with cosmic implications. In *Oresteia*, as a result of the interaction of gods and mortals, more constructive relations among gods and between gods and mortals are achieved. In *Oedipus at Colonus*, the hero at the moment of death achieves divine or semi-divine status. It is because the *Aeneid* is a *commedia*, a visionary epic, a drama of election and of the transition from mortal to immortal, that what we think of as the "story," the narrative of events in time from the fall of Troy to the death of Turnus, is so much less immediate than the story in Homeric epic.

In the Homeric poems the boundaries between the different spheres of reality are firmly observed—mortal and god, dream and waking, present and future, life and death, image and reality. Though the Homeric gods behave more like mortals than do those of Vergil and though their contacts with mortals are more direct, it is a condition of heroism in the Homeric poems that the transition from mortality to divinity is not made.[11] In the *Aeneid,* with the traversing of the intraversable barrier between mortal and immortal, all other boundaries also break down. Which is primary in the opening episode of Book 1, the "real" events of the story, Venus "storming" to Jupiter, and a subsequent storm in nature which Neptune calms, or the event to which Neptune's action is compared, the statesman in the forum, calming the violence of the mob by force of words alone? The subject matter of the poem, the attempt to master *furor* in human affairs, is more explicit in the simile than in the episodes.[12] Here both the boundary between image and "reality" and the boundary between legendary past and Roman present have been blurred. The figure of speech preempts our attention as having equal or greater reality than the mythological story event, both because of its thematic immediacy and because of its air of contemporary Roman reality. It makes us unusually conscious of a fact some storytellers would like us to forget, though it is true of all stories, that the story itself, like the many kinds of images it incorporates—figures of speech, dreams, visions, descriptions of works of art—is itself also an image, an artifact.

❖   ❖   ❖

The contrasting ways in which Odysseus and Aeneas establish contact with the dead provide an illustration of how in the story itself spheres that Homer keeps distinct tend to interpenetrate.[13] Odysseus, accompanied by his men, goes to the mouth of Hades. He does not enter the realm of the dead, but brings the souls out, and by making them drink blood, temporarily restores them to this world. Then he extorts information from them—information primarily about events of this world up to and including the manner of his own death. Later he narrates the whole story to the Phaeacians. Aeneas, in the flesh, actually enters the world of the spirit. In doing so, he violates the order of nature, whose revulsion is registered by earthquakes and howling dogs, by Charon's objections, and by the groaning of his boat under the weight of living flesh. No companion of Aeneas shares the adventure. Only the Sibyl accompanies him. Like Odysseus he encounters and is enlightened by figures from his personal past and learns about the fate of various types of mortals in Hades, but unlike Odysseus, Aeneas never speaks to anyone of his journey to Hades. The contrast with Odysseus would, I think, not be lost on a Roman reader. What happened beyond the boundary that separates the living and the dead is incommunicable. Election means isolation, loss of community, and surrender of all human ties.[14] Aeneas acquires no practical information about his personal future in Italy. The first part of Anchises' twofold message is a powerful affirmation of the primacy of the spirit—a vision of the soul imprisoned in the body, hampered and contaminated by matter, ultimately, after many incarnations, released forever from the ordeal of rebirth, to become pure ethereal flame. Only after this does Anchises speak about the future—not Aeneas' future, but the future of the souls standing on the shores of Lethe waiting to return to the dark prison of matter—a future of glorious exertion and achievement, but marred by *furor*, and ending on a note of heartbreak, as all achievement in this world must, if we take Anchises' exposition of the primacy of spirit seriously.[15] Information about Aeneas' own future is summarized in three lines at the end of the encounter (890–92). They mention wars to be fought and *labores* to come, but nothing about his personal fate. In contrast to Odysseus, who remains in this world as he receives practical information about his future and has impressed on him that the only real life for mortals is life in the body, Aeneas penetrates into the other world and receives a few dark hints about his own future in this world; a prophecy of a Roman future in which glory is mixed with tragedy; and a vision of an afterlife, more real, more intense, and infinitely more blessed, than anything life in the body has to offer. Both in the message itself and in the circumstances of its reception barriers between spheres of reality which are absolute in the Homeric poems have become traversable.

To ignore the implications for the Roman story of Anchises' description of the soul's vicissitudes, as most critics do, or to explain them away as Otis does, as merely a literary device for introducing the future Romans, or to claim, with Johnson and Gordon Williams, that Vergil denies or "subverts" the vision of transcendence, seems to me to overlook a principal reason for the poem's enduring poetic power—the complex and subtle integration of disparate, even conflicting, elements into a single coherent vision of a cosmos permeated by *pietas*.[16] Though Vergil, like Plato, makes it clear that his myths of the afterlife are not to be taken literally, must we assume that in this moment of high poetry at the climax of the central element of his poem, Vergil did not mean them to be taken *seriously?* Klingner (492), speaking of Aeneas' question about the *dira cupido* ["dire longing"] (721) of the souls waiting to be born, perhaps intuits the lurking contradiction in not taking the implications of Anchises' answer seriously when he says that never before has anyone "begun the praise of a state, of a history, in such a way as to question the entire value of earthly existence." In fact Anchises' answer, both his picture of corrupting matter and his prophecy of Roman greatness, puts earthly existence in an even darker light than Aeneas' question. Roman achievement is repeatedly marked by tragedy, violence, and fratricidal strife, and is seen in the perspective of a doctrine that subordinates this world to the world of the spirit.

If Vergil did mean Anchises' vision of the relation of matter and spirit to be taken seriously, the flawed and partial nature of the Roman achievement as presented here and elsewhere in the *Aeneid* is an inevitable effect of contact with matter (6.730–32; cf. also 2.604–6 where the same verb *hebeto* ["to blunt or dull"] is used), but the vision is not repudiated. The golden age can never be fully realized in this world, but the actions, the *labores*, by which Roman *imperium* ["empire, power"] is extended are indeed glorious. It is they, not their flawed outcome, that are celebrated and are to serve as an inspiration to Aeneas to undertake similar *labores*.

We should perhaps think of the way the soul of Scipio Africanus, instructing his grandson on the mysteries of the universe, uses the cosmic perspective to belittle all (even Roman) history and earthly dominion and represents life in the body as an obligation, a *munus* ["service"] imposed by the gods. The highest form of this *munus* is service to humanity through service to the state, without regard to fame or recognition in this world, its reward blessedness in the next life.[17] Or we might consider Krishna, in the *Bhagavad Gita*, instructing Prince Arjuna, who is shrinking from engaging in a fratricidal battle, on the importance, in the cosmic scheme, of selfless action without reference to its fruits. It is just such action (*labor*) that Aeneas is destined to undertake when he accepts the divine summons to lead the Trojans in fratricidal war against the Latins. For both Aeneas and Arjuna the most significant outcome of acceptance is a state of soul that qualifies them for the company of the gods (see further 134–6 below). The *labores* of the hero prepare the soul for a golden age that is realized only in the realm of the spirit.

The opening simile and Aeneas' voyage to Hades are two of many possible examples of ways in which Vergil breaks down barriers between spheres of reality which Homer keeps distinct. This breakdown of barriers is, I suggest, one of Vergil's chief means of conveying the timelessness and universality of the struggle to found Rome, a way of showing us that the actual Rome of any particular time is not the subject, but the material of the *Aeneid*. Rome must be founded in each generation. The subject is not the founding of a city that will realize the golden age of peace and brotherhood in this world, but the struggle, the *labores,* of those who undertake the glorious but impossible mission, whose only reward is to become worthy to participate in the golden age in the next world. Not only the story of Aeneas, but Rome itself is subordinate to this struggle.[18]

If the action is to be interpreted in this way, how are we to understand the traditional mythological machinery of epic that structures that action? How are the metaphysical and the mythological theology related? It is important to recognize that Anchises' speech is not a philosophical treatise but a Platonizing poetized vision of the transcendent reality of soul — of the cosmos as an organism animated by soul, of individual souls imprisoned in bodies, dulled and corrupted by their contact with matter, of an afterlife in which souls after long periods of purgation are either reborn to undergo another cycle of life in the body or, completely purified, are exempted from the cycle of births and achieve the status of pure spirit in some unspecified, immaterial "heaven" (see above, 126–7 and below, 130–1).

✧ ✧ ✧

There is, therefore,…no detailed correspondence, only a loose similarity, between the mythological theology that structures the poem and the metaphysical theology of Anchises' vision. The cult of deified heroes from Hercules to Augustus with its suggestion of deities to whom the worshipper can relate as persons is not a literal representation of the idea of divinity as pure spirit, purged of matter and exempt from the cycle of births, any more than Vergil's, or Plato's, mythological Hades is a literal representation of what souls must actually experience in the afterlife. Vergil's myths like Plato's resist all attempts to reduce them to theoretical statements. They are not disguised metaphysics but a way of giving fictional reality to the vision that infuses the poem. The myths, which in terms of the central vision cannot be true, nevertheless convincingly actualize that vision as a poetic fusion. The poet's illusionistic skill, which can make things simultaneously true and not true, causes the mythological and metaphysical, like so many other spheres of reality in the poem, to interpenetrate.

The richest support for this interpretation of the *Aeneid* as a visionary poem of transcendence is to be found in the content and technique of Books 5 through 8. Until recently these books have been more studied for their contribution to Roman antiquities than for their contribution to the *Aeneid,* and, with the exception of Book 6, they are generally neglected in the classroom. The reason, of course, is their static effect, the absence of personal dramas like those of Dido and Turnus, and of events which advance the "story." They contain even more supernatural events and less of what we think of as story than the rest of the *Aeneid*. But, as most contemporary critics would agree, the focus on story is too one-sided an approach to Vergil's many-layered narrative. Through its systems of imagery and symbolism, its integration of myth, philosophy, religion, and history, past and present, art and reality, the poem makes a statement about Rome's place in the cosmos that the story itself could not encompass.[19] In Books 5 through 8 there is an even denser concentration of these and similar devices than in the rest of the *Aeneid*.

In the system of symmetries that divides the *Aeneid* into three tetralogies, these central books constitute both the pivot of the action and its visionary core. Books 1 through 4, the fall of Troy and the wanderings, are framed by the tragedy of Dido. Here Aeneas, resisting election, is reluctant and forgetful of his mission. In 9 through 12 the war in Italy is framed by the tragedy of Turnus. Here Aeneas, having renounced all personal aims, is totally dedicated to his mission. It is in the central tetralogy, between these two major story elements, that in spite of their lack of episode, the pivotal event of the poem gradually transpires as Aeneas makes the transition from reluctant mortal to consecrated future god in a process of progressive illumination and reorientation which culminates in the acceptance of election.[20]

The beginning of Book 5 and the end of Book 8 are an index of the nature of that transition. In the first eight lines of Book 5, Aeneas, as he sails toward Italy, is described as *certus*, steady of purpose, after his earlier vacillations, but still looking back (*respiciens*) as he contemplates the flames of Dido's pyre without understanding what they mean. He takes the advice of Palinurus, who has his hand on the tiller, and goes *with* the wind (the first suggestion that he is no longer going against the order of things) towards his father's grave in Sicily (8–34).[21] The reunion with his father is in stages, first at the grave, then in the dream instructing him to make the journey to Hades, finally in the encounter in the other world. At the end of Book 8 (729–31) Aeneas is no longer reluctant or doubtful, but he is still uncomprehending (*ignarus*) of the future now, as he was of the past in Book 5. He accepts his mother's gift of the arms with solemn wonder and joy, and shoulders the shield with its images of the Roman future as a burden of *pietas*. He has been transformed from the hesitant, still dependent, barely forward-moving person of the beginning of Book 5 to the bearer of the Roman future. He has also gone from his human father to his divine mother.[22] For the rest of the action his purpose never falters.

At the beginning of Book 5 Aeneas, for all his *pietas*, is still in and of this world, but in Book 5, as he commemorates his dead father, he manifests an involvement with the other world that is new and becomes progressively stronger. Signs of this involvement are the celebration of commemorative rites and games in Anchises' honor; the manifestation of Anchises' spirit as a snake (84–93) and in a dream (722–42), where, as in the encounter with his mother (1.406–9) and with the shade of Creusa (2.790–95), Aeneas' longing for an embrace is thwarted; and the establishment of cults of Venus and Anchises near the newly founded city of Acesta (759–61).[23] This is the beginning of a movement of withdrawal and return that is completed only at the end of Book 8.

There is another well-known system of symmetries in which actions, images, and themes of the first half of the poem are paralleled, book for book, in the second half of the poem, with the result that the narrative itself, from the fall of Troy to the death of Turnus, like the larger vision of Rome's multiple foundings which that narrative encompasses, is characterized by rhythmic cyclical recurrence.[24] In addition this structure causes references to the end and the beginning of the poem to be concentrated and juxtaposed in the central tetralogy, as Books 5 and 6 look forward to 11 and 12 while Books 7 and 8 look back to 1 and 2. Book 5 with its funeral ritual, anticipates the funerals of Book 11; the glories of Rome in arms and the untimely death of Marcellus in Book 6 look forward to the glorious battles of Aeneas in Book 12 and the untimely death of Turnus. In Book 7, on the other hand, the landing on a strange shore, the hospitality offered by the Latins and the opening of the gates of war by Juno, look back to the landing in Africa, to Dido's hospitality, and Jupiter's prophecy of the closing of the gates of war. In Book 8, the visit to the site of Rome, the city coming into life, and the decision to undertake the new *labor*, the war in Italy, that is precipitated by the portent of the thunderbolt and the arms blazing in the sky (520–28) look back to the dying city of Book 2 and the beginning of the *labores*, the decision to abandon Troy, that is precipitated by the portent of the thunderbolt and the shooting star (692–98). And just as Book 8 ends with the shouldering of the burden of the future, *attollens umeris famamque et fata nepotum*, "lifting on his shoulders the fame and destiny of his descendants," Book 2 ends with the shouldering of the burden of the past, *cessi et sublato montes genitore petivi*, "I submitted, and lifting up my father sought the mountains."[25] These systems of symmetries attenuate the narrative in these books and contribute to their atmosphere of timelessness by bringing together in the center the beginning and the end of the poem.

There is still another set of symmetries, that is less often discussed, that of concentric circles, in which 1 and 12, 2 and 11, 3 and 10, etc. echo each other.[26] The echoes in 5 through 8 are concentrated and intensified by proximity. At the absolute center of the poem in Books 6 and 7 are two very different landings on Italian soil, one leading into the underworld and the other leading into primitive Latium. These two landings are framed by the contrasting cities of 5 and 8. In Book 5, Acesta in Sicily is founded by Aeneas for those too old and weary to go on to the struggles in Italy. This city of the past is balanced in Book 8 by the vision of the city of the future, at the site of Rome on the Palatine. Even more than in the rest of the *Aeneid*, in Books 5 through 8 the many worlds and themes of the poem are brought together by these schemes of symmetry.[27] The story is attenuated, distinctions of time and place, art and life, this world and the next, are blurred as Vergil concentrates his poem's meanings in these central books to create a comprehensive vision of the never-completed process of "founding" Rome.

A principal reason for the static effect of these books is the unusually frequent use of the standard epic device of the list, and of certain other kinds of description which are basically annotated and expanded lists.[28] Vergil uses this device as another means of blurring the boundaries between different spheres of reality. Its concentrated use in 5 through 8 makes it possible to present the vision of the Roman mission simultaneously through richly Italian scenes and incidents and outside time and space.

These lists and descriptions are permeated with a sense of the Italian landscape, history, religion, and folkways, so that, in the central books the vision of Italy, past and to come, is presented in a way that is concrete as well as visionary. Primitive Italy and Augustan Italy coexist as vehicles of a timeless vision.

✧ ✧ ✧

Book 6 is a series of lists. The description of Apollo's temple at Cumae begins with an account of Daedalus' escape from Crete on wings of his own contriving. It is followed by an ecphrasis — a list of scenes represented by Daedalus on the doors of the temple: the murder of Androgeus; the devouring monster in the maze, the offspring of Pasiphae's bestial love (*Veneris monimenta nefandae,* 26), to whom the Athenian youths are to be sacrificed; Ariadne's redemptive love (*magnum...amorem* ["great...love"], 28) that can persuade Daedalus to reveal the means of escape from the maze and the monster. The list ends with an allusion to a scene the artist failed to complete — the flight and fall of Icarus. The maze, the love that dooms mortals to bestiality or rescues them from the beast and guides them out of the maze to freedom, the wings that bear them skyward or fail and let them fall to earth, are thematic images in Plato's descriptions of the soul's ordeals in its struggles to escape the prison of the flesh and become "equal to the gods."[29] At the moment when Vergil is about to show us Aeneas successfully negotiating the underworld maze with its devouring monsters and learning how the soul may ultimately escape the constraints of earth, that, like a maze, bewilder and disorient the soul, he gives us Daedalus, a fellow artist, who holds the clue to the maze and is the contriver of the means of flight. No one, so far as I know, has included the analogies between Plato's description in *Phaedrus* of the experiences of the winged soul and Vergil's version of the story of Daedalus and Icarus among the Platonic echoes to be noted in Book 6. The more obvious Platonic evocations elsewhere in the book make such an allusion probable.

Ecphrasis, here and elsewhere in the poem, has an effect similar to that of the opening simile. It is one of several means of blurring boundaries between different spheres of existence, and, in particular, by blurring the boundary between art and reality it draws attention to the fact that the story itself is only another artifact. This effect is more pronounced here than in the simile, both because the sculpture on the doors is more obviously an artifact and because the role of Daedalus, the artist, is stressed. Like the scene in the Roman forum of the simile, like the scenes from the Trojan war on Juno's temple in Carthage, and, as we shall shortly see, like the scenes on Aeneas' shield, the scenes on the doors of Apollo's temple are as much a part of the totality of events that constitute the *Aeneid* as are the events of the narrative proper, and no more and no less fictive than they. Daedalus' narrative is time-bound in story terms since it connects a recent legendary past with Aeneas' story, but timeless in its intimations of the nature and destiny of the soul and what that implies about Aeneas' mission.

Further lists or near-lists mark the rest of Book 6. Aeneas' itinerary in Hades is a variation on a list, in which Aeneas encounters his personal past in inverse order, Palinurus, Dido, Deiphobus.[30] At the mouth of Tartarus the Sibyl recites a list of crimes against *pietas,* and of famous sinners and their punishments. Finally, in a non-chronological listing, the unborn heroes of the Roman future are shown. The order of the list is contrived to juxtapose past and future: Romulus, Rome's first founder, with Augustus, Rome's latest founder; Caesar and Pompey, the destroyers the Republic, with the early creators of the Republic; and the third-century B.C. Marcellus with his first-century descendant.[31]

In Book 7 we shift from the no time and no place of Book 6 to primitive Italy. This world is thrown into chaos — a chaos that perhaps suggests the chaos that convulsed Italy in Vergil's own time — by the incursion of a creature from the world that Aeneas invaded in Book 6. Allecto's triple mission, to Amata, to Turnus, and to the Latins has, in its reiterated motifs, some elements of a list. It is soon followed by another list. The Latin catalogue evokes simultaneously the Georgic landscape of contemporary Italy with its cities, fields, vineyards, and gardens, and the primitive Italian world of lands without names, as Anchises had described it (6.776), of woods and streams and wild tribes. It culminates in a description of Turnus and his arms, and of Camilla, each of whom in a different way sums up the process of transformation of the almost idyllic harmony of primitive Italy, which we see in the first third of that book, into the bestial and uncontrolled violence that breaks out under the impact of Allecto. Turnus with the monster chimaera on his helmet flaring with his moods, and Io on his shield, already metamorphosed into a beast, suggests the violence and instability of the Latin world. Camilla, the very last note of the book, in her mixture of freedom and innocence with warlike savagery, is the emblem of that doomed, primitive world that the Trojans have disrupted. Allusions to Circe frame and punctuate this book of bestial transformations (10–20, 187–91, 282, 799).[32]

In Book 8 as in Book 6 we have a walk through a landscape, this time the site of Rome that is to be, the wooded hills and grassy valleys that will become the Capitol, the Forum, the Esquiline, and the Palatine, where Augustus will one day have his dwelling, presently occupied by the thatched hut of King Evander. The boundaries between past and present are blurred as the splendors of Augustan Rome are superimposed on Evander's primitive settlement.

This walk, too, like the walk through Hades, is soon followed by a vision that is also a list, presented in an ecphrasis even more extended and detailed than that in which the Platonizing vision at the beginning of Book 6 is presented. It takes the form of scenes from future Roman history in chronological order, on the miraculous shield. They are described as *res Italas Romanorumque triumphos* (626), "Italian events and Roman triumphs." Though all but the first scene have some connection with a Roman victory, only two, the Gauls' attack on the Capitol and the battle of Actium and the triple triumph of 29 B.C., focus on the military aspect of the event. As in the victories in the games of Book 5, in all these victories, including the last, *pietas* has a crucial part. In addition to military prowess each scene commemorates some demonstration of singular devotion, to family, to country, to gods, which saves Rome from some form of violence and destructiveness (*furor*), as Hercules saved Pallanteum from Cacus. Even Actium seems to be won by the gods of Rome, who are putting the Egyptian gods to flight, rather than by the military skill of Augustus, who stands transfigured in the stern of his ship, a living emblem of *pietas*, companioned by his fellow Romans and the gods that Aeneas brought from Troy, with the symbol of filial devotion, the star of Julius, flaming in the sky above him (679–81).[33] The reenactment on the shield of the struggle of *pietas* and *furor* at successive stages of the city's development is a reminder that this struggle, this *labor,* is never finished in this world.

With each scene on the shield, from the wolf in the Lupercal tenderly cherishing her natural foes, two human infants, to Augustus enthroned on the threshold of the temple of Apollo receiving the submission of the peoples of the empire, the scope of *pietas* widens. Devotion to family, the Sabine women's reverence for both the marriage bond and the bond of blood, and their appeal to husbands and fathers in the name of children and grandchildren, as Vergil's audience would have known, was the cause of the union of Sabines and Roman that concludes the Sabine episode (Livy 1.9, 13). The failure to reverence another kind of bond, Mettus' betrayal of the treaty that united Albans and Romans after the conquest of Alba, is the reason for his hideous fate (Livy 1.23, 27–28). Devotion to country causes Rome's defiance of Porsenna and the extraordinary acts of bravery of Horatius and Cloelia (Livy 2.10, 13). Devotion to the gods, the sparing of Juno's geese during the siege-induced famine, saves the Capitol from the Gauls (Livy 5.47), a devotion further illustrated by the rites of the Salii and Luperci, and by the Roman matrons who contributed their gold ornaments to help complete Apollo's promised thank offering (Livy 5.25). This historical section ends with two Roman exemplars of the destiny of the souls of *pii* and *impii* ["the pious and the impious"], Cato in Elysium giving laws to the *pii*, and Catiline in Tartarus, like Mettus suffering a traitor's fate. To place Cato, whose struggles on behalf of Rome came to nothing, in Elysium, perhaps awaiting rebirth like the future Roman heroes of Book 6, is another suggestion that the criterion of spiritual progress is the *labor* itself, regardless of its outcome. This glimpse of the afterlife just before the final climactic scenes on the shield puts Roman deeds in this world in the cosmic perspective of Anchises' vision.

In the concluding tripartite section all these types of devotion are summed up in Augustus, confronting in battle under his father's sign the forces of chaos and darkness arrayed against Rome, then fulfilling his vow to the gods of Italy by building or rebuilding their temples in Rome. The assimilation of the vanquished enemy into the Roman sphere, to which the Sabine treaty and the treachery of Mettus refer, is completed in the final scene in which the Gauls (Morini) and all the other conquered peoples acknowledge Augustus' sovereignty. For this theme of reconciliation, which is implicit in every scene, the scene of Romulus and Remus and the wolf, and its verbal reminiscence of Lucretius' Venus instilling peace by subduing Mars (1.31–37), is emblematic. Even this final scene depicts not the golden age on earth but one more precarious triumph in the recurrent struggle of *pietas* and *furor*. Again, in the representation on the shield of the future triumphs of *pietas* the boundaries between past and present become blurred as the poet superimposes the vision of Augustus' triumph on earlier Roman history. In addition, the image of the transfigured Augustus at the same time that it looks back to the transfiguration of Achilles in *Iliad* 18.201ff. looks both forward in story terms, and back in terms of history (for Vergil's audience as well as for us) to the transfiguration of Aeneas on the stern of his ship in Book 10 (260–75).[34] As with the images on the doors of Apollo's temple, Vergil, by repeated verbal reminders, keeps us constantly aware that these events too are images, artifacts, the work of the artist Vulcan, *haud vatum ignarus venturique inscius aevi* ["not ignorant in prophecy nor unknowing of the age to come"] (626–27). The merging of art and reality that characterizes Vergilian ecphrasis is particularly marked here, as though to draw attention to the evanescence of the actual events that embody the climactic vision.

In the context of this series of visions and illuminations in the central tetralogy Aeneas' gradual reorientation, his progression from reluctant to tentative to committed, takes place. Book 5 ends his dependence on Anchises and Anchises' surrogate Palinurus, disposes of the weary elders, and takes the vital youngsters to Italy. In Book 6 Aeneas renews contact with his father and receives the strengthening vision of the next world as well as of this one, the vision of the future of the soul as well as the vision of the Roman future. In Book 7 the activation of the underworld forces that begins with the visit to Hades gathers momentum as primitive Italy's almost idyllic harmony with nature is jarred by the arrival of the civilized Trojans and then thrown into chaos when Juno calls up Allecto.

In Book 8 the transformation of chaos into order begins. At the feast of the deified Hercules at the *ara maxima* ["greatest altar"] Evander recalls how the hero rescued the tiny civilized community of Pallanteum from the underworld fire-monster Cacus. Fire, both destructive and creative, is engaged on both sides of the struggle to achieve order and civilization. Vulcan, repeatedly called *ignipotens* ["powerful with fire"], is both the father of the "half man" (194) Cacus who preys on Pallanteum, and the creator of the shield, the emblem of civilization. Hercules subdues Cacus, *incendia vana vomentem* ["spewing useless fires"] (259), by letting in the light of heaven (247); and love, described as flame (389) and compared to fire from heaven (lightning 391–92), impels Vulcan to harness subterranean Cyclopean fire to forge the shield on which is depicted Augustus, savior and civilizer, *geminas cui tempora flammas / laeta vomunt* ["whose joyful temples spew twin flames"] (680–81). Fire epitomizes the force that uncontrolled destroys order but when organized by Hercules, hymned as *non rationis egentem* ["not lacking in reason"] (299), or Vulcan, the artist, saves civilization from chaos and makes possible the work of art that is its ultimate expression.[35]

Evander links Aeneas with the deified Hercules, civilizer and savior, bringer of light and order, subduer of the fire-monster, and simultaneously signals his readiness for deification, as he welcomes him into his humble hut.… The climax of this process of deification, the pivot of the whole poem, comes when, as Aeneas hesitates at the prospect of accepting the leadership of a fratricidal war, Venus gives the fiery sign in the form of the lightning bolt in a clear sky (523–29; lightning bolts are also the work of the Cyclopes in their underground forge, 426–32), and Aeneas responds: *ego poscor Olympo* "I am summoned by heaven" (533). It is to this acceptance of election that all the actions and all the visions of the poem have been leading. By this ultimate act of *pietas,* of surrender to the will of the gods, he becomes their willing, though still uncomprehending instrument. Wlosok compares this moment in the poem to a consecration.[36]

In the Homeric poems Zeus' thunderbolt, with which he enforces cosmic order and implements fate, when not wielded by Zeus himself, is entrusted to Apollo or Athena as his deputies. That Venus should act as minister of fate and communicator of Jove's will is one of several signs of a revolutionized cosmos—a cosmos in which not only does Venus replace Apollo and Athena as Jove's deputy, but Venus herself is radically transformed from Homer's wayward, unwarlike, lawless Aphrodite, to a goddess both of battles and of wifely and maternal *pietas.* In addition in Books 7 through 12 Venus presides over and repeatedly intervenes to facilitate the action as Jove's surrogate and intermediary, the embodiment of *pietas* that is the basis of the *maior rerum ordo* ["a greater order of events"] that is coming to birth (7.44). Perhaps her role as implementer of Jove's purpose is the principal reason for the invocation of Erato, the muse of love poetry, in the introduction to Book 7.[37] In Books 1 through 6 her role is more that of personal helper in the manner of Athena to Odysseus, though there are foreshadowings of this later role in the unveiling of the gods at work (2.589–633) and in her bestowal of the golden bough (6.190–211), the talisman that signals divine recognition that Aeneas, through *pietas,* is qualified to cross the barrier between the living and the dead. If we are to take the invocation to Erato seriously all the battles of the second half of the *Aeneid,* not just those in which Venus participates directly, take place under her sign.

But if the second half of the *Aeneid* is to be conceived as love poetry it is because love and the love goddess have, like so much else in the *Aeneid,* been transformed.[38] And yet she is still the goddess of passionate love, as her epithet *laeta* (*philomeidês* ["loving laughter"]), her intervention with Dido, and above all the scene of lovemaking with Vulcan make clear.[39] And in that scene, less than 200 lines before she gives Aeneas the sign from heaven, she also, metaphorically, wields the thunderbolt. For the flame of passion which courses through Vulcan is compared to lightning accompanied by thunder coursing through the clouds (8.388–92). In another characteristic blurring of the boundaries between image and reality the simile links the power that enforces fate to the power of passion, not the lawless passion of Greek Aphrodite, but passion in the context of conjugal love and *pietas*. Catullus widened the meaning of *pietas* to include passion (e.g., 58, 72, 76, 87, 109). Vergil, by associating it not only with passion but also with Jove's thunderbolt, transforms this richer notion of *pietas* into a cosmic force. For the fire of the thunderbolt wielded by Venus in the *Aeneid*, unlike the defiant and disruptive fires of Eros' torches and arrows in Hellenistic love poetry, is passion in the service of a creative and evolving cosmos.[40] The simile in the love scene of Venus and Vulcan prepares us to see the sign that Venus gives her son as indicating the integration of *pietas*, which has now coopted and transformed the procreative principle, into the system of the cosmos.

This process of cosmic evolution arising out of the interaction of gods and mortals and gods and gods in the struggle to found Rome, and resulting in the incorporation into the cosmic order of a new, more humane element, is noted by many scholars. Boyancé explicitly calls this element *pietas*. Pöschl speaks of love and a new kind of humanity, Haeker of two orders of passion, one natural, one spiritual, that inform creation. Wlosok refers to a theodicy *among the gods*, and describes Venus as the incorporation and consecration of the humane qualities in the cosmos.[41] The cosmic power of love in its two aspects as passion and as *pietas* has some precedent in Greek literature. Passion as a cosmic force, personified in Eros/Aphrodite, is a commonplace from Hesiod on, and love also appears as the facilitator of a spiritual process, for example in Euripides' praise of Athens (*Med.* 824–45), Sophocles' Colonus ode (*O.C* 669–94), and above all in Plato's *Symposium* and *Phaedrus*.

After Aeneas' acceptance of the sign of election, as complement and completion of the vision received from his father by a stream in a valley of Elysium, he receives, in the form of a shield forged, under the stimulus of physical passion, in subterranean fires, the *non enarrabile textum*, "the indescribable fabric," of the future, from his mother by a stream in a valley of this world (605–25).[42] Achilles' acceptance of the heroic obligation to return to battle entitles him to receive the divine arms procured by his mother, but also, as both mother and son know, it seals the mortal fate that will separate them forever. Aeneas' acceptance of his heroic obligation to lead the war against the Latins confirms his title to the divine arms and admits him for the first time to his mother's embrace (615). This embrace (the only one between god and mortal in the *Aeneid*) evokes the longed-for embrace that Venus denies him in Book 1 (405–10), and the embraces that the conditions of mortality make impossible between Aeneas and Creusa in Book 2 (790–94) and Aeneas and Anchises in Books 5 (740–42) and 6 (697–702). Though Aeneas himself seems scarcely to realize it (see 124 and 129, above), it validates him as a future god. It is the final sign that by accepting election he has won the privilege of crossing the impassable barrier that separates gods and mortals.[43]

Notes

*This essay is affectionately, admiringly, gratefully, dedicated to Louise Adams Holland. Her generous sharing of her rare ability to join literary discernment to fundamental scholarship, philological, archaeological, cultural, has helped to shape and enrich my reading of Vergil throughout my scholarly life. My special thanks to Eleanor Leach for learned and penetrating advice at various stages of this study; to Michael Putnam for encouraging me in this venture outside my own fields; to my colleagues Lydia Lenaghan, Matthew

Santirocco, and James Zetzel, the editor of *TAPA* 116 (1986), for invaluable criticism of the final version; and to Mark Daniel Hopke for indispensable scholarly and editorial assistance. I have also profited from stimulating contributions by audiences at Brown University and Boston University in 1983, and at the American Academy in Rome in 1984, where I presented earlier forms of the essay.

[1]The following frequently cited works are referred to by author's name; date of publication is added when needed for clarity. W. P. Basson, *Pivotal Catalogues in the Aeneid* (Amsterdam 1978); Gerhard Binder, *Aeneas und Augustus: Interpretationen zum 8. Buch der Aeneis* (Meisenheim am Glan 1971); Pierre Boyancé, *La Religion de Virgile* (Paris 1963); W. A. Camps, *An Introduction to Vergil's Aeneid* (Oxford 1969); Mario A. Di Cesare, *The Altar and the City: A Reading of Vergil's Aeneid* (New York 1974); Theodore Haeker, *Virgil, Father of the West*, trans. A. W. Wheen (Near York 1934; German ed. Leipzig 1931); Friedrich Klingner, *Virgil: Bucolica, Georgica, Aeneis* (Zurich 1967); Brooks Otis, *Virgil: A Study in Civilized Poetry* (Oxford, 1963); Viktor Pöschl, *The Art of Vergil: Image and Symbol in the Aeneid*, trans. Gerda Seligson (Ann Arbor, 1962; German eds. Innsbruck and Vienna 1950[1], Darmstadt 1964[2]); id. "Das Zeichen der Venus und die Gestalt des Aeneas," *Hermeneia: Festschrift Otto Regenbogen zum 60. Geburstag* (Heidelberg 1952) 135–43; Michael Putnam, *The Poetry of the Aeneid* (Cambridge, Mass. 1965); A. Setaioli, *Alcuni aspetti del VI libro dell'Eneide* (Bologna 1970); Agathe Thornton, *The Living Universe: Gods and Men in Virgil's Aeneid*, Mnemosyne Suppl. 46 (Leiden 1976); Gordon Williams, *Technique and Ideas in the Aeneid* (New Haven 1983); Antonie Wlosok, *Die Göttin Venus in Vergils Aeneis* (Heidelberg 1967). References to the *Aeneid* are from *P. Vergili Maronis Opera*, ed. R. A. B. Mynors (Oxford 1969). The translations in the text are my own.

[2]Seth L. Schein, *The Mortal Hero: An Introduction to Homer's Iliad* (Berkeley, Los Angeles and London 1984).

❖ ❖ ❖

[3]For Hercules in the *Aeneid* and in Augustan ideology as theme, image, and prototype of the savior and ruler who achieves godhood, see note 5 below. On the fundamental importance of *labor* see Haeker 46–51, 79–80, 89, 109–12. See below, note 5, for Hercules as prototype of the hero who undertakes *labores*. The symbolic, even sacred, aspect of Aeneas' quest is frequently commented on. See particularly the pages in Otis cited below, note 5, and his overview in Ch. 8; also Boyancé, "Le Sens cosmique de Virgile," *REL* 32/33 (1954–55) 220–49; and notes 7, 9, 15–18 below.

[4]On the transition from mortal to divine and the primacy of spirit over matter see below, 125–9, 135.

[5]*Patterns of Time in Vergil* (Hamden, Conn. 1978) 87. See also 67–88 for the dark side of Roman history in the prophecies of the *Aeneid*. The ideas of multiple foundings of Rome, and of deification as a reward for saving the city, were not unfamiliar to Vergil's audience. See S. Weinstock, *Divus Julius* (Oxford 1971) 162–91. On Hercules as the prototype of Rome's mythological and historical savior-rulers destined for godhood see G. K. Galinsky, *The Herakles Theme: The Adaptations of the Hero in Literature from Homer to the Twentieth Century* (Oxford 1972) 131–49; also the more specialized discussions in V. Buchheit, *Vergil über die Sendung Roms* (Heidelberg 1963) 116–32; Otis 220, note 1, 302, 317, 330–38, 342; Wlosok 66–67 with her notes 53–55; W. Heilmann, "Aeneas und Evander im achten Buch der *Aeneis*" *Gymnasium* 78 (1971) 76–89, Binder 62–65, 118–22, 137–49, 152, 157–69, 271–73; Basson 70 with notes 134 and 135; Bernadette Liou-Gille, *Cultes "héroïques" romains: Les fondateurs* (Paris 1980) 15–83.

[6]Pöschl (1962) 23–24, 27. Compare Basson's more literal interpretation (25). A. E. Housman claims, *CR* 10 (1906) 44–45, that *extra sidera tellus extra anni solisque vias* refers not to extraterrestrial regions but to lands on the surface of the earth "south of the zodiac and the ecliptic," and reflects the fact that "the poets...do not always remember that the zodiac is oblique." The fact that other poets make this mistake, if they do, does not prove that Vergil does. In the case of a poet as steeped in philosophical learning as Vergil such an error is intrinsically unlikely. W. J. N. Rudd, "The Idea of Empire in the *Aeneid*," *Hermathena* 134 (Summer 1983) 35–50 is a needed reminder of the indispensable role that Vergil assigns to force and power, but disregards these and all other passages that suggest a moral and spiritual dimension to Roman rule.

[7]Most editors seem to take the reconciliation as symbolic, e.g., *P. Vergili Maronis Aeneidos Liber Primus*, ed. R. G. Austin (Oxford 1971) and Virgil, *Aeneid 1–6*, ed. R. D. Williams (London

and New York 1972) ad loc. Servius on 1.276 is more literal. He explains the presence of Remus in 292 as an allusion to the custom, begun in obedience to an oracle commanding the propitiation of the murdered bother, of placing a *sella curulis* and all the other insignia of royalty for Remus beside Romulus when he performed in his kingly role. He implies here, and more explicitly in his comment on 1.292, that Vergil tries to avoid a reminder of the fratricide. Basson 31-33 tries to solve the "problem" through allegory. Relying on Servius ad loc. he identifies Quirinus as Augustus and Remus as Agrippa. Like Servius he does away with the allusion to fratricide, i.e., civil war, and with it the idea of universal brotherhood. Wlosok recognizes that for Aeneas idyllic peace is realized only after death (144-45) but sees the Augustan regime as its realization on earth (passim). For different approaches to how and if the vision can be fulfilled see notes 9 and 15 below.

[8]When Cicero is indirectly alluded to in the echoes of Scipio's dream, 6.702-55 (see above, 127), and in the reference to the exposed heads of Cacus' victims, 8.195-96, and to Catiline in Tartarus, 8.668-69, it is hard to avoid remembering that he was one of Augustus' more notable victims.

[9]The visionary and spiritual aspect of the *Aeneid* is not overlooked by recent scholars. Only Buchheit (above, note 5), though he does not neglect the gods, comes close to disregarding the way Vergil incorporates them in his religious-philosophical scheme. One group, which includes Adam Parry, "The Two Voices of the *Aeneid*," *Arion* 2.4 (1963) 66-80; Putnam; Kenneth Quinn, *Virgil's Aeneid: A Critical Description* (London 1968); Di Cesare; Ralph Johnson, *Darkness Visible: A Study of Vergil's Aeneid* (Berkeley, Los Angeles, and London 1976); M. Owen Lee, *Fathers and Sons In Vergil's Aeneid: Tum Genitor Natum* (Albany 1979); and Gordon Williams, asserts that Vergil presents the vision of the new golden age as unattained or unattainable, whether because of human nature or the nature of things in general. Another group, which includes Haeker (whose wide knowledge of literature and religion makes him sensitive to aspects of Vergil often overlooked by philologists); Pöschl (1962 and 1952); Boyancé (above, note 3), also (1963), and "Sur le discours d'Anchise *(L'Enéide* VI. 724-751)," *Hommages à G. Dumezil* (Brussels 1960) 60-76; G. N. Knauer, *Die Aeneis und Homer*, Hypomnemata 7 (Göttingen 1964); Otis; Klingner; Wlosok (1967), also "Et poeticae figmentum et philosophiae veritatem," *Listy filologike* 106 (1983) 13-19, and "Vergil als Theologe: Iuppiter-pater omnipotens," *Gymnasium* 90 (1983) 187-202; Binder; Setaioli; Thornton; and Donald H. Mills, "'Sacred Space' in Vergil s *Aeneid*," *Vergilius* 29 (1983) 34-46, though they differ significantly in emphasis and detail, adhere to the more traditional critical view that Vergil presents the story of Rome as in some sense leading to fulfillment of that vision. R. D. Williams, "Virgil and Rome: A Lecture to the Virgil Society," *The Augustan Age* 3 (1983) 95-108, with some qualification, takes his position with this second group. J. A. Hanson, "*Vergil*," *Ancient Writers: Greece and Rome*, ed. T. James Luce (New York 1982) 693-97 is illuminating on the question of whether or not Vergil represents Augustan Rome as the new golden age, and sees the poem as ending in ambiguity. R. D. Williams, *Vergil*, Greece and Rome: New Surveys in the Classics I (Oxford 1967) is a balanced survey of these and other aspects of Vergil scholarship. Wlosok's survey, also very informative, "Vergil in der Forschung," *Gymnasium* 80 (1973) 129-51, focuses mainly on these two approaches. None of these scholars, not even Haeker, locates the fulfillment of the vision of the new golden age in the world of the spirit. Friedrich Solmson, "Greek Ideas of the Hereafter in Virgil's Roman Epic," *Proceedings of the American Philosophical Society* 112 (1968) 8-14 and "The World of the Dead in Book 6 of the *Aeneid*," *CP* 67 (1972) 31-41 takes Anchises' affirmation of the primacy of the spirit as representing Vergil's real beliefs, but thinks the poet allows these to be muted by the celebration of the Roman mission in this world. Charles Segal, "Art and the Hero: Participation, Detachment and Narrative Point of View in *Aeneid* 1," *Arethusa* 14.1 (1981) 67-83, especially 81, *perhaps* leaves it to the reader to infer transcendence. See further above 125-8 with notes 11, 15-18.

[10]C. J. Herington, "Aeschylus: The Last Phase," *Arion* 4 (1965) 387-403.

[11]See Boyancé 23-29 and note 2.

[12]The pervasive technical terminology of Roman government, politics, warfare, marriage, documented by John Sarkissian, "The Idea of Roman *Imperium* in *Aeneid* 1.50-296," *Augustan Age* 4 (1985) 51-56, reinforces the impression that the simile takes precedence over the story. For the possibility that the simile refers to an actual occasion on which Cato prevented a riot see R. D. Williams (above, note 7) ad loc.

[13]Book 6, both because of its subject matter and because, as Knauer points out (above note 9) 107, it is the only example of an entire book of Vergil modeled on an entire book of Homer, provides an exceptionally good opportunity for an extended comparison of the two poets' treatment of the boundaries between spheres of reality. My discussion adds another dimension to Pöschl's view that, in spite of the overall parallels with *Od.* 11, *Aen.* 6 is "the most Vergilian" of the first six books, (1962) 28. See also Boyancé 142–74; R. D. Williams, "The Sixth Book of the *Aeneid*," *G&R* 11 (1964) 48–63; Setaioli 7–9; Camps Ch. 9 on the contrasts between *Aen.* 6 and *Od.* 11.

[14]On Aeneas' initial hesitation and forgetfulness in the first part of the poem see G. E. Duckworth, "The Architecture of the *Aeneid*," *AJP* 75 (1954) 1–15; on his loneliness and progressive isolation and his renunciation of earthly goals see Wlosok 24, 18, 144; also Di Cesare 236–39 and Elizabeth Belfiore, "Ter Frustra Comprensa: Embraces in the *Aeneid*," *Phoenix* 38 (1984) 19–30.

[15]For the pervasiveness of this gloomy note see Mack (above, note 5) 67–88. Of those who argue that the doctrines expounded by Anchises are to be taken seriously and have meaning in terms of the poem as a whole Solmsen (1968 and 1972; above, note 9) is the most explicit about the primacy of the spirit. However he sidesteps the implications of this doctrine for Roman history and contents himself with pointing out that the end of Anchises' revelation of the future emphasizes the sorrows of this world rather than the joys of the next, (1972) 41. Klingner; Wlosok (1967) and two 1983 articles (above, note 9); Thornton 60–69 and passim; Mills (above note 9); R. D. Williams (above, note 9) expand on, refine, and deepen the view of Pöschl (1962) and Boyancé (above, notes 3 and 9), also (1963) that Vergil presents Roman history as the unfolding of the divine will (fate). Though the action is cosmic the goal is realized in the earthly city of Augustan Rome. There is no suggestion of a transcendent goal or, except in Williams, of a falling short of the ideal, though the cost in human suffering is often dwelt on. Lee, though he emphasizes the reality and profundity of Anchises' description of the cosmos (above, note 9) 152, and argues that it "will be fulfilled in Rome" (64, also 158), still draws an oddly negative conclusion in terms of the poem as a whole. Though the epic represents a cosmic struggle the cosmos is "flawed" (163–67), and the hero "fails" (140–56, 163–64). Lee misreads the review of heroes as a guarantee to Aeneas of immortality in the form of rebirth as Romulus and Augustus (65, 152), taking no account of the fact that each of these heroes is destined for godhood (i.e., exemption from the cycle of births) in his own right (see above, 128). Haeker does not deal with the details of Anchises' doctrine of the soul. He emphasizes transcendence more than any other scholar, but even he affirms Rome as the fulfillment of the ideal (78).

[16]Otis 301; Johnson (above, note 9) 89–91, 107–11, and passim; Gordon Williams 131, 161–62, 213, 242–43. See also Putnam 192. Di Cesare like Otis, but for different reasons, drains the passage of religious or philosophical meaning, 113–17. The view, which goes back to Norden, that this passage has no serious religious or philosophical intent, is explicitly contested by Boyancé (1963) 173–74, also (above, note 3) 247–48 and (above, note 9) 62; Klingner 491; and Wlosok (above, note 9) 14. See also R. D. Williams (above, note 13), and Setaioli 15–16, 37–52. It is somewhat paradoxical that Otis, who sees the heart of the *Aeneid* as an individual and cosmic spiritual struggle, should so emphatically dissociate the vision of the soul's vicissitude in the cosmos from this struggle. It is more usual for critics who emphasize the visionary aspects of the poem to see this passage as integral to their interpretations. See notes 9 and 15 above.

[17]Cicero *de Republica* 6.19–23, ed. K. Ziegler (Leipzig 1969). See Setaioli 46–52 following R. Lamacchia, "Ciceros Somnium Scipionis und das sechste Buch der *Aeneis*," *RhM* 108 (1964) 261–78. Though both scholars argue that Vergil reflects this Ciceronian view they regard Roman dominion in this world as integral to the performance of the obligation. See also Camps 89–99 for discussion of the many Ciceronian parallels in 6.679–751. He too tends to deemphasize Anchises' spiritual message.

[18]Though Boyancé 14–15 recognizes that the religious-philosophical aspect of the *Aeneid* might cause "un moderne" to raise the question of which came first for Vergil, the divine or Rome, he argues that this view is anachronistic. Vergil would not have subordinated this world to the next since for the Romans the gods existed only as gods of the city. This underestimates the influence on Vergil of the religious-philosophic tradition that goes back at least to Pythagoras and Parmenides and finds notable expression in Plato and, among Romans, in "Scipio's Dream."

The Christianizing readings of J. N Hritzu, "A New and Broader Interpretation of the Ideality of Aeneas," *CW* 39 (1945–46) 98–103, 106–10, and Haeker 82–91, 109–14, and passim do indeed imply such subordination, but Hritzu does not engage with the details of the text on which such an interpretation must rest, and neither takes sufficient account of Roman religious and philosophic views. Gordon Williams 232–43 also sees all Roman history, including the Augustan Age, as "incidental" to the main ideas of the *Aeneid* — for him not the vision of the soul's vicissitudes and ultimate destination, but the vision of the human condition as painful and ephemeral. For details see 127 above. Any reading of the *Aeneid* that assigns a secondary role to Roman history implies a cyclical view of history as endless recurrence (though not without progression). See K. W. Gransden, *Virgil's Iliad: An Essay on Epic Narrative* (Cambridge 1984) 43 and at above, 124–5.

[19]On the secondary importance of the "story" in the *Aeneid* generally, see Johnson (above, note 9) 36, 89; on many-layered structure, above, 125–8 and notes 15–17.

[20]G. E. Duckworth, "The Architecture of the *Aeneid*," *AJP* 75 (1954) 1-15 and "The *Aeneid* as a Trilogy," *TAPA* 88 (1957) 1–10, provides useful summaries and elaborations on this and other systems of symmetry detected by scholars in the *Aeneid*. See also Otis 227–28, 320–63, 392; Hanson (above note 9) 697; and Thornton, who provides a convenient survey (149) and her own analysis of the action of the poem as structured by a series of cosmic movements (70–148). Camps Ch. 6 discusses some of the correspondences pointed out above, 125–130, and others which I have not mentioned, and discounts their thematic significance, 58. Pöschl (1962) 59–60 and (1952) 140–41 comments on the transitional nature of the central books and on 8.520–40 as a major turning point in Aeneas' development and in the action. See also Duckworth (1957) 6–7 and "Fate and Free Will in Vergil's *Aeneid*," *CJ* 51 (1956) 357–64; Putnam 101; Klingner 536, 541–42; Wlosok 123–27; Heilmann (above, note 5) 87–89; Thornton 117; Hanson (above, note 9) 694. Otis 223, 308, 313–16 considers the end of Book 6 a major turning point after which there is no change or development in Aeneas, but says Book 8 marks "the moment when the passive spectator or endurer becomes the active possessor of his history," 331–32. See further 133–5, above.

[21]Pöschl (1962) 48 emphasizes the importance of *certus*, and of the winds as symbols of destiny. Thornton 97 interprets the winds as a form of divine guidance.

[22]Lee (above, note 9) 115–18, 152 argues that the fundamental transition for Aeneas is the archetypal one from mother to father. He does not take into account that in Books 7–12 Venus is not only Aeneas' protector, but also his main inspiration and stimulus. See Pöschl (1952) 141 on signs of hesitation in *Aen.* 8.520–24, also Klingner 535–36; Thornton 117.

[23]The involvement with the afterlife is reinforced by a proliferation of words associated with the dead, *ossa, cineres, animae, umbrae* (Boyancé 149, citing J. Bayet).

[24]For discussion and bibliography on this basic structure see Duckworth (above, note 20 [1954]) 5–7, 11. Buchheit (above, note 5) 173–90 gives a detailed presentation of the correspondences between Books 1 and 7. His view (192) that this twofold division rules out the tripartite structure referred to above, 129, seems unnecessarily rigid and literalist. As Duckworth (above, note 20 [1957]) 3–5, 9 and Camps 59–60 recognize, different kinds of symmetries can coexist. Like the many levels of reference they contribute richness and resonance to this most complex of poems.

[25]Klingner 536 and P. T. Eden, *A Commentary on Vergil: Aeneid VIII* (Leiden 1975) xxi, comment on the similar impact of these portents in Books 2 and 8. The parallelism between the endings is noted by Duckworth (above, note 20 [1954]) 12 and Di Cesare 156.

[26]I have not found any systematic demonstration of this particular structure, which I have worked out in some detail. Framing devices like the two swan portents (1.390–400 and 12.247–56) and Jupiter's interview with Venus in 1.223–96 and with Juno in 12.791–842, with the verbal echo *olli subridens* (1.254, 12.830), are frequently remarked on. Another system of rings that omits Book 1 and has Book 7 as its center is pointed out by Otis 217.

[27]Camps 57–60 discusses this scheme (in which he includes Book 9) of concentrating themes in the center of the poem. See also Hansen (above, note 9) 694 and K. Reckford, "Latent Tragedy in *Aeneid* VII, 1–285," *AJP* 82 (1961) 252–61, passim but particularly 253–54.

[28]Basson analyzes four principal lists (1.257ff., 6.752ff., 7.641ff., 10.163ff.). He does not deal with the other lists discussed here or the implications of their concentration in Books 5–8.

See also Pöschl (1962) 28; R. J. Rowland, Jr., "Books of Lists: Observations on Vergil's *Aeneid,* Books vi–viii," *Augustan Age* 1 (1982) 20–25; Duckworth (above, note 20 [1957]) 6.

✧ ✧ ✧

[29]R. D. Williams (above, note 7) 459–60, citing W. F. J. Knight, *Cumaean Gates* (Oxford 1936), emphasizes the world-wide association of the maze with the realm of the dead and its use as a means of separating out the elect, but does not consider the implications for the *Aeneid* of the maze image's Platonic associations. Raimund J. Quiter, *Aeneas und die Sibylle: Die rituellen Motive im sechsten Buch der Aeneis,* Beiträge zur klassischen Philologie 162 (Königstein/Ts. 1984) includes a detailed study of the maze as a symbol of the underworld. It has come to my attention as this goes to the printer; I regret that I have been unable to locate a copy. Ronna Burger's *The Phaedo: A Platonic Labyrinth,* (New Haven 1984) is the first (I think probably not the final) exploration of Plato's use of the maze in *Phaedo* as emblematic both for the progress of the discussion and for Socrates' imminent journey from this world to the next. For a more general discussion of Vergil's use of Plato's myths of the afterlife in Book 6, see J. Pearson, "Vergil's 'Divine Vision' (*Aeneid* 4.238–244 and 6.724–751)," *CP* 56 (1961) 33–38, and Setaioli 9–15. For bibliography and other connections and implications of the story on the temple doors see William Fitzgerald, "Aeneas, Daedalus and the Labyrinth," *Arethusa* 17 (1984) 51–65; Eleanor Leach, *The Rhetoric of Space* (Princeton 1988) 350, 353–58; and Otis 284–85.

[30]See Otis 290–97 and R. D. Williams (above, note 7) 458–59 on Aeneas' encounter with his own past in Hades.

[31]On the structure and rationale of this list see Basson 44–93. R. D. Williams (above, note 13) 59–62 also notes the juxtaposition of Romulus with Augustus and of Republican heroes with Caesar and Pompey.

[32]Circe's functions in *Aen.* 7 are explored by Charles Segal, "Circean Temptations: Homer, Vergil, Ovid," *TAPA* 99 (1968) 419–42, particularly 428–36. He notes the connection of the first three references with the bestial transformations of the Latins but does not mention the fourth allusion (*Circaeumque iugum,* 799) or the beast metamorphosis on Turnus' shield (789–92). Thornton 106 and Buchheit (above, note 5) 76 discuss 7.10–20 only in relation to past temptations of Aeneas and the Trojans. Both writers (Thornton 115; Buchheit 109, 115) see Turnus' shield device as emblematic of his own transformation, but neither comments on the recurrent references to Circe or the transformation of the whole Latin people. Di Cesare 126 sees Circe as introducing the "love-death motif" of Books 7–12. Reckford (above, note 27) 255, 263, 266 sees the Circaean metamorphoses of Book 7 as symbolizing the "dehumanizing passion" that rages through Book 7–12.

[33]See Binder 150–282 for discussion of almost every aspect of the shield. Di Cesare's interpretation of the shield as a monument to the destructive violence that is a precondition of "achievement," 150–56, overlooks the fact, noted by Binder, that each struggle on the shield saves Rome from some form of *furor.* Binder 224 characterizes Octavian's struggle with Antony as *pius.* See also Wlosok 128–38 and Klingner 540–42 for the way the shield epitomizes this struggle.

[34]Binder 224–25. Wlosok 129–31 stresses the way the shield evokes events of the *Aeneid* as well as those of later Roman history.

[35]As Binder 267 and Duckworth (above, note 20 [1957]) 361 point out, fire's two aspects exemplify Horace's *vis temperata* and *vis consili expers* (*Odes* 3.4.65–67). See also B. M. W. Knox's treatment of the creative and destructive aspects of fire in Book 2, "The Serpent and the Flame: The Imagery of the Second Book of the *Aeneid,*" *AJP* 61 (1950) 379–400.

[36]145 with her note 84. On Book 8 as a major turning point see above 129 with notes 20 and 22. Pöschl (1952) 138–40 articulates most fully Aeneas' recognition and acceptance of a divine summons to a war ordained by fate with all the renunciation of personal goals that that entails. See also Putnam 134; Eden (above, note 25) xxi–xxii; Klingner 541; and 124 above.

[37]On Apollo and Athena as traditional wielders of the thunderbolt see Eden (above note 25) on 8.435 and 522. Basson 98–101 summarizes the controversy over whether Erato is invoked simply as the muse in a generalized sense, as Servius ad loc. suggests, or specifically as the patron of love poetry. In the second case the reference is usually explained by the rivalry of Turnus and Aeneas for Lavinia. See F. A. Todd, "Virgil's Invocation of Erato," *CR*

45 (1931) 216–18 and Reckford (above, note 27) 257. Many scholars feel, rightly I believe, that this love triangle is not prominent enough for this to be the whole explanation. Di Cesare 126, however, sees Erato, like Circe (above, note 32), underscoring the "love–death motif" of Books 7–12.

[38]For Venus' transformation, see Wlosok 145–46, also Thornton 117; for the connections of her maternal and war-like aspects with her role as *genetrix* and *victrix* in Roman cult and in the family cult of the *gens Julia* Wlosok 116–39; K. G. Galinsky, *Aeneas, Sicily and Rome* (Princeton 1969) 169–241; Weinstock (above, note 5) 15–18, 80–91.

[39]On *laeta* as *philomeidês* see Wlosok 11–12, 95–97; on *Cupido* Thornton 87. Although Lucretius does not use *laeta* as an epithet of Venus its use here may also be intended to suggest Lucretius' Venus, who represents the basic procreative force of the cosmos. This and the observation on Lucretius in note 43, I owe to a reminder by my colleague Lydia Lenaghan. Vergil himself frequently uses *laetus* in its commonest Lucretian sense of "fertile, teeming" (e.g., *Georg.* 1.1, 1.325, 2.236, 2.252; *Aen.* 2.306, 3.220). Venus' two aspects as exemplar of cosmic generation and of *pietas* are implicit in Haeker's description (39–41) of the two orders of passion, the natural and the spiritual, in Vergil's poetry. See further note 43 below.

[40]According to Plutarch *Alcibiades* 16, Alcibiades disgusted and shocked Athenians of the better sort by sporting, instead of some family emblem, an *Eros Keraunophoros* as a shield device. The transfiguration of Peisthetairos at the end of *Birds* as a winged erotic god casting thunderbolts left and right may be intended to suggest an outrageous image. William Arrowsmith's demonstration of the pervasive eroticism of *Birds*, "Aristophanes' *Birds*: The Fantasy Politics of Eros," *Arion* n.s. 1 (1973) 119–67, gives credibility to this suggestion. Fire is the traditional implement of Eros, and so of Aphrodite, who often works through him. Both in art and literature however, when he appropriates the weapons of another god they are usually those of Herakles not Zeus.

[41]Boyancé 76–82; Pöschl (1962) 15–16, (1952) passim, particularly 143; Wlosok, 83, 144–46. Di Cesare, while he interprets the thunderbolt simile as indicating Venus' connection with Jupiter's cosmic power (152), characteristically treats the whole love scene as one of "brutal sex-and-violence" in preparation for "the violence of reality [that] is moving in on Arcadia" (154). Vergil's view of Venus as embodying the *pietas* that determines the evolution of the cosmos may owe something to Lucretius' use of Venus to represent the creative principle of the universe that can overcome violence and destructiveness. See above, note 39.

[42]The parallelism of these two scenes, with the verbal echo, *in valle reducta* (6.703, 8.609), is commented on by Otis 341, Putnam 146–47, Di Cesare 111–12, and most fully by Elizabeth Belfiore, (above, note 14) 26–27.

[43]The failed embraces of the *Aeneid* are frequently commented on (see Di Cesare, above note 1 and Belfiore, above, note 14). Wlosok, 86–88, 110–12 points out that the denial of the embrace in 1.405–10 is a sign that Aeneas and Venus belong to different spheres of reality. She is one of the few critics who discuss the granting of the embrace, which she characterizes as an indication of the "accord between goddess and hero that becomes fully evident" in Books 7–12, 144 with note 15. She argues that Aeneas' deification means attainment of fellowship with the gods in heaven and a share in their peace and blessedness through the agency of Venus and as a reward for *pietas*, and that enjoyment of that peace and blessedness can occur only after death. She stops just short of interpreting the embrace as confirmation of Aeneas' fitness to enter that world. On Aeneas' deification see also above 123–124, 127–128.

John Frederick Nims

GOLDEN NUMBERS
ON NATURE AND FORM

The notion that numbers and art are profoundly connected may seem odd to us at first, if we think of numbers as belonging to "objective" science and art to the realm of "subjectivity." In fact, the connections are close. In architecture and music, for example, number, form, and beauty operate together. Also, for ancient Greek and Roman thinkers, mathematical order was related to philosophical order. In poetry, number underlies the design of individual lines along patterns of beats and measures and also the structure of lines and sections. Nims explores a phenomenon in mathematics called the Fibonacci series, in which "each number is the sum of the two preceding ones: 1, 1, 2, 3, 5, 8," etc. He tells us that that series occurs in nature, for example in the sunflower and the nautilus shell. Using *Aeneid* 4.416–36, Nims demonstrates the way the series seems also to occur in the poetry of Vergil. Even more important than the particular system involved, Nims says, is the fact that pattern and precision, form generally, are full partners in art and are perhaps even a source of its power. (Ed.)

If we leaf through a book of verse we notice immediately that poetry, unlike prose, favors special conformations; it likes to arrange itself in shapes on the page. These shapes in space originally represented shapes in time—shapes to be heard if we were listening to a recitation rather than looking at a book.

In its love for shapeliness and proportion, poetry is like mathematics. Many readers, however, believe that poetry and mathematics are opposed in spirit. Such readers may be repelled by the pages that follow, with their drawings that seem to be straight out of Euclid. But no mathematical background is required—there are no problems to solve. The drawings are only to marvel at. And to be seen as analogies: they are really telling us something about the nature of poetry, and about nature itself.

To decide in advance that a poem will have seventeen syllables or fourteen lines or that it will be constructed in stanzaic units of this or that size or shape may seem arbitrary and artificial. When a poem begins to germinate in the poet's mind, could it not grow simply and naturally, the way a flower grows, instead of being forced to follow a pattern? This seems a good question—but it shows little knowledge of how flowers do grow. Nature has been working on its flowers for some millions of years; a close look at them, as at anything in the natural world, will show why Pythagoras said that all things are number, why Plato said that God always geometrizes.

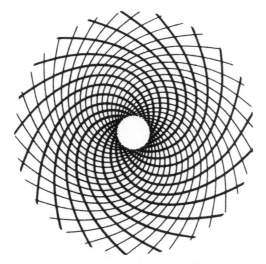

Spiral Pattern in the Sunflower.

If we take a close look at the head of a sunflower, we see two sets of spirals whirling in opposite directions. The florets that make it are not of any random number. Typically, there are twenty-one going clockwise and thirty-four going counterclockwise—numbers that a mathematician would come on with a thrill of recognition. They belong to the series of "golden numbers" called the Fibonacci sequence (he was a thirteenth-century Italian mathematician), in which each number is the sum of the two preceding ones: 1, 1, 2, 3, 5, 8, 13, 21, 34, 55 and so on. Although the sequence may look like a man-made curiosity, it turns up again and again in nature—in the way rabbits breed, in the generation of bees, in the number and pattern of leaves or petals on certain plants, in the spirals of the sunflower. The sequence has been used by modern artists in placing units in their paintings, and by modern musicians in planning the durations within their rhythms.

A further strangeness about the series is that the ratio between consecutive numbers, after the first few, remains about the same coming closer and closer to a stabilization in which the smaller number is to the larger as .618 is to 1. This .618 ratio—familiar to the ancient Greeks and to most designers, artists, and architects ever since—is that of the discovery of the golden section, a way of proportioning dimensions so that the parts (many believe) have the most aesthetically pleasing relation to each other and to the whole.

In this division, the lesser part is to the greater as the greater is to the whole: $CB : AC :: AC : AB$.

It is also a ratio we have perceived, without being aware of it, in many things in nature. The human body, besides having bilateral symmetry, seems to have proportioned itself in accordance with the golden section. The length from the top of the head to the navel and the length from the navel to the toes have the ratio of about

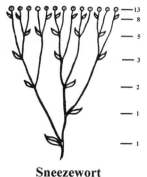

Sneezewort

.618 to 1. These two divisions are subdivided. The length from navel to knee is to the length from knee to sole as 1 to .618. In reverse order, navel to throat and throat to top of head are related as 1 to .618. The architect Le Corbusier, who has planned buildings on the basis of the golden section, has even devised a scale for designers based on the proportions of the human body.

If bodily proportions might have given the Greeks a feeling for the golden section, geometry would have suggested it with more precision. The mysterious appeal of the ancient pentagram, or "endless knot," one of the most famous of all magic signs, owes much to its play of proportion. This star-shaped figure fairly glitters with its two hundred .618's. B cuts both AC and AD so as to give golden sections. BE is .618 of AB, and so on. The followers of Pythagoras used the pentagram as their secret sign. It stood not only for health and love but for the human body itself, which was thought to be organized in fives: five senses, four limbs and a head, five fingers (their three bones having the golden proportion).

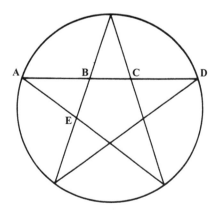

Since the pentagram also stood for the letters in the name "Jesus," it was thought to be an object of fear to hellish spirits. When Mephistopheles finds the pentagram's *Drudenfuss*, or "wizard's foot," drawn on Faust's threshold, it takes some trickery to get by it. Its shape—as with good poems—is its power. In the pentagram—as in good poems—mathematics and magic come together. We are affected by precise relationships we are not conscious of.

If we take a line divided according to the golden section, bend the shorter part upward, and then complete the rectangle, we have the golden rectangle with its "divine proportion," which, with the section itself, is supposed to have had an important influence on ancient art and architecture, determining, it may be, the structure of the pyramids and of the Parthenon, which fits neatly into it. Certainly it made itself felt in the Renaissance (Da Vinci made use of it) and ever since, right down to the architecture of Le Corbusier and the art of Seurat and Mondrian. In 1912 one group of artists even exhibited in Paris as the "Golden Section" painters. It was with them that Marcel Duchamp first showed his *Nude Descending a Staircase*. We can still find this proportion in modern buildings and in many common objects—envelopes, playing cards, magazines. Perhaps we like this rectangle because its proportions correspond with our oval field of vision.

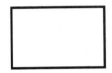

The golden rectangle has been called, with something like Oriental mysteriousness, "the rectangle of the whirling squares." If we divide it by the golden section so that one part is a square, the smaller area will itself be a second golden rectangle within the first (A). If we divide the smaller rectangle in the same way, the same thing will happen—another square, another golden rectangle (B). We can continue in this way, making smaller and smaller squares as we whirl around clockwise. If we then connect, with an evenly curving line, corresponding points of all the squares (C), we will have one of the most beautiful curves in mathematics and one of the most beautiful lines in nature—the logarithmic spiral, whose allure moved one admirer to ask that it be engraved on his tombstone.

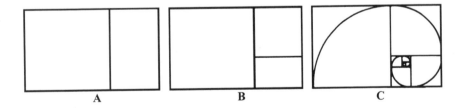

A   B   C

This graceful curve, which seems to have been artificially constructed at a drawing board, probably appears most spectacularly in the nautilus seashell, a favorite of collectors. As the creature in the seashell grows, it moves onward, in a spiral, into larger and larger chambers, all of them having the same proportions. Oliver Wendell Holmes found a moral here, which he expressed, by means of a stanza form that itself expands, in "The Chambered Nautilus."

> Build thee more stately mansions, O my soul,
> As the swift seasons roll!
> Leave thy low-vaulted past!

> Let each new temple, nobler than the last,
> Shut thee from heaven with a dome more vast
>   Till thou at last art free,
> Leaving thine outgrown shell by life's unresting sea.

We find this same curve in the sunflower head and the daisy, in the pine cone and the pineapple, all of which have their opposing spirals in Fibonacci numbers. We find it where the time element of living growth has left its shape on matter — in the curling horns of mountain goats, in the tusks of elephants, in the claws of a cat, the beak of a parrot. It appears in transitory fashion in the coil of an elephant's trunk or a monkey's tail, in a lock of hair falling naturally.

Part of the pleasure we feel in contemplating this spiral may come from our awareness of its continuous proportion, which, in a world of change, gives us the reassurance of what remains similar to itself. Certain well-managed patterns in poetry may have an analogous effect.

Poets cannot hope to work with the geometrical precision of nature. Most trust their own sense of proportion, developed from study, contemplation, and exercise. But Dante does give a mathematical framework to his *Divine Comedy*. And Vergil, Dante's guide, appears to have made an almost unbelievable use of the proportions of the golden section and the Fibonacci numbers (as they were later named).[1] In Book IV of the *Aeneid* [lines 416–436], for example, Dido, seeing she is about to be deserted by her lover Aeneas, asks her sister Anna to go and plead with him. This is a passionate moment, but not so passionate that Vergil lets his mathematical composition get out of control. He describes the scene in sections of 5, 8, and 13 lines — all numbers in the basic Fibonacci sequence.

13 { 8 {
> Look, Anna, all that scurrying on the seashore,
> Crowds everywhere, sails restless for the wind,
> The sailors, glad to go, arranging garlands.
> Well, as I saw this trouble brewing once,
> So, sister, I'll endure it. Just one thing   5
> That you could do in kindness. It was you
> That liar was polite to, liked to talk with.
> You knew his ways, and how to manage with him.

13 { 5 {
> Go, dear; go coax a little. Tell His Arrogance
> I wasn't there at Aulis when those Greeks   10
> Swore death to all the Trojans; didn't send
> Warships to Troy; and didn't kill his father.
> Why won't he even listen when I speak?

8 {
> Where is he rushing off to? Let him do
> His love a final favor: wait for friendly   15
> Weather and easier sailing. Once he loved me —
> I don't ask that again; won't block his glorious
> Future. I only ask: a quiet interval.
> Time to get used to suffering, used to grief.
> Pity your sister. Say it's all I'm asking.   20
> Say I'll return his favor — with my life.

Anna's visit to Aeneas is described in the section that follows—in exactly thirteen lines. These two passages would prove nothing. But when we are told that more than a thousand such correspondences have been found in the *Aeneid*, it does begin to look as if Vergil constructed his episodes like little equations and then related them like larger equations of the same proportions, so that his whole work is a kind of mathematical symphony, as orderly as the music of Bach.

Contrived as this intricacy may seem to be, we can hardly call it artificial. Nature—in the seashell, in the daisy, in a lock of hair—far outdoes our artists in the use of mathematical symmetry. All that matters, in any art, is that the calculation and effort should not show, that we see the ease and elegance of the achievement but not the labor that went into it. It is important to realize that imposing a form is not in any way unnatural—Parthenon and nautilus owe their beauty to the same kind of mathematical harmony.

William Blake once wrote: "Without Minute Neatness of Execution the Sublime cannot Exist! Grandeur of ideas is founded on Precision of Ideas." Yeats saw no contradiction between calculated precision and human passion. He once praised Lady Gregory's house as a place in which "passion and precision have been one." He insisted to a friend that "the very essence of genius, of whatever kind, is precision."

❖ ❖ ❖

[T]here is nothing unnatural in our desire to find form and pattern in our experience. We can hardly keep from doing so. When we look at the starry skies, all we really see are swarms of bright specks. But we have never been content to see that way. We see hunters and great bears and rocking chairs and dippers. Or we see figures like lions and scorpions and fish, which we name Leo and Scorpio and Pisces, relating them to long-dead languages. We like to believe there are connections between these imaginary creatures and the temperament and fate of human beings born under them. Everywhere we like to find the reassurance of form.

❖ ❖ ❖

Notes

[1]George E. Duckworth, *Structural Patterns and Proportions in Vergil's* Aeneid (Ann Arbor: University of Michigan Press, 1962).

George E. Duckworth

THE ARCHITECTURE OF THE *AENEID*

Duckworth's article on the large-scale design, or architecture, of the *Aeneid* redirects our reading of the poem from the intricacies of language and line to the panorama of the work as a whole. With Duckworth's help, we can observe Vergil build meaning across the expanse of his epic. Duckworth charts correspondences among the poem's three thirds and especially between the two halves, as well as other structural patterns. His analysis invites us to consider the connection between form and meaning. Duckworth concludes that the *Aeneid*'s elaborate structure is apt support to the thematic complexity of the poem, in which "so many threads [are] inextricably and harmoniously interwoven." (Ed.)

All readers of the *Aeneid* are conscious of the attention which Vergil has given to the structural framework of his poem. Each book is a unit, but each fits into its place as a part of a greater unity and contributes meaning to the epic as a whole. The poet's efforts to achieve variety, symmetry, and contrast have been noted by many Vergilian scholars both in small episodes and in the larger portions of his work.[1] But the tendency, unfortunately all too prevalent, to look upon the *Aeneid* as a Roman *Odyssey* of wanderings followed by a less interesting Roman *Iliad* of war has distorted and obscured the structure of the poem for many readers. Mackail is correct in saying that "neither of the two halves, Books I–VI and Books VII–XII, is a substantive epic by itself," that the whole poem "is a continuous and ordered movement towards which the successive scenes are subordinated."[2] The last six books form, as Vergil himself states (VII, 44 f.), a *maior rerum ordo*, a *maius opus* ["greater order of things (or story), a greater task"]; they have far greater unity and coherence than the first six books, and only in them can the true meaning and purpose of the poet be seen.[3]

The title of this paper will recall that of a lecture by R. S. Conway which he published more than twenty years ago,[4] and the resemblance of title is intentional. Much that I wish to say derives from and is an expansion of Conway's views concerning the alternation and the correspondence of the various books. According to Conway, Vergil's "love of alternation has shaped the structure of the *Aeneid* in two ways: (a) by the contrast which the poet has made between every pair of consecutive Books, and (b) by the correspondence and contrast between each of the Books in the first half of the poem and the Book in the corresponding place in the second half."[5]

❖ ❖ ❖

George E. Duckworth, "The Architecture of the *Aeneid*," *American Journal of Philology* 75 (1954) 1–15. Reprinted by permission of The Johns Hopkins University Press.

To support his theory that the books of the second half correspond to those of the first half, Conway lists numerous similarities and contrasts,[6] of which the following seem the most significant:

I and VII: arrival in a strange land; friendship offered

II and VIII: each the story of a city — one destroyed by Greeks, the other to be founded with the help of Greeks

III and IX: Aeneas inactive and action centers around Anchises (III): Aeneas absent and action centers around Ascanius (IX)

IV and X: Aeneas in action — conflict between love and duty (IV); conflict with the enemy (X)

V and XI: each begins with funeral ceremonies and ends with death — Palinurus (V) and Camilla (XI)

VI and XII: Aeneas receives his commission in VI, executes it in XII.

As Conway says, these parallel features seem too numerous to be due merely to accident.

Conway looks upon VI as the "crowning Book, which Vergil has placed in the centre, to unite all that stand before it and all that stand after"; it is "the keystone of the whole poem" and "contributes a sense of unity to the epic."[7] Aeneas' visit to the underworld is thus very different in function as well as in content from that of Odysseus' interview of the shades in the *Odyssey,* an incidental episode which lacks the philosophical, religious, and national significance which Vergil has given to *Aeneid* VI.

A re-examination of Conway's position seems necessary, for in recent years several Vergilian scholars have made new and interesting contributions to the study of the structure of the *Aeneid.* Tracy analyzes I–VI, showing how each book has a distinct pattern, with its own thematic treatment and balanced arrangement of moods, with color and tone values set in deliberate contrast.[8] Mendell makes clear that Catullus and the neoterics had a definite influence upon Vergil's workmanship in the *Aeneid,* inasmuch as many episodes in the epic reveal a symmetrical framing of the action around a central focal point, usually a significant speech or a scene of emotional tension.[9]

Pöschl in his excellent book on the poetic art of Vergil points out instances of symmetry and contrast between the two halves of the poem, especially in I and VII, the opening scenes of which he considers symbolic of each half;[10] the *Aeneid* as a whole he divides into three parts of four books each, with an alternation of light and shadow: I–IV (storm, fall of Troy, loss of homeland, death of Dido) are dark; the middle portion shines with light (the games of V, the vision of Roman glory in VI, the description of Italian troops in VII, the triumph of Augustus in VIII); the last third (IX–XII) portrays the darkness and tragedy of war. "Dunkel — Licht — Dunkel: dies also ist der Rhythmus, der das Epos in seiner Gesamtheit beherrscht" ["dark — light — dark: this therefore is the rhythm that the epic governs in its totality"].[11] In spite of possible reservations,[12] the existence of this major rhythm — or at least this threefold division — can scarcely be doubted; IV brings to an end the story of Dido and Carthage, and the main conflict in Italy does not begin until IX, while patriotic and national themes occupy a large part of the central portion of the poem, with the high points at the ends of VI and VIII. Such an over-all design does not, however, invalidate the similarities and contrasts found by Conway in the individual books.

✧ ✧ ✧

The possible existence of overlapping and inter-locking designs should not be ignored, and the ability of different scholars to see quite dissimilar schemes[13] merely gives added testimony of the structural richness of the epic.

✧ ✧ ✧

Vergil's own description of VII–XII as a *maius opus* implies that I–VI are an enriched and amplified prelude to his main theme, and Perret's careful and interesting analysis of VII–XII has presented additional proof of the attention which Vergil gave to the structure and content of the second half of the poem. Brilliant characterizations are numerous — Mezentius, Lausus, Pallas, Nisus, Euryalus, Camilla, and, above all, Turnus. The outstanding episodes — Aeneas' visit to the site of Rome, the tragic deaths of Nisus and Euryalus, the slaying of Pallas with its fateful result for Turnus himself, the defeat of the wounded Mezentius as he attempts to avenge his son's death — are all firmly embedded in the main structure and are essential parts of it. Two of the greatest single books of the *Aeneid* are undoubtedly IV and VI, and the latter, as we have already seen, is great not only for its content but because of its central position in the structure of the whole. But what of X and XII? These two books must rank high in any consideration of the poem as a whole. X pictures the tragic deaths of Pallas, Lausus, and Mezentius and provides an effective counterpart to Dido's suicide in IV — the tragedy of war balancing the tragedy of love. Mackail compares XII with II, IV, and VI and says that the final book "reaches an even higher point of artistic achievement and marks the utmost of what poetry can do, in its dramatic value, its masterly construction, and its faultless diction and rhythm."[14] Even those who do not rate XII so highly must admit that it provides an effective and dramatic conclusion to the poem and serves as an adequate balance for VI.

In the first half of the poem, I and IV are separated by II and III (Aeneas' narrative); in like manner VII and X are separated by VIII and IX (Aeneas' absence). V is an interlude between the tragedy of IV and the seriousness of VI, and similarly XI provides a lessening of tension between the tragic fighting in X and the final conflict in XII. The grouping of the books is therefore as follows:

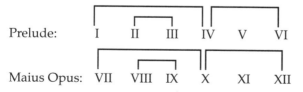

Whereas this scheme for the first half resembles that of Perret in part, the second half is very different and, what is more important, it is an exact counterpart of the first half. This supports Conway's view of the correspondence of the books in each half.

Vergil has composed his epic in two large parallel panels, with an alternating rise and fall of tension and with each book of the second panel balancing that of the first. The twelve books of the *Aeneid* may be presented in the following diagrammatic form:[15]

I	Juno and storm
	II DESTRUCTION OF TROY
	III Interlude (of wandering)
	IV TRAGEDY OF LOVE
	V Games (lessening of tension)
	VI FUTURE REVEALED
VII	Juno and war
	VIII BIRTH OF ROME
	IX Interlude (at Trojan camp)
	X TRAGEDY OF WAR
	XI Truce (lessening of tension)
	XII FUTURE ASSURED

I agree that VI is the keystone, the focal point of the poem as a whole, but it should not be isolated between two contrasted panels; it forms the climax of the first panel, as XII concludes the second. The diagram presented above reveals the manner in which the books of the second panel balance those of the first, but to gain an adequate impression of the numerous parallelisms and contrasts which exist within each pair of corresponding books, a more detailed analysis will be necessary. The parallel columns which follow give the similarities and contrasts (including those of Conway) and illustrate dramatic rise and fall of the action:

I	VII
Juno and storm	Juno and war
Arrival in strange land	Arrival in strange land
Trojans already known	Trojans already known
Friendship offered	Friendship offered
Ilioneus speaks for Aeneas	Ilioneus speaks for Aeneas
Omens and prophecies aid reception	Omens and prophecies aid reception
Juno arouses storm with aid of Aeolus	Juno arouses war with aid of Allecto
Venus prevails over Juno	Juno prevails over Venus
Movement of book — misery to happiness	Movement of book — happiness to misery

II	VIII
DESTRUCTION OF TROY	BIRTH OF ROME
Story of Carthage interrupted	Story of Trojan camp interrupted
Greeks destroy	Greeks help to found
Trojans suffer from Greeks	Trojans profit from Greeks
Helplessness of aged Priam	Helpfulness of aged Evander
Aeneas center of stage	Aeneas center of stage
Ascanius — fire about head, comet	Augustus — fire about head, comet
At end, Aeneas carries on shoulders his father (symbolic of past)	At end, Aeneas carries on shoulder the shield (picture of future)

III	IX
Interlude (of wandering)	Interlude (at Trojan camp)

Aeneas has minor role	Aeneas absent
Anchises important	Ascanius important
Helenus and Andromache (joyful episode)	Nisus and Euryalus (tragic episode)
Escape from danger — Cyclops, Scylla, Charybdis	Escape from danger — Turnus in camp

IV	X
TRAGEDY OF LOVE — DIDO	TRAGEDY OF WAR — PALLAS, LAUSUS, MEZENTIUS

Venus and Juno (agreement)	Venus and Juno (conflict)
Inner conflict of Aeneas	Outer conflict of Aeneas
Affection yields to duty	Pity yields to justice
culpa ["fault"] of Dido — results in death	*culpa* ["fault"] of Turnus — leads to death in XII
Turning point — Aeneas' decision to depart and effect on Dido	Turning point — death of Pallas and effect on Aeneas
At end, suicide of Dido — cannot live without Aeneas	At end, death of wounded Mezentius — cannot live without Lausus

V	XI
Lessening of tension — Games	Lessening of tension — Truce

Funeral games	Burial of dead
Aeneas quiets disputes	Latinus unable to avert dissension
Increase of tension — burning of ships	Increase of tension — renewal of fighting
At end, death of Palinurus	At end, death of Camilla

VI	XII
FUTURE REVEALED	FUTURE ASSURED

Aeneas receives his commission	Aeneas fulfills his commission
Dramatic progression — retardations and suspense, climaxed by revelation of Rome's destiny	Dramatic treatment of combat — retardations and suspense, climaxed by victory of Aeneas
Anchises reveals later Roman history	Reconciliation of Jupiter and Juno creates later Roman people
At end, death of Marcellus consecrates new order	At end, death of Turnus seals doom of old order

The existence of so many similarities and contrasts in books of such varied subject-matter is an amazing fact....We find here the symmetry and contrast and alternation of tension which are peculiarly characteristic of Vergil. Furthermore, not only do we have (again to use Conway's phrase) an alternation of lighter and more serious books, but a second type of alternation may now be seen: in the numerous contrasts and similarities which in the corresponding books of each half, the similarities appear to predominate in I and VII, III and IX, V and XI, i. e., in the odd-numbered books, whereas in II and VIII, IV and X, VI and XII the contrasts seem more numerous. Apparently the *Aeneid* contains a far more subtle fusion of Conway's two principles of alternation and correspondence than he himself realized.

Perret considers the miracle of the *Aeneid* to be Vergil's ability to treat three themes simultaneously — (1) the legendary narrative of Aeneas, (2) themes and personages of Roman history, and (3) the praise of the achievements of Augustus.[16] The poem is both an epic of Trojan Aeneas and an epic of Augustan Rome;[17] perhaps, as Rand suggests, it is also an expression of Vergil's ideal empire — "an empire founded on justice, righteousness, law and order, religion and an ultimate peace."[18] In such an epic symbolism is inevitable.[19] Aeneas is Aeneas, but at times he is Augustus (cf. his promise in VI, 69 ff. to erect a temple to Apollo); he is also the ideal ruler who displays the *virtus, clementia, iustitia,* and *pietas* ["courage, mercy, justice, and piety"] which were ascribed to Augustus by the Senate and the Roman people;[20] Aeneas is even viewed as symbolic of suffering mankind fulfilling an unknown destiny.[21]

In a work of such magnitude, with so many threads inextricably and harmoniously interwoven, it should occasion no surprise that so elaborate a basic design of symmetry and contrast underlies the structure of the poem. But this does not mean that Vergil gave excessive attention to details and consequently neglected the effect of the whole. I disagree, therefore, with Tracy when he says that "Vergil would appear to have made the mistake of fussiness,"[22] and when he prefers to use the word "pattern," i. e., detailed craftsmanship, rather than "design," which suggests a broader structural conception. The structural framework of the poem, as we see it in the parallel columns submitted above, indicates that the whole conception stands out boldly and that Vergil was master of his material, in large features as in small.[23] The poem's architecture, or "design," when properly understood, is one more proof of Vergil's supreme achievement as an epic poet.

Notes

[1] Cf., e. g., H. W. Prescott, *The Development of Virgil's Art* (Chicago, 1927), p. 440, on the arrangement of material in Books VII–XII: "His artistic aims in this distribution may be comprehended in the two words, symmetry and variety."

[2] J. W. Mackail, "The *Aeneid* as a Work of Art," *C.J.*, XXVI (1930–31), p. 14.

[3] Cf. G. E. Duckworth, "Turnus as a Tragic Character," *Vergilius*, 4 (1940), p. 5. On the value of the last six books, see also W. H. Alexander, "Maius Opus," *Univ. Cal. Pub. Class. Philol.*, XIV (1951), pp. 193–214.

[4] "The Architecture of the Epic," *Harvard Lectures* on *the Vergilian Age* (Cambridge, Mass., 1928), pp. 129–49. This was a revision of an earlier lecture on the same subject which appeared in *Bull. John Rylands Library*, IX (1925), pp. 481–500. All references to Conway, unless otherwise specified, will be to the *Harvard Lectures on the Vergilian Age*.

[5] *Op. cit.*, p. 139.

❖ ❖ ❖

[6] *Harvard Lectures on the Vergilian Age*, pp. 139 f.

[7] *Op. cit.*, p. 143. Cf. also Prescott, *op. cit.*, pp. 360 f.

[8] H. L. Tracy, "The Pattern of Vergil's *Aeneid* I–VI," *Phoenix*, IV (1950), pp. 1–8.

[9] C. W. Mendell, "The Influence of the Epyllion on the *Aeneid*," *Yale Class. Stud.*, XII (1951), pp. 203–26; cf. especially pp. 223 f., where the entire eleventh book is arranged around three focal points — Aeneas' appeal for peace (100–138), Latinus' speech (302–335), and the deeds of Camilla (648–724).

[10]V. Pöschl, *Die Dichtkunst Virgils. Bild und Symbol in der Äneis* (Innsbruck, 1950), pp. 46 ff. Pöschl believes that the conflict between Jupiter and Juno in I is symbolic of the struggle "zwischen Licht und Finsternis, zwischen Idee und Leidenschaft, Geist und Natur, Ordnung und Chaos" (p. 31) and that this conflict is repeated in the conflict between Aeneas and Dido and in that between Aeneas and Turnus; "der römische Gott, der römische Held und der römische Kaiser sind Inkarnationen der gleichen Idee" (*ibid.*).

[11]*Op. cit.,* p. 280.

[12]Cf. Tracy, *op. cit.,* pp. 4 f., on the darkness and gloom of VI. Are the activity of Allecto and the outbreak of war in VII to be looked upon as light rather than darkness? In the third section of the poem, is no light to be seen in Aeneas' victories in X and XII?

✧ ✧ ✧

[13]To illustrate from a shorter passage, cf. the pattern of the Latin catalogue in VII as analyzed by B. Brotherton ("Vergil's Catalogue of the Latin Forces," *T.A.P.A.,* LXII [1931], pp. 192–202) and by E. A. Hahn ("Vergil's Catalogue of the Latin Forces: A Reply to Professor Brotherton," *T.A.P.A.,* LXIII [1932], pp. lxii f.). Miss Brotherton finds in the catalogue twelve groups of forces, with the last six paralleling the first six in reverse order; Miss Hahn rejects this and favors a more straightforward alternation of important and unimportant leaders.

✧ ✧ ✧

[14]*Op. cit.,* p. 17.

[15]The headings in capitals both here and in the parallel columns below indicate the more significant books (those with even numbers).

✧ ✧ ✧

[16]*Op. cit.,* p. 89.

[17]For instance, in VIII Aeneas visits the site of Rome, then the Pallanteum of the Arcadians, but it is Augustus' Rome that is suggested to the reader by the walk with Evander; cf. P. Grimal, "La promenade d'Évandre et d'Énée à la lumière des fouilles récentes," *R.E.A.,* L (1948), pp. 348–51.

[18]E. K. Rand, *The Building of Eternal Rome* (Cambridge, Mass., 1943), p. 61.

[19]On the distinction between symbolism and allegory, cf. Pöschl, *op. cit.,* pp. 36 f.; Perret, *op. cit.,* pp. 93 f.

[20]*Res Gestae,* 34, 2.

[21]Cf. Alexander, *op. cit.,* pp. 212 f.; see also J. N. Hritzu, "A New and Broader Interpretation of the Ideality of Aeneas," *C.W.,* XXXIX (1945–46), pp. 98–103, 106–10. Hritzu looks upon the *Aeneid* as "an universal epic of the Iliad and Odyssey of man…striving to fulfill his divine mission of the gaining of the kingdom of heaven and the salvation of his own soul" (pp. 108 f.). Such a view resembles rather closely the various allegorical interpretations of the *Aeneid* which were prevalent in the Middle Ages.

[22]*Op. cit.,* p. 7. Tracy's failure to see an over-all design may result in part from the fact that he limited his useful discussion of contrasting moods and tone values to I–VI.

[23]We cannot assume that the contrasts and parallels mentioned above have resulted merely from Vergil's subconscious feeling for balance and symmetry. They are too numerous and too striking. The balancing of the contrasting books in each half of the epic must be the result of deliberate design and was perhaps worked out before Vergil began to write, at the time when his material was arranged in a prose outline; cf. the *Suetonian Life,* 23: *Aeneida prosa prius oratione formatam digestamque in XII libros particulatim componere instituit, prout liberet quidque, et nihil in ordinem arripiens.*

Adam Parry

THE TWO VOICES OF VIRGIL'S *AENEID*

In one of the most influential essays on the *Aeneid* in the last thirty-five years, Parry articulates a fundamental characteristic of Vergil's poetry. Even as Vergil constructs a vision of the glorious public future of Rome, he gives equal voice to the suffering incurred in the private realm to achieve the public vision. These "two voices" are present throughout the *Aeneid*, reflecting on each other and causing the reader to keep them both in mind. Parry analyzes a brief passage at *Aeneid* 7.759–60, describing its meticulous artfulness and also its effect: to evoke a sense of mourning on the part of the Italian countryside at the arrival of the Trojans and the war they bring. From these lines, Parry expands his interpretation to the *Aeneid* as a whole. (Ed.)

I want to begin with the particular. Sometimes we come upon a short passage in a poetic work we know well, a passage we have never particularly noticed before, and all at once, as a kind of epiphany, the essential mood of the author seems to be contained in it. Here is a candidate for such a passage in the *Aeneid*.

There is at the end of book 7 a kind of *Catalogue of Ships,* a muster or roll-call of the Latin leaders and their forces as they are arrayed against Aeneas in the long war which occupies the last books of the poem. One of these leaders is a quite obscure figure named Umbro. The Catalogue is an Homeric form, and Virgil here exploits it in the Homeric fashion, drawing out a ringing sense of power from place-names, epithets of landscape and valor, names of heroes. He endeavors further, again in the Homeric fashion, to give individuality within the sense of multitude by singling out some characteristic of each Latin warrior, a device the *Aeneid* has yet more need of than the *Iliad,* since Virgil has behind him no tradition of Latin song which could give the audience a previous familiarity with the heroes he names.

So Umbro comes from the Marruvian people, and he is most valiant: *fortissimus Umbro.* And he is a priest, who possesses the art of shedding sleep over fierce serpents. But—and here we catch the Homeric pathos—his herbs and his incantation could not save *him,* wounded by the Dardanian spear. Virgil then closes the brief scene with a beautiful lamentation:

> For you the grove of Angitia mourned, and Fucinus' glassy waters,
> And the clear lakes.

> Te nemus Angitiae, vitrea te Fucinus unda,
> Te liquidi flevere lacus.

Adam Parry, "The Two Voices of Virgil's *Aeneid*," *Arion* II.4 (1963) 66–80. Reprinted by permission of Catherine Parry Marcial.

If we could understand wholly the reasons for this lamentation, so elaborate within its brevity, and what makes it so poignant, and why it is so Virgilian, we should, I think, have grasped much of Virgil's art. First, something I can talk about a little but not translate, there is the absolute mastery of rhetoric. We have a *tricolon,* three successive noun-phrases, here in *asyndeton,* that is, with no grammatical connectives, joined to one verb, *flevere, mourned;* and this device combined with *apostrophe:* the dead warrior is suddenly addressed in the second person. The pronoun *te, you,* is repeated thrice, each time in the beginning of one of the three elements of the tricolon, a repetition we call *anaphora.* So much is developed but standard rhetoric. Virgil's mastery consists not in that, but in the subtle variations of it we see here. The three nouns are all a little different. The first is a grove with the name of the goddess to whom it is sacred in the possessive singular: *nemus Angitiae, the grove of Angitia.* The second is the name of a nearby lake, Fucinus, qualified by a noun and adjective: *Fucinus with glassy wave, vitrea Fucinus unda.* The third, beginning another hexameter line, is a common noun *lacus, lakes,* in the plural, with an adjective only: *liquidi lacus, transparent lakes.* The first two nouns are opposed to the third by being names of places. The second and third are opposed to the first by having adjectives and by having adjective and noun separated, whereas *the grove of Angitia, nemus Angitiae,* comes together. But the first and third are also opposed to the second by the variation of the *anaphora: te, you,* embodying the directness of lamentation, begins the first phrase: *Te nemus Angitiae...Te* is repeated in the second phrase, but its directness is modulated, softened, by its coming second in the phrase, after the adjective *vitrea, glassy: vitrea te Fucinus unda.* Then in the third phrase, the tonic note is struck again: *Te liquidi flevere lacus.* And finally, the verse accent falls on the first *te* and the third, but not on the second:

Te nemus Angitiae, vitrea te Fucinus unda,
Te liquidi flevere lacus.

["For you the grove of Angitia mourned, and Fucinus' glassy waters,
And the clear lakes."]

If this analysis seems too microcosmic, let me say that Virgil may not be, surely is not, the greatest poet who ever lived; but that in this mastery of the disposition of words within a formal pattern, he has no rivals. The effect of the variation within the symmetry is first to establish a rhythm, whose value might finally have to be analyzed in musical terms; and second, to add emotion to the lines. The tricolon with anaphora is a strong formal device, appropriate to the sounds of public lamentation. The variations, like a gentle yielding within the firm tripartite structure, add the note of genuine grief, invest the far-off place names with something of what used to be called the lyric cry.

For it is the place-names in this passage that show us how Virgil has departed from his Homeric model. The Homeric lines the commentators cite here occur in the Catalogue of the Trojans at the end of book 2 of the *Iliad:* "The forces from Mysia were led by Chromius and by Ennomus, a diviner of birds. But his birds did not keep *him* from black death. He was to be slain by the hands of swift Achilles at the river, where many another Trojan fell." The moment of death, and the great slaughter of the Trojans when Achilles returned to battle, is the picture we are left with.

Or again this, from the fifth book of the *Iliad:* "Menelaus son of Atreus caught with his sharp spear Strophius' son Scamandrius, a great hunter. Artemis herself had taught him how to down all the wildlife that the woods nourish. But the huntress goddess Artemis did him no good then, nor did his mastery with the bow for which he was so famous. The son of Atreus, killer Menelaus, struck him with the spear as he fled before him, right between the shoulders, and drove the point out through his chest. And he fell forward, and his armor rang as he fell." Again, and more emphatically in a typical passage such as this, the bitter irony of Homer leaves us with the image of the instant death of the man: the glory of Scamandrius when he lived and was famed as a hunter, then the uselessness of what he was as death comes upon him.

Virgil in the lines about Umbro imitates these scenes. But the image he leaves us with is not a fallen warrior, but a mourning landscape. The dramatic preoccupation of Homer with the single man and the single instant of time gives way to an echoing appeal to the Italian countryside, and an appeal strengthened in wholly unhomeric fashion by historical associations.

The place-names invoked by Virgil, Marravium, Lake Fucinus, the grove of the goddess Angitia, are from the Marsian country, hill country to the east of Rome, where a few generations earlier than Virgil a tough and warlike Italian people, the Marsi, had lived in independence, as Roman allies. In the Italian or Marsic war of 91–88 B.C., they had been defeated by Rome, and though they had gained citizenship, they had effectively lost their independence. To Virgil, this people represented the original Italian stock....They were somehow more Italian than the Romans themselves. Proud, independent, with local traditions hallowed by the names they had given to the countryside, they succumbed inevitably to the expansion of Roman power. The explicit message of the *Aeneid* claims that Rome was a happy reconciliation of the natural virtues of the local Italian peoples and the civilized might of the Trojans who came to found the new city. But the tragic movement of the last books of the poem carries a different suggestion: that the formation of Rome's empire involved the loss of the pristine purity of Italy. Thus the plot of the closing books of the poem centers on Turnus, Aeneas' antagonist, who is made the embodiment of a simple valor and love of honor which cannot survive the complex forces of civilization.

In this light we can understand the form which the lamentation for Umbro takes. Umbro himself is not important. He is no more than a made-up name. The real pathos is for the places that mourn him. They are the true victims of Aeneas' war, and in saying that they weep, Virgil calls on us to weep for what to his mind made an earlier Italy fresh and true.

The lamentation of the ancient hallowed places of the Marsi strikes a characteristic Virgilian note of melancholy and nostalgia, a note produced by the personal accents of sorrow over human and heroic values lost. But equally characteristic is the aesthetic resolution of the lines. The lament is presented to us as an object of artistic contemplation. By this I mean not simply that the lines are beautiful, for that is no distinguishing feature of Virgil. Nor do I refer to the vulgar concepts of "word-painting" or "scenic values," concepts often invoked in Virgilian criticism. The unexpected epithets *vitrea, glassy,* and *liquidi, clear,* do not, I think, "paint a picture" for us. But they do create a sense of sublimation, a conscious feeling that the raw emotions of grief have been subsumed in an artistic finality of vision. Not only the death of Umbro but also the loss of Italy itself is at last replaced by an image of bright and clear waters. The word *vitrea* in the middle of the lamentation is particularly noteworthy, for its connotations are those of an artifact. It is as if Virgil were telling us that the way to resolve our personal sorrow over the losses of history is to regard these losses in the same mood as we would a beautifully wrought vessel of clear glass. The perfection of the lines itself imposes a kind of artistic detachment, and we are put in the position of Aeneas himself, as he sees, in Carthage, the destruction of Troy represented as paintings in a gallery of art.

These paintings remind Aeneas of all that has been, of the *tears of human things*; and at the same time, Virgil tells us, they fill him with hope. In a larger way, the whole poem is such a painting. It is about history, but its purpose is not to tell us that history is good, or for that matter that it is bad. Its purpose is rather to impose on us an attitude that can take into account all in history that is both good and bad, and can regard it with the purer emotions of artistic detachment, so that we are given a higher consolation, and sorrow itself becomes a thing to be desired.

Let us now consider the poem from a wider point of view. Here we take care not to let orthodox interpretations of the *Aeneid* obscure our sense of what it really is. The nostalgia for the heroic and Latin past, the pervasive sadness, the regretful sense of the limitations of human action in a world where you've got to end up on the right side or perish, the frequent elegiac note so apparently uncalled for in a panegyric of Roman greatness — like the passage at the end of book 5 which describes the drowning of the good pilot Palinurus in dark and forgetful waters just before the Trojans reach Italy — the continual opposition of a personal voice which comes to us as if it were Virgil's own to the public voice of Roman success: all this I think is felt by every attentive reader of the poem. But most readers, in making a final judgment on the *Aeneid,* feel nonetheless constrained to put forth a hypothetical "Roman reader" whose eyes were quite unused to the melting mood. *He* would have taken the poem ultimately as a great work of Augustan propaganda, clapped his hands when Aeneas abandons the overemotional Dido, and approved with little qualification the steady march of the Roman state to world dominion and the Principate of Augustus as we see these institutions mirrored in Anchises' speech in book 6 and in Juno's renunciation in book 12. This, we are told, is how we should read the poem. After all, what was Augustus giving Virgil all those gold-pieces for?

So Mr. Kevin Guinach, the Rinehart translator, after putting forth these views, adds: "From this it must not be inferred that Virgil was a hireling.... It is fairer to suppose that he was an ardent admirer of the First Citizen and his policies, and sought to promote the reconstruction that Augustus had in mind." Apropos of Dido he says: "The ancient Romans did not read this episode as tearfully as we do.... From the Roman point of view, Dido was the aggressor in her marriage with Aeneas, an intolerable assumption of a male prerogative." Moreover, he tells us, the Roman would have condemned her for breaking her vow to her first husband, dead these many years. Consider the case of Vestal Virgins....

But what, on the simple glorification of Rome interpretation, do we make of some of the finest passages of the *Aeneid*? What we find, again and again, is not a sense of triumph, but a sense of loss. Consider the three lines at the end of book 2 which describe Aeneas' attempts to embrace the ghost of his wife:

> Three times I tried to put my arms around her
> And three times her image fled my arms' embrace,
> As light as the winds; as fleeting as a dream.

Like the lines about the fallen warrior, these lines derive from an earlier literary tradition. And again a comparison with this tradition will tell us something about the *Aeneid*. Virgil has two Homeric passages in mind, one in the twenty-third book of the *Iliad* where Achilles tries to embrace the hollow wraith of Patroclus:

> So spoke Achilles, and reached for him, but could not
> seize him, and the spirit went underground, like vapor,
> with a thin cry. And Achilles started awake, in amazement,
> and drove his hands together, and spoke, and his words were sorrowful:
> Ah me! even in the house of Hades there is left something of us,
> a soul and an image, but there is no real heart of life in it!

And a passage from the eleventh book of the *Odyssey*, where Odysseus in the Underworld attempts to embrace the shade of his mother:

> I bit my lip
> rising perplexed, with longing to embrace her,
> and tried three times,
> but she went sifting through my arms, impalpable
> as shadows are, and wavering like a dream.
> And this embittered all the pain I bore…

So the Virgilian passage first of all serves to reinforce the identification, operative throughout the poem, of Aeneas with the heroes of Homer. But the identification only sets in relief the differences. Virgil's lines are characteristic of the whole mood of his poem, the sadness, the loss, the frustration, the sense of the insubstantiality of what could be palpable and satisfying. Virgil emphasizes the *image* — the word *imago* ends the second line; and we can think of countless like passages, such as the appearance of Aeneas' mother in book 1, not recognized until after she has fled. The Homeric heroes are made angry by these signs of what lies beyond our physical existence. Achilles *drives* his hands together, Odysseus is *embittered*, that this kind of frustration should be added to his troubles. The Homeric hero, however beleaguered by fate, loves and enjoys the warmth of life, and his course of action includes a protest against the evanescence of mortality. But the sense of emptiness is the very heart of the Virgilian mood. After the three lines I have quoted, Aeneas goes on simply:

> The night was over; I went back to my comrades.

And the third of the three lines

> As light as the winds, as fleeting as a dream

receives a delicate emphasis, partly due to the two different words for *as*

> *Par* levibus ventis, volucrique *simillima* somno

that blurs the contours of our waking senses and gives the line a force of poignant resignation absent from both Homeric passages.

One other passage here, which I will speak of again later on. Aeneas comforts his men after the storm in book 1 with a famous phrase:

Forsan et haec olim meminisse iuvabit.
Some day perhaps remembering this too will be a pleasure.

Lifted again from the *Odyssey*. But the Homeric line is quite unmemorable. Odysseus says to his men that some day their troubles now will be a memory. He means only, they will be in the past, don't be overcome by them now. Virgil has made one clear change: the word *iuvabit: it will be a pleasure,* which makes a commonplace idea into a profoundly touching one. Not I would insist, because Virgil is a greater poet, but because the kind of sentiment that stands out in the *Aeneid* is different from the kind that stands out in the *Odyssey*.

How much in general is Aeneas like the Greek heroes? We know from the first line that he is cast in the role of Achilles and Odysseus:

Arms and the man I sing...

The *arms* are of course the *Iliad*, the *man* is the *Odyssey*. And the first six books of the *Aeneid* retrace the wanderings of Odysseus, the wars of the last six books follow the example of the *Iliad*. But the examples are not followed closely. The *Odyssey* goes on after its first line to tell us about the single man Odysseus; the *Iliad* goes on to describe the quarrel that was the first step in the tragedy of Achilles. The *Aeneid* moves from Aeneas straightway to something larger than himself—Rome:

that man who was tossed about on land and sea
and suffered much in war until
he built his city, brought the gods to Latium
from whence the Alban Fathers, the towering walls of Rome.

Aeneas from the start is absorbed in his own destiny, a destiny which does not ultimately relate to him, but to something later, larger, and less personal: the high walls of Rome, stony and grand, the Augustan Empire. And throughout he has no choice. Aeneas never asserts himself like Odysseus. He is always the victim of forces greater than himself, and the one lesson he must learn is, not to resist them. The second book of the poem drills him thoroughly in this lesson. The word Aeneas keeps using, as he tells of the night Troy fell, is *obstipui*: I was *dumbfounded*, shocked into silence. Again and again he tries to assert himself, to act as a hero, and again and again he fails. He leads a band of desperate Trojans against the Greeks, but it all turns sour. The Trojans dress up as Greeks, an unheroic stratagem which works for a while, but then their own countrymen mistake them, and Trojans slaughter each other, while Aeneas himself ends up on the roof of Priam's palace, passive spectator of the terrible violations within. A key passage is the one in which Aeneas is about to kill Helen. At least the personal, if not entirely heroic, emotion of revenge can be satisfied. But his mother stops him, not with a personal plea, as Athena checks Achilles in the *Iliad*, but by revealing for an instant the gods at work destroying the city. Against such overwhelming forces as these, individual feeling has no place. Aeneas must do the *right* thing, the thing destiny demands, and sneak away from Troy.

One of the effects, then, of the epic identifications of Aeneas is ironic contrast: he is cast in a role which it is his tragedy not to be able to fulfill. Let us now consider another kind of identification: the historical ones. As well as being cast as Odysseus and Achilles, Aeneas has to be the emperor Augustus. Of many passages, this one in the third book particularly contributes to setting up the connection. Aeneas and his men coast along the western shore of Greece and stop at Actium, where there is a temple of Apollo. There they hold games and Aeneas fastens to the door of the temple spoils taken from the Greeks with the inscription THESE ARMS FROM THE GREEK VICTORS. The reason for this action in this place is that Augustus had won his great victory over Antony and Cleopatra a few years earlier at Actium. He had instituted games in honor of his victory, and he liked to identify himself with Apollo. Moreover THE GREEK VICTORS, who are now vanquished, represent the armies of Antony, who recruited his forces from the eastern Mediterranean, whereas Augustus made himself the champion of Italy. So that the victory Aeneas somewhat illogically claims here by dedicating Greek spoils prefigures the victory that was to establish the power of Augustus.

Some striking verbal parallels confirm the connection, and give us as well insight into Virgil's technique. At the beginning of book 3, Aeneas sets sail from Troy.

> I am borne forth an exile onto the high seas
> With my comrades, my son, the Penates and the Great Gods
>
> Cum sociis natoque Penatibus et Magnis Dis.

The exact meaning of the phrase *the Penates and the Great Gods* is obscure. But it is clear that they are some sort of cult statues of Troy, destined to become cult statues of the New Troy, or Rome. The oddity of the phrase in fact helps us to remember it—the Romans liked their religious language to be obscure—and so does its remarkable thudding rhythm: *Penatibus et Magnis Dis.* This is Aeneas in his sacral character as bearer of the divine charter of Troy

At the end of book 8, Vulcan makes a shield for Aeneas, and on it are engraved scenes from subsequent Roman history. One of these scenes depicts the Battle of Actium:

> On one side stands Augustus Caesar leading Italians into battle,
> With the Fathers (i.e., the Senate), the People, the Penates and the Great
>   Gods
>
> Cum patribus populoque, Penatibus et Magnis Dis.

Aeneas' shield shows the future version of himself.

But Aeneas is not just Augustus. There is also the possibility of his being Augustus' bitter enemy, Mark Antony. Such is the identification we are led to make when, in the fourth book, he has become the consort of Dido, queen of Carthage. Thus the contemptuous description of him by Iarbas, his rival for Dido's love, "that Paris with his effeminate retinue," closely matches the image of Antony and Cleopatra with their corrupt eastern armies which Augustus created for Roman morale.

And Dido is Cleopatra. When she is about to die, she is said to be *pale with imminent death, pallida morte futura.* Cleopatra, in her own person, is described on Aeneas' shield in book 8 as *paling before imminent death, pallentem morte futura.*

To understand the meaning in the poem of these historical identifications, we must first consider more fully the figure of Aeneas. We learn from the second line of the poem that he is a man *exiled by fate, fato profugus,* and we soon learn that fate has for Aeneas implications that go beyond his personal journey through life. He is a man blessed — or is it cursed? — with a mission. The mission is no less than to be the founder of the most powerful state known to history; and so his every act and his every passion, all that he does, all that he feels and all that happens to him is in the light or under the shadow of this immense prophetic future of which he, by no choice of his own, is the representative elected by the gods. Every experience he passes through, therefore, has a significance greater than the events an ordinary man's life could possibly have. Every place he visits acquires an eternal fame of one kind or another. Every action he performs, every word he speaks, is fraught with consequences of which he himself can only dimly perceive the enormity.

This sense of pregnant greatness in every detail of experience is impressed on us too by the rhetorical exaggeration which pervades the *Aeneid,* and by the unrealism of many of its incidents. Juno's wrath in book 1 is magnified far beyond Poseidon's resentment in the *Odyssey;* Athena's punishment of the lesser Ajax, which Juno would like to inflict upon Aeneas, is enlarged into a cosmic destruction. When there are storms, the waves rise up and lash the heavens. Dido is supposed to have arrived in Africa not long before with a small band of refugees; but already the construction of a tremendous city — the later Carthage, of course — can be seen, complete with temples and art-galleries. Aeneas is moving through a world where everything is a symbol of something larger than itself. The layers of literary and historical allusion reinforce this sense of expansion in space and time which every monumental hexameter verse imposes on the reader.

The potentialities of ages and empires are alive in the smallest details of the *Aeneid,* and Aeneas has been made into the keystone of it all. The inconceivable destiny of Rome rests upon his shoulders. The *Aeneid* can give a literal meaning to that cliché. So line 32 of the first book:

Tantae molis erat Romanam condere gentem
It was a thing of so much *weight* to found the Roman race.

Aeneas can only leave Troy by carrying his aged father upon his shoulders. And Anchises is more than Aeneas' father. He is the burden of destiny itself. Thus in book 6 it is he who unfolds the panorama of Roman history to his son who has descended to the Nether World to hear him. And at the end of book 8, Virgil insists on Aeneas' rôle as bearer of destiny. The shield which Vulcan makes for him corresponds to the one he made for Achilles in the *Iliad.* Only Achilles' shield was adorned with generic pictures of life: a city at peace, a city at war, a scene of harvest, a scene of dancing, and so on. Aeneas' shield is adorned with scenes from Roman history, history which is future to him — it is here that we read of Augustus at the Battle of Actium — and as he puts it on, Virgil says:

He marvels at the scenes, events unknown to him,
And lays upon his shoulder the fame and fate of his descendants

Attollens umero famamque et fata nepotum.

The burden may well be a heavy one to bear, particularly if the bearer of it himself is permitted only an occasional prophetic glimpse into its meaning. And when such a glimpse is permitted him, it is likely to be anything but reassuring.

Bella, horrida bella…

Wars, hideous wars! the Sibyl shrieks at him when he questions her in book 6. "You will get to Latium, all right," she tells him, "but you will wish you had never come!" *Sed non et venisse volent.* "Go, seek your Italy!" Dido tells him, and then prophesies: "Let him beg for help in his own land, and when he has accepted the terms of a shameful peace, let him not enjoy his realm, or that light he has prayed for, but

fall before his time, and lie unburied on the sands

Sed cadat ante diem mediaque inhumatus harena,

whereby Aeneas is included in an almost obsessively recurrent series of images of disgraceful and nameless death.

Labor, ignorance and suffering are Aeneas' most faithful companions on his journey to Rome. And at once to intensify his own suffering and lack of fulfillment and to magnify the destiny he is serving, Aeneas must witness the happiness and success of others. In the third book he visits his kinsman Helenus in Epirus, and there he sees a copy of Troy, laid out in miniature. Aeneas is at first hopeful as he asks the prophetic Helenus for advice: "Now tell me, for I have divine sanction for all I do, and the gods have promised me a happy course, tell me the labors I must undergo, and the dangers I must avoid." But a little later, when Anchises enters, and he must set sail again, Aeneas falls into despair: "May you live happy, for your destiny is accomplished; but we are called from one fate to another…You have peace, you have no need to plow up the sea and follow forever the forever receding shores of Italy."

Arva neque Ausoniae semper cedentia retro
Quaerenda.

What this and other like passages impress upon us is something subtly at variance with the stated theme of the poem. Instead of an arduous but certain journey to a fixed and glorious goal, there arises, and gathers strength, a suggestion that the true end of the Trojan and Roman labors will never arrive. It is not that Aeneas will literally never arrive in Latium, found a city, and win his wars. That is as certain as it is that Odysseus will return to Ithaca. But everything in the *Odyssey* prepares us for a fuller end to Odysseus' labors: we are made always to expect his reinstatement in kingship, home, honor and happiness. In the *Aeneid* every prophecy and every episode prepares us for the contrary: Aeneas' end, it is suggested will see him as far from his fulfillment as his beginning. This other Italy will never cease receding into the distance.

There is another dimension to Aeneas' suffering as the bearer of too vast a destiny. Aeneas cannot live his own life. An agent of powers at once high and impersonal, he is successively denied all the attributes of a hero, and even of a man. His every utterance perforce contains a note of history, rather than of individuality. He cannot be himself, because he is wired for sound for all the centuries to come, a fact that is reflected in the speeches of the *Aeneid*. The sonorous lines tend to come out as perfect epigrams, ready to be lifted out of their context and applied to an indefinite number of parallel situations. Aeneas arrives in Carthage and sees the busy construction of the city.

O Fortunate you, whose walls already rise!

he cries out.

O fortunati, quorum iam moenia surgunt!

The line is memorable, too memorable perhaps for spontaneity. What Virgil has done is to turn to peculiar account what is at once the weakness and the glory of much of Latin verse: its monumentality, and its concomitant lack of dramatic illusion.

But Aeneas' failure as a hero goes deeper than the formality of his speech. As he makes his way through the first six books, we see him successively divested of every personal quality which makes a man into a hero. We have seen how the weight of his mission is made to overwhelm him at the very beginning of the poem. In the second book, he is in a situation which above all calls for self-sacrifice in the heat of battle. But this is precisely what he is kept from doing. Hector appears to him in a dream and tells him not to die for his country, but to flee. "For if Troy could have been saved," the ghost says almost with condescension, "my right arm would have saved it." We understand that Aeneas' words in the first book, when he was overwhelmed by the storm, have a deeper meaning than the parallel lines of the *Odyssey*: "O thrice and four times happy, you who fell at Troy!" Odysseus spoke out of a momentary despair. Aeneas' words are true for all his life. His personal ties too are not kept intact: in his haste to get his father and the state gods out of Troy, he leaves his wife behind; and when he returns to fetch her, she is an empty phantom, who can comfort him only with another prophecy.

But the most dramatic episode and the one in which Aeneas most loses his claims to heroism is the fourth book. The tragedy of Dido is lucid and deeply moving. But the judgment it leads us to make on Aeneas needs some comment. Generations of Latin teachers have felt it necessary to defend Aeneas from the charge of having been a cad. Modern readers are romantic, but a Roman reader would have known that Aeneas did the right thing. So the student is asked to forsake his own experience of the poem for that of a hypothetical Roman. Another theory is that Virgil somehow fell in love with, and was carried away by, his own heroine. But we cannot explain Virgil by assuming that he did not intend to write as he did. It is clear that on the contrary Virgil deliberately presented Dido as a heroine, and Aeneas as an inglorious deserter. Dido's speeches are passionate, and, in their operatic way, ring utterly true. Aeneas can apologize only by urging that his will is not his own. "If I had had my way," he tells her, "I would never have left Troy to come here at all." "I would never have fallen in love with you in the first place," he seems to mean. "I follow Italy not of my own choice." *Italiam non sponte sequor.* Of course he is right. Aeneas' will is not his own, and the episode in Carthage is his last attempt to assert himself as an individual and not as the agent of an institution. And in his failure, he loses his claim even to the humbler of the heroic virtues. For piety, in the Roman sense, meant devotion to persons as well as the state. "Unhappy Dido!" the queen about to die cries out, "is it now his impious deeds become clear to you? They should have before, when you made him your partner in rule. See now his pledge of faith, this man who carries about his gods, and his ancient father on his back." For pious Aeneas, as he is called, and calls himself, throughout, cannot maintain even his piety in a personal way.

Two later passages serve to emphasize this. At the beginning of the fifth book, the Trojans sail to Italy, troubled by the death-fires they see back in Carthage. "For they knew what a woman is capable of, when insane with the grief of her love dishonored." The Latin is perhaps more blunt. Dido's love was literally *defiled, polluto amore*, and Aeneas is its defiler. Later, in the Underworld in book 6, Aeneas meets Dido. He wants reconciliation now, and begs forgiveness. "I did not know the strength of your love for me," he says. Again the implication is clear. Aeneas did not know, because he could not feel the same love for her; because he is not master of himself, but the servant of an abstract destiny. Dido, speechless in anger, turns away. Aeneas is modeled on Odysseus here, and Dido's shade is the shade of Ajax in book 11 of the *Odyssey*. Virgil strengthens the emotions this scene creates in us by recalling the one scene in the *Odyssey* where Odysseus meets a hero greater than himself, and is put to shame by his silence.

But Dido, we remember, is also Cleopatra, and we must consider the meaning of that identification. Dido-Cleopatra is the sworn enemy of Rome:

Rise thou forth from my bones, some avenger!
Exoriare aliquis nostris ex ossibus ultor!

invoking the fell shades of Hannibal; but she is a tragic heroine. Aeneas, on the other hand, could have been, and for a while seemed to be, Antony, losing a world for love. Only he must in the end be Augustus, losing love and honor for a dubious world. The *Aeneid*, the supposed panegyric of Augustus and great propaganda-piece of the new régime, has turned into something quite different. The processes of history are presented as inevitable, as indeed they are, but the value of what they achieve is cast into doubt. Virgil continually insists on the public glory of the Roman achievement, the establishment of peace and order and civilization, that *dominion without end* which Jupiter tells Venus he has given the Romans:

Imperium sine fine dedi.

But he insists equally on the terrible price one must pay for this glory. More than blood, sweat and tears, something more precious is continually being lost by the necessary process; human freedom, love, personal loyalty, all the qualities which the heroes of Homer represent, are lost in the service of what is grand, monumental and impersonal: the Roman State.

The sixth book sets the seal on Aeneas' renunciation of himself. What gives it a depth so much greater than the corresponding book of the *Odyssey* is the unmistakable impression we have that Aeneas has not only gone into the Underworld: he has in some way himself died. He descends carrying the Golden Bough, a symbol of splendor and lifelessness.[1] The bough glitters and it *crackles in the wind:*

...sic leni crepitabat brattea vento.

It sheds, Virgil says, a strange discolored aura of gold; and it is compared to the mistletoe, a *parasitic plant, quod non sua seminat arbos*, a plant with no vital connection to the tree to which it clings. A powerful contrast to the culminating image of the *Odyssey*, that great hidden rooted tree from which the bed-chamber, the house and the kingship of Odysseus draw continuous and organic life.

Aeneas moves through the world of the dead. He listens, again the passive spectator, to the famous Roman policy speech of Anchises, a speech full of eagles and trumpets and a speech renouncing the very things Virgil as a man prized most:

Let others fashion the lifelike image from bronze and marble;
Let others have the palm of eloquence;
Let others describe the wheeling constellations of heaven;
Thy duty, O Roman, is to rule...

Tu regere imperio populos, Romane, memento...

When he emerges, so strangely, from the ivory gate of false dreams, he is no longer a living man, but one who has at last understood his mission, and become identified with it. Peace and order are to be had, but Aeneas will not enjoy them, for their price is life itself.

And yet there is something left which is deeper than all this. It is the capacity of the human being to suffer. We hear two distinct voices in the *Aeneid*, a public voice of triumph, and a private voice of regret. The private voice, the personal emotions of a man, is never allowed to motivate action. But it is nonetheless everywhere present. For Aeneas, after all, is something more than an Odysseus manqué, or a prototype of Augustus and myriads of Roman leaders. He is man himself; not man as the brilliant free agent of Homer's world, but man of a later stage in civilization, man in a metropolitan and imperial world, man in a world where the State is supreme. He cannot resist the forces of history, or even deny them; but he can be capable of human suffering, and this is where the personal voice asserts itself.

Someday these things too will be pleasant to think back on

Forsan et haec olim meminisse iuvabit

he tells his comrades in book 1. The implication is that when the great abstract goal is finally somehow reached, these present sufferings, seen in retrospect, will be more precious than it.

And so this pleasure, the only true pleasure left to Aeneas in a life of betrayals of the self, is envisaged as art. The sufferings of the Trojans, as Aeneas sees them in Carthage, have become fixed in art, literally: they are paintings. And it is here first, Virgil tells us, that Aeneas began to hope for a kind of salvation. Here he can look back on his own losses, and see them as made beautiful and given universal meaning because human art has transfigured them. "Look here!" he cries. "There is Priam; there are tears for suffering, and the limitations of life can touch the heart."

Sunt lacrimae rerum et mentem mortalia tangunt.

The pleasure felt here by Aeneas in the midst of his reawakened grief is the essential paradox and the great human insight of the *Aeneid,* a poem as much about the *imperium* of art as about the *imperium* of Rome. The images in Carthage make Aeneas feel Priam's death not less deeply, but more. At the same time they are a redemption of past suffering, partly because they remove one element of the nightmare: final obscurity and namelessness, partly because they mean that we have found a form in which we can see suffering itself clearly. The brightness of the image and the power of pleasurable vision it confers, consoles for the pain of what it represents.

The pleasure of art in fact gives value to the pain itself, because tragic experience is the content of this art. Virgil continues the scene in the art gallery: "He spoke, and with deep sorrow, and many lamentations, fed his soul on the empty pictures."

Atque animum pictura pascit inani.

Empty – inani – is the key-word here. Consider again how many times Virgil creates his most touching scenes by dwelling on how something substantial becomes empty and insubstantial: the phantom of Creusa, old fallen Troy, the apparition of Venus in book 1, the shade of Dido in the Underworld, the lost pledge to Evander, the outraged life of Turnus. *Inanis* is the very word that describes the tears Aeneas sheds upon leaving Carthage and Dido: "His mind was unmoved; the tears he wept were empty." That is, *of no avail*.

Mens immota manet; lacrimae volvuntur inanes.

Aeneas' tragedy is that he cannot be a hero, being in the service of an impersonal power. What saves him as a man is that all the glory of the solid achievement which he is serving, all the satisfaction of "having arrived" in Italy means less to him than his own sense of personal loss. The *Aeneid* enforces the fine paradox that all the wonders of the most powerful institution the world has ever known are not necessarily of greater importance than the emptiness of human suffering.

Notes

[1]See R. A. Brooks, "Discolor Aura," *American Journal of Philology*, LXXIV (1953), 260–80, the best article on the *Aeneid* to date.

Robert Gurval

'NO, VIRGIL, NO': THE BATTLE OF ACTIUM ON THE SHIELD OF AENEAS

In *Actium and Augustus: The Politics and Emotions of the Civil War*, Gurval asks about the effects on Roman culture of that decisive battle. The chapter excerpted here, "'No, Virgil, No': The Battle of Actium on the Shield of Aeneas," contains Gurval's reading of the description of the shield, at *Aeneid* 8.626–731. He begins by pointing out the conventional interpretation of the passage as one of the few "shining and untarnished moments of hope and glory" within the epic. His analysis reveals instead complex shades of meaning and conflicted feelings, which Vergil created through his choices and arrangement of the episodes depicted on the shield. Gurval concludes that the description of the shield did not so much support an existing Augustan propaganda as it created the understanding of the event in the Augustan age. (Ed.)

INTRODUCTION

On the second day of September in 31 B.C.E., the heir to the political legacy and name of Julius Caesar defeated the joint naval forces of Antony and Cleopatra off the coast of northwestern Greece. The outcome of the battle was not immediate, but the confrontation proved decisive and momentous. The vanquished pair fled to Egypt, and after seven tense days of protracted negotiations, the nineteen Roman legions that Antony had left behind at Actium surrendered to Octavian on equal terms with the victorious side. Foreign allies abandoned what was perceived as the losing cause and declared their allegiance to the victor. With the capture of Alexandria in the following year, Antony and the Egyptian queen were forced to commit suicide, and Octavian emerged as the sole and undisputed ruler of the Roman world. Peace was firmly established and officially proclaimed by the formal closure of the Temple of Janus. The Senate graciously rewarded the victor on his return to Italy with an accumulation of extraordinary honors, titles, and privileges. A political regime, which later generations would call the Augustan Principate, gradually evolved and, with it, a system of government that endured for more than four centuries. The Roman Empire had begun.

Actium constitutes a potent and enduring turning point in the course of Roman history and indeed of Western civilization. The significance of this victory hardly needs any long defense or complex explanation. Subsequent generations have not failed to recognize the serious consequences of the battle and to render their own verdict and individual bias. From the fawning Tiberian chronicler, who exclaimed that he could not record all the blessings that one day of fighting brought forth to the world,[1] to the more censorious author of the *Annales,* who viewed Octavian's victory at Actium as the lamentable sign of a failing Republic's demise,[2] to the later Greek historian of the Severan Age, who marked the date of the military engagement as the beginning of a new political regime in Rome,[3] the judgment of posterity is firm and unequivocal: Actium signals the commencement of a new era.

❖ ❖ ❖

CHAPTER FIVE

No, Virgil, no:
Not even the first of the Romans can learn
His Roman history in the future tense,
Not even to serve your political turn:
Hindsight as foresight makes no sense.

How was your shield-making god to explain
Why his masterpiece, his grand panorama
Of scenes from the coming historical drama
Of an unborn nation, war after war,
All the birthdays needed to preordain
The Octavius the world was waiting for,
Should so abruptly, mysteriously stop,
What cause should he show why he didn't foresee
The future beyond 31 B.C....

In these opening verses from Auden's "Secondary Epic,"[1] the twentieth century berates the greatest of the Roman poets. No, not even Vergil can make us believe the scenes of a glorious Roman future transposed to the decorative panels of the shield of Aeneas. What disturbed Auden about the nature of the Vergilian shield has disturbed many readers of the *Aeneid.* As the modern poet protested, Roman history did not "so abruptly, mysteriously stop" on that fateful day in September of 31 B.C.E. in the troubled waters of the Ambracian Gulf, or even two years later, in Rome, on those hot August days during the lavish spectacle and show of the Augustan triumphal ceremony. The might and authority of Rome would not always extend over the race of the Nomads and the arrow-bearing Geloni, from the double-horned Rhine to the indignant Araxes. Despite the prophecy of Jupiter, the imperium of Rome was not made without end. Auden scornfully disparaged the images that he viewed on the shield as manifestations of extreme nationalism and Roman imperialism, branding the celebrated passage at the end of the eighth book of the *Aeneid* as the poet's "political turn."

Almost two centuries earlier, G. E. Lessing had also objected to what he reckoned as the patriotic pride of the Roman poet.

The shield of Aeneas is therefore, in fact, an interpolation, intended solely to flatter the pride of the Romans; a foreign brook with which the poet seeks to give fresh movement to his stream....Homer makes Vulcan devise decorations, because he is to make a shield worthy of a divine workman. Virgil seems to make him fashion the shield for the sake of the decorations,

since he deems these of sufficient importance to deserve a special description long after the shield is finished.[2]

In his famous essay on originality and imitation of art, Lessing turned to consider
Vergil's depiction of the shield only to find the means for an unflattering comparison
between the two epic poets. For Lessing, the Homeric shield represented on its
broad surface the beauty and marvel of the universe, the whole range of human
experience and achievement. The tragedy of Achilles subsumed the universal dilemma
of mortal man. In contrast, the Vergilian shield seemed static and frigid, a series of
curiously selected scenes, empty of vitality, emotion, and universal appeal.[3] The
Roman poet failed to copy the noble example set before him. Patriotic pride and
political propaganda make poor craftsmen of poetry.
    More recent critics of the *Aeneid* have prudently avoided subjective comparisons
between Homer and Vergil and have refrained from censure of Roman patriotism
and politics; instead, scholars have sought to analyze the shield of Aeneas on its
own literary terms, on the basis of the themes and techniques that Vergil employs
in the epic. The description of the hero's shield has been viewed as part of the poet's
intentions to link the mythic past of Troy with the political reality of Augustan
Rome. The shield complements the prophecy of Jupiter to Venus (1.257–96) and the
pageant of Roman heroes in the underworld (6.756–886) in the content and tone of
its message; it is the culmination of Vergil's efforts to link Caesar Augustus with the
poem's hero, Trojan Aeneas.

> The Augustan reader of the book recognizes the meaningful continuity of
> Roman history in the parallels between the experiences of Aeneas and the
> events of Roman history, especially those of the Augustan Age: he sees in
> Aeneas the complementary figure to Augustus.[4]

Since the early 1960s, however, the *Aeneid* has been read as an ambiguous or, at
times, profoundly pessimistic epic.[5] The so-called Harvard school of Vergilian criticism
revolutionized the traditional view of the poem. Critics stressed the distinction between
the poet's voices in the *Aeneid*, "a public voice of triumph, and a private voice of
regret."[6] Throughout the epic, from Aeneas' tragic flight from Troy to his arrival in
Latium, where he must wage a war against Turnus and the Italians, the bright image
of glory and victory is marred by the harsh reality of individual tragedy and defeat.
Vergil's *Aeneid* embraces and at the same time defies Homeric models, constructing
a new type of hero—pious, dutiful, and deliberative. His final victory for the cause,
the angry killing of Turnus, is also viewed in terms of a personal defeat. Individual
studies on the poem's potent symbolism, recurring imagery, and allusive echoes
have converged in interpretations of a dark and irrational Vergilian world.[7] But
the heavy pendulum of literary interpretation ever swings. In response to such
pessimistic readings of the *Aeneid,* critics have forcefully resurrected a positive and
propagandistic message of the poem, particularly in search for philosophical justi-
fications for the hero's anger and Turnus' mournful descent into the underworld in
the last verses of the epic.[8]
    Nonetheless, throughout these evolving critical perceptions of the *Aeneid,* its
underlying messages and mixed sentiments, the judgment on the shield of Aeneas
has surprisingly remained fixed; the passage is deemed as one of the few shining and
untarnished moments of hope and glory, a detached and uncomplicated expression

of the poet's patriotic pride and his optimism for the future. Those critics who are inclined toward the more somber and pessimistic interpretations of the poem refrain from extended analysis[9] or prefer to extract the whole passage from the context of the *Aeneid* and to view the poet's gesture to Augustus and his victory at Actium as a reluctant obligation, an expression of sincere jubilation, or a moment of delusion. To many readers, the *ecphrasis* ["description"] of the hero's shield suggests what the *Aeneid* could have been if Vergil had composed a panegyric epic.

✧ ✧ ✧

The focus of this chapter is the Vergilian treatment of the battle at Actium and the victor's triple triumph ceremony that closes the poet's *ecphrasis* of the shield....[M]y primary intent is to examine the Vergilian passage in the context of the epic, without the presumption of the poet's purpose or public obligation to the Augustan regime. The contribution of Vergil's *Aeneid* to the glorification of Actium and its victor should not be undervalued or denied. What should not be assumed with such assurance, however, is that Augustus actually sought or expected the attention bestowed on this final victory in civil war or that the epic poet intended his description of Actium to be read as a manifesto of Roman might and imperial glory. I argue that, however much we may search in vain for the expectations of contemporaries and strive to assess the literary objectives or success of the poet, the shield's *ecphrasis* at the end of the eighth book of Vergil's *Aeneid* served more to mold a new "Augustan" conception and ideology of the Actian victory than to endorse or transmit any prior propaganda of the battle.

✧ ✧ ✧

The Vergilian shield is a much more complex and critical reflection on Rome, past and present, than any absolute expression of national pride or unrestrained eulogy of Augustan might and authority. A subtle tension pervades within and among the individual scenes, building from the narrative momentum and subjective emotion of each passage and resulting in what Viktor Pöschl once characterized as the basic truth of Vergilian art and the essence of the poem, "a sequence of moods, a series of changing sensations."[10] The shield of Aeneas culminates in Actium and Augustan triumph, a culmination that ultimately must be judged by this series of historical scenes viewed in rapid succession and with fluctuating emotions and conflicting passions.

Introduction to the Shield
illic res Italas Romanorumque triumphos
haud vatum ignarus venturique inscius aevi
fecerat ignipotens, illic genus omne futurae
stirpis ab Ascanio pugnataque in ordine bella.

(8.626–29)

There the history of Italy and the triumphs of the Romans,
not ignorant of the prophets or unknowing of the coming age,
the lord of fire had fashioned, there all the generations of the
stock born from Ascanius and the wars fought in succession.

Romulus and Remus
fecerat et viridi fetam Mavortis in antro
procubuisse lupam, geminos huic ubera circum
ludere pendentis pueros et lambere matrem
impavidos, illam tereti cervice reflexa
mulcere alternos et corpora fingere lingua.

(8.630–34)

He had fashioned too, outstretched in the green cave of Mars,
the mother wolf, and the twins, hanging around her teats
as they played like boys and licked their mother
without fear; bending back her smooth neck, she
fondles one and the other and shapes their bodies with her tongue.

✧ ✧ ✧

Catiline and Cato
                 hinc procul addit
Tartareas etiam sedes, alta ostia Ditis,
et scelerum poenas, et te, Catilina, minaci
pendentem scopulo Furiarumque ora trementem,
secretosque pios, his dantem iura Catonem.

(8.666–70)

                At a distance from this he added
too the dwellings of Tartarus, the lofty portals of Dis,
and the punishments of the wicked, and you, Catiline, hanging
on a menacing crag and trembling at the faces of the Furies,
and far apart the pious, and giving laws to them, Cato.

The first scene of the hero's shield depicts the infants Romulus and Remus. The she-wolf has recently given birth; she permits the twin boys to play about her and to draw her milk without fear; with her smooth neck bent back, she fondles the boys, first one, then the other, and she fashions their bodies with her tongue. She is called by the poet a mother (*matrem,* line 632). The savage nature of the wolf has been tamed, man and beast are reconciled in a manner evocative of the peace from the Saturnian Golden Age or Evander's Latium. Critics have compared the passage to the opening invocation to the mother of Aeneas in Lucretius' *de Rerum Natura* where the goddess of Love seduces the savage spirit of Mars.[11] There are also possible echoes of Ennius' treatment of early Rome (*lupus femina feta repente,* Vahlen *Ann.* 68).[12] The opening scene testifies to the important role Mars plays in the origins of Rome. The emphatic genitive *Mavortis* ["of Mars"] links the green cave with Mars, the father of the infant twins. But the focus of the poet's description is not on the birth of the twins or their paternal ancestry but on the "mothering" by the wolf and the innocent play of the boys, a scene vividly expressed in literal, figurative, and symbolic terms. Before a Vergilian reader might contemplate the implications of this striking image where the boys lick (*lambere*) the animal's teats and the wolf fashions (*fingere*) their bodies with her tongue, the poet shifts to Rome in line 635. The play of the boys yields to the actions of men. The mention of *Romam* serves as a chronological as well as geographical transition, an allusion to the foundation of the city where Romulus killed his brother in anger; nonetheless, the poet refrains from an explicit commentary.

✧ ✧ ✧

[After the stories of the rape of the Sabine women, the punishment of Mettus, of Porsenna and the Aeneadae, and the attack of the Gauls, the description on the shield shifts] abruptly to Tartarus and a scene of eternal punishments and rewards (8.666–70). The choice of the two figures who are seen, Catiline and Cato, is puzzling. The great generals of the late Republic — Marius, Sulla, Pompey, and Caesar — and their military triumphs, as well as the heroes of the wars against Carthage, Spain, and Greece, are passed over in silence. More surprising, however, is the poet's decision to include the realm of Tartarus on the hero's shield. Not merely a Homeric imitation or a physical description of the cosmos, the gloomy setting in the underworld affects our perception of the two characters. The one receives his punishment from the Furies; the other gives laws among the pious. Evil is punished, and virtue is rewarded. The contrasting situations would thus seem to fit neatly into the standard interpretations of the passage. But this somewhat narrow viewpoint ignores the emphasis and detail of the poet's words.

We hear first of Tartarus (the adjective *Tartareas* introduces us to the sudden and dramatic change in scene) and the lofty portals of Dis. The punishment of the wicked follows, and for the second time in these opening scenes, the poet focuses our attention on an individual by a second-person apostrophe (the first apostrophe was to Mettus in line 643). Again, the poet's address, almost an appeal or warning, is directed to a figure of moral failure. The horrid fate of Catiline is revealed in the following verse. While the guilt of the failed conspirator is unambiguous and presumed, his appearance on the shield can only serve to remind the Vergilian reader of those forces of discord and civil conflict that so often haunted the recent past. The sudden emergence of Cato, however, makes this bitter memory of civil war more implicit and immediate. His name dramatically concludes line 670 and marks an astonishing finale to the scene in Tartarus. In any other context, the phrase *dantem iura Catonem* ["and Cato giving laws"] might seem to refer to the conservative senator Cato Censor rather than to his equally distinguished descendant Cato Uticensis. At least the name would be ambiguous.[13] Here, however, coupled with Catiline, this Cato must surely be the enemy of Julius Caesar who committed suicide rather than live under a tyrant. Vergil's praise of Cato is not unique in contemporary poetry (cf. *Catonis / nobile letum* ["Cato's noble death"] in Horace *Odes* 1.12.35–36 and *praeter atrocem animum Catonis* ["except Cato's fierce spirit"] in *Odes* 2.1.24). It would be simplistic and misleading, however, to see Cato's name as the bold manifestation of a poet's lingering Republican sentient. The deliberate and striking contrast with Catiline, a fitting symbol of rebellion, extols the vanquished opponent of Caesar as an emblem of justice and authority. The emphatic addition of Cato, evoking in the minds of contemporary readers painful memories of civil conflict and defeat, concludes the fleeting and illusory glimpses of Roman history and leads directly to the centerpiece of the shield — the battle at Actium and the subsequent triumph by Caesar Augustus.

The scenes depicted on the hero's shield proceed in a swift and uneven movement. Vergil compels his reader to shift back and forth, up and down around the armor's edges before focusing on the dramatic centerpiece. The progression of historic events is chronological but eclectic and uneven. The focus of the shield of Aeneas is Italy (*res Italas* ["the history of Italy"] begins the poet's explanation of the shield's scenes in line 626); the themes are war and conquest in the story of Rome's expansion in the Italian peninsula and the incorporation of its neighboring peoples and former enemies. The Sabines, the Albans, the Etruscans, and even the invading Gauls of northern Italy are destined to be part of the Roman nation. That the battle at Actium would be the culmination of this poetic arrangement of fleeting images and historic personages must come as a startling development to any Vergilian reader; nothing in the preliminary scenes on the shield's periphery would signal to any Roman contemporary that Actium was the centerpiece of the hero's armor. Too often critics seek to explain how these initial scenes on the shield (8.630–70) correspond to the message of Augustan victory and triumph; it seems at least as reasonable, if not more prudent, to inquire how the confrontation at Actium relates to the encircling images of warfare, treachery, and civil conflict that visually and emotionally prepare the reader for the dramatic centerpiece.

The Battle of Actium
haec inter tumidi late maris ibat imago
aurea, sed fluctu spumabant caerula cano,
et circum argento clari delphines in orbem
aequora verrebant caudis aestumque secabant.
in medio classis aeratas, Actia bella,
cernere erat, totumque instructo Marte videres
fervere Leucaten auroque effulgere fluctus.
hinc Augustus agens Italos in proelia Caesar
cum patribus populoque, penatibus et magnis dis,
stans celsa in puppi, geminas cui tempora flammas
laeta vomunt patriumque aperitur vertice sidus.
parte alia ventis et dis Agrippa secundis
arduus agmen agens, cui, belli insigne superbum,
tempora navali fulgent rostrata corona.
hinc ope barbarica variisque Antonius armis,
victor ab Aurorae populis et litore rubro,
Aegyptum virisque Orientis et ultima secum
Bactra vehit, sequiturque—nefas—Aegyptia coniunx.
una omnes ruere ac totum spumare reductis
convulsum remis rostrisque tridentibus aequor.
alta petunt; pelago credas innare revulsas
Cycladas aut montis concurrere montibus altos,
tanta mole viri turritis puppibus instant.
stuppea flamma manu telisque volatile ferrum
spargitur, arva nova Neptunia caede rubescunt.
regina in mediis patrio vocat agmina sistro,
necdum etiam geminos a tergo respicit anguis.
omnigenumque deum monstra et latrator Anubis
contra Neptunum et Venerem contraque Minervam
tela tenent. saevit medio in certamine Mavors
caelatus ferro, tristesque ex aethere Dirae,
et scissa gaudens vadit Discordia palla,

quam cum sanguineo sequitur Bellona flagello.
Actius haec cernens arcum intendebat Apollo
desuper; omnis eo terrore Aegyptus et Indi,
omnis Arabs, omnes vertebant terga Sabaei.
ipsa videbatur ventis regina vocatis
vela dare et laxos iam iamque immittere funis.
illam inter caedes pallentem morte futura
fecerat ignipotens undis et Iapyge ferri,
contra autem magno maerentem corpore Nilum
pandentemque sinus et tota veste vocantem
caeruleum in gremium latebrosaque flumina victos.

                                                          (8.671–713)

Amid these scenes, an image of the swollen sea surged far around,
fashioned in gold, but dark blue waves foamed with white billows,
and all around, dolphins, shining with silver, swept the seas
in a circle and cut the swell with their tails.
In the middle, the brazen ships, the battle at Actium,
were in view, and you would see all Leucate ablaze
with Mars in array, and the waves gleam with gold.
On one side, Caesar Augustus, leading the Italians into battle,
with the senators and people, with the Penates and great gods,
stands on the lofty stern, his brow in joy spews forth twin flames,
and the star of his father appears above his head.
Elsewhere, Agrippa, with the winds and gods in his favor,
towers above and leads the column of ships; his brow gleams,
beaked with a naval crown, the proud ornament of war.
On the other side, Antony with barbaric wealth and varied arms,
the victor from the peoples of the Dawn and Red Sea,
bringing with him Egypt and the strength of the Orient
and remote Bactra, and there follows — the shame! — his Egyptian wife.
All rush together, and the expanse of the sea is torn up
and foams from the pulling of oars and three-pronged beaks;
they seek the open sea; you would think the Cyclades, uprooted,
swam in the sea or mountains rushed against mountains on high;
      with such a massive force the men press against the turreted sterns.
From their hands, flaming tow and weapons of flying steel
are scattered; the fields of Neptune redden with fresh slaughter.
The queen, in the middle, calls the lines with her ancestral rattle,
not even yet does she see behind her the twin snakes.
Monstrous gods of every kind and barking Anubis
hold weapons against Neptune and Venus, against Minerva.
In the very middle of the battle rages Mars,
engraved in iron, and the grim Dirae from above,
and Discord advances, exultant in her torn garb,
and behind her Bellona follows with bloody whip.
Actian Apollo, watching the battle, bent back his bow
from above, and at this terror, all Egypt and India,
all Arabians, all Sabaeans turned their backs in flight.

The queen herself was seen calling the winds and
spreading sails and just now releasing the slackened ropes.
The god of fire had depicted her amid the slaughter,
pale with approaching death, carried by the waves and Iapyx.
And opposite her the Nile, his great body in mourning,
expanded his folds and with his whole raiment summoned
into his dark blue bosom and hidden streams the conquered.

✧ ✧ ✧

An image of the swollen sea introduces Actium in line 671. The adjective *tumidi*
["swollen"] might at first suggest a storm or disturbance at sea (cf. the *tumida aequora*
["swollen seas"] Neptune calms after the storm scene in book 1, line 142), but Vergil
refrains from developing this initial suggestion. Instead, the reader learns that the
image of the sea is golden. *Aurea* ["golden"] emphatically begins line 672. Dark
blue waves foam with billows of white; dolphins, brilliant with silver, sweep the
waters in a circle and cut through the swell with their fins. In this opening description of the marine setting, Vergil sets before us once again, as in the initial scene of
the green cave with the twins and she-wolf of Mars, a brief glimpse of apparent
calm, natural beauty, and innocent wonder. The poet's enthusiasm for the vibrant
colors of the ocean, for the frolic of dolphins amid the foaming swirl, can only
beguile us with its beauty, but such beauty beguiles us for the short span of four
verses. Suddenly, in line 675, the image of playful sport gives way, and in the middle,
we can perceive the brazen ships of war, the battle of Actium. *Actia bella* ["Actian
wars"] identifies the scene. The poet's subsequent words revoke the emotion and
peace of the opening verses.

As critics remind us, there is much in the shield's description of the Actian
conflict to suggest Vergil's intentions to link Aeneas with Augustus. The phrase
"standing on the lofty stern" (*stans celsa in puppi*) recurs in book 10 (line 261) to
describe Aeneas, who, from high above, beholds the camp of the Trojans on his
return to battle. And there too flames surround the head of the Trojan hero, denoting
the mark of divine favor, just as they appear on the head of Augustus. Tempted as
we may be to make this connection between the two, and not only tempted but
compelled by the verbal echoes here and in other passages to make this connection,
nonetheless, we are also alerted to the strange irony of this future moment of proud
Roman glory when Augustus leads into battle not the sons of Romulus and not the
race of its Trojan founder but the Italians (*Italos*), the very people against whom
Aeneas is about to wage his war in Latium. His is a war, as the poet reminds us
more than once in the epic, that the Trojan hero enters with nothing but reluctance
for what he knows to be its final senselessness and waste.

The *hinc* ["on one side"] of line 678 is answered by another in line 685. The enemy of Augustus is named; he is Antony. This identification is a stunning revelation,
stunning when perceived in the context of the almost total suppression of that name
in the descriptions of Actium by contemporary poets. Among the Augustan poets,
Horace nowhere mentions the name of Antony. In *Epode* 9 he is the unnamed *hostis*
["enemy"]. He is passed over without even a suggestion of his presence in the famous Cleopatra Ode (1.37). And everywhere else in Horace, there is a hushed silence about Antony — and about Actium. Propertius refers to Antony, to his notorious love affair with the Egyptian queen, and to his ultimate fate in only two pas-

sages: by the epithet *dux* ["leader"] in 2.16.37–40, where he describes the waters at Actium filled with the futile groans of his condemned soldiers; and explicitly by Antony's *nomen* ["name"] in 3.9.56, where he refers to his suicide at Alexandria. In *Elegy* 4.6, the poem whose action is the counterpart to this scene in Vergil, Propertius is strangely reticent and refrains from including Antony's involvement in the naval battle.

Antony is introduced into the Vergilian scene of battle by name; he is described, however, as an Eastern potentate and an enemy of Rome. He carries with him the opulence of the Orient and its varied strength. But in the beginning of line 686, the poet also calls Antony *victor*, an impressive and ironic epithet for a man who will soon be defeated in one of the most significant battles in Western civilization. He leads with him Egypt, the strength of the East, and the farthest land of Bactra. His Egyptian wife follows, the *nefas* ["the shame!"], as the poet emphatically interjects — a perverse counterpart to the ally of Augustus, Marcus Agrippa. All Italy supports the just cause of Augustus. Antony is no longer Roman; instead, he is an Eastern king and lover. The Egyptian woman who follows is called his wife.

Historians and literary critics alike refer to this passage as the culmination of the official view on the Actian conflict in the propaganda terms of East versus West, the unmediated slander and deceit of a victorious regime. The confidence of the claim is surprising, since neither Horace nor Propertius interprets the battle as a mighty struggle between opposing civilizations or geographic areas. The enemies of Rome are a woman, Egypt, and a band of eunuchs. And though the evidence is fragmentary, this seems to be the force of Octavian's propaganda against Antony before the war.[14] I have already suggested the irony in the fact that the descendant of Trojan Aeneas is leading Aeneas' enemy (*Italos*) into battle. The description of Antony strangely corresponds in more than one respect to the situation of the hero in Italy. Both men are the objects of unfair and harsh ridicule because of their Eastern habits: Antony — by the propaganda of Augustus, and Aeneas, on several occasions throughout the epic — by Iarbas, the African king, in book 4 (4.215–18); by Remulus Numanus, the brother-in-law of Turnus, in book 9 (9.598–620); and finally in a savage attack by Turnus himself in the opening of book 12.

> ...da sternere corpus
> loricamque manu valida lacerare revulsam
> semiviri Phrygis et foedare in pulvere crinis
> vibratos calido ferro murraque madentis.

> (12.97–100)

> ...grant to me to lay low his body
> and with a powerful blow to tear away and shatter the breastplate
> of this effeminate Phrygian and to defile his hair in the dust,
> curled by the hot iron and drenched with myrrh.

The selected manner of Vergil's description of the Eastern forces of Antony offers the reader a pointed reference to an earlier scene in the epic. The phrase *ope barbarica* ["with barbaric wealth"] in 8.685, which introduces us to Antony before we even hear his Roman name, recalls the once proud grandeur of Troy and its fall. The adjective *barbaricus*, which Vergil reserves for only two occasions in the *Aeneid*, formerly described the doorposts of Priam's palace, doorposts proud with barbaric gold and spoils.

barbarico postes auro spoliisque superbi
procubuere

                                                                            (2.504–5)

doorposts, haughty in barbaric gold and spoils,
fell down

Vergil describes the doorposts as proud just before they fell forward in ruin
(*procubuere*), hurled down by the flames of destruction.[15] A foreign and royal bride
is destined for the Trojan hero in his new homeland. Amid the destruction of Troy,
the shade of Creusa foretold to her husband that a kingdom and royal wife (*regia
coniunx*, 2.783–84) awaited him in Hesperia. And in the sixth book of the epic, the
Sibyl prophesied ominously how a foreign wife (*coniunx hospita*) and a foreign marriage (*externi thalami*) would once again be the cause of so much evil to the Trojans.

causa mali tanti coniunx iterum hospita Teucris
externique iterum thalami.

                                                                            (6.93–94)

the cause of such evil to the Trojans is again an alien bride
and again a foreign marriage.

Oddly, therefore, both antagonists in the battle of Actium, as they are depicted by
the poet on the shield, seem to anticipate the single protagonist of the epic, Aeneas
himself. Vergil denies us any straightforward and uncomplicated allegorical reading,
any simple equation that matches Augustus with Aeneas. The complexity and overlapping of allusions confuse the claims of the opposing sides and mark an uneasy
introduction into the scene of battle.

In 8.689–703, a fierce struggle ensues, cosmic in its dimensions, as if islands
moved in conflict or as if tall mountains clashed. The fields of Neptune grow red
with fresh slaughter. The metaphor is found in Ennius ([*pont*]*i caerula prata* ["the
dark blue fields of the sea"], Vahlen *Ann.* 143) and Cicero (*Neptunia prata* ["Neptunian fields"], *Arat.* 129), but the imagery of color is uniquely Vergilian.

✧ ✧ ✧

From the reddening of the Neptunian fields, we come to the figure of Cleopatra,
who appears amid the battle lines, calling the host with her native *sistrum* ["rattle"].
Cleopatra's active participation in the campaign and battle dominated subsequent
Augustan propaganda. But Vergil does not insert into the midst of the Actian battle
the brief glimpse of this woman only to serve as a medium of further abuse and
scorn. The *Aegyptia coniunx* ["Egyptian wife"] of Antony is now called *regina*, the
queen. On hearing the mention of *regina,* we might think back to the first of the two
queens of the *Aeneid,* the Carthaginian queen whose love affair with Aeneas threatened the promise and destiny of Rome, the tragic and lovely Dido. And we may
think of the second *regina* of the epic, the wife of aged Latinus, whose maddened
opposition to the marriage of her daughter to Aeneas, even now as we come to the
end of the eighth book, threatens the welfare of her city and makes necessary the
armor Aeneas requires. Like Dido and Amata, the Egyptian queen is also fated to

die. Twin snakes lurk ominously and unseen behind her, foreshadowing her approaching death. It is a sudden and surprising shift in tone to the passage. Throughout the *Aeneid*, snakes represent the supernatural forces of evil and destruction, especially when they appear in pairs.[16] Twin snakes (*gemini anguis*) threaten the life of the infant Hercules earlier in book 8 (line 289). In book 7 (line 450), they project from the hair of the Fury Allecto, as she sounds her whip and hurls her torch at Turnus. And in the most dramatic and frightening appearance of these creatures in the *Aeneid*, twin serpents with huge coils and scaly backs emerge from the peaceful depths of the sea and make their way for the shores of Troy, bearing death to the priest Laocoön and his young sons (2.203–4). Here, on the shield, the twin snakes that forebode the death of the Egyptian queen are known only to the reader. Vergil has intensified the pathos of the moment by the subjective disclosure that the queen does not foresee her death; the queen does not yet look behind her to see the agents of her destruction (*necdum etiam...respicit* ["not even yet does she look behind"]).

Gods of every strange and monstrous form wage war against the Olympian deities. Neptune, Venus, and Minerva oppose the barking Anubis. Philip Hardie explores in full the Gigantomachic aspects of the battle of Actium in the shield's *ecphrasis* ["description"].[17] Hardie's cosmic and cosmogonic interpretation of the passage supports the popular view that Vergil offers on the hero's shield a pure and uplifting vision of Roman imperialism and eternal dominion, the triumph of Western civilization over the barbaric East, the victory of order and reason over the forces of chaos and discord. And herein lies the cause of Auden's caustic wit and serious complaint in "Secondary Epic," whose opening verses introduced this chapter. The painful experience of two world wars had made the twentieth-century poet especially distrustful of the fraudulent and boastful claims of extreme nationalism, imperial power, and manifest destiny. The symbolic aspects of the poet's elevation of the war between Caesar's heir and Antony into a struggle of cosmic dimensions, and the profound implications of this symbolism, are obvious to readers of the *Aeneid*, whether ancient or modern. And yet such symbols are often disappointing and never quite as clear and one-dimensional in Vergil as some might expect them to be.

Much has been said, and much more inferred, by critics about the ideological and propagandistic dichotomies that underlie the opposing forces depicted on the hero's shield: "reasoned order" vs. "directionless irrationality."[18] Apollo represents reason and wisdom. Even Minerva in line 699 has been understood as the Athenian goddess of wisdom and prudence.[19] Mars, the Dirae, and Discordia represent the enemy forces of disorder and madness. The final victory of Augustus over Antony assures the universal order. However attractive this view may be, the poet's description of the fighting cannot support this idealized portrait; instead, it rejects the simplicity and neatness of such an interpretation. The gods that represent the senselessness, violence, and destruction of war are not allied with Antony and his Eastern throng; they are not the foreign enemies opposed to Augustus and the Italians; and they do not belong to one group or the other, to one political faction or ideology. Mars, the grim Dirae, Discordia, and Bellona contend in the very middle of the Actian struggle (*medio in certamine* ["in the middle of the battle"], line 700). The madness of war is not partisan; it does not choose sides, and it rejects the appropriate distinctions between ally and foe, Roman and barbarian. Instead, the fury engulfs both sides and all combatants. And as so often happens in the second half of the *Aeneid*, moral convictions and proud assertions of righteous causes ultimately give way and lose their validity in the course of fighting on the battlefield.

Apollo Actius enters suddenly into the scene of confrontation (line 704). The Egyptians, Indians, Arabs, and Sabaeans flee in terror at the sight. The enemy is defeated, and the Romans are victorious. This is the first appearance in extant Latin literature of Apollo Actius, the god who assures the victory at Actium. Horace ignores the role of the god in his treatment of the battle (*Epode* 9), and Propertius composed his aetiological hymn on the Temple of Palatine Apollo and the battle at Actium (*Elegy* 4.6) after the publication of the *Aeneid* and perhaps in direct response to the epic description of the battle on the Vergilian shield. His earlier poem (*Elegy* 3.11) alluded indirectly to the god's role in the battle in a closing address, but there Propertius called on Apollo Leucadius, not Apollo Actius. In Vergil's characterization of the Actian battle, the god plays a dramatic and crucial role, though this fact is neither surprising nor extraordinary in the context of an epic scene where the divine forces of each side have already been arrayed by the poet. Vergil attributes the victory to the intervention of the god and his archery, and later the triumphator sits on the threshold of the god's temple in Rome during the procession of conquered nations (*ipse sedens niveo candentis limine Phoebi* ["as himself sitting on the snowy white threshold of shining Apollo"] line 720). The Augustan victory is divinely sanctioned and won. Apollo usurps the role of presiding deity over the naval battle and the triumphal celebrations.

The poet's emphasis on Apollo's role in the battle should not be understood (or need not be explained) as the reflection of an Augustan attitude toward the battle or as the ultimate expression of a contemporary political ideology. To be sure, at Nicopolis, near the site of the naval battle, the proud victor acknowledged his gratitude to Apollo by the enlargement of the god's temple and the exaltation of local games to an "Olympian" status. Yet the dedicatory inscription to Octavian's Actian "campsite memorial," the elaborate display of captured ships' prows, surprisingly excludes the role of Apollo in the battle and instead grants thanksgiving offerings to Neptune and Mars for the victory on land and sea. In Rome, the returning conqueror celebrated a triple triumph; and earlier in the same year, the Senate closed the doors of the temple of Janus. There seems to be no prominence or attention bestowed on Apollo during these occasions. As I have argued previously, Octavian did not take any official or overt steps at this time to associate the Temple of Apollo on the Palatine with his victory at Actium. Neither Horace in his *Odes* nor Propertius in his first three books of *Elegies* alludes to the Augustan temple's public connections with Actium before the epic poet. The Vergilian representation of battle, the victory of Roman might and morals over the allied peoples of the "barbaric" East, and the subsequent union and assimilation of these formerly hostile cultures, prefigured in the triumphal ceremonies described in lines 714–27, anticipate the resolution of the conflict between Aeneas, the *Troianus dux* ["Trojan leader"], and Turnus, the leader of the Italians, at the end of the epic. The implications of the poet's decision to exalt the final episode of Roman civil war into a heroic struggle, divinely fought and won by the aid of Apollo, are serious, profound, and immediate.

❖ ❖ ❖

Amid the slaughter of battle (*inter caedes,* line 709), the queen appears, pale with the signs of her own approaching death. If Vergil sought to make us think back to Dido in the prior brief glimpse of the queen, calling the host with her native *sistrum* ["rattle"], he compels us to do so now. The phrase *pallida morte futura* ["pale with approaching death"] occurs in the tragic scene in the fourth book where Dido is about to fall on the sword of her Dardanian lover (4.644). For the second time in the passage, the poet alludes to the future death of the Egyptian queen. Cleopatra's death is imminent, but the craftsman/god (*ignipotens*) ["god of fire"] allows us to see her only in flight. The final three verses in the treatment of the battle (lines 711–13) suddenly shift the scene to Egypt, to an image of the mighty Nile in grief. The river god is seen mourning with his great body, extending his folds, and calling with his whole robe. The object of this mournful embrace into his dark blue bosom and hidden streams is postponed. We are expecting through the three verses that it is the queen whom the Nile will receive into his folds. The verse concludes surprisingly and emphatically with *victos* ["the conquered"]. The plight of the Egyptian queen is extended to include all the conquered.

❖ ❖ ❖

At the end of his "Secondary Epic," Auden's mocking tone becomes more serious.

No, Virgil, no:
Behind your verse so masterfully made
We hear the weeping of a Muse betrayed.

Auden's charge of betrayal prejudges the Roman poet and his intentions in the *Aeneid* and convicts him of jingoistic patriotism and nineteenth-century nationalism. The final scene on the Vergilian shield, however, discloses a more complex image of Actium and Augustan triumph. Linking Actium with the past, Vergil places the battle as the culmination of a long series of wars and Roman triumphs. But the poet also complicates his reader's emotions as the displays of righteous pride and public jubilation fail to eclipse the episodes of cruel violence, irrational strife, and individual sorrow. The Vergilian concept of victory, not only on the hero's shield, but throughout his national epic, is more often perceived in terms of defeat. Public triumph and joy inevitably give way to private loss and suffering. The reality of civil war behind the Actian facade prefigures the conflict of the epic's final four books, the fierce struggle between Trojan Aeneas and Italian Turnus, the representative leaders of two races who are destined to be one. While the Roman poet gave eloquent and sincere expression to the promise and hope of a bright Augustan future, he could not forget the misery and loss inflicted in the still recent past.

Vergil concludes the eighth book with Aeneas' reaction to the scenes on the shield.

Talia per clipeum Volcani, dona parentis,
miratur rerumque ignarus imagine gaudet,
attollens umero famamque et fata nepotum.

(8.729–31)

He marvels at such scenes on Vulcan's shield, the gift of his mother,
and though ignorant of the events, he rejoices in their pictures,
uplifting on his shoulder the fame and fortunes of his descendants.

Aeneas marvels and rejoices at the images on the shield; he is also ignorant. Placed in the center of the verse, the adjective *ignarus* ["ignorant"] is emphatic and meaningful.

The ignorance of the hero looks back to the poet's introduction of the shield's description and offers a stark contrast to the divine craftsman's knowledge (*haud...ignarus* ["not ignorant"], 8.627). The hero of the *Aeneid* rejoices, though he cannot fully comprehend the message of the shield's elaborate artwork, which reveals the outcome of his much proclaimed destiny and the grandeur that is due to Rome and Augustus.[20] The *ignarus* Aeneas inspects the future of his race; Vergil's omniscient reader reviews his own past. The difference in perspective perhaps reflects the complex attitude of the poet toward his subject, a mixture of emotions and conflicting passions. Vergil looked forward to the fulfillment of Aeneas' destiny, the final suppression of the madness and violence of war.

> Furor impius intus
> saeva sedens super arma et centum vinctus aënis
> post tergum nodis fremet horridus ore cruento.
>
> (1.294–96)

> within, impious Furor,
> sitting above the savage arms, bound with a hundred brazen knots
> behind his back, will roar horribly with his mouth dripping blood.

But despite the hundred brazen chains and firm imprisonment, the impious monster roars, and his mouth is still bloody. Even the establishment of peace and Augustan rule cannot remove this memory and suppress this continuing fear.

The epic poet profoundly shaped and defined anew the contemporary perception of Actium. Like Horace and Propertius, Vergil recognized the painful reality of Roman civil war (*Antonius* ["Antony"] in line 685 is explicit recognition, even if he is described as a foreign king) and expressed feelings of shame and disgust (*nefas* ["shame"] in line 688 derives from the shocking fact that the Roman married a foreign woman; *Aegyptia coniunx* ["Egyptian wife"] immediately follows the exclamation and emphatically closes the line). The clash of brazen ships in the Actian sea is a powerful and symbolic climax to the early history of Rome, represented as a continuous succession of wars and the conflict of peoples in Italy. For Vergil, the battle at Actium is neither a national crusade against Egypt to thwart the regal ambitions of the dissolute and seductive queen, as hostile propaganda distorted Rome's enemy, nor a political struggle between former allies and their adherents for supreme power and authority in Rome, as every contemporary painfully realized. Vergil's Actium mixes elements of both truth and falsehood, history and legend, propaganda and pathos. The poet's almost mythic interpretation of the past results in a mighty clash of cultures, a Roman victory over barbarian foes, supported and achieved by the assistance of the Olympian gods. To the contemporary reader of the *Aeneid,* the victory can be seen not only as a spontaneous occasion of celebration but as the fulfillment of dreams, the final cessation of hostilities, and the embarkation of a new age. The god of archery, who looks favorably on Aeneas and the Trojan race, has secured the Augustan victory with his bow. It is the last act in the destiny of the epic's hero, the motivating impulse and theme of the *Aeneid.*

The symbolic framework of Vergil's *Aeneid* did not so much reflect a public image of Actium as it created or redefined the role of this victory in Augustan political culture. Vergil gave Augustus and his regime what Actium had previously lacked, not simply poetic expression and epic grandeur (what any composer of hackneyed verses might provide), but political interpretation, meaning, and import. Viewed from the perspective of more than a decade that witnessed an enduring, if at times fragile, political success, the Augustan victory entered the Roman public consciousness as a critical moment of a collective history and national culture, what Auden disparaged as the poet's "grand panorama" of history without end. To seek the political or private concerns that motivated the epic poet in his narrative discourse on the hero's shield is a vain and disconcerting effort. Individual readers, whether ancient or modern, make their own judgments on the message and meaning of the *Aeneid*. With his untimely death in September of 19 B.C.E. Vergil left behind a great poem and, with it, the impetus of something powerful, alluring, and unreal—a political myth of Augustus and Actium.

✧ ✧ ✧

Notes

INTRODUCTION

[1]Vell. 2.86.1: *quid ille dies terrarum orbi praestiterit, ex quo in quem statum pervenerit fortuna publica, quis in hoc transcursu tam artati operis exprimere audeat?*

[2]Tac. *Ann.* 1.3.7: *iuniores post Actiacam victoriam, etiam senes plerique inter bella civium nati: quotus quisque reliquus qui rem publicam vidisset?* And *Hist.* 1.1: *postquam bellatum apud Actium atque omnem potentiam ad unum conferri pacis interfuit, magna illa ingenia cessere.*

[3]Dio 51.1.1-2: τοιαύτη τις ἡ ναυμαχία αὐτῶν τῇ δευτέρᾳ τοῦ Σεπτεμβρίου ἐγένετο. τοῦτο δὲ οὐκ ἄλλως εἶπον (οὐδὲ γὰρ εἴωθα αὐτὸ ποιεῖν) ἀλλ᾽ ὅτι τότε πρῶτον ὁ Καῖσαρ τὸ κράτος πᾶν μόνος ἔσχεν, ὥστε καὶ τὴν ἀπαρίθμησιν τῶν τῆς μοναρχίας αὐτοῦ ἐτῶν ἀπ᾽ ἐκείνης τῆς ἡμέρας ἀκριβοῦσθαι.

CHAPTER FIVE

[1]W. H. Auden, "Secondary Epic," in *Homage to Clio* (New York, 1955).

[2]G. E. Lessing, *Laocoon* (1776); trans. E. Frothingham (Boston, 1890), 116–17.

[3]Cf. P. Hardie, *Virgil's Aeneid: Cosmos and Imperium* (Oxford, 1986), 336–46, on the criticism of the shield since Lessing and on the close relationship of the Vergilian shield to the Homeric model. In response to the recent efforts by scholars to emphasize the profound differences between the two epic shield descriptions, Hardie argues that the Shield of Achilles is the "central model" for the Shield of Aeneas, and that the Vergilian shield merges the cosmic setting with the history of Rome by an "ideological equation of *cosmos* and *imperium*." For a sober criticism of Hardie's interpretation, see the review by J. Griffin, *JRS* 78 (1988), 229–33. Griffin raises serious doubts about the meaning of the "Gigantomachic" echoes that, as Hardie contends, pervade Vergil's *Aeneid*. Neither a clear nor a consistent pattern emerges in the examples Hardie cites, and more often an arresting ambiguity and blurring of sharp contrasts shape the epic poet's characterization of the hero's struggles.

[4]G. Binder, *Aeneas und Augustus. Interpretationen zum 8. Buch der Aeneis*, Beiträge zur klassischen Philologie 38 (Meisenheim am Glan, 1971), 152 (author's translation).

[5]For an informative survey of the trends in Vergilian scholarship since the nineteenth century, see S. J. Harrison, "Some Views of the *Aeneid* in the Twentieth Century," in *Oxford Readings in Vergil's Aeneid*, ed. S. J. Harrison (Oxford and New York, 1990), 1–20. Cf. also W. R. Johnson, *Darkness Visible: A Study of Vergil's Aeneid* (Berkeley and Los Angeles, 1976), 1–22.

[6]A. Parry, "The Two Voices of Vergil's *Aeneid*," *Arion* 2.4 (1963), 79.

[7]W. R. Johnson's *Darkness Visible* emphasized the violence and cruelty of Juno's intervention in human affairs. His eloquent and sensitive discussion gives perhaps the fullest expression to the pessimistic view of the *Aeneid*.

[8]For this reactionary view, see especially K. Galinsky, "The Anger of Aeneas," *AJP* 109 (1988), 321–48, and H. P. Stahl, "The Death of Turnus: Augustan Vergil and the Political Rival," in *Between Republic and Empire*, 174–211.

[9]Apart from the commentaries on the eighth book of the *Aeneid*, the most detailed discussions or individual studies on the shield's *ecphrasis* are by scholars who have emphasized the patriotic and uncomplicated tone of the passage; see especially C. Becker, "Der Schild des Aeneas," *WS* 77 (1964), 111–27; Binder, *Aeneas und Augustus*, 150–282; and Hardie, *Virgil's Aeneid*, 336–76, whose original and provocative work on the poet's incorporation of cosmological models in his conceptualization of Roman history and Augustan imperialism represented a new direction in Vergilian scholarship. For an imaginative realization of the illustrations and their placement on an actual shield, cf. D. A. West, "*Cernere erat*: The Shield of Aeneas," *PVS* 15 (1975–76), 1–7; reprinted in *Oxford Readings in Vergil's Aeneid*, 295–304.

✧ ✧ ✧

[10]V. Pöschl, *The Art of Vergil: Image and Symbol in the Aeneid*, trans. G. Seligson (Ann Arbor, Mich., 1962), 140; originally published as *Die Dichtkunst Virgils. Bild und Symbol in der Äneis* (Innsbruck-Vienna, 1950).

[11]Cf. Putnam, *Poetry of the Aeneid*, 147–49, who observes an implicit allusion to Lucretius in this opening scene.

[12]Serv. *Comm. in Verg. Aen.* 8.631: *sane totus hic locus Ennianus est.*

✧ ✧ ✧

[13]Cf. D. C. Feeney's illuminating discussion on the ambiguity in the name *Scipiadas* in *Aen.* 6.843 in "History and Revelation in Vergil's Underworld," *PCPS* 32 (1986), 13–14. Feeney persuasively argues that the poet's pointed description in verses 842–43 offers multiple identifications and allusions to four generations of Scipiones.

[14]For Octavian's propaganda against Antony, see K. Scott, "Political Propaganda of 44–30 B.C.," and, more recently, P. Wallmann, *Triumviri Rei Publicae Constituendae. Untersuchungen zur politischen Propaganda im Zweiten Triumvirat (43–30 v. Chr.)* (Frankfurt, 1989), 249–350.

[15]It has been plausibly suggested that Vergil borrowed the phrase *ope barbarica* from Ennius. The phrase occurs not in Ennius' epic, the *Annales*, but in one of his tragedies, the *Andromacha*. Here too Ennius employs it to describe the splendor that was once of Troy (*O pater, o patria, o Priami domus / saeptum altisono cardine templum / vidi ego te adstante[m] ope barbarica / tectis caelatis laqueatis / auro eboro instructam regifice*, Vahlen *Scenica* 92–96).

[16]For a discussion of the passages where twin snakes appear in the *Aeneid*, cf. Binder, *Aeneas und Augustus*, 241–42.

[17]Hardie, *Virgil's Aeneid*, 336–76.

[18]The phrases come from David Quint's stimulating essay on the influence of the shield's *ecphrasis* upon modern European epic in *Epic and Empire: Politics and Generic Form from Virgil to Milton* (Princeton, 1993), 37. In the catalog that he has arranged for the binary oppositions underlying the poet's description of the Actian battle, Quint attributes the gods representing chaos (Mars, Dirae, and Discordia) to the forces of Antony and Cleopatra, even though Vergil places them directly in the midst of the two battle lines (*medio in certamine*, line 700), and though nothing in the poet's description of the god or the events of battle supports the view that Apollo serves as a symbol of cosmic order and rationality.

[19]Hardie, *Virgil's Aeneid*, 99, is tempted to see the goddess Minerva as the "representative of reason and wisdom, fighting on the side of the legitimate champion of Rome." He implausibly suggests that the Pheidian statue of the goddess in the Parthenon, whose shield depicted reliefs of an Amazonomachy and Gigantomachy on its exterior and interior panels, respectively, influenced the poet's decision to include Minerva among the fighting Olympian participants. For such an interpretation, see R. Cohon, "Vergil and Pheidias: The Shield of Aeneas and of Athena Parthenos," *Vergilius* 37 (1991), 22–30.

✧ ✧ ✧

[20]See Johnson, *Darkness Visible*, 111–14, for an illuminating analysis of "the wonder, the ignorance, and the joy"; cf. Hardie, *Virgil's Aeneid*, 369–76, who examines Aeneas' "Atlantean" shouldering of the cosmic shield.

GRIEVING MOTHERS
AND THE COSTS OF ATTACHMENT

Wiltshire's book, *Public and Private in Vergil's Aeneid*, from which the selection here is taken, extends Parry's observation about public and private voices into a study of the whole epic. In this excerpt from the chapter, "Grieving Mothers and the Costs of Attachment," Wiltshire analyzes the story of Nisus and Euryalus in book 9, particularly in passages at lines 216–218, 283–292, 296–302, 481–92, with reference as well to the pair's first appearance in book 5. In addition, comparing the simile of the wolf at *Aeneid* 9.59–64 with its Homeric model, Wiltshire observes that Vergil introduces the mother of the animal young into the Homeric simile, "beyond the necessity of the context." Vergil also uses the mother image later in the book and elsewhere in the poem, notably regarding the Vulcan scene in book 8 and Juturna in book 12. Wiltshire concludes that, in reference to many of the deaths in the epic, Vergil "introduces the 'lesser' world of affiliative bonds and sacrificial affection," in significant contrast to the conventional heroic context. (Ed.)

> Women and poets see the truth
>   arrive,
> Then it is acted out,
> The lives are lost, and all the
>   newsboys shout.
>   MURIEL RUKEYSER

*C*arolyn Heilbrun writes of the tendency of men longing for the honor of a past culture to fail to mention the costs of that culture to women.[1] Vergil is the clear exception who does not forget. In every book of the *Aeneid,* whether in simile, allusion, or narrative detail, the persistent laments of mothers bear witness to the importance of human attachments and the consequences of violence to those bonds. Vergil affirms the private claims of the close community, of family and maintenance of the cycles of life, as inseparable from the heroic achievements of history and Rome.

MOTHERS IN THE SIMILES

Often what is most distinctive about him emerges when Vergil is working within the frame of his tradition, especially the Homeric tradition. The epic similes of the

Reprinted from PUBLIC & PRIVATE IN VERGIL'S *AENEID*, by Susan Ford Wiltshire (Amherst: University of Massachusetts Press, 1989), copyright © 1989 by The University of Massachusetts Press.

Aeneid frequently provide evidence of the poet's concern with the plight of mothers. At 9.59–64 Turnus is compared with a wolf stalking a sheepfold for prey, while the Trojans, following the orders of the absent Aeneas, hover inside the walls. The wolf rages at the lambs just out of reach, maddened by prolonged hunger and thirst.

> Just as a wolf, pelted by wind and rain, prowls at
> midnight around the crowded sheepfold, howling at
> the fencerails. The lambs bleat from their safe place
> under their mothers, while the wolf, fierce and
> unslaked in his fury, rages at them out of reach,
> driven wild by his long-unfilled hunger and throat
> thirsty for blood.

> ac veluti pleno lupus insidiatus ovili
> cum fremit ad caulas ventos perpessus et imbris
> nocte super media; tuti sub matribus agni
> balatum exercent, ille asper et improbus ira
> saevit in absentis; collecta fatigat edendi
> ex longo rabies et siccae sanguine fauces
> 9.59–64

The figure is familiar from Homer. At *Iliad* 11.548–55 Ajax is likened to a hungry lion, harrying the oxen fenced in their pens; the same simile is attached to Menelaus at *Iliad* 17.657–64. Sarpedon is seen as a lion stalking the sheepfolds as he attacks the Trojan defenses at *Iliad* 12.299–306. Similar analogies are made of the Myrmidons as wolves at *Iliad* 16.156–63 and of Odysseus as a lion after oxen or sheep at *Odyssey* 6.130–34. In none of these cases, however, does Homer make any mention of mothers or their young. All other components of Vergil's simile are precedented in their Homeric models except the bleating lambs under their mothers: *tuti sub matribus agni / balatum exercent* ["The lambs bleat from their safe place under their mothers"] (9.61–62).

As if to underscore his variant, Vergil reintroduces the motif later in the same book. Turnus is still the predator, seizing the young Lycus and tearing him from the safety of the Trojan walls just as an eagle seizes a hare or a wolf seizes a lamb:

> Just as when an eagle of Jove flies to the sky with a
> hare or a snowy white swan in its talons, or when a
> wolf of Mars steals a lamb from its pens, sought by its
> mother with many bleatings.

> qualis ubi aut leporem aut candenti corpore cycnum
> sustulit alta petens pedibus Iovis armiger uncis,
> quaesitum aut matri multis balatibus agnum
> Martius a stabulis rapuit lupus.
> 9.563–66

Again, the simile incorporates more than is necessary to the characterization of Turnus as a ravening warrior. Lycus may quite appropriately be seen as the seized lamb, but at no point does the lament of the bereft dam intersect with the substance of the narrative. The grieving mother is a Vergilian gloss on the entire scene, an expression of the awareness that there are consequences to violence and that it is mothers by whom these consequences are borne.

In other similes, too, reference is made to mothers beyond the necessity of the context.

✧ ✧ ✧

In Book 12, Juturna's dartings on the battlefield in aid of her brother Turnus are compared with those of a swallow flying about the halls of an atrium:

> As when a black swallow flies through the expanses of
> a rich man's abode, searching the high colonnades for
> bits and morsels for her chirping brood, singing now
> around the empty porticoes, now by the quiet pools:

> nigra velut magnas domini cum divitis aedes
> pervolat et pennis alta atria lustrat hirundo
> pabula parva legens nidisque loquacibus escas,
> et nunc porticibus vacuis, nunc umida circum
> stagna sonat:
> 12.437–77

Juturna has taken on the guise of Metiscus, Turnus's driver, and dashes all over the field in her effort to confuse the issue and save Turnus from death. The point of comparison is the swift, darting motion of both swallow and sister. Many elements in the simile, however, do not correspond.[2] The narrative context is martial, but the setting of the simile is domestic. *Magnas, divitis, aedes,* and *alta atria* ["expanses," "rich," "abode," "high colonades"] all evoke a richness far distant from the present scene; the *umida stagna* are quiet pools inconsonant with the din of battle. Most striking of all is the detailed description of the mother's efforts to find food for her young: *pabula parva legens nidisque loquacibus escas* ["searching for bits and morsels for her chirping brood"]. Line 475, with its carefully worked alliteration, euphony, and diction, becomes the centerpiece of the simile.

The noncorresponding elements are instructive. By interposing such a simile in this context, Vergil contrasts war with peace, chaos with tranquility. But he does more than that, for the swallow is portrayed not only as a peaceful creature but also in the process of feeding her young, nurturing the next generation. This cyclical activity interjected into the linear events of the battle emphasizes the difference between them. The sister Juturna and the mother swallow demonstrate the importance of sustaining life even in the middle of war.

A similar effect occurs in the startling simile in Book 8, in which Vulcan is compared with a faithful, dutiful wife:

> When the first ease of the passing night rouses the
> sleeper, straightway a woman whose lot it is to
> support a modest existence by spinning and weaving
> stirs the ashes and slumbering coals so as to add hours
> from the night to the time of her toil. She pushes her

helpers to finish the day's work by lamplight; her
labor keeps her home chaste for her husband and
nurtures her children. With the same intent and
alacrity the smithy god rises from his couch to take up
the tools of his trade.

> Inde ubi prima quies medio iam noctis abactae
> curriculo expulerat somnum, cum femina primum,
> cui tolerare colo vitam tenuique Minerva
> impositum, cinerem et sopitos suscitat ignis
> noctem addens operi, famulasque ad lumina longo
> exercet penso, castum ut servare cubile
> coniugis et possit parvos educere natos:
> haud secus ignipotens nec tempore segnior illo
> mollibus e stratis opera ad fabrilia surgit.
> 8.407–15

The obligation of raising young children (*parvos educere natos*) is made emphatic by
its place at the end of the simile. Conjugal duty forms the primary comparison
(*coniugis* ["of his wife"], 406; *coniugis* ["for her husband"], 413), but once again the
simile signifies more. Vulcan's piety will result in the production of weaponry for
war for Aeneas, but the process of its preparation is compared with the domestic
tasks required daily of mothers in order to raise their young. Although Vergil did
not create this image out of nothing,[3] it is striking in its context. Williams speaks of
the sympathy and pathos here,[4] but there is more than mere pathos: with this collocation Vergil once again inserts directly into war and the preparation for war a
poignant reminder of responsibilities to care for the next generation.

❖ ❖ ❖

THE MOTHER OF EURYALUS

Only one mother among the Trojan survivors is prepared to face history by
enduring the journey to its end. We do not even know her name, only that she is the
mother of Euryalus. We are partially prepared for her lament at the death of her son
in Book 9 by the revolt of the other Trojan women in Book 5. While Ascanius is
leading his young peers through their equestrian paces, the women, keeping their
place but not their peace, are in a mutinous state. Even before Juno sends Iris, in the
guise of the old woman Beroe, to provoke them into setting fire to the ships, they
are grieving the limits of their endurance. Their desolation, hardened now by the
death of Anchises, oppresses them as they think of the seas yet to be crossed:

> But at a distance alone on the seashore the Trojan
> women grieved the dead Anchises, weeping too as
> they glared together at the ominous sea. The same
> thought was shared by all, weary as they were of the
> waves and the water still to be sailed: They prayed for
> a home, dreading the toil of another journey at sea.

at procul in sola secretae Troades acta
amissum Anchisen flebant, cunctaeque profundum
pontum aspectabant flentes. heu tot vada fessis
et tantum superesse maris, vox omnibus una;
urbem orant, taedet pelagi perferre laborem.
5.613–17

Procul, sola, and *secretae* ["at a distance," "alone," "separate"] in the first line all point to the isolation of the women; the parallel metrical patterns, similar elisions, and repetition of *flebant* and *flentes* ["grieved," "weeping"] in the following two lines underscore the extent of their despair. They are weary of the sea, weary of effort, weary of enduring; their prayer is for a city — now it hardly matters where. The mother of Euryalus is not mentioned by name as being among the Troades, but her presence is implicit in the *vox omnibus una* ["The same thought was shared by all"] of line 616.

What the other mothers want is not a homeland but a home, and it is a home that they get: *hic domus est...vobis* ["here is your home"], announces Beroe/Iris at 5.638. The former is a political achievement, the latter a private arrangement. It is the second that is worked out in the settlement with Acestes. Those who choose to stay, says Vergil, are those who have no need of fame: *animos nil magnae laudis egentis* ["spirits that lack any need of great fame"] (5.751).[5]

We do not know why the mother of Euryalus chose to endure the hard journey to Italy, but Vergil prepares for the impact of her son's death by repeated references to her even before Nisus and Euryalus set out on their ill-fated expedition. Nisus, the elder of the pair, poses the excursion in the first place but later tries to dissuade Euryalus from joining him. His grounds are several: as the younger, Euryalus should survive to redeem Nisus's body and offer the final rites, should anything go wrong; in addition, the death of Nisus alone would not cause so much suffering for Euryalus's mother, who alone foreswore safe settlement in Sicily in order to follow her son:

Nor would I be cause of so much grief for your
mother, my lad, who alone of all mothers dared to
follow you here, scorning the safe walls of Acestes.

neu matri miserae tanti sim causa doloris,
quae te sola, puer, multis e matribus ausa
persequitur, magni nec moenia curat Acestae.
9.216–18

This episode is crucial in the maturing of Ascanius. As the pair approaches the caucus of Trojan leaders, trying to determine what move to make next, it is Iulus who admits them and orders Nisus to speak. Iulus is fully in control throughout the passage, functioning effectively as a substitute for his absent father, Aeneas. He exercises the power of gift-giving by his promises to Nisus of spoils won by his father, including, significantly, a crater given him by Dido, together with future booty to be won in Italy: Turnus's horse and armor, women, prisoners, land. His promise to Euryalus is a more personal one, the assurance of a future relationship between them as close friends and agemates, the glory of one accruing to both whether in war or peace (9.275–80). Euryalus's response might be interpreted as an adroit evasion, in view of his relationship with Nisus. More to the point is his larger concern for his mother:

> Beyond all else I beg of you this
> one favor: my aged mother is with me, a woman of
> Priam's race, who in her grief at my going would not
> remain home in Troy nor settle in the realm of
> Acestes. Without speaking I am leaving her now,
> unaware of the perils I face (I swear by night and
> your right hand), for I cannot bear the tears of a
> mother. But you, I beg, take care of her and support
> her when she's left all alone. Allow me to take from
> you this one hope, and bravely I'll face every danger.

> sed te super omnia dona
> unum oro: genetrix Priami de gente vetusta
> est mihi, quam miseram tenuit non Ilia tellus
> mecum excedentem, non moenia regis Acestae.
> hanc ego nunc ignaram huius quodcumque pericli
> inque salutatam linquo (nox et tua testis
> dextera), quod nequeam lacrimas perferre parentis.
> at tu, oro, solare inopem et succurre relictae.
> hanc sine me spem ferre tui, audentior ibo
> in casus omnis.
> 9.283–92

Euryalus's request of Ascanius returns attention to parental and filial ties. The contrast between the gifts Ascanius offers and the one for which Euryalus yearns is stark: ... *super omnia dona /unum oro* ["Beyond all else I beg this one favor"]. The mother is commended to Ascanius first through the obligations of family relationship: Servius comments that the mention of her kinship with Priam is apt in that Ascanius is the grandson of Priam through Creusa.[6] Neither Troy nor the settlement in Sicily dissuaded her from following her son, miserable as she emphatically was from the outset.[7] *Hanc* and *ego* ["her," "I"] are juxtaposed only in the text of line 287; the separation of child from parent is made more emphatic by the long hyperbaton of *ego* and *linquo* ["I am leaving"] and by the startling tmesis of *inque salutatam* ["and unaddressed"] in line 288. Euryalus feels such great anxiety at his sudden departure that he justifies it by saying that he cannot bear his mother's tears. His own audacity, he says, will be enhanced if Ascanius is able to promise solace for the mother about to be bereaved: "Allow me to take from you this one hope, and bravely I'll face every danger" (9.291–92).

The mesh of the personal with the public here, the connecting of family bonds with martial exploit, inverts the Homeric pattern in a striking way. Hector fights in the *Iliad* in spite of the sanctions evoked by his wife, mother, and father, the people nearest to him. Achilles fights in spite of the grief of his mother, certain as they both are of the consequences. In the end the warrior ethic for them both is highly personalistic and separable from the fabric of family relationships. Both, of course, are repeatedly summoned into battle by insults done to them, harm done to an intimate friend such as Patroclus, for example, or to such a brother as Polydorus, but the controlling motivation is always finally the hero's own honor, his own estimation of his position and worth.

In the Nisus-Euryalus episode Vergil maintains parity between family and fame, between bond and achievement. The two do not merge, their coexistence is not even peaceful — it cannot be — but the claims of one on the other are powerful and exacting. The impact of Euryalus's request upon the Trojans is so great that they weep. Iulus is stricken because the plea reminds him of the devotion he feels for his father as his own sole surviving parent: *ante omnis pulcher Iulus, / atque animum patriae strinxit pietatis imago* ["before everyone lovely Iulus, / and the image of familial piety touched his spirit"] (9.293–94).

Thus, instead of discounting familial claims, Iulus accepts and incorporates them. The only proper reward for such a dangerous mission, he assures Euryalus, is that only the name "Creusa" shall be lacking in Iulus's future relationship with Euryalus's mother. Further, the prizes he has promised will go to her if Euryalus should not survive:

> "Be assured that your rewards will correspond to your
> risk. Your mother shall be as a mother to me, lacking
> only the name of 'Creusa.' No small reward suffices
> for such a parent. Whatever the outcome of this
> venture, I swear by my life, as my father always
> swore, that the honors I promised you upon a safe
> return shall remain in trust for your mother and heirs."

> "sponde digna tuis ingentibus omnia coeptis.
> namque erit ista mihi genetrix nomenque Creusae
> solum defuerit, nec partum gratia talem
> parva manet. casus factum quicumque sequentur,
> per caput hoc iuro, per quod pater ante solebat:
> quae tibi polliceor reduci rebusque secundis,
> haec eadem matrique tuae generique manebunt."
> 9.296–302

Nisus and Euryalus imitate the heroic action of the *Iliad*. The difference between heroic action in Homer's poem and Vergil's is that in the *Aeneid,* mothers mourn. As Fama ["Rumor"] brings the report to the mother of Euryalus that her son has died, a chill terror overwhelms her and the shuttle drops from her hands.

Weaving is traditionally the work of women in antiquity, and the reference here brings to mind an important Homeric precedent. In *Iliad* 22 a relatively insignificant Trojan woman, a princess of some sort perhaps but nameless, similarly drops her shuttle, as does Andromache upon learning of the death of her Hector.[8] But another part of the passage reminds us also of Dido and the losses incurred in Book 4. The scream of Euryalus's mother (*femineo ululatu* ["with a female scream"], 9.477) is the same as those echoing over Book 4 (168, 609, 667); she is *infelix* ["unlucky"] (9.477), just as is Dido, and like her, she tears her hair (4.590, 9.478) as she rushes to the walls, mindless of men and arms: *non illa virum, non illa pericli / telorumque memor* ["not mindful she of men, nor of danger / or arms"] (9.479–80). For this mother the official themes of the epic — *arma virumque cano* ["arms and the man I sing"] — cease to exist. She experiences only the costs.

The mother's grief takes the form of unanswerable questions (as did Dido's at 4.590–604) as she addresses her son:

> Is this you I gaze upon, Euryalus? You the final
> respite of my own old age, have you chosen to leave
> me alone, cruel son? Was it not permitted to a grief-
> stricken mother to say a final farewell as you
> embarked on such perils? Ah, now you lie in a foreign
> field, booty for the dogs and vultures of Latium! I,
> your mother, could not attend your rites, close your
> eyes, wash your wounds, cover you for a shroud with
> the cloak I was working night and day to complete, a
> solace of weaving for my old woman's grief. Where
> shall I go? What land now will hold your torn limbs
> and poor corpse? Is this all that is left of you, son, for
> me? Was it for this that I followed you over land and sea?

> hunc ego te, Euryale, aspicio? tune ille senectae
> sera meae requies, potuisti linquere solam,
> crudelis? nec te sub tanta pericula missum
> adfari extremum miserae data copia matri?
> heu, terra ignota canibus data praeda Latinis
> alitibusque iaces! nec te tua funere mater
> produxi pressive oculos aut vulnera lavi,
> veste tegens tibi quam noctes festina diesque
> urgebam, et tela curas solabar anilis.
> quo sequar? aut quae nunc artus avulsaque membra
> et funus lacerum tellus habet? hoc mihi de te
> nate, refers? hoc sum terraque marique secuta?
> 9.481–92

Vergil lavishes elaborate detail on the mother's lament. Lines 484 and 485 startle with their disparate similarities—the metrical pattern precisely the same, elisions occurring in the same position, but the sentiments contradicting each other: the first, the thwarting of a final farewell; the second, the boy's body as booty for Latin dogs in a foreign field.

The contiguity of *ego / te* ["I / you"] is especially poignant. These two words appear together seven times in the *Aeneid*, four times in contexts in which separation by death has occurred or is pending. In 4.333 Aeneas begins his final address to Dido with *ego te*; in 6.692 the shade of the dead Anchises addresses Aeneas in the same terms; finally, in a scene closely paralleling the grief of Euryalus's mother, Amata in Book 12 implores Turnus not to resist the Trojans further: *"Turne, per has ego te lacrimas…unum oro"* ["Turnus, by these tears of mine you…I pray one thing"] (12.56 and 60). Turnus, like Euryalus, is perceived by a mother as the surety for her old age—*senectae…requies* (12.57–58). The proximity of the pronouns in each case makes more emphatic the break in the relationship.

The term *crudelis* ["cruel"] exacerbates the sense of separation. Aeneas charged his mother with cruelty in Book 1 when he needed human contact and she offered only triviality: *crudelis tu quoque* ["cruel, you too"], 1.407. *Crudelis* is Dido's epithet for Aeneas when she learns of his imminent departure (4.311). Anna cries *crudelis* as well (4.681) as she comprehends the suicide of her sister. Again, it is Aeneas himself who is *crudelis* (4.661), the cruel Dardanian whom Dido curses at her death. The words *Dardanus* and *mortis* ["of death"] bracket line 4.662.

Among the stages of the grieving process is negotiation, and for a moment the mother of Euryalus engages in the "if only" questions of her loss. Why, she asks, was she not permitted to say goodbye to her son as he embarked upon such great perils? Why could she not have conducted his last rites herself? Why could she not have covered his body with the cloak she had been weaving for him?

WOMEN'S WORK, WOMEN'S GIFTS

In the ancient world, gift-giving between or among men is a public transaction. In the *Aeneid,* gifts given by women extend the sphere of the private domain. Among men, the status of individuals is at stake with the gift; women's gifts replace competition with community. One form of gift-giving manipulates power; the other repairs the social fabric.

The cloak woven by Euryalus's mother is not the first connection Vergil makes, nor will it be the last, between death and the handwork of women. The garments given by Andromache to Ascanius, surely woven originally for her son Astyanax, were embroidered with designs in gold thread: *fert picturatas auri subtemine vestis* ["she brings garments embroidered with gold thread"] (3.483). When Aeneas kills Lausus in Book 10, he plunges his sword through the boy's tunic, similarly woven with gold by his mother: *transiit...tunicam molli mater quam neverat auro* ["it passed through...the tunic that his mother had woven with soft gold"] (10.817–18). Finally, Pallas's shroud will be two matching coats, made for Aeneas by Dido and worked with patterns of gold:

> Then Aeneas brought forth two cloaks heavy with
> purple and gold, which Dido once, long ago, made for
> him joyfully with her own hands, embroidered finely
> with gold.

> tum geminas vestis auroque ostroque rigentis
> extulit Aeneas, quas illi laeta laborum
> ipsa suis quondam manibus Sidonia Dido
> fecerat et tenui telas discreverat auro.
> 11.72–75

In each of these cases the private world of family affections — of women's work and women's love — intrudes into the events of history. War and the costs of history are hateful to those who give birth and nurture.[9] Honor and empire will finally bring Euryalus, Lausus, and Pallas to their deaths. None of these deaths, however, does Vergil leave unattended. Into each of them he introduces the "lesser" world of affiliative bonds and sacrificial affection, represented by beautiful garments woven by loving hands.

In the *Aeneid* the world's good is death to mothers and others who cherish community. But the detail Vergil lavishes on the mourning of those deaths attaches both meaning and questions to the grief. The suffering of mothers measures the achievements of heroes by the losses they cost.

❖ ❖ ❖

Notes

[1]Carolyn Heilbrun, *Reinventing Womanhood* (New York, 1979), 135.

❖ ❖ ❖

[2]R. D. Williams, ed., *The Aeneid of Virgil, Books 7-12* (Basingstoke and London, 1972), points out that the proportion of nonsimilar elements is unusually large: 469, *ad* 12.47ff.

[3]Partial precedents occur at Homer, *Il.* 12.433f.; Apoll. Rhod. 4.1062ff., 3.291ff.

[4]Williams, ed., *Aeneid 7-12*, 255, *ad* 8.408ff.

❖ ❖ ❖

[5]Only too late did they decide that they wanted to leave after all: *fugae perferre laborem* (5.769).

[6]Serv., *Aen. ad loc* 9.282: *nam Ascanius nepos est Priami per Creusam.*

[7]Serv., *Aen. ad loc* 9.283: *quae sic impatienter diligit filium.*

[8]*Iliad* 22.448.

[9]Elizabeth Block, "The Theme of Parents and Children in the *Aeneid*," *Ramus* 9.2 (1980), 130, explains: "Vergil uses children, and the relationship of protection and vulnerability between parents and children, symbolically in the *Aeneid* to represent the future and its debt to the past; at the same time, he uses the child as symbol of the sacrifice that is necessary to this future...." See also the discussion of Grace Starry West, "Andromache and Dido," *American Journal of Philology* 104 (1983), 257-67.

Herbert W. Benario

THE TENTH BOOK OF THE AENEID

Benario's reading of book 10 follows Vergil's language closely, and he places the book within the context of the work as a whole. *Aeneid* 10 is especially important because it lays the groundwork for the story of Pallas, Evander's son. Evander entrusted Pallas to Aeneas, and Pallas was later killed by Turnus. Pallas became, through Aeneas' memory of him, the cause of Turnus' death at the end of the poem. The way readers understand the hero Aeneas in these relationships is central to interpretations of the work. (Ed.)

In the vast range of Vergilian studies, the tenth book of the Aeneid has been more completely ignored than any of its companions.[1] A review of the bibliographies of Mambelli and Duckworth[2] reveals how little attention has been devoted to the book that contains several of Vergil's finest scenes, and comprehensive studies of the author and his work tend to treat it with a certain disdain. It is my belief, however, that it deserves better than that.

I am not here concerned with the structure, the architecture of the book; this has recently been often and well treated.[3] I shall rather comment upon some of the things that the poet says and to what they may allude.

The book opens with a *concilium deorum* ["council of the gods"] (1–117); the second word of the first line is *interea* ["meanwhile"], indicating the simultaneity of this scene with action in the previous book.[4] Nowhere else in the poem do the gods meet in assembly; such a lofty beginning bespeaks the importance of the book. First Jupiter complains that the other gods have ignored his instructions to stay out of the conflict on earth; then Venus and Juno plead their respective claims, and Jupiter concludes by displaying seeming neutrality: *fata viam invenient* ["the fates will find the way"] (113).[5] He of course knows what *necessitas* ["necessity"] will bring. There is not much great poetry in this scene, but there are several striking effects.

Venus' plea recalls both the Sibyl's vision to Aeneas and Jupiter's own prophecy to her. Venus laments that a second army (27) opposes the Trojans, although the Sibyl had forecast this (6.88–90) and Aeneas had not been surprised or shocked by the revelation (6.103–5). Venus certainly knew the difficulties that her son would have to face, but she expresses resentment here, unfairly, and compounds her emotional outburst by adding Tydides to the enemies of the Trojans. Her plea, calculated to win Jupiter's sympathy rather than to withstand argument, is demolished almost point by point by Juno, who has much the better of the argument. Jupiter tacitly

---

Herbert Benario, "The Tenth Book of the *Aeneid*," *Transactions of the American Philological Association* 98 (1967) 23–36. Reprinted by permission of the American Philological Association.

admits this, since he does not here speak out for the side that he knows will triumph and that he himself favors.

As her last bidding, Venus requests that she be allowed to save Ascanius from the debacle. She no longer asks to do the same for Aeneas (perhaps because she now fears him lost: *si* ["if"] in 44). Her dream is reduced from the lofty hopes of empire to the salvation of her grandson: *nil super imperio moveor* ["I am not moved by empire"] (42). Here is her great concession, and here is her great rebuke of Jupiter, for in words reminiscent of the latter's promise of empire, *imperium sine fine dedi* ["I gave empire without end"] (1.279), she now denies his promise and her hope.[6] The metrical pattern of the two clauses is identical. At this point, it seems that the great task that was the founding of the Roman race has ended abortively, beleaguered in the Trojan camp.

Juno's response is considerably briefer and much more powerful than Venus' whining, and the reaction of the remaining gods, their doubts and hesitation, is presented in a passage rendered weighty and majestic by frequent instances of alliteration (96–103). Nor do Jupiter's remarks disappoint the expectation of gravity. The key lines are 107–8, marked by the effect of the spondaic beginning of 107, underscored by the three monosyllabic words that appear first, the initial *q*'s, the unusual form *secat* ["follows"], the rare monosyllabic line ending, the unusual metrical pattern of the last three words,[7] the archaic form *fuat* ["if he be"], and the uncommon elision in the fifth foot.

Line 118 begins with another *interea* ["meanwhile"], to shift the reader's attention to the contemporaneous struggle on earth. Aeneas is returning during the night with the newly-won Etruscan allies, and himself holds the helm, with Pallas at his side (159–62).

The relationship between the two that is indicated by these lines is of the utmost importance. Evander, on the site of Pallanteum, had entrusted his son to Aeneas with these words (8.514–17):

> hunc tibi praeterea, spes et solacia nostri,
> Pallanta adiungam; sub te tolerare magistro
> militiam et grave Martis opus, tua cernere facta
> adsuescat, primis et te miretur ab annis.

> ["I shall entrust him to you, moreover, my hope and comfort, Pallas; take him under your guidance, let him learn to endure war and the weighty work of Mars, to watch your deeds, let him admire you from his early years."]

Pallas here is learning from the older man, and also, like Dido (1.753–56), is asking about Aeneas' experiences and sufferings in the past. Only those with whom Aeneas becomes deeply involved emotionally bid him relate his *infandum dolorem* ["unspeakable grief"] (2.3). Aeneas stands *in loco parentis* ["in the place of a parent"] to Pallas: he is *pater* ["father"], Pallas is *filius* and *contubernalis* ["son" and "tent-mate"], and Aeneas is fully conscious of the trust shown him, for after the death of Pallas, who is to him a maturer Ascanius, his first thoughts are of that faith and trust (515–17):

> Pallas, Euander, in ipsis
> omnia sunt oculis, mensae quas advena primas
> tunc adiit, dextraeque datae.

["Pallas, Evander, everything is before his eyes, the tables to which he first came as a stranger, the right hands given."]

There thus seems to be no doubt in Vergil's mind about the relationship of the two. Aeneas is as deeply wounded as he would be by the loss of his own son.[8]

Pallas, however, has not yet had the opportunity to prove himself worthy of the highest esteem. This he will be able to do only in battle, and Vergil proceeds to set the scene for this. He invokes the Muses to assist him in the enumeration of the Etruscan forces (163–214), and the next section resumes the narrative. Aeneas, the new Palinurus, is visited by supernatural beings as Palinurus had been by Somnus ["Sleep"] at the end of Book 5; the outcome in the former instance had been fatal, here it is joyful and optimistic. Palinurus is put to sleep, Cymodocea makes certain that Aeneas is awake. The parallel is obvious (cf. 5.852–53 and 217–18). And Somnus, disguised as Phorbas, addresses Palinurus as *Iaside* ["son of Iasus"] (5.843), while Cymodocea does not use the patronymic *Anchisiade* ["son of Anchises"],[9] but the even loftier substitute indicating Aeneas' divine parentage, *deum gens* ["race of the gods"] (228), which gains in emphasis from the monosyllabic line ending.

When Cymodocea finishes her story and report of events, Aeneas, although not fully aware of the import of the occurrence (*inscius* ["unknowing"], 249), prays to Cybele for her favor and support. Then follows the first scene to have immediate effect upon the struggle between the Trojans and the Italian forces: the return of Aeneas and his assumption of command. He orders his company to prepare themselves for battle and then shows himself at a distance to his besieged followers (258–62). He stands high in the prow, *stans celsa in puppi*, exactly as the great figure sculpted on the shield that he brandishes on his left arm; Augustus, *stans celsa in puppi* (8.680), goes against the enemy toward destined triumph.[10] So, we know, Aeneas will triumph too; the victory may be delayed, but it will come.[11]

Turnus, however, is not dismayed, even by the flames that mark Aeneas' helmet and shield.[12] He displays his accustomed bravado but no indication of understanding that the outcome may depend upon more than his own prowess (*audentis Fortuna iuvat* ["Fortune favors those who dare"], 284). Aeneas' allies then land, inspired by Tarchon's eager ramming of his ship against the shore, and are met by a spirited resistance led by Turnus himself.

An Homeric battle scene follows; killing is routine, bodies pile up, Aeneas, basically passive, hurls weapon after weapon. But the outcome is inconclusive; neither side has an advantage, and the siege of the Trojan camp has not been broken (360–61):

haud aliter Troianae acies aciesque Latinae
concurrunt, haeret pede pes densusque viro vir.

["not otherwise do the Trojan lines and the lines of Latins rush together, foot clings to foot and, close together, man to man."]

To a large degree, the book thus far has been only expository; little or nothing has been presented to engage the emotions. The story of the poem has not advanced at all, with the sole, yet important, exception of Aeneas' return to the battlefield. The remainder of the book is largely devoted to three of Vergil's finest character portrayals, and it is these, to my mind, that give the book its qualities of greatness.

The deadlock of line 361 is immediately broken by the arrival of the Arcadian cavalry, under the leadership of Pallas, who, we must assume, had gone, after landing with Aeneas, to join the horsemen who had traveled overland. His hero's role begins at once and he occupies stage-center until 509.

The cavalry, forced to fight afoot by the unfavorable terrain, are being routed until Pallas, by word and deed, causes them to recover their spirit. His first words mark his quality (369–78); the words *patriae* in 371 and *patria* in 374 ["father's, fatherland"], although different parts of speech, have the same larger sense. Pallas fights for family and country in the same way that Aeneas does; personal glory, though sought, is secondary. When he is first introduced in Book 8, he is characterized as *audax* ["daring"] (110), and he now displays his eager boldness in battle, *haec ait, et medius densos prorumpit in hostis* ["thus he speaks, and dashes directly into the midst of the enemy close arrayed"] (379) and *ire prior Pallas, si qua fors adiuvet ausum / viribus imparibus* ["Pallas goes first, if any fortune would aid him, brave in unequal strength"] (458–59).

Pallas' aristeia turns the tide (397–98); he is described here, and also in 426, as a *vir* ["man, warrior"], a misleading designation, for he is a *vir* only in relation to his inferiors, not to his betters. The picture that Vergil draws of him is of a *iuvenis*, a young man sent to do a man's job, to which his strength is not equal. But here the *vir* is aided by the *omnis virtus* ["entire valor"] of the allies (410) and then he kills his last man, Halaesus.

There now appears a match for Pallas, a perfect match in every respect, Lausus, in some senses the most winning character Vergil drew in the entire poem. His good looks and his skill in taming horses and hunting wild beasts have already been mentioned, but emphasis was placed upon his misfortune in having Mezentius as his father (7.649–54). Here, unfrightened by Pallas' prowess, he rallies his forces, *pars ingens belli* ["a huge part of the battle"] (427). The scales on both sides are now in balance, *ducibusque et viribus aequis* ["equal in leaders and men"] (431). These words can be construed in a double sense; the more obvious is that the *agmina* ["troop lines"] have equal strength and leaders who are worthy of each other. Or we may see herein an instance of hendiadys, referring to the comparable ability of the two young men. This equality is emphasized by *hinc...hinc* ["from here...from here"] and by their similar fates (433–38):

> hinc Pallas instat et urget,
> hinc contra Lausus, nec multum discrepat aetas,
> egregii forma, sed quis Fortuna negarat
> in patriam reditus. ipsos concurrere passus
> haud tamen inter se magni regnator Olympi;
> mox illos sua fata manent maiore sub hoste.

["From here Pallas presses and pursues, from here on the other side Lausus, not much apart in age, excellent in form, but to both Fortune denies the return home. The ruler of great Olympus does not permit them though to engage battle with each other; soon their fates will await each of them at the hand of a greater foe."]

The first of these greater foes enters at once, summoned by his sister Juturna. Turnus, with his customary arrogance, claims Pallas as his due and—here is the dreadful thing—wishes Evander present to witness his son's death (441–43).

Pallas, however, displays no fear and is the first to cast his weapon. But against Turnus he fights *viribus imparibus* ["with unequal strength"] (459), and his great enterprise is doomed, in spite of a prayer to his father's guest-friend, Hercules (460–61). Hercules listens and pours forth tears (*lacrimasque effundit inanis* ["he pours forth ineffectual tears"], 465), which emphasize the woe and misery of human existence, recalling perhaps the most poignant line in the entire poem, *sunt lacrimae rerum et mentem mortalia tangunt* ["there are tears for the world and mortal events touch the soul"] (1.462), and Aeneas' own steadfast despair against the railing of Dido (4.449). Hercules is unable to postpone or avert the impending death. So too Aeneas, likewise a guest-friend of Evander (516–17), is unable to be present at the crucial moment of Pallas' warring career.

Jupiter's solace of his son is grave, reminding him of the limits of human life, but also showing how one may "survive" after death (467–72). This passage evokes the language of Lucretius (1.76–77) and forecasts the afterlife that Pallas will enjoy (cf. *quisque suos patimur manis* ["each of us suffers his own spirit"], 6.743). The second half of 468 and the first half of 469 recall the Sibyl's sombre words about the accessibility of the underworld (6.128–29).

Pallas hurls his spear with great strength (*magnis viribus*, 474) and follows up with his sword. But to no avail. His spear fails to kill, and Turnus' pierces his breast. Turnus hands the body over to the Arcadians for burial; his last words speak of the high price Evander has paid for Aeneas' friendship (494–5). Then he strips Pallas of his armor, reversing the latter's wish (462–63), but he is unaware of the doom that he will bring upon himself by having won the baldric, and the poet permits himself one of his rare apostrophes (501–2):

nescia mens hominum fati sortisque futurae
et servare modum rebus sublata secundis!

["Mind of men, ignorant of fate and future fortune, nor to preserve moderation, when enjoying favoring times!"]

And yet what Turnus has done is customary under the rites of war;[13] Pallas would have stripped him had he had the chance. In Book 12, at the very end, when Aeneas is on the verge of sparing Turnus, the booty of this battle reminds him of the debt that he owes Evander and his son, and of the obligation that he had undertaken to revenge the latter's death. These are Evander's words (11.177–81):

quod vitam moror invisam Pallante perempto
dextera causa tua est, Turnum natoque patrique
quam debere vides. meritis vacat hic tibi solus
fortunaeque locus. non vitae gaudia quaero,
nec fas, sed nato manis perferre sub imos.

["That I drag out my life, hateful with Pallas gone, your right hand is the cause, which you see owes Turnus to son and father. One opportunity remains for your merits and fortune. I seek no joy in life, that is not granted, but to bring news to my son among the shades deep below."]

The bond of *fides* ["faithfulness"], established in Book 8 and of which Evander here reminds Aeneas, is satisfied and redeemed by the conclusion of the poem. Yet, in spite of the urgency of this *fides*, the internal struggle in Aeneas' mind and emotions that raged while he stood over Turnus might have been won by his sense of *humanitas* ["humanity"] had he not at that very moment been reminded of Pallas.

The news of Turnus' triumph reaches Aeneas at once, and he is immediately transformed.[14] He becomes a demon on the battlefield, with his purpose being to reach Turnus, whereas before his efforts had been random and essentially passive. He first captures eight youths to be reserved for sacrifice at Pallas' pyre, a singularly Homeric touch found nowhere else in the poem. Pallas is Aeneas' Patroclus, whose death changes the entire aspect of the conflict. At the end of the scene the Trojans burst from the camp; the siege is at last broken (604–5).

The scene now returns to Olympus. Jupiter sarcastically chides Juno by intimating that the Trojans' current success is indeed due to Venus' support rather than their own prowess (607–10). His tone has the desired effect upon his sister-wife, and she, in a complete reversal from the beginning of the book, is reduced to pleading, as Venus had then been. Subserviently, she addresses him as *pulcherrime coniunx* ["most handsome husband"] and *omnipotens* ["all powerful"], and intimates that her one desire now regarding the war is to save Turnus (613–16). Her words *pugnae subducere Turnum* ["to withdraw Turnus from battle"] echo Venus' desire to save at least Ascanius from disaster (46–47). Hercules had hoped that Pallas could be saved (464 ff.), but that was not permitted. Yet Turnus cannot be allowed to die at this point, for there would be no tragedy in the death of one marked by arrogance and haughtiness, who had not yet begun to attain a bit of wisdom by personal suffering.

Jupiter therefore allows Turnus' fate to be postponed, and Juno straightway descends to earth to rescue Turnus by fashioning an image of Aeneas—the image, unlike the man, without strength (*sine viribus*, 636)—which Turnus eagerly pursues. He challenges "Aeneas" to stand and fight (649), while only a few lines later, Vergil makes Turnus' mocking tone rebound upon himself, when the real Aeneas hunts the missing foe (663). Finally Turnus, when on shipboard, although he does not fully understand what has happened (he is *ignarus rerum* ["ignorant of events"] [666] about the past as Aeneas was about the future [*rerumque ignarus*] at the end of Book 8), rages violently in his despair, and longs for death so that his honor will be spared reproach (676–79). His emotional state, emphasized by the verb *fluctuat* ["wavers"] (680), is equated to the changeability of the sea (683), but all his efforts are thwarted by Juno, and he arrives at the city of his father Daunus. The void created by his absence is filled at once, at Jupiter's instance, by Mezentius, the best warrior on the Italian side after Turnus himself. Juno removes one hero to save him for a later day; Jupiter brings another forward for his last day on earth.

In Book 7, Mezentius and Lausus had been introduced together; Mezentius' violent nature and lack of respect for the gods are his trademarks (7.647–48). Here too he advances violently and precipitates a unanimous reaction of weapons and hate (689–92):

at Iovis interea monitis Mezentius ardens
succedit pugnae Teucrosque invadit ovantis.
concurrunt Tyrrhenae acies atque omnibus uni,
uni odiisque viro telisque frequentibus instant.

["But meanwhile at Zeus' warning Mezentius burning engages battle and attacks the rejoicing Trojans. The Tyrrhene lines charge together, in unison against one, against one man they press in hatred with relentless weapons."]

The chiasmus of *omnibus uni, / uni odiis* ["in unison against one, against one man in hatred"] emphasizes the loathing with which he is held and makes his relations with his son, soon to be brought out so strikingly, all the more unexpected. He now enters upon a great aristeia, and presents the armor from one of his first victims to Lausus, soon to face Aeneas; Lausus is, in his physical presence, a vicarious Turnus. Mezentius' behavior is compared to that of a wild boar, which no one dares to approach; all attack him from a distance; there are none who do not hate him (714–16). His successes conclude with the killing of Orodes, *pars belli haud temnenda* ["a part of the battle not to be slighted"] (737), who, with his last breath, warns Mezentius that his moment will soon come too. Mezentius, surprisingly, says that Jupiter will look out for his future, a strange remark for a *contemptor divum* ["one contemptuous of the gods"] (742–44). The death of Orodes is perhaps meant to forecast that of Lausus, himself *pars ingens belli* ["a significant part of the war"] (427).

Once again, as at 361, the battle is deadlocked (755–61). The balance of these lines is noteworthy, both in choice of vocabulary and in word placement. Everything indicates the equality of the two sides, in exploit and in suffering. It is a deadlock that can be broken only by a meeting of champions, and, as Mezentius rages like Orion over the field, Aeneas prepares to meet him.

Now, for the first time on Italian soil, we see Aeneas actually fighting an opponent worthy of him. Mezentius' spearcast bounces off Aeneas' divinely made shield and kills his companion Antores. Aeneas, here designated *pius* ["pious"] (783) to contrast him with Mezentius, whose prayer for success had been to his own right hand and weapon (773–74), has greater success in turn; his spear lodges in Mezentius' groin, but does not have the force to prove fatal. Aeneas gleefully and eagerly (*laetus...fervidus*, 787–88) draws his sword to despatch his crippled enemy.

Aeneas thinks Mezentius defenseless; he has not reckoned with the latter's son. Lausus, deeply affected by his father's plight, interjects himself into the struggle, to cover his father's withdrawal. It is an exploit brief in duration, but one that time, reaching far into the future, will not forget. Vergil here allows himself another personal intrusion into the narrative (791–93). These lines remind us of his similar eulogy of Euryalus and Nisus (9.446–49).

Lausus' feelings for his father (*cari genitoris* ["dear father"], 789) introduce a factor not even hinted at before. Mezentius, a monster to all others, is a father who evokes the deepest emotions in his son; and it is a relationship that is fully reciprocated, as we shall soon see. It may be that herein Vergil denies what he had earlier said, that Lausus deserved a better father (7.654). For the two were clearly very close, and this relationship is suggested by the positioning of the words for father and son as Mezentius makes good his escape (799–800):

> socii magno clamore sequuntur,
> dum genitor nati parma protectus abiret.

["his allies follow with a great roar, until the father, protected with the son's shield, could get away."]

Aeneas is outraged and finds himself suddenly on the defensive (802). The abruptness of the monosyllabic line ending indicates the harshness of Aeneas' position. Weapons rain upon him as hail in a storm, while he tries to persuade Lausus to withdraw from his path (810–12):

sustinet et Lausum increpitat Lausoque minatur:
"quo moriture ruis maioraque viribus audes?
fallit te incautum pietas tua."

["He endures and shouts at Lausus and warns him: why are you rushing,
you who will die, and dare trials too great for your strength? Your devotion misleads you, incautious."]

Aeneas, the epitome of *pietas* ["piety, devotion"], so often throughout the poem
called *pius* ["pious"], recognizes the excellence of the young man, recognizes too
that his own strength is far too great for Mezentius' son and defender. In his mind, he
may well have pictured Ascanius at some time fighting for him, or Pallas protecting
Evander, or himself succoring Anchises. But Lausus does not withdraw, he waxes
even more violent; Aeneas' patience runs out, as do the threads of Lausus' life, and
Aeneas' sword, made by a god, pierces the tunic made by Lausus' mother. Another
in Vergil's great line of young people dying before their time has fallen (812–20).

Not until this book has Aeneas become *saevus* ["cruel"];[15] yet, in spite of his
violent emotion, he is not deprived of his humanity. His involvement with the end
of Lausus is indicated by the bracketing of Aeneas by *medium* and *iuvenem* ["midpart,
youth"] in 816. Lausus' death is underscored by the similarity of *recondit* and *reliquit*
["buried, left"], in final position in the line. The sombreness of the scene is intimated
by the abundant alliteration.

Aeneas' reaction to his triumph over Lausus is totally different from Turnus'
after the slaying of Pallas. There is no boasting, no vaunting, only compassion, the
compassion that none but a father can feel (821–32); and it is this relationship that
the patronymic *Anchisiades* ["son of Anchises"][16] emphasizes. Line 824 is a para-
phrase of 9.294, *atque animum patriae strinxit pietatis imago* ["and the image of a son's
devotion pierced his spirit"], where Ascanius is touched by Euryalus' devotion to
his mother. The two lines are in essentials the same, and must rank as one of Vergil's
finest statements of what his poem is, at least in part, ultimately about, the affection
of human being for human being. Aeneas then, in 825, takes his leave of Lausus in
words recalling those of Anchises addressed to Marcellus, *heu, miserande puer, si qua
fata aspera rumpas* ["alas, pitiful youth, if by chance you could break your harsh
fates"] (6.882), and anticipating his own last farewell to Pallas (11.42–44):

" tene" inquit "miserande puer, cum laeta veniret,
invidit Fortuna mihi, ne regna videres
nostra neque ad sedes victor veherere paternas?"

["Was it you" he says "youth to be pitied, that Fortune withheld from me,
when it was propitious, that you would not see our kingdom, nor a victor
be conveyed to your father's abode?"]

These are the three main characters[17] whom Vergil addresses as *miserande* ["to
be pitied"]; the link among the three seems even stronger than merely linguistic.
Both Pallas and Lausus represent Marcellus; they, however, die with the glory of
achievement, which in Marcellus' case was never attained, only forecast.[18]

In the meantime, Mezentius escapes to the bank of the river Tiber, where he
begins to recover a bit from his wound and the shock caused thereby. But all the

time he is as concerned about his son as about himself (839–43). The frequentative *rogitat* ["he keeps asking"] shows his worry, as does the adjective *maesti* ["mournful"]. But, before any news can be brought him, the body of Lausus appears, borne by companions whose grief is underscored by the initial spondaic *flentes* ["weeping"], followed by a decided pause; and Lausus himself is described in the remainder of the line, with three successive spondees, alliterative pairs, chiasmus of case, and repetition of *ingens* ["huge"] in different cases. Mezentius had feared as much (*praesaga mali mens* ["his mind presaging ill fortune"]), but the realization is no less hard.

He at once pours forth his pain in terms of self-reproach (846–56); the disjointed order of the first line, with its double alliteration, leads up to the emphatic position of the words *quem genui* ["whom I sired"], preceding a definite break in the line. The first words of the next line are similarly set off by their position before the caesura; their dread meaning, of life won at the cost of death, underscores Mezentius' terrible anguish. The remainder of this line, together with the next, is, for him, the moment of truth and the realization of what his past life has really meant to himself and his son. Wounded by Lausus' death as he could have been in no other way, his only wish is to join Lausus in the underworld; his return to face Aeneas is thus inevitable.[19]

One should not, however, balance Mezentius' return with Turnus' failure to do so.[20] Mezentius is master of his actions, whereas Turnus' withdrawal from battle was divinely caused, and his efforts to return to the battlefield were thwarted by the same divinity. It is not Turnus' will, or lack thereof, that comes into question here. Nor would this book have been the appropriate place for Turnus and Aeneas to meet in the final combat. Turnus has not yet begun to recognize that he is wrong; this realization comes only in the last two books, beginning with the attack of Drances, after which he is largely on the defensive. Death without understanding would be the opposite of tragic; he must first suffer, as did Achilles, and as does Mezentius, for whom life holds no further attraction. Turnus too will return, when the occasion is right.

After his resolve, Mezentius painfully raises himself and eagerly (*haud deiectus* ["not diverted"], 858) orders his horse to be brought. It is quite clear that the animal was, other than Lausus, the only object of the old man's affection, and his gentleness with the horse shows us further the sympathetic side of the man so hated by all (860–66). Then, driven by passion (*aestuat ingens, / uno in corde pudor mixtoque insania luctu* ["enormous shame surges in one heart, and madness mixed with grief"] 870–71), he calls upon Aeneas to face him, which the latter eagerly does. As Mezentius before had invoked his own power to aid him (773–74), here Aeneas calls upon the great gods and bids Mezentius come forward (875–76). His response is what we now expect, a mixture of savagery and tenderness; the two sides of the old man are displayed in unison (878–82):

> ille autem: "quid me erepto, saevissime, nato
> terres? haec via sola fuit qua perdere posses:
> nec mortem horremus nec divum parcimus ulli.
> desine, nam venio moriturus et haec tibi porto
> dona prius.

["Then he: why are you frightening me, most cruel man, now that my son is gone? This was the only way that you could ruin me. We do not shudder at death nor defer to any of the gods. Stop it, I come about to die and I bring these gifts to you first."]

Only Aeneas in the entire poem, and he only here, is addressed as *saevissime* ["most cruel"]. He is so to Mezentius because he destroyed the old man's desire for life in the only way possible, through his son.

The book is almost at its end. Mezentius, mounted, rides around Aeneas firing his weapons, until Aeneas slays the horse that pins his rider as he falls. Aeneas then stands over his foe and chides him (897–898), but Mezentius retains his dignity and composure, and begs only that his body be spared for burial and thus escape the wrath of his foes. The customs of war are harsh, harsh are men's deaths; Mezentius requests no more than Lausus had received (900–2):

> "hostis amare, quid increpitas mortemque minaris?
> nullum in caede nefas, nec sic ad proelia veni,
> nec tecum meus haec pepigit mihi foedera Lausus."

["Bitter enemy, why are you challenging me with death and threats? There is no crime in slaughter, I did not come thus to the battle, nor did my Lausus make any agreement with you for me."]

The crucial word here is *meus* ["my"]. It represents all that had existed between father and son, who will now everlastingly be together. This was Mezentius' wish, and he intentionally offers his neck as an easy target to Aeneas' blow.

Mezentius and Turnus are different in one other respect, a sense of awareness of reality and the future. Throughout the book, Vergil frequently uses adjectives of knowledge and ignorance. Turnus' actions after the death of Pallas provoke Vergil's remarks about the *nescia mens hominum* ["the unknowing mind of men"] (501), and when he is rescued by Juno he is *ignarus rerum* ["ignorant of events"] (666). But Mezentius foresaw much, if not all; he anticipated the death of his son (*praesaga mens* ["a mind presaging"], 843), and he knew full well what death would bring (*haud inscius* ["not unknowing"], 907). The passing of Mezentius closes the Lausus episode; the story of Pallas, however, will not conclude until the very end of the twelfth book, when Aeneas, satisfying the vow implied in 11.177–81, will comfort the *manes* ["shades"] of the youth. The great passion[21] set under way in the charged tenth book will thus at last be assuaged.[22]

Notes

[1] V. Ussani, "Il decimo libro dell' 'Eneide'," *Studi Virgiliani* (Roma 1932) 2.235–53, furnishes very little detail. F. Klingner, *Virgil: Bucolica Georgica Aeneis* (Zürich and Stuttgart 1967) devotes one chapter (566–81) to Book 10.

[2] G. Mambelli, *Gli studi virgiliani nel secolo xx* (Firenze 1940), and G. E. Duckworth, "Recent Work on Vergil (1940–1956)," *CW* 51 (1957–58) 89 ff., 123 ff., 151 ff., 185 ff., 228 ff., and "Recent Work on Vergil (1957–63)," *CW* 57 (1963–64) 193–228.

[3] See e.g. K. Büchner, *P. Vergilius Maro: Der Dichter der Römer* (Stuttgart 1956) 387–94; G. E. Duckworth, "The Architecture of the *Aeneid*," *AJP* 75 (1954) 1–15, "The *Aeneid* as a Trilogy," *TAPA* 88 (1957) 1–10, "Tripartite Structure in the *Aeneid*," *Vergilius* 7 (1961) 2–11; B. Otis, *Virgil: A Study in Civilized Poetry* (Oxford 1963) 352.

[4]For the problems of time and chronology involved in this book and its relation with Books 8 and 9, see, most recently, Büchner (above, note 3) 390. Vergil nowhere else presents scenes simultaneous with others elsewhere in the poem; his presentation otherwise is consecutive. Very valuable is G. E. Duckworth, "The Chronology of Aeneid VIII–X," *AJP* 59 (1938) 135–44. See also O. W. Reinmuth, "Vergil's Use of *Interea:* a Study of the Treatment of Contemporaneous Events in Roman Epic," *AJP* 54 (1933) 323–39, particularly 325–27 and 336–37.

[5] See the remarks of G. E. Duckworth, "Fate and Free Will in Vergil's *Aeneid*," *CJ* 51 (1955–56) 361.

[6]So too Klingner (above, note 1) 572: "In Wirklichkeit ist der halb trotzig, halb wehklagend ausgesprochene Verzicht auf das verheissene Reich...der schärfste Zwang, mit dem sie Jupiter zusetzt: soll er sich doch hörig der Juno beugen und seinen Weltplan der Geschichte umstossen!"

[7]On these last two points, see E. G. O'Neill, Jr., "Word-Accents and Final Syllables in Latin Verse," *TAPA* 71 (1940) 338–40.

[8]I thus cannot agree with Otis (above, note 3) 361, who says "the picture of Pallas lacks the emotional connotations required to explain his supposed hold on Aeneas."

[9]See E. A. Hahn, "Note on Vergil's Use of Anchisiades," *CW* 14 (1920–21) 3: "In my opinion the poet bestows this name upon his hero only when he wishes subtly to indicate Aeneas' relation to his father."

[10]J. R. Bacon, "Aeneas in Wonderland: A Study of Aeneid VIII," *CR* 53 (1939) 102, comments upon this clause: "The words ... are also full of allusive significance.... It is a symbol of the hope of fulfillment of his destiny."

[11]Otis (above, note 3) 355 does not note the repetition of these crucial words from the eighth book; rather he says that "Virgil uses with great éclat the simile applied by Apollonius to Jason. Aeneas is like the bane-bringing star Sirius or — as Virgil himself adds — like a red comet in the night; both foretell bad news, such as Aeneas undoubtedly is to the Latins." But surely it is more logical to see Aeneas' antecedent at this crucial moment in the picture of Augustus rather than in the shallow Jason.

[12]Lines 270 ff. recall 8.680–81, and suggest another link with Augustus. The passage in Book 8 echoes the omens concerning Ascanius in 2.682 ff. and 692 ff.

[13]On this theme in Vergil see R. Hornsby, "The Armor of the Slain," *PQ* 45 (1966) 347–59.

[14]Cf. R. S. Conway, "Vergil's Creative Art," *PBA* 17 (1931) 28: "[The secret of the book] lies in the story of Pallas and its effects, which, though indeed they reach out beyond the Book, make the turning-point of its story. So far as I know no commentator has yet realized what Vergil has indicated by repeated emphasis, the complete difference which the death of Pallas makes in Aeneas himself." The same view had been stated earlier in his *Harvard Lectures on the Vergilian Age* (Cambridge, Mass., 1928) 135–36.

[15]J. W. Mackail, *The Aeneid* (Oxford 1930), note *ad loc.*: "It should not escape notice that the epithet *saevus*, 'furious,' is never applied to Aeneas until he has been wrought up to extreme passion by the death of Pallas; thenceforward it becomes almost habitual, to emphasize that his grief and anger are unextinguishable except by the death of Turnus."

[16]T. R. Glover, *Virgil*[3] (London n.d.) 223–24: "Lausus is but a boy — *puer* — but he has done what Aeneas did himself years before, he has saved his father — the patronymic *Anchisiades* is not without purpose — and now all the honour that a hero can pay to a hero Aeneas will render to Lausus. *Pietas* covers his feeling for Lausus as well as his feeling for Anchises."

[17] Only one other, Cydon in 10.327, is so addressed.

[18]I think Otis (above, note 3) 351 is too narrow in his view when he says, "The death of Pallas is a tragedy of sorts — Pallas is the great Marcellus figure of the poem — but, like Marcellus himself, he is also an *exemplum virtutis* who in dying rouses the very forces that bring victory." The ultimate question, however, is not one of victory but of humanity. Otis is more generous to Lausus on p. 354, where Pallas and Lausus are called "the noble Marcelli of each side." V. Pöschl, *The Art of Vergil*, tr. Gerda Seligson (Ann Arbor 1962) 106, sees deeper when he says: "Pallas and especially Lausus and Mezentius are tragic figures because they fall not only through the fatality of war, but because they attract their destinies through the grandeur of their souls."

[19]Cf. Conway (above, note 14) 28: "[Mezentius] is brought to realize the truth and confess it, but not through the prospect of his own death—note this Vergilian touch; it is the death of his son that has pierced his armour and brings him to repentance."

[20]As does Otis (above, note 3) 360, who says that "This 'return' of Mezentius is of course the pointed obverse of Turnus' non-return."

[21]It is the greatest passion that Aeneas feels throughout the poem, next to his feelings for Dido. His action in covering Pallas' body with a robe woven by Dido herself (11.72–77) underscores his similar emotions toward them.

[22]This paper has profited from the comments and suggestions of Miss Bertha Tilly, Prof. Robert B. Lloyd, the Association's Editor, and its anonymous referee. Responsibility for the views expressed, however, is mine alone.

THE SONS OF IASUS
AND THE END OF THE *AENEID*

In his article, Lee uses the musical idea of the development and recapitulation of themes to study a passage in book 12, at lines 384–429, in which Aeneas is wounded. Lee names this passage a "recapitulation" of a section at the end of book 5, the death of Palinurus. Lee points out that in book 12, Palinurus and Iapyx, the doctor who tends Aeneas, seem to be brothers, sons of Iasus. Lee analyzes their role with reference to Aeneas, especially regarding figurative father/son relationships. This passage prepares the reader for Aeneas' only direct address to his literal son, Ascanius, in lines 435–36. Lee connects these small passages to images of flowers throughout the poem, especially the golden bough and its "hesitation." He ends with a look at Aeneas' final hesitation before he kills Turnus, in Vergil's "shocking and abrupt conclusion" to his poem. (Ed.)

*O*ne of the features of music as it has developed in the West is the repetition of themes, and the recapitulation of them—often across considerable stretches of time—in new keys, with new instrumentation and new harmonization. In abstract music, this feature has likely found its highest expression in the sonata-form movements of Haydn, Mozart, and Beethoven. In dramatic music, the high-point is probably Wagner's *Ring*, where hundreds of musical motifs, associated with characters, ideas, and emotions, are manipulated through some fifteen hours of playing time. By the final pages of a Beethoven symphonic movement or a Wagner music drama, a theme has been used in so many ways and in so many contexts, and in combination with so many other themes, that its restatement at the close has the effect of being a summation and fulfillment.

Of all Latin authors, Virgil I think comes closest to working along these lines. He writes, of course, on a scale that allows it, and he has inherited from Homer the mandate to repeat and recapitulate. But while Homer's recapitulations are usually the word-for-word repetitions of the *aoidos* ["bard"], Virgil's are stated in new words and new combinations, and carry special subjective or emotive weight, and are tensed towards some high-point, some movement's end, to which they will contribute.

There is a passage in Book 12 of the *Aeneid* which illustrates this to some degree. As it is not an overly familiar passage, it may be summarized here. Aeneas has been struck in the thigh by an arrow. He is brought back to camp wounded, supported by his son Ascanius, and Mnestheus, and the ever-present Achates. Bleeding, stumbling, leaning on his great spear, he calls impatiently for someone to cut his wound open and extract the arrow, and send him back to battle. But the efforts of the doctor

M. Own Lee, "The Sons of Iasus and the End of the *Aeneid*," *Augustan Age* 1 (1981) 13–16. Reprinted by permission of M. Own Lee, St. Michael's College, University of Toronto.

who attends him are to no avail. The arrow is lodged too deep in the flesh. And all the time the battle is going badly. The cries of the dying echo around the tent. Then suddenly the pain stops, the blood ceases to flow from the wound, and the doctor finds that the arrow of its own accord follows his hand as he draws it from the flesh. He cries out that more than medical skill has wrought this wonder. He is right. None of those present knows, but Venus, unable to bear her son's pain, has with motherly tenderness plucked the healing herb dittany on Mount Ida and brought it, veiled in a mist, to the Trojan camp, and plunged it into the water the doctor was using.

This passage (12.384–429) is a recapitulation. It restates several motifs from the end of Book 5. There, in a much more familiar passage, Aeneas is within easy sailing distance of his promised land, Italy, and yet his goddess mother knows that cruel gods pursue her son, and have blown him off course before. She asks Neptune to give the Trojan fleet safe passage, and he agrees, provided one life be given for many. The life taken is that of Aeneas' helmsman, Palinurus. High in the stern, he is enchanted by the mistclad god of sleep, hesitates for a moment, and drops to his death in the sea, taking the rudder with him (5.779–871).

We note first that, in each of the two passages, Venus intervenes out of maternal concern for her son (*exercita curis*: 5.779; *concussa dolore*: 12.411 ["troubled with cares, struck with grief"]); that Somnus ["Sleep"], like Venus, comes veiled in mist; that Palinurus, like the dittany stalk, plunges into the water; that the rudderless ship, like the arrow from the flesh, moves of its own accord over the sea. These links are more suggested than stressed, and they are not exact parallels. But they are there.

Next we note that Palinurus, the helmsman in Book 5, and Iapyx, the doctor in Book 12, are or appear to be brothers, sons of Iasus. Vergil establishes this cross-reference more directly than the others, addressing Palinurus in the initial word *Iaside* ["son of Iasus"] in 5.843 and referring to Iapyx as *Iasides* ["son of Iasus"], the initial word in 12.392. Further, in each of the two sons' lives there is a sacrifice, the kind of selfless action expected of the *pii* ["the pious"] in this epic of *pietas* ["piety"]. Palinurus' comes at the end of his life and is involuntary. It is visited upon him *insonti* ["innocent"] (841) and *cunctanti* ["hesitating"] (856). Iapyx, on the other hand, has made his self-sacrifice voluntarily, and at the beginning of his life: Vergil tells us that Iapyx was in his youth loved by Apollo, and offered any of the god's arts and skills as a reward, and that Iapyx chose, not prophecy or archery or music — things which a young man might want to have — but rather what Vergil calls *mutas artes*, the quiet arts, of medicine. Iapyx wanted to tend his aged father, and to put off for as long as possible the day of his father's death. We note the similarities and the differences in the motivic stories of the two brothers: Palinurus' life is taken, in *inopina quies* ["unexpected quiet"] (5.857); Iapyx's is voluntarily dedicated to *mutas artes* (12.397).

Next we note that both sacrifices are beneficial to Aeneas. Each son of Iasus is, in his way, a healer (*iaomai*, I heal, appears to be the root of the patronymic). And here we come to the subtlest and the most beautiful of the correspondences. Aeneas is a father, in a figurative sense, to each of the sons of Iasus. His lament for Palinurus, lost to the sea at the end of Book 5, is immediately recast at the beginning of Book 6, where Daedalus laments the loss of his son Icarus to the sea. Captain and lost helmsman are figured in myth as father and lost son. Correspondingly, in Book 12 Aeneas is figured as father to Iapyx: he is healed by the hand of the one who chose medicine above all other gifts so he could prolong the life of his father.

Virgil is too subtle an artist to make all the correspondences explicit, or even to make them exact. I think, though, that he hoped they would keep working in the mind of the reader, especially the father-son relationship. For it is at this point in Book 12, as the *figurative* son exclaims that a miracle has been wrought, that Aeneas claps on his armor, embraces his *flesh-and-blood* son, kisses him through the visor of his helmet, and speaks one of the great passages in the poem. It is, in fact, the only time in all the poem that Virgil gives us Aeneas' actual words to Ascanius:

> Disce, puer, virtutem ex me verumque laborem
> fortunam ex aliis (12. 435-6).

> "Learn from me, my boy, what it is to be a man and to suffer.
> Learn from others what it is to be happy."

These lines would be memorable even in a context less well prepared. As it is, they come like the climax after a recapitulation in music. One reads them with the sacrifices of the two figurative sons Palinurus and Iapyx in one's consciousness. And one reflects that, of all the sons we meet in the poem, only the son to whom these lines are spoken, only Ascanius, is not sacrificed. Euryalus, Lausus, and Pallas have already fallen. Marcellus, who stands symbol for them all in the vision of the future in Book 6, will also die young. And at the very moment that Aeneas is being healed of his wound, Virgil tells us, the cries of young men falling in battle echo around him:

> it tristis ad aethera clamor
> bellantum iuvenum et duro sub Marte cadentum (12.409-10).

> ["The sad clamor of the warring youths goes to the skies, and also of those falling beneath the harsh war god, Mars."]

These correspondences are reinforced by recurrent flower-images: Euryalus in death is compared to poppies weighted with rain, and Pallas at his state funeral to a culled violet; lilies are scattered from full hands at the envisioned death of Marcellus; as the young men fall in battle around him, Iapyx is aided by the dittany stalk plucked by Venus; Palinurus is lulled to sleep on the stern by a dewy branch Somnus ["Sleep"] has brought from Lethe ["Forgetfulness"]; and it is while preparing the funeral pyre of yet another fallen victim, Misenus, that Aeneas sights and plucks the growth that is central to all of these, the Golden Bough itself.

There is something of that magic bough in our episodes of the two sons of Iasus. In Book 6, Aeneas is told that the Golden Bough is impossible to pluck for those not destined, easy for those who are: Iapyx must, in Book 12, tug away at the arrow unsuccessfully, only to have it come forth of its own accord at heaven's will. In Book 6, when Aeneas does pluck the Golden Bough, it is neither impossible nor easy for him—the bough hesitates (*cunctantem*); Palinurus, in Book 5, hesitates (*cunctanti*) before he falls.

And are all these various motifs tensed, as in some great piece of music, towards a final summation? I think so. There is one last feature in the passage on Iapyx that I should like to note: the choice. The little vignette about Iapyx preserves an old legend about Aeneas himself that Virgil did not use when he might have, in Book 2. According to the legend, on the night Troy fell, the victorious Greeks were so impressed with Aeneas that they spared his life, offered to let him go free, and gave him a choice of any treasure he wanted to take with him from the fallen city.

Aeneas chose his father. Virgil probably decided against the story (preserved by, among others, Servius on *Aeneid* 2.636) because it would make his hero too dependent on his Greek conquerors. But the story was too good not to use somewhere, and Virgil recast it in Book 12 for Iapyx: given a choice of all the gifts of Apollo, Iapyx chose the gift that would most help his father.

We turn to the last page of the poem, the final recapitulation. Here too we have the maternal intervention of Venus. She plucks Aeneas' spear from an olive tree sacred to those saved from shipwreck. Here, too, as Aeneas poises that spear to slay the prostrate Turnus, he hesitates; again, we have that tantalizing word *cunctantem* (12. 940). Here, above all, we have the father-son relationship: Turnus asks Aeneas for mercy in the name of his father. And Aeneas is presented with a choice — to kill or to spare. Everything we have noted, and much more, is tensed towards the final statement, the final resolution of the Leitmotivs ["recurrent themes"] — and Aeneas makes his choice. He forgets the words his father spoke when he gave him his mission in Book 6 — *parcere subiectis* ["spare the humbled"]. He does not, as legend and our expectations of him make us think he will, choose his father. For he is suddenly reminded of a figurative son, sacrificed for him. Remembering Pallas — and Marcellus and Misenus and Lausus and the sons of Iasus and what he had said to his own son Ascanius — he kills.

It is a shocking and abrupt conclusion. It has not pleased many. But it is carefully prepared. And the way one reads the stories of the sons in that final recapitulation is the way one, in the end, reads the father, and the *Aeneid* itself.

DESECRATION AND EXPIATION
AS A THEME IN THE *AENEID*

Petter begins his article facing squarely the issue of conflicting interpretations with respect to the meaning of the end of the *Aeneid*. He analyzes Aeneas' anger in killing Turnus in terms of unwritten laws of moral order in the Greek and Roman worlds, terming violations of that moral order "desecrations" and several responses to them in the poem "expiations." Petter than analyzes three stages of desecrations and expiations in the *Aeneid*, the first stage being the fall of Troy in book 2 and the second stage, the Hercules/Cacus episode in book 8. The third stage concerns the relationship between Turnus and Aeneas. In Petter's view, when Aeneas kills Turnus he expiates a series of desecrations accumulated from the beginning of the poem. (Ed.)

"The reaction he [Vergil] wants to prompt is plain. We must condemn the sudden rage that causes Aeneas to kill Turnus...[1]

"Nothing could be more false...than to say: 'The reaction [Vergil] wants to prompt is plain. We must condemn the sudden rage that causes Aeneas to kill Turnus'."[2]

These quotations, from two authorities, document the sharp disagreement that prevails in the evaluation of Aeneas' conduct and character in Vergil's *Aeneid*. On the one hand, a long tradition of interpretation of Aeneas' conduct and character, represented by Gordon Williams, has found Aeneas to be a hero guided by lofty ideals which explain and justify his actions. On the other hand, a more recent trend, represented by Quinn,[3] finds at least some of Aeneas' conduct to be blameworthy, e.g., in the cases of Dido and Turnus. In his conflict with Turnus a personal, uncontrolled anger overwhelms Aeneas, and he kills him brutally and mercilessly. Aeneas' anger, as it is manifest in his conduct toward Turnus, has become an object of intense scrutiny,[4] and the question is raised what role this anger plays in the totality of the development of Aeneas' character within his personal history.[5]

In this study I seek to demonstrate that this anger is born of a moral reaction against a violation of the moral order recognized universally in the Greco-Roman world as a body of unwritten law — the *ius moribus constitutum* ["law established by custom"]. The Turnus episode constitutes only one of a series of such moral conflicts, and the other instances in the series provide an interpretive framework for the Turnus episode.

Gerald J. Petter, "Desecration and Expiation in the *Aeneid*," *Vergilius* 40 (1994) 76–84. Reprinted by permission of Gerald J. Petter, Ph.D.

For convenience I identify violations of the moral order with the term "desecration." Desecrations are most frequently denoted in the *Aeneid* by the terms '*scelus*' ["crime"] and '*nefas*' ["wicked, unholy"], but other circumlocutions are also employed. Desecrations call for moral responses which should variously effect penalty, retribution, restitution, and purification. These responses I designate by the term "expiation." They are intended to thwart or remove the agent of desecration and thus to restore to integrity the violated moral order.[6]

In the *Aeneid* a series of desecrations and expiations divides into three stages distinguished by increasingly clear discernment of the fact of desecration and by the relative effectuality of the expiation in each instance of desecration. In the first stage (I) several desecrations are not clearly discerned by Aeneas and none is effectually expiated. In the second stage (II), which has only one pivotal instance, the desecration is discerned and the expiation is effectual, but effectual only in a provisional, didactic sense. In the third stage (III) the desecration is discerned and the expiation is effectual and conclusive: it restores to integrity the moral order which was violated by the series of previous desecrations. The exposition presented here will follow the theme of desecration and expiation through the three stages, and will interpret the Aeneas/Turnus episode as an episode of desecration and expiation.

(I) In the first stage a number of desecrations occur in conjunction with the fall of Troy. Aeneas learns of the gravity of desecration by its consequences, is moved to distinguish and identify it when it occurs, and learns the necessity of a response commensurate to the desecration.

The first of these desecrations occurs at the beginning of Aeneas' saga. This beginning is in Book 2 rather than in Book 1, for in the opening lines of Book 2, Aeneas begins his tale at its temporal beginning. The moral problem is introduced in the first instance in the figure of the wooden horse. The horse is holy (*sacrum*, 2.230), a gift (*donum, dona*, 2.31, 36, 49) to a deity (*votum* ["votive offering"], 2.17); yet it is an instrument of treachery (*insidias, crimine* ["trickery, crime"], 2.65), a deadly (*exitiale*, 2.31) gift, a gift which destroys rather than honors. The horse is a *monstrum* ["monster"] (2.245),[7] a denatured mongrel, an entity which offends against the moral order inherent in the cosmos. The treachery which the Greeks accomplish through this horse, precisely by virtue of its character as a sacred gift, is a *scelus* (2.106), a desecration.

Sinon, the horse's advocate (2.57–198), complements its nefarious character. Sinon explains that the horse is a holy object, devoted to a goddess to assuage her wrath aroused by previous desecrations committed by the Greeks. Not only are Sinon's words treacherous, but, like the gift of the horse, he raises that treachery to the level of desecration by swearing an oath (2.154–9). As the treachery in the horse is packaged in a sacred object, so Sinon's treacherous words are packaged in a sacred oath. The horse presents the Trojans with the urgent necessity of distinguishing desecration when it is ambiguous or concealed; only thus can it be responded to appropriately. This they failed to do; their mind was unclear (2.54) .

Enter Laocoon, who is a priest (2.201) and hence holy. He realizes that the horse is evil and reacts against the evil by hurling his spear at it (2.40–56). His act is justified, even required, if the horse is an instance and agent of desecration. On the other hand, if the horse is in fact a sacred object, a gift to a goddess, then Laocoon's violence against the horse is a *scelus* (2.229), a desecration. Laocoon's act is thus ambiguous.[8] But the act is not only ambiguous, it is ineffectual; Laocoon only blemishes the horse, he does not destroy it.

Laocoon is attacked by two serpents (2.199–233) and another instance of this same moral ambiguity is generated. If Laocoon's violence to the sacred horse was a desecration, the attack of the serpents is a just reaction. If, however, Laocoon's attack was against an evil horse, and thus justified, the serpents' attack upon Laocoon, the priest, is a desecration. Similar to the horse, Laocoon and the serpents are, for the Trojans, a lesson in the need to discern correctly the presence of desecration even as it may be disguised as sanctity. Only when desecration is recognized can it be responded to appropriately.[9]

The motifs of desecration and expiation are present yet again in the scene of the collapse of the city (2.506–58). King Priam is weak and feeble, crouching near an altar (*ara* 2.513), protected by its inviolability (*sacra...in sede* ["on the sacred site"], 2.525). Into his presence comes his son Polites, pursued by Pyrrhus. Pyrrhus kills the son before the eyes of the father; this act is identified as a *scelus* (2.535); it is a defilement (*foedasti* ["you defiled"], 2.539), a desecration. As Priam reacts he identifies the religious, moral motive in his reaction (2.535–39)—he is an ally of the gods (*di...persolvant...et...reddant* ["may the gods...pay...and...repay"] 2.536–38). The thrust of his spear at the evil Pyrrhus is weak and ineffectual. Priam dies at the hand of Pyrrhus, in yet another desecration: Pyrrhus kills him as he is clinging to an altar, which should render Priam immune (2.525, 550–53). His demise as symbolic head of the city concludes the sequence of events which constitute the fall of the city.

Thus the fall of Troy is marked by a series of confrontations of moral forces evincing the motifs of desecration and expiation.[10] The desecrations are characterized by ambiguity[11] and the Trojans demonstrate a general inability to discern them correctly (2.54–56). Some attempts at expiation occur, but they are all ineffectual; the agents of the desecrations continue their evil existence.

These desecrations and expiations pose a pronounced moral problem which accompanies Aeneas as he flees Troy: he must recognize and identify desecration, and having recognized it he must react commensurately. Early in his flight he learns a grim lesson in the continuing consequences of unexpiated desecration. He flees to Thrace, intending to establish himself there (3.16–18), but Thrace is unsuited for his planned kingdom (3.24–68). Polydorus, a son of Priam, was murdered there in an act of treachery, a violation of the rights of a guest (3.61), a violation against *fas* ["divine law"] (3.55), i.e. a desecration. As a consequence Aeneas may not stay, lest he make himself a partner to the *scelus* ["crime"] (*parce...scelerare* ["refrain from...desecrating"], 3.42). He must continue his flight because of the unexpiated desecration.

(II) In 1966 G. K. Galinsky[12] evaluated the Hercules/Cacus episode (8.184–275). He argued that the conflicts between two pairs of antagonists (Hercules/Cacus, Aeneas/Turnus) represent the moral conflict of good with evil. The conflict between Hercules and Cacus is in fact another instance of desecration and expiation. Cacus' appearance and behavior express evil; he belches fire, he eats humans and hangs their heads on his doorpost. He is a wily trickster, a *monstrum* (8.198),[13] who cannot refrain from any *scelus* ["crime"] (8.206) which is within his power to attempt. Hercules is passing through the region and is entitled to the rights of a guest from the residents of the area; instead the *monstrum* violates the guest and his guest-rights by stealing his guest's cattle, a desecration. Hercules reacts and again the outcome appears uncertain. Three times he inspects the area; three times he attempts to enter the cave; three times he fails; having failed he desists, exhausted (8.230–3). But neither can he tolerate the desecration unavenged. His subsequent behavior brings new clarity to the problem of desecration and expiation. He renews the attack and with one final—Herculean!—effort rips open the cave from the rear, then enters and closes with Cacus. This attack does not leave, at its conclusion, a superficially wounded evil force; rather, it leaves a *cadaver* ["corpse"] (8.264). This instance of conflict does not issue in a banishment and flight; rather it issues in the erection of an altar which will guarantee the permanent memory of the one whose expiation of the desecration was effectual (8.268–72).

This effectual resolution of the moral problem in the Hercules/Cacus episode is a pivotal point in the evolution of the theme of desecration and expiation. But the Hercules/Cacus episode is only a story narrated to Aeneas; it is not an event which shaped his life; it constitutes a stage of provisional, didactic resolution of the moral problem.

(III) In the third and final stage in this evolution Aeneas will definitively resolve the moral problem which constituted the background of his flight from Troy. This occurs in Aeneas' personal closure with Turnus which begins when Turnus kills Pallas and is completed when Aeneas kills Turnus. Vergil presents this conflict as an instance of desecration and expiation. In this conjunction the previous series enlightens the final conflict and the final conflict in turn illuminates that series. In his conflict with Turnus Aeneas will come to moral clarity, attain moral resolve, and effect the necessary moral solution: a commensurate and conclusive expiation.

Turnus, who has already broken a solemn treaty, has been joined by Mezentius, the desecrator (7.648; 8.483–5, 489). Aeneas resolves to advance against them both. Aeneas becomes a conscious and purposive agent of restoration to integrity of the violated moral order. Allied to Aeneas in this purpose is Pallas, son of Evander.

During the subsequent conflict between the two opposing forces, Turnus seeks Pallas for personal combat and kills him (10.439–509). Although the conflict is between two *unequals* (a lion and bull fighting *viribus imparibus* ["with unequal strength"], 10.454–5, 459), it entails no violation of the mores of war. Though Pallas' death certainly touched upon Aeneas' sense of responsibility, it was not due to irresponsibility on Aeneas' part; it is simply one more battlefield tragedy, justifiable by the rules of combat.

But Vergil presents Pallas' death from another perspective. As Turnus advances against Pallas he expresses explicitly that he intends not so much the death of Pallas as the ruin of his father, Evander, through the death of the son (10.443, 491–2). Thereby this death becomes something other than a typical battlefield casualty and this explains Aeneas' reaction both immediately and at the close of the epic.[14] This feature must therefore be examined more closely.

Aeneas left Troy in the company of his father Anchises and his son Ascanius (2.721–29). His relationships to his father and his son were fundamental to his character and consciousness. Aeneas is not only devoted to them, he realizes his relationships to his father and his son are realities in the moral/religious dimension of life and a violation of them would be *nefas* ["wicked, unholy"] (2.658). Each generation in the succession of generations (3.98) is the "hope" (*spes*, 4.274, 12.168) of the preceding generation. As Ascanius was Aeneas' "hope," and Aeneas was Anchises' "hope," each a pledge for the other's future, so Pallas was Evander's "hope" (*spes*, 8.514), a pledge for Evander's future and thus also his comfort (*solacia*, 8.514). This bond between human generations is not only a fact in human life, it enjoys the gods' jealousy and protection, and therefore it requires reverence from the human side. The paternal/filial relationship in its inviolability could serve as the foundation of oaths (4.357, 9.300), and the sanctity of this relationship had made Pyrrhus' murder of Polites a desecration (2.535–9). When Turnus states that he wishes he could kill Pallas before the eyes of his father (10.443) and thus dash the father's hope, he commits the same desecration of which Pyrrhus had made himself guilty.

After Turnus has killed Pallas from this motive, Aeneas begins to seek out Turnus personally as being a desecrator, i.e., as one guilty of *hybris*.[15] Therefore, Aeneas responds not only with the "elemental cruelty" and ferocity which are normal to the warrior, he responds with an engaged moral consciousness, aroused by the desecration, and a corresponding heightened intensity. This was the kind of intensity with which Hercules responded to the treachery of Cacus, viz., *furiis* ["with rage"] (8.219) and *fervidus ira* ["heated with anger"] (8.230); Aeneas now responds with the same intensity (*furit, furens* ["he rages, raging"], 10.545, 604).

Because he cannot immediately lay hold of Turnus, Aeneas commences with Turnus' comrades whom he treats as parties to the desecration.[16] He seizes eight of Turnus' comrades whom he means not simply to kill from a military motive but whom he means to *sacrifice* (*immolet*, 10.519) from a moral/religious motive. When one of the enemy, Magus, appeals to Aeneas for mercy on the basis of paternal/filial piety, on the basis of the "hope" (10.524) which Ascanius constitutes for Aeneas, Aeneas rejects the appeal outright. Turnus, so Aeneas declares, has abrogated the normal rules of the battlefield (*belli commercia Turnus sustulit ista* ["these conditions of warfare Turnus put aside"], 10.532–3), and has placed the interactions on another plane where other values obtain. Aeneas kills Magus, declaring that the sanctity of that relationship requires this response in these particular circumstances (10.534).[17] Aeneas' present conduct is now not forbidden but rather required by his relationship to Anchises and Ascanius/Iulus (10.534); Aeneas is *pius* ["dutiful"] (10.591) precisely in these actions.[18]

The general conflict between the Trojans and the Latins continues until in Book XII it comes to a climax in the episode in which Aeneas meets Turnus in single combat (12.697–952). The facts are relatively simple but the secondary literature has recognized virtually unanimously that the event retrojects a certain meaning upon the entire epic.[19] If, as I have sought to trace them, the motifs of desecration and expiation in the epic at large are now sufficiently clear, this final event is unmistakably an instance of those motifs. When the wounded Turnus pleads for mercy he addresses Aeneas:

> miseri te si qua parentis
> tangere cura potest, oro (fuit et tibi talis
> Anchises genitor), Dauni miserere senectae,
> et me seu corpus spoliatum lumine mavis
> redde meis.
> (12.932–6)

["If any sympathy for a wretched parent can touch you, I pray (you had such a father too, Anchises), pity Daunus, his old age, and return me, or if you prefer, my body bereft of light, to my people."]

Turnus appeals to Aeneas to honor the sanctity of the paternal/filial relationship. Aeneas begins to relent:

> stetit acer in armis
> Aeneas volvens oculos dextramque repressit;

et iam iamque magis cunctantem flectere sermo
coeperat

(12.938-41)

["Fierce in his arms stood Aeneas, rolling his eyes, and he restrained his right hand; now more and more, as he was hesitating, the speech began to sway him."]

Suddenly he spies Pallas' belt on Turnus' shoulder (12.941-4). As he dwells on it, fury inflames him and he kills Turnus with one blow (12.946-52), crying out: "Pallas te hoc vulnere, Pallas immolat, et poenam scelerato ex sanguine sumit" ["With this blow, Pallas sacrifices you, Pallas, and exacts punishment for desecrated blood"] (12.948-9). The words *Pallas, immolat, poenam, scelerato* ["Pallas, sacrifices, punishment, desecrated"] (12.949), indicate that the death results from a moral/religious motive, that the death is an expiation of a desecration, and the words point the reader to Pallas as the agent of this death.

What happened to Aeneas when he saw Pallas' belt on Turnus' shoulder? Why did the sight of the belt so profoundly affect his disposition? Turnus had taken Pallas' belt for himself as booty. In itself this was a violation of a code of conduct for the battlefield; Turnus should have dedicated the belt as a trophy. But, in the description of Turnus' act of stripping the belt from Pallas, Vergil had directed the reader's attention not so much to the belt as to the scene engraved on the belt (10.495-500), a scene which Vergil identifies as *nefas* ["wicked, unholy"] (10.497). When Aeneas sees Pallas' belt on Turnus' shoulder he does not see only an article of armor; he focuses on the scene engraved on the belt.[20]

The scene engraved on Pallas' belt was the collective murder of the sons of Aegyptus. This murder was peculiarly treacherous, for it was committed by their traitorous brides on their wedding night (10.497-8). It was thus a desecration (*nefas* 10.497) against the sacred vows and the sacred trust of marriage.

The reader must ask: what is the significance of the scene on the belt when the belt is worn by Pallas? Pallas was advancing to war, in the place of his father, specifically to expiate the desecrations of Mezentius. Thus the belt is a kind of banner which states that Pallas is a preventer and expiator of desecration.

When Turnus took the belt from Pallas, he also "appropriated the desecration" (*rapiens...nefas*, 10.496-7) engraved on the belt. Also Turnus, when wearing the belt, wears a banner; in Turnus' case the banner states that he is a desecrator. Given the motive from which he had killed Pallas, he had forfeited every right to appeal in his own interest to the sanctity of the paternal/filial relationship. But he is now making precisely such an appeal to Aeneas (12.932-6). This is another instance of the terrible ambiguity which characterized the wooden horse and Sinon, the ambiguity created when desecration cloaks itself in sanctity. The scene on the belt, in conjunction with the content of Turnus' appeal at that moment, raises Aeneas' moral consciousness to a new height.[21] In this conjunction Aeneas must have further recalled the desecration in the case of Polites and Priam, a desecration which sealed finally the fall of Troy. The desecrations committed against Pallas Athena and against the Trojans at Troy were still awaiting, in some sense, their expiation. Pallas' belt was a reminder of all this. Indeed, the belt was a *saevi monimenta doloris* ["reminder of a cruel grief"] (12.945).

When Aeneas relates his story from its beginning (*incipiam* ["I will begin"], 2.13), he introduces immediately the ominous name 'Pallas' (2.15); it is not a coincidence that this is also the last name mentioned in the entire epic (12.948). The words, "Pallas...Pallas sacrifices you" (12.948-9), conjoin this last event with events at the very beginning of the narrative. Aeneas' own moral consciousness at the moment of Turnus' death gives the death the character of an expiation. But since Pallas is, with Aeneas, also the agent of the sacrifice of Turnus, Pallas' character as an avenger of desecration is vindicated. But further, in the death of Turnus not only is the desecration attaching to the death of Pallas the son of Evander expiated; so also is the desecration attaching to the death of Polites the son of Priam; so also is the desecration attaching to the great horse, which bears a connection to another "Pallas" (*pro Palladio* ["for the Palladium, the image of Pallas"], 2.183); so also is the original desecration of Pallas Athena by the Greeks. The words "Pallas,...Pallas sacrifices you" hint at the agency of not only Pallas, the son of Evander, but also Pallas Athena or even the horse. In an ultimate sense Vergil may wish the reader to recognize that all the "Pallases" together with Aeneas are agents of the death of Turnus. They are agents of an expiation of previous desecrations, and when Aeneas kills Turnus the reaction against desecration is finally resolute and effectual. Expiation has restored to integrity the moral order which continued to bear the injury of desecrations left unexpiated. *Therefore* Aeneas' flight is ended and, hence, the end of the epic.[22]

Notes

[1] K. Quinn, *Virgil's Aeneid: A Critical Description* (Ann Arbor 1968) 273.

[2] G. Williams, *Technique and Ideas in the Aeneid* (New Haven 1983) 225.

[3] H.-P. Stahl, "Aeneas, an 'Unheroic' Hero?" *Arethusa* 14 (1981) 157-86, identifies those who represent this trend as an "American school" (p. 157, n. 2) and lists the dates of the several monographs through which the school has acquired its identity. Stahl dates the birth of the school c. 1960 (p. 157). For a more extensive account of the trends in interpretation see S. J. Harrison, "Some Views of the *Aeneid* in the Twentieth Century," in *Oxford Readings in Vergil's Aeneid*, ed. S. J. Harrison (Oxford 1990) 1–20.

[4] See, e.g., K. Galinsky, "The Anger of Aeneas," *AJPh* 109 (1988) 321–48.

[5] The question specifically of a development of Aeneas' character is treated by T. Fuhrer "Aeneas: a Study in Character Development," *G&R* 38 (1989) 63–72. This article is useful also for the résumé it presents of other answers to the question.

[6] "The *Aeneid* is sometimes referred to as a religious poem, but perhaps it would be better described as a document of religious history," states W. Camps, (*An Introduction to Virgil's Aeneid* [Oxford 1969] 47). Whether one decides it is a "religious poem" or a "document of religious history," desecration and expiation are elements of the moral/religious content.

[7] The *Oxford Latin Dictionary* lists the meanings of the word '*monstrum*' under five headings, four of which include references to entities which violate the norm of their nature. The wooden horse is an entity contrary to its own nature: to produce detriment and death is contrary to the nature of something which is sacred and which is a gift. For a discussion of the meaning of the term '*monstrum*,' cf. J. V. Luce, "Cleopatra as *Fatale Monstrum*," *CQ* 13 (1963) 251-7. Luce's study is devoted to the use of the term in Horace, but is enlightening on the meaning of the term generally. A monstrum is an entity not only of a certain mythical, but also of a certain moral, quality.

[8] S. V. Tracy, "Laocoon's Guilt," *AJPh* 108 (1987) 451-4, discusses the ambiguity of Laocoon's act.

[9] It may be noted parenthetically that Vergil's presentation of this episode explicitly leaves open the interpretation that Laocoon was not killed, though his sons apparently were. The brief simile at 2.223-4 compares the cries of Laocoon not to the cries of a dying animal, but to the cries of an injured animal which flees the one who injures it. The conjunction '*at*' (2.225) then marks the discrepancy between the apparent intention of the serpents and their failure

to accomplish their intention. Such a version of the Laocoon episode, a version in which Laocoon does not die, is preserved also by Apollodorus (*Bibl.*, v.18). The point is not crucial to the general thesis being advanced here; but if, according to Vergil's simile (2.223–4), Laocoon was not killed by the serpents, his escape is another instance of ineffectual expiation.

[10]These desecrations as instrumental causes in the fall of the city are of course part of a larger, more complex group of causes. The complexity of the issue may be seen from the discussion in K. W. Gransden, "The Fall of Troy," *G&R*, 32 (1985) 60–72. The point at present is not to present an exhaustive list of the causes of the city's fall, but only to point to the presence of these desecrations as contributing causes.

[11]"Moral ambiguity" in the *Aeneid* is treated by Williams (note 2) ch. 8. But Williams means by "moral ambiguity" a "mixture of motives" in one person, a different notion than is being presented here. Cf. also Galinsky, (note 4 above) 322.

[12]G. K. Galinsky, "The Hercules-Cacus Episode in *Aeneid* viii," *AJPh* 87 (1966) 18–51.

[13]Cf. note 7.

[14]The episodes of the death of Pallas with Aeneas' reaction (in Bk. X) and of the death of Turnus (in Bk. XII) have generated intense interpretive debate and markedly different interpretations (cf. notes 1 & 2 for examples). A convenient review of the many interpretations of the episode may be found in P. Burnell, "The Death of Turnus and Roman Morality," *G&R*, 34 (1987) 186–200. It is not the purpose of this article expressly to dispute any of the extant interpretations, though some difference with them is inevitable. The treatments by both Quinn and Williams, and by others of the "schools" (note 3) they represent, are illuminating, and I am indebted to all.

[15]This word is used by Quinn (note 1) 326, though he discerns the hybris in a different aspect of Turnus' act.

[16]The relationship of the *Aeneid* to the *Iliad* and the *Odyssey* has long been an object of study in the secondary, scholarly literature. The monograph by G. Knauer, *Die Aeneis und Homer* (Göttingen 1964), has collected, and assessed the results of, much previous research and has advanced beyond those results. In the Pallas/Turnus/Aeneas episode, here under discussion, Knauer (pp. 298–305, 316–327) draws lines of reference between the *Aeneid* and Homer's two epics. Though the various and numerous Homeric precedents illumine the *Aeneid*, the ultimate meaning of the *Aeneid* is a creation of its author. Aeneas' wrath toward Turnus and the Latins is reminiscent of Odysseus' wrath toward the suitors and of Achilles' wrath toward Hector and the Trojans, but the motives of Odysseus and Achilles must not simply be transposed onto Aeneas. Aeneas' motives must be discerned from within the *Aeneid*.

[17]Cf. K. Gransden, *Virgil's Iliad: An Essay on Epic Narrative* (Cambridge 1984) 200–1. Aeneas is acting in two aspects of the life of his band, in two capacities which in the Republic were assigned to specific offices. As leader in this situation of armed conflict he embraces responsibilities which were later assigned to the *imperator*; as the one who embraces and effects the moral/religious obligations representatively for his people he embraces responsibilities later assigned to the *pontifex*. Though of course Aeneas does not have these titles, these two offices might be said already to coalesce in his person.

[18]"A man is *pius* in relation to his father and his son, the gods he bears, and the civilization he serves," states M. Owen Lee, (in *Fathers and Sons in Virgil's Aeneid: Tum Genitor Natum* [Albany 1979] 45).

[19]Cf. P. Burnell (note 14).

[20]K. Quinn, (note 1) 274–276, in his explanation of the final scene of the epic, assumed that not only the belt as a reminder of Pallas, but specifically the desecration on the belt, explain Aeneas' reaction. But Quinn treats the desecration on the belt apart from the person wearing the belt and apart from the history of desecration in the epic in general. Consequently Quinn's explanation lacks a substantive attachment to the rest of the epic. When the other instances of desecration are considered, the motive for action which the desecration on the belt engenders in Aeneas can be much more clearly identified and defined. An interesting contribution to the interpretation of the desecration on the belt is made by G. Dimock Jr., "The Mistake of Aeneas," *The Yale Review* 46 (1975) 334–56. Also Dimock finds that the desecration on the belt, as much or more than the belt itself, determines Aeneas' reaction.

[21]Note the explanation of Camps (note 6 above) 39. He states, "It is dramatically effective that the sword-belt should later become the cause of Turnus' own death by reawakening

Aeneas' anger when he is about to spare him; but the effect is one of poetic justice not of moral retribution."

[22]The *Aeneid* contains other instances of desecrations, as the term is used in this paper, which have not been included in this discussion: e.g., the abuse of the corpses of Euryalus and Nisus (9.465–7); the offense against the sacred tree of Faunus (12.766–71). Such instances are not treated in this paper since the topic of this paper is not desecrations *per se*, but only those desecrations which the text makes instrumental in the emergence of Aeneas' consciousness that his mission in life is, among other things, to uphold the moral order as an expiator of desecrations.

Michael C. J. Putnam

DAEDALUS, VIRGIL, AND THE END OF ART

The final essay in Part I returns us from the end of the *Aeneid* to a crucial moment at the midpoint of the poem, as Aeneas prepares to enter the Underworld. Vergil introduces book 6 through a seeming digression, the story of Daedalus and his son Icarus, depicted on the doors of the temple of Apollo at lines 14–37. Putnam reads the Daedalus story as "a metaphor of the progress of any artist." He helps us see that Vergil has created an opportunity for himself as an artist to talk about the meaning of his art within his poem, especially art's power to deceive. Through a close reading of the passage, Putnam brings us back again from the middle to the end, interpreting Aeneas' last act in light of the grief for art's limitations that we read in the story of Daedalus. (Ed.)

My text is Virgil's version of the story of Daedalus, from the opening of *Aeneid* 6.[1] Aeneas confronts this tale on reaching Cumae in search of the Sibyl. It is told in a series of tableaux on the doors of a temple dedicated to Apollo by the artisan-sculptor himself after his safe arrival in Italy. This is the only occasion in ancient literature where an artist is described as constructing his literal, which in this case is also to say his spiritual, or psychic, biography. As such I take it as a metaphor for the progress of any artist, for his imaginative diary, as it were. My thesis will be that in certain essential ways the tale of Daedalus, crafted by himself, sets up a typology that is mirrored in the ethical artistry practiced by Aeneas from standards set him by his father toward the end of the same book. After parading before his son a host of future Roman heroes, most of them distinguished for their military prowess, Anchises summarizes what he foresees as Rome's special genius. It will not lie in any unique brilliance as sculptors in bronze or stone, or as orators or astronomers, but in their accomplishment as governing warriors, in their moral usage of political power:

"tu regere imperio populos, Romane, memento
(hae tibi erunt artes), pacique imponere morem,
parcere subiectis et debellare superbos."[2]

["Remember, Roman, to rule peoples with your power (for you, these will be your arts), and to establish a custom for peace, to spare the suppliants and to war down the proud."]

Michael C. J. Putnam, "Daedalus, Virgil, and the End of Art," *American Journal of Philology* 108.2 (1987) 173–198. Reprinted by permission of The Johns Hopkins University Press.

This is the Roman "artistry" set up for Aeneas to model himself against in the epic's second half.

But I would go still further in drawing analogies from the *vita* ["life"] of Daedalus and suggest that it reveals something, first, of the narrator's spirit as he outlines Aeneas' progress, and then also of the intelligence of the poet Virgil working within the demands of a strict generic tradition. Aeneas who has himself, like Daedalus, just completed an extraordinary journey, is not allowed by the Sibyl to meditate on even the most simplistic parallels between himself and the Cretan inventor. She brusquely whisks her charge away from what she styles *spectacula*, sights presumably purveying only aesthetic delight. But Virgil's reader, with his privileged, unheroic leisure for contemplation, is under the obligation to respond not only — as Aeneas might have — to the sculptured encapsulation of an artist's life but to what Aeneas does not know, to the emotions of the artist in the crafting and of the narrator in the telling.

Here is the story as told by Virgil at *Aeneid* 6.14–37:

> Daedalus, ut fama est, fugiens Minoia regna
> praepetibus pennis ausus se credere caelo   15
> insuetum per iter gelidas enauit ad Arctos,
> Chalcidicaque leuis tandem super astitit arce.
> redditus his primum terris tibi, Phoebe, sacrauit
> remigium alarum posuitque immania templa.
> in foribus letum Androgeo; tum pendere poenas   20
> Cecropidae iussi (miserum!) septena quotannis
> corpora natorum; stat ductis sortibus urna.
> contra elata mari respondet Cnosia tellus:
> hic crudelis amor tauri suppostaque furto
> Pasiphae mixtumque genus prolesque biformis   25
> Minotaurus inest, Veneris monimenta nefandae,
> hic labor ille domus et inextricabilis error;
> magnum reginae sed enim miseratus amorem
> Daedalus ipse dolos tecti ambagesque resoluit,
> caeca regens filo uestigia. tu quoque magnam   30
> partem opere in tanto, sineret dolor, Icare, haberes.
> bis conatus erat casus effingere in auro,
> bis patriae cecidere manus. quin protinus omnia
> perlegerent oculis, ni iam praemissus Achates
> adforet atque una Phoebi Triuiaeque sacerdos,   35
> Deiphobe Glauci, fatur quae talia regi:
> "non hoc ista sibi tempus spectacula poscit;…"

["Daedalus, according to the story, fleeing the Minoan kingdom on swift wings, having dared to trust himself to the sky [15], swam through the unfamiliar path to the cold north and finally, stood lightly on the Chalcidian height. On his return, first to these lands, to you Phoebus he sanctified the rigging of his wings and built a huge temple. On the doors is the death of Androgeus; [20] then the children of Cecrops ordered (alas!) to pay the price of seven bodies of sons each year; there stands the urn with the lots sorted. Opposite, raised from the sea, faces the Cnosian land: here is the cruel love for a bull and Pasiphae mated in secret and the mixed breed and two-formed offspring [25], the Minotaur, reminder of the unspeakable passion; here the labor, the house and the inextricable maze. But then, taking pity on the queen's mighty love, Daedalus himself unravelled the tricks of the house and its windings, leading unseeing footsteps with a thread. [30] You too would have a great part in such a work, Icarus, if grief allowed. Twice he had tried to craft your fall in gold, twice your father's hand fell. Indeed continuing they would have surveyed everything with their eyes, had not Achates, sent ahead, come back and with him the priestess of Phoebus and Trivia [35], Deiphobe, daughter of Glaucus, who speaks as follows to the king: 'not these sights does this moment demand;...'"]

The story divides itself into five parts: introduction (Daedalus' arrival in Italy), first segment of sculpture devoted to events at Athens, counterbalancing Cretan exploits, the story of Ariadne and the address to Icarus. There is a climactic heightening of emotion on the part of both artist and the narrator of his tale as the story progresses, leading in the final episode to the artist's inability to create. Let us watch this happening by examining each section in more detail.

At the start, through the phrase *ut fama est* ["according to the story"], the narrator seems hyperconscious of putting things before us. By recreating someone else's report and not, it would seem, inventing his own version of the Daedalus story, he distances us in time while apparently disclaiming any direct involvement on his part in the telling.[3] Yet even in this introduction the narrator betrays a certain empathy with his version of Daedalus which suggests a deep understanding of his subject's imaginative ways. Daedalus, as the Cretan vignette makes clear, is a dealer in duplicity, an inventor of hybrid objects that cater to the furtive in their recipients and in their turn create further hybrids—a fake beast enclosing a true human (Pasiphae inside the replica of a cow) that begets a man-animal the Minotaur. The narrator anticipates this proclivity even now in his own poetic inventiveness. He replaces visual duplicity with verbal contrivance, exchanging the craftsman's dualistic artifact with the poet's ambiguous metaphor by seeing Daedalus, the human aviator, as swimmer through the heavens. The terrestrial creature, though airborne, is made poetically to deal (like Aeneas for much of the preceding story of his epic) with a watery element, and dedicate on return to earth the oarage of his wings.[4]

The narrator is a discerning critic of Daedalus' adventures in two other ways. One is a simple matter of rhetoric. By apostrophizing Apollo he, as it were, mimics Daedalus, claiming himself to share the emotion Daedalus felt on safe return to earth and voiced in gesture of thanks to Phoebus Apollo. But address to the god as Phoebus proves the narrator privy to the myth of Daedalus on a deeper level. Daedalus ends his adventuring on a spot sacred to Apollo, where Aeneas will hear prophecy of his, and Rome's, future through the god's mouthpiece, Deiphobe, the Sibyl. But Apollo the sun god played an important role in Daedalus' recent life. By steering a course toward the chill Bears, Daedalus saved himself from the fate of Icarus whose wings melted as he drew too near the sun's heat. The artisan of hybrids, who turns himself and his offspring into men-birds, loses his son in the process of artistic experimentation.

But there is also a hint, in the verb *enavit* ["he swam"] and the very phrase *gelidas Arctos* ["the cold north"], of a certain insouciance on the part of Daedalus. By swimming free of danger toward northern cold he followed the proper procedures for survival, but his child Icarus either was not taught, or at least was not able to practice, them.[5] To put it another way, both Daedalus within this initial segment of the narrative and the narrator expounding his tale, seem in different senses careless — and leave the reader thus far unaware — that more than one person was involved in this strange itinerary. Because there is no mention of Icarus and no hint of Daedalus' role as father, the reader remains with the impression, which the narrator's metaphors abet, that Daedalus thinks largely of his invention and the clever manipulation of it, not of its human consequences.

The narrator therefore gives us a foretaste of circularity in his rendering of the tale, preparing us for the address to Icarus at the end. But neither at the start nor at the conclusion of the episode is the actual death of Icarus mentioned, a fact which invites the reader to fill in the text, to exercise his own imagination recreating and contemplating the most poignant incident in Daedalus' biography. In his role as father Daedalus is a double artistic failure, first incapable of completely imitating nature, then unable to mime the disastrous results of this inadequacy.

Though they now forthrightly continue the theme of sons killed or sacrificed, the initial sculptures proper, devoted to events in Athens, are treated as matters of fact, save in one respect. There is no word for the act of crafting and the only object mentioned, the urn, was not of Daedalus' making. The exception is the exclamation *miserum* (alas! dreadful!). From its placement in the middle of line 21 and therefore at the center of the three lines, it serves as emotional commentary on the whole segment. But to whom the emotion is imputed remains ambiguous. Is it that experienced by the suffering Athenians? Is it Daedalus' response as he contemplates the results of his handiwork (or, in his mind's eye, the events themselves), or Aeneas', examining the sculpture? Is it the reaction of the narrator sharing the same sensations, or of the reader being taught them in his turn? For one verbal moment, even in the most "detached" segment of Daedalus' tale, narrator, characters and audience are united in empathy.[6]

The first Cretan segment is even more nominal, but now the list of characters and emotions concentrates specifically on Daedalus' art. His is an inventiveness which articulates subterfuge and doubleness, that tangibly fosters sexual perversity, and harbors its results, a man-bull, in a labyrinthine dwelling that is both labor and error.[7] It exemplifies the intensity of craftsmanship that imprisons the misformed product of human-animal passion in a maze symbolizing, like its contents, the troubling results of a "wandering" of the emotions. Pasiphae's double "error" receives its artistic complement from Daedalus' tricky fabrication.[8] Thus far in his tale Daedalus' art is dangerous only for its receivers.

The second Cretan scene brings a series of abrupt changes. Though the labyrinth remains an essential part of the plot, we turn from one queen, Pasiphae, to another, her unnamed daughter, Ariadne, and from a cruel love to another labeled simply "mighty." But the viewer-reader is also appropriately disoriented. We know from what follows that the Ariadne episode is part of the tableaux of sculptural reliefs. But Daedalus has suddenly, and Virgil brilliantly, led us from his *curriculum vitae* as guileful artisan to his role as apparently dispassionate reappraiser of the effects of that art. He becomes the undoer of his own trickery, an undoing we can hear in the sound of line 29:

Daedalus ipse dolos tecti ambagesque resolvit,...

["Daedalus himself unravelled the tricks of the house and its windings,..."]

Daedalus, who reprojects his artistic self through *ipse dolos* ["himself the tricks"],
the labyrinth's wiliness, now straightens its windings and lightens its darkening
ways. But dispassionate is far too mild a word. Through poetry's magic Daedalus
actually becomes Ariadne. She is the *regina* ["queen"] and she it was who, through
Daedalus' gift of thread, directed the steps of Theseus out from the maze after killing the Minotaur.[9] Yet, according to Virgil-Daedalus, we find him *regens* ["leading"], taking her emotional and physical role by linguistic sleight of hand. The reason for this empathy, as the artist unwinds his own artistry and foregoes his own
self-made heritage of deception, is pity. Pity is the response that transforms the
apparently aloof artistic deceiver into the emotional resolver of his own deceits. It is
this response in himself that he would now monumentalize.[10]

His own poet-monumentalizer is equally forward. He puts no word of crafting
into his own presentation. Nothing intervenes to prevent the reader from the stated
actuality of Daedalus' experience.[11] By contrast to the preceding episode, then, this
tableau is *vivant* ["living"]. Frozen re-presentation yields to active experience, as
we are made to share directly in the artist's suffering. We are Daedalus but, because
he is one with his protagonist, we are Virgil as well, uttering through the power of
words what cannot be expressed in sculpture.

Finally, we leave the triply fictive world of poet imagining artist crafting
himself in art to look more simply at the artist's inability to create. We find him
unable to bring to aesthetic completion the delineation in sculpture of an event
which in itself, to the artist as experiencer, remained a subject of sorrow, rousing
emotion unsatisfied and therefore incomplete. As an interested third party,
Daedalus could be shown to share in Ariadne's feelings, ruling with her out of
pity her lover's steps. The death of Icarus is a deeper matter. It is the death of a
son from the misuse of his father's artistry and for which the father's artistic but
duplicitous heroizing must bear some responsibility. As he did in the case of
Ariadne, the narrator draws a lexical connection between artist and subject. But
the artist who there rules the queen he depicts (*regina-regens*) now fails in his
vocation. Because of Icarus' attempt to emulate his father as man-bird, he suffered
a mortal fall, and the contemplation of this mischance (the Latin *casus* ["fall, mischance"] plays on both literal and figurative senses) caused his father's hands twice
to fall as he attempted to monumentalize it.[12]

Here the empathy of the narrator, which has been building from the opening
segment, is most fully expressed. As in the initial apostrophe to Phoebus Apollo, he
seems to adopt the voice of Daedalus. There his cry was in thanksgiving. Here his
words are uttered in sorrow. But in fact so strong is the narrator's involvement that
he replaces Daedalus entirely so as to address Icarus directly in explanation of his
father's artistic failure. In so doing, in replacing the sculptor-father, the poet's narrator becomes a Daedalian figure, bringing Icarus and his father's frustrating grief
before us in the permanence of words.

We have therefore, in one of Virgil's richest poetic moments, a study in artistic
incompletion that is extraordinarily complete as a poetic act. The incompletion, the
tale within the tale, is Daedalus' and it results from a gradual heightening of his
emotional participation. In the last three episodes of Daedalus' story as Virgil tells
it, the only ones where the artisan is directly involved, we watch him first as aloof
artificer of duplicity, constructing monsters to create further monsters. His empathy grows, and his characterization as artist disappears, as he shows himself (and is
shown) pitying Ariadne and as a result unravelling his own artistic stratagems

(which, I take it, is not only to show himself powerful over his own art but also, perhaps, even to admit fallibilities in that art). Finally he becomes the victim of *dolor* ["grief, anguish"], of the spasm of grief for his lost son, and this distress results in his inability to create at all. Death renders this artist artless. Daedalus' final honesty, his deepest response to natural feelings, brings artistic barrenness as well as a final powerlessness. But this very gesture of unfulfillment becomes, through Virgil's narration of it, the perfecting element of a poet's holistic enterprise. One artist's failure through passion is the subject of another's successful finishing of his art.

My thesis is that this treatment by one artist of the spiritual biography of another serves as paradigm of the Virgilian career and of the equally tripartite division of the *Aeneid* as a poetic entity, and that it is particularly enlightening for the reader probing the meaning of the epic's conclusion. It is important for my argument to remember that the *Aeneid* begins and ends with acts sparked by *dolor* ["grief, anguish"]. At line 9 of the first book we find Juno, Aeneas' divine arch enemy and emblem of irrationality, *dolens*, aggrieved, as she launches this hero, noteworthy for his *pietas* ["piety"], into a sea of troubles. Sixteen lines later we are told in greater detail of the *causae irarum saevique dolores*, the sources of her wrath and fierce anguish that now spur her on to violence. In balance, eight lines from the epic's conclusion we learn of the *saevus dolor*, the fierce anguish which Aeneas experienced at the death of Pallas. Recollection of this event, aroused by sight of the belt Pallas had worn, now on the suppliant Turnus, who had killed him earlier in battle, drives Aeneas to a frenzy of rage (he is described as "set aflame by furies and terrible in his wrath"). In this paroxysm he slays his antagonist whose soul flees under the shades as the epic comes to its abrupt end. I have proposed elsewhere, from several angles, that Aeneas' final deed turns him into a Juno figure, in other words that he becomes a personification, not of his much touted *pietas* based on his father's injunction to *clementia* ["clemency"] for the beaten down, but of its opposite, Junonian anger.[13] The subsequent pages will further defend this contention.

First, Daedalus and the Virgilian career, and Daedalus and the structure of the *Aeneid*. In two cryptic lines near the start of the second book of his *Georgics* Virgil in his own voice addresses his patron Maecenas:

...non hic te carmine ficto
atque per ambages et longa exorsa tenebo.[14]

["I will not hold you here with an invented song and through windings and long beginnings."]

This definition of casuistic poetry may apply to work Virgil anticipates for his later career, but more likely it is his way of looking back to his first work, the *Eclogues*. Certainly no other poems in Latin, with their many layers of symbolism and multivalent masquerades, could more justly claim the epithets fictive and ambiguous. The rich later history of pastoral poetry as a vehicle for necessary indirection of statement looks back in honor to its primarily Virgilian source.

As Virgil, Daedalus-like, leads his poetry out of the *ambages* ["windings, ambiguities"] of pastoral and into the greater openness and availability of didactic, his poetic voice moves from playful to serious and he from poet as implicit deceiver to poet as explicit pitier. His opening prayer to Augustus asks Caesar to nod approval to his bold beginnings:

ignarosque viae mecum miseratus agrestis
ingredere...[15]

["having pitied with me the country folk ignorant of the path, begin..."]

Pity creates poetry with the Daedalian power of Ariadne's thread, capable, through teaching, of directing those unsure of the path they tread. The immediate result, as the poet and his farmer set out on their interactive labors, is that new spring arrives, snow melts and "the crumbling clod has broken itself up" (*resolvit*) under the power of the west wind.[16] Pity's poetry has also Daedalus' power to resolve nature's seasonal dilemmas and set the farmer firmly on his arduous road.

Last in the Virgilian career comes the poetry of *dolor* ["anguish"]. The *Aeneid* seems the impersonal epic of one man's pious journey toward accomplishment, mirroring *in parvo* ["in miniature"] the future achievements of imperial Rome as it rises to unparalleled greatness under Augustus. But it is also, as we have seen and will further observe, a passion-ridden poem whose final deed of violence stemming from anguish and anger leaves open as many questions as it answers. It leaves dissatisfied the reader's expectations of praise for Aeneas' most memorable action as model for Rome's glorious enterprise to come, and instead completes a cycle based on *dolor,* that is, on an emotion founded in discontent and battening on deprivation. Like Virgil's history of Daedalus it is a brilliantly complete poem ending on premonitions of artistic incompletion.

For the *Aeneid* itself also has the rhythms of a Daedalian undertaking. As one of the most highly ordered of poems, the possibilities for imaginative structuring it offers to the reader are numerous. We gain pleasure, as we approach the epic in linear fashion, from sensing books grouped as pairs or trios, or from savoring a balance between the epic's halves, as they open out in clear echoes of book 1 in book 7. We may also acknowledge Virgil's grand chiasmus, where opening anticipates closure. We then focus centrally on the powerful linkage between books 6 and 7 which begins with address to Caieta, Aeneas' nurse, another in the host of those, especially prominent in the preceding book, who gain real death and dubious immortality for being in Aeneas' entourage.

I would like here to reconsider what has long been observed as the *Aeneid's* tripartite division.[17] We could distinguish the three movements as follows: books 1–4, which take us topographically and temporally from Troy to Carthage and revolve on Aeneas' meeting with Dido; books 5–8, as we move from Sicily, to Cumae, to Tibermouth, which contain Aeneas' two great revelations of the future, from his father in the Underworld and on the shield of Vulcan; books 9–12, which deal primarily with the war for supremacy in Latium and, in particular, with Aeneas' confrontation with Turnus.

After the pattern Virgil has Daedalus establish for himself, the first segment of the *Aeneid* is rich with exemplification of deceit. As recreated for us in Aeneas' words, the wooden horse, Troy's equivalent of Pasiphae's cow, is, save for the shield of Aeneas, the single most memorable artifact in the *Aeneid*, notable for its Daedalian duplicity and duality.[18] (It is at once alive and dead, a wooden object, fashioned as an animal, pregnant with a human brood. As objects both cow and horse are marvelous on the outside, deceptive on the inside. They can, even should, be viewed as Virgil's epic can be read. Past a veneer of artificial charm—in regard to the *Aeneid* the veneer is partially manufactured of our idealizing expectations—lie, in all cases, terrible truths). The second part of Aeneas' narrative is also riddled with the monstral and the biform, with a plant that drips with human blood, Harpies who are at once birds or maidens or goddesses, Scylla (part human, part fish, part wolf), the man-mountain Etna and the mountain-man Polyphemus.

But it is the story of Aeneas, especially as it merges with Dido's, to which I want to call attention.[19] Venus, divinity of love and mother of Aeneas, arrives on the scene in the disguise of the virgin-goddess Diana. She soon hides her son in a cloud, as he makes his way into Carthage, and his beauty is said to be his mother's artifice (grace added by craftsmen to ivory is the poet's simile, gold embellishing silver or marble) as he bursts from its enclosure. But counterfeiting is once again her province, her "new arts" (*novas artis*) in the narrator's words, as she replaces Ascanius with Cupid in preparation for the temptation of Dido.

The pretendings of Aeneas, as orchestrated by Virgil, are more elaborate. The most patent example is his gift-giving. He offers to Dido Helen's cloak and the scepter of Ilione, which is to say his presence brings her, from Helen, illicit love leading to her city's symbolic razing by fire, from Ilione, suicide. His relation to the sculptures on Juno's temple which he sees in Carthage's midst is more subtle. They depict scenes from Troy's fall which summarize Homer or intervene between the story line of the *Iliad* and Aeneas' own tale. Aeneas and Achates take them as evidence of Dido's sympathy for human suffering. The reader, aware of their connection with Juno and her vengeful proclivities, looks at them in other ways. Their great figure is Achilles. He appears directly in three of their episodes, indirectly in three others, primarily as a killer, of Troilus, Hector, Memnon and Penthesilea. By the end of the epic, Aeneas will become in part an Achilles, pitilessly killing his Latin Hector, Turnus. The equation here is more understated. By continuing on the tale of Troy in his narrative to Dido, Aeneas becomes active as well as passive, participant in events but their passionate recaller as well. His verbal artisanship, in other words, takes up where the sculptures left off yet also becomes part of the seduction of Dido.[20] The destruction of Troy, which he suffers as a character within his narrative, leads inevitably to the destruction of Dido which his very act of narration helps to cause.

The lexical, symbolic or imagistic continuum from the end of book 1, through Aeneas' narrative, to the masterful delineation of Dido's downfall in the fourth book needs only brief documentation. Cupid's fake words (*simulata verba*, 1.710) lead directly to the faking of the wooden horse (*simulant*, 2.17), which in turn anticipates Aeneas' attempts at dissimulation (*dissimulant*, 4.291) which Dido unmasks in her first words addressed to him after his decision to depart:

"dissimulare etiam sperasti, perfide, tantum
posse nefas...?"[21]

["did you even hope to be able to disguise, faithless one, such great wickedness...?"]

It is an easy transition from the *doli*, the wiles of Venus and Cupid, in book 1, to the deceits of the Greeks in book 2 as executed by Sinon and the horse, to the deception of Aeneas which Dido uncloaks. The symbolic flames with which Venus plans to gird Dido become the destructive arson of Troy and then the triple fires of book 4 — the metaphoric ardor of her love, her literal burning on the pyre which, as we have seen, is visualized as the burning of Carthage, the queen as city demolished by a concatenation of circumstances.

It is not necessary to argue yet again the moral fine-points of a tragic adventure where ignorance and knowledge play intermeshed roles, and human weaknesses make its characters easy prey for divine machinations as well as self-deceptions. I want only to suggest that in detail and in general the constancy of deceit in the story-line of *Aeneid* 1–4 finds its parallel in the exploits of Daedalus as artificer. The particularities and their consequences press the connection between Pasiphae and Dido. Pasiphae's love is *crudelis* ["cruel"] and this is the adjective Dido twice applies to her absconding lover. Just as the Cretan queen's erotic adventure is based on a strategem which is also a hiding (*furto*), so also, in the narrator's words, Dido ponders a furtive love (*furtivum amorem*), and it is against accusations of trickery (*furto*) from her that Aeneas must defend himself. Finally, the Minotaur, symbol of Pasiphae's "unspeakable passion" (*Veneris monimenta nefandae*) has its more tangible counterpart in Aeneas' trappings and their marriage, "all the reminders of that unspeakable man" (*nefandi/cuncta viri monimenta*) which Dido will set aflame along with herself.

The generalities, on the other hand, center as we have seen on the artificers rather than on their products. They define Aeneas, and the narrator of his tale, as Daedalus figures. Both particular points of contact and more broad equations persist in the second segment of Virgil's scheme. Critics have remarked on the abruptness with which Ariadne is introduced into the narrative at line 28. She is not named and, though she was a princess, she was certainly not, at least not at that moment in her eventful life, a *regina* ["queen"]. This apparent discontinuity, however, is actually a brilliant transition when we pursue our projection of the plot of Daedalus' psychological progress on to the *Aeneid*'s triple divisions. For, if in the life of Daedalus we move from Pasiphae to Ariadne, in the artistic development of the *Aeneid* we stay with Dido, who need not be renamed and who remains the poem's great *regina*.[22] The difference is that, in the second movement of the *Aeneid*, her *crudelis amor* ["cruel love"] (now become *magnum amorem* ["a great love"]) is resolved. When Aeneas sees her in the Underworld, in the company of those "whom harsh love has gnawed through with cruel wasting" (*quos durus amor crudeli tabe peredit*), she scorns him, fleeing into a shady grove:

> …coniunx ubi pristinus illi
> respondit curis aequatque Sychaeus amorem.[23]

> ["…where her original husband, Sychaeus, responds to her cares and equals her love."]

Differentiation leading to suicide has yielded, in book 6, to reciprocation and balance.

Yet we have been readied for this denouement earlier. At the conclusion of book 4, as we prepare to leave the epic's initial third for its central articulation, we have Virgil's first, enormously moving example of pity for suffering leading to its resolution. The moment is Dido's death:

> Tum Iuno omnipotens longum miserata dolorem
> difficilisque obitus Irim demisit Olympo
> quae luctantem animam nexosque resolveret artus.[24]

> ["Then Juno all powerful, who pitied her long suffering and the difficult passing, sent Iris down from Olympus, to release her struggling soul and binding limbs."]

At the end pity releases the troubled queen from her enmeshed body, which is to say from the deceits of what Anchises is soon to call the blind prison which confines us within the toils of our destructive emotions.[25]

There is another Daedalian resolution, centering on book 6, that belongs more exactly to Aeneas. The literal labyrinth of Daedalus' manufacture (*hic labor ille domus* ["here the labor, the house"]) becomes now symbolic, but equally present, in the hero's effortful life as he faces the prospect of descending, alive into the world of the dead and returning whence he came. *Hoc opus, hic labor est* "this the task, this the effort," says the Sibyl.[26] As preparation for this undertaking, Aeneas must attend to the *horrendas ambages*, the fearful enigmas of the seeress' utterances which correspond to the palpable but no less devious windings (*ambages*) of the Minotaur's dwelling. The Daedalian "threads" that bring resolutions to Aeneas' quandary are manifold. They consist not only in a growing clarity to the Sibyl's words but in the person of the Sibyl herself who will serve as guide through the Underworld's paths. He is, however, given further assistance by a series of talismans, first, the birds of his mother, then the golden bough—a very Daedalian object, serving now to open out rather than close in, to undeceive instead of dupe—his chief passport, to which the birds direct his traces. Finally we have the words of the poet Musaeus to whom the priestess turns for help in the search for Anchises.

If deceit is the chief impulse behind Daedalus' initial fabrications, pity rules him in their undoing. Though Aeneas does address Dido in his first words to her as the only person to have taken pity on the Trojans' sufferings, it is a virtue noticeably absent from the first four books. Yet here once more it is our changing viewpoint on the figure of Dido that helps us make the transition from segment to segment. At 4.369–70 she speaks to her former lover as if he were already absent:

num fletu ingemuit nostro? num lumina flexit?
num lacrimas victus dedit aut miseratus amantem est?[27]

["Did he groan at my weeping? Did he turn his eyes? Did he, overcome, shed tears or pity her who loved him?"]

This, we remember, is exactly what Aeneas does do here in the Underworld, though she refuses to respond to his plea for words:

prosequitur lacrimis longe et miseratur euntem.[28]

["he follows her in tears at a distance and pities her as she goes."]

Aeneas has now performed the great act of which Dido had earlier found him negligent. He himself has—at last, and too late—also pitied the queen's love (*reginae...miseratus amorem*).

He had come to this emotion, for the first time in the epic, in the fifth book, which opens the *Aeneid*'s second of three divisions. There, at the end of the footrace, Aeneas pities the unfortunate Salius who had slipped during the competition.[29] It is an emotion that he must receive as much as offer during this middle segment of the epic. He pities the unburied who are forced to wait at length before crossing the Styx. Yet he is also himself subject to three notable acts of pity during these books, from Jupiter, who saves his fleet, from the Sibyl and her inspirer, to both of whom he must pray, and from the Tiber in book 8. For this reach of the epic is Aeneas' most extended period of dependence which proves at the same time to initiate him, and the reader of his saga, into the most elaborate revelations of the future. Pity of Sibyl and of river god leads him, one, to his father, the other, to the site of future Rome. Anchises parades before him future Roman heroic greats and gives him his ethical commission. Evander's tour of Pallanteum anticipates the grand city to come, and the shield, which Venus brings to Aeneas at Caere, concludes book 8 with another series of visions into heroic action, the *non ennarrabile textum* ["unnarratable fabric"] of Roman history.

In details, then, and from a larger viewpoint, during the second segment of the epic Virgil has his hero put behind him the deceitful, artifice-ridden atmosphere of the initial quartet of books. He replaces it with a portrait of the artisan-hero as pitier. Aeneas undoes his own dissimulations, or those thrust upon him, while the mazey mysteries that lead him to Rome's future are tantalizingly unraveled for him by others who offer him their rich solace in turn.

The last third of the epic can be treated more briefly. Its plot is the war in Latium, but the narrator tells a singularly purposeless tale. The omniscient reader knows from occasional prophecies that Aeneas will become overlord of Latium and marry Lavinia. But the fullness of the narrative dwells on the relentless futility and unceasing loss that war engenders. It furnishes a catalogue of deaths, especially those of the young whose lives have been cut off near their starts. We think immediately of Nisus and Euryalus, of Pallas and Lausus, of Camilla and finally of Turnus. The rampage of slaughter that Aeneas embarks on after Pallas' death, in which he kills with equal indiscrimination suppliant and priest, takes its last victim in his primary antagonist who is wearing Pallas' belt. Yet for all his *violentia* ["violence"] and pride our sympathies lie at the end with Turnus, not with the titular hero, with Turnus beaten down by Jupiter's minion Fury and by the inner furies which set Aeneas at the last ablaze.

One of the framing emotions of this last quartet of books, as it is of the epic as a whole, is *dolor* ["anguish"]. We find it in Turnus near the opening of book 9 as he casts a greedy eye on the leaderless Trojans penned within their camp:

> ignescunt irae, duris dolor ossibus ardet.[30]

> ["anger ignites, anguish burns in his hard bones."]

Or, soon again, in a speech of exhortation to his colleagues:

> "sunt et mea contra
> fata mihi, ferro sceleratam exscindere gentem
> coniuge praerepta; nec solos tangit Atrides
> iste dolor, solisque licet capere arma Mycenis…"[31]

> ["There are my fates too in opposition, to extinguish with my sword the criminal race, my bride stolen; such anguish does not touch the sons of Atreus alone, nor is it only Mycenae which can seize arms…"]

It is remarkable how much of the same language recurs in the counter-balancing moment of anger with which the epic concludes. Aeneas, in his final words, accuses

Turnus of possessing *scelerato sanguine*, criminal blood. The reader could presume that a variation of the reason Turnus gives for his own *dolor* ["anguish"] — that Lavinia, his Helen, has been torn from him — is applicable also now to Aeneas poised to kill because of the *dolor* aroused by the death of Pallas. In any case, though the last appearance of *dolor* doubly rounds out the epic to a splendid rhetorical and psychological moment of closure, it is, in senses that transcend mere personal feelings, an extraordinarily unfulfilling, not to say devastating, emotion. Turnus asks for pity and Aeneas does hesitate, as if he were preparing to respond with sympathy and practice *clementia* ["clemency"].[32] For Aeneas to grant pity through clemency, though it might appear an unheroic act by Homeric standards, would be for Virgil to round out the poem spiritually. He does not — cannot, perhaps — allow himself the luxury.[33]

I would like, in conclusion, to look in more detail at reasons why *dolor* leaves Aeneas-Daedalus-Virgil with his (their, if you prefer) heroic-artistic-poetic fabrication unfinished. First Aeneas-Daedalus. The ethical artistry imposed on Roman might, pursuing its political ends, was summarized, as we have seen, by Anchises to his son near the end of their meeting in the Underworld. The nub of his command, which he addresses to Aeneas as *Romane* ["Roman"], ancestor of and paradigm for his distinguished race, is to remember to spare the suppliant and war down the proud. By the end of the poem proud Turnus has been battled into abject submission, but, for whatever deep-seated reason, Aeneas does not spare him. He does not, finally, recall his father's admonition. Instead, in the narrator's words, he drank in the reminders of his fierce grief (*saevi monimenta doloris*) and, in an access of fury and rage, buries his sword in his opponent's chest. *Dolor* initiates Aeneas' final act. In so doing it gives the lie to Roman pretensions toward clemency, toward an artistic morality that reincorporates an antagonist, abased but living, into the civic community. Aeneas' attack of *dolor* proves the impossibility of realizing in fact Anchises' exhortation. In this case to complete is to idealize, to idealize is to dream untruths.[34]

Secondly we must pursue the analogy of Virgil, the creator of the *Aeneid*, and Daedalus. We are not now concerned with Aeneas' emotions as they undermine Roman political artisanship but with the imagination that shapes such an ending. My thesis is that Virgil deliberately leaves his poem incomplete, vis-à-vis the epic genre as he inherited it, as if the *Aeneid* were to serve as one final, magnificent metaphor — one masterful artistic symbol — for the incompletions in Roman, which is to say human, life. Let me illustrate my point with brief reminders of the plot endings of four other epics of which three (the *Iliad*, the *Odyssey* and the *Argonautica* of Apollonius Rhodius)[35] precede the *Aeneid*, while the other, Statius' *Thebaid*, follows.

First the *Iliad*. The bulk of its last book is taken up with the reconciliation scene between Priam and Achilles, but its last moments are devoted to the aftermath of the burning of Hector's body:

> And when they [the people of Troy] were assembled together, first they quenched with flaming wine all the pyre, so far as the fire's might had come upon it, and thereafter his brethren and his comrades gathered the white bones, mourning, and big tears flowed over down their cheeks. The bones they took and placed in a golden urn, covering them over with soft purple robes, and quickly laid the urn in a hollow grave, and covered it over with great close-set stones. Then with speed heaped they the mound, and round about were watchers set on every side, lest the well-greaved

Achaeans should set upon them before the time. And when they had piled the barrow they want back, and gathering together duly feasted a glorious feast in the palace of Priam, the king fostered of Zeus. On this wise held they the funeral for horse-taming Hector.

The completion of a life demarcates the completion of a poem. The careful rituals of burial and feast, that bring the funeral of Hector to conclusion with communal ceremony, are complemented by the perfection of the epic that describes them, by poetry's own exacting ritual.

The twenty-fourth book of the *Odyssey* finds its hero taking revenge with bloody slaughter on the suitors of Penelope. But the ending turns this thirst for vengeance around. Zeus says to Athene in heaven:

> "Now that goodly Odysseus has taken vengeance on the wooers, let them swear a solemn oath, and let him be king all his days, and let us on our part bring about a forgetting of the slaying of their sons and brothers; and let them love one another as before, and let wealth and peace abound."

Thus, as Odysseus is preparing to kill the suitors' relatives bent, in their turn, on revenge, Athene speaks to him, bringing the epic to end:

> "Son of Laertes, sprung from Zeus, Odysseus of many devices, stay your hand, and make the strife of equal war to cease, lest haply the son of Cronos be wroth with you, even Zeus, whose voice is borne afar."
>
> So spoke Athena, and he obeyed, and was glad at heart. Then for all time to come a solemn covenant betwixt the twain was made by Pallas Athene, daughter of Zeus, who bears the aegis, in the likeness of Mentor both in form and in voice.

Forgiveness, reconciliation, a commitment to peace and a statement by the narrator of an eternal pact to assure it—these are the gestures with which the *Odyssey* ends. Reintegration of society betokens poetic wholeness, and vice versa. Content and imagination are one.[36]

The ending of the *Argonautica* is simpler still as the singer speaks in his own voice:

> For now I have come to the glorious end of your toils; for no adventure befell you as you came home from Aegina, and no tempest of wind opposed you; but quietly did you skirt the Cecropian land and Aulis inside of Euboea and the Opuntian cities of the Locrians, and gladly did you step forth upon the beach of Pagasae.

Just as the Argonauts bring their journey to completion by returning whence they started, so the singer, proclaiming direct control over the matter of his verse, brings his own poetic voyage to a parallel stop.

Unfortunately we lack the final lines of any pre-Virgilian Latin epics. We must therefore jump in our survey to silver Latin and in particular to Statius who, at the end of his only completed epic, the *Thebaid*, directly acknowledges his indebtedness to Virgil. He finishes with an address to his own book:

vive, precor; nec tu divinam Aeneida tempta,
sed longe sequere et vestigia semper adora.
mox, tibi si quis adhuc praetendit nubila livor,
occidet, et meriti post me referentur honores.

["Live, I pray; do not compete with the divine *Aeneid*, but follow from afar
and adore always its footsteps. Soon, if any envy still spreads its clouds, it
will perish, and after my life, deserved honors will follow."]

The ending of the narrative proper, which precedes the speaker's *sphragis* ["seal"], is
equally important for our purposes. After the hideous carnage of civil strife and Theseus'
killing of Creon (the equivalent moment to the end of the *Aeneid*), who had refused to
allow the dead to be buried, the warring factions forge a treaty as the women rejoice in
the Athenian leader's calming presence. The epic's plot ends with due display of mourning for the fallen and with some of Statius' most beautiful (and most Virgilian) lines. I
could not tell, says the speaker, even if I had a hundred voices, of all the cries of grief:

Arcada quo planctu genetrix Erymanthia clamet,
Arcada, consumpto servantem sanguine vultus,
Arcada, quem geminae pariter flevere cohortes.
vix novus ista furor veniensque implesset Apollo,
et mea iam longo meruit ratis aequore portum.[37]

["With what lamenting, the Arcadian, his Erymanthian mother cried, the
Arcadian, who preserved his visage although his blood was lost, the
Arcadian, over whom twin cohorts wept equally. Scarcely would such new
madness and Apollo's approach have sufficed, and my boat now long at
sea deserves its port."]

Though he gives them new turns, especially in his elaboration of the autobiographical
"seal," Statius essentially clings to the closure patterns of his generic inheritance. In
fact he combines elements from the endings of all three Greek epics — ceremonies of
lamentation from the *Iliad*, the *Odyssey*'s call for forgiveness and reconciliation, and
Apollonius Rhodius' self-projection as traveller, appropriately completing at once
his poetic journey and the heroic voyage it had sung.

It is important to notice not so much how influential Greek epic remains upon
Statius' conclusion but how clearly the *Aeneid*'s finale is absent as an imaginative
force on this most Virgilian of poets while he wrote his *envoi* ["closing"]. Hence to
my point. In terms of its Greek epic past and its Roman poetic progeny, Virgil's
Aeneid is a strikingly incomplete poem.[38] Its ending is equivalent to Achilles' killing
of Hector, to the death of the suitors in the *Odyssey* or of Creon in the *Thebaid*. No
Iliadic mourning breaks the spell of Aeneas' inexorable blood-lust.[39] Reconciliations
akin to the *Odyssey*'s are mouthed in heaven but form no part in human action, as
victor kills suppliant. Turning to the end of the *Argonautica*, which has its spiritual
kinship to the *Odyssey*'s conclusion, we do not find in the *Aeneid* any equivalent
satisfactions. No wife is given Aeneas in a marriage ceremony that might give the
epic's quasi-tragic ending a comic twist. Nor is there a speaking "I," proud of his
accomplishment, who could at least abstract us at the end from the lived experience of the violence his story tells into the imagination that fostered it.

We will never know what Daedalian *dolor* ["grief, anguish"] within Virgil caused him to leave his epic so generically incomplete. (The ancient lives tell us that at his death Virgil had failed only to apply his *ultima manus*, his finishing touch, to the poem, not that it remained deficient in any substantial way.) But I have a suggestion. Critics have long since, and quite correctly, sensed a parallel between Icarus and the many people who die as they follow in the wake of Aeneas. I listed earlier the most prominent losses in the last quartet of books and it is well to remember that books 2 through 5 all end with deaths, of Creusa, Anchises, Dido, and Palinurus. The clearest parallel structurally, however, is with the death of Marcellus, the son of Augustus' sister and his adopted heir, whose funeral is described at the end of the sixth book.[40] It is as if the poet were saying that the Roman mission cannot go forward without loss of life, that the reality of death ever looms as a counterbalance to progress.

What critics have not stressed is the concomitant parallel between Aeneas and Daedalus. To do so is to turn from deaths suffered as the price of empire to placing responsibility for those deaths.[41] The artisan loses his son from his overreaching. Aeneas loses Pallas but he also kills Turnus. These deaths receive the final emphasis which is on causes as much as on results, on the perpetrator as much as on its victims.

The conclusion of the *Aeneid*, then, doubly uncloaks the deceptiveness of art. Aeneas cannot fulfill his father's idealizing, and therefore deceptive, vision of Rome, and Virgil, the artisan of his tale, cannot show him as so doing. Aeneas' final killing of Turnus differs from Daedalus' loss of Icarus essentially for being active instead of passive. Each demonstrates nature's final, Pyrrhic, triumph over art.

We may be meant to think that, as he crafted the *Aeneid*, in the process of writing, of practicing his own art, Virgil followed his own voyage of self-discovery and came with full assurance to see *dolor*, the immediacy of suffering, frustration, resentment, as an overriding presence in human life and therefore in his creative life. His plot-line, which mimes and reproduces the artist's growing inwardness, suggests a paradox: when, in the course of his experience an artist foregoes his natural role as trickster, and relieves his art of duplicity, in favor of truth of expression, his artifact, as his life's work, is an apparent failure. To idealize is to envision wholeness in self and society, to claim consistency in their patternings. It is to twist the tragic divisiveness of life's irrationality into comic returns, reconciliations, renewals. But Virgil, by ending his epic with two consequential acts of resentment, the one resulting in violence, the other from having to accept that violence, does not finally idealize. His final artifice is the sham of foregoing art.

In sum, Virgil does, idiosyncratically, complete the *Aeneid* just as he completes with growing emotion the tale of Daedalus' inability to create. This carefully, brilliantly flawed wholeness is perhaps his passionate way of saying that art's feigned orderings do not, cannot, claim to control the uncontrollable. For a poet of consummate honesty the truths of nature, Virgil would seem to say, are ever triumphant over the soothing trickery of art, however seductively its practitioners pattern their wares. For the art that supplants deceit with honesty, that composes life's imperfections, that unthreads its own labyrinthine text, not piety, or even pity, is possible, only the final, perfecting deficiencies of anger and sorrow.[42]

Notes

[1]The most recent discussions of the Daedalus episode are by V. Pöschl ("Die Tempeltüren des Dädalus in der Aeneis [6.14–33]," *WJA* n.f. I [1975] 119–33) who sees it as exemplifying

the failure of art when the artist confronts the truth of his suffering; C. Weber ("Gallus' Grynium and Virgil's Cumae," *ARCM* 1 [1978] 45–76) for whom the sequence serves as model for a miniature epyllion; and W. Fitzgerald ("Aeneas, Daedalus and the Labyrinth," *Arethusa* 17 [1984] 51–65). Fitzgerald's important essay views the two major segments of the tale as illustrating the change from "a finished work of art" to "the narrative of Daedalus, unfrozen and released into history" (54). In his earlier discussion (*Die Dichtkunst Virgils* [Innsbruck 1950] 244–46 = *The Art of Vergil*, trans. G. Seligson [Ann Arbor 1962] 149–50), Pöschl draws analogies between Aeneas and Daedalus. Both are exiles, both offer pity at crucial moments (Daedalus for Ariadne, Aeneas for Dido), both exemplify *pietas* (Daedalus' love for Icarus is parallel, according to Pöschl, to Aeneas' yearning for Anchises with whom he is soon to be reunited). See also Weber, op. cit., 40, n. 33.

   Such analogies are further developed by C. P. Segal in his sympathetic analysis of these lines ("*Aeternum per saecula nomen*, the golden bough and the tragedy of history: Part I," *Arion* 4 [1965] 617–57, especially 642–45). For Segal Daedalus "foreshadows the sufferings of the individual in the mythical, not the historical world, sufferings which lead to no lasting fruition in history, hence no transcendence of death."

   The legend of Daedalus has been treated in depth by F. Frontisi-Ducroux (*Dédale: mythologie de l'artisan en grèce ancienne* [Paris 1975]) and by J. K. Koerner (*Die Suche nach dem Labyrinth* [Frankfurt 1983]) who draws analogies between Daedalus and the modern mind dealing with its labyrinthine past while at the same time drawn toward self-sufficient flights into the a-historical and the novel. Cf. also the remarks on Daedalus as typifying "the artist as magician" by E. Kris and O. Kurz in *Legend, Myth, and Magic in the Image of the Artist* [New Haven 1979] 66–71.

   [2]6.851–53.

   [3]The authoritative discussion of the phrase *ut fama est* is by Norden (*P. Vergilius Maro: Aeneis Buch VI* [repr. Stuttgart 1957] *ad loc.*). The variations on tradition which it implies are numerous. Foremost is the connection of Daedalus with Italy. Writers of the generation before Virgil return Daedalus to earth either in Sicily (Dio. Sic. 4.78) or Sardinia (Sall. *Hist.* fr. 2.7 [Maurenbrecher] from, among others, Servius on 1.14). By having him aim directly for Cumae, Virgil emphasizes the parallel with Aeneas which will gradually grow clearer as the ecphrasis evolves.

   By feigning to repeat tradition unemotionally and then significantly varying it, the narrator claims control over the history of his subject. The poet does the same generically. Virgil's model for Aeneas' arrival at Cumae as prelude to his visit to the underworld is the opening of book 11 of the *Odyssey* where Odysseus reaches the land of the Cimmerians and immediately conjures up the spirits of the dead. No ecphrasis intervenes (re. G. Knauer, *Die Aeneis und Homer* [Hypomnemata 9: Göttingen 1979] 130, n. 1). Therefore, even where Daedalus seems as yet indifferent to, or even unaware of, his loss, the narrator-poet is very involved with the tale so as to mould Daedalus, to make the sculptor his own artifact, to impress his stamp of originality on his artisan-hero. If Daedalus deepens his emotional involvement in his subjects over time, as he sets about the crafting of his psychic biography, the narrator has a deep imaginative commitment from the start.

   [4]According to R. G. Austin (ed., *P. Vergili Maronis: Aeneidos Liber Sextus* [Oxford 1977] on 18, following Norden on 18f.) the dedication to Apollo "marks his gratitude for a safe landing and also his retirement from air-travel, in the manner of many Greek dedicatory epigrams…" But these strange oar-wings are also an offering for passing safely through the god's province in which men do not ordinarily trespass. (Virgil's only other use of the phrase *remigium/remigio alarum* is to describe the means of Mercury's descent from heaven at *Aen.* 1.301. The repetition here suggests a momentary equivalence between god and mortal who ascribes to the supernatural.) The over-reacher might be expected to pay a penalty for challenging Apollo in his territory. The passive *redditus* implies that throughout this stage of his adventures Daedalus has in fact been the god's subject. Virgil may portray him as flying *praepetibus pinnis*, but Horace, in an ode of which Servius twice reminds us (on 15 and 18), sees the means of his journey as *pinnis non homini datis* (*c.* 1.3.35). Perhaps the implication is that Phoebus Apollo does claim recompense, in the form of Icarus, for earth-bound man's sally into the skies, for momentary human arrogation of divinity. As god-man, the ultimate in spiritual hybridization, the Orphic artist, fulfilling for an instant his imagination's divine claims, suffers a profound human loss.

By forcing us even here to meditate on the negative demands of progress, Virgil reminds us that, in the unfolding epic story, it has not been long since Neptune exacted *unum caput* (5.815), one life for the safe completion of Aeneas' journey to Italy through the god's watery element.

[5]*OLD* (*s.v.* 1b) would translate *enavit* here as "to fly forth," but it is more enriching within the context to take the meaning as a metaphorical example of the dictionary's first definition: "to swim out or forth; (esp.) to escape by swimming; swim to safety." But, since Daedalus escaped the danger and the (pointedly) unnamed Icarus did not, the reader should rightly sense ambiguities in *praepetibus* and *levis.*

The first is an augural word, discussed in detail in relation to these lines by Aulus Gellius (*N.A.* 7.6). It appears four times in Ennius (Gellius mentions two instances) and lends a tone of majesty to the description of the artisan's epic accomplishment. As a term in augury it means "propitious," the opposite (according to Gellius' source, Figulus' *Augurii Privati*) of *infera* which he defines as a low-flying, less auspicious appearance. Its etymology is from *prae-peto,* "forward-seeking." As Gellius (followed closely by Servius on 6.15) expounds the meaning, the word becomes closely complementary to *enavit*:

idcirco Daedali pennas "praepetes" dixit, quoniam ex locis in quibus
periculum metuebat in loca tutiora pervenerat.

The reader, wondering why the narrator does not have Daedalus here include Icarus in his daring, sees *praepes* as "well-omened" (at least for Daedalus!), as "flying directly ahead" (without a concern for the tragic events occurring behind?), and as "lofty" (unlike Icarus who, after rising too high, fell into the sea?). *Levis,* then, while primarily defining Daedalus' nimbleness, hints at a certain fickleness as well. Physical dexterity (or artistic talent, for that matter) does not necessarily ally itself with stability of mind.

[6]Even here Virgil may possibly be alluding to Aeneas' tale. The seven bodies (*septena corpora*) of sons sent to Crete each year by the Athenians are reviewed shortly later in the *septem iuvencos* (38), the seven bullocks and the same number of heifers which Aeneas must now present to Apollo and Trivia. As the two myths follow their parallel progress, human offering is replaced by animal but in each case sacrifice is essential.

[7]The standard article on Daedalus' labyrinth and its resonances for Virgil is by P. J. Enk, "De Labyrinthi Imagine in Foribus Templi Cumani Inscripta," *Mnemosyne,* ser. 4.11 (1958) 322–30.

[8]The language is close to *Aen.* 7.282–83 where the horses given by Latinus to Aeneas are described as coming

illorum de gente patri quos daedala Circe
supposita de matre nothos furata creavit.

Aen. 6.24 and 7.283 document Virgil's only uses of the perfect participle of *suppono* in a sexual sense, and *furata* (7.283) echoes *furto* (6.24). The connection is further secured by Circe's epithet *daedala.* Circe is prone to the same erotic supposititiousness and "thievery" as the Athenian artificer. This supposititiousness is both literal and figurative. To "put under" sexually is fraudulently to replace the usual with the unexpected. The resulting miscegenation is, in book 7, between mortal and immortal (in the animal kingdom), in book 6, between human and animal. In each case generic mixing, as performed by Circe and Daedalus and recreated by the latter in sculpture, is typically Daedalian. Circe's hybrid horses anticipate the figures on the armor of Turnus: a Chimaera on his helmet (7.783–84) which, like Circe's horses (*spirantis naribus ignem,* 281), spouts fire (*efflantem faucibus ignis*), and Io in the process of metamorphosis from human into animal, *iam saetis obsita, iam bos.* Hybridization and metamorphosis complement each other in both instances. The latter, especially metamorphosis down from a higher to a lower sensibility, typifies book 7 as a whole (lines 660–61, e.g., offer an example of the furtive "mixing" of god and mortal). I trace the book's patterns of metamorphosis in further detail in "*Aeneid* 7 and the *Aeneid,*" *AJP* 91 (1970) 408–30 = *Essays on Latin Lyric, Elegy, and Epic* (Princeton 1982). On the association of Turnus and the Minotaur see P. duBois, *History, Rhetorical Description and the Epic* (Cambridge, England 1982) 39f., part of a thoughtful discussion of Daedalus' sculptures.

⁹It remains deliberately ambiguous whether *caeca vestigia* refer to the unseeing steps of Theseus or to the Labyrinth's dark path. Support for the former proposition comes from Catullus' reference to Theseus' *errabunda vestigia* (64.113) and from later imitations (re. Austin on 30), for the latter from Virgil's earlier description of the Labyrinth with its dark walls (*caecis parietibus, Aen.* 5.589) and from the sentence structure whose logic suggests a sequence from *ambages* to *caeca vestigia*. In either case the artisan is directly involved though his duplex activity lends different shades of meaning to *regens*. He becomes Ariadne and empathetically "leads" her lover to safety, or "straightens" the windings of his Labyrinth, unravelling the unravellable out of pity. *Inextricabilis* (27), Varro's coinage to describe Porsena's Etruscan labyrinth (Pliny *H.N.* 36.91), helps define the Labyrinth's puzzlement and toils, and adds a further dimension to Catullus' parallel, *inobservabilis* (64.115, itself a coinage), whose point is absorbed into Virgil's *caeca*. Virgil's Daedalus first creates, and then solves, the problems of his "text."

The influence of Catullus 64 on the Daedalus episode as a whole, most recently treated by Weber (op. cit. 47, 50–51), deserves still further study. It begins with similarities between the Argonauts and Daedalus through the primacy of their daring (there is a common emphasis on nimbleness, oarage and swimming in both initial episodes), develops in close parallels between the poets' treatments of Androgeos (64.77–83; *Aen.* 6.20–22) and the Labyrinth (64.113–15; *Aen.* 6.28–30), and concludes with loss. In Catullus the loss is double. Ariadne loses Theseus, Theseus Aegeus. In Virgil Daedalus misses Icarus alone.

¹⁰Perhaps the artist unravels his artistry, out of manifest pity, to abet the love of others for fear that it might bring doom on himself. At the least his uniting of two other lovers anticipates the loss of love in his own life. (For the relation of pity and fear, see P. Pucci, *The Violence of Pity* [Cornell 1980] especially 169–74.)

¹¹This point is valid for the ecphrasis as a whole. We are earlier made aware of the placement of the sculptures (*in foribus*), of the dynamic interrelationship between episodes (*respondet*), of the specifics of location within a scene (*hic...hic*). The absence of a word for crafting in the Ariadne vignette is particularly telling. Because the Icarus scene could not be started we assume that Ariadne's story, which precedes it, was brought to completion, but nothing in the narrative attends to this. Instead, while Daedalus implements the penultimate, and the second most emotional, episode in his artistic biography, the narrator of his tale shows him in the emotional act of unravelling his past art, not in the dispassionate formation of it. Even here, though we are led to presume one act of artistic fulfillment, emotion directly undoes the mind's creation.

¹²Though Virgil on three other occasions repeats *bis* in a line or between adjacent lines (*Aen.* 2.218; 6.134; 9.799–800), only once elsewhere does he employ it in anaphora at the opening of contiguous verses, 11.629–30, which is also the only instance where the two uses of *bis* contrast with rather than reinforce each other. The context is the ebb and flow of war which in turn, if we look at the last four books as a whole, analogizes its futility.

The parallel with 6.134–35, where the Sibyl remarks on Aeneas' *cupido*

> his Stygios innare lacus, bis nigra videre
> Tartara...

no doubt strengthens the bond between Daedalus and Aeneas. Though Aeneas does in fact complete his underworld journey, where Daedalus fails to finish his sculpture, the verbal interconnection may be one of Virgil's several subtle ways in book 6 of questioning the success of Aeneas', or Rome's, enterprise. There is, however, a later moment in book 6 with an even richer correlation to lines 32–33. When Aeneas finally reaches Anchises, son tries to embrace father (6.700–701):

> ter conatus ibi collo dare bracchia circum;
> ter frustra comprensa manus effugit imago...

The lines are repeated from book 2 (792–93) where Aeneas fails in his attempt to clasp the ghost of Creusa. Both events document the hero's inability throughout the epic to achieve emotional fulfillment (he does embrace his mother at 8.615 but at her insistence, not his). As critics note, Daedalus' inability to sculpt Icarus after two attempts may be modeled on Odysseus' triple attempt, and triple failure (*Od.* 11.206–208) to embrace the spirit of his mother (re. Pöschl, "Die Tempeltüren," 121; Fitzgerald, 63, n. 18). This, of course, was Virgil's model in the episodes of book 2 and 6 (the imitation, in the case of the latter, has most recently been noted by Austin ad loc.). But further potential meanings of this last anticipation in the Daedalus story of the later narrative of book 6 must not be overlooked. If Daedalus cannot perfect the loss of his son in art, can Aeneas finally fulfill the *pietas* owed to Anchises, especially given the strong need for *clementia* with which his father overlays his future loyalty?

It is noteworthy that the fall of Icarus is alluded to only by paranomasia in the word *casus*. The fall of Daedalus' hands, however, suggests that now, finally, the artisan experiences a version of his son's misfortune. Father becomes son. The son's physical fall is reiterated in the father's emotional collapse. Empathetically, literal death is the death of art.

[13] I examine the reasoning behind Aeneas' actions at this crucial moment in "The Hesitation of Aeneas," *Atti del Convegno mondiale scientifico di studi su Virgilio* (Milan 1984) 2.233–52.

[14] *Geo.* 2.45–46.

[15] *Geo.* 1.41–42.

[16] *Geo.* 1.44.

[17] See especially G. Duckworth, "The *Aeneid* as a Trilogy," *TAPA* 88 (1957) 1–10, revised and expanded in *Structural Patterns and Proportions in Vergil's Aeneid* (Ann Arbor 1962) 11–13.

[18] The parallels between the wooden horse and Daedalus' cow and Labyrinth are noteworthy. In each case they include *doli* (2.44), accompanied by the supportive wiles of Thymoetes, Sinon, Epeos—the Daedalian *doli fabricator* (264)—and the Greeks (34, 62, 152, 196, 252), trickery (18, 258), and *error* (48). In both instances a hybrid animal produces a monstrous birth. Both the cow and horse are mounted on wheels as they implement their subterfuge (Dio. Sic. 4.77, Apollodorus 3.1.4, for the cow; *Aen.* 2.235–36, for the horse). Daedalus' gift to Pasiphae therefore resembles the Greeks' gift to Minerva, the *innuptae donum exitiale Minervae* (2.31), which the art of the goddess has helped produce (*divina Palladis arte*, 15). At this stage of his career and in this particular instance, Daedalus anticipates both duplicitous Greeks and crafty Minerva as they bring into being the *machina…feta armis* (2.237–38), the horse and its destructive brood.

[19] Allusions to deceit begin, in book 1, at 130 where Neptune becomes aware of the *doli* and *irae* of his sister Juno. Out of 18 uses of *dolus* in the *Aeneid*, 10 are in books 1–4

[20] Dido, in this matter as in others, is an accomplice in her own downfall, asking, at the end of book 1 (750–52), for Aeneas to retell the known as well as the novel in Troy's demise, and reiterating the request as her tragic love deepens (4.77–79).

Yet, whereas the sculptures of book 1 lead diachronically toward Aeneas' narrative, as he "sculpts" Troy's fall and manages Dido's death, and the shield of book 8 details Rome's future in linear progression, Daedalus' artistry analogizes the whole of the epic on several levels, offering a series of synchronic paradigms. The two longer ecphraseis, by dwelling, in the first instance, on Aeneas' response, in the second, on Vulcan's craftsmanship, retain a strong specific point of focus that the Daedalian sculptures, with their lack of concern with the crafter at work or the viewer reacting, carefully forego.

Aeneas' perception of the sculptures on Juno's temple is discussed, with great sensitivity, by W. R. Johnson (*Darkness Visible* [Berkeley 1976] 99–105). By contrast with the earlier episode, the narrator does not allow us to learn how far in his examination of Daedalus' sculptures Aeneas had proceeded (*quin protinus omnia perlegerent oculis, ni…*, 33–34), though we presume that his "reading" was near to completion. In any case only narrator and reader, not the poem's protagonists, know of Daedalus' final suffering (see p. 224 above). But perhaps a similar event will occur in Aeneas' life. At the moment in book 8 when Aeneas is about to set out from Pallanteum, taking himself and Pallas to war, we find him and Achates "pondering many hardships with sad heart" (*multa…dura suo tristi cum corde putabant*, 8.522). To break his spell of contemplation Venus sends as sign a lightning-bolt and resounding thunder (*iterum atque iterum fragor increpat ingens*, 527). Aeneas will not explain what *casus* (533) this betokens, only that he must go into battle. But he may already sense the loss of Pallas with its many ramifications of incompletion in his life. It is a *fragor* (493), three times heard in Avernus, which, in the fourth *Georgic*, signals Eurydice's death caused by the *furor* (495) of Orpheus. The reader schooled in Virgil's symbolic modes is prepared to await a parallel misfortune as the *Aeneid* draws to a close and Aeneas, potential artist of Rome, undoes his work by his own version of madness.

[21]4.305–306.

[22]Looked at within the bounds of books 1–4, the story of Dido shares common ground with that of Daedalus and, partially, of Aeneas. It begins with double artistic accomplishment—an extraordinary city being built with a magnificent temple at its heart, a disciplined civilization arising to bring order to the territory around it—and ends with a series of *dolores* (419, 474, 547, 679, and the death agony at 693; cf. the uses of *doleo* at 393 and 434). These destroy, literally, the queen and, symbolically, the city she had founded. Pöschl (*Die Dichtkunst*, 246 and note = *The Art of Vergil*, 150 and 207, n. 17) recognizes the parallel between Ariadne and Dido *regina*. See n. 1 above.

[23]6.473–74.

[24]4.693–95.

[25]The complex *resolveret* is simplified shortly later in *solvo* (703). For Dido here, as for Pasiphae, passion creates the need for subterfuge, for *doli* (663) which only augment and finalize the *doli* of Venus and Juno which initiate her tragedy (95, 128) and of Aeneas who furthers it (296, the narrator's word). In Daedalus' artistic, which is to say psychic, life, *doli* precede *dolor*. For Dido *dolor* both anticipates and is precipitated by her resort to *doli* (see n. 22 above). The release of Dido from her entrapment, cares and body unmeshed at once (*me…his exsolvite curis* she cries to Aeneas' *dulces exuviae*, at 652) is the reader's release into the second third of the epic. Aeneas is the major Daedalian figure in Dido's life, but it is Virgil who frees her from his text.

[26]Fitzgerald (63, n. 13) sees a probable connection between Labyrinth and underworld. The link is strengthened by appeal to the Sibyl's definition of Aeneas' labor (128):

> sed revocare gradum superasque evadere ad auras…

Though Aeneas' "mad enterprise" (*insano…labori*; 135) works on the vertical plane while the Labyrinth presents a horizontal complexity, the parallels between the two adventures, where the hero must enter treacherous territory, engage in an arduous challenge or challenges, and return out alive, are suggestive. They are supported by the narrator's striking, ironic designation—and presumably Daedalus' depiction—of the Labyrinth as a *domus*. It will not be long before Aeneas will cross the *atri ianua Ditis* (127) and enter the *vestibulum* (273) in order to make his way *per…domos Ditis* (269).

Among the monsters Aeneas must soon thereafter pass by are *Scyllae biformes* (286). (Virgil's only two uses of the word are at 25 and here.) It will not be long before he crosses the *inremeabilis unda* of the Styx (425), an adjective used of the *error* of the Labyrinth at 5.591 and akin to the rare *inextricabilis* at 6.27. These difficulties past, Aeneas, as we shall see, continues his Daedalian enterprise with his pity for Dido and with his manifold inability to embrace his father.

[27]Cf. also Dido's plea to Aeneas at 4.318—*miserere domus labentis*—and her later command to Anna, *miserere sororis* (435).

[28]6.476.

[29]5.350–54.

[30]9.66.

[31]9.136–39.

[32]See n. 13 above.

[33]If we pursue the analogy between Daedalus and Aeneas as we reach the poem's conclusion, we could say that in terms of life's terminations the two are successful. Each has reached a goal. Daedalus gains Cumae and constructs a notable artifact (*immania templa*), an awesome temple to Apollo. Aeneas, too, has come to Italy and defeated the enemy who, presumably, has stood in the way of his founding the Roman race. But to turn biographical completions into art, to make them appear as art, is for each a different, highly inconclusive matter.

[34]By the end of his epic Aeneas could also be seen as an Icarus figure, the most palpable sign of his father's failed artistry, realistic proof of how idealizing are Anchises' notions of *clementia*. (We remember that it is Anchises, not Aeneas, who initiates the sparing of

Achaemenides in the epic's third book.) Daedalus' *dolor*, yearning for his lost son which may well include resentment and self-hatred also, results only in artistic incompletion. Aeneas' *dolor*, where loss is directly linked to the Furies' fires, to *saevitia* and *ira*, leads to a resentful, passionate killing with far more complex intimations of failure.

Forgetful Aeneas is made to mimic careless Icarus with the forceful difference, of course, that Aeneas lives on. For him, in Virgil's richly ironic narrative, survival is the equivalent of over-reaching Icarus' plummeting into the sea, and this survival means the end of his father's art.

The "celestial" plot of the *Aeneid* concludes with Jupiter yielding to Juno's demand that all things Trojan submerge their identity in the Latin present and future. What follows, there-fore, up to the epic's last lines, is in fact the intellectual birth of Rome, as Aeneas becomes, according to his father's definition, *Romanus* (6.851). Two actions are paramount. First, Jupiter coopts the Dirae to warn Juturna and her brother of the latter's impending death. Second, Aeneas kills Turnus. In the first deed heaven summons hell to motivate earthly doings for the last time in the epic but for the first, one could surmise, in Virgil's Roman history, as history's cycle starts anew. The second, Aeneas' concluding deed, becomes the initial Roman action. Motivated by inner furies, it betokens a continuum of passion and anger, portending the impossibility of any new aesthetic or ethical wholeness.

[35] The translations of the *Iliad*, *Odyssey*, and *Argonautica* passages are from the Loeb series, adapted slightly: *Homer, The Iliad: Books XIII–XXIV*, trans. A. T. Murray (Cambridge, MA: Harvard University Press, 1993) 623; *Homer, The Odyssey: In Two Volumes, II*, trans. A. T. Murray (Cambridge, MA: Harvard University Press, 1980) 443; *Apollonius Rhodius, The Argonautica*, trans. R. C. Seaton (London: William Heinemann, 1912) 415.

[36] The case for the authenticity of the *Odyssey* from 23.297 to the end is argued persua-sively by C. Moulton, "The End of the Odyssey," *GRBS* 15 (1974) 153-69.

[37] 12.803–808. His beloved Virgil is here on Statius' mind, but the Virgil not of the *Aeneid* but of *Georgic* 4 (525–27).

[38] The abrupt conclusion of *De Rerum Natura* offers the closest parallel in earlier litera-ture to the end of the *Aeneid*. I strongly support the view of Diskin Clay (*Lucretius and Epicurus* [Ithaca 1983] 251) that Virgil's "grim and unresolved" finale deliberately echoes both the style and tone of his great predecessor.

[39] The reversals of the *Iliad* in the *Aeneid* deserve separate study. The *Aeneid* ends in one respect where the *Iliad* begins. Achilles' anger at the start of the *Iliad* turns to forgiveness at the end. The story of Aeneas, on the other hand, begins with the hero's suppression of *dolor* (1.209), for hardships experienced in the past, and ends with his outburst of *dolor* over the loss of Pallas. In at least one episode of the *Aeneid* the reversal directly concerns Achilles. In Pyrrhus' vengeful killing of Priam, Achilles' anger lives on. It too, of course, is an emotion that spurs on Aeneas to his final deed (*ira terribilis* is the narrator's characterization of Aeneas immediately before his final speech, 12.946–47). Is it mere coincidence that Helenus bestows the *arma Neoptolemi* (3.469) on Aeneas as his parting gift?

[40] The parallel is developed with sensitivity by C. P. Segal ("*Aeternum per saecula nomen*, the golden bough and the tragedy of history: Part II," *Arion* 5 [1966] 34–72, especially 50–52). Cf. also H. Rutledge ("Vergil's Daedalus," *CJ* 62 [1967] 311) and Pöschl ("Die Tempeltüren," 120).

[41] Fitzgerald (note 1 above, 54) rightly notes that Daedalus' tale delivers him "from the past [that his artwork first encapsulated] into the painful and unfinished world of history." He pursues his insight by concluding that Aeneas, as Daedalus, is forced into a tragic history "that forfeits the comfort of closure."

[42] The truth of Aeneas' emotions at the end of book 12, as in the Helen episode in book 2, leads to artistic inconclusions, in the first instance because the text (2.567–88) would be ex-punged by, and nearly lost because of, Varius and Tucca, in the second because it leads not to potential elimination but to aspects of incompletion. The first episode suggests, too early and too strongly, it might have been said, the truth of the hero's emotionality. The second cannot be argued away, though its author sought to destroy it as part of his whole epic. It forms a special complement to the first. Virgil stops at a moment of the greatest honesty which demonstrates Anchises' model to be one based on wishful thinking while Aeneas' violent response to Turnus and the emotional thrust behind it speak the truth. This truth brings about, literally and splendidly, the end of art.

The Uses of Tradition and
the Making of Meaning

VIRGIL: A STUDY IN CIVILIZED POETRY

Readers have always known that Vergil borrowed heavily from Homer's *Iliad* and *Odyssey* in creating the *Aeneid*. Indeed, he has often been criticized for being an imitator, not an original artist. Otis shows us in two ways how original his "borrowings" in fact were. First, he explains that literary theories in the first century B.C.E. explicitly opposed the creation of large-scale heroic works like the *Aeneid*. Second, Otis demonstrates exactly how Vergil's borrowing worked, through a detailed analysis of a passage at *Aeneid* 5.315–42 and its Homeric "source," *Iliad* 23.757–83, two descriptions of foot races. That analysis reveals the fundamental, poetic difference between Vergil's style, which Otis names "subjective," and that of Homeric epic. Otis locates in Vergil's work the presence of new emotional, psychological content, sometimes in a character, sometimes on the part of the narrator or author, and more usually in "a subtle blend of both." It is in this new style, and the poetic and interpretive possibilities it opens up, that Otis discovers Vergil's "modernity," giving the *Aeneid* "vastly more in common with contemporary New York than with [ancient] Mycenae or Tiryns." (Ed.)

CHAPTER 1
THE MYSTERY OF THE *AENEID*

Virgil died at the seaport of Brundisium on 21 September 19 B.C. All his plans for a prolonged residence abroad had been interrupted by his meeting with Augustus at Athens, his subsequent sunstroke at Megara and his hasty return to Italy and death. His projected three-year revision of the *Aeneid* in the retirement of Greece and Asia had been disastrously cut short. Yet Virgil had either foreseen or provided for the contingency: on leaving Italy for Greece, he had instructed Varius to burn the *Aeneid* 'if anything should happen to him.' On his death-bed, he seems to have wavered a little: he asked for the manuscript in order to burn it, yet he did not insist when no one complied with his request.[1] We must, I think, see in this instruction and this uncertainty more than the morbid doubts of a perfectionist or the ostentatious modesty of one who secretly expected his wish to be ignored. The *Aeneid* was a colossal *tour de force,* unprecedented in both its aim and its execution. Virgil felt he could not let it out into the world without the most elaborate revision.

We can gather as much from the little we know about its composition. When Augustus once requested a sample of the poem, Virgil replied that he had nothing to show that was worthy of Augustus' attention: the very attempt had begun to look like madness, such was its scope, such the preliminary studies that it required.[2]

Finally, after reiterated requests, Virgil did read Augustus three books (2, 4, 6) but it seems quite clear from Donatus' account that the requests had to be very pressing indeed.[3] We do not even require Donatus' famous description of Virgil's method of composition—the prose outline, the utter lack of continuity in the actual writing, the tiny daily quota of verses, the constant revision—to understand the terrible difficulty of the task.[4] It was not, to judge by all the appearances, the kind of reluctance that delayed the completion of *Faust* – a sheer inability to come to terms with the poetic *daimon* – but the very magnitude and scope of the work itself.

Yet no one, surely, can seriously doubt the wisdom of Augustus, Varius and Tucca in publishing the *Aeneid*. Whatever its difficulties and its rough spots, it had actually reached a stage of sufficient completion to reveal the poet's intention, and more—his conquest of those difficulties that had so baffled him, and his attainment of that magnitude, that poetic ὕψος ["height"], which he had thought so presumptuous. This has been vaguely sensed by generations of readers and critics, though Virgil has had his detractors, especially among romantically inclined nineteenth-century Germans; but it has not yet been clearly understood. It is only when one tries to grasp the self-imposed difficulties, the almost preposterous ambition of the Augustan poet, that one can begin to appreciate the poem and perhaps to see *how* it was after all possible.

We can state at once the character of his task by saying that Virgil did what no one else had done before him and no one was able to do after him. The *Aeneid* is, in one sense, an imitation of Homer: it is based on the *Iliad* and *Odyssey* not only in its Homeric plot and incidents but in its choice of an heroic date and milieu. Virgil was thus the first and only poet truly to recreate the heroic-age epic in an urban civilization. There had been many—there were to be more—second-rate imitations of Homeric or Homeric-style epic. But these were all anachronisms betraying at every joint their obsolete and imitative substance. There were to be other great and authentic epics but these, like the Germanic eddas, are themselves the original products of other heroic ages or, like the *Divine Comedy* and *Paradise Lost*, are deliberate departures from the theme and the mood of heroic-age epic. Only the *Aeneid* aspired to be both heroic and civilized, both remote and contemporary, both Homeric and Augustan. This was precisely the 'mad' undertaking in which Virgil succeeded. It is our task and problem to explain how it was possible.

The fact with which previous attempts to explain this achievement have not really reckoned is quite simply the law of obsolescence in literature. In all literature, but most especially in Greek literature, the literary genre or form is inseparably attached to a particular age. The age of epic yielded to the age of personal and choral lyric, this to tragedy, tragedy to comedy and the prose forms. There were overlappings and transitions but no essential reversals: apart from learned and uninspired imitations, the course of literary development was quite as definite as that in any other field. The change from the rudimentary *polis* ["city-state"] of Homer to the democratic-imperialistic *polis* of Pericles and the vast *metropolis* of the Ptolemies was no less great than the change from the *Iliad* to Thucydides, or from Pindar to Callimachus, and no less irreversible. It is thus wholly false to account for Virgil's achievement in terms of his imitative predecessors—the fact that many before him tried and miserably failed to write like Homer—or to 'explain' the *Aeneid* by the Augustans' proclaimed desire to revive the classical Greek genres (as if the thought could guarantee the deed) or by their ardent wish to praise Augustus in true Homeric fashion (again the thought and the deed). None of these 'reasons' explains anything. Nor does it help to declare that the *Aeneid* is a different kind of epic from Homer's, if one does not also explain how the difference accounts for Virgil's success. What did he do that Homer did not do, so that in the doing an obvious 'imitation' of Homer could become the true epic of a metropolis that has vastly more in common with contemporary New York than with Mycenae or Tiryns?

This is a question to which modern classical scholarship has produced no satisfactory answer. It has been relatively easy to show the un-Homeric character of Virgil's technique (though even here it was not until 1902 that Richard Heinze really collected and analysed the evidence). We can now see the difference between Homer's *oral* and Virgil's *literary* or written style. We can understand, at least partially, the devices by which Virgil connected his two ages; his use of prophecy and prophetic revelation, his combination of Homeric and old Roman legend. We can also see the evident influence of Stoic philosophy and allegory on both the human and the divine sections of the poem. But all this says little about the essential problem—the use of Homer to produce a genuine Roman epic or the very fact that this *imitation* is also a great poem in its own right.

Nor can the problem be disposed of by an easy submission to the inexplicable ways of genius. Any great literary work is bound to contain a residue of mystery, but the mystery of the *Aeneid* is much more than a residue. Virgil was not just another genius. Shakespeare, Sophocles, Homer himself took their form, their *genre* fresh from the hands of a line of predecessors: they added the master's touch, but only to a vital tradition which was in fact ripe for them. Virgil had no such living genre to work on. He was, indeed, reviving, giving new breath and life to a form some seven hundred years obsolete. This was a quite new thing in literature. We ought to be able to penetrate part of the secret by which this unexampled metamorphosis was accomplished.

❖ ❖ ❖

CHAPTER III
THE SUBJECTIVE STYLE

So far...we have tried to show the novelty of the *Aeneid*, the absence of a living epic tradition on which Virgil could draw. He was directed by Horace and others to return to Homer yet his Alexandrine and neoteric training had made clear the difficulty — perhaps the impossibility — of any such attempt. Yet somehow he did it: the *Aeneid* exists as the tangible proof of his achievement. Thus our problem is to see what the *Aeneid* is, by what innovations of thought or diction the old could be renewed, Homer could be made Roman and Augustan. Obviously, this can be no superficial task: we must look beneath all matters of technique and arrangement to the very texture of Virgil's style and language. Previous scholarship has gone a certain way — men like Heinze and Pöschl have pointed to some essential elements of the *Aeneid*'s style — but very much still remains to be done.

We must begin with some rather close textual analysis. Let us first consider a brief piece of narrative (the foot race: *Aeneid* 5.315-42) and its Homeric model (*Iliad* 23.757-83). The difference between the Virgilian and Homeric races is evident. We can see this best by looking closely at the accidental fall of Nisus and Ajax. In Homer, it is the result of Odysseus' prayer to his patron goddess, Athene. This is quite clear to Ajax (Oilean) whom the reader already knows as the companion of Telamonian Ajax, the ancient rival of Odysseus. It is all part of an old story of bad relations between Athene and the two Ajaxes. But Virgil's characters are unknowns: he has

Aeneid 5.315–42

315 Haec ubi dicta, locum capiunt signoque repente
corripiunt spatia audito limenque relinquunt,
effusi nimbo similes; simul ultima signant.
Primus abit longeque ante omnia corpora Nisus
emicat, et ventis et fulminis ocior alis;
320 proximus huic, longo sed proximus intervallo,
insequitur Salius; spatio post deinde relicto
tertius Euryalus;
Euryalumque Helymus sequitur: quo deinde sub ipso
ecce volat calcemque terit iam calce Diores
325 incumbens umero; spatia et si plura supersint,
transeat elapsus prior ambiguumque relinquat.
Iamque fere spatio extremo fessique sub ipsam
finem adventabant, levi cum sanguine Nisus
labitur infelix, caesis ut forte iuvencis
330 fusus humum viridisque super madefecerat herbas.
Hic iuvenis iam victor ovans vestigia presso
haud tenuit titubata solo, sed pronus in ipso
concidit immundoque firmo sacroque cruore,
non tamen Euryali, non ille oblitus amorum:
335 nam sese opposuit Salio per lubrica surgens,
ille autem spissa iacuit revolutus harena.
Emicat Euryalus et munere victor amici
prima tenet plausuque volat fremituque secundo;
post Helymus subit et nunc tertia palma Diores.
340 Hic totum caveae consessum ingentis et ora
prima patrum magnis Salius clamoribus implet
342 ereptumque dolo reddi sibi poscit honorem.

---

to create, as it were, a dramatic situation out of the race itself. So he makes Nisus' slip the means of Euryalus' victory: the defeat of the unimportant Salius is quite secondary to the demonstration of Nisus' affection for his friend. The race is thus *dramatic* (at least three of the participants seemed at one time possible winners) and above all a drama determined by the inner motivation (Nisus' love for Euryalus) of the main or deciding participant. Homer's race is not dramatic in this sense: there is no true peripety or reversal arising out of the action itself; Athene is rather a quite extraneous figure who is introduced to decide the event by *force majeure* ["a greater force"]. Nor is there much dramatic suspense; we know that Odysseus wants to win and that his appeal to Athene will be heeded. In Virgil, the unexpected tripping of Salius completely changes the expected outcome: the friendship of Nisus and Euryalus, unlike the rivalry of Ajax and Odysseus, achieves a truly dramatic result. Virgil in brief has written a 'psycho-drama'; Homer a simple narrative.

All this is a familiar story ever since Richard Heinze's famous analysis of Virgil's games.[5] What has *not* been so clearly seen is the extent to which Virgil's psycho-dramatic approach governs the smallest details of his language. Thus, comparing the Homeric and Virgilian passages, we can note at once the following differences:

315   This said, they take their place and quick at the signal's blast
       They devour the course: and are well off the mark
       Like a swift cloud burst: their eyes upon their goal.
       First far beyond the other runners Nisus goes away.
       He flashes faster than the winds or winged thunder bolt.
320   Next to him but next by a long interval
       Follows Salius: finally then after another space
       The third, Euryalus.
       Helymus follows Euryalus: and then right on his track
       Look! Diores flies and almost gets his heel
325   Straining upon him: and if there'd been more room
       He would have gone ahead or left the race in doubt.
       And now almost at the end and near exhaustion point
       They were coming to the goal, when Nisus on slick ground
       Slips, the unlucky, for a bullock's blood had there
330   Been shed and had made the grass slippery and wet.
       Here the young man—so sure of victory—could not keep
       His footing as he rocked and reeled, then headlong
       Down he went in the foul mud and sacred gore.
334   Yet not Euryalus, yet not his love did he forget
335   For he threw himself on Salius, rising from where he slipped
       And Salius now lay wallowing in the trodden sand.
       Euryalus then flashes by, victor by his friend's gift,
       And takes first place as he flies on to much applause and cheers.
       Next Helymus comes in second; Diores is third.
340   Then the whole amphitheatre's broad expanse with Salius' cries
       Is filled: with shouts he begs the chieftains to give back
342   The honour snatched from him only by deceitful trick.

---

1. The Virgilian narrative shifts the sentence subject as little as possible. The subject of lines 315–17 is the *runners* (plural): *capiunt, corripiunt, relinquunt, signant* ["they take," "devour," "are well off," "their eyes upon"]. Then the subject shifts to the individual runners in order: Nisus (318–19: *abit, emicat* ["he goes away," "he flashes"]), Salius (320–1), Euryalus, Helymus, Diores. From 327–35 the subject is Nisus. In 336 it shifts logically enough to Salius (*ille* ["that one"]) and in 337 to Euryalus. In other words, we have as subject first the runners as a group, then each runner in his relative position at the start of the race, then Nisus again (quite logically since his fall shifts the race order), Salius (as Nisus trips him) and lastly Euryalus and the other two winners (Helymus, Diores) in the order of victory.

In contrast, Homer does not attempt to preserve any logical succession of subjects. Thus in line 757 the subject is plural (στὰν ["they stood"]) but it shifts in the same line to Achilles; in the next to the impersonal δρόμος ["the course"], then in 759 to the runners, Ajax and Odysseus. The simile (760–3) breaks the narrative but Odysseus is the grammatical subject of 765 though our attention is equally divided between him and Ajax. In 765 Ajax is referred to only by the pronoun οἱ ["his/to him"] while Odysseus is mentioned by name with the epithet δῖος ["noble"]. In 766

757   Then they stood in a row and Achilles showed them the limits.
            The course was laid out to the turn-point. Swiftly thereafter
            Out started Oileus' son: right after him rushed Odysseus,
760   Close to him as the weaver's beam is close to the bosom
            Of some woman fair-breasted as deftly with fingers she draweth
            The shuttle over the warps and very near does she hold it
            Near to her breast: so then did Odysseus run close and behind
            He beat up the dust with his feet before it had settled
765   And on Ajax' head the noble Odysseus was breathing,
            Ever swift running. And for him all the Achaeans did shout
            As he strove for the victory and accosted him as he sped onward.
            But when they reached the final lap of the contest, straight-way Odysseus
            Prayed to Athene, the gleaming-eyed, in his bosom:
770   'Hear me, goddess, come aider benevolent, help now my feet!'
            So he spoke praying. And Pallas Athene heard him.
            Light made she his feet and his limbs and his hands above them
            But when they just were about to secure the prize,
            Then Ajax slipped as he ran — for Athene upset him —
775   There where was spread the gore of the slaughtered, loud-mouthed bulls
            Which for Patroclus, the swift-footed Achilles had sacrificed,
777   And this was the gore Ajax' mouth and nostrils were filled with.
            Thus gained the prize-bowl, the much-braving Odysseus
            As he came first in: but the ox seized glorious Ajax
780   And he stood holding its horn in his fingers
            Spewing forth gore as he spoke to the Argives as follows:
            'Ah! fie! The goddess tripped me and always before this
783   Just like a mother she stands by Odysseus and helps him.'

---

the subject shifts again, this time to the Achaeans (cheering on Odysseus). In 768 it is the runners again, then in the same line Odysseus. In 770 we have his single line prayer to Athene (with Athene as subject). It shifts, 773–7, from the runners (collective) to Ajax, to Athene again and (disregarding the relative clauses) to Ajax. Thereafter it alternates between Ajax and Odysseus with θεά (goddess) the subject of the two line quote of Ajax at the end (782–3).

     2. The Homeric narrative is broken (as Virgil's is not) by two quotations (of one and two lines).

     3. The Homeric narrative contains one (relatively) long simile (3–4 lines); the Virgilian, only brief phrase-similes in 317 (*nimbo similes* ["like a swift cloud burst"]) and 319 (*ventis et fulminis ocior alis* ["faster than the winds or winged thunder bolt"]).

     4. The Homeric narrative contains a number of traditional epithets and patronymics (δῖος Ὀδυσσεύς ["noble Odysseus"] (3 times)) πόδας ὠκὺς Ἀχιλλεύς, φαίδιμος Αἴας ["swift-footed Achilles," "glorious Ajax"], &c. In Virgil Nisus is called *infelix, iuvenis, victor* ["unlucky," "young man," "victor"] but these are really descriptive adjectives rather than epithets.

Homer, *Iliad* 23.757–83

757 στὰν δὲ μεταστοιχί· σήμηνε δὲ τέρματ' Ἀχιλλεύς.
τοῖσι δ' ἀπὸ νύσσης τέτατο δρόμος· ὦκα δ' ἔπειτα
ἔκφερ' Ὀϊλιάδης· ἐπὶ δ' ὤρνυτο δῖος Ὀδυσσεὺς
760 ἄγχι μάλ', ὡς ὅτε τίς τε γυναικὸς ἐϋζώνοιο
στήθεός ἐστι κανών, ὅν τ' εὖ μάλα χερσὶ τανύσσῃ
πηνίον ἐξέλκουσα παρὲκ μίτον, ἀγχόθι δ' ἴσχει
στήθεος· ὡς Ὀδυσεὺς θέεν ἐγγύθεν, αὐτὰρ ὄπισθεν
ἴχνια τύπτε πόδεσσι πάρος κόνιν ἀμφιχυθῆναι·
765 κὰδ δ' ἄρα οἱ κεφαλῆς χέ' ἀϋτμένα δῖος Ὀδυσσεὺς
αἰεὶ ῥίμφα θέων· ἴαχον δ' ἐπὶ πάντες Ἀχαιοὶ
νίκης ἱεμένῳ, μάλα δὲ σπεύδοντι κέλευον.
ἀλλ' ὅτε δὴ πύματον τέλεον δρόμον, αὐτίκ' Ὀδυσσεὺς
εὔχετ' Ἀθηναίῃ γλαυκώπιδι ὃν κατὰ θυμόν·
770 "κλῦθι, θεά, ἀγαθή μοι ἐπίρροθος ἐλθὲ ποδοῖιν."
ὡς ἔφατ' εὐχόμενος· τοῦ δ' ἔκλυε Παλλὰς Ἀθήνη,
γυῖα δ' ἔθηκεν ἐλαφρά, πόδας καὶ χεῖρας ὕπερθεν.
ἀλλ' ὅτε δὴ τάχ' ἔμελλον ἐπαΐξασθαι ἄεθλον,
ἔνθ' Αἴας μὲν ὄλισθε θέων —βλάψεν γὰρ Ἀθήνη—
775 τῇ ῥα βοῶν κέχυτ' ὄνθος ἀποκταμένων ἐριμύκων,
οὓς ἐπὶ Πατρόκλῳ πέφνεν πόδας ὠκὺς Ἀχιλλεύς·
ἐν δ' ὄνθου βοέου πλῆτο στόμα τε ῥῖνάς τε·
κρητῆρ' αὖτ' ἀνάειρε πολύτλας δῖος Ὀδυσσεύς,
ὡς ἦλθε φθάμενος· ὁ δὲ βοῦν ἕλε φαίδιμος Αἴας.
780 στῆ δὲ κέρας μετὰ χερσὶν ἔχων βοὸς ἀγραύλοιο,
ὄνθον ἀποπτύων, μετὰ δ' Ἀργείοισιν ἔειπεν·
"ὢ πόποι, ἦ μ' ἔβλαψε θεὰ πόδας, ἣ τὸ πάρος περ
783 μήτηρ ὡς Ὀδυσῆϊ παρίσταται ἠδ' ἐπαρήγει."

---

5. All Homeric verbs are simple aorists or perfects and aoristic imperfects (στὰν, σήμηνε, ὄρνυτο, θέεν, τύπτε, ἴαχον ["stood," "showed," "rushed," "did run," "beat up," "did shout"]. The only exception is ἴσχει ["does hold"] (l. 762). There is obviously no exact temporal demarcation of the narrative. In Virgil the use of the tenses is most exact and telling: note, e.g. the presents of 315–17 (*capiunt, corripiunt, relinquunt* ["they seize," "run quickly," "leave"]) and thereafter (*abit, emicat, insequitur, volat, terit* ["he goes away," "flashes," "follows," "flies," "rubs/almost gets"]), the future-less-vivid condition of 325–26, the exact imperfect of 328 (to bring out the contrasted present, *labitur* ["slips"], of 329). Finally there are the perfects of 332, 333–6 and again the presents (*emicat, tenet, volat, subit* ["he flashes," "takes," "flies," "comes"]) of 337–9. Here the vivid present of the actual running is contrasted with the imperfect (*adventabant* ["they were coming"] 328), explaining the incompleteness of the race, and the perfects (332–6), expressing the falls of Nisus and Salius (which of course abruptly remove them from the race).

6. The Virgilian passage is full of words which describe the feeling of the runners: note such verbs as *corripiunt spatia, emicat, volat* ["they devour the course," "he flashes," "he flies"], such adjectives and adjectival phrases as *infelix, non ille*

oblitus amorum, iuvenis victor ovans ["unlucky," "not his love did he forget," "the young man so sure of victory"]. In contrast the Homeric verbs and adjectives are quite ordinary and objective: στὰν, ὄρνυτο, θέεν, τέλεον, εὔχετο ["they stood," "he rushed," "he did run," "they reached," "he prayed"]. The one indication of feeling is the phrase νίκης ἱεμένῳ ["as he strove for victory"] of line 767 but this is pretty neutral: all know that Odysseus wants to win. As remarked, the epithets are strictly traditional. Phrases like ῥίμφα θέων and μάλα δὲ σπεύδοντι ["ever swift running," "sped onward"] merely accent the *speed* of the race, not the emotion of the runners.

    7. The use of subordinate clauses and participles is less immediately indicative. Homer uses three ὅτε ["when"] clauses, a ὡς ["so"] clause (for the simile) and a πάρος ["before"] clause (with the infinitive). There are ten participles though most of these are of the simplest kind (e.g. θέων ["running"] used twice, ἔχων, ἀποπτύων, σπεύδοντι ["holding," "spewing forth," "speeding"]). In general the sentence structure is very simple (short sentences with concrete subjects and action verbs). The Virgilian narrative, as befits the rapid subject, has a number of verbs (*capiunt, corripiunt, emicat, volat, terit, &c.*) and short rapid sentences. But it also has a conditional subjunctive, an *ut* ["as"] indicative clause and a number (4) of ablative absolutes. The difference here is not revealed by the statistics though Virgil uses fewer dependent clauses than Homer: the point is that the dependent clauses in Virgil are *deliberate* interruptions of the action as the clauses in Homer are not. Thus the condition of lines 325–6 expresses the unfulfilled intention of Diores, obviously an exception to the movement of the rest of the passage; the *ut* ["as"] clause of line 329 is introduced to show by the pluperfect *madefecerat* ["had made wet"] that the blood had been shed on the ground *before* the race. (Note that Virgil has here an impersonal subject, *sanguis* ["blood"] (understood) rather than, as in Homer, a concrete individual. The slayer of the cattle is an unimportant detail which would merely distract the reader's attention.)

    8. A metrical analysis of the two passages shows clearly that Virgil is using every device to focus the reader's attention on those aspects of the narrative he wants to emphasize: this is not so in Homer. Note, e.g. the line (320):

$$- \cup \; \cup / - \; - /- \; - \; / \; - \cup \; \cup /- \; -/- \; -$$
proximus huic longo sed proximus intervallo.

["next to him but next by a long interval"]

    The striking fifth foot spondee here vividly expresses the distance between Salius and Nisus. The repetition of the *proximus* ["next"] and the inclusion of the second *proximus* between *longo* ["long"] and *intervallo* ["interval"] are very deliberate; so are the caesurae in the second and third feet which emphasize *longo* and the clash of prose and metrical stresses in *longo* as opposed to their agreement in the double *proximus*. In contrast to the fading Salius we have the gaining Diores:

$$- \; \cup \; \cup /- \; -/- \quad \cup \; \cup /- -/ \; - \; \cup \cup /- -$$
ecce volat calcemque terit iam calce Diores

["Look! Diores flies and almost gets his heel"]

Here the alternate dactyls and spondees, the tripartite division (caesurae in the second and fourth feet) and the repetition *calcem calce* ["heel"] produce the effect of rhythmic speed. Similar analyses could be made of, e.g. lines 319, 325, 328, 335, 336, 337. All this, however, is of less importance than the strictly psychological effect which Virgil gets through sound and rhythm. Note, e.g.

329
$$- \cup \cup / - - / -$$
labitur infelix

331
$$- \cup \ \cup / - - \ / - \cup \cup / -$$
hic iuvenis iam victor ovans

334
$$- \cup \ \cup \ / - \ \cup\cup / - \ - / - \ - / - \cup \cup \ / - \cup$$
non tamen Euryali, non ille oblitus amorum

["slips, the unlucky"
"Here the young man—so sure of victory"
"Yet not Euryalus, yet not his love did he forget"]

It is clear that the three longs of *infelix* ["unlucky"] (329) with the following main caesura and the preceding diaeresis form a deliberate contrast to the rapid truncated *labitur* ["he slips"]. Again line 331 expresses the triumphant feeling of Nisus. In 334 the metrical emphasis of *Euryali* and *ille* ["he"], the repetition of *non* ["not"], the two spondaic feet (3 and 4), the alliteration and the long *i* sounds in *Euryali* and *oblitus* ["forget"], enhance the emotional effect. In its context the line is very striking for it slows up the rapid movement to focus a vivid light on the pathetic feeling which Virgil wishes to accent. In the Homeric passage, in contrast, I find it most difficult to be certain that any metrical effect is really intended. The frequency with which lines end in such ready-made phrases as δῖος Ὀδυσσεύς, Παλλὰς Ἀθήνη, φαίδιμος Αἴας ["noble Odysseus," "Pallas Athena," "glorious Ajax"] seems to exclude the artful, Virgilian kind of onomatopoeia.[6]

These points of comparison suffice I think to bring out the striking differences between the two styles. Obviously Virgil's technique is far more deliberate and knowing than Homer's but this fact hardly needs demonstration. The point of interest is why and with what intent Virgil was so deliberate. Heinze has suggested the answer in saying that Virgil puts himself in the place of his characters and narrates through them. Virgil takes the point of view either of a specific character (Nisus, Diores, Euryalus, &c.) or of himself as interested spectator. Actually he takes both at once in a very subtle and rather complicated way. As we have seen, his centre of interest is the friendship of Nisus and Euryalus. Thus his emphasis is not (as is Homer's) on the race as an objective event but on the psychological relation of Nisus and Euryalus.

All the points we have adduced—the relative continuity of grammatical subject, the absence of quotations, the shortness of the similes, the absence of traditional epithets, the abundance of words with feeling tone, the deliberateness of the grammatical structure, the artful onomatopoeia—receive their adequate explanation when we note that they are all necessitated by Virgil's subjective method and attitude. Virgil is constantly conscious of himself inside his characters; he thinks through them and for them. In the passage in question he identifies himself successively with the runners as a whole (315–17), with Nisus, then with the others (but specifically with Diores) and then again with Nisus though his attention reverts at the end to Euryalus, Salius and the rest. But he also makes it clear that he himself feels most deeply for Nisus and shares Nisus' noble affection for Euryalus: Nisus is *infelix* ["unlucky"] but he does not forget his friend. Virgil thus enters the *psyche* of each runner in turn to emerge with a final judgment or *parti pris*. Such a procedure supplies dramatic unity to the narrative as a whole. Each runner (at least all who interest Virgil at all) has his own view of the race but all these views are comprehended and unified in Virgil's view. He is doubly subjective — first in the *empathy* with which he shares the emotions of each runner, second in his own, *personal reaction* to their emotions. Such things as the shift of the subject and the use of tense are thus clues to the movement of the poet's feeling. There is a precise correspondence of grammatical structure and emotion which cannot be broken by direct quotations or relatively long similes (as in Homer). We can see, for example, the emotional content of tense differentiation when we consider a consecutive series of verbs in the passage, as, e.g. lines 327–33: iamque sub ipsam finem *adventabant* cum...Nisus...*labitur*. Hic iuvenis iam victor *ovans* vestigia haud tenuit...sed pronus *concidit* ["And now *they were coming* to the goal when...Nisus...*slips*." "Here the young man" already *celebrating* as victor "could not keep his footing...but headlong *down he went*"].

The most obvious key to Virgil's 'psychological identification' of himself with the characters is the tell-tale phrase or word which either describes the character's feelings or Virgil's own feeling for him or — what is nearest to the fact — a subtle blend of both. These phrases also gain a large part of their effectiveness from their metrical position: the 'sound track' is always indispensable to the film proper. But the chief point to make about them is that they act as a means of *special* emphasis. Virgil's art is altogether too subtle to rely on them as the regular vehicles of his subjectivist method: his sympathy and personal feeling is in fact expressed by a series of devices far less obvious than overt editorializing such as e.g. the use of tenses, caesurae, vowel sounds, &c., as set forth above.

Let us consider in this connection lines 324–6:

> ecce volat calcemque terit iam calce Diores
> incumbens umero; spatia et si plura supersint
> transeat elapsus prior ambiguumque relinquat.

> ["Look! Diores flies and almost gets his heel
> Straining upon him: and if there'd been more room
> He would have gone ahead or left the race in doubt."]

Is Virgil here describing the race of Diores objectively or does he identify himself with Diores? The latter is nearer the truth but we feel, nevertheless, that the identification is in no sense close or unambiguous. Thus the future-less-vivid clause can represent either Virgil's or Diores' point of view but neither is sharply discriminated. The *ecce* ["look!"] singles Diores out from the others for a moment only. What Virgil really wants us to grasp is that the race is close, that even the last might have been first. Diores is thus mainly a means of heightening the tension: it would have been quite distracting for Virgil to have identified himself with him too obviously. But Nisus is different: he is the true centre of attention and Virgil quite deliberately takes his point of view in the metrically impressive line 334:

> non tamen Euryali, non ille oblitus amorum

> ["Yet not Euryalus, yet not his love did he forget"]

But he does more than this: he makes explicit his own feeling for Nisus in the obviously 'finger pointing' epithet *infelix* ["unlucky"] of line 329. The poet cannot at this point contain his own sympathy: it bursts out directly and thus gives climactic emphasis to the feeling in which the whole passage is drenched.

The radical difference between Homer and Virgil here is of course very obvious. Each is effective in his own way but each achieves a quite dissimilar effect. Homer is indifferent to the devices by which Virgil obtains subjective concentration of the narrative: he shifts his subjects almost at random, he relies on the relatively colourless aorist tense, his grammatical structure is loose and he puts in details (e.g. the relatively lengthy simile of weaving and the identification of the slayer of the cattle in line 776) which add nothing essential to the narrative. But his greater objectivity makes for much more vivid and clear characterizations. Thus even this brief passage brings out the feeling between Odysseus and Ajax and something of Ajax's character (cf. especially his two-line speech 782-3). We grasp at once his sturdy independence of the gods and his attitude towards Athene's partiality to Odysseus. We have no doubt that here is a man with his own characteristic point of view though we in no sense identify ourselves with him or see him through the poet's emotions toward him. The *disadvantage* – if it can be called such – of Virgil's subjective approach is revealed in this contrast: his empathetic or sympathetic relation to his characters gives them a certain ambiguity; we are never sure when he is simply describing the character's feelings or putting his own feelings into the character – he actually seems to do both things – and we thus lose the sense of the character's objective reality. Homer's Ajax is real: he stands on his own feet and speaks his own thoughts. But Virgil's Nisus is much less real for he has not gotten fully away from his creator: he is a source of emotion (a pathetic instance) rather than a tangible human being in a tangible environment.

Broadly speaking the principles discovered in the analysis of Homer's and Virgil's foot-races hold for most of the other passages in which we can clearly identify the Homeric original or model of Virgil. We must of course allow for the special situations with which Virgil is dealing. Thus the fact that he avoids direct quotations in the account of the foot-race does not, of course, mean that he does not elsewhere make extensive use of quotation. But it is the very essence of his 'empathetic' and dramatico-psychological method to take the special dramatic situation into full account: there are places where the set speech of epic is appropriate and there are places (e.g. the footrace) where it is not.

❖ ❖ ❖

So far then we have uncovered certain characteristics of the Virgilian epic style: the empathy and sympathy revealed in sentence structure, tense differentiation, metric, and choice of words and similes; the 'editorial' intrusion of the author by 'finger-pointing' epithet, explicit declaration of *parti pris* and the implicit bias of his language; the relative absence of objective characters, speaking their own words and with emotions distinct from those of their author. This is a *subjective* style: Homer's in contrast is *objective*. Virgil *concentrates* on an object or purpose which dominates his characters and, to some extent his readers; Homer, though he actually tells his story with great art, always gives the illusion that he is letting his characters speak and act for themselves in a narrative big enough and leisurely enough to give them the scope and independence they need. We must now try to see how Virgil used this subjective style, how it enabled him to give a quite new content and meaning to Homeric material.

❖ ❖ ❖

Notes

[1]Cf. *Vita Donati* (35): Anno aetatis quinquagesimo secundo inpositurus Aeneidi summam manum statuit in Graeciam et in Asiam secedere triennioque continuo nihil amplius quam emendare, ut reliqua vita tantum philosophiae vacaret. Sed cum ingressus iter Athenis occurrisset Augusto ab oriente Romam revertenti destinaretque non absistere atque etiam una redire, dum Megara vicinum oppidum ferventissimo sole cognoscit, languorem nactus est eumque non intermissa navigatione auxit ita, ut gravior aliquanto Brundisium appelleret, ubi diebus paucis obiit XI Kal. Octobr. Cn. Sentio Q. Lucretio coss. (39): Egerat cum Vario, priusquam Italia decederet, ut, si quid sibi accidisset, Aeneida combureret; at is facturum se pernegarat; igitur in extrema valetudine assidue scrinia desideravit crematurus ipse; verum nemine offerente nihil quidem nominatim de ea cavit.

[2]Letter to Augustus (Macrobius, *Sat.* 1.24.11): De Aenea quidem meo, si mehercle iam dignum auribus haberem tuis, libenter mitterem, sed tanta inchoata res est, ut paene vitio mentis tantum opus ingressus mihi videar cum praesertim, ut scis, alia quoque studia ad id opus multoque potiora impendam.

[3]*Vita Donati*, 31–32

[4]*Vita Donati*, 22–24

❖ ❖ ❖

[5]Heinze, Chapter 4.

[6]Milman Parry, *L'epithète traditionelle dans Homère* (1928) has well shown the difference between a metric based on the ready-made patterns of the traditional *name-epithets* or *formulae* and the quite different *literary* metric of Apollonius (*Argonautica*) or Virgil. See esp. pp. 30–44 and the revealing tables on pp. 38–40, 50–51. But Parry does not discriminate between the metrics of Virgil and Apollonius: the important differences between them are in fact irrelevant to his purpose (to show the nature of *Homer's* oral style). It may be said here that Parry's emphasis on the *difference* between *oral* and *literary* epic style *as such* has tended to obscure the equally important difference between Greek and Latin epic *as such*.

❖ ❖ ❖

Michael C. J. Putnam

THE LYRIC GENIUS OF THE *AENEID*

The favored poetic style in Vergil's day was short, light, learned verse. The poet Catullus, Vergil's near contemporary, was a master practitioner of that style. In this article, Putnam demonstrates how thoroughly Vergil integrated into his heroic epic the stylistic attributes that were its presumed antithesis. Putnam does this by tracing the allusions to one poem of Catullus, number 11, throughout the latter half of the *Aeneid*. He then analyzes one passage of the epic, the meeting of Aeneas and his father Anchises in the Underworld at 6.687–94, for its allusions to several poems of Catullus. Putnam's analysis helps us understand more fully the way Vergil transformed the style and emotive content of epic by incorporating into it the lyric voice. Lyric content asks "the reader to pause and to compare contexts." That capacity for reflection is the "more general effect of lyricization" that marks the *Aeneid* as a whole. (Ed.)

Ralph Johnson, in his searching book *The Idea of Lyric*, speaks of Virgil as "the supreme master of lyrical disguises."[1] He is, of course, absolutely correct, and I would like to explore some of the devices that Virgil uses to "lyricize" his epic, [notably]…his use of allusion, in particular of allusion to the poetry of Catullus.…

Allusivity…is by nature an anti-narrative gesture. It forces the reader to linger and gain a frisson of pleasure, in epic's case, not from description of the excited propulsion of events but from an act of intellectual recognition and inner reflection. We take a moment to watch the mirroring of one previous poetic context upon another subsequent to it which compounds the latter's importance and signification.

My particular focus will be the pervasive influence of the poetry of Catullus upon Virgil's text.[2] This phenomenon is nothing new to scholars of the *Aeneid*, especially where the sixty-fourth poem of the Catullan corpus is concerned. Nevertheless I will attempt to look at it afresh from two angles. I will first observe how, and why, he takes echoes of one poem of Catullus, number 11, and spreads them across the final reaches of his poem. I will suggest that Virgil's bows to this extraordinary lyric reflect a spiritual evolution in the epic itself as it progresses from its central segments, with their commanding glimpses of incipient Roman majesty, to the perpetual sense of loss and presence of brutality that suffuses the final quartet of books.

I will then shift from diffusion to concentration and take a moment of some intensity in Virgil's poem, the initial lines of Aeneas's meeting with his father in the Underworld, and examine how, as he wrote, Virgil drew upon a series of Catullan texts, asking the reader to pause, and pause again, for the contemplation of the

Michael C. J. Putnam, "The Lyric Genius of the *Aeneid*," *Arion*, Third Series 3.2 & 3 (1995/1996) 81–101. Reprinted by permission of Michael C. J. Putnam.

means by which careful echoes of other imaginative contexts affect the dynamism of Virgil's own. I will use these illustrations as springboards not to theorize further on allusivity as a poetic device but to comment yet again on the deeply subjective nature of Virgil's art as it molds what is assumed to be an essentially objective genre of poetry.

✧ ✧ ✧

I...turn...to one of Catullus's lyric masterpieces, the eleventh poem of the polymetrics, written in Sapphic stanzas, and observe its potency over a broad reach of the *Aeneid*. It...was a major force on Virgil's imagination, and the manner in which he projects this influence has, I think, something to tell us of at least one way which Virgil would have us read his epic. I quote the poem in full:

> Furi et Aureli, comites Catulli,
> sive in extremos penetrabit Indos,
> litus ut longe resonante Eoa
>   tunditur unda,
>
> sive in Hyrcanos Arabasve molles,
> seu Sagas sagittiferosve Parthos,
> sive quae septemgeminus colorat
>   aequora Nilus,
>
> sive trans altas gradietur Alpes,
> Caesaris visens monimenta magni,
> Gallicum Rhenum horribile aequor ulti-
>   mosque Britannos,
>
> omnia haec, quaecumque feret voluntas
> caelitum, temptare simul parati,
> pauca nuntiate meae puellae
>   non bona dicta.
>
> cum suis vivat valeatque moechis,
> quos simul complexa tenet trecentos,
> nullum amans vere, sed identidem omnium
>   ilia rumpens;
>
> nec meum respectet, ut ante, amorem,
> qui illius culpa cecidit velut prati
> ultimi flos, praetereunte postquam
>   tactus aratro est.

Furius and Aurelius, companions of Catullus, whether he will penetrate the farthest Indi, where the shore is beaten by the far-resounding eastern wave, or the Hyrcani or the soft Arabians, whether the Sagae or arrow-bearing Parthians, whether the seas which seven-twinned Nile dyes, whether he will march over the lofty Alps, viewing the memorials of mighty

Caesar, the Gallic Rhine, the bristling water and remotest Britons — all these things, prepared to test together whatever the will of the gods shall bring: announce a few words, not pleasant, to my girl. Let her live and flourish with her adulterers, whom she holds in her embrace, three hundred at once, loving no one of them truly but again and again breaking the groins of all. And let her not look for my love, as before, which by her fault has fallen like a flower of the remotest meadow after it has been touched by a passing plough.

This extraordinary poem offers a study of two diverse worlds and the challenge of their juxtaposition. The realm that the speaking "Catullus" ponders entering, in the putative company of Furius and Aurelius, reflects the extent of Roman power expressed in geographical terms. To name is to control and we follow place after place in the east, south and northwest, the victims or targets of the imperial ambitions of Pompey (presumably) and Caesar (certainly). We revel in a boundless, public sphere of topographical grandeur where omnipresent activity and dynamism are couched in terms of sexual mastery (*penetrabit, tunditur*) ["he will penetrate," "is beaten"] and conveyed in grandiloquent language (*sagittiferos, septemgeminus*) ["arrow-bearing," "seven-twinned"] that pushes lyric to the borders of epic. The same intensity spills over into the second segment of the poem where Rome's territorial acquisitiveness merges with, and is reinterpreted by, the omnivorous sexual greed of Lesbia, and lyric for a moment takes on yet another shade, this time the *maledicta* ["harsh words, curses"] of the iamb and invective. But the fourth stanza, in the change from *omnia* to *pauca* ["all," "a few"], also anticipates the larger metamorphosis that overcomes the poem as it progresses to a conclusion. As we shift from the limitless rapacity of Rome and Lesbia, from the *omnium ilia* ["the groins of all"] that she ruptures to her particular destructiveness of the speaker's love, of the *nullum* ["no one"] who cannot receive her true affection because it is non-existent, we leave behind literal description for one of Catullus's most brilliant symbolic analogies. From the farthest Britons we turn to a flower of the farthest meadow, but now also we have at the end the passive private helplessness of Catullus's love likened to a vulnerable, virginal flower that suffers "touching," even though at the meadow's most distant remove. .

The paradoxes in this finale are many. Faultless love, for Catullus, is something inviolate, uncontaminated. His masculine sexuality, before Lesbia's ubiquitous cupidity had revealed itself, is metaphorized as something both feminine and pre-sexual. But what remains finally with the reader is a picture of both physical and spiritual hurt and victimization, where the enormity of Rome's political ravening, resumed in Lesbia's careless, cold, gluttonous physicality, is focused on a single emblem of helplessness whose curious distinctiveness is obliterated by grander, more impersonal forces than a lone, motionless flower can withstand or muster energy with which to respond.

Let us now turn to examples of when and how Virgil in the *Aeneid* betrays the influence of this extraordinary poem. I will follow the allusions book by book because the sequential development will prove important. Virgil begins in Book 6, with a series of references contained within Anchises' expansive survey for his son of future Roman political and military accomplishment. The first comes in an analogy where the extent of Rome's dominion is compared to the number of people the Magna Mater ["Great Mother"] holds in her embrace (6.786–7):

...centum complexa nepotes,
omnis caelicolas, omnis supera alta tenentis.

...clutching a hundred descendants, all the dwellers in the sky, all who hold heaven's heights.

Here we are not far from Lesbia, *complexa tenet trecentos* ["holding three hundred in embrace"].[3]

Virgil then has Anchises, in his survey, turn to the *Indos* ["the Indi"] (794), to "the trembling mouths of seven-twinned Nile" (*septemgemini...trepida ostia Nili*, 800)[4] and, finally, closer to home, to Caesar and Pompey (830-1):

aggeribus socer Alpinis atque arce Monoeci
descendens, gener adversis instructus Eois.

the father-in-law swooping down from Alpine heights and the citadel of Monoecus, the son-in-law furnished with troops from the East against his enemy.

Virgil draws the collocation of *socer* and *gener* ["father-in law," "son-in-law"], and a touch of that poem's irony, from Catullus 29 (24) where the two relatives are apostrophized as incorporations of Roman immorality. His bows here are more oblique, *aggeribus Alpinis* ["Alpine heights"] picking up *altas Alpes* ["lofty Alps"], natural eminences which Caesar remakes as his own fortifications, and *Eois* ["eastern"] paralleling Catullus's use of the adjective and reminding us of Pompey's associations with the East that began with his campaigns against Mithridates.

We next meet Catullus 11 in *Aeneid 7* at the moment before Juno breaks open the *Belli portae* ["gates of War"] to initiate war in Latium. As preface, the narrator takes the custom down to present-day Rome when this "greatest of states" makes war not against herself in civil strife but against foreign enemies (7.603-6):

...cum prima movent in proelia Martem
sive Getis inferre manu lacrimabile bellum
Hyrcanisve Arabisve parant, seu tendere ad Indos
Auroramque sequi Parthosque reposcere signa...

...when they first stir Mars to battle, whether their hands prepare to bring tearful battle to the Getae or Hyrcanians or Arabians or to march against the Indi and follow the Dawn and demand their standards of the Parthians...

In the space of lines 605-6 Virgil names the *Hyrcani*, *Arabes*, and *Parthi*, peoples whom Catullus likewise compresses into two lines, with the addition of the *Indi* whom Catullus had mentioned three lines previously.

Catullus 11 also makes an important appearance in Book 8, during the final scene on the shield of Aeneas. We are perhaps meant to find allusion to Catullus's *ultimos Britannos* ["remotest Britons"] in the *ultima Bactra* ["remotest Bactra"] (687-8) that Antony draws with him to fight at Actium. We certainly sense the earlier poet's strong presence in the last four lines of the ekphrasis, listing the conquered peoples who pay obeisance to Octavian on the steps of his new, resplendent temple to Apollo (8.725-8):

hic Lelegas Carasque sagittiferosque Gelonos
finxerat; Euphrates ibat iam mollior undis,
extremique hominum Morini, Rhenusque bicornis,
indomitique Dahae, et pontem indignatus Araxes.

Here [Vulcan] had fashioned the Leleges and Carians and arrow-bearing
Gelonians; the Euphrates was moving now gentler with its waves, and the
Morini, farthest of men, the double-horned Rhine, the untamed Dahae and
the Araxes, aggrieved at its bridge.

Line 725 offers the second appearance in Latin letters of the adjective *sagittifer* ["arrow-bearing"]. The *undis* ["waves"] of the Euphrates recall Catullus's *Eoa...unda* ["eastern wave"] just as *extremi Morini* ["farthest Morini"] are a reminder of *extremos Indos* ["farthest Indi"] (11.2). Line 727 contains the only mention of the Rhine in the *Aeneid*.[5]

The influence of the opening stanzas of Catullus also spills over into the initial lines of *Aeneid* 9. At line 10 Virgil, evoking Catullus's equation of sexual with military control, has Iris tell Turnus of how Aeneas "has penetrated to the farthest cities of Corythus" (*extremas Corythi penetravit ad urbes*). And in the book's first simile (30–1) we find the movement of Turnus's army compared to the Ganges "rising high with its seven calm streams" (*ceu septem surgens sedatis amnibus altus*) and the Nile—a clear case of transfer with *septemgeminus* ["seven-twinned"] in the background.

But before turning to the epic's final four books it is best to summarize what we have so far seen of Virgil's allusions to Catullus 11. The first thing to note is that hitherto in our survey we have seen no allusions to the last stanza of Catullus's poem. Secondly, we should observe the similarities in the contexts of the allusions in *Aeneid* 6–8. All look to the Rome of the late Republic or early Empire. This is accomplished in Book 6 through the agency of Anchises' clairvoyant words, in Book 7 during a piece of aetiological explanation on the narrator's part that takes us from mythic Latium to Augustan foreign policy, and in Book 8 as we leap to Rome of 28 B.C.E. by means of the magic of ekphrasis. As in Catullus's poem itself, Virgil's allusions deal with the recent history of Roman power. They catalogue, in name after name, her portentous accomplishment (and suggest, in the case of Anchises' speech, with an irony that surfaces clearly from time to time, parallels with Lesbia's pantophagy) and her sweeping dominion.

But Book 9 marks a turning point in Virgil's reception of Catullus 11. The opening references, as we have seen, do return our thoughts to the lyric's initial stanzas though they now grace activity not in some imagined future but in the poem's mythic foreground, as Aeneas and Turnus prepare for war. But Book 9 marks another critical juncture as well. After the opening lines of the book the initial stanzas of poem 11 disappear from the *Aeneid* to be replaced by two long-noticed allusions to the poem's conclusion. The first and more pointed occurs later in the book as blood spurts from the limbs of dead Euryalus and his neck collapses on his shoulders (435–6):

purpureus veluti cum flos succisus aratro
languescit moriens...

just as when a purple flower, cut down by a plough, droops and dies...

The second is less direct verbally but serves, nevertheless, to keep alive the same analogy. It, too, occurs, like its poetic forebear, in a simile, now in the eleventh book, describing the recently killed Pallas as (68–9)

> qualem virgineo demessum pollice florem
> seu mollis violae seu languentis hyacinthi...

> like a flower sheared by the thumb of a virgin, either of soft violet or drooping hyacinth...[6]

As we turn in the *Aeneid* from visions of the fruits of Rome's future acquisition of world dominion to the immediacy of battling in Latium, we also follow the course of Catullus's lyric as we move from public grandeur (or grandiosity) to private hurt, to the many individual losses of youth in war. We supplant love or, better, sexuality with death and instead of deflowering as analogy for marriage we have the flower cut down as symbol for androgynous youth devirginated by the violence of mortal wound. Catullus 11, in Virgil's adoptions, therefore proffers an important intellectual and spiritual map of the *Aeneid*, showing how the Augustan poet utilizes his great predecessor to make us turn from idealizing vistas of Roman glory to the lived horrors of human brutality. Or, to put the matter in terms of genres, by his linear survey of Catullus 11 Virgil in a special way personalizes the *Aeneid*, putting final stress, where Catullus does, on the immediacy and the problematics of human emotionality, not on the impersonal prowess of empire and its dreams of future glory. It is with stress on man's passional side, not on Rome's achievement, that the epic ends.

Let me expand on this briefly by using a recent definition of the lyric offered by the critic and poet, Joseph Brodsky. He writes, "Scrutiny and interpretation are the gist of any intense human interplay, and of love in particular. They are also the most powerful source of literature: of fiction (which is by and large about betrayal) and, above all, of lyric poetry where one is trying to figure out the beloved and what makes her/him tick."[7]

Virgil's refractions of Catullus's extraordinary lyric take this "scrutiny" and spread it out as a larger glow over a grand stretch of epic time. From Catullus we have a focused moment of apprehension and apprehending, of mental and emotional deepening as we move from the possibilities of escape from love's hideous travails to the horrors of its immediate destructiveness. In Virgil's hands this emotional evolution suffers metamorphosis into an overarching survey, first of future Roman, historical pretensions, then of the present losses that Roman *imperium* ["empire"] brings in its wake.

Catullus's Roman world, the world that initiates his poem, like Virgil's to follow, in the descriptions of *Aeneid* 6 and 8, offers a synoptic glimpse of time to come. Its power is built on namings, those proclamations of control and ownership. It anticipates journeying through a realm which the traveller possesses because he shares in the vigor of Rome, of a Caesar or a Pompey. But when contemporary immediacy becomes paramount, as it does again in the *Aeneid*'s last quartet of books and at the end of Catullus's brilliant poem, we engage finally with individual suffering and hurt. In both instances, as lyric leaves behind its foray into epic impersonality and vastness, and as epic absorbs lyric's concentrated affectivity, apparent eulogy of *imperium* yields to acknowledgement of human emotions and to the particulars of loss.

Merely drawing this parallel might seem to violate my own definition of lyric as characterized by compression and intensity, since Virgil alludes throughout the *Aeneid* to a single Catullan poem. Perhaps so, but Virgil may be up to something more generically challenging than he is regularly allowed. By making the progress in his majestic epic from the public vistas of future Roman glory to the private anguish that war brings parallel the circumscribed scope of Catullus's lyric, by having the hurt of *eris* ["strife"] reviewed as the injuriousness of *eros* ["love"], he lyricizes his poem in a most powerful way and puts the emphasis where most readers now sense it, on the darkness of the human spirit and its ambitions.

We have been studying an example of what I earlier called the diffusion of a Catullan lyric throughout Virgil's text. I would like to end by observing a largely opposite phenomenon, the presence of a series of allusions to Catullus concentrated by Virgil in a single passage. Out of several possible instances I have chosen the moment when Aeneas comes upon his father in the Underworld, in particular Anchises' speech of greeting which I quote in full (6. 687–94):

'venisti tandem, tuaque exspectata parenti
vicit iter durum pietas? datur ora tueri,
nate, tua et notas audire et reddere voces?
sic equidem ducebam animo rebarque futurum
tempora dinumerans, nec me mea cura fefellit.
quas ego te terras et quanta per aequora vectum
accipio! quantis iactatum, nate, periclis!
quam metui ne quid Libyae tibi regna nocerent!'

"Have you come at last, and has your devotion, presumed by your father, won out over the hardship of the journey? Am I allowed, my son, to view your features, and to hear your familiar voice and to reply? This is certainly what I worked out in my mind, what I thought would happen as I counted time's passage, nor has my anxiety misled me. Over what lands and through what seas have you travelled to my welcome! By what great perils, my son, were you tossed! How I feared that the kingdoms of Libya might do you some harm."

There follows one of the most moving scenes in the epic where Aeneas asks for his father's embrace and, weeping, attempts three times in vain to grasp his disembodied form.

The two most salient parallels with Catullus have regularly been cited by critics. The phrase *notas audire et reddere voces* ["to hear your familiar voice and reply"] comes from a moment in Catullus 64 during Ariadne's great soliloquy of lament where she addresses the breezes (165–6):

'...quae nullis sensibus auctae
nec missas audire queunt nec reddere voces...'

"...which, furnished with no feelings, can neither hear the words that I utter nor reply..."

Ariadne, abandoned and alone, has become, through Virgil's recollection, Anchises whose object of affection has returned to him and with whom he can in fact have a conversation.[8] Equally direct is the allusion that the sentence *quas ego te terras et quanta per aequora vectum / accipio!* ["over what lands and through what seas have you travelled to my welcome!"] makes to the opening lines of Catullus's poem 101:

> Multas per gentes et multa per aequora vectus
>   advenio...

> Having travelled through many peoples and over many seas I reach my destination...

Poem 101 is a lamentation where the epigram itself is the funerary offering of Catullus to his dead brother.[9] One of its most moving aspects is its projection as a dialogue — the poet's "I" addressing the deceased "you" — incapable of implementation. There can be no discourse with mute ashes. Here again Virgil appears to reverse Catullus's tonality. By a *coup de maître* ["master stroke"] he "reanimates" Catullus's dead brother in the form of Anchises who, by a happy quirk of fortune, can in fact be visited in the Underworld and with whom Aeneas can have the dialogue withheld from Catullus in the world above. Through both Catullan reminiscences Virgil takes the inability to communicate, because of desertion or death, and makes it possible again.[10]

But the opening line of Anchises' speech, I would propose, also contains two further brief but significant echoes of Catullus. The words *tandem* and *expectata* ["at last," "presumed"] appear in the second line of Catullus 62, modifying Vesper, the Evening Star whose sudden appearance, for the male chorus, announces the beginning of the marriage ceremony:

> Vesper adest, iuvenes, consurgite: Vesper Olympo
> expectata diu vix tandem lumina tollit.

> The Evening Star has appeared, youths, rise up. The Evening Star, long awaited, is at last just raising its light from heaven.

If we transfer the symbolism from epithalamium to epic, Vesper's advent becomes Aeneas and his vaunted *pietas* ["devotion"], arrived not to satisfy eager lovers but to bring joy to a father who had literally been counting the days for a reunion with his son.

Finally, we have the speech's opening verb, *venisti* ["have you come"]. A single word may seem a slim thread on which to hang the weight of allusion, but a particular circumstance warrants the claim here. This is the only occasion in the corpus of his writings that Virgil uses this form of *venio* ["I come"]. The same holds true for Catullus, vis-à-vis the two appearances of the word in a single poem of his, the ninth. Though they do not occur in the first line, as in the case of Anchises' speech, they do initiate lines 3 and 5. I quote the poem in full:

> Verani, omnibus e meis amicis
> antistans mihi milibus trecentis,
> venistine domum ad tuos penates
> fratresque unanimos anumque matrem?
> venisti. o mihi nuntii beati!
> visam te incolumem audiamque Hiberum

narrantem loca, facta, nationes,
ut mos est tuus, applicansque collum
iucundum os oculosque suaviabor.
o quantum est hominum beatiorum,
quid me laetius est beatiusve?

Veranius, of all my friends preferred to me over three hundred thousand, have you come home to your household gods and to your like-minded brothers and your aged mother? You have come! O happy news to me! I will gaze on you safe and sound and I will hear you telling of the places, deeds, tribes of the Hiberi, as is your wont, and clinging to your neck I will kiss your sweet face and eyes. O, of all men of the happier sort, who is gladder or happier than I?

In the previous three allusions to Catullus I have discussed in the speech of Anchises, the relationships that Virgil overlays upon his text are of lover with lover, father with son and, implicitly, future husband with future wife. Here it is of friend with friend. Catullus's speaker is like Anchises anticipating what actually happens in the *Aeneid* – the arrival of someone beloved, after a series of adventures, safely back to another person who matters deeply. But there is one jarring difference between the two selections which I would suggest is a primary reason for Virgil's cooptation. Both passages are extremely sensual. In Catullus we move, in the speaker's eager expectation, from his seeing and hearing to clutching Veranius's neck and kissing his mouth and eyes. The same physicality is present throughout the meeting of Aeneas and Anchises. Virgil draws attention to Anchises' hands, cheeks, and mouth (*ore*) before he speaks. Anchises himself likewise mentions Aeneas's face (*ora*). Aeneas in turn pleads with his father to grasp his right hand and hold him in his embrace (*amplexu*, 698, is cognate with Catullus's *applicans* ["clinging"]). Finally in the subsequent narration we have mention again of Aeneas's *ora* and the hands by which he attempts to clasp his father's neck (there are forms of *os* and *collum* ["face," "neck"] in the adjacent lines 8–9 in Catullus as well).

But the last segment of the episode points up the startling, carefully contrived discrepancies between the two passages. There can be no physical contact in the world of ghosts, no possibility for living son to embrace dead father. This fact points to further levels of intent in the allusions to poems 64 and 101 of Catullus. Both the Catullan poems deal with the horror of separation and with discourse apparently cut off forever or only resumed in one-sided fashion. It is this notion that Virgil chooses to emphasize in contrast to Catullus 9. Dialogue is momentarily, magically ensured between father and son but the possibility of further fulfillment is evanescent while the future looks to separation, loss, and a type of death.

Finally we might also note the implicit presence of Dido for the final time in the book in the last line allotted to Anchises (694):

quam metui ne quid Libyae tibi regna nocerent!

["How I feared that the kingdoms of Libya might do you some harm!"]

This line draws our attention back to Aeneas's initial appeal to Apollo, reminding him

… magnas obeuntia terras
tot maria intravi duce te penitusque repostas
Massylum gentis praetentaque Syrtibus arva… (58–60)

Under your guidance I have entered so many seas skirting great lands and
the far withdrawn tribes of the Massyli and fields fringed by the Syrtes…

Though mention of seas and races has a faint echo again of the opening of Catullus
101, the presence of Catullus is not directly felt in either quotation, and Aeneas's
words — *terras…maria, duce te* – ["lands…seas, under your guidance"] smack largely
of conquest and power. In particular, he seems to dwell more on a hero's dangers
than on any emotional threats that might claim reference to lyric.

Yet the very indirection of Anchises' statement calls attention to itself and
therefore to his past fears that Dido might deflect Aeneas from his mission. And
this implication in turn reminds us of the dangers, throughout the poem, of the
erotic as a source of irrationality. But there is also a latent irony here. The strong
juxtaposition of *ego* and *te* ["I, you"] in the words Virgil gives Anchises and the
replacement of Catullus's *advenio* ["I reach my destination"] with the more tactile
accipio "[I receive you, to my welcome"] suggest that some physical union might
be possible between father and son because dialogue has recommenced. But even
this embrace, though it lacks the hazards of carnality, is incapable of fruition.
Learning of the idealistic side of the future Roman moral mission is only imagin-
able in the incorporeal world of the dead, undergoing their process of emotional
purgation, where no physical contact, however much desired by either or both
parties, is possible. Spiritual insight and erotic fulfillment would seem, for Virgil,
to be mutually exclusive.

A survey of Book 6 as a whole, however, suggests that it is Aeneas who primarily
fosters the lyric mode whereas Anchises is the purveyor of the stuff of epic, parading
before his son the shades of the Roman political and military future. The exhortation
to face what is to come, that is, to initiate the saga of incipient Rome, lies not with
Aeneas, who sees return to life as fostered only by a *dira cupido* ["dread desire"],
but by Anchises. Though Anchises displays emotion upon seeing his son, it is the
latter who seeks an embrace impossible to fulfill. And it is the ghost of Anchises
who tells of martial ghosts to come and who dismisses both son and Sibyl back into
the world of reality through the ivory gate of opaque dreams.

We must also remember that it is the appearance of Dido in the book's center
that elicits from Virgil, through the mouth of his hero, the book's most prominent
(and most discussed) allusion to Catullus. When Aeneas announces (6.460)

invitus, regina, tuo de litore cessi

— unwilling, queen, I withdrew from your shore —

he is, of course, echoing words Catullus puts into the mouth of the lock of Berenice,
snipped from the head of her mistress and wafted heavenwards:

invite, o regina, tuo de vertice cessi.[11]

— unwilling, o queen, I took my leave from your head.

There are those who see some pertness in the lock's exclamation slip over into Aeneas's words so that the potential diminution in his heroic stature which comparison with a lock of hair might suggest is supplemented by cynicism of tone. But I take the emotion behind both utterances seriously, in each case bringing back to mind a separation that was deeply troubling. In having Anchises express his worry about the danger which Dido presented, Virgil has us recall her recent appearance to Aeneas and with this comes, secondarily, a last reminder of Catullus in this cluster of recollections. As for Dido, she may not have been able to intervene between father and son but she remains a powerful presence, through both direct and indirect references, in the epic's final sextet of books.

In summary, as son meets father in one of the most emotional moments of the epic's story line, poetic son reveals with a special intensity the influence of one of his major poetic forebears. Even allusion to Homer is an act of lyricizing, asking the reader to pause and to compare contexts. When the references are to Catullus the force of the gesture is redoubled. Perhaps this is a form of rivalry. But cooptation here is also an act of imaginative embrace. Virgil makes no attempt to better or to supercede his Republican predecessor. Rather he allows him to permeate, and therefore to strongly mark, his text so as to infuse it with a special emotionality that belongs to his particular lyric genius.

This richness of allusion is paralleled in Canto 30 of Dante's *Purgatorio* where the departure of Virgil from the pilgrim's side is accompanied by the most lavish set of allusions to Virgilian texts in the *Commedia*.[12] The many references to Catullus in the description of the meeting of Anchises and Aeneas serve two purposes. Each Catullan context has something individual to tell us about Virgil's purposes. But the accumulation, especially when the predecessor in question happens to be Catullus, aims toward the more general effect of lyricization that I have been seeking to define. Narrative time stops at one of the epic's most emotional moments and allusion redoubles the impact of such a pause. By being made to watch so closely the initiation of a highly unusual meeting of father and son, we tend also the better to keep the evolution of the whole of that encounter in mind. We follow the ambiguities of Anchises' overview of future Rome, and with Aeneas we ponder his father's maxim, uttered at a climactic moment in Book 6, to war down the prideful and spare the humbled.[13]

At the very end of the poem it is the epic mode of anger and revenge, the ongoing humanness which regularly complements the exercise of power, the suggestion that civil strife is ever renewable, that rules events, not the lyric's pause to react with sorrow or joy at life's losses and fulfillments or, in the case of Aeneas before his final deed, to contemplate for more than a moment a defeated hero at his mercy. But perhaps the final essence of the poem is thus also lyric, dwelling on individual emotion and its repeatability. The words of Anchises, which enjoin an act of *clementia* ["mercy"] that would symbolically initiate Rome's new era and bring its epic to a conclusion of novel ethical force and grandeur, will prove impossible for the passionate hero to implement. It is Catullus in Virgil who has helped us linger again over their importance.

Notes

[1]W. R. Johnson *The Idea of Lyric* (Berkeley 1982), 149. We might also take note of W. H. Auden's more general remark, "A verbal art like poetry is reflective; it stops to think," quoted by Robert Craft, *New York Review of Books*, November 3, 1994, 57.

❖ ❖ ❖

[2]From the large bibliography on the subject of the influence of Catullus on the *Aeneid* I would single out the following: F. P. Simpson, ed., *Select Poems of Catullus* (London 1879), xxxviii–ix; E. K. Rand "Catullus and the Augustans," *HSCP* 17 (1906), 15–30; L. Herrmann "Le poème 64 de Catulle et Virgile," *REL* 8 (1930), 211–22; R. E. H. Westendorp Boerma "Vergil's Debt to Catullus," *Acta Classica* 1 (1958), 51–63; D. H. Abel "Ariadne and Dido," *CB* 38 (1962), 57–61; G. Gonnelli "Presenza di Catullo in Virgilio," *GIF* 15 (1962), 225–53; D. Knecht "Virgile et ses modèles latins," *L'Antiquité Classique* 32 (1963), 491–512, especially 501–3; G. Kilroy "The Dido Episode and the Sixty-Fourth Poem of Catullus," *SO* 44 (1969), 48–60; J. Ferguson "Catullus and Virgil," *PVS* 11 (1971–2), 25–47; M. Wigodsky *Vergil and Early Latin Poetry* (*Hermes Einzelschrift* 24 [Wiesbaden 1972]), especially 126–31; J. Glenn "The Blinded Cyclops: *Lumen Ademptum* (*Aen.* 3.658)," *CP* 69 (1974), 37–8; S. V. Tracy "Catullan Echoes in *Aeneid* 6.333–36," *AJP* 98 (1977), 20–3; R. Schmiel "A Virgilian Formula," *Vergilius* 25 (1979), 37–40; B. Arkins "New Approaches to Virgil," *Latomus* 45 (1986), 33–42.

❖ ❖ ❖

[3]See M. C. J. Putnam "Catullus 11 and Virgil *Aen.* 6.786–7," *Vergilius* 35 (1989), 28–30.

[4]Cf. *centumgeminus Briareus* (6.287).

[5]*Indi* and *Arabes* are mentioned in adjacent lines at *Aen.* 8.705–6.

[6]The allusions are often noted. See, e.g., Ferguson (*op. cit.* n. 2), 34–5.

[7]*The New Yorker*, September 26, 1994, 75–6.

[8]Virgil uses the phrase *veras audire et reddere voces* at *Aen.* 1.409 in a context that is carefully complementary to the episode in Book 6. In the earlier episode Aeneas has wished to embrace his mother who flees from his approach. It, too, is richly allusive, with careful bows to *Eclogue* 8 as well as to the fourth book of *De Rerum Natura*.

[9]This particular echo has been discussed most recently by Ferguson (32–3), Tracy and Schmiel (*op. cit.* n. 2). See also G. B. Conte *The Rhetoric of Imitation* (Ithaca 1986), 34 n. 2.

[10]We should note that poem 101 was already on Virgil's mind in the writing of *Aeneid* 6, for the phrase *more parentum* (101.7) recurs at 6.223, each concluding its line. There is another clear echo of the opening of 101 at *Aen.* 11.97–8.

[11]66.39. On this famous echo see most recently P. A. Johnston "Dido, Berenice, and Arsinoe: *Aeneid* 6.460," *AJP* 108 (1987), 649–54, with bibliography in n. 1, 649.

[12]On allusions to Virgil's poetry at the moment of his literal departure from Dante's text see M. Putnam "Virgil's Inferno," *MD* 20–21 (1988), 165–202, reprinted in *The Poetry of Allusion*, ed. R. Jacoff and J. Schnapp (Stanford 1991), 94–112, especially 107–12.

In this context it is worth quoting the remark of Ezra Pound (*The Spirit of Romance* [New York 1952], 153), "The *Divina Commedia* must not be considered as an epic; to compare it with epic poems is usually unprofitable. It is in a sense lyric, the tremendous lyric of the subjective Dante…"

[13]*Aen.* 6.853.

Annabel Patterson

PASTORAL AND IDEOLOGY
INTRODUCTION

Starting with the first five lines of the first poem of Vergil's first work, the *Eclogues*, written from about 42–37 B.C.E., Patterson investigates the role of the author in the work of poetry. She studies the meaning and function of the pronouns in these lines and thus of the characters and their relation to the poet. Vergil's book of ten short pastoral poems, modeled on the work of the third-century B.C.E. Greek poet Theocritus, has been influential throughout the history of European literature, and Patterson is especially interested in their reception. She argues that "what people think of Virgil's *Eclogues* is a key to their own cultural assumptions, because the text was so structured as to provoke, consciously or unconsciously, an ideological response," particularly as revealed through people's assumptions about art. She concludes the essay with a discussion of the twentieth-century novel *The Death of Virgil* by Hermann Broch, a refugee from Nazi Europe, who, like writers before him, "interprets the *Eclogues* in light of his own situation." The discussion of the author function is the point of entry to the "role of the intellectual in society," an issue as important for Vergil as it is for us. (Ed.)

More than two thousand years ago, certain privileged Roman readers unrolled a "book" of poems and encountered the following greeting:

Tityre, tu patulae recubans sub tegmine fagi
silvestrem tenui musam meditaris avena;
nos patriae finis et dulcia linquimus arva.
nos patriam fugimus; tu, Tityre, lentus in umbra
formosam resonare doces Amaryllida silvas.[1]

You, Tityrus, reclining under the spreading shelter of the beech, meditate pastoral poetics on your slender pipe; we are leaving the borders of our country and its sweet fields. We are in flight from our fatherland; you, Tityrus, relaxed in the shade, teach the woods to echo the name of fair Amaryllis.[2]

These lines have been echoing ever since; not, I would argue, because of their graceful memorability, but because those Roman readers faced, even in these first five lines, a challenge that has remained intensely audible. Almost every word in this apparently translucent opening is overdetermined, making demands on interpretation that translators in every generation have wrestled with, only to the dissatisfaction of the new translators who follow with wrestlings of their own. Among the most pressing textual exigencies are the relationships between the pronouns, so insistent in their chiastic structure, "tu...nos...nos...tu" ["you...we...we...you"]; the presence of those Greek names, Tityrus and Amaryllis, which invite speculation into Virgil's recall of Theocritus, and hence the full meaning of *resonare,* echo; and the question of how to translate *silvestrem...musam meditaris,* which permits a more cerebral response than its equally permissible alternative, "practice woodland music." Neither option, however, is innocent. Each carries with it a rival theory of pastoral.

...[I]t is the first [issue], the relationship between "tu" and "nos," that most economically represents this book's concerns. Modern thought has done much for the status of the pronoun, and particularly for the Latinate "ego" ["I"], with its privileged status in the various disciplines that seek to define (or to erase) subjectivity. "Est 'ego' qui *dit* 'ego,'" ["That person is an 'I' who *says* 'I'"] writes, for example, Emile Benveniste, developing an argument for the linguistic expression both of subjectivity and of its essentially dialogic nature.[3] But Virgil, who also begins with dialogue, indicates in his opening statement the limitations of a discourse centered on the first person singular. The relational structure of the first eclogue is not between the ego and its audience but between "tu" and "nos," a plural that immediately confronts the reader with a choice of identifications. If *I* is normally the index of subjectivity, and *you* the audience who permits its expression, *we* is the sign of community, of some common communicative ground. But here, as Virgil insists by his *contrastive* positioning of the pronouns, the *we* represented by Meliboeus must exclude the *you* represented by Tityrus. And every other aspect of those first five lines explains and passionately justifies that exclusion. While the selfhood of Tityrus is associated with reflection (*meditaris*), with echoes, with song, with literary allusion, and especially with leisure and protection, the community to which Meliboeus belongs is connected to (at the moment of its severance from) the most value-laden word in Roman culture, the *patria* ["fatherland"], subsuming the concepts of origin, national identity, and home. To which of these sets of values should Virgil's readers (by definition here, readers of poetry) be expected to affiliate themselves?

As the dialogue continues, the ethical indeterminacy posited in its opening lines steadily increases. We learn that the community at risk, for whom Meliboeus claims to speak, does not "flee" the land of their fathers voluntarily, but rather that they have been expelled by an apparently unjust military force:

> impius haec tam culta novalia miles habebit,
> barbarus has segetes. en quo discordia cives
> produxit miseros: his nos consevimus agros!

(lines 70–72)

Shall the impious soldier possess these well-tilled grounds? A barbarian possess these crops? See where fighting has brought our miserable countrymen. See for whom we have sown our fields!

In these lines, especially as their implications were developed in the ninth eclogue, the ground was laid for early recognition that Virgilian pastoral referred to something other than itself, and specifically to the historical circumstances in which it was produced — the last phases of the civil war between Brutus and Cassius, representing the old republic, and Antony and Octavian, agents and heirs of Caesarian centrism. Here, too, words that Roman culture had already saturated with value competed with each other, *impius* and *barbarus* ["impious," "barbarian"] in apparently oxymoronic proximity to *miles* (member of a disciplined armed force), *discordia* ["discord"] undoing the *corporate* semantics of *cives* ["citizens"]. Thousands of years of scholarly quarreling as to how much of recent Roman history was embedded in the *Eclogues*, and why it matters, have not resolved the tensions here established — between words whose social function, we may suppose, was normally to go unexamined.

The status of Tityrus also becomes increasingly problematic. However we read the dialogue, it speaks dramatically of the barriers that inhibit the exchange of values or even of information. Questions go unanswered. Listeners do not listen. Especially, many commentators have felt, Tityrus fails to attend to the obvious, if indirect, appeals for his sympathy and concern. So oblivious is he of the responsibilities of the fortunate toward the unfortunate that he misses the ethical force of Meliboeus's pronouns, declaring, in defiance of all evidence to the contrary, that "deus *nobis* haec otia fecit" ("a god gives *us* this leisure"). The ambiguity of *deus* ["a god"] as the source of protected leisure and the continued enjoyment of one's patrimony is intensified at the opening of the sixth eclogue, where, in eight lines full of allusions to the opening of the first, Virgil attaches the speaking ego to himself; elliptically suggests his reasons for writing pastoral at such a time; names a god, Apollo, as his somewhat playful superego; and identifies himself as Tityrus:

> Prima Syracosia dignata est ludere versu
> nostra neque erubuit silvas habitare Thalea.
> cum canerem reges et proelia, Cynthius aurem
> vellit et admonuit: "pastorem, Tityre, pinguis
> pascere oportet ovis, deductum dicere carmen."
> nunc ego (namque super tibi erunt qui dicere laudes,
> Vare, tuas cupiant et tristia condere bella)
> agrestem tenui meditabor harundine Musam.
> non iniussa cano.

> From the beginning our Thalea deigned to amuse herself with Sicilian verse, nor did she blush to inhabit the woods. When I would sing of kings and battles, Apollo tweaked my ear and warned me: "A shepherd, Tityrus, ought to feed fat sheep, to sing a slender song." Now I (for there will be plenty who wish to sing your praises, Varus, and to celebrate melancholy wars) will meditate the country Muse on my narrow reed. I do not sing unbidden.

So, astonishingly, Virgil lays claim to the character of the protégé whose limitations the opening dialogue had exposed; the Tityrus of the first poem must be recognized retrospectively as one aspect of the *authorial* ego, and his pastoral project, however externally or transcendentally authorized, as supported precisely by his exclusiveness, his difference from the civic "we" who are dispossessed.

We may recognize these maneuvers, pronominal and nominal play, as one of the earliest analyses we have of the problematic author-function defined by Michel Foucault, but operating here, manifestly, to thicken rather than to erase the historical presence of a writer. The very deviousness of the ploys by which "persons" are represented in the *Eclogues* invites our forming the most basic questions about authorship — questions about how an artist survives in society and what are his obligations: to his fellow citizens, to his patrons, to himself. Especially in Eclogue 6, we can see the relevance to Virgil of Foucault's notion of a link between authorship as a convention or strategy, and a controlling state authority.[4] The naming of one actual Roman patron, Varus, supports the inference that the god who controls the media, here and in Eclogue 1, is Octavian. And by throwing into structural and linguistic question the location of his own voice throughout the ten poems, Virgil effectively demonstrated how a writer can *protect* himself by dismemberment, how he can best assert his ownership of the text by a wickedly shifting authorial presence. Servius was the first to observe that Tityrus sometimes functions as an authorial persona and sometimes merely as the name of a Greek shepherd. The sign "Menalcas" behaves in the same unsettling way, being attached to singers of very different character in Eclogues 3 and 5, and in Eclogue 9 denoting the master singer (again, perhaps, Virgil) whose significance in this poem is marked by his physical absence from it, his songs recorded only in fragments, those fragments carefully balanced between echoes of Theocritus and allusions to recent Roman history. Menalcas, then, is a name for Virgil to invest *momentarily* with his own cultural ambitions: his desire to reinvent the Greek pastoral in the Roman historical context, and his doubts (expressed also in the lament of Moeris for his loss of voice and memory) that the fusion can be managed, or that Rome and its current leaders deserve it. But Menalcas's absence from the ninth eclogue is not the disabling absence of a deconstructive theory of language. The poem speaks of doubt and vocational anxiety, but it ends on a note of pragmatism:

> Desine plura, puer, et quod nunc instat agamus;
> carmine tum melius, cum venerit ipse, canemus.

> No more singing, boy; let us do what needs to be done now; when he himself comes, then we will sing better songs.

The contrast between doing and singing at the end of the ninth eclogue retains, therefore, the possibility that singing is doing. It alerts us to the argument woven through the *Eclogues* as to whether poetry has a social function, and if so, where it rates on the scale of social usefulness. At one end of the argument stand the lovelorn, idle Corydon of Eclogue 2 and his counterpart Gallus in Eclogue 10, the former defined by his attraction to "formosus Alexis ["lovely Alexis"]," both belonging to a pastoral in which formal and aesthetic properties count for almost everything, provided the mirror of art does not lie, "si numquam fallit imago." Yet even this poem, with its reduction of *otium* ["leisure"] to solipsism, ends with the self-injunction to "at least do something useful," and so points against itself to the limited instrumentality of Eclogue 9, whose saddest moment is Moeris's complaint that poetry has not *worked* to protect its singers from a hostile environment:

> carmina tantum
> nostra valent, Lycida, tela inter Martia quantum
> Chaonias dicunt aquila veniente columbas.

> (lines 11–13)

Our songs, Lycidas, are worth about as much in wartime as, so the saying goes, the Chaonian doves when the eagle comes.

These lines would later become a trope of humanist discourse. In their own context they point to the other most obviously provocative aspect of the *Eclogues;* that the tight network of cross-references between them only serves to accentuate their generic disparities, the doubts at the heart of Virgil's pastoral theory.

Critics from Servius onward have tried to account for the striking variations in tone and range, dealing in oppositions such as serious/light, high/low, idyllic/ironic, Theocritean/Roman, or "forward-looking, peaceful, conciliatory, and patriotic" versus "neoteric, ambiguous, or polemic."[5] Virgil himself invited such activity by his cryptic suggestion, at the opening of Eclogue 4, that the pastoral could have both gradations of seriousness and political relevance: he there proposed to sing a *little* more grandly ("paulo maiora canamus"), producing a silvan song worthy of a consul's attention ("silvae sint consule dignae"). But, as the history of his reception shows, he absolutely prevented any neat decisions as to how the eclogues might be rearranged in preferential order. To recognize Eclogues 2, 3, 7, and 8 as directly modeled on Theocritus, while Eclogues 1, 4, 5, 9, and 10 require a Roman perspective, is not to determine their relative value, a question that would not only be hotly debated ever after but that would bring to the surface, for all later readers, their own ideological requirements. For some early Christian readers, the series was only worthy of preservation for the sake of the messianic fourth eclogue; for others, Virgil's higher mood extended also to Silenus's account of creation in the sixth eclogue and to the lament for Daphnis in the fifth; while for others, all complexity, whether political or philosophical, was hopelessly out of place in pastoral, and only the Theocritean songs of love or lovely grief deserved imitation. All such revealing decisions — revealing of *their* authors' cultural premises — were set in motion by the dialectical structure that Virgil bequeathed to us, an ancient poetics no less elliptical than those of Plato and Aristotle, and one that has been, I would argue, at least as influential.

✧ ✧ ✧

Europeans have never lost interest in this remarkable collection of short poems[,] and...[a] certain drive (the Freudian term is not misplaced)...has kept them coming back to it again and again. I shall here argue that what people think of Virgil's *Eclogues* is a key to their own cultural assumptions, because the text was so structured as to provoke, consciously or unconsciously, an ideological response.

By *ideology* I mean both a more capacious and a less totalizing concept than is sometimes invoked by that term: not only the dominant structure of beliefs in a society, but also the singular view (heterodox, subversive, maverick); not only the biases inherent in class differentiation and structured by large-scale, long-term economics, but also the lonely strictures of personal ambition or its restraint; and, especially, sets of aesthetic or metaphysical premises, whether held at large or idiosyncratically. For aesthetic beliefs are seldom fully insulated from the first two categories and frequently serve as acceptable metaphors for them.

Among the competing ideologies proleptically displayed in the *Eclogues* are Roman republicanism, the classic statement of the claims of the many to equal consideration; the counter-claim of the privileged few to special treatment on the grounds of special talent; the hegemonic needs of the holders of power for cultural authentication; the responsibility of the intellectual for providing that authentication, in the interests of stability; the value of political or social stability in nurturing the arts; the responsibility of the intellectual for telling the whole truth, in the interests of social justice; the intellectual's claim to personal autonomy. At various stages in European cultural history one or more of these positions has become dominant in a society or at least among those most able to establish themselves as its spokesmen, and among the most powerful ideologies in our own century has been the position that literature, and pastoral in particular, is or should be nonideological. This book charts the growth of that view from the eighteenth century onward, while at the same time attempting to show both that it has consistently been challenged by thinkers and artists of stature, and that it is no less "political" in intention and effect than opinions whose exile it has sought.

✧ ✧ ✧

One particularly distinguished example [of the applicability of what follows to ourselves] comes from our own century: Hermann Broch's *Death of Virgil,* a lyric novel conceived in the 1930s as an essay on the death of culture. An Austrian intellectual who in 1938 fled from the Nazis and whose work was banned in Germany until 1945, when *Der Tod des Vergil* appeared both there and in America, Broch is a powerful instance of the writer in exile, a Meliboeus, as it were, of a later and greater expropriation.[6] But the connection with the *Eclogues* goes deeper than analogy. It is true that the *Death of Virgil* focuses whatever narrative it contains on the *Aeneid,* on the question of whether Virgil will persist in his dying determination to destroy the unfinished poem or whether he will, as actually happens, bequeath it to his friends, along with its carefully unwritten dedication to Augustus. But Broch's characterization of Virgil as author and, indeed, his novel's central debate depend on a profoundly inventive (yet not unprecedented) reading of the *Eclogues.*

For Broch, Virgil as author was explicable primarily as a peasant, but one who had come to conceptualize his own origins, or, as the second georgic has it, to know his own happiness. Early in the novel, as the invalid poet is carried from the port at Brundisium up to the imperial palace, he is torn between pastoral and political impulses. A scent of lumber makes him think

> of forests, of olive groves, the bucolic peace from which he himself a
> peasant's son had emerged, the peace of his constant nostalgia and of his
> earth-bound, earth-bent, always earthly longing, the peace to which his
> song had been dedicated since days of yore, oh the peace of his longing,
> unattainable; and as if this lack of attainment reflected itself here, as if
> everywhere it must come to be the image of his selfhood, this peace was
> constrained here between stones, subserviated and misused for ambition,
> for gain, for bribery, for headlong greed, for worldliness, for servitude, for
> discord.[7]

The novel's lyric movement will be to resolve this conflict through a series of visionary memories, on the one hand, and on the other, by Virgil's debating with the emperor the meaning of his own work.

Like many earlier writers, though with infinitely greater provocation, Broch interprets the *Eclogues* in the light of his own situation. Watching the war in Europe from the safety of the United States, writing his novel with the support of a Guggenheim Fellowship, he found the meaning of Virgil's career in the *Eclogues,* and the meaning of the *Eclogues* in Eclogue 4, with its prophecies of peace in one's own time and the desuetude of nostalgia.[8] It was this vision that empowered Broch's Virgil in his last confrontation with Augustus and permitted him to challenge the emperor's view that the *Aeneid* was his greatest, because most Roman, work. The fourth eclogue, in that argument, is reinterpreted *not* as Augustus would have it, as a statement that "the glory of the ages had been fulfilled by our time" (p. 336), but as a new provisional statement poised between epochs and already receding before the "stronger metaphor" of a new perception. "In the kingdom of that perception the sword will come to be superfluous" (p. 360), Broch's dying Virgil is capable of asserting, and his Augustus, grasping its radical (transgressive) spiritualism, remarks: "These are extremely dangerous and novel ideas, Virgil: they are derogatory to the state" (p. 377).

Yet to focus on the confrontation between poet and emperor, between transcendence and historical pragmatism, art and politics, pastoral and epic, is to oversimplify. This spoken debate comes late in the novel, as if narrative and dramatic modes can only reappear in a last moment of "normal" lucidity prior to death; and it is preceded by wave after wave of lyric self-analysis, during which Virgil takes, if one can put it so sharply, the other side of the argument. Watching the slaves rowing, he muses on the probable fate of the *Aeneid:* "Nothing availed the poet, he could right no wrongs; he is heeded only if he extols the world, never if he portrays it as it is…only the agreeable things would be extracted from it, and…there was neither danger nor hope that the exhortations would be heeded" (p. 15). Meditating on his own dependency as an intellectual, a man "who had never fought for anything," he knows himself as a man "endowed, fed, and kept by Asinius Pollio and by Augustus — they who had fought for Rome" (p. 244). And, most importantly, forcing himself in interior monologue to scrutinize his aesthetics, Broch's Virgil (and, surely, Broch himself), contemplated one of the most obvious dangers facing the pastoral lyric (and even the lyric novel):

> he knew also that the beauty of the symbol, were it ever so precise in its reality, was never its own excuse for being, that whenever such was the case, whenever beauty existed for its own sake, there art was attacked at its very roots…there was only intoxication with empty forms and empty words, whereby art through this lack of discrimination and even of fidelity, was reduced to un-art, and poetry to mere literarity.
>
> (pp. 141–42)

The pleasure of the text and the allure of constant revision (a terrible insight, this one) are temptations in the same family as the final temptation for the artist: to destroy the *Aeneid* because it is less than perfect.[9] Passing beyond it, Virgil allows himself to become the *Aeneid*'s author, an act of submission to history marked by the dictation of his "will" and its formal dating, "at Brundisium, the ninth day before the calends of October in the seven hundredth and thirtieth year after the founding of the city of Rome" (p. 432).

My own version of pastoral, also written from a protected position, with the help of a Guggenheim Fellowship and other institutional supports, but without any of the shocks and hazards that must have stimulated Broch's return to Virgil, is an imperfect contribution to the topic he embraced with such self-analytical rigor: the long debate on the author-function, the role of the intellectual in society, and the cultural work that pastoral, as a metaphoric poetics, has apparently being doing. It should already be clear that the structural neutrality I aim for is undermined by a commitment to a socially conscious, or rather self-consciously social, aesthetic. Such self-contradictions are endemic to our profession, and I make no apology for mine....As usual, Virgil (and one of his readers) said it for me. In Fielding's *Tom Jones* (book 8, chapter 4) Partridge the ex-schoolmaster has a habit of classical allusion, which leads the hero to remark, "I find, Friend, you are a scholar." "A poor one," was the reply, "non omnia possumus omnes." His source was Virgil's eighth eclogue; his citation, a phrase that had become a commonplace of humanist scholarship;[10] its sensible if self-forgiving meaning: we cannot all do everything.

Notes

[1] The Latin text cited throughout is that of R. A. B. Mynors (Oxford, 1969), as modified by Paul Alpers, *The Singer of the Eclogues: A Study of Virgilian Pastoral* (Berkeley, Los Angeles, London, 1979). Readers unfamiliar with Virgil may find the subject easiest of approach through Alpers's attractive and useful volume, with its text facing a "new" verse translation, and a commentary highly sensitive to differences of opinion.

[2] Unless otherwise specified, all translations from the *Eclogues* and other non-English texts are my own.

[3] Emile Benveniste, *Problèmes de linguistique générale* (Paris, 1966), p. 260.

[4] Michel Foucault, "What Is an Author?" in *Language, Counter-Memory, Practice,* trans. Donald Bouchard and Sherry Simon (Ithaca, N.Y., 1977), pp. 124–25.

[5] Brooks Otis, *Virgil: A Study in Civilized Poetry* (Oxford, 1964), p. 130.

✧ ✧ ✧

[6] For Broch's circumstances, including his abandonment of "a well-established career as industrialist, engineer and director of a Viennese textile concern for philosophy and letters," see R. Hinton Thomas, "The Novels of Hermann Broch," *Cambridge Journal* 6 (1953): 591–604; for Broch's own account of his novel's evolution, see H. J. Weigand, "Broch's *Death of Vergil:* Program Notes," *PMLA* 62 (1947): 551–54; and for an essay on its contributions to poetics and cultural history, see Lawrence Lipking, *The Life of the Poet: Beginning and Ending Poetic Careers* (Chicago and London, 1981), pp. 130–37.

[7] *The Death of Virgil,* trans. Jean Starr Untermeyer (New York, 1965), p. 36.

[8] On the role of the fourth eclogue in Broch's thought, see Timm Collmann, *Zeit und Geschichte in Hermann Brochs Roman "Der Tod des Vergil"* (Bonn, 1967), pp. 159–64. The novel is also saturated with allusions to, quotations from, and interpretations of other eclogues: see *Death of Virgil,* pp. 65, 251, 273, 281, 301, 305, 412. Significantly, Broch assumes a political context for the *Eclogues,* referring (p. 305) to their connection with the Treaty of Brundisium; and his Virgil confesses that, despite his own homoerotic experiences, the second eclogue "had not come to be love-song, but an Eclogue of thanks for Asinius Pollio, dealing but in a most negligible way with love in a longed-for landscape" (p. 251).

[9] Lipking, *Life of the Poet,* p. 135, cites Broch on the analogy between Virgil's vocational *angst* and his own: "I have renounced the thought of completing the book in a genuinely artistic way, because in this time of horrors I could not dare to put still more years into a work that, with each additional page, would have become increasingly esoteric."

[10] Eclogue 8.63; it is also cited by Broch, *Death of Virgil,* p. 281.

William W. Batstone

ON THE SURFACE OF THE *GEORGICS*

The *Georgics*, Vergil's second work, written in the period 37–30 B.C.E., is part of a tradition of ancient didactic or instructive poetry that stems from about 700 B.C.E. and the Greek poet Hesiod. The four books of the *Georgics* offer advice on tending the soil, planting crops, raising cattle, and keeping bees. At the same time, the *Georgics*, like the *Eclogues* before it and the *Aeneid* to come, by injecting the world of contemporary Rome into the poetry, also questions poetry's role in history. Batstone's article analyzes the first five lines of *Georgics* 1 and a later passage, 1.43–46, using a technique called reader-response theory, which helps us analyse the way an author creates for readers or listeners an experience of interaction with the words of the poem. In the two passages he has selected, Batstone analyzes the expectations Vergil creates and then modifies, and the questions raised by the "shifting surface" of Vergil's poetry. The didactic lessons of the *Georgics* are not only about agriculture then, but also "about thinking (not merely knowing) and feeling," through the "continually shifting interplay of different perspectives, revisions and changing meanings." Vergil, Batstone says, "makes his audience large and insists that they contain multitudes." (Ed.)

This paper is about a way of reading, especially of reading the *Georgics*. It falls under the rubric of reader-response criticism,[1] and, consequently, its general perspective will not be wholly new to classics. For, the surprises and suspense a reader feels, and the revised assumptions he/she makes, at the level of narrative events, have for some time been recognized aspects of a classical text.[2] In the past 20 years of criticism in English literature, however, the reader's experience in creating provisional meanings has been examined at quite subtle levels within a sentence.[3] In this paper, I will combine an argument that Latin readers, like English readers, form expectations and arrive at provisional meanings as soon as they can, even within phrases, with a descriptive analysis of two programmatic passages from *Georgics I*. I hope to show that readers' provisional syntactic and lexical assumptions can in general be an important part of their experience as readers and in particular are an essential part of the value of the *Georgics*.

We can take as a model for this approach an analysis of the opening lines of [a] Shakespearean [sonnet]. I use [this example] from English poetry because we may more readily trust our responses as readers when the language is our own and because we can rely upon the subtle and perceptive analysis which Stephen Booth has offered of these poems.[4] The 15th sonnet begins with a potentially misleading construction: "When I consider everything that grows." It seems to be a complete

William W. Batstone, "On the Surface of the *Georgics*," *Arethusa* 21 (1988)2, 227–254. Reprinted by permission of The Johns Hopkins University Press.

syntactical unit, with a simple subject-verb-object: the poet considers all growing things. Line 2, however, undoes this interpretation: "When I consider everything that grows / Holds in perfection but a little moment." The reader must, when he comes upon "Holds," revise his assumption that "everything" was the object of "consider." "Everything" now appears to be the subject in an indirect discourse construction.

This mistake, however, is not merely an error. The reader's misinterpretation of line 1 is significant in two ways: first, because the originally complete construction itself held, as it were, its own "perfection" but a little moment. Thus, the reader experiences the mutability of which the line speaks. Second, because, when the reader comes to the end of Sonnet 15 and its consideration of "this huge stage," "the stars," "men, as plants," "the selfsame sky," "youth" and "time," the reader has, in a non-trivial sense, considered "everything that grows." Thus, the original interpretation, which first seemed to be an error, turns out by a second revision not to be an error at all.

✧ ✧ ✧

In Latin any discussion of the misinterpretation of syntax and meaning may meet with some initial resistance. It runs counter to the tendency of our commentaries, which are designed to help the reader avoid mistaken interpretations. But, perhaps more important, there is the specific objection and caution that the Latin language may create expectations more slowly than English. The discussion that follows tries to weave together practical demonstration and theoretical argument,[5] ...[in] two programmatic passages from the *Georgics*.... I hope to indicate that for the Latin reader, as for the English reader, it is the observable tendency of the human mind to make sense, or provisional sense, out of a combination of events, shapes or words at the simplest level as soon as it can,[6] and that a poet like Vergil relies upon this tendency in fairly subtle ways: a mistaken interpretation may be an important part of the aesthetic and interpretative experience of a reader, and, so, part of a poem's expressive content.

Georgic I (1–5)

Quid faciat laetas segetes, quo sidere terram
vertere, Maecenas, ulmisque adiungere vitis
conveniat, quae cura boum, qui cultus habendo
sit pecori, apibus quanta experientia parcis,
hinc canere incipiam.

["What makes the cornfields joyful, under what star to turn the earth, Maecenas, and when it is a good time to attach vines to elms, what the care of cattle is and what the practice for keeping flocks, for thrifty bees how great the efforts, from here I will begin to sing."]

Traditional commentary tells us that *faciat, conveniat* and *sit* ["makes," "is a good time," "is"] are subjunctives in indirect questions dependent upon *hinc canere incipiam* ["from here I will begin to sing"]. True, but does the reader know this when he reads line 1? In a small way, like Aeneas when he hears the Harpies' prophecy in *Aeneid*

III, the reader must make whatever sense he can, for he will be reading for four more lines before he comes to *hinc canere incipiam*. For some duration of time, then, we do not have three subjunctives in indirect questions, but three freestanding subjunctives. All are in emphatic verse positions and so are "marked." Vergil, therefore, does not begin by saying, "What makes joyful cornfields...this is the beginning of my song." He begins by saying, "What should make joyful cornfields?" or "What could make joyful cornfields?" A jussive or potential question which engages and surprises the reader, and, most of all, suggests some uncertainty about the actual result.[7]

The *Georgics*, then, begins with a series of questions about potential or propriety. The uncertainty of which these questions speak is, in a sense, never resolved in the *Georgics*, as, for instance, the final answer to *quid faciat laetas segetes* is the prayer with which the first *Georgic* ends. In another sense, these questions reveal larger and more important questions about the very science that should underlie *didaxis* ["instruction"]. For, the answer to questions like "What does make joyful cornfields?" is ultimately knowable only in an historical sense: "what did?" Theoretically, until all contingencies are controlled, there are only the questions "What could make joyful cornfields?" and "What should make joyful cornfields?" and "How do we handle that ambiguous boundary between what should be, what could be, and what is and will be?" In *Georgic I*, the storm of civil war may be the final destroyer of agriculture (*squalent abductis arva colonis* ["the lands lie neglected, the farmers led away"], I 507), but should not be (*satis iam pridem* ["enough now for a long time"], I 501). The boundary is acknowledged in prayer: *di patrii Indigetes et Romule Vestaque mater*...["native gods of the fatherland, and Romulus and mother Vesta"] (I 498). This kind of uncertainty has also been long apparent in the divergent interpretations of the *Georgics*. One thinks especially of the varied interpretations of Orpheus and Aristaeus: What, there, should have been, or could have been?

Quid faciat laetas segetes ["what makes the cornfields joyful"]? My description of the reader's response may be thought to raise the question of the so-called "second-reading." What happens when the reader knows that the subjunctives are subordinate? There are two answers. First, as with the Shakespeare [sonnet] quoted above, the reader may choose or not choose to notice the poem's shifting syntax, even when he knows what the final interpretation will be. Since it is a matter of choice, one cannot, therefore, argue that the subjunctives will necessarily be unambiguously subordinate. One can only declare one's decision to read them subordinately by *fiat*.[8] Second, even when the reader comes to line 5, *hinc canere incipiam* ["from here I will begin to sing"], he cannot merely decide that his provisional interpretation of *faciat, conveniat,* and *sit* ["makes," "is a good time, is"] was absolutely wrong. As jussive or potential subjunctives in direct discourse, the subjunctives remain in indirect discourse. The question of their interpretation is not solved by *incipiam*.[9] *Incipiam* only adds the further fact that they may have stood all along for indicatives,[10] and then warns the reader that, whatever his current provisional interpretation, this is only the beginning.[11] Syntactically and denotatively the opening lines uncover and are about uncovering proliferating contingencies and contexts. They introduce Vergil's agricultural pantheon: a dazzling concatenation of influences which extends the world of Vergilian georgic well beyond the world of Varro's *concilium deorum* ["council of the gods"].

My comments so far have proceeded at the level of clauses and potential sentences; they are analogous to the comments above on "When I consider everything that grows." Vergil, however, does more: the first potential sense-unit the reader hears is an idiomatic expression of aporia ["questioning"]: *quid faciat* – "What should he do?" The reader soon sees that *quid* ["what"] is the subject and *laetas segetes* ["joyful cornfields"] the object of *faciat* ["makes"]. Two questions arise then: first, can we isolate this "phrase" and speak of the fleeting assumptions it provokes and, second, what is the value of pointing to those assumptions?

❖ ❖ ❖

Like Shakespeare's consideration of everything that grows, [the phrase *quid faciat*] first appears as a syntactical unit....We offer in summary form our evidence that Vergil wanted his audience to hear, however briefly, this expression of helplessness. 1) As mentioned above, the phrase is idiomatic, which means that it fulfills immediately a gestalt, and, coming at a caesura, is potentially a *kolon* ["clause"]. 2) It is also programmatic for the *Georgics,* where science and *techne* ["skill"] are never sufficient in themselves and never solve man's larger problems. The phrase itself will reoccur in the imperfect jussive subjunctive less than 100 lines from the end of the poem: as he contemplates Orpheus' grief and failure, Vergil's voice joins that of Proteus (another poet who fails to give practical advice) in a cry to sympathy: *quid faceret?* ["what was he to do?"] (IV 504). 3) The normal position of factitive verbs in Latin is immediately after the predicate; in fact, they may be said to mark the predicate.[12] This is the result of Indo-European *enklesis* ["inflection"] of verbs, and, while not everywhere operative in Latin, it should also be significant that neither Lucretius, Ovid, Cicero, Livy or elsewhere Vergil himself ever writes *quid faciat* or its equivalent and means *quid* to be the subject of the verb.[13] 4) The first clause of the *Georgics* can be written in any order, providing that *quid* comes first, and it will still scan. Consequently, Vergil must be said to have rejected expressions like *quid segetes laetas faciat* and *quid segetes faciat laetas,*[14] which would have avoided what Quintilian calls *ambiguum* ["ambiguity"]. In sum, then, we have arguments from idiom and thematic propriety, normal Latin word-order, and possible alternative expressions, all of which point to the appearance of *quid faciat* as a phrase of shifting value in Vergil's composition of aporia. As "What should he do" becomes "What should make joyful cornfields,"[15] a phrase of aporia becomes the locus of a reader's error and so of the reader's aporia (but, given the word order, what was he to do?). All of this is still within the four lines of questions which are not really questions but statements about what will be answered (or are they?), and *that,* Vergil says, is only the beginning of his song.

❖ ❖ ❖

I come now to my second example from the beginning of *Georgic I.* Together, my two examples from the *Georgics,* both from traditionally programmatic passages, are representative of the surface Vergil creates and suggest not just the fact of provisional meanings but something of their value and the aesthetic density of Vergil's surface.[16]

Georgic I (43–46)

Vere novo, gelidus canis cum montibus umor
liquitur et Zephyro putris se glaeba resolvit,

depresso incipiat iam tum mihi taurus aratro
ingemere et sulco attritus splendescere vomer.

["In early spring, when chill water flows from white mountains, and the
loamy clod of earth crumbles at the west wind, with the plow deep-driven,
now then let my bull begin to groan and the plow become shiny, worn by
the furrow."]

While most commentaries emphasize the need for work,[17] it should be noted
that the first two lines paint a leisurely and affective picture of the newness of spring.
Montibus ["mountains"], when it first appears in the sequence "chill - white - mountains
- water" is construed as a locatival ablative. With the appearance of *liquitur* ["flows
from"] it begins to seem separative: "When chill water flows from the white mountains." This impression, well recorded in scholarly commentaries and translations,[18]
is no doubt aided by the echo of *liqui* (from *linquo*) ["to leave"] and the reader's
shifting attention. As "place where," a point of stasis, turns into "place from which,"
the reader's mental eye with its stable gaze on the white mountains (plural and in
the distance) has been set in motion and comes to look at the clod (singular and at
one's feet). Traditional interpretation, if it notices such "ambiguities" as *montibus*,
uses a formalistic and static terminology. For instance, one might say that *montibus*
is to be understood *apo koinou* ["as belonging in two phrases"]. But, as one reads the
verse, when *montibus* first appears, it is naturally locatival; with *liquitur*, the static
secure "place where" dissolves, at least potentially, into a "place from which." In
this small way, as spring is itself a process in time which sets things in motion and
changes them,[19] so Vergil's description requires a sense of changing syntax.
     Against this background, the emphasis on work in v. 45 comes as an intrusion.
It also requires some interpretative renegotiations. *Putris glaeba* ["loamy clod"] is
no longer the squishy loam that clogs the feet: it is the friable land, and land which
the plow will make friable. The descriptive impulse, contemplative in origin, which
doubles the *cum*-clauses ["when"-clauses] is reduced to *cum*'s lexical and indicative
marking: *cum*-temporal.[20] Is spring being described and evoked? or is necessary
action being dated? Both; the poetry creates in its diachronic process the conflict
and connection between the two, and, in so doing, catches the reader off guard.[21]
Let me elaborate further.
     At the denotative level, in line 45 the time to begin is past: the action of *depresso*
["deep pressed"] must be already completed.[22] This denotative aspect of the line is,
again, complemented by the reader's experience. Work is urgent, and the reader is
already behind. *Depresso* appears, but what should be depressed? And with *incipiat*
["would begin"] we are already beginning a second action. Furthermore, *depresso*,
since it appears first in its clause, seems to be part of an absolute construction. The
natural assumption is that the farmer is to begin a second action after pressing
something down. *iam tum mihi* ["now then my"] underscores the urgency and the
objectivity of the precept. In this context, when *taurus* ["bull"] appears, all the denotative
urgency confronts an error: the subject of *incipiat* ["would begin"] was not, after all,
the presupposed farmer, but an unmentioned "bull." There was a prior context to
be negotiated with *depresso* – and the need to negotiate a prior context will become
itself an explicit part of the *didaxis* in 5 lines: *ac prius ignotum ferro quam scindimus
aequor* ["and before we split the unknown plain with the iron plow"] (v. 50).[23] This
error requires two simultaneous responses: as the reader changes his assumptions

about the subject of *incipiut*, he must add to his previous imaginations enough context to get the bull into the field (that is, he must bring the bull out of the barn, yoke him up, lead him out, all this in order to have already pushed in the plow). In the process, the implied agent of *depresso aratro* ["the deep-driven plow"] changes.[24]

At the moment, then, that work intrudes upon the contemplative pleasures of Vergil's description of spring, the reader is also required to perform a substantial number of mental operations both in the assimilation of the content, which means a prior context, and in the assimilation and revision of the grammar. This process continues when *ingemere* ["to groan"] at the beginning of line 46 requires that the phrase *depresso aratro* be again reconstrued, now as a dative with *ingemere*: "let the bull begin to groan at the deep-driven plow." Thus, as the attention of the reader now shifts from the actions (depressing and beginning) and things (plow and bull) of line 45 to the *pathemata* (groaning) of line 46 the grammar and syntax also shift.

❖ ❖ ❖

By itself Vergil's shifting surface might be only a pretty aesthetic effect.[25] But it has measurable consequences. Vergil's injunctions, at the literal level, are Catonic: they are about the ox's hard work and about indifference to the ox's groan. It is in part because line 46 intrudes on the reader's own enjoyment of a description of spring, because *depresso aratro* seemed at first to have only the farmer as agent, and because these provisional interpretations join the fictive reader/farmer and his experience to the bull that commentaries speak of the farmer's own difficult labors and of Vergil's (and presumably the reader's) sympathy for the ox.[26] One must add, of course, that sympathy and distress remain in the commentaries because elsewhere Vergil does show sympathy for nature, for the beasts of burden as well as the farmers who burden the beasts. This conflict between sympathy and hardness is here part of the larger effect of the passage: from the affective and slowly shifting effects of spring, to the intrusion of time and labor, to the bull's groan and the promise of *splendescere* ["become shiny"], the opening lines are about conflict and context and the fullness of the moment.

The *Georgics* are a rich poem. They continually say that everything they consider is not one thing but always many things. And they not only say this; they make their reader participate in an experience of mutability and shifting perspectives. The poem's surface speaks of and imitates *varietas* ["diversity"], which is not merely aesthetic, but epistemological and ethical. It is, after all, the way in which things are like a number of things and the number of things each one is like that determines each thing's unique particularity. Similarly, it is the number of thoughts we can and do think about things, the number of ways we feel, that tells us both who we are and what the world we live in is like.[27]

The continually shifting interplay of different perspectives, revisions and changing meanings is a large part of what Vergil creates. This is, of course, anti-didactic, if *didaxis* tells us what's what and how you do this and that. But, in another sense, it is didactic: it is about thinking (not merely knowing[28]) and feeling. When what to do, *quid faciat*, raises questions of what we know, what we should do, and how we feel about knowledge and action,[29] we begin to see why Dryden was moved to call the *Georgics* "the best poem by the best poet." Vergil's poem uses a reader's expectations and provisional meanings continually to remind us of the number of different ways we think and feel about what surrounds us and about what should be done.

Whether it is the bees of Book IV, that paradigm for *civitas* ["civic community, the state"] which is a failed paradigm, perhaps no paradigm at all, perhaps a paradigm for how paradigms fail, or the peculiar tensions of Aristaeus and Orpheus, or the vines of Book II and Bacchus, Vergil never settles for a reductive *didaxis*. In another expansive poem, Walt Whitman wrote, "Do I contradict myself? Very well, then, I contradict myself." He continued, "I am large and contain multitudes." Vergil makes his audience large and insists that they contain multitudes.[30]

Notes

[1]Important theoretical discussions may be found in Fish 1970; Fish 1980; and Iser 1978. An extensive annotated bibliography may be found in Tompkins 1980.233–272. The reader should be warned, however, that this is not a theoretical paper. My "reader" is, in a sense, prior to the sophisticated studies of Fish, Iser and others; "he" is based more on probable linguistic responses than on a theory of aesthetic response.

[2]The more formalistic aspects of Stanley Fish, for instance, provide the basis for Block 1981; see also Warden 1980. Shortly after this paper was accepted *Arethusa* devoted an issue, *Audience-Oriented Criticism and the Classics* 19.2 (1986), exclusively to "audience response" criticism, which bespeaks its increasing familiarity to Classicists. The issue includes a useful general bibliography, pp. 111–114.

[3]The essential and exemplary study is Booth 1969; see also the practical criticism of Fish 1967.

[4]See Booth 1969. His subsequent edition with analytic commentary of Shakespeare's *Sonnets*, Booth 1977, attempts to recover for the twentieth century reader the experience of a Renaissance reader. Much of that "Preface" is relevant to this study. I am indebted throughout to his readings for my comments.

❖ ❖ ❖

[5]This form of discussion is perhaps inevitable with this subject matter. See Fish 1980. 356–372.

[6]This is considered one of the "laws" of gestalt psychology. See Katz 1950.24–29.

[7]This uncertainty with regard to the result is mirrored in the uncertain specification of the subjunctives (jussive or potential) and in the unexpected, indeed unprecedented, beginning of a didactic poem with questions—regardless of whether the questions are direct or indirect. Vergil's opening l. deprives the reader of sure generic or syntactic "footings"; 2. speaks itself of uncertain results; 3. is itself, finally, not resolved, that is, does not result in any certain interpretation: see below on *hinc canere incipiam*.

[8]Quintilian, when he notes that ambiguity can be removed by a pause (VII 9.11), implicitly recognizes that 1. a "director's hand" is at work in these matters, and 2. one can also read in such a way as to preserve ambiguity in these instances. Any reader can try it out on the lines for Sonnet 15 discussed above.

[9]One cannot help but note that here, despite the fact that formal and propriety pressures insist that *incipiam* is a future, the verb form itself is tantalizingly ambiguous.

[10]If Vergil had begun with a controlling and introductory verb, the subjunctives would have been already expected when they appeared. Thus, except for the force of their "marked" position in the hexameter line, and, ultimately from the spirit and content of the *Georgics* as a whole, one would expect them to "stand for" original indicatives. A different order of words would have avoided any problem of "misinterpretation." However, even a different order of words would not have changed the fact that *hinc* is not *de his rebus:* Vergil stresses beginning, not closure; see Putnam 1980.17. The subject matter and the eventual entanglements, even the final goal, are as obscure (and as clear) as they are in any of the beginnings life offers us or which we choose for ourselves.

[11]A full analytic commentary would note another interpretation of *quid faciat laetas segetes:* "Why make joyful cornfields?" Besides being within the potential interpretations of the Latin, the possibility is thematic. As a further extension of aporia, the question implies that there is no purpose to making happy cornfields. Compare I 104ff.: *quid dicam...?* After the fetching

account of a small success, *ecce*, 108, the reason for the question, "Why?," is that one cannot always gain a practical advantage from practical instruction: *praesertim incertis si mensibus,*115. If the farmer's failure in the face of unpredictable storms prompts the question, "Why tell of the farmer's labors?," the helplessness of the farmer faced with the storms of civil war at the end of *Georgic I* should justify the parallel, though fleeting, aporia of "Why make joyful crops?" One may also note that at I 311 ff., Vergil begins, *quid tempestates…dicam*? Vergil continually questions the effectiveness and propriety of his own *didaxis*. Cp. *Possum multa tibi veterum praecepta referre, / ni refugis tenuisque piget cognoscere curas* I 176–177.

❖ ❖ ❖

[12]For the general principle involved, see Murgia 1981.304–305.

[13]Based upon Roberts 1977; Deferrari 1939; Merguet 1877; Packard 1968; and Warwick 1975.

[14]The first is the norm for prose; the second for a poem like Horace's *Ars Poetica*. Both avoid ambiguity.

[15]The phrase *laetas segetes* is, as is often noted, a common metaphor from the farmer's idiom. The commentaries, however, are all too eager to drop the matter after having noted that fact. Several questions arise: what is a farmer's metaphor doing in a Callimachean poem? Is it merely a farmer's idiom here? Does *laetas* mean rich, fertile, happy? How is this happiness related to human happiness? We should note that we only know that the phrase is a farmer's idiom because Cicero chose to discuss it as a metaphor: thus, even in the vernacular, the metaphoric nature of the expression was noteworthy; see Cic. *de Or.* III 38. Even *segetes* is tantalizingly vague: field, sown field, field of corn or corn crop? The aporia does not end when *quid faciat*, a strange way to begin a poem, turns out to be different from what its initial gestalt suggests.

❖ ❖ ❖

[16]In these days when the semiotic referent of texts is brought into question and when all thought and all *poemata* are treated as signs (often signs reflecting signs), this kind of discussion has a special significance. It insists that in some ways Vergil, or any poet and artist, does not create a sign (= *signans*, symbol, index, etc.), but a thing in itself. While one may disagree about one's experience of that thing, or even its importance in the life of the community as a whole, and while one may always use it, as one may use anything, as a sign, the thing itself remains "dumb as old medallions to the thumb." This quote, from Archibald MacLeish's "Ars Poetica," intentionally places my remarks within the aesthetic concerns of Pierce's icons, and Langer's "expressive forms."

[17]There is nothing but an emphasis on "Mühe und Plage und harte Gewalt" in Conington 1898, Page 1898, Richter 1957, Wilkinson 1969, and Klingner 1963. Page's comment *ad v.* is indicative: "Notice the force of *depresso, ingemere, attritus, splendescere*: from the very first Virgil emphasizes strongly the necessity of hard work." Miles 1980.70–71 speaks of the "eloquent evocation of spring," and Putnam 1980.26 has a sense of the "appropriate freshness."

[18]Locatival according to Wilkinson, Miles, Bovie, Dryden, and Klingner; separative in Conington, Putnam, Lewis, Jermyn, Saint-Denis, and Fairclough (Loeb translation). The fact that none of the scholars remarks on the difference (although Conington does offer a note and a parallel for his interpretation) says something about the ease with which the reader is led to shift his interpretation.

[19]See the pretty little e. e. cummings' poem which ends: "spring is like a perhaps / Hand in a window / (carefully to / and from moving New and / Old things, while / people stare carefully / moving a perhaps / fraction of flower here placing / an inch of air there) and / / without breaking anything." Vergil's lines, less ostentatiously, do what cummings' lines do and say.

[20]The subtle movement in the *cum*-clauses itself deserves some comment: *liquitur*, present indicative, is followed by *resolvit*, either present or perfect. Thus while the passage tends to generalize, it also tends to refer to time-past. The ambiguous form of *resolvit* is an apt introduction to *iam tum*. See Page's gloss (at v. 42): "without waiting a moment longer." Page is right; the reader has been waiting while the time for action has been slipping from the present to the past.

[21]After the leisurely movement of 43–44, *depresso incipiat* is not merely surprising, it is contradictory. In Xenophon's *Oeconomicus* (20.16–19), a passage which illustrates the Hesiodic virtues of *labor* and timely action, the lazy and worthless worker, a pastoral figure (see

Rosenmeyer 1973.73–74) which does not belong in *Georgic*, is compared to an idle wayfarer who never gets anywhere because he pauses to enjoy the view and chase breezes. Here, Vergil forces his reader to "catch up," as it were, after chasing the breezes of Zephyr. On the use of the word Zephyr in Latin, see Quintilian, *I.O.* xii. 10.28: *nescio quo modo velut hilarior protinus renidet oratio.*

[22]*Tum* itself emphasizes pastness, even though here its primary function is to step away from the affective quality of lines 43–44 and to stress the impersonal precept and the temporal urgency.

[23]See above on *quid faciat.* The *Georgics* begin *in medias res*, both syntactically and didactically. As I argue in my dissertation, this is at least in part because there are, after all, no beginnings which do not take place *in mediis rebus*, rife with conflicting claims and assorted patterns.

[24]In fact, the agent may be either the farmer or the bull, but only because Vergil has postponed the subject. The verse creates the presence of the farmer's mutual labor through the error it fosters.

✧ ✧ ✧

[25]Such an evaluation does not mean that *qua* "pretty aesthetic effect" it is not worth noting. It certainly is, for Vergil's creation in effects like this is continually casting Hellenistic *otium* and poetic *labor* into contexts that are redolent of Cato, of Roman *negotium* and poetic *nugae*. Something of the complex voices of the *Georgics* is suggested by Johnson 1981.

[26]Both farmer and ox, of course, cooperate in driving the plow into the ground. Their labors, just like their groans, are joined as much in Vergil's ambiguity as in real life. Page's comment (also cited above) is telling: "Notice the force of *depresso, ingemere, attritus, splendescere:* from the very first Virgil emphasises strongly the necessity of hard work." True, but literally Vergil says that the ox groans, and it is probably the ox that depresses the plow, and certainly the ox who wears away the rust, and, finally, *splendescere* has more sheen than *labor.*

[27]In terms of recent literary theory, this statement is a partial response to the deconstructive critique of presence and its Saussurean emphasis upon the differential nature of semiotic systems and its consequent concern with *différence.* In terms of recent advances in cognitive science, it is relevant to point out that the model inherent in my description is that of the neural "computer," not the digital, calculating computer, and that of the hologram: both of which seem to represent more accurately than earlier models the way people "think."

[28]See Arendt 1978 for an elaboration of the distinction and its importance both politically and philosophically. Her preface, 3–16, elaborates the distinction between thinking and knowing with reference to Heidegger: "Thinking does not bring knowledge as do the sciences. Thinking does not produce usable practical wisdom. Thinking does not solve the riddles of the universe. Thinking does not endow us directly with the power to act." Somewhere she herself says, "Knowing will never know what thinking is doing."

[29]Another programmatic example of this at the denotative level may be found in the fifth line of the *didaxis* proper of *Georgic I: illa seges demum votis respondet avari / agricolae, bis quae solem, bis frigora sensit,* 47–48. Where Hesiod introduced his *didaxis* with the propositional security of two kinds of *eris*, Vergil offers his reader not just the ethical problem Hesiod secures but the fact that the various kinds of *avaritia* are a problem and create insecurity. *Avari agricolae* is both an interpretive and an ethical problem, and that statement is true of both life and Vergil's text. By giving his reader only *avari agricolae* and by declining to give us Hesiod's clear ethical perspective, Vergil asks his reader to know more about *avaritia* than its two kinds; and that includes knowing that there are more than two kinds.

[30]What to do, as practical *didaxis*, presupposes clarity of purpose (i.e., the question is, how to succeed) and discrete means to choose among. In the *Georgics*, it is especially purpose (enjoyment, virtue, success, contemplation, *otium*) and means (always entangled in the prior context) which Vergil complicates and obscures as much as he develops and elucidates them. Ultimately this feature of the poem accounts for Wilkinson's assertion that the poem is a descriptive poem and his emphasis on variety, for Klingner's perception that everything in the poem is related through varied connections to everything else, for Boyle's conviction, Boyle 1979.5, that "Paradox is the *Georgics* primary mode," for Miles' argument that the poem makes a dialectical kind of progress, and for the general uncertainty about whether the *Georgics* are a single poem or the poem is itself a plurality.

BIBLIOGRAPHY

Arendt, Hannah. 1978. *The Life of the Mind*, one vol. ed., *One: Thinking*. New York.

Block, E. 1981. *The Effects of Divine Manifestation on the Reader's Perspective in Vergil's Aeneid.* New York.

Booth, Stephen. 1969. *An Essay on Shakespeare's Sonnets*. New Haven.

———— 1977. *Shakespeare's Sonnets*, Edited with Analytic Commentary. New Haven.

Boyle, A. J. 1979. "Introduction," *Virgil's Ascraean Song: Ramus Essays on the Georgics*, 1–6. Melbourne.

Conington, J. H. Nettleship and F. Haverfield, edd., 1898. *The Works of Virgil*, vol. 1, 5th ed. London.

Deferrari, R. J. *et al.* 1939. *A Concordance of Ovid*. Washington.

Fish, Stanley. 1967. *Surprised by Sin: The Reader in Paradise Lost*. London and New York.

———— 1970. "Literature in the Reader: Affective Stylistics," *New Literary History* 2.123 ff.

———— 1980. *Is there a Text in this Class? The Authority of Interpretive Communities*. Cambridge, Mass.

Iser, Wolfgang. 1978. *The Act of Reading: A Theory of Aesthetic Response*. Baltimore.

Johnson, W. Ralph. 1981. "The Broken World: Virgil and his Augustus," *Arethusa* 14 (1981) 49–56.

Katz, David. 1950. *Gestalt Psychology*, Robert Tyson, tr. New York.

Klingner, F. 1963. *Virgils Georgica*. Zürich.

Merguet, H. 1877. *Lexikon zu den Reden des Cicero*. Jena.

Miles, Gary B. 1980. *Virgil's Georgics: A New Interpretation*. Berkeley.

Murgia, C. E. 1981. "Analyzing Cicero's Style," *CPh* 76 (1981) 301–313.

Packard, David. 1968. *A Concordance to Livy*. Cambridge, Mass.

Page, T. E. 1898. *P. Vergili Maronis Bucolica et Georgica*. London.

Putnam, Michael C. J. 1980. *Virgil's Poem of the Earth*. Princeton.

Richter, K. 1957. *Vergil, Georgica*. Munich.

Roberts, Louis. 1977. *A Concordance of Lucretius*. New York.

Rosenmeyer, Thomas G. 1973. *The Green Cabinet: Theocritus and the European Pastoral Lyric.* Berkeley.

Tompkins, Jane P. 1980. *Reader Response Criticism: From Formalism to Post-Structuralism*. Baltimore.

Warden, John. 1980. *Fallax Opus: Poet and Reader in the Elegies of Propertius, Phoenix* Supplementary Volume 14. Toronto.

Warwick, H. H. 1975. *A Vergil Concordance*. Minneapolis.

Wilkinson, L. P. 1969. *The Georgics of Vergil*. Cambridge.

HOMAGE TO VIRGIL

Fantazzi's brief overview of the uses to which subsequent ages have put Vergil's works starts with the chilling reminder of Mussolini's World War II Fascist propaganda, which referred to Vergil's works. Fantazzi discusses Vergil's Christian interpreters in the Middle Ages, who saw that "the first appearance of Virgil's poetry coincided with that same *kairos*, or propitious moment of time, that favoured the coming of Christ." Fantazzi turns next to the profound relationship between Dante and Vergil, presenting evidence within Dante's works of his veneration of Vergil. Matthew Arnold in the ninetheenth century and T. S. Eliot in the twentieth were both highly influential and represent changing attitudes about the value of Vergil's poetry. Fantazzi's final example comes from Hermann Broch's novel, *The Death of Virgil*. Themes in Broch's novel recapitulate the pre-Christian guide, the artist despairing of the uses history would make of his work, and concerns over his poem's imperfection. Fantazzi asks us to wonder how we can reconcile the divergent views this one poet's work inspires, a crucial question for many readers. (Ed.)

*O*n or about the Ides of October fifty-three years ago, scholars and lovers of poetry met together in various parts of the world to celebrate the birth of Publius Vergilius Maro, a very auspicious birth indeed for poetry and civilization, and, according to the ancient biographers, one that was attended by certain miraculous events. In that commemorative year special ceremonies were held in Virgil's native city of Mantua at the Accademia Virgiliana, at which learned 'interventi,' as they are termed in Italian, were delivered by professors from all over Europe. It is interesting to note in the published proceedings that one professor, at least, gave an official address on the significance of Virgil for 'la nuova Italia' ["the new Italy"], by which he meant not the Italy of the Risorgimento, the usual meaning of that phrase, but the nascent Fascist state of Italy.[1] He took advantage of the occasion to illustrate how the new regime was restoring the traditional values of the people of Italy and fulfilling the imperial destiny of Rome, of which Virgil had sung. The evocation of ancient Rome and the adaptation of Virgilian tags for patriotic purposes were, of course, favorite devices of Fascist propaganda, climaxing in the Augustan exhibition of *romanità* ["Romanness"] in 1937 and Mussolini's famous speech delivered from the balcony of Palazzo Venezia, in which he conjured up for his enthralled hearers 'la riapparizione dell'Impero sui colli fatali di Roma' ["the reappearance of the Empire upon the fateful hills of Rome"].

Charles Fantazzi, "Homage to Virgil," *Vergilius* 29 (1983) 1–11. Reprinted by permission of Charles Fantazzi.

Fortunately such strident nationalism is absent from the celebrations in Italy and elsewhere in the bimillennium of the poet's death. While the commemorations of 1930 honoured the beginning of a brief span of mortal existence, in 1982 we commemorated the two-thousandth year of the poet's long afterlife, or *Nachleben*, which will undoubtedly continue as long as books are read, and as long as a poet's voice can be heard amid the chaotic din of modern life. Unlike Horace, Virgil never dared to immortalize or monumentalize himself in so many words, although his shade became used to veneration early in his afterlife. We are told that his birthday and death were celebrated with sacrifices at his tomb soon after his death; Seneca regarded him as an oracle; Hadrian is said to have consulted the *sortes vergilianae* ["Vergilian prophesies"], and as Juvenal tells us, schoolboys in the next century were carrying their grimy copies of the *Aeneid* to school in the early morning light.

In rendering homage to Virgil's continued living presence in the Western World I should like to touch very briefly on a few specific moments of his immortality. Virgil has always appealed to both the simple and the sophisticated, as the seer and sorcerer of popular legend and as the storehouse of antiquarian lore and epitome of all learning. But what assured his privileged status throughout the Middle Ages was something of an accident, although in some respects it may be regarded as a planned accident, brought about by Virgil's Christian interpreters. The *Fourth Eclogue* is a poem instinct with the air of prophecy. Virgil designed it to be so, and his mysterious, prophetic utterance was interpreted to support many an imperial claim in the first centuries after its composition.[2] The most famous and influential of these interpretations was Constantine's official recognition of the poem as a prophecy of the coming of Christ in a Good Friday sermon, which the historian Eusebius of Caesarea appended to his life of the emperor.[3] A substantial portion of the poem, lines 21 to 45, had already been turned to the uses of Christian apologetics by Lactantius,[4] who used this excerpt from the poem to signify the condition of the world after the coming of Christ, attributing to Virgil a privileged vision granted by the divine Spirit. Constantine's allegorical commentary on the poem, however, canonized Virgil for the reading of the faithful for all succeeding centuries. The poet laureate of Rome was thus formally enshrined as a prophet of the Christian dispensation, and became "a liaison between the old world and the new," as T. S. Eliot remarked.[5] As the first appearance of Virgil's poetry coincided with that same *kairos*, or propitious moment of time, that favoured the coming of Christ, so this second historical accident gave new impetus to his acceptance in the Christian world. While continuing to be sacred to the old religion, he also became the prophet of the Christian empire. He appeared together with the Sibyls and the Hebrew prophets in mystery plays and was generally regarded as a bearer of revelation.

Another rather fortuitous event, Saint Paul's stop at Pozzuoli on the way to Rome, gave rise to the legend of his visiting the tomb of Virgil there, reinforcing the Christian affinities of the poet in the popular imagination. As Italian travellers will readily know, the supposed tomb of Virgil lies in what was once a quiet recess of the promontory of Posillipo, the Greek equivalent of Sans-Souci, but now overlooking the hectic traffic pouring in and out of the tunnel to Pozzuoli. A fragment of an early liturgical sequence re-evokes this visit in the lovely meter of the *Stabat Mater*.[6]

Ad Maronis mausoleum
ductus, fudit super eum

piae rorem lacrimae.
Quemne, inquit, reddidissem
si te vivum invenissem,
poetarum maxime.

John Addington Symonds' translation into the same meter in English is deservedly famous:

When to Maro's tomb they brought him,
tender grief and pity wrought him
to bedew the stone with tears.
'What a saint might I have crowned thee
had I only living found thee,
poet first and without peers.'

A more permanent link in the perpetuation of the Christian Virgil was forged by one of his greatest pagan admirers, Macrobius. In a passage of the *Commentarii in Somnium Scipionis* ["Commentaries on the Dream of Scipio"] he opened the floodgates to a tradition of Christian allegorization of Virgil that would continue well into the Renaissance: "et Vergilius profitetur...ut geminae doctrinae observationes praestiterit et poeticae figmentum et philosophiae veritatem"[7] ["even Vergil...states that he provides observations of twofold teaching, both the fiction of poetry and the truth of philosophy"]. For the pagan writer imbued with Neo-Platonic doctrine the *Aeneid* was a source book for all scientific and philosophical truth. As he goes on to say, nature withheld her secrets from the uncouth senses of men and wished that they be revealed only by prudent individuals so that she would not show herself even to initiates. Such a doctrine could easily be converted into Christian terms and the first to do so in a sustained treatise was the Christian apologist Fulgentius in his *Expositio Virgilianae continentiae*[8] ["Exposition of Vergil's Hidden Sense"]. According to his interpretation, the first five books of the *Aeneid* represent the five stages of human life — infancy, boyhood, adolescence, young manhood and maturity, while the sixth book is an allegory of the acquisition of wisdom. In the 'exposition' of the latent truths contained in the pagan writer Fulgentius diligently insists that Virgil was indeed pagan in his beliefs but unwittingly inspired by the Christian God. As the narrator points out the Christian parallels to the shade of Virgil, the Roman poet expresses his frequent astonishment, denying that such doctrines were ever known to him.

While Fulgentius' treatment is openly Christianizing, a much later allegorization, the commentary of Bernard Silvester on the first six books of the *Aeneid*, is a more philosophical harmonization of both pagan commentators and Christian mythographers, with some rather ingenious exegeses of its own. The wanderings of Aeneas are construed as an exemplary tale of those who pursue wisdom by erroneous paths. Underneath the wrappings or *integumenta* of the Virgilian epic is the odyssey of the human soul imprisoned in the body: "quid agat vel quid patiatur humanus spiritus in humano corpore temporaliter positus"[9] ["what the human spirit does or suffers, placed temporarily in the human body"]. The commentary on the sixth book is a recapitulation of all that preceded, the review and rectification of errors committed in the past. It is only when Aeneas has passed through the grove of Trivia and is about to enter the temple of Apollo, iam subeunt Triviae lucos atque aurea tecta

(*Aen.* 6.13)

["now they pass under the grove of Trivia and the golden roof"]

that the soul is liberated from the dominion of the senses and may pass from earthly knowledge to the repository of true philosophy.

Such readings of the Virgilian *Nekyia* ["meeting with the dead"] emanating from the school of Chartres in the twelfth century and from other medieval centers of learning lie behind Dante's great *poema sacro* ["sacred poem"], as his son Pietro mentions in his commentary.[10] Dante becomes another Aeneas with Virgil at his side in his journey to the nether regions. What distinguishes this journey from previous penetrations of the underworld is the personal guidance given by one poet to another. The link between them is eternal Rome, which Virgil's hero was privileged by highest heaven to found, and which would become the seat of St. Peter:

Ch' e' fu dell'alma Roma e di suo impero
nell'empireo ciel per padre eletto:
    la quale e `l quale, a voler dir lo vero,
fu stabilita per lo loco santo
u' siede il successor del maggior Piero.

(*Inferno* 2.20–24)

["Since he was chosen as father of hallowed Rome and her empire in the lofty, Empyrean regions of the heavens, both of which, to tell the truth, were established as the holy place where sits the successor of great Peter."]

The meeting of Dante and Virgil in the first canto of the *Inferno* is perhaps the most momentous encounter in all of Western literature.[11] What is difficult for the modern reader to sense fully is that Dante saw Virgil as a real person, one whom he knew intimately from his diligent study and reading of the poet. As Dante makes his way across the *selva oscura* ["dark forest"], he discerns the shadowy figure of one who through long silence seemed faint "chi per lungo silenzio parea fioco." (*Inferno* 1.63) Most commentators interpret this description allegorically to mean that the voice of reason symbolized by Virgil had grown faint in the pilgrim's consciousness. I should rather interpret it more literally to mean that in preceding centuries the full and true message of Virgil and of Rome had been lost, but that now in this meeting of two poets and two worlds, new life would arise. Never has one poet paid homage to another with such sincere and profound emotion:

"Or se' tu quel Virgilio e quella fonte
che spandi di parlar sì largo fiume?"
rispuos' io lui con vergognosa fronte
"O degli altri poeti onore e lume,
vagliami `l lungo studio e 'l grande amore
che m'ha fatto cercar lo tuo volume.
Tu se' lo mio maestro e 'l mio autore
tu se' solo colui da cui io tolsi
lo bello stilo che m'ha fatto onore."

(*Inferno* 1.79–87)

["'Are you then that Vergil, that fountain that spreads forth so ample a stream of speech?' I answered with shame on my brow, 'O honor and light of other poets, may my long study and great love, which made me search your volume, avail me. You are my master and my author, you alone are he from whom I took the beautiful style that has won me honor.'"]

Virgil is not only Dante's master in style, but his authority in all branches of knowledge second only to the scriptures. From Virgil's passing accolade of the Trojan hero Riphaeus as *justissimus unus* ["the one who is the most just"], Dante sees fit to place him in heaven as a beneficiary of divine grace. In Dante's conception, the poet Statius was converted to Christianity from his illumined reading of the *Fourth Eclogue* and acknowledges his debt to his benefactor in the beautiful line:

Per te poeta fui, per te cristiano.

(*Purgatorio* 22.73)

["Through you I was a poet, through you a Christian."]

At the summit of Purgatory in the earthly paradise, as Virgil is about to take silent leave of his companion, Dante pays him the supreme homage of having a chorus of angels intone a line from the *Aeneid* that was spoken by Anchises in rendering homage to the shade of Marcellus:

Manibus date lilia plenis.

(*Aen.* 6.883, *Purgatorio* 30.21)

["give lilies with full hands"]

Then, as Beatrice appears, he turns to Virgil, this time refashioning another famous line from the *Aeneid*:

Conosco i segni dell'antica fiamma,

(*Purgatorio* 30.48)

["I recognize the signs of the ancient flame"]

reminiscent of 'Agnosco veteris vestigia flammae' ["I recognize the traces of the old flame"] (*Aen.* 4.23). But Virgil has already silently departed as Dante is about to enter into the spheres of Paradise. There is no formal parting, but in another deft act of homage to his master Dante laments the disappearance of his guide in a disconsolate triple invocation of his name, recalling the pitiful cries of Orpheus in the Fourth Book of the *Georgics*.

Dante's encounter with Virgil was still a fact of profound significance for one of the great poets of our own eclectic age, T. S. Eliot. In 1944 he delivered a presidential address to the Virgil Society of London entitled "What is a Classic?"[12] The question purposely recalled a causerie of Sainte-Beuve on the same theme 'Qu'est-ce qu'un classique' ["What is a classic?"], which drew the taunts of a Jacobin audience at the Collège de France in 1850. The French critic called Virgil "le poète de la Latinité tout entière" ["the poet of the entire Latin world"], saying that he had given a new form not only to poetry but to civility, and that all later European culture descended from him in a direct line. It was more plausible for a Frenchman to insist upon the continuity of the Latin tradition, but Eliot was not abashed to make the same claim, referring to Virgil as the still point of that tradition. The quality that Eliot insists on in the essay is summed up in the word maturity, maturity of a civilization, maturity of a language and a literature, grown to full stature through the work of a succession of writers who have brought them to the point where the hand of the master-poet alone is awaited. Without being aware of it, Virgil was that poet. He appeared at a moment in the development of the Latin language when a uniquely classical poet was possible, and by the perfection of his art exhausted the possibilities of the language in which he wrote. In Eliot's view it was left to Dante to transfer the essential qualities of that language and style into the *volgare illustre,* "the perfection of a common language," which while still near enough in feeling to medieval Latin was able to open the way for national literatures in the vernacular languages.

Such is the official, orthodox view of Virgil as a kind of continuous immutable force in Western letters, that has prevailed almost unchallenged through the centuries. But there is another side, as we all know, a darker side more consonant with the present age. It has been alluded to with greater frequency in recent decades, but even in the hey-day of Victorianism, these more dreamy and melancholic qualities of the Roman poet were singled out for criticism by Matthew Arnold in his inaugural address from the Chair of Poetry at Oxford entitled 'The Modern Element in Literature,' almost in direct refutation of the ideas expressed by Sainte-Beuve three years previously. He says in part:

> Over the whole of the great poem of Virgil, over the whole *Aeneid,* there rests an ineffable melancholy; not a rigid, a moody gloom, like the melancholy of Lucretius: no, a sweet, a touching sadness, but still a sadness; a melancholy which is at once a source of charm in the poem, and a testimony of its incompleteness. Virgil, as Niebuhr has well said, expressed no affected self-disparagement, but the jaunting, the irresistible, self-dissatisfaction of his heart, when he desired on his death-bed that his poem might be destroyed. A man of the most delicate genius, the most rich learning, but of weak health, of the most sensitive nature, in a great and overwhelming world; conscious, at heart, of his inadequacy for the thorough spiritual mastery of that world and its interpretation in a work of art; conscious of this inadequacy — the one inadequacy, the one weak place in the mighty Roman nature! This suffering, this graceful-minded, this finely gifted man is the most beautiful, the most attractive figure in literary history; but he is not the adequate interpreter of the great period of Rome.[13]

The key word here is adequate. Arnold, and many others with him, were more taken by the adequacy and the rationality of Periclean Athens and its "utmost energy of mature manhood" (a different kind of maturity, to be sure, than that envisioned by Eliot for the perennial classic). In one of the best books dedicated to Virgil in recent times, W. R. Johnson identifies in modern approaches to the poet a Harvard pessimistic school, chiefly Wendell Clausen and Adam Parry, the young Harvard scholar who met such a tragic end. According to Johnson, this school emphasizes "Virgil's infatuation with twilight moods, with blurred images, and with haunted, half-enacted interviews and confrontations that disintegrate before our eyes just as we begin to perceive them."[14]

To illustrate this peculiarly twentieth-century *Stimmungskunst* ["mood art"] one could not choose a better example than Hermann Broch's rhapsodic and prolix account of Virgil's last eighteen hours, a fantasmagoria on the 'inadequacy' that Arnold intuited. The *Death of Virgil* is a difficult, even exasperating book, but it is an important testimony of the continued presence of Virgil even at such a critical moment in the history of the West as the rise of Fascism.

✧ ✧ ✧

Broch imagines Virgil being borne by slaves in a sedan chair, through the milling crowd up the winding alleys of the slums of Brindisi. He is so nauseated by the stench and obscene taunts, the *Unheil* ["unwholesome havoc"] of the masses, that he must veil his countenance and sink back into the litter. This shrinking away from the seamier aspects of life gives him a sudden intimation of how selectively he has filtered human experience as poet laureate of Rome despite his yearnings to see life whole. A stark terror invades his being, and a numbness (*Erstarrung*) grips his feeble members. He feels that his life has been squandered, diverted into a labyrinth of error and disappointment. The *Aeneid* becomes for him the supreme symbol of imperfection, the target of all his frustrations and of all human limitation.

✧ ✧ ✧

He is driven to examine his own artistic creed and performance, and finds himself gravely wanting. Like Orpheus and like his own hero, Aeneas, he experiences the truth of his own lines:

> facilis descensus Averno:
> sed revocare gradum superasque evadere ad auras,
> hoc opus, hic labor est.
>
> (*Aen.* 6. 126, 128–9)

["easy the descent to Avernus (the Underworld): but to recall one's path and come out to the upper air, this is the task, this the labor."]

In a world shot through with rottenness and fraud he realizes that he has woven a tissue of false dreams and hollow pretences. Instead of fulfilling his mission as a civilizing poet he has dallied with beauty and yielded to self-complacency and self-intoxication, a servant of non-art (*Unkunst*) and literariness.[15]

✧ ✧ ✧

With this inner drama of contrition or mortification (*Verknirschung*) played out, the stage is set for the operation of grace....He is in a realm divested of individual memory and the guilt-laden language of man, a world of pure forms....It is given to Virgil to see the dawn of things to come, the Christian dispensation, but neither to herald it nor to give it shape.

✧ ✧ ✧

At one point the boy [accompanying him] hails the unique role allotted to Virgil in the evolving drama of salvation: "You saw the beginning, Virgil, but you yourself are not yet the beginning; you heard the voice, Virgil, but you yourself are not yet the voice; you felt the heart of creation beating, but you yourself are not yet the heart; you are the eternal guide, who himself does not reach the goal: you will be immortal, immortal as guide, not yet and yet already, your lot at every turn of time."[16] It seems clear that Virgil is here depicted as the future guide of Dante, a link between the pagan and the Christian era and perhaps also as a guide at a much later turning point in time, the aftermath of the Second World War.

✧ ✧ ✧

Broch's heavy Wagnerian chords drown out the more subtle music of the Virgilian hexameter. Yet the central theme, the dilemma of the artist, the fear that the poet's life's work has been sterile and artificial is worthy of our consideration. Themes of darkness, destructiveness and disintegration do insert themselves in the Virgilian narrative. One seems to discern a controlled despair, which does not affect the flow of the current, but is nonetheless present. The world Virgil describes is already old. Homer's world was younger and gods still walked the earth. Aeneas, unlike Achilles and Odysseus, is darkened by destiny. Robert Lowell went as far as to call him a man of sorrows. He wins his quest, but at terrible cost and sacrifice. Not only a *mauvaise conscience* ["bad conscience"], as Broch intuited, but the sadness engendered by the unresolved conflict between human *pietas* ["piety"] and the arbitrary ruthlessness of the gods could have tempted Virgil to despair. How can this pessimistic view be reconciled with the traditional acceptance of Virgil, as Eliot eulogized him, as the poet of reason and order, of empire and glorious destiny? It is simply to impose our own allegory upon the poem, as ages and generations have done before us. The majestic sadness of the seer and the uncertainties that plagued him to the end despite his great faith appeal to our disillusioned age, which has all but lost faith.

To close on an elegiac note I should like to quote some lines from a lovely lyric, which I happened upon but recently. The epigraph comes from another poem written by a poetess named V. R. Lang, who died in 1956.

> I wore this very dress
> The night that Virgil died.

The new poem continues:

> I was there and I remember the brown brocade
> With pearls like tears gleaming on the bodice.
> We lounged at court, at ease, on lavender cushions,
> Toasting Augustus, when Maecenas brought the news.
> I remember you held his wrinkled ringless hands,
> Gazing deep for comfort in his ancient eyes,
> Avoiding relevant words. He looked like Death.
> You rose to depart, draped like an autumn goddess,
> The jewel I gave you burning at your throat,
> And fainted. I caught you as you drifted down.
> But, you were no friend to Virgil, wrote him no poems.
> The hurt was deeper. Once we stood in the Forum

And stared at a pompous hearse. Your beautiful eyes,
Full of the tears of the ages, said everything dies.[17]

Yet again the evocation of Virgil's *lacrimae rerum* ["tears of the ages"] conjures up
the Roman poet's still, sad music, which continues to haunt the Western world. As
our civilization drifts ever further from its cultural moorings, let us remember Virgil
and still trust him as a guide in our mortal wanderings.[18]

Notes

[1]P. E. Santangelo, "Virgilio e lo spirito della nuova Italia," *Atti e memorie della reale
Accademia Virgiliana di Mantova* 22 (1931) 19–49.

[2]A convenient summary of these interpretations is given in Harold Mattingly, "Virgil's
Fourth Eclogue," *Journal of the Warburg and Courtauld Institutes* 10 (1947) 14–19.

[3]*The Nicene and Post-Nicene Fathers of the Christian Church* (Grand Rapids 1952) series 2,
vol. 1, 561–80.

[4]*Divinae institutiones* 7.24.

[5]T. S. Eliot, "Virgil and the Christian World," in *Poetry and Poets* (New York 1957) 123.

[6]The poem is found in a flyleaf of Petrarch's Virgil at the Ambrosiana and in a few later
versions studied by Professor Bernard Peebles, to whom I owe my first acquaintance with
these lines. Cf. Bernard Peebles, "The *Ad Maronis mausoleum*. Petrarch's Virgil and two fifteenth-
century manuscripts," in *Classical Medieval and Renaissance Studies in Honor of B. L. Ullman*
(Rome 1964) vol. 2, 169–198.

[7]*Commentarii in Somnium Scipionis* 1.9.8, ed. Willis (Leipzig 1970) 41.

[8]Fulgentius, *Opera* ed. Rudolf Helm (Leipzig 1898) 83–107. The use of the word *continentia*
in the meaning of a "hidden sense" is found also in Macrobius, *Commentarii in Somnium
Scipionis* 1.6.28.

[9]*Commentum Bernardi Silvestris super sex libros Eneidos* ed. W. Riedel (Greifswald 1924) 3.

[10]Giorgio Padovan, "Tradizione e fortuna del commento all' *Eneide di Bernardo Silvestre*,"
Italia medioevale e umanistica 3 (1960) 240.

[11]Cf. Ernst Robert Curtius, *European Literature and the Latin Middle Ages* (New York 1953) 358.

[12]T. S. Eliot, *Poetry and Poets* (New York 1957) 53–71.

[13]*Matthew Arnold on the Classical Tradition*, ed. R. H. Super (Ann Arbor 1960) 35–36.

[14]W. R. Johnson, *Darkness Visible* (Berkeley 1976) 12.

✧ ✧ ✧

[15]All translations of Broch are my own, rather than those of the official English version
by Jean Starr Untermeyer.

[16]"Du sahest den Anfang, Vergil, bist selber noch nicht der Anfang, du hörtest die Stimme,
Vergil, bist selber noch nicht die Stimme, du fühltest das Schöpfungsherz pochen, bist selber
noch nicht das Herz, du bist der ewige Führer, der selber das Ziel nicht erreicht: unsterblich
wirst du sein, unsterblich als Führer, noch nicht und doch schon, dein Los an jeder Wende
der Zeit" (258–9).

✧ ✧ ✧

[17]Mac Hammond, ["In memory of V. R. Lang (1924–1956)"] in *The Horse Opera and Other
Poems* (Columbus 1966) 35.

[18]This is a revised and expanded version of a paper delivered to the Detroit Classical
Association in October 1981.

THE POETRY OF ALLUSION
INTRODUCTION

The topic of borrowings and searches for sources will be familiar to readers of the *Aeneid*. In this essay, Jacoff and Schnapp take up the issue regarding not Vergil's borrowings from other authors but another poet's borrowings from him, the thirteenth- to fourteenth-century Italian poet Dante, author of *The Divine Comedy*. For Dante, Vergil's works were canonical, as were Homer's for Vergil. What interests Jacoff and Schnapp is not just the identification of Dante's individual borrowings from Vergil but how Dante reworked them from their original context into his own very different poem. They study Dante in "conversation" with Vergil, across many centuries, even disputing with him. They go so far as to characterize the conversation as one of "continual subversion and revisionary rewriting," in which "Virgil's authority is simultaneously affirmed and denied, built up and undermined." Through this strenuous artistic relationship, the issue of literary influence broadens into questions about "the overlap and opposition between Christian and classical culture." (Ed.)

V irgil and Ovid offer an optimal unit for examining issues of literary influence and imitation in Dante's *Commedia:* Virgil, because he is Dante's explicit authorial model, his primary guide and literary "father"; Ovid, because he is second only to Virgil in the number of allusions Dante makes to his works and because he is repeatedly presented by Dante as the principal literary countermodel of the Dantean Virgil.

✧ ✧ ✧

The question of allusion in Dante has traditionally been studied within the framework of *Quellenforschung* (the pursuit of sources). With sometimes invaluable results, Dante's commentators have proceeded on the assumption that a given allusion recalls a single locus in a source-text. The reader's task has thus been defined as that of determining the single source and ascertaining its appropriateness to the poetic context. The notion of "borrowing" that lies at the heart of such an approach is insufficient, however, to describe the processes of textual realignment characteristically at work in Dante's text. Identifying the source is only a first step; by returning to the original context of the source and then examining its implications one begins to see the ways in which Dante's citations are often dialogic or even confrontational.

✧ ✧ ✧

Adapted from THE POETRY OF ALLUSION: VIRGIL AND OVID IN DANTE'S 'COMMEDIA', edited by Rachel Jacoff and Jeffrey T. Schnapp, with permission of the publishers, Stanford University Press. © 1991 by the Board of Trustees of the Leland Stanford Junior University.

[T]he central question remains that of the meaning of the allusions studied. Although diverse answers are proposed to that question, what is striking overall is how Dante repeatedly thematizes the relationship of his text to its predecessors in the process of citation, a practice Thomas Greene has usefully called "heuristic imitation."

✧ ✧ ✧

Virgil in Dante

The opening cantos of the *Inferno* establish Virgil's role as the pilgrim's guide while simultaneously suggesting, through a variety of echoes and allusions, the centrality of Virgil's epic to Dante's creation of his own poem. The representation of Virgil as a literary character and of the *Aeneid* as a model epic are therefore to some extent reciprocal or coincident. As character, Virgil is accorded homage and treated with tender affection in scenes of increasing intensity; as father, mother, pedagogue, and guide, he is granted sufficient authority to have been read as a personification of Reason by centuries of commentators. The *Aeneid*, too, receives special homage: Dante uses the same language for its seminality that he employs for Scripture, and the word "autore" is reserved exclusively for Virgil and the "author" of Holy Scripture. Dante insists on the importance of Virgil's text in literary, moral, and spiritual terms, especially in the encounter with Statius in *Purgatorio* 21–22.

Nonetheless, Virgil, both as a character and as a textual presence, is subject to continual subversion and revisionary rewriting. Virgil's authority is simultaneously affirmed and denied, built up and undermined. This doubleness brings into ever sharper focus the poignant and finally unresolvable tension between Dante's devotion to the *Aeneid* and his conviction that its author is not and cannot be saved. The allusions studied in the present volume often crystallize this tension, and in so doing, they place the narrowly literary issue of imitation within a broader historical frame: that of the overlap and opposition between Christian and classical culture.

For Dante, who had no direct access to Homer, the *Aeneid* was by definition *the* canonic epic model. With passionate conviction, Dante viewed the *Aeneid* less as a "mere" poetic fable than as the sacred scripture of ancient Rome, the record of the exodus of the Trojans into the promised land in which the empire would achieve its providentially ordained dominion. The historical and quasi-scriptural authority of Virgil's poem was of crucial importance because it granted legitimacy to Dante's claim that the *Commedia*, even though composed in the humble Tuscan vernacular of the fourteenth century, might also be vested with similar authority and prophetic force. At the same time, Dante regularly reminds us of the *Aeneid's* limitations, and indeed of the incompleteness of all pagan sources of knowledge. In this context, he invokes the centrality of Christian revelation necessarily absent from Virgil's text and the pre-Christian world. This he accomplishes by playing the *Aeneid* off against the text of Scripture, whose "verace Autore" (true Author; *Par.* 26.40) is regularly invoked as the *Commedia's* true and ultimate model author.

With respect to the *Commedia*, then, Virgil's epic occupies an ambivalent position. On the one hand, it appears as an absolute poetic model, as the very emblem of what literature can aspire to and accomplish. On the other, it is seen as so firmly rooted in the soil of history that its vision must remain tragically partial. The net result is Dante's notion that the *Aeneid* is open to — and, indeed, requires — the sort of retrospective critique, revision, and fulfillment proposed in the *Commedia*.

Dante's reading of the *Aeneid* bears certain affinities with that developed by Virgil scholars such as Adam Parry, Michael Putnam, Ralph Johnson, and Gian Biagio Conte, who emphasize the epic's tragic dimension. Postwar scholarship has repeatedly pointed to the subtle presence of multiple (and even contradictory) perspectives within the *Aeneid*'s larger narrative, as well as to Virgil's deep awareness of the terrible human cost incurred in founding the Roman imperial state. Dante was as haunted by the specter of civil war as Virgil and envisaged a near-identical solution to the threat of perpetual internecine strife: an imperial monarch, half-man and half-god, poised above the warring interests and cupidities of the citizenry. But, unlike Virgil, Dante was fated to remain the poet of an imperial vacuum; and in the absence of any actual or probable world monarch he had even less desire than Virgil to rend the ideological veil of empire. Dante strove to further buttress the theory of universal monarchy by placing it within a Christian theology of history and granting it divine sanction. This theological emphasis, however, entails a challenge to Roman conceptions of human and civil worth. Persuaded that the unanswerable finality of death calls into question the human achievements the *Acneid* honors, Dante counterposes to them a promise of Christian consolation alien to Virgil's poem and his world.

The connection between Dante's Christian epic and its Roman predecessor may also be thought of as a drama of fathers and sons, wherein the pagan father is eventually replaced by a Christian (Cacciaguida) who grants his son the vocation to compose a Christian epic that will supplant Virgil's. The two texts are placed in a relation of promise and fulfillment, following the model of the Christian reading of Hebrew scripture. Virgil's poem becomes a provisionally sacred text analogous to the Old Testament book of Exodus. As the inspired narrative of the Trojan's pilgrimage, it is granted its "true" intelligibility not from within, but rather from a hermeneutic point *external* to the text itself. The perspective of the Christ event — and by implication Dante's Christian poem — is posited as the ultimate arbiter of its significance.

By remotivating the idea of Virgil as a proto-Christian prophet, Dante succeeds in rescuing the *Aeneid* (and with it the political ideals of the Roman empire) from the powerful critique proposed in Augustine's *City of God*. But he also sets up Virgil's inevitable displacement. Just as the Old Testament "must" give way to the New, so Virgil "must" give way to Beatrice, classical tragedy to Christian comedy. In *Purgatorio* 30 the author of the Roman book of exodus is left standing on the edge of Eden like a pagan Moses on the bank of the Jordan, unable to cross over into the promised land.

✧ ✧ ✧

John E. Rexine

REVIEW: *VIRGIL AND THE TEMPEST:*
THE POLITICS OF IMITATION

Rexine's book review considers the argument that in *The Tempest* Shakespeare used the first six books of the *Aeneid* as a creative foil to position himself within a contemporary and potentially dangerous political argument about absolutist theories and practices of monarchy, under the reign of James I (1603–25). By combining and reassembling episodes from the *Aeneid* in the play, "[c]ontemporary culture is seen reworked in the Shakespearean reworking of Vergilian structures." Rexine finds that the book he is reviewing offers "a powerful example of the profound relationship between one great poet and another — and a superb example of the creative use of the classical tradition by one of the creative geniuses of English literature." (Ed.)

John Rexine, review of Donna B. Hamilton, *Virgil and The Tempest: The Politics of Imitation.* Columbus: Ohio State University Press, 1990. Pp. xvi + 185. clothbound, $30.00.

Virgil and the Tempest* will undoubtedly be of primary interest to Shakespearean scholars but it will also be of great interest to students of the Classical tradition, and especially to students of Virgil who can examine firsthand how important Virgil was to the Renaissance and in particular to English literature. Donna Hamilton, who teaches English at the University of Maryland, College Park, offers the reader a fully documented, richly illustrated assessment of Shakespeare's *Tempest*, which has often been pointed to as supporting the absolutist theories and policies of King James I—a view that Hamilton challenges and replaces with the thesis that Shakespeare [used] the rhetorical skill of indirection, a skill that guaranteed safety, respect, and power for the author [and] at the same time [was a skill] that a writer could use in the politics of opposition as well as in the politics of *apologia*. The unique contribution of this book is to show that "In *The Tempest,* Shakespeare situates his writing between two authorities, the poet Virgil and the monarch James I, each the possessor of a set of symbols and idioms that Shakespeare reappropriates for himself.... In the case of Virgil this means rewriting the *Aeneid* to suit a new time, a new situation; in the case of James, it means repeating the King's language about rule in a manner which also changes that language" (p. ix). The direct consequence is to present a strong case for Shakespeare's having constructed an argument for constitutionalism, as that ideology most directly in competition with absolutism. Even though there has been no known text with a narrative line that persuasively matches the plot by Shakespeare, we are informed by the author that there has been a growing consensus that there are undeniable links between the *Aeneid* and *The*

Review of Donna B. Hamilton, *Virgil and the Tempest: The Politics of Imitation*, by John E. Rexine, first appeared in *Vergilius* 38 (1990) 146–149. Reprinted by permission of Michael Rexine.

Tempest, most obviously from Books 1–6 of the *Aeneid.* Donna Hamilton tries to show that "Shakespeare's involvement in the Virgilian idiom surpasses that of allusion and echo, and that his investment in Virgil's text is so great as to constitute a formal and rhetorical imitation of the major narrative kernels of *Aeneid* 1–6. Moreover, Shakespeare's management of the Virgilian idiom is matched by an equally thorough encompassment of the contemporary discourse about monarchy — a discourse that, especially in 1610, took the form of debate as King and Parliament argued about the limits of royal power, and thus the respective merits of absolutism and constitutionalism. Shakespeare, then, is involved both in demonstrating his mastery of the poetic discourse and in responding to the master discourses of high politics" (pp. x–xi).

❖ ❖ ❖

Donna Hamilton sees *The Tempest* as "a work that is a formal imitation of the first six books of the *Aeneid,* both in its larger theme and structure and in its smaller details of vocabulary and syntax" (p. 4). Shakespeare is shown to have placed himself between Virgil and his own times within the conventions of masque and romance that promoted the epideictic strategies of the Renaissance which were used by poets to comment on ideological controversies and to offer noncontroversial rhetorical stances that were politically proper and circumspect. Shakespeare very deftly used Virgil. Johannes Sturm in *Nobilitas liberata* ["Nobility liberated"], published in German in 1549 and available in English translation in 1570 under the title *A Ritch Storehouse or Treasure for Nobilitye and Gentlemen,* taught students how "to imitate" Virgil, among others, with the emphasis on the process of reading and analyzing the text to be imitated and on the alternative methods for transforming the text into something new. In *The Tempest* Shakespeare offers us something new, what Hamilton describes as leading to "defiguration" (by conceptualizing a text and articulating its art) that, in turn, leads to "figuration." Shakespeare does not borrow Virgilian plots but uses them to respond to his own textual variation (in this sense, he imitates Virgil). Examples can be drawn from his use of the Laocoon episode (I); the tempest and reaction of Aeneas to being shipwrecked (II); the Trojan horse conspiracy (IV); the episodes in the Lower World and Elysium (VI). Also, the use of a series of conspiracy plots (Prospero's expulsion from Milan; Antonio and Sebastian's plot to overthrow Alonso; Caliban's plot to overthrow Prospero) [is] all patterned on Virgil's story of how the Greeks conquered Troy. Shakespeare is shown to combine more than one Virgilian pattern and even to disassemble parts of the pattern. Contemporary culture is seen reworked in the Shakespearean reworking of Virgilian structures.

In *The Tempest,* Ferdinand is reworked as a chaste Aeneas. [By] 1611, the date of *The Tempest,*…the question of how much power a king should have [had been] vigorously debated [for more than three centuries]. Hamilton goes into detail about this debate. She argues that "the political discourse, especially of 1610, is represented by Shakespeare in fictional constructs that imitate the language — that is, the metaphors, idioms, and rhetoric that James was using to represent his identity (the king as god, father, head of a microcosm) as well as rhetorical structures that the opposition parliamentarians were using to represent the identity they felt they would acquire as subjects to such a king (the subject in bondage and servitude)" (p. 48). Prospero with his magical and transcendent powers stands in relation to Ariel and Caliban as does King James to his subjects. And just as Ariel and Caliban express their desire for freedom, their metaphors, idioms, and rhetoric correspond to that of the Commons' expression of the subjects' right to freedom, their right to express their grievances, and their fears of "restraint" (by the King), and loss of property. Hamilton sees Shakespeare making an argument for constitutionalism. The *Suprema Potestas* ["Supreme Power"] of the king was being disputed by the House of Commons. Caliban, we are told, represents the displanted natives of Virginia or Ireland, but also the English fear of being made slaves in their own country. Prospero legitimizes the position of constitutionalism which also involves the legitimization of the position of the opposition to excessive royal authority. Implicit, too, is a critique of colonization which is strongly linked to imperialist monarchy and colonial subjection. As an Augustan imperialist text, the *Aeneid* can be viewed as the archetypical colonizing text of all time—a paradigm for the expansion and transmission of culture and ideology from one place to another (Hamilton cites Richard Waswo in this regard).

Focusing on the three spectacles of the harpy banquet scene, the betrothal masque, and the glistering apparel scene, Hamilton finds here the language of the masque—a substitution for the heroic language of the Virgilian epic (paradoxically represented as the use of the king's own language). Virgil's text is shown to be "handled discontinuously, yields to conflation, recombination, and change" (p. 73) with reason and discipline stressed. Caliban becomes an Aeneas stripped of his *pietas* ["piety"], one whose behavior disrupts normative standards. Ferdinand embodies that reciprocity by way of a love relationship in which both parties (Ferdinand and Miranda) gain freedom by being bound to each other in mutual obligation and achieving perfect harmony. Miranda is linked to Venus, thus not only fueling Ferdinand's passion but leading him to divine knowledge, while Prospero, who has arranged the love and assigned the tasks, stresses that "The love proceeds visually and linguistically within the context of patriarchal guidance, and thus also within the context of the language of absolutism, to which patriarchy and its analogous metaphors of dominance and subordination were central" (p. 99). King James again!

We come then to refiguration. Shakespeare has chosen the language of love and marriage (mutuality and not equality) to parallel the language of constitutionalism and contract. In *The Tempest* the power of restraint can be seen in Prospero who effectively encourages a constitutionalism that is inherent in a godlike and fatherlike figure who elects to give up his transcendent power, who knows how to dispense mercy, and learns to accommodate himself to the tensions present in a king-subject relationship. This involves a sacrifice for a higher cause, similar to the sacrifices Aeneas has to make for the fulfillment of his destiny. Prospero comes through as noble and heroic. Sovereignty and liberty are reconciled. Donna Hamilton's highly appropriate, concluding words are: "The poet who imitated Virgil and has, in the same work, intervened in national politics ends his play gracefully and yet with authority. The closing language, however humble, invokes the authority of Virgil, which Shakespeare has made his own" (p. 137).

Donna Hamilton's *Virgil and The Tempest* is an incredibly compact and at the same time highly brilliant book. Even if there are those who will, for one reason or another, not agree with her arguments, her analysis is extremely orderly, her documentation impressive, and her illustrations to support her arguments telling. For the classicist and the Virgilian student and scholar, she offers a powerful example of the profound relationship between one great poet and another and a superb example of the creative use of the classical tradition by one of the creative geniuses of English literature.

Barbara Kiefer Lewalski

PARADISE LOST AS ENCYCLOPEDIC EPIC: THE USES OF LITERARY FORMS

Milton's artistic debt to Vergil is as well known as Dante's. Lewalski is concerned with a pervasive phenomenon in Milton's *Paradise Lost*: his use of a repertoire of literary genres within the epic frame. In the literary thinking of the Renaissance, Lewalski explains, epic was imagined as a microcosm in which a literary universe could operate. Indeed, genre could be deployed to "provide a range of culturally defined perspectives upon the matter of the poem," much as Vergil invested his epic with both dramatic and lyric content. Lewalski argues that Milton's use of genre is an interpretative key, a "rhetorical and symbolic vocabulary shared by poet and reader." In this light, Milton's relationship to Vergil, like that of Dante and Shakespeare, is one of both direct borrowing and also a similar, subtle manipulation of artistic form. (Ed.)

P*aradise Lost* is preeminently a poem about knowing and choosing—for the Miltonic Bard, for his characters, for the reader. I intend to argue that the ground for many of these choices is Milton's own choice and rhetorical use of a panoply of literary forms, with their accumulated freight of shared cultural significances.

Readers have long recognized that *Paradise Lost* is an epic whose closest structural affinities are to Virgil's *Aeneid,* and that it undertakes to redefine classical heroism in Christian terms.[1] We now recognize as well the influence of epic traditions and the presence of epic features other than Virgilian. Among the poem's Homeric elements are its Iliadic subject, the death and woe resulting from an act of disobedience; the portrayal of Satan as an Achillean hero motivated by a sense of injured merit and also as an Odyssean hero of wiles and craft; the description of Satan's perilous Odyssey to find a new homeland; and the battle scenes in heaven.[2] The poem also incorporates a Hesiodic gigantomachy; numerous Ovidian metamorphoses; an Ariostan Paradise of Fools; Spenserian allegorical figures (Sin and Death); a romance garden of love in which a hero and heroine must withstand a dragon of sorts; and a poetic hexaemeron in the tradition of Du Bartas.[3] Moreover, because heroic values have been so profoundly transvalued in *Paradise Lost,* the poem is sometimes assigned to categories beyond epic: pseudomorph, prophetic poem, apocalypse, anti-epic, transcendent epic.[4]

Dramatic elements have also been identified within the epic form: some vestiges of Milton's early sketches for a drama entitled *Adam Unparadiz'd*; some structural affinities to contemporary epics in five "acts," such as Davenant's *Gondibert*; and tragic protagonists who fall from happiness to misery through *hamartia* ["an error, failure"]. Other dramatic features include the tragic soliloquies of Satan and Adam, recalling those of Faustus and Macbeth; the morality-play "Parliament of Heaven" sequence; the scene of domestic farce in which Satan first vehemently repudiates and then fawns upon his reprehensible offspring, Sin and Death; the scenes of domestic tragedy that present Adam and Eve's quarrel, Fall, mutual recriminations (and later, reconciliation); and the tragic masques or pageants portraying the sins and miseries of human history.[5]

The panoply of kinds includes pastoral: landscape descriptions of an Arcadian "happy rural seat of various view" (4.247); eclogue-like passages presenting the *otium* ["quiet, peace"] of Heaven and unfallen Eden; scenes of light georgic gardening activity.[6] Also, the several varieties of embedded lyrics in the poem have received some critical attention: celebratory odes, psalmic hymns of praise and thanksgiving, submerged sonnets, epithalamia ["marriage songs"], love lyrics (*aubade* ["a morning song"], nocturne, sonnet), laments, and complaints.[7] There are also many rhetorical and dialogic kinds which have not been much studied from the perspective of genre: Satan's several political orations; God's judicial oration defending his ways; the parliamentary debate in hell over war and peace; the Satan-Abdiel debate over God's right of sovereignty; a treatise on astronomical systems; a dialogue on human nature between God and Adam and another on love between Raphael and Adam; a lecture on Christian historiography; Satan's temptation speech to Eve in the style and manner of "some Orator renown'd / In *Athens* or free *Rome*" (9.670–71).[8]

If we ask why Milton incorporated so complete a spectrum of literary forms and genres in *Paradise Lost,* a partial answer must be that much Renaissance critical theory supports the notion of epic as a heterocosm or compendium of subjects, forms, and styles. According to the major Renaissance genre theorist, Julius-Caesar Scaliger, epic is both a mixed form and "the chiefest of all forms"; it is "catholic in the range of subject-matter," and it supplies "the universal controlling rules for the composition of each other kind."[9] Homer's epics, as Rosalie Colie has reminded us, were widely recognized as the source and origin of all arts and sciences—philosophy, mathematics, history, geography, military art, religion, hymnic praise, rhetoric, and much more—and, accordingly, as the source of all literary forms.[10] Out of Homer, said his great English translator George Chapman (citing Petrarch), "all Arts [are] deduced, confirmed or illustrated," and by reason of this inclusiveness, Homer can best instruct all kinds of people—kings, soldiers, counsellors, fathers, husbands, wives, lovers, friends.[11] Scaliger, on the other hand, considered the *Aeneid* to be the supreme epic, presenting the very "*ideas* of things…just as they might be taken from nature itself," only more perfect.[12] Moreover, ancient and Renaissance tradition recognized the Bible as epic-like in its comprehension of all history, all subject matters, and many genres—law, history, prophecy, heroic poetry, psalm, allegory, proverb, hymn, sermon, epistle, tragedy, tragicomedy, and more.[13]

Many Renaissance theorists also called attention to specific amalgams in the great poems of the tradition. The close parallel Aristotle drew between epic and tragedy, and his description of the plot of the *Iliad* as "pathetic," laid the groundwork for the common Renaissance view of it as a tragic epic. In this vein, William Webbe traced the origins of tragedy to the *Iliad* and the origins of comedy to the *Odyssey.* Giraldi Cinthio identified romance elements (characters, wonders, *copia* ["plenitude"]) in the *Odyssey* and the *Metamorphoses,* and Jacopo Mazzoni discussed Dante's *Commedia* as both comedy and epic. Puttenham (following Scaliger) emphasized the historical dimension in the epics of Homer and Virgil and classified them as one species of a larger category, of historical poems.[14] And Sidney, the major literary theorist in Renaissance England, attributed a specific moral effect to each of the poetic kinds and defended their mixture: "if severed they be good, the conjunction cannot be hurtfull."[15]

Responding to this tradition, Renaissance poets devised epics on inclusivist lines. Noting that Homer and Virgil had intermingled all forms and styles in their great epics, Tasso (with obvious reference to his own *Gerusalemme Liberata* ["Jerusalem Delivered"]) claimed that Renaissance heroic poems incorporated an even greater range and variety of subject matter, imaging that of the created universe itself:

> The great poet (who is called divine for no other reason than that as he resembles the supreme Artificer in his workings he comes to participate in his divinity) can form a poem in which, as in a little world, one may read here of armies assembling, here of battles on land or sea, here of conquests of cities, skirmishes and duels, here of jousts, here descriptions of hunger and thirst, here tempests, fires, prodigies, there of celestial and infernal councils, there seditions, there discord, wanderings, adventures, enchantments, deeds of cruelty, daring, courtesy, generosity, there the fortunes of love, now happy, now sad, now joyous, now pitiful.[16]

And the major sixteenth-century English narratives with claims to epic status — Sidney's *New Arcadia* and Spenser's *Faerie Queene* — were quite obviously mixtures of epic, romance, pastoral, allegory, and song.

Contemporary theory and practice, it seems clear, gave Milton ample warrant to conclude that an epic comprehending the entire spectrum of kinds and subjects would be most doctrinal and exemplary to a nation, and would also have best claim to inclusion in the company he expressly sought for such a work — the *Iliad*, the *Odyssey*, the *Aeneid*, the *Gerusalemme Liberata*, and the Bible.[17] In this study, however, I do not undertake to enumerate and extend the list of kinds that can be located in Milton's epic, but rather to address the more important question of just how Milton employs generic inclusiveness to accomplish his poetic purposes. I shall be attending to the ways in which Milton uses topoi, thematic and structural signs, and allusions to particular exemplars to evoke a very broad spectrum of kinds and modes.

My central proposition is that genre choices, changes, and transformations provide a range of culturally defined perspectives upon the matter of the poem, and thereby serve Milton the poet in several ways: as an indispensable vehicle for his own artistic perception; as a fundamental means of accommodating his subject to his audience; and as a major rhetorical strategy for educating that audience. This argument engages some major issues in contemporary Milton criticism — intertextuality, the springs of poetic creativity and authority, the responses of the reader — but in terms supplied by Renaissance poetics and rhetorical theory. This vantage point invites revision of some current views of Milton and his epic.

Though I consider many specific allusions, and the subtexts and "infracontexts" they invoke,[18] I do not employ the contemporary vocabulary of intertextuality to discuss such allusions because I am concerned here with conscious artistic choices, with Milton's deliberate orchestrations within the echo chamber of language. Also, my argument proposes that the manifold allusions in *Paradise Lost* function most significantly as generic topoi, to activate and develop various generic paradigms within that poem. To use Thomas Greene's terms,[19] I argue that Milton's imitative and allusive strategies are essentially heuristic, and that the conventions of literary genre and mode constitute a primary element of his poem's *mundus significans* ["signifying world"] – the rhetorical and symbolic vocabulary shared by poet and reader.

In addition, though I focus upon Milton's engagement with literary precursors I do not find that engagement characterized by anxiety, struggle, transumption, or triumph.[20] And though I take Milton's conception of himself as poet-prophet to be central to his poetics, I do not find him claiming the direct divine inspiration or the transcendent visions afforded the biblical prophets.[21] Again, though I analyze readers' responses to *Paradise Lost*,[22] my emphasis falls upon the author as rhetor, employing carefully designed literary strategies to elicit these responses. But I do not see Milton as a rigorous and punitive teacher, forcing readers into frequent and inevitable mistakes in reading and thereby causing them to recognize and reenact their own fallenness. To my mind, he embodies instead the pedagogic ideal in *Of Education*, advancing his readers' understanding through a literary regimen at once intellectually demanding and delightful.[23]

✧ ✧ ✧

...The formidable array of conventional genres and modes in *Paradise Lost* testifies to Milton's awareness that he can only see and tell of things invisible by using the familiar forms which literary art supplies to his own imagination and that of his readers. It testifies also to his belief that he can teach most effectively by building upon and letting his readers refine their developed responses to the values and assumptions about man, nature, language, heroism, virtue, pleasure, work, and love that have long been associated with the several genres and literary modes.

Notes

[1] See especially C. M. Bowra, *From Virgil to Milton* (London: Macmillan, 1944); Davis P. Harding, *The Club of Hercules: Studies in the Classical Background of Paradise Lost* (Urbana: Univ. of Illinois Press, 1962); John M. Steadman, *Milton and the Renaissance Hero* (Oxford: Clarendon Press, 1967); K. W. Gransden, "Paradise Lost and the *Aeneid*," *EIC* 17 (1967), 281–303; Mario A. Di Cesare, "*Paradise Lost* and Epic Tradition," *Milton Studies* 1 (1969), 31–50; Francis C. Blessington, *Paradise Lost and the Classical Epic* (Boston and London: Routledge & Kegan Paul, 1979); G. K. Hunter, *Paradise Lost* (London: George Allen & Unwin, 1980).

[2] See, e.g., Martin Mueller, "*Paradise Lost* and the *Iliad*," *CLS* 6 (1969), 292–316; Steadman, *Milton and the Renaissance Hero*, and *Milton's Epic Characters: Image and Idol* (Chapel Hill: Univ. of North Carolina Press, 1968); Manoocher Aryanpur, "*Paradise Lost* and the *Odyssey*," *TSLL* 9 (1967), 151–66; Neil Forsyth, "Homer in Milton: The Attendance Motif and the Graces," *CL* 33 (1981), 137–55; Philip Damon, "*Paradise Lost* as Homeric Epic" (Paper presented at the 100th Annual Meeting of the Modern Language Association, New York, December 27–30, 1983); Blessington, *Paradise Lost and Classical Epic*; Hunter, *Paradise Lost*.

[3] See, e.g., Merritt Y. Hughes, "Milton's Celestial Battles and the Theogonies," in *Studies in Honor of T. W. Baldwin*, ed. Don C. Allen (Urbana: Univ. of Illinois Press, 1958), pp. 237–53; rpt. in *Ten Perspectives on Milton* (New Haven: Yale Univ. Press, 1965), pp. 196–219; Stella Purce Revard, *The War in Heaven: Paradise Lost and the Tradition of Satan's Rebellion* (Ithaca and London: Cornell Univ. Press, 1980); Davis P. Harding, *Milton and the Renaissance Ovid* (Urbana: Univ. of Illinois Press, 1946); Louis L. Martz, "*Paradise Lost*: Figurations of Ovid," in *Poet of Exile: A Study of Milton's Poetry* (New Haven and London: Yale Univ. Press, 1980), pp. 203–44; Irene Samuel, *Dante and Milton: The Commedia and Paradise Lost* (Ithaca and London: Cornell Univ. Press, 1966); A. Bartlett Giamatti, *The Earthly Paradise and the Renaissance Epic* (Princeton:

Princeton Univ. Press, 1966); Merritt Y. Hughes, "Milton's Limbo of Vanities," and Wayne Shumacher, "*Paradise Lost* and the Italian Epic Tradition," in *Th' Upright Heart and Pure*, ed. Amadeus P. Fiore (Pittsburgh: Duquesne Univ. Press, 1967), pp. 7–24 and 87–100; Edward Weismiller, "Materials Dark and Crude: A Partial Genealogy for Milton's Satan," *HLQ* 31 (1967), 75–93; Edwin Greenlaw, "Spenser's Influence on *Paradise Lost*," *SP* 17 (1920), 320–59; A. Kent Hieatt, "Spenser and Milton," in *Chaucer, Spenser, Milton: Mythopoeic Continuities and Tranformations* (Montreal and London: McGill-Queen's Univ. Press, 1975), pp. 153–270; Kathleen Williams, "Milton, Greatest Spenserian," in *Milton and the Line of Vision*, ed . Joseph A. Wittreich (Madison: Univ. of Wisconsin Press, 1975), pp. 25–55; Patricia A. Parker, *Inescapable Romance: Studies in the Poetics of a Mode* (Princeton: Princeton Univ. Press, 1975), pp. 114–58; George C. Taylor, *Milton's Use of Du Bartas* (1934; rpt. New York: Octagon Books, 1967); J. M. Evans, *Paradise Lost and the Genesis Tradition* (Oxford: Clarendon Press, 1968).

[4]See, e.g., John M. Steadman, "The Epic as Pseudomorph: Methodology in Milton Studies," *Milton Studies* 7 (1973), 3–25; Joseph A. Wittreich, "Milton and the Tradition of Prophecy," in *Milton and the Line of Vision*, pp. 97–142; Michael Fixler, "The Apocalypse Within *Paradise Lost*," in *New Essays on Paradise Lost*, ed. Thomas Kranidas (Berkeley: Univ. of California Press, 1969), pp. 131–78; T. J. B. Spencer, "*Paradise Lost*: The Anti-Epic," in *Approaches to Paradise Lost: The York Tercentenary Lectures*, ed. C. A. Patrides (Toronto: Univ. of Toronto Press, 1968); Harold E. Toliver, "Milton's Household Epic," *Milton Studies* 9 (1976), 105–20; Joan Webber, *Milton and His Epic Tradition* (Seattle and London: Univ. of Washington Press, 1979). The presence and effects of *genera mixta* in *Paradise Lost* is the burden of several essays (by Earl Miner, Joseph Wittreich, Barbara K. Lewalski, Balachandra Rajan, Richard S. Ide, and Thomas Amorose) in the collection edited by Ide and Wittreich, *Composite Orders: The Genres of Milton's Last Poems, Milton Studies* 17 (Pittsburgh: Univ. of Pittsburgh Press, 1983).

[5]See, e.g., James Holly Hanford, "The Dramatic Element in *Paradise Lost*," *SP* 14 (1917), 178–95, rpt. *in John Milton: Poet and Humanist*, ed. John S. Diekhoff (Cleveland: Western Reserve Univ. Press, 1966), pp. 224–43; Arthur E. Barker, "Structural Pattern in *Paradise Lost*," *PQ* 28 (1949), 16–36; Ernest Sirluck, *Paradise Lost: A Deliberate Epic* (Cambridge: W. Heffer, 1967); Roger E. Rollin, "*Paradise Lost*: 'Tragical-Comical-Historical-Pastoral,'" *Milton Studies* 5 (1973), 3–37; John M. Steadman, *Epic and Tragic Structure in Paradise Lost* (Chicago: Univ. of Chicago Press, 1976); F. T. Prince, "Milton and the Theatrical Sublime," in *Approaches to Paradise Lost*, ed. Patrides, pp. 53–63; John G. Demaray, *Milton's Theatrical Epic: The Invention and Design of Paradise Lost* (Cambridge and London: Harvard Univ. Press, 1980); Thomas Kranidas, "Adam and Eve in the Garden: A Study of *Paradise Lost*, Book V," *SEL* 4 (1964), 71–83; Alwin Thaler, "Shakespearean Recollections in Milton: A Summing Up," in *Shakespeare and Our World* (Knoxville: Univ. of Tennessee Press, 1966), pp. 139–227; Helen Gardner, "Milton's Satan and the Theme of Damnation in Elizabethan Tragedy," *E&S* 1 (1948), 46–66, rpt. in *A Reading of Paradise Lost* (Oxford: Clarendon Press, 1965), pp. 99–120; Marshall Grossman, "Dramatic Structure and Emotive Pattern in the Fall: *Paradise Lost* IX," *Milton Studies* 13 (1979), 201–19; Richard S. Ide, "On the Uses of Elizabethan Drama: The Revaluation of Epic in *Paradise Lost*," *Milton Studies* 17 (1983), 121–40; Hunter, *Paradise Lost*, pp. 72–95.

[6]The major study is John R. Knott's *Milton's Pastoral Vision: An Approach to Paradise Lost* (Chicago and London: Chicago Univ. Press, 1971). See also Joseph E. Duncan, *Milton's Earthly Paradise: A Historical Study of Eden* (Minneapolis: Univ. of Minnesota Press, 1972); William Empson, "Milton and Bentley: The Pastoral of the Innocence of Man and Nature," in *Some Versions of Pastoral* (London: Chatto & Windus, 1935), pp. 149–94; Northrop Frye, *The Return of Eden* (Toronto: Univ. of Toronto Press, 1965); Roy Daniells, "A Happy Rural Seat of Various View," in *Paradise Lost: A Tercentenary Tribute*, ed. Balachandra Rajan (Toronto: Univ. of Toronto Press, 1967), pp. 3–17; G. Stanley Koehler, "Milton and the Art of Landscape," *Milton Studies* 8 (1975), 3–40; Barbara K. Lewalski, "Innocence and Experience in Milton's Eden," in *New Essays on Paradise Lost*, ed. Kranidas, pp. 86–117; Rollin, "'Tragical-Comical-Historical- Pastoral.'"

[7]See, e.g., Joseph Summers, *The Muse's Method: An Introduction to Paradise Lost* (Cambridge: Harvard Univ. Press, 1962), pp. 71–86; Donald Davie, "Syntax and Music in *Paradise Lost*," in *The Living Milton*, ed. Frank Kermode (London: Routledge & Kegan Paul, 1960), pp. 70–84; William Haller, "Hail, Wedded Love," *ELH* 13 (1946), 79–97; Gary M. McCown, "Milton and the Epic Epithalamium," *Milton Studies* 5 (1973), 39–66; John Demaray, "Love's Epic Revel in *Paradise Lost*: A Theatrical Vision of Marriage," *MLQ* 38 (1977), 3–20; Lee M. Johnson, "Milton's

Blank Verse Sonnets," *Milton Studies* 5 (1973), 129–53; A. K. Nardo, "The Submerged Sonnet as Lyric Moment in Miltonic Epic," *Genre* 9 (1976), 21–35; Richard M. Bridges, "Milton's Original Psalm," *Milton Quarterly* 14 (1980), 12–21; Judy L. Van Sickle, "Song as Structure and Symbol in Four Poems of John Milton" (Ph.D. diss., Brown Univ., 1980), pp. 190–267; Sara Thorne-Thomsen, "Milton's 'adven'rous Song': Lyric Genres in *Paradise Lost*" (Ph.D. diss., Brown Univ. 1985).

⁸See, e.g., J. B. Broadbent, *Some Graver Subject: An Essay on Paradise Lost* (London: Chatto & Windus, 1960), pp. 110–20; Broadbent, "Milton's Rhetoric," *MP* 56 (1958–59), 224–42; John M. Steadman, "'Semblance of Worth': Pandaemonium and Deliberative Oratory," *Neophilologus* 48 (1964), 159–76, rpt. in *Milton's Epic Characters*, 241–62; Steadman, "Ethos and Dianoia: Character and Rhetoric in *Paradise Lost*," in *Language and Style in Milton*, ed. R. D. Emma and John T. Shawcross (New York: Ungar, 1967), pp. 193–232; Dennis Burden, *The Logical Epic: A Study of the Argument of Paradise Lost* (Cambridge: Harvard Univ. Press; London: Routledge & Kegan Paul, 1967); Irene Samuel, "The Dialogue in Heaven: A Reconsideration of *Paradise Lost* III.1–417," *PMLA* 72 (1957), 601–11; Samuel, "Milton on the Province of Rhetoric," *Milton Studies* 10 (1977), 177–93; Elaine B. Safer, "The Use of Contraries; Milton's Adaptation of Dialectic in *Paradise Lost*," *Ariel* 2 (1981), 55–69; H. R. MacCallum, "Milton and Sacred History, Books XI–XII of *Paradise Lost*," in *Essays in English Literature from the Renaissance to the Victorian Age, Presented to A. S. P. Woodhouse*, ed. M. Maclure and F. W. Watt (Toronto: Univ. of Toronto Press, 1964), pp. 149–68; John M. Major, "Milton's View of Rhetoric," *SP* 64 (1967), 685–711; Francis Blessington, "Autotheodicy: The Father as Orator in *Paradise Lost*," *Cithera: Essays in the Judaeo-Christian Tradition* 14 (1975), 49–60.

⁹Julius-Caesar Scaliger, *Poetices libri septem*, I.3, III.25 (Geneva, 1561), pp. 5, 113; trans. F. M. Padelford, *Select Translations from Scaliger's Poetics* (New York: Holt, 1905), pp. 20, 54.

¹⁰Rosalie L. Colie, *The Resources of Kind: Genre-Theory in the Renaissance*, ed. Barbara K. Lewalski (Berkeley: Univ. of California Press, 1973), pp. 22–23.

¹¹Chapman, "The Preface to the Reader," *Homer's Iliad*, in *Chapman's Homer*, ed. Allardyce Nicoll, 2 vols. (Princeton: Princeton Univ. Press, 1967), 1:14; "To the Understander," *Achilles Shield* (1598), in *Chapman's Homer*, ed. Nicoll, 1:549.

¹²Scaliger, *Poetices*, III.25, p. 113, Padelford, p. 52.

¹³For a survey of this "biblical poetics" tradition, see Lewalski, *Milton's Brief Epic: The Genre, Meaning, and Art of Paradise Regained* (Providence: Brown Univ. Press; London: Methuen, 1966), pp. 10–36, and *Protestant Poetics and the Seventeenth-Century Religious Lyric* (Princeton: Princeton Univ. Press, 1979), pp. 31–71. Also, Joseph A. Wittreich, *Visionary Poetics: Milton's Tradition and His Legacy* (San Marino: Huntington Library, 1979), pp. 9–26.

¹⁴Aristode, *Poetics* 1459b.8–1460b.5, 1461b.26–1462b.19, trans. S. H. Butcher, *Aristotle's Theory of Poetry and Fine Art*, 4th ed. (1932, rpt. New York: Dover, 1951), pp. 90–97, 106–11; William Webbe, *A Discourse of English Poetrie* (1586), in *Elizabethan Critical Essays*, ed. G. G. Smith, 2 vols. (Oxford: Oxford Univ. Press, 1971), 1:249; Giovambattista Giraldi Cinthio, *Discorso intorno al comporre dei romanzi, delle comedie, e delle tragedie* (Venice, 1554), ed. and trans. Henry L. Snuggs, *On Romances* (Lexington: Univ. of Kentucky Press, 1968), pp. 53, 57; Jacopo Mazzoni, *Della difesa della Comedia di Dante* (Cesena, 1587–1588), cited in Bernard Weinberg, *A History of Literary Criticism of the Italian Renaissance*, 2 vols. (Chicago: Univ. of Chicago Press, 1961), 2:877–83; George Puttenham, *The Arte of English Poesie* (London, 1589), pp. 31–34; Scaliger, *Poetices*, I.2, p. 5; Padelford, pp. 16–17.

¹⁵Sidney, *The Defense of Poesie* (London, 1595), sig. E 3ᵥ.

¹⁶Torquato Tasso, *Discorso del poema eroico* (Naples, 1594); *Discourses on the Heroic Poem*, trans. Mariella Cavalchini and Irene Samuel (Oxford, 1973), p. 78. See also pp. 76–77, 191–95.

¹⁷In the Preface to Book 2, *The Reason of Church Government*, *CPW*, 1:813.

¹⁸For an impressive study of intertexuality with reference to ten major "vertical context systems" or "infracontexts," present in *Paradise Lost* but not necessarily by conscious authorial design, see Claes Schaar, *The Full-Voic'd Quire Below: Vertical Context Systems in Paradise Lost*, Lund Studies in English, 60 (Lund: C. W. K. Gleerup, 1982).

¹⁹Thomas M. Greene, *The Light in Troy: Imitation and Dismay in Renaissance Poetry* (New Haven and London: Yale Univ. Press, 1982), esp. pp. 20–27, 32–43.

²⁰For the counter-argument see Harold Bloom, *A Map of Misreading* (New York: Oxford Univ. Press, 1975).

[21]For counter-arguments, see William Kerrigan, *The Prophetic Milton* (Charlottesville: Univ. of Virginia Press, 1974); Wittreich, *Visionary Poetics;* and John Guillory, *Poetic Authority: Spenser, Milton, and Literary History* (New York: Columbia Univ. Press, 1984).

[22]For various reader-response approaches, see Stanley Fish, *Surprised by Sin: The Reader in Paradise Lost* (London: Macmillan; New York: St. Martins, 1967); Robert Crosman, *Reading Paradise Lost* (Bloomington and London: Indiana Univ. Press, 1980); Maureen Quilligan, *Milton's Spenser: The Politics of Reading* (Ithaca and London: Cornell Univ. Press, 1983).

[23]*Of Education, CPW,* 2:366–79. For the counter-argument, see Fish, *Surprised by Sin.*

Erich S. Gruen

CULTURAL FICTIONS AND CULTURAL IDENTITY

Gruen confronts the issue of multiculturalism in classical studies with the reminder that the ancient Mediterranean world was a vastly diverse society, and he urges classicists not to retreat into defensiveness but instead to consider multiculturalism "a challenge and a stimulus, an occasion to reach out to concerns that swirl about the academy." In this essay, Gruen, taking his own advice, discusses the formation of cultural identity, "the development of a cultural consciousness through experience with and by reference to other cultures." He uses two examples, ancient Jewish culture and the circumstances that led ancient Rome to adopt Troy as its ancestor, in an explicit and intentional process of self-created identity. Regarding Rome, he reaches back to the fourth-century B.C.E., when the issue of Roman origins was far from settled and the Trojan choice had not reached "canonical status." He asks: "Why did the Romans, in their own estimation, become Trojans rather than Greeks?" Gruen's recounting of the cultural choices made by Rome is a lesson in the maleability of history and cultural identity. (Ed.)

Presidential Address 1992
New Orleans, Louisiana

*C*ultural identity is a hot topic in the academy these days. The phenomenon has swept through the halls of ivy. Courses, curricula, programs, and departments have undergone wholesale transformation in recent years. The affirmation of ethnic, racial, or religious roots has translated itself into new catalogue offerings, lecture series, majors, undergraduate degrees, and graduate specializations—not to mention scholarly conferences by the score. At Berkeley, an Ethnic Studies Division encompasses separate units for African-American studies, Native American studies, Asian-American studies, and Chicano studies, each offering a raft of courses and seminars. Nor is this an instance where Berkeley is so far in the vanguard as to have lost claim to representative status. In fact, the reshaping of academic disciplines in terms of cultural identity is a nationwide development, firmly entrenched in numerous institutions and in process of implementation in many others.

Where does the Classics fit into this? Sadly, our discipline too often regards the development as a threat, girding its loins for retrenchment or resistance. And, sadder still, Classics frequently supplies a prime target for attack, labelled as the quintessential representative of elitism, the custodian of western tradition, the pillar of Eurocentrism. The current drive for multiculturalism appears in this light as the

Erich S. Gruen, "Cultural Fictions and Cultural Identity," was originally published in *Transactions of the American Philological Association* 123 (1993) 1–14 and is reprinted here by permission of the American Philological Association.

enemy, a menace to those old dead languages, that bygone civilization, that one-dimensional and stodgy academic pursuit that largely studies and is studied by aging white males of European extraction.

Certainly our discipline does not need additional enemies. At a time when tight-fisted administrators face budgetary shortfalls and receive directives to cut expenditures, Classics departments become inviting victims. Too many programs have already been reduced, amalgamated, or eliminated, too many individuals reckoned as expendable. This is hardly the time for retreat into the bunker, a rear-guard action to preserve hoary values against the presumed barbarian. Multiculturalism should, in fact, serve as a challenge and a stimulus, an occasion to reach out to concerns that swirl about the academy.

❖   ❖   ❖

The proposition that multiculturalism and the study of classical antiquity are somehow at cross-purposes strikes me as peculiar and paradoxical. Few societies have ever been more multicultural than those clustered about the Mediterranean. The worlds of the ancient Near East, Greece, and Rome encompassed a bewildering range and diversity of peoples, races, colors, languages, attitudes, conventions, and beliefs. As Dio Chrysostom observed, with reference to the population of Alexandria in the late 1st or early 2nd century C.E., the inhabitants consisted of Greeks, Italians, Syrians, Libyans, Cilicians, Ethiopians, Arabs, Bactrians, Scythians, Persians, and Indians (*Orat.* 32.40). No need to devise artificial constructs in order to meet the tests of political correctnesss or to stave off the predatory dean. Far from being a threat to the study of antiquity, multiculturalism stands at its very core. This is precisely the area that can and should excite research, writing, and instruction—without defensiveness and without romanticizing.[1] The ancient world did not constitute a melting pot, some congenial mixing bowl that blended and integrated its pieces to form the origins of western civilization. The ingredients came from east as well as west, from north as well as south. And the differences among ancient societies are at least as striking as the similarities, the confrontations at least as significant as any assimilation. A sense of cultural identity, after all, can hardly take form unless defined against or with reference to other cultures.

The treatment of cultural identity as applied to ancient societies in recent years has not always been salutary. Emphasis can be misplaced, and false or unproductive issues have taken precedence. Take, for instance, the matter of cultural theft. Who stole what from whom? A singularly pointless debate. Cultures do not become impoverished if their creations are borrowed by others. This is no zero-sum game. Interaction enriches the legacy, rather than diminishing the contributors. Or, to cite another bustling enterprise, excessive energy has been expended in searching out origins. Our understanding of the Hellenic achievement is no more enhanced by postulating an occupation of Boeotia by the Hyksos than by belief in a Dorian invasion of the Peloponnese. Speculation along these lines can rapidly degenerate into polemics, with unwelcome overtones of politics and ideology. A decision on whether or not Cleopatra was black would bring us no insight into her character or accomplishment—let alone those of contemporary blacks, whites, Greeks, of Egyptians.[2] Or consider a different line of inquiry that is quite familiar: the tracing of cultural influences from one society to another. That has long been a staple item of classical scholarship, and it can occasionally be fruitful and interesting. But it generally presupposes a rather passive recipient, thus posing a distinction between cultural benefactor and beneficiary. It also implies an unspoken privileging of one culture over another. And it ignores or suppresses what should capture attention: the dynamics of the interchange and the active transformation of a cultural inheritance into a new entity.[3]

Emphasis needs to be shifted. I want to place stress on the development of a cultural consciousness through experience with and by reference to other cultures. Antiquity supplies an especially rich repository for such an investigation. How did ancient societies come to articulate their own identities? The question presents numerous difficulties and stumbling-blocks. One topic of inquiry, however, may bring some useful results. I refer to the manipulation of myths, the reshaping of traditions, the elaboration of legends, fictions, and inventions, the recasting of ostensibly alien cultural legacies with the aim of defining or reinforcing a distinctive cultural character. Research into this subject encounters intricate and involved tales of national origins, of borrowings, kinship, and interconnections among societies, of common heritage, and of intercultural associations.

Scholarly interpretation of such stories, of course, has a long history. But it has not always taken the most promising direction. That is to say, interpreters have exercised undue ingenuity in attempting to determine the historicity of these tales, efforts that can be debated endlessly without approaching a consensus. Yet the stories are no less intriguing—indeed more so—if they are imaginative inventions. For they thereby raise the more important questions about motives for adoption and adaptation of the fables, the context in which they were framed, the attitudes they reveal toward other cultures, and the role they played in forming a people's sense of cultural distinctiveness.

The present occasion forbids a detailed exploration of this topic. But certain revealing examples can bring it into vivid focus. I want to pursue the matter on two fronts, one quite familiar to Classicists, the other rather less so. It might be noted...that neither one involves the debate about the origins of Greek civilization or the competing claims of Egyptians, Semites, and Indo-Europeans on those origins. Rather, I look first at the legends of Rome's connection with Troy, and then at some of the fascinating tales that associate the Jews with the traditions and peoples of Greece. Each represents an illuminating case of appropriation and adaptation of alien traditions, in order, on the one hand, to establish a place within a broader cultural framework and, on the other, to assert superiority within it.

First, Rome and Troy.[4] It is no secret that the legends associating the forebears of Rome with the survivors of the Trojan War were conceived by Greek writers and intellectuals. They generated what was later to become the canonical tradition on Rome's beginnings. The orthodox tale, of course, has the city derive from a settlement of Trojan refugees, remnants of a people defeated by the Achaean expedition that sacked Troy. Aeneas holds center stage in this version, leader of the Trojans who survived that calamity and who, after countless setbacks and detours, successfully reached the shores of Italy. The progeny of Aeneas eventually carried out their destiny, the founding of Rome, via the cities of Lavinium and Alba Longa. Vergil's *Aeneid* enshrines the tale, and Livy's history encapsulates it.

What is not so well known, however, is the fact that this version took quite a long time before it attained canonical status and that it had some very different and very strong competitors along the way. The earliest Hellenic explanations, in fact, had Greeks themselves, not Trojans, as the ancestors of Rome. As might be expected, the stories began to take shape in the era of Greek colonization, a process that naturally sparked Hellenic interest in the west. Greeks, in characteristic fashion, inclined to interpret the western past in light of their own national traditions. The circumstances would readily call attention to legends like the western adventures of Herakles or the settler-heroes of the *Nostoi* ["journeys home"] – most particularly, the wanderings of Odysseus.

One intriguing item appears very early in the record. The concluding lines of Hesiod's *Theogony* register the union of Odysseus and Circe, a union that produced as offspring Agrius and Latinus, future rulers over the Tyrrhenians (1011–1016). Those lines disclose early Hellenic interest in central Italy, possibly Etruria and certainly Latium, and the introduction of those lands into the Greek legendary complex. More significant, Odysseus takes the role of ultimate ancestor to the rulers of those regions. The passage appropriately exemplifies the Greek penchant for reshaping foreign experiences by imposing Hellenic lore.

A strong Greek component continued to cling to the legends of Rome's beginnings. Heracleides Ponticus, for instance, a pupil of Plato writing in the mid 4th century B.C.E., referred to Rome simply as a "Greek city" (Plut. *Cam.* 22.2). Aristotle himself endorsed a version that had Achaean, not Trojan, warriors driven by storm to Italy while trying to return home after the fall of Troy. They got no further. Their ships were burned, an act of defiance by the Trojan women brought as captives from Troy. The stranded Achaeans had to remain in Italy and took up permanent residence in a site which Aristotle called "Latinium" (D.H. 1.72.3–4). Aristotle's pupil Heracleides Lembos was more precise: the shipwrecked Achaeans settled a city on the Tiber named for the woman who had set their ships ablaze, Rhome (Festus, 329 L).

The foregoing are but a small sample of the abundant tales of Rome's origins that trace those origins to Greek founders. The phenomenon is a familiar one, a form of Hellenic cultural imperialism, a spinning out of tales in accord with Greek legends, and ascription of foreign cities to Greek colonists – a standard characteristic of the Hellenic mentality.

That ingredient had a tenacious quality. One finds it still present and, in even more vivid form, in a contemporary of Vergil and Livy, the Greek rhetorician and historian Dionysius of Halicarnassus. For Dionysius Rome was a Greek city many times over. He postulated successive waves of migrants from the east: Arcadians, Pelasgians, yet more Arcadians, then the followers of Herakles (1.31, 41–44, 60, 89). Dionysius engaged in a form of Hellenic overkill, swamping Rome with eastern settlers in order to reinforce its role as torch-bearer of Greek civilization. He even went so far as to have Romulus defend the rape of the Sabine women by assuring the victims that this constituted hallowed Hellenic practice (2.30).

The orthodox version that has Aeneas as ancestor of Rome is, in fact, a later and, initially at least, a less prevalent one. It appears among Sicilian Greek writers who propagated the tales of Trojan migrants to their island. Western Greeks, on the edges of the Hellenic world, had a special incentive to attach their own pedigrees to the great legends that grew out of the epic tradition and that had served to define a common Greek culture. And when such writers perceived Romans expanding their influence into the Greek-speaking areas of central and southern Italy in the 4th century B.C.E., they extended those tales to encompass the new emerging power. It is not surprising that the earliest extant historians to associate Aeneas with the origins of Rome are Sicilian historians (Gruen 14–16).

The traditions subsequently overlap, becoming amalgamated or blended in confusing fashion. The eponymous creation Roma or Rhome took on a number of roles in the hands of various creative writers. Some gave her solid Greek lineage as granddaughter of Herakles, or Telemachus, or Odysseus. Others made her wife of Aeneas or Ascanius, or granddaughter of Aeneas.[5] One bizarre combination of traditions has Aeneas come to Italy together with Odysseus and become founder of the city which he designated as Rome, taking the name from one of the Trojan women who set fire to the ships (D.H. 1.72.2). That version evidently patches together a variety of independent traditions: the western migration of Odysseus, the flight of Aeneas, the burning of ships after return from Troy, and the foundation story of Rome.

All of these tales derive from the Hellenic imagination. But it is the Roman response to which I seek to call attention. When Greek accounts of Rome's origins first impinged upon Roman consciousness, they came, as we have seen, in several different varieties. And many of them gave a greater role to Achaean than to Trojan heroes. Yet it was the Trojan tale that eventually prevailed, an outcome that could not have been forecast from the beginning. How does one explain it? Why did the Romans, in their own estimation, become Trojans rather than Greeks? The question goes to the heart of Rome's cultural awakening and its own sense of identity.

The canonical tale in its full blown form associated Rome most closely with two Latin towns: Lavinium and Alba Longa. As the story has it, Aeneas established a Trojan settlement at Lavinium, and, after an interval of thirty years, his son Ascanius departed to found a new city at Alba Longa. Ascanius thereby instituted the line of Alban kings who reigned for three centuries until the birth of the twins Romulus and Remus who would be the creators of Rome. The special prestige accorded to the Latin towns in this narrative supplies a vital clue.

Appropriation of the legend by Rome can reasonably be set in the late 4th century B.C.E. That period brought a convergence of political and cultural circumstances that made the Trojan connection in a Latin context particularly attractive. This was the era in which Rome defeated the forces of the Latin League and extended military and political control over the cities of Latium. It was also the era in which Rome spread its influence into Campania and entered into diplomatic relations with Greek cities like Naples. The time proved propitious for adoption of the fables that linked Rome and Latin cities to the heritage of the Hellenic past. Rome found especially welcome benefits in the legends. They lent a cultural legitimacy to its position of authority in Latium. Rome was now heir to the region's glorious past — not just its conqueror and suzerain but its cultural curator. And, equally important, the assimilation of the legends announced a connector with the Hellenic world, thereby to validate Rome's association with the Greek cities of Italy (Gruen 26–29).

This brings us back then to the central question. Why did the Romans choose to consider themselves as descendants of Trojans rather than Greeks? Were they drawn to Aeneas rather than to Odysseus because the latter had a reputation for sly shrewdness, a dubious quality, whereas the former exemplified *pietas* ["piety, duty"], the preeminent Roman virtue? An unsatisfactory solution. The Romans were not shopping for heroes in some divine supermarket, weighing respective qualities and selecting their favorite. The embrace of Troy had more subtle and more significant meaning. It enabled Rome to associate itself with the rich and complex fabric of Hellenic tradition, thus to enter that wider cultural world, just as it had entered the wider political world. But at the same time it announced Rome's distinctiveness from the dominant element in that world.[6] Rome's literate classes welcomed incorporation into the cultural legacy of Hellas — but preferred to carve out their own niche within it. They thereby sharpened a sense of their identity and laid the foundations for a national character.

Troy supplied an especially attractive ingredient in that endeavor. The celebrated Trojan past lay in remote antiquity, its people no longer extant, the city but a shell of its former self. Troy, unlike Greece, persisted as a symbol, not a current reality. So Rome ran no risk of identification with any contemporary folk whose defects would be all too evident — and all too embarrassing. The Romans could mold the ancient Trojans to suit their own ends. As in so much else, they astutely converted Hellenic traditions to meet their own political and cultural purposes. In short, the successful and enduring version that made Trojans the forebears of Rome owed its origin to Greek inventiveness, but its reformulation to Latin ingenuity. The Greeks imposed the Trojan legend upon the west as a form of Hellenic cultural imperialism, only to see it appropriated by the westerner as a means to define and convey a Roman cultural identity.

The embrace of Troy made its mark on the international scene during the next century and more. That development has led scholars to render a familiar negative verdict on Roman character. Rome, so it is asserted, exploited the Trojan legend in order to facilitate interventionism and expansionism in the Greek east (e.g., Momigliano 453). Such a verdict misplaces the emphasis and misconceives the motivation. The Romans had larger aims in view: they advertised this association to announce their credentials as legitimate participants in a broader Mediterranean civilization. To that end, for example, they installed a temple to Venus Erycina on the Capitoline in 215, a cult whose origins lay in Sicilian Eryx where, so legend had it, Aeneas had dedicated a shrine to his mother.[7] Similarly, the Romans transferred the worship of Magna Mater ["Great Mother"], protective deity of the Trojans, from her locus on Mt. Ida to her new home on the Palatine. The striking festival inaugurated for the goddess exhibited the high value that Romans placed upon public proclamation of their cultural legacy.[8] Roman commanders in the east reinforced that objective when they made a point of offering sacrifice to shrines in Ilium. The gesture was accompanied by carefully orchestrated and mutual expressions of joy delivered by Romans and Ilians at the common heritage that bound them to one another (Liv. 37.9.7, 37.1–3). Such acts had purposes other than conventional aggrandizement. Contemporary Ilium was an utterly insignificant town that could hardly supply substantive assistance to expansionism. Nor is it likely that other Greek cities would render allegiance to Rome on the basis of a Trojan connection. The symbolic connotations took precedence — and the cultural, rather than the political, meaning was central. Rome shunned the label of barbarian and struck the pose of heir and standard-bearer of an antique civilization shared by Trojans and Achaeans. The words of T. Quinctius Flamininus, victor over Philip V of Macedon and self-proclaimed liberator of Greeks, epitomized the posture. Flamininus dedicated precious objects at Delphi inscribed with his own verses in Greek, reminding the Hellenes that their liberation had come at the hands of a descendant of Aeneas (Plut. *Flam.* 12.6–7). That is a significant image. Flamininus had no military goals to achieve with this gesture; Roman martial supremacy had already been established. The conjunction of Greek freedom and Trojan ancestry delivered a different message. Flamininus not only enunciated Rome's claim to a place in the cultivated community of the Mediterranean but he declared Rome's centrality as the protector of that heritage.

The Jews approached Hellenism from an angle quite different from that of the Romans. The Romans, of course, held a political and military ascendancy. But the greater their success in those arenas, the more urgently they asserted an antique connection to that cultural world which they had, in fact, only recently entered. The Jews, on the other hand, constituted a numerical minority in the Diaspora and a subordinate state at home, dependent on the suzerainty of greater powers. Yet they too staked a claim on a shared cultural lineage with Hellenic society. And they too, like the Romans, propagated tales that both associated themselves with Greek traditions and reaffirmed their own special character.

✧ ✧ ✧

[Most] telling…are the fictions that accommodate Jewish traditions to Hellenic culture. And, as one might expect, the Jewish contribution in these stories takes central place. A noteworthy example exists in the fable composed by the Egyptian-Jewish writer Artapanus in the 3rd or 2nd century B.C.E. It depicts Moses not in the conventional mode as great lawgiver to the Israelites. Rather he appears as author of most of the religious and cultural practices of other peoples, including the introduction of animal worship to the Egyptians and of circumcision to the Ethiopians. For the Greeks, according to Artapanus, Moses was a revered figure, identified with the mythical Greek poet Mousaios, reckoned as the teacher of Orpheus, and even made equivalent to Hermes in his capacity as patron of literature and the arts (Eus. *PE* 9.8.1–2; Clement, *Strom.* 1.154.2–3). So Moses emerges here as culture hero, a source of inspiration to Hebrews, Greeks, and Egyptians alike.

The 2nd century Alexandrian Jew Aristobulus focused more pointedly upon Hellenic culture and its putative Judaic roots. He had read widely in the works of Greek authors—including some that they probably never wrote. And he repeatedly ascribed the wisdom and insights found therein to the Jewish lore that they must have been familiar with. So, Plato found the source for his *Laws* in the Pentateuch, Pythagorean philosophy was an adaptation of Hebraic doctrine, Orpheus imitated Moses in his verses on the Hieros Logos ["Holy Word"], all Greek philosophy with a monotheistic tinge derived from the Bible, and the Jewish reverence for the Sabbath found its way into the verses of Homer and Hesiod (Eus. *PE* 7.32.16–18; 13.12.1–16). Never mind that the Septuagint was not composed until the Hellenistic period. Aristobulus simply postulated some earlier unknown translation of the Pentateuch into Greek, so as to have its doctrines available to Hellenic poets and philosophers of the archaic and classical eras (Eus. *PE* 13.12.1). Once more the assimilation is not of Judaism to Hellenism, but the other way around.

The reinterpretation of authentic statements and the invention of spurious utterances affords valuable insight into the motives of Jews learned in Hellenic literature and lore. Their activity goes beyond what is conventionally termed apologetic writing. This is no mere defensive posturing by a subordinate minority in an alien world. The Jews, to be sure, were in no position to challenge the political supremacy of Hellenic powers—nor did they do so. Indeed, many of the stories reaffirm that supremacy. But by selectively appropriating Hellenic culture, they redefined it in their own image, thus not only asserting their place in the larger community but articulating their cultural identity in terms intelligible to that community.

On this broad level, therefore, Romans and Jews each gave their own spin to Hellenism. The cultivated elite among both peoples welcomed Hellenic traditions but reshaped them to sharpen their own identity and declare their own primacy. Two final illustrations can underscore the point.

First, from the Roman side. When that crusty old conservative, Cato the Elder, visited Athens, he came as a Roman officer in the campaign against Antiochus III. He delivered an address to the Athenian assembly, a brief and pointed speech in Latin, knowing full well that no one in the audience could understand a word of it. He then had a subordinate deliver a translation of that speech in Greek. The Greek version took twice as long to say the same thing. Cato thus exhibited the inferiority of Hellenic rhetoric to the forceful brevity of the Latin language. But he did more than that. He let it be known that he could have delivered the speech in Greek, had he wished to do so (Plut. *Cato* 12.4–5). Whatever the truth of that claim, it emphasized that the Romans held the upper hand. Unlike his monolingual audience, so Cato implied, Romans had mastered both tongues, had the option of employing either, and chose the superior one. Rome's cultural confidence matched its military might.

Now, a final Jewish illustration, a quite irresistible one. As the story has it, a Ptolemaic army conducting a march to the Red Sea included a number of Jewish soldiers. Among them was a certain Jewish archer named Mosollamus. In the course of the march, the whole company halted because a bird was spotted overhead. The Greek seer who accompanied the army wished to observe its movements so as to be able to forecast what was in store. He proceeded to explain the rules that governed his divination: if the bird stays still, the army ought to wait; if it flies forward, the forces should advance; if it flies backward, the troops better retreat. When Mosollamus, the Jewish archer, heard this, he drew his bow and shot the bird dead. Of course, the Greeks were horrified, turned on Mosollamus with fury, and demanded an explanation. "Look," he said, "if this bird was so smart and could predict the future, how come he didn't know I was going to shoot him?" (Jos. *Ap.* 1.201–204). The setting of the story is authentic enough. Jewish soldiers served in the army of the superior power, the Ptolemaic rulers of Egypt, as participants in the larger Hellenistic enterprise. But the point of the tale, of course, lies elsewhere. The hard-headed, pragmatic Jew, like Cato the Elder, has gained familiarity with Greek practices — only to mock their fatuous superstition. The Jews have the upper hand not only in spirituality but even in street-smarts.

These diverse and miscellaneous examples share a common theme. In the heterogeneous society of the Hellenistic world, peoples strove to articulate their special qualities with reference to the dominant culture, but without succumbing to it. Indeed, it was precisely the ability to accommodate to that culture that supplied the tools whereby to express a distinct identity.

There is a lesson here for multicultural studies that hardly needs to be spelled out. A secure sense of one's own cultural identity depends upon engaging seriously with other cultures, gaining close familiarity with them, and perhaps even exploiting them to one's own advantage. The ancients did so all the time — or whenever they could. Ancient societies defined themselves by reference to "the other," but did so most effectively by expropriating "the other." That subject can stimulate some exciting research. And it will also play in the classroom — an extra dividend. Multiculturalism, in short, far from being a menace to the study of antiquity, is integral to it. This is not the periphery of our discipline but stands at the very heart of it. And it offers us as compelling a case as we can make, to administrators and to ourselves, for the enduring importance and the richness of our field.

Notes

[1] The wise words of Molly Myerowitz Levine, "Multiculturalism and the Classics," *Arethusa* 25 (1992) 215–220, deserve attention.

[2] Reference, of course, is to the heated debate still raging over Martin Bernal's ambitious, admirably learned, occasionally brilliant, and productively provocative *Black Athena*, a projected multi-volume work, of which two have appeared: *Black Athena: The Afroasiatic Roots of Classical Civilization*, vol. 1: *The Fabrication of Ancient Greece, 1785–1985* (New Brunswick 1987); vol. 2: *The Archaeological and Documentary Evidence* (New Brunswick 1991). Numerous discussions and disputes have found their way into print, with Bernal frequently offering rebuttal. See, especially, *The Challenge of 'Black Athena,'* special issue, *Arethusa* (1989), ed. by M. M. Levine and J. Peradotto; and a range of articles in *Journal of Mediterranean Archaeology* 3 (1990). Note also the trenchant remarks of Edith Hall, "When is a Myth not a Myth? Bernal's 'Ancient Model'," *Arethusa* 25 (1992) 181–201, with Bernal's response, 203–214. A valuable bibliography on the controversy may be found in M. M. Levine, "The Use and Abuse of Black Athena," *AHR* 97 (1992) 440–460.

[3] Cf. the salutary comments of H. van Staden, "Affinities and Elisions: Helen and Hellenocentrism," *Isis* 83 (1992) 578–595.

[4] For what follows, see the much fuller treatment in E. S. Gruen, *Culture and National Identity in Republican Rome* (Ithaca 1992) 6–51.

[5] Plut. *Rom.* 2.1–3; D. H. 1.72.6; Festus, 326, 328L; Servius, ad *Aen.* 1.273.

[6] Cf. A. Momigliano, *Settimo contributo alla storia degli studi classici e del mondo antico* (Rome 1984) 109, 447, 459.

[7] Liv. 22.9.7–10, 10.10; 23.30.13–14, 31.9.

[8] Sources and discussion in Gruen, *Studies in Greek Culture and Roman Policy* (Leiden 1990) 5–33.

✧ ✧ ✧

Meyer Reinhold

THE AMERICANIZATION OF VERGIL, FROM COLONIAL TIMES TO 1882

The founders of the United States, who were steeped in classical learning, saw many analogies between their experience and that of the ancients, especially the Romans. Reinhold introduces us to what could seem a paradox, however. The reception of Vergil's *Aeneid* in the colonial and early Republican period was not for the most part positive. Indeed, what Reinhold recounts is the "intensity of the rejection of him," despite what seems to us "such potentially transferable themes as the birth of a new nation in a new land, the wanderings of a divinely guided people led by a man of destiny, and the struggle between the Trojan pilgrims and the native Italic peoples." Instead, the early settlers identified with the apparently simple or agrarian tales in Vergil's *Eclogues* and *Georgics*, their "idyllic landscapes and fantasies,"and "rural values and moral exaltation of agriculture." The changing uses of Vergil's works, in the United States and elsewhere, focuses a valuable lens on the meaning of his works and the cultural and historical understandings of their readers. (Ed.)

When I was sixteen, I had my first love affair—with a book. It was Vergil's *Aeneid*—and I haven't been the same since. But I wasn't as precocious as Tennyson, who said in his famous tribute to Vergil, "I that loved thee since my days began." It was not love at first sight with me. I worked hard at it, a labor without love at first, learning the poetic forms and usages, the new vocabulary, the dactylic hexameter, using a text that was edited by a man who was later to be my beloved teacher in graduate school at Columbia University, Charles Knapp. But one day something happened to me, suddenly, unexpectedly, in a sort of blazing light of understanding. I can remember the classroom, and where I sat, and the teacher, blond, chubby Miss Ethel Lacey. In a sudden revelation I seemed to experience total, immediate communion with Rome's greatest poet.

I tell you this personal confession about my lifelong love affair with Vergil because had I been a student of Latin in America from 1635 (when the Boston Latin School was founded) to about 1900, my affection for Vergil's poetry would assuredly have not come about. For over 250 years Vergil's works were, in unbroken continuity, read, studied, agonized over by generations of American youths who went through the academic curriculum in the colonial and early national grammar schools, academies, high schools, and colleges. From the beginning of American liberal education the *Aeneid* was required as preparation for all college-bound students. Ability to translate and parse Vergil was written into the entrance requirements of Harvard, Yale and other colonial colleges, and then of the numerous colleges that sprang up

---

Meyer Reinhold, "The Americanization of Aeneas, from Colonial Times to 1882," *Augustan Age* 6 (1987) 207–18. Reprinted by permission of Meyer Reinhold.

like mushrooms in the first century of the national period. Accordingly, all college preparatory schools (and in many cases private tutors in New England and the southern plantation mansions) included the *Aeneid* in their curriculum of studies. In the college curricula of the seventeenth, eighteenth, and nineteenth centuries Vergil continued to be required study: college students read the *Eclogues* and the *Georgics*.[1]

I must tell you that out of this year after year exposure to Vergil American teenagers and youths harbored memories of Vergil that were quite distasteful for the rest of their lives. How could this have happened so consistently to one of the world's greatest poets? Well, the text of the *Aeneid* unfortunately as taught and studied in the earlier secondary schools and even the later academic high schools well into the beginning of the twentieth century, served the function of a classroom cadaver for academic vivisection and autopsy by teacher and students. It was used for drilling grammar, for construing and parsing Latin, for scansion of the verses in the dactylic hexameter. Day after day, the students prepared a fixed number of lines, and in the classroom recitation read a few lines for the teacher metrically, gave the case or mood and reason for the grammar of every word, the principal parts of every verb, and received a recitation grade. It was a formal exercise in memory, grammar, forms, rules, and discipline, but assuredly not an aesthetic experience or guidance to the radiant beauty and the profound thought of Vergil. It is safe to say that the teachers themselves, with rare exceptions, even most college teachers, did not understand the magic of Vergil or his insights. They were drill masters.

❖ ❖ ❖

To add to this woe, the textbooks employed in teaching Vergil's works were not conducive to the development of understanding and appreciation of Vergil as literary artist and philosopher-poet. Decade after decade school texts of Vergil were far beyond the capacity of young boys, even of young men. For many decades the Delphin edition in a popular text by Charles de la Rue, S.J. (Ruaeus) held the field. All the notes, even the Preface, were in Latin. At the other extreme were texts that were so simplified and provided the students with so many crutches that they effectively destroyed initiative and challenge in the students. The popular Vergil by the English classicist Davidson (there were numerous editions in America) gave first the Latin text, then on the same page the Latin in the order of the sense, and also on the very same page a literal prose translation, with very brief notes.

This is not to say that outside the drudgery of the schools and colleges Vergil's works were not appreciated. Many Americans indeed read Vergil, but they were likely to use Dryden's translation of the *Aeneid*, a version that is more English Dryden than Roman Vergil. It might interest you to know that it was not until the beginning of the twentieth century that an America translation of the *Aeneid* was composed. Yet creative energies on the *Aeneid* were expended not on efforts to provide enlightenment on and appreciation of Vergil's works, but on comic imitations—on travesties and parodies. The most notorious of these was a travesty of Book IV of the *Aeneid* by one Rowland Rugely in 1774.

Here is how it begins:

Aeneas finish'd here his ditty
Of old King Priam and his city:

The Trojans at a tale so deep,
And wondrous roving, fell—asleep
But not the Queen...

At the end of the book, when Dido commits suicide, after Aeneas abandons love for
duty, Juno sends down Iris to liberate her tragic soul by cutting off a lock of her hair.
Here is the indignity Dido suffers at Rugely's hands:

"And thus I set at liberty
Your restless headstrong soul—die."
This said—she gave a lusty pluck at
The lock, and Dido kick'd the bucket.[2]

If you compare the dominant place Vergil had in the hearts of most educated Europeans ever since his untimely death in 19 B.C.E, you will appreciate the intensity of
the rejection of him by Americans. It is also true, by the way, that in Latin America
in this period, translations, imitations, echoes of Vergil abound in the literature and
scholarship of Mexico, Guatemala, Cuba, Venezuela, Chile, Argentina.[3] Not so in
our country.

The absence of such influences and acceptance of the *Aeneid* among Americans
is especially curious because the Roman epic might have provided them with such
potentially transferable themes as the birth of a new nation in a new land, the wanderings of a divinely guided people led by a man of destiny, and the struggle between
the Trojan pilgrims and the native Italic peoples—these did not, in general, leave
their mark on American thought and literature. Compare, for example, ... the splendid opera with libretto and music by Hector Berlioz, *Les Troyens* ["*The Trojans*"], that
was such a triumph in the middle of the nineteenth-century, and, long before, Henry
Purcell's exquisite *Dido and Aeneas.*

I might tell you that some early American painters were inspired by the *Aeneid*
with its abundance of pictorial imagery (a recent critic called it "painterly"). For
example, Washington Allston, about 1800–1850, painted some scenes from the *Aeneid*,
the most noteworthy of which are "Aeneas and Achates Come Ashore," and "Dido
and Anna," the latter depicting familial love as more durable than the passionate
love of Dido for Aeneas. About 1820 Joshua Shaw did the gorgeous scene of "Dido
and Aeneas Departing for the Hunt." Later William Page, ca. 1860, painted "Venus
Guiding Aeneas and the Trojans," with emphasis on the beauty and perfection of
Venus rather than on the mission of Aeneas.[4]

But, by and large, the epic themes and the grandeur of the *Aeneid* were not in
tune with American life and thought. There is no doubt, however, that the agrarian
and pastoral models provided by the *Eclogues* and *Georgics* were. Many aspects of
American life in colonial and early national times attracted Americans to the idyllic
landscapes and fantasies of the *Eclogues* and the rural values and moral exaltation
of agriculture in the *Georgics*. Especially appealing were the universal messages of
the *Eclogues*, *omnia vincit Amor*, "Love conquers all," and of the Georgics, *omnia vicit
labor*, "Work conquered all." In this connection the appeal to Americans of Horace's
"Sabine Farm" ideal was very strong; and among the classical models, culled from
antiquity for imitation, was the Roman idealization of the virtuous
farmer-citizen-soldier, and the role model of Cincinnatus. And there were many
early American Cincinnatuses: Washington, Jefferson, John Adams, John Jay. There

was the message of the work ethic and the rewards of labor in the *Georgics*; and the ideal of a rural retreat (like Monticello) as refuge from the city, with its dual perils of immoral temptations and physical dangers, was widespread among Americans from New England to the Southern plantation aristocracy. This vision remained as a strong pastoral theme in our literature until the industrial revolution, and for this Vergil's *Eclogues* was the authentic fountainhead. This is why, though the *Aeneid* remained virtually untried by American translators, versions and imitations of the *Eclogues* and *Georgics* were quite frequent.[5]

The influence of the *Georgics* is to be found, e.g., in the first American novel about life in rural New England. It is a work by Royall Tyler, *The Algerine Captive*, published in 1797. The hero is a youth named Updike Underhill, son of a struggling farmer. He was sent to school to prepare for college, and for years studied only Greek and Latin. Because of family difficulties Updike was called back to the farm to pitch in and help the home folks. Here he proceeded to give Greek names to all the farming implements, and to recite hexameter verses, like Orpheus, to the cattle to soothe them and increase the yield of milk. The only book he ever took with him to the fields was a copy of Vergil. One day, after rereading the end of the *Georgics* he tried to apply the practical knowledge he had acquired from that didactic poem: he killed a cow, and, to add to the family income, tried to raise out of it a swarm of bees, after the manner of Vergil. But, of course, it failed, and Updike was sent back from the farm to school, where he would do less damage to the family.[6]

Still, the positive influences of Vergil on early Americana should not be understated. For example, the famous New England Puritan Cotton Mather in his *Magnalia Christi Americana* ["The Great American Achievements of Christ"] begins his account of the epic dimensions of the achievements of the Puritan Founding Fathers by an analogy to the *Aeneid*: "I write the wonder of the Christian religion, flying from the Depravations of Europe to the American Strand." His readers would recognize the opening of the *Aeneid*: *Arma virumque cano, Troiae qui primus ab oris* ["I sing of arms and a man, who was the first from the shores of Troy..."]. In his tribute to his great teacher at the Boston Latin School, the venerable Ezekiel Cheever, Mather wrote, "Our Master...us from Virgil did to David train."[7]...Thomas Jefferson and John Adams, the best classical scholars of their time, had but a superficial understanding of Vergil. In a famous lament on the intrusion of practical politics into his "supreme delights," —i.e., the pursuit of knowledge, in which the "classic pages" were for him "a rich source of delight," Jefferson, when he was Secretary of State wrote: "But as we advance in life...things fall off one by one, and I suspect that we are left with Homer and Virgil, perhaps with Homer alone."[8] But in his voluminous letters, essays, and speeches there are many references to Homer but hardly any evidence of his great love of Vergil.

John Adams' interest in Vergil lasted all his life, and this was quite varied and vocal. Once he wrote to himself (in a still unpublished notebook among the Adams Papers in the Massachusetts Historical Society Library): The "*Aeneid* is like a well-ordered Garden, where it is impossible to find any Part unadorned, or to cast our Eyes upon a single Spot that does not produce some beautiful Plant or Flower." With his own love of country life, Adams commented: "In his *Georgics* he has given us a Collection of the most delightful Landskips that can be made out of Field and Woods, Herds of Cattle, and Swarms of Bees." And he recognized that poetic genius has been exhibited "in a surprising degree by Milton, and Shakespeare, Homer and Virgil."[9]

For the Revolutionary generation political science was in the forefront, and the cult of antiquity was at its height in the "Golden Age" of classical learning in America. Thus the Founding Fathers ransacked the Roman and Greek classics for republican models and classical virtues, and in a modest way Vergil has made a lasting contribution to our national image. It was at this time that the Great Seal of the United States was created, with mottoes taken from Vergil. One of the consultants of the committee that drew up the design was Charles Thomson, Secretary of Congress. He had been a teacher of Latin in Philadelphia, and was later eulogized by Ashbel Green, President of Princeton College, as "one of the best classical scholars our country has ever produced." The seal, now on the obverse of our dollar bill, contains three Vergilian phrases: *annuit coeptis* ["he approved the undertakings"] (from the *Aeneid* and *Georgics*); *novus ordo seclorum* ["a new order of the ages"] (adapted from the Fourth Eclogue); and *e pluribus unum* ["from many, one"] (adapted from the minor poem *Moretum* attributed to Vergil). These mottoes, embodying as they did a statement of the classical heritage and humanistic origins of the first modern republic, would have been understood only by educated Americans of the time. Today it would have meaning to very few educated Americans.

❖ ❖ ❖

The prevailing hostility to and dismissal of Vergil was, however, the dominant judgement. Rejection of him was caused, in part, by deeply felt reservations on religious, moral, and political grounds. For example, in the seventeenth century Robert Calef of Boston condemned "the pernicious works of pagan learning in Virgil, Ovid, and Homer," and he defended his own religious and social views with, "If I err, I may be shown it from Scriptures or sound reasoning, and not by quotations from out of Virgil."[10] In 1769 a teacher at the Friends Latin School in Philadelphia, one John Wilson, fired by moral and religious objections to the classical curriculum, resigned from his position, and wrote in a letter to the Overseers of the school that instruction in classical authors was "the grossest absurdity that ever was practiced. It has contributed more to promote Ignorance, Lewdness & Profanity, in our Youth than anything I know...Will the Lasciviousness of Ovid teach them Chastity? the Epicurean Horace Sobriety?...the impudent Juvenal Modesty? the atheistick Lucretius Devotion? & tho' Virgil commonly is excepted from this guilty line yet his representing the Ungrateful Lustful Perfidious Aeneas as the particular Friend and Favorite of Heaven are shocking to every System of Morality."[11] Strong words, indeed! But similar objections to the pagan writers, including Vergil, erupted time and time again.

In another sector of the population American pragmatists in their quest for useful knowledge recommended a cautious attitude toward the study of the classics. In New York, for example, the brilliant William Livingston (later the Governor of New Jersey) wrote in 1768: "We want hands...more than heads. The most intimate acquaintance with the classics will not move our oaks nor a taste for the *Georgics* cultivate our lands."[12]

But the most sustained challenge to the reputation of Vergil in America came in the early national period, when rising American nationalism spurred a vigorous debate on the classics. There arose a clamor for the immediate creation of a native literature, and manifestoes were issued that depreciated the great literary models of antiquity, and denounced slavish imitation of them as absolute standards in literature, indeed as slavish chains upon creative originality in America. In 1772 Timothy Dwight (later President of Yale) early in his career repudiated the conventional view that "Homer and Virgil...were sent into the world to give Laws to all other authors." In 1785 he published his huge Biblical epic, *The Conquest of Canaan*. This poem, about 10,000 lines, on the Biblical hero Joshua, was the first American epic. With it Dwight sought to replace Homer's *Iliad* among Americans. Similarly, in 1807 Joel Barlow's American epic *The Columbiad* was composed to supersede the *Aeneid*. Barlow's epic was intended deliberately to serve as an important contribution to an original national literature. In his Preface he unleashed a vigorous assault on both Homer and Vergil. The classical authors, Barlow asserted, served to inculcate glorification of war, support for the divine right of kings; and they promoted military booty, violence, and false notions of honor. "The moral tendency of the *Aeneid* of Virgil is nearly as pernicious as the *Iliad* of Homer." "Virgil," he concluded, "wrote and felt like a subject, not like a citizen. The real design of his poem was to encourage, like Homer, the great system of military depredation." Yet Barlow clung to a Vergilian echo: "I sing of the mariner who first unfurled / An eastern banner o'er the western world." Do I have to tell you that Dwight's epic is virtually unknown today? I can tell you that Joel Barlow's work remains one of the most dismal failures in the history of American poetry.[13]

❖ ❖ ❖

In the 1830s, in the face of waning influence of classical symbols and thought in America, the militant South Carolinian minister, the brilliant anti-classicist Thomas Smith Grimke (beloved brother of abolitionists Sarah and Angelina Grimke), moved by religious and patriotic fervor, dismissed Vergil (and Homer, as well) for not providing useful knowledge of proper edification for Americans. "As for their morals, who would be willing to have a son, or brother, like...the mean and treacherous Aeneas, the hero of the *Aeneid*, if indeed it has a hero." Grimke condemned Aeneas not only for meanness but for ingratitude and perfidy toward Dido, and, above all, for killing Turnus. "The beauties of Shakespeare are worth all the beauties of Homer and Virgil." Instead of the classical epics of Homer and Vergil, Americans should read *Paradise Lost* and *Paradise Regained* of Milton. "I do not doubt that *Paradise Lost* is worth the *Iliad*, *Odyssey*, and the *Aeneid* all together; there is more sublime and rich and beautiful descriptive poetry even in Childe Harold than half a dozen *Georgics*." Indeed, in a Phi Beta Kappa address he gave at Yale in 1830 he proclaimed: "I would rather read that great impeccable and glorious poem *Gertrude of Wyoming* than the Fourth Book of the *Aeneid*."[14] Now this poem, you should know, was not an American work at all, but by Thomas Campbell, a Scot who had never set foot in America, but was a sympathizer of the American Revolution. The poem is a long romanticized narrative, in Spenserian stanzas, of the Wyoming Valley massacre in 1778 in western Pennsylvania in the Susquehanna River country, based on events involving American patriots battling Loyalists and Indians, with resultant brutalities on both sides. The poem created quite a sensation in America—it was even edited for publication on this side of the Atlantic by Washington Irving. The poem opens with the bland line: "On Susquehanna's side, fair Wyoming." Campbell had an admiring biographer, whose judgement on this poem was that it is "a third-rate poem containing a few first-rate lines."[15]

But the stock of Vergil was far different in the Adams family. John Adams' love of Vergil remained a legacy, as it were, for generations. When John Quincy Adams was a student he translated all of the *Eclogues* into his notebooks, and commented, "What a difference between this study and that of a dry, barren, Greek Grammar." In 1808 he wrote of the *Georgics* that the poem was "the most perfect composition that ever issued from the mind of man," and he praised its "transcendent excellence." Some passages in the *Georgics*, he wrote, "have been the special delight of twenty centuries..., and will enchant the ear of harmony and transfix the soul of fancy as long as taste and sentiment shall last among mankind." John Quincy Adams had six bronze busts in his study in Quincy, which he called his "Household Gods." One of these was Vergil.[16]

It is from the Adams family that we get the most extensive appreciation of Vergil in America during the nineteenth-century. It is to be found in the diary of John Adams' grandson, Charles Francis Adams. After studying Vergil as a student with daily lessons, he decided in 1832 to read all of Vergil's works systematically, in Latin, of course. About the *Eclogues* he commented that "they are fine specimens of the highest polish of which verse is susceptible." The *Georgics*, which he read through in less than a week, he praised as [a] "model of that species of composition, a sign of which is that all subsequent times have only imitated them." In five weeks he read through the entire *Aeneid*. About Vergil's epic he wrote, "It is a very great mistake committed to make boys or men to read Virgil first and Homer afterward." He never deviated from his disapproval of Aeneas' conduct in Book IV. "The pious Aeneas is little better than a rascal for the desertion of Dido after seducing her." Taken as a whole, however, he wrote about the *Aeneid* that it "is an honour to the human intellect for imagination, for perfect harmony, for beauty, and there is moral in it, so far at least as the Ancients allowed themselves to have moral."[17]

❖ ❖ ❖

As for American women, most of them got no education at all. But if the family could afford it, some were exposed to "female education," and rarely had the opportunity to read, or have any knowledge of Vergil, except in translation by Dryden. We surely would have had vigorous reaction to the Aeneas-Dido affair. There were exceptions. Aaron Burr's brilliant daughter Theodosia Burr was one. And Margaret Fuller, that great nineteenth-century American feminist, in the early part of the century received a full rigorous "masculine education." An only child, and a very precocious one, she was given by her father a liberal education. At the age of seven, she was already reading Vergil, Horace, and Ovid in Latin, and at the age of ten had reached Book V of Vergil's *Aeneid*. In a letter to her father, who supervised every step of her education, she wrote "In my last lesson I got the whole of the Fourth Book."[18] This at a time when study of the classics by women was considered "unsexual," detrimental to their chances of finding a proper husband, and, in any case, not compatible with their role in society and the perceived limited intellectual capacities of women. It was not until decades later, with the founding of Oberlin College and a number of women's colleges, especially Smith, Wellesley, and Vassar, that women began to study Vergil "like men."

About the middle of the nineteenth-century Henry Thoreau found Vergil a leading inspiration in his thought, for descriptions of nature, for man's closeness to the soil, the idyllic pastoral life, and even the concept of a golden age. He found in the *Eclogues*, in particular, confirmation of the eternal sameness of human beings. "I would read Vergil," he wrote, "if only that I might be reminded of the identity of human nature in all ages...It was the same world, and the same men inhabited it."[19]

But, by the last decades of the nineteenth-century classical learning had ceased to perform its age-old function of humanistic education, of providing moral, political, aesthetic models. Classical scholars took over the field. Indeed, the first scholarly studies on Vergil's poetic works were published just about the time in the nineteenth-century when the nineteenth centenary of Vergil's death came 'round, in the early 1880s. But nowhere in America was notice taken to commemorate the passing of Rome's greatest poet, the man whom Paul Claudel, Nobel prize winner, called "the greatest genius who ever lived." How different it was in 1930, the 2000th anniversary of the birth of Vergil — how well I remember the events of that year! And how different it was at the bimillennial commemoration in 1981 of his death. But in 1881 no American classical scholar, no teacher of the classics, no American poet was moved to remember Vergil, as Tennyson did that year in England in his stately ode "To Roman Virgil," "Wielder of the stateliest measure ever moulded by the lips of man."

Today, as the result of the numerous and enlightening contributions of the last hundred years by American scholars and teachers, there exists an invitation to many of our youth to understand Vergil profoundly and to "fall in love" with his poetry. I have had many students who, whether in a Latin course, or in the reading of all of the *Aeneid* in a course in the classics in translation, had a better understanding in a short time than most Americans who for centuries were compelled to construe and parse Vergil. What a waste! The splendid textbooks now available, our many superb teachers in our secondary schools and our colleges and universities, have opened up for students the opportunity to appreciate not only the beauty and virtuosity of Vergil's poetry, but his tenderness and compassion for the human condition. Yes, there is violence, cruelty, and man's inhumanity to man, and the horrors of war in the *Aeneid*, but it is also "the epic of grief." We now understand that in Vergil's poetry there is overwhelming pity for human suffering (*sunt lacrimae rerum* ["the tears of the world"] can embrace *sunt lacrimae Romae* ["the tears of Rome"]), and even profound doubts about his beloved Rome's imperial policies (*parcere subjectis et debellare superbos* ["spare those brought low and war down the proud"] betrays Rome's arrogance and her demand that her *majestas*, i.e., "greaterness," be everywhere acknowledged). There is in Vergil pity for the deaths especially of young people, and grave doubts about the price of progress as the Romans understood it. (After all, the *pax Romana* ["the Roman peace"] was based on military might, with Rome as the policeman of the world, and Augustus as *princeps pacis* ["prince of peace"] was one of the adroitly fashioned myths of the propaganda of Augustus' public relations staff). As Bowra has put it, "The poem of imperial Rome closes not with a patriotic paean or a hope of high national achievements but with the sadness of a young man's death." And Letters puts it beautifully: "Thus the *Aeneid* that opened with a cry of trumpets, dies away with a sigh."[20] It is, I believe, Vergil's agonized doubts about the realities of Rome's imperial policies that motivated his death-bed request that the manuscript of the *Aeneid* be burned.

If there is one grand positive theme that one might take away from the study of the *Aeneid*, despite the doubts and ambivalence of Vergil, it is the advice that an old man, Aeneas' father Anchises, gives him in his journey of "errors" to warn him agains backsliding: *perge modo*, "keep going!"

Notes

[1]Pauline Holmes, *A Tercentenary History of the Boston Latin School 1635–1935* (Cambridge: Harvard University Press, 1935) 256–60, 264, 287, 330–31; Frederick Rudolph, *Curriculum: A*

History of the American Undergraduate Course of Study Since 1636 (San Francisco: Jossey-Bass, 1977) 29–39; Meyer Reinhold, *The Classick Pages: Classical Reading of Eighteenth-Century Americans* (University Park: Pennsylvania State University Press, 1975) 5–6; Idem, *Classica Americana: The Greek and Roman Heritage in the United States* (Detroit: Wayne State University Press, 1984) 25–28.

❖ ❖ ❖

[2]*The Story of Aeneas and Dido Burlesqued* (Charleston, 1774).

[3]Tom B. Jones, "Classics in Colonial Hispanic America," *TAPhA* 70 (1939), 37–45; A. G. Rostropo, "*Virgilio en la America Latina,*" *Colombo* 22 (1930) 1–5.

[4]I am indebted here to the paper of Robert M. Wilhelm on "Vergilian Themes in American Painting: Hesperia in America," given at the panel on "The Classical Tradition in the Arts of America" at the annual meeting of the American Philological Association in Washington, D.C., December, 1985.

[5]Douglass G. Adair, "The Intellectual Origins of Jeffersonian Democracy: Republicanism, the Class Struggle, and the Virtuous Farmer" (Diss., Yale University, 1943) i–ii, 27–30, 69–95, 272–295; Leo Marx, *The Machine in the Garden and the Pastoral Ideal in America* (New York: Oxford University Press, 1969) 3; Lewis P. Simpson, *The Dispossessed Garden: Pastoral History in Southern Literature* (Athens: University of Georgia Press, 1975) 1–3; Clarence Gohden, "Old Virginia *Georgics,*" *Southern Literary Journal* 11 (1978) 44–53.

[6]*The Algerine Captive*, ed. Joseph B. Moore (Gainesville: Scholars Facsimiles and Reprints, 1967) 41–42.

[7]Cotton Mather, *Magnalia Christi Americana*, Books I & II, ed. Kenneth B. Murdock (Cambridge, Ma.: Harvard University Press, 1977), 45, 89–90, 107, 200; Idem, *Corderius Americanus* (Boston: Borne, 1708) 31; Leo M. Kaiser, "On the Latin Verse Passages in Cotton Mather's *Magnalia Christi Americana,*" *Early American Literature* 10 (1976–1977) 301–306.

❖ ❖ ❖

[8]*Writings of Thomas Jefferson* (Washington, D.C.: Memorial Edition, 1905) Vol. 18, 448.

[9]Manuscript at the Massachusetts Historical Society Library, Adams Family Papers, Microfilm Reel 187, 31–38; *Diary and Autobiography of John Adams*, ed. L. H. Butterfield (Cambridge, Ma.: Harvard University Press, 1962) Vol. I, 37–38, 41; *The Earliest Diary of John Adams* (Cambridge, Ma.: Harvard University Press, 1965) 68, 72–73, 76.

❖ ❖ ❖

[10]Richard M. Gummere, *Seven Wise Men of Colonial America* (Cambridge, Ma.: Harvard University Press, 1967) 23.

[11]James Mulhern, *A History of Secondary Education in Pennsylvania* (Philadelphia: University of Pennsylvania Press, 1933) 43–44, 122.

[12]*A Letter to the Right Reverend in God, John, Bishop of Landaff* (New York, 1768) 23–24.

[13]Timothy Dwight, *A Dissertation on the Harmony, Eloquence, and Poetry of the Bible* (New Haven: Green, 1772); Joel Barlow, *The Columbiad*, 2 Vols. (Philadelphia: Conrad, Lucas, 1809) Vol. I, v–vii; Vol. II, 184–195.

❖ ❖ ❖

[14]Thomas Smith Grimke, *Oration on American Education* (Cincinnati: Drake, 1835) 16–17, 39; *Oration...before the Connecticut Alpha of the Phi Beta Kappa Society...Sept. 17, 1830* (New Haven: Howe, 1831).

[15]H. C. Hadden, *Thomas Campbell* (Edinburgh: Oliphant, Anderson, and Ferrier, 1899) 97.

[16]John Quincy Adams, in Port Folio 3 (1803) 43–44, 50–51, 58–59, 66–68; Linda K. Kerber and Walter J. Morris, "Politics and Literature: The Adams Family and the Port Folio," *William and Mary Quarterly* 23 (1966) 455–456.

[17]*Diary of Charles Francis Adams*, ed. Aida di Pace Donald and David Donald (Cambridge, Ma.: Harvard University Press, 1964–1968) Vol. 1, 4–7; Vol. 3, vii; Vol. 4, 114, 247–79; Vol. 5, 147–150, 174, 213, 250.

[18]Meyer Reinhold, "Margaret Fuller and Classical Learning," *Annual Bulletin of the Classical Association of New England* 81 (1986) 21–22.

[19]Ethel Seybold, *Thoreau: The Quest and the Classics* (New Haven: Yale University Press, 1951) 16, 29, 37, 55, 121–123.

[20]C. M. Bowra, *From Vergil to Milton* (London: Macmillan, 1945) 47; F. J. H. Letters, *Vergil* (New York: Sheed & Ward, 1946) 156.

TO MAECENAS

It is a telling commentary that the story of the classical tradition in the United States among slaves and African-Americans is little known. Phillis Wheatley was a west African brought to Boston as a child in 1761 through the slave trade. Bought by the Wheatley family and tutored by the family's daughter, she seems to have received as good an education, including Latin, as any women had at the time. She began writing poetry early and was known widely, in the United States and England, although some people disbelieved that a slave girl could evidence such learning. Her poem, "To Maecenas," is suffused with classical references, naming Homer, Vergil and Terence, the north African playwright of ancient Latin comedies. Maecenas was the great friend of Augustus and patron to the literary circle of which Vergil was a member. (Ed.)

TO MAECENAS

MAECENAS, you beneath the myrtle shade,
Read o'er what poets sung, and shepherds play'd.
What felt those poets but you feel the same?
Does not your soul possess the sacred flame?
Their noble strains your equal genius shares
In softer language, and diviner airs.

    While *Homer* paints lo! circumfus'd in air,
Celestial Gods in mortal forms appear;
Swift as they move hear each recess rebound,
Heav'n quakes, earth trembles, and the shores resound.
Great Sire of verse, before my mortal eyes,
The lightnings blaze across the vaulted skies,
And, as the thunder shakes the heav'nly plains,
A deep-felt horror thrills through all my veins.
When gentler strains demand thy graceful song,
The length'ning line moves languishing along.
When great *Patroclus* courts *Achilles'* aid,
The grateful tribute of my tears is paid;
Prone on the shore he feels the pangs of love,
And stern *Pelides* tend'rest passions move.

From THE POEMS OF PHILLIS WHEATLEY edited by Julian D. Mason, Jr. Copyright © 1966, 1989 by the University of North Carolina Press. Used by permission of the publisher.

Great *Maro's* strain in heav'nly numbers flows,
The *Nine* inspire, and all the bosom glows.
O could I rival shine and *Virgil's* page,
Or claim the *Muses* with the *Mantuan* Sage;
Soon the same beauties should my mind adorn,
And the same ardors in my soul should burn:
Then should my song in bolder notes arise,
And all my numbers pleasingly surprize;
But here I sit, and mourn a grov'ling mind,
That fain would mount, and ride upon the wind.

Not you, my friend, these plaintive strains become,
Not you, whose bosom is the *Muses* home;
When they from tow'ring *Helicon* retire,
They fan in you the bright immortal fire,
But I less happy, cannot raise the song,
The fault'ring music dies upon my tongue.

The happier *Terence** all the choir inspir'd,
His soul replenish'd, and his bosom fir'd;
But say, ye *Muses*, why this partial grace,
To one alone of *Afric's* sable race;
From age to age transmitting thus his name
With the first glory in the rolls of fame?

Thy virtues, great *Maecenas*! shall be sung
In praise of him, from whom those virtues sprung:
While blooming wreaths around thy temples spread,
I'll snatch a laurel from thine honour'd head,
While you indulgent smile upon the deed.

As long as *Thames* in streams majestic flows,
Or *Naiads* in their cozy beds repose,
While Phoebus reigns above the starry train,
While bright *Aurora* purples o'er the main,
So long, great Sir, the muse thy praise shall sing,
So long thy praise shall make *Parnassus* ring:
Then grant, *Maecenas*, thy paternal rays,
Hear me propitious, and defend my lays.

*He was *African* by birth.

W. R. Johnson

ELIOT'S MYTH AND VERGIL'S FICTIONS

Two essays by important English men of letters, Matthew Arnold and T. S. Eliot, nineteenth- and twentieth-century authors respectively, express opposing views of the value of Vergil's *Aeneid*. W. R. Johnson uses Arnold's and Eliot's essays as entry points to reveal the range of contemporary responses to the epic, from optimistic to pessimistic interpretations. In so doing, Johnson identifies the habit of reading the poem as a "political and cultural allegory," with readers projecting onto the work their own faith or anxiety about history and human nature in an effort to learn, in effect, what Vergil might be saying about the "unity and salvation of *our* civilization." Johnson finds both approaches wanting, by reducing a work of vital fictions to a rigid, absolute myth. Instead, Johnson proposes that we learn from Vergil to condition ourselves to an "uncommitted mediation," the ability that Vergil's work teaches "to live with, to live richly with, our weakness and our ignorance." (Ed.)

> ...*as every half-truth at length produces the contradiction of itself in the opposite half-truth.*
>
> D. H. LAWRENCE

> *Myth operates within the diagrams of ritual, which presupposes total and adequate explanations of things as they are and were; it is a sequence of radically unchangeable gestures. Fictions are for finding things out, and they change as the needs of sense-making change. Myths are the agents of stability, fictions are the agents of change. Myths call for absolute, fictions for conditional assent. Myths make sense in terms of a lost order of time, illud tempus ["that time"] as Eliade calls it; fictions, if successful, make sense of the here and now, hoc tempus ["this time"].*[1]

It may seem an injustice that Eliot should be made to serve as the instigator of a wild-goose chase that, in a sense, he only strayed into and out of accidentally. But he cast himself as the defender of the grand orthodoxies. He glories in that role, and so it is not wholly unfair that he should be taken as a representative figure when we examine the major approaches to Vergil that developed during the age of Eliot, that period between the two wars (and a little before and a little after) when Western civilization was lost and reviled and recovered and sentimentalized with all the passion and imprecision that the millennistic sensibility is capable of. My object in this essay is to sketch the fortunes of Vergil's reputation in the last century and a half with a view to showing that the *Aeneid*, having been reduced from a

---

W. R. Johnson, *Darkness Visible: A Study in Vergil's Aeneid*, "Eliot's Myth and Vergil's Fictions," 1–22. University of California Press, 1976. Reprinted by permission of W. R. Johnson.

poem to a myth, was first rejected as a bad myth and then exalted as the good European (Western) myth, and that the habit of reading the poem as a political and cultural allegory (however much the debate over the meaning of the allegory alters its direction) persists to the present day, obscuring the quality of the poetry and limiting, disastrously, the range and depths of the poem. Having briefly surveyed the general outlines of this reductive allegorical approach to the poem and having described and assessed the results of this approach in its most recent flowering, I shall attempt to show how and why the *Aeneid*, in all the complexity and rich con-figuration of its multiple allegories and its dialectical movement, will not allow its living fictions to be transformed into a dead myth—into Eliot's *Aeneid*, the emblem of a vanishing, vanished world whose death the young Eliot announced and whose rebirth the middle-aged and elder Eliot, not to his discredit, undertook to fabricate. What follows may seem tendentious, frivolous, unfair. I can only plead that, having come to find that the myth of Vergil is as dangerous as it is unreal, I grow ever more certain that the fictions of Vergil remain as potent and as useful as they were when, out of the courage of his despair, he struggled to imagine them.

1

The history of how the *Aeneid*—or, to be more precise, the history of how the first six books of the *Aeneid*—became essentially a high-school textbook in the nineteenth century and in the first half of the twentieth century is a droll and complicated affair. The broad outlines of this story are fairly well known, but the significance of the story, for a variety of reasons, is generally ignored. Parts of its meaning are amusingly discussed by Ogilvie and brilliantly defined by R. D. Williams,[2] but so far as I know there is no methodical study of the entire story, perhaps because it is not only funny and complex but also faintly depressing. In the interests of brevity and at the risk of oversimplification, I suggest that the major reasons for the demo-tion of the *Aeneid* from a great living epic to the role of co-drudge with Xenophon, Nepos, and the *Gallic Wars* were Homer *redivivus* ["revived"] (again) and the Roman-tics, poets and professors alike (it was once the fashion for young living professors to read the work of recently dead poets). Vergil's main problem after the French Revolution was that he was clearly the darling of the neoclassical establishment. The late eighteenth-century Homer, on the other hand, a dim adumbration of our free-spirited Yugoslavian minstrels, did not have the misfortune of being literate, and he was not intimately connected with Roman Europe. This Homer, however he changed in the course of the Romantic generations, was here to stay; and Vergil, standard-bearer of the hated old order, had to go.

The French and the Italians (and, because of cultural lag, the Americans) remained tepidly loyal to Vergil, but the English and the Germans had no vested interest in the myth of *Roma aeterna* ["eternal Rome"] and, delighted by the final failure of the Latin Middle Ages (the vernacular Middle Ages were rediscovered along with the unlatinized Homer), they shifted their gaze from the exhausted and oppressive rubble of Rome and the ruins of Aquinas' Paris to the old, new glories of the Acropolis. There is a fresh dry irony in the fact that the teen-age Nietzsche was just about to enter high school as Matthew Arnold was giving his inaugural address, "The Modern Element in Literature," from the Chair of Poetry at Oxford; for different as these two poets were in temperament, achievement, and destiny, it tingles one's spine to hear the words, though not of course the music, of Nietzsche's Hellenic revelations in the staid accents of the Scholar-Gypsy on his best behavior:

> Now, the peculiar characteristic of the highest literature — the poetry — of the fifth century in Greece before the Christian era, is its *adequacy*; the peculiar characteristic of the poetry of Sophocles is its consummate, its unrivalled *adequacy*; that it represents the highly developed human nature of that age — human nature developed in a number of directions, politically, socially, religiously, morally developed — in its completest and most harmonious development in all these directions; while there is shed over this poetry the charm of that noble serenity which always accompanies true insight. If in the body of the Athenians of that time there was, as we have said, the utmost energy of mature manhood, public and private; the most entire freedom, the most unprejudiced and intelligent observation of human affairs — in Sophocles there is the same energy, the same maturity, the same freedom, the same intelligent observation; but all of these idealized and glorified by the grace and light shed over them from the noblest poetical feeling. And therefore I have ventured to say of Sophocles that he 'saw life steadily, and saw it whole.' Well may we understand how Pericles — how the great statesman whose aim it was, it has been said, 'to realize in Athens the idea which he had conceived of human greatness' and who partly succeeded in his aim — should have been drawn to the poet whose works are the noblest reflection of his success.

Some of what Arnold is saying here is that Pericles could qualify as Victoria's prime minister, and that he and Sophocles and lots of their contemporaries could wear the school tie without dishonoring it, mingle without indecorum with other old boys. "Adequacy" is obviously a key word in this passage, as it is throughout Arnold's lecture, and to "adequacy" we shall turn in a moment; other key words are "energy," "maturity" (a word that we shall see on prominent display in Eliot's lecture on Vergil), "freedom," and "intelligence." Nietzsche will be focusing on the same concepts some fifteen years later, and he will be pinning his argument about the insuperable greatness of the pre-Socratic Greeks on the same texts — Aeschylus, Sophocles, and Thucydides — the last of whom Arnold deems the perfect historian for Pericles and his achievement, even as he finds Sophocles the perfect poetic celebrant of Periclean grandeur. But the sickly German recluse will see more clearly than the muscular English Christian what "the utmost energy of manhood" meant in fifth-century Athens. In his cultivated self-deception, Arnold worshipped the will to power under the illusion that he was merely paying homage to the ideals and the realities of "human greatness." Whatever illusions Nietzsche labored under — and when he was at his best (which was astonishingly often) they were few — the realities of the imperial sensibility did not moisten his eyes when the trumpets and the drums played *dulce et decorum* ["sweet and proper"]. Nietzsche did not read his Thucydides sentimentally, and he, like Milton (though obviously for very different reasons), knew that alliances between pagan and Christian culture were few, delicate, and uncertain. But Arnold, who is pagan *malgré-lui* ["in spite of himself"] and unawares, is as busy as Nietzsche in welcoming the modern, that is to say, the post-Christian and neo-pagan era. For this new world Arnold, like Nietzsche, finds abundant models in Periclean Athens; unlike Nietzsche, who liked Rome only for Horace and for Sallust (who furnished the equipment for French epigrammatic style), Arnold is willing to admit that the Rome of Cicero and Augustus is very modern indeed, is perhaps even more modern than fifth-century Athens: it shows vividly "the utmost energy of mature manhood" in combination with "cultivation of mind and intelligence"; it qualifies, that is to say, as a successful empire. But the literature of Rome, unlike the literature of Periclean Athens, is inadequate to its modern greatness. Lucretius, for instance, frequently manifests "depression and ennui" (is he thinking of the dreadful things that are being written, across the Channel, in Paris?), and so he is modern, but in a wrong, negative way. "Yes, Lucretius is modern; but is he adequate? And how can a man adequately interpret the activity of his age when he is not in sympathy with it? Think of the varied, the abundant, the wide spectacle of Roman life in his day; think of the fulness of occupation, its energy of effort." Yes; read Lily Ross Taylor; then think of the spectacle; then reread Lucretius. But let us pass from Arnold's scoutmasterly condemnation of the Lucretian exhortation to *lathe biōsas* ["live unnoticed"] to his evaluation of the adequacy of Vergil:

> Over the whole of the great poem of Virgil, over the whole *Aeneid*, there rests an ineffable melancholy; not a rigid, a moody gloom, like the melancholy of Lucretius: no, a sweet, a touching sadness, but still a sadness; a melancholy which is at once a source of charm in the poem, and a testimony of its incompleteness. Virgil, as Niebuhr has well said, expressed no affected self-disparagement, but the haunting, the irresistible, self-dissatisfaction of his heart, when he desired on his death-bed that his poem might be destroyed. A man of the most delicate genius, the most rich learning, but of weak health, of the most sensitive nature, in a great and overwhelming world; conscious, at heart, of his inadequacy for the thorough spiritual mastery of that world and its interpretation in a work of art; conscious of this inadequacy—the one inadequacy, the one weak place in the mighty Roman nature! This suffering, this graceful-minded, this finely gifted man is the most beautiful, the most attractive figure in literary history; but he is not the adequate interpretor of the great period of Rome.

This is, of course, the kiss of death. I do not mean that Arnold is singly responsible for the decline of Vergil's reputation, nor do I think that his diagnosis of Vergil's "weakness" is altogether incorrect, since in my final chapter I shall be saying rather similar things, though for quite different reasons. Nor should we take occasion to wax merry over the follies of British imperialism; it is hardly the place of an American to castigate another nation's dreams of glory, since if Americans can read "The Modern Element in Literature" and see what Arnold's comparisons between Periclean Athens and Victorian England really mean, and are chilled by what they read, it is only because we too are the people our parents warned us about.

I emphasize Arnold's lecture for two reasons. First, Arnold clearly frames an attitude toward the *Aeneid* that was popular for more than a century, and he is representative of a majority opinion that, though it was seldom voiced so elegantly or so shrewdly, was not effectively countered by voices from the minority until Klingner, Büchner, Pöschl, and Otis.[3] Second, if Arnold is wrong here, he has nevertheless seen, however dimly, the heart of the matter. In its negative way, his judgment on, and description of, Vergil's poem foreshadows the findings of a major contemporary school of Vergilian criticism. Members of this school, to whose views I shall presently turn, also find Vergil's epic essentially melancholy and his world over-whelming, but they nevertheless find Vergil, because of his special gifts and special limitations, as adequate to his world as any poet can be.

Since Arnold had found Vergil inadequate to the task of expressing the great-ness of the Roman Empire, Eliot, who both loved and resented the sage whose mantle he spent most of his adult life snatching and donning, naturally found that Vergil was adequate not only to expressing the greatness of the Roman Empire but also to defining the greatness of Western civilization. In other words, both in "What Is a Classic?" and in "Vergil and the Christian World," Eliot restores Vergil to the position from which Arnold had carefully exiled him. These two essays are not samples of Eliot's most inspired criticism (I at least can find nothing in them that is not more passionately and more precisely said by Haecker in his *Vergil, Vater des Abendlands* [*"Vergil, Father of the West"*], a book which Eliot conspicuously praises in the second of these essays[4]), but they were delivered and published at a time when Eliot's reputation was at its zenith and when his audience was as captivated as it was enormous. His fans in the forties, old and new alike, were doubtless more interested in the man who had written *The Wasteland* and *A Cooking Egg* than they were in the prophet who recalled them to kneel at the Mantuan's shrine, but German critics were more than merely polite in their reception of Eliot's remarks on Vergil. Here was the Urwastelander himself, proudly displaying some of the fragments he had come upon in his retreat from modernism, lifting up the *Aeneid* on his shoulders as he struggled onward toward the twenty-first century. This was something to write home to the learned journals about. This was a catch. Büchner and Pöschl, both of whom were at this time engaged in serious and fruitful reevaluations of the *Aeneid*, record Vergil's readmission into the ranks of the blessed with solemn thanks-giving.[5] Büchner and Pöschl had not learned anything new from Eliot; they found nothing useful in him that they could not have found in Haecker. So they ignore the fantastic fudge that makes up most of what he has to say about Vergil ("A classic can only occur when a civilization is mature; when a language and a literature are mature; and it must be the work of a mature mind," etc.) and concentrate their attention on the conclusions rather than the proofs: "Virgil acquires the centrality of the unique classic; he is at the centre of European civilization, in a position which no other poet can share or usurp. The Roman Empire and the Latin language were not any empire and language but an empire and a language with a unique destiny in relation to ourselves; and the poet in whom that Empire and that language came to consciousness and expression is a poet of unique destiny." Home run with the bases loaded! This is what Büchner and Pöschl needed: a living and authentic *Weltdichter* ["world poet"] vouching for the authenticity of a dead, and in recent times dubious, *Weltdichter*. Homer, Sophocles, and Pericles, it turned out, had not ushered us into the twentieth century. Maybe our grandfathers had got it wrong. Maybe we should read about *labor* ["labor"] and *pietas* ["piety, duty"] for ourselves.

Down, malice, down! Even if we grant that this is Eliot not at his best, the instinct of the German critics in focusing on Eliot's reaffirmation was both natural and correct, nor was Eliot's act of homage foolish. In his remarks on Vergil he addresses himself to a problem that inevitably engrossed the attention of Western intellectuals (and particularly European, as opposed to American and Soviet, intellectuals) after the end of World War II. How was Europe to become reunified in the aftermath of what seemed, and very probably was, the most massive disintegration it had suffered in many centuries? The center had not held —had, in fact, failed to hold disastrously.

Where was a new center to be found? The question is not really a literary one, and Eliot obscures the question by giving it a literary answer (that obscuring is essentially the subject of my essay since by obscuring the political question he obscures the poem), but Eliot was, after all, a literary man and literary answers were what he had to give. Vergil had guided Dante; Dante, through the late twenties, through the thirties, and into the forties had guided Eliot. So, in the hour of supreme crisis, it is not strange to find Eliot announcing that it is Vergil who stands at the center of European civilization, and it is not strange to find, so wild are the changes, the super Englishman reaffirming the primacy of the Roman Empire and the Latin language. It is clear that politicians and financiers were not much interested in what Eliot had to say about Vergil; even the younger generation of modernists (Sartre, for example, and even the young Auden—but the case of Auden would soon begin to change) seem not to have paid attention to Eliot's call for unity. But for European classicists—and particularly for German classicists—Eliot's recommitment to Vergil, his reassertion of Vergil's central place in the image of Europe's essential and unending unity was a heartening and necessary event. Thus, though Eliot's lectures on Vergil may seem dated to us now, though they fail of the boldness and the precision that articulate his major critical essays, it is worth our remembering that when these fine German critics set about the task of reevaluating Vergil, it was Eliot's authority that they offered as an earnest of their own aims and methods because Eliot, at the height of his prestige, had said not merely to classicists but to the literate world that the greatness of Vergil's poetry was to be measured by the truth of his vision of *Roma aeterna* ["eternal Rome"].

2

It is the nature of that vision, its truth or falsity, that has tended to engross the attention of Vergil's critics since the forties. This is, of course, an old concern for readers of the *Aeneid*, but the urgency of Eliot and his most sympathetic listeners seems new in the intensity of its almost audible question, What is Vergil also saying about the unity and the salvation of *our* civilization?[6] Many generations flatter themselves that they are the apocalyptic generation, and other generations who have found or thought that they have found the barbarians at their gates most likely read the *Aeneid* as Eliot and his listeners have been reading it. But the events of this century constrain admirers of *Roma aeterna* to temper their enthusiasm for *imperium sine fine dedi* ["I gave empire without end"], to pay more attention to the blessings of peace and to the *anima naturaliter Christiana* ["spirit naturally Christian"] than to the grandeur of empire. In this reformulation of what *Roma aeterna* means, victory (and of course conquest) yields to "love of order" in a way that most Romans and even Gibbon himself might find somewhat maudlin. But beyond this softening, this christening, of the concept of Rome and her empire, this magnification of Vergil's own compassions and charities, the events of this century have caused some readers of the *Aeneid* to redefine Vergil's attitude to *imperium* ["empire"] in a quite radical way: what these readers have understood is that the problem is not so much that the barbarians are at the gates or even within the gates, but rather that we are ourselves the barbarians. Both those who trust in the concept of *imperium* and those who distrust and dread it even in its softer aspects have been forced to review the Roman Empire and Vergil's epic from a dizzy and frightening vantage point, from this planet in this century.

There are, then, at present two quite distinct schools of Vergilian criticism that seek to explain and to justify the *Aeneid* by constructing for it two radically opposed political allegories. The major achievement of the essentially optimistic European school has been to show that what had been taken as Vergil's chief defects might better be seen as his particular virtues. What had been named a slavish or incompetent dependence on Homer becomes in their hands a brilliant recreation, a thorough and fresh rethinking of Homeric problems and Homeric solutions. For them, the genre of epic is not so much artificially resuscitated by Vergil as it is reinvented. If, for instance, a constant complaint throughout the nineteenth and much of the twentieth century had been that Aeneas is a poor excuse for a hero, the European school counters that it is not a question of Aeneas' failing as a hero but a question of Vergil's rethinking the concept of heroism which was a process that entailed a distillation of post-Socratic ethical speculation and that implied some criticism of the Homeric concept of heroism. In Aeneas we do not have some paltry Hellenistic epigone, clumsy and frightened and embarrassed as he bumbles about in armor too heavy and too huge for him; rather, we have an authentic Stoic (or perhaps Epicurean, or Academic, or Pythagorean — the sect hardly matters) who struggles from the old, primitive code and the mindless, amoral jungle into the clear sunshine of the Augustan enlightenment: *humanitas, pietas, ratio, salus* ["humanity, piety, reason, security"]. Not the old shame-culture or even the old guilt-culture; rather the world where conscience, compassion, reason, and free will matter. The tendency to emphasize the growth of Aeneas' resolve and character had begun at the turn of the century, but the achievement of demonstrating not only Stoic resolve but also pre-Christian sensitivity and compassion is (in modern times) a fairly recent one; this demonstration required, above all else, that the last six books of the *Aeneid* be read as carefully as the first six books had been read. When these later books began being scrutinized, Aeneas became less priggish, less stupid, more complex and his real dilemmas and his real inner conflicts came into sharp focus. In short, with the readings of this school we begin to glimpse profound tensions between the brutal nasty world Aeneas moves in and the virtues and ideals, which are as complex as they are strong and dramatic, that his character expresses; these virtues and ideals shine ever brighter as the darkness of the chaos that menaces him and what he stands for increases in the accelerated and violent tempos of the last six books of the poem. This gentle power that survives the onslaughts of darkness and disaster is a fit vehicle for the kind of empire that, in these readings of the poem, the *Aeneid* exists to celebrate. Thus, for Pöschl and the school to which he belongs, Aeneas and his *muthos* ["myth"] are capable of signifying not merely a temporal equilibrium, a historical triumph of virtue over unreason, but also, in a way that all myths of empire require, a transcendental cosmic order; for in this reading of the poem, the political allegory is sanctioned by Homer's vision of the unity of nature as well as by Cicero's vision of the unity of the *civitas* ["civic community, state"].[7]

This philosophical epic, then, becomes a kind of compendium of all that is best in the poetry, history, philosophy, and theology of the Graeco-Roman world (a notion that is more elaborately defined by Knauer[8]), and in this way it becomes, as Eliot had hinted, the *Weltgedicht* ["world poem"] without rival before or since. If Aeneas is less vital, less single-minded than Achilles, Hector, or Odysseus, well, that is because the concept of heroism changes constantly, and perhaps the concept that Vergil formulated poetically a few decades before the birth of Christ was more civilized than any concept that Homer could possibly have shaped (the Homer-Vergil debate sometimes rears its head in this reading of the poem, though usually in a rather oblique way[9]). If Vergil's style is less unified than Homer's, more charged with lyrical wavering, more prone to indeterminate clarities, well, that is perhaps because the world that Vergil has to express and wants to express is a more complicated and more subtle world than the world that was available to Homer. Finally, even if we grant that Vergil's poem is less dramatic than Homer's on its surface, that Aeneas and the other figures in the poem seem somewhat dim, somewhat overwhelmed by the vastness of the fate which moves them and toward which they move, well, that is perhaps because Vergil himself was fated to live and work in a crucial moment in Western history when History itself, the birth and death of nations, the concept of national destiny, and, finally, the high price of civilization, were questions that could at last be fashioned with a fair amount of precision. Such questions as these, at least in the forms that Vergil encountered them, could not be asked until a Thucydides or a Polybius had hammered them out of the harsh, intractable experience of Greek and Roman history, and, indeed, they are not questions that Homer would be likely to take an interest in, even if they could be explained to him. For Homer human action is not a progression in time and space but an aspect of things as they are in eternity, a vibrant *coincidentia oppositorum* ["coincidence of opposites"] that catches the light and holds it.

The studies of Vergil's inner and outer forms which reaffirm both the unique greatness of his poem and his role as a maker of the myth of Europe evidence precision and vigor of imagination that are almost unparalleled in contemporary Latin studies. This school of Vergilian criticism has ventured on a tremendously difficult task and has performed it with extraordinary success, so it is with real diffidence that I turn from the strengths of this school to its weaknesses. Those weaknesses can best be described by their being contrasted with the strengths of the somewhat pessimistic Harvard school.[10] In this reading of the poem the superior virtues and the high ideals of Aeneas are sometimes grudgingly allowed him, but he is in the wrong poem. His being in the wrong poem furnishes it with a kind of tragic greatness that calls into question not only the heroisms of Homer's poems but also Augustan heroism and indeed any heroism. The presence of the Stoic or the Epicurean sage on the Homeric battlefield creates a *concordia discors* ["discordant harmony"] that is clearly wrong for a celebration of *Roma aeterna* ["eternal Rome"] and evades any possible kind of good resolution to the conflicts the poem mirrors. The historical and the metaphysical stakes in this race between order and disorder are too high, and the hero, the order, and the disorder are all gathered up into, and at last devoured by, an implacable and unintelligible nihilism. It is worth noting that this reading of the poem seems to begin its real history at just about the time that Pöschl, Klingner, and Büchner were producing their important reevaluations of the *Aeneid*, but Brooks and, later, Adam Parry seem not to be listening to Eliot but rather to the news from the Left Bank or to Auden's *The Age of Anxiety*, that wild and scandalously neglected masterpiece which captures its era and outlives it. As politically sensitive as the critics of the rival school, these critics had read their Syme and their Taylor as closely as they read the front pages of their newspapers, and for them the value, much less the grandeur, of the Roman Empire was not taken for granted. For them Pöschl's version of the "Augustan idea of Rome," whether inside or outside Vergil's poem, was utterly problematic. What did Vergil think of Augustus? What did he think of the Roman Empire? Is he not, at the very least, ambivalent in his attitude toward the Augustan peace? Is the poem not considerably darker than Eliot and Pöschl had suggested?

This school's difficulties with the *Aeneid* as political allegory that celebrates not only Rome, but the Graeco-Roman concept of Cosmos as well, are nourished by a deep sensitivity to what Arnold had experienced profoundly but had misidentified and misnamed: Vergil's "melancholy," his "sweet, touching sadness." Brooks, Parry, Clausen, and Putnam have all written telling descriptions of Vergil's infatuation with twilight moods, with blurred images, with haunted, half-enacted interviews and confrontations that disintegrate before our eyes just as we begin to perceive them. Again and again, and often on the edge of a sharply etched dramatic moment, clarity and conflict are sacrificed to *Stimmungskunst* ["mood art"], and the actors, now iridescent phantoms that dwindle into unrealities, dramatize only the fact of illusion. In place of Homer's clarities of scene and articulations of action, in place of "the healing centrality"[11] toward which those clarities and articulations flow, Vergil offers images and actions that promise completions and harmonies but that seldom deliver them. And the vanishing surface of the poem, the light and outlines that fail, the actions and the confrontations that end unachieved, faithfully reflect not only the political but also the metaphysical depths of the poem. For Pöschl and Otis and other critics of the European school, the order, the stability, and the goodness of the empire that Vergil imagines in the *Aeneid* are reflections of a Homeric, a Platonic, a Ciceronian cosmos wherein evil and the disorders that Juno sets in motion and of which she is symbolic are seen finally as part of a larger pattern, are seen, that is to say, not as evils or disorders at all. Pöschl and Knauer seem to think that an educated Roman of Vergil's time, having Homer, the tragedians, Plato, and Aristotle at his fingertips, will find strength and comfort in the great syntheses of the heroic age, the tragic age, and the final age of the Greek enlightenment. That is a possible way of looking at the meaning of classical humanism in Vergil's age, but the poised rationalism of Cicero's *De republica* ["On the Republic"] needs to be balanced against the more pressed, more tentative, more uncertain tone of the late philosophical works. And we want to remember, too, how E. R. Dodds characterizes the last century [B.C.E.] in the final chapter of his *The Greeks and the Irrational*:

> Many students of this subject [he is talking about astrology] have seen in the first century B.C. the decisive period of *Weltwende* ["turning poing in history"], the period when the tide of rationalism, which for the past hundred years had flowed ever more sluggishly, had finally expended its force and begins to retreat. There is no doubt that all the philosophical schools save the Epicurean took a new direction at this time. The old religious dualism of mind and matter, God and Nature, the soul and appetite, which rationalists had striven to overcome, reasserts itself in fresh forms with fresh vigor. In the new unorthodox Stoicism of Posidonius this dualism appears as a tension of opposites within the unified cosmos and the unified nature of the old Stoa.[12]

In respect of intellectual climate, then, it is possible to see in Vergil's time not an age of faith but the beginning of the age of anxiety that Dodds went on to describe. It is against these intuitions of a terrible dualism that the *Aeneid* should be viewed. Few readers of the *Iliad* today would seriously maintain that Homer's world is one of primeval simplicity, but the complexities of his powerful and dynamic world are gathered into an adumbration of the great affirmations of unity and intelligibility that we encounter in the classical moment of Greek philosophy. Vergil's world, on the other hand, prefigures (it does not affirm) a world where matter and reason and unity *may* be only illusions, where madness and discord *may* be the only realities, here below, in space and time.

It is with this aspect of the *Aeneid* that the European school has the most difficulty, toward which it shows the least sensitivity. If Aeneas is not only symbolic of classical rational freedom but is also himself, in his *muthos* ["myth"], possessed of rational freedom, why do we last view him as a victim of the very anger and madness that he has so gallantly opposed throughout the poem? Has the champion of Western civilization triumphed? Over his foes, yes; over the immediate evils that Juno has designed, yes. But over what Juno is and wants and stands for? I think the general design and in particular the closure of the poem argue against Aeneas' victory over those evils.[13]

Buchheit, who has written what seems to me one of the finest works that the European school has produced, correctly sees that Juno cannot be written off as a minor aberrancy in an otherwise perfect universe and demonstrates that she is the central figure in the poem's structure, but he is nevertheless satisfied with her reconciliation with Jupiter and to Fate.[14] But that reconciliation...is fraught with difficulties, some of which I sketch briefly here. The curse that Dido puts on Rome will be fulfilled with a vengeance long after she and Aeneas are dead, and there is a special irony in Jupiter's prophecy of the Punic Wars in Book 10 (11–15):

adveniet iustum pugnae (ne arcessite) tempus,
cum fera Karthago Romanis arcibus olim
exitium magnum atque Alpes immittet apertas:
tum certare odiis, tum res rapuisse licebit.
nunc sinite et placitum laeti componite foedus.

The fitting time for battle will yet come
(and soon enough without your hurrying)
when savage Carthage will unleash its hate
and ruin on the towers of Rome, unlock
the Alps against them: then it will be right
to rage and fight and ravage everything.
Now it is time to stop, to give your glad
assent to what I want: a league of peace.

For the cunning, malevolent fiend of the *Aeneid* has no connection but their common type-scene with the silly, charming, sensual lady of the *Iliad*. Hera's capitulation is real enough because her anger, or rather her petulance, is skin deep; but the anger of Juno, which is close to being the central theme of the *Aeneid*, is in her heart and in her blood; it cannot be altered even by the ritual of *evocatio* ["summoning"] that Jupiter himself performs and that reads like a grim parody of Athena's transfiguration of the Furies in Aeschylus. No less sinister in this regard is the appearance of the Dira whom Jupiter sends against Turnus. The figure of Allecto, a kind of outdoing of Lyssa in Euripides' *Herakles*, is bad enough: the satanic in the service of the divine. But in Book 12, the satanic Dira at the throne of Jupiter is herself somehow divine, and this connection between the Dira and Jupiter lends to the closing scenes of the epic a peculiarly desperate horror — it is almost as if Jupiter himself had come under the spell of Juno. And feeling the horror of this perversion of justice and the savagery of the Dira's attack on Turnus, one looks back a few hundred lines to what had then seemed an innocently formulaic and rhetorical statement of *aporia* ["questioning"] in the invocation to Jupiter:

quis mihi nunc tot acerba deus, quis carmine caedes
diversas obitumque ducum, quos aequore toto
inque vicem nunc Turnus agit, nunc Troius heros,
expediat? tanton placuit concurrere motu,
Iuppiter, aeterna gentis in pace futuras?

(12.500–504)

What god can now unfold for me in song
all of the bitterness and butchery
and deaths of chieftains — driven now by Turnus,
now by the Trojan hero, each in turn
throughout that field? O Jupiter, was it
your will that nations destined to eternal
peace should have clashed in such tremendous turmoil?

The question posed here neatly echoes the desperate question, the cry of anguish, with which the poem had begun: *tantaene animis caelestibus irae* ["Is there such great rage in heavenly minds"]? There was no answer then; there is none now. Until the coming of the Dira, this question, like the first question, might seem merely rhetorical, and the universe of the *Aeneid* might seem the enlightened, free, and intelligible universe that a Plato or a Zeno bore witness to; after the coming of the Dira, these questions continue to sound and they will not cease: they reverberate with an endless disintegration of reality, with the dull despairing silence that haunts Turnus as he flees from sure destruction. And so the poem ends, with a taste of ashes and death, and one hopes that life is only a nightmare that we wake from, and we pray only that reality is at last unreal. This is not to say that Aeneas is not heroic in precisely the way that his champions claim him to be: he is a deeply humane and profoundly good man; he is also fearless and courageous, as powerful and as energetic as he is compassionate and gentle. But what this poem says is that, in a universe where Juno holds sway, even these qualities are not enough. It is a terrifying poem.

The major weakness of the Harvard school is, as I see it, that it is obviously rooted in our peculiarly contemporary brand of pessimism. It is hard to imagine how this reading of the poem could exist without the support of our agnostic and atheistic existentialisms. And it is therefore only too possible that such readings of the poem project back upon Vergil a taste for the cult of failure and for the sense of the absurd and the meaningless that ancients, even the ancients that Dodds characterizes so well, would have found all but incomprehensible. Furthermore, it is clearly impossible to ignore Vergil's very real (if qualified) admiration for Augustus, his hope for political salvation, his desire to believe in cosmic order, and, failing a strong faith in human nature, his reverence for human dignity.

So the debate stands — a sober, cautious celebration of human beings and the cosmos they inhabit countered by a deeply pessimistic lamentation for the human condition. I confess that I favor the second reading, chiefly because it tries to deal with the world in which Vergil shaped his fictions and does not project the symbolic world in the poem back onto the difficult world that he lived and wrote in. And I also admit that I am grateful for and deeply influenced by the first reading and am troubled by what I am sure are the uncertainties of the second. The question then is: Are we now trapped into choosing one over the other? Until recently I have thought so but am now increasingly tempted to say, A plague on both your houses. What triggers my skepticism about both positions and continues to nourish that skepticism has been precisely set forth by Jaspers:

> Visions of universal harmony can function as ciphers. Their beauty appeals to us at certain moments, but soon we come to question their truth. At all times two ciphers have been current. One is expressed in the philosophical view that the world and all things in it are governed by a fundamental harmony; the other, in the view that the world originated in deviltry and that its existence is a fraud. Both must be rejected. They are only to be taken as symbolic expression or as ciphers of a passing experience; apart from this they have no validity.[15]

I wonder if critics of both schools of Vergilian criticism that I have described have not been essentially engaged in attempting to fix and order their own moods about disorder and order by freezing the dialectical rhythms of this poem in the static shape of one or the other of Jaspers' ciphers. The question, Can our civilization be saved? is, I suppose, valid enough, and one can often understand why we are prompted to ask it with urgency and sometimes with more than urgency. But it is both unreasonable and unfair to Vergil to ask him to answer this question for us, and that, I submit, is what readers of the *Aeneid*, particularly in the last few decades, have been asking him to do. It is an unreasonable question to ask Vergil because Vergil does not know any more about the answer than we do; furthermore, when we ask this question of Vergil, we usually, by the manner in which we frame our question, predetermine the answer he will give us in an outrageously subjective way. Poets, of course, are not less vain than professors or men and women in the streets, and not a few poets, therefore, have succumbed to the temptation of giving their opinions on current events, thereby degenerating from poets into *vates* ["prophets"] and bards. Dante certainly felt this temptation from time to time; Milton was not above it; nor was Goethe, nor Arnold, nor Eliot, nor even Ginsberg. Vergil was clearly tempted, yielded a bit too much, and then finally yielded no more; he defused the splendid, silly, dangerous myth and used what was left of the myth to make his somber and nourishing fictions.

3

ad evidentiam itaque dicendorum sciendum est, quod
istius operis non est simplex sensus, immo dici
potest polysemum, hoc est plurium sensuum; nam
alius sensus est qui habetur per literam, alius
est qui habetur per significata per literam.

(Dante to Can Grande, 8)

For a clear understanding of what I am saying here, therefore, you should know that this poem yields no single meaning; rather, it might best be described as being *polysemous*, that is, as being possessed of several meanings. For in its literal aspect it offers one kind of meaning, but in its metaphorical aspects (allegorical, moral, anagogical) it offers another kind of meaning, which is manifested through the literal aspect.

Littera gesta docet, quod credas allegoria,
moralis quod agas, quo tendas anagogia.

(Nicholas of Lyra)

The literal portion tells the sequence of fictional or historical events; the allegorical tells what you should believe to be true about the nature of reality; the moral tells what you should do (and not do) in living your life; the anagogical tells what the purpose of your earthly life is, the goal of your pilgrimage through this world.

Few contemporary readers of the *Aeneid* would deny that the poem is in some sense *polysemous*, but it is our habit, if not in fact our nature, to make myths out of poems as we make myths out of other realities—because it is easier and usually more comforting to make myths than to think thoughts and to feel feelings accurately. Even when we are willing or eager to admit the complexities of *allegoria*, we want always to say, But, of course, the *real* meaning of the poem is....[16] It is this lust for the real meaning, the real solution (as if a poem were a problem or even a crime) that persuades us to forget that most great poems are polysematic to an extraordinary degree and that whenever we ignore this fact we are probably about to turn a fiction (that is to say, a polysematic configuration) into a convenient and probably an intensely private cipher. In so transforming fiction into myth, and into private myth at that, we all but make certain that we will not, cannot hear much of what the poet is trying to show us or tell us, or, beyond the showing and telling, prepare us for. I am not arguing here against the truth or the uses of myth, but I am insisting that myths, which are as dangerous as they are necessary for the private religious life, belong to the chapel, the launching-pad, the vegetable garden, the football field, the beauty contest—in short, to the public and social religious life where the truths that shape our existence can be recovered, believed, and lived in order that members of the community can gain the patterns of confidence necessary for the continuation and enrichment of human life in the society. Myths have no place in poems except as a part of the raw materials out of which the poetry is imagined by the poet. The use of poetic fictions is to exercise our spirits, to make us think and feel more precisely and more abundantly than we normally think and feel by reminding us vividly of the beauties and the hazards of our existence. When we reduce living fictions to dead, fake myths, we are perverting the nature of both myth and poetry, and we are cheating ourselves of the real blessings that myth and poetry, in their separate and very different ways, can confer on us. If we need myth in our lives (and we do, and one way or another we find it), we should go off to the mass, or the dance floor, or the playing field, or the county fair, or the Thanksgiving Day dinner table, or the golf course, or the stock market (in short, to the myth or myths of our choice), wherever myths are alive and well and beneficial. If we want the solace and the strength of religion, I suppose we learn to go into our secret names and learn to pray. If we want poetry we rush into the delights and dangers that the great poets have furnished us as pure gifts. But if we persist in trying to convert poetry into religion and myth, our sustenance will be ersatz ritual, ersatz theology, ersatz ethics, and ersatz politics. And we shall perish of real hunger from illusory food.

✧ ✧ ✧

The *Aeneid* is, as has been seen through the ages, a political allegory, but it is not merely positive in its political connotations, and it is no less a metaphysical and also a moral allegory. Not three allegories moving parallel, separate and independently, but three allegories moving interdependently, at once harmonious and dissonant, shaping iridescent fictions that force us to ponder for ourselves the shapes they configure. *Tis aēthēs krasis*, some extraordinary mixture — the phrase is by another master of allegory, Plato, describing another mystery that defies language that will not submit to the disciplines of multiple and interdependent allegory (*Phaedo* 59A).

> ...There is a dark
> Inscrutable workmanship that reconciles
> Discordant elements, makes them cling together
> In one society.

But as Wordsworth sometimes (inevitably) forgot, the "society" so formed remains unnamable and invisible and unknowable apart from the intricate reconciliation in which, and by virtue of which, it exists. If we call the "society" of the *Aeneid* a political allegory (or, what is the same thing, if we call it a symbolic poem about Rome and Augustus), we have not mere prose (there is no such thing as mere prose), but bad prose (which the *Aeneid* is not). The free and powerful fictions of Vergil's poem do not explain to us or resolve for us the problems of man's fantasies about bondage in time or his fantasies about freedom from time, but they bring the existence of those fantasies and the danger of those fantasies into clear focus. So far from existing for the sake of myths, which pretend to give us explanations of the human condition, the fictions of the *Aeneid* use myths to discredit myth's unwarranted and hazardous claims. It is ironic that a poem that has among its aims the banishing of myth should gain and hold much of its esteem because it is mistaken for a myth; but poetry has always been misused in one way or another and has survived, its integrity undiminished and its proper powers unbroken, and the *Aeneid* has survived and will survive the irony of being confused with its opposite. The unique interplay between courage and despair that enforms this poem is proof against all efforts to hear in its tempos and cadences only our own good luck or bad luck, to imprint upon the poem our personal guess about what reality is or means. The bold justice and the unpersuadable honesty of these fictions require that we learn to suspend our beliefs, to put aside our craving for final answers, and to learn, by experiencing and absorbing the exact impartiality of these fictions, to live with, to live richly with, our weakness and our ignorance.

What Vergil offers in this poem that other poets do not is a passionate, grieving, but uncommitted meditation on man's nature and on the possibilities and impossibilities of his fate. It is the free and open dialectic of Vergil's polysematic fictions that makes possible this kind of meditation, and we misread the poem and refuse the wisdom (it is not knowledge) that Vergil makes possible for us (he cannot bestow it on us) when we reduce his many allegories to one allegory and pervert his good fictions to bad myths.

Notes

[1]F. Kermode, *The Sense of an Ending: Studies in the Theory of Fiction* (Oxford, 1967), 39.

[2]Ogilvie, *Greek and Roman Studies in England from 1600 to 1914* (London, 1964); R. D. Williams, in *Virgil*, ed. D. R. Dudley (London, 1969), 119–139.

[3]The extent of the Homerists' triumph may be measured by the feebleness of D. Comparetti's challenge to Teuffel (*Virgil in the Middle Ages*, trans. Beneche [London, 1895], 13); by Conington's polite but chilly allusions to the arrogant victors (*Commentary* [London, 1876], 2:2f.); by J. Henry's oblique petulance (*e.g.*, "Homer, the Paragon of Perfection," *Aeneidea* [London, 1873], 1:9); and by Mackail's wonderful refusal to notice that there was any controversy (see the introduction to his fine edition of the *Aeneid* [Oxford, 1930], *passim*). This tactic of refuting "the old German prejudice" (see M. L. Clarke's review of Pöschl in *CR* 65 [1951]: 178) by ignoring it is prevalent in what now seems the rather undernourished pro-Vergilian criticism of D. L. Drew, *The Allegory of the Aeneid* (Oxford, 1977); R. S. Conway, *The Vergilian Age* (Cambridge, Mass., 1928); C. N. Cochrane, *Christianity and Classical Culture: A Study of Thought and Action from Augustus to Augustine* (Oxford, 1940, 1957); E. K. Rand, *The Building of Eternal Rome* (Cambridge, Mass., 1943); in this regard see also the remarks and bibliography by T. E. Wright in the new edition of M. Platnauer's *Fifty Years of Classical Scholarship (and Twelve)* (London, 1968), 387–415. A. Cartault ignores the controversy also, in his remarkable *L'art de Virgile dans l'Enéide* (Paris, 1926), and he can almost afford to ignore it. A. Bellessort (*Virgile* [Paris, 1920], 327–331) calls attention to what the Germans have been up to, and are up to, with futile hysteria. The "renascence" may be properly said to begin in the early thirties in Germany, Austria, and Switzerland (see H. Opperman's introduction to his collection, *Weg zu Vergil* [Darmstadt, 1963]; and F. Klingner, "Wiederentdeckung eines Dichters," in *Römische Geisteswelt* [Wiesbaden, 1953], 177–214 for good sketches of the history of the renewal). But it is not until these works that the renascence gets into full swing: V. Pöschl, *Die Dichtkunst Vergils* (Innsbruck, Vienna, 1950) = *The Art of Vergil*, trans. Seligson (Ann Arbor, 1962); K. Büchner, *P. Vergilius Maro* (Stuttgart, 1961 = Pauly Wissowa 2.8.1021–1486); F. Klingner, 155–176, 215–235 (the second essay dates from 1930); see his sound estimate of Heinze (224–226); B. Otis, *Vergil: A Study in Civilized Poetry* (Oxford, 1964).

[4]Leipzig, 1931; Munich, 1967, trans. Wheen (London, 1934). For a generous discussion of Eliot's use of Vergil, see F. Kermode's lecture, "The Classic," *University of Denver Quarterly* 9, no. 1 (Spring 1974): 1–33.

[5]Pöschl (n. 3), 22 (Seligson, 176, n. 11); Büchner (n. 3), 441. See Opperman (n. 3), xii; a German translation of "What Is a Classic?" begins his collection.

[6]For the antiquity and the perdurability of the political allegory, see the remarks of Comparetti (n. 3) on T. C. Donatus, 61; L. Proudfoot, *Dryden's Aeneid and Its Seventeenth Century Predecessors* (Manchester, 1960), 258 ff; G. K. Galinksy, *Aeneas, Sicily, and Rome* (Princeton, 1969), 49–54, 165–167; G. Binder, *Aeneas und Augustus: Interpretationen zum 8. Buch der Aeneis*, Beiträge zur Klassischen Philologie 38 (Meisenheim am Glan, 1971) *passim*. For excellent arguments against the centrality of political allegory, see Cartault (n. 3), 35–36; and W. S. Anderson, *The Art of the Aeneid* (Englewood Cliffs, N.J., 1969), 18–19. For the apolitical allegorical tradition, see Comparetti (n. 3), 116–118; and, on Bernardus Silvestris, W. Wetherbee, *Platonism and Poetry in the Twelfth Century* (Princeton, 1972), 105–111. Drew's book (n. 3) has been very influential in reasserting the centrality of the political allegory; see also Conway (n. 3), 145–146 and Rand (n. 3), 57–58, 197–202.

[7]See Pöschl (n. 3), 39 (Seligson, 23).

[8]G. Knauer, *Die Aeneis und Homer*, Hypomnemata 7 (Göttingen, 1964): 345–359, and "Vergil's *Aeneid* and Homer," *GRBS* 5 (1964): 61–84. Knauer's book is immensely valuable as a reference work; his conclusions are usefully questioned by M. Wigodsky, *Vergil and Early Latin Poetry*, Hermes Einzelschriften 24 (Wiesbaden, 1972), 8 ff., and B. Otis, "The Originality of the *Aeneid*," in *Virgil*, ed. Dudley (n. 2), 28.

[9]K. Quinn, for example, speaks of Homer's "old soldiers' yarns," but that sort of thing is rare in the conduct of the old debate (see Quinn's *Vergil's Aeneid: A Critical Description* [Ann Arbor, 1968], 53; for similar remarks, see 284–288).

[10]I label it in this fashion because the major works that cluster about this reading of the poem were written by critics who have been associated with classics at Harvard from the late

forties to the present at some time or other: Brooks, Clausen, Adam Parry, Putnam. Some of the emphases of this school are wildly adumbrated, almost as if in caricature, by F. Sforza, "The Problem of Vergil," *CR* 49 (1935): 97–108. The central works are, in order of publication: R. A. Brooks, "*Discolor Aura*: Reflections of a Golden Bough," *AJP* 74 (1953): 260–280; A. Parry, "The Two Voices of Vergil's *Aeneid*," *Arion* 2.4 (1963): 66–80; W. Clausen, "An Interpretation of the *Aeneid*," *HSCP* 68 (1964): 139–147; M. J. Putnam, *The Poetry of the Aeneid* (Cambridge, Mass, 1965). Independent of these works, yet not alien to some of their central concerns, are the cool deliberations of L. A. MacKay, "Hero and Theme in the *Aeneid*," *TAPA* 94 (1963): 157–166.

[11]See J. R. Wilson, "Action and Emotion in Aeneas," *G&R* 16.1 (1969): 75.

[12]Berkeley and Los Angeles, 1951, 247. The European school may be correct in emphasizing once again that the *Aeneid* in some sense adumbrates the coming of Christianity, but this kind of emphasis should be so qualified as to remind us that the matrix of early Christianity is the world of the other mystery religions, the dread and the desperate hope, the failure of nerve, the intuition of the prevalence of evil, the disgust with the flesh, the world, and time — in short, an almost total and almost hysterical rejection of pagan rationalism and the pagan belief in the goodness and eternity of nature. Vergil's imagination of the dualism is the more terrifying because he does not bother with crude materialisms; the oppositions are spiritual (see R. C. Zaehner's exact formulations in *Concordant Discord* [Oxford, 1970], 389 ff.

[13]Haecker (n. 4) deals with the problem of evil in this poem — that is to say, with what Juno means in it — by blaming Allecto. Eliot deals with the evils by dismissing Turnus as "a man without a destiny." (Cartault [n. 3] is specially fine in his understanding of Turnus [864–865, 893–894].) Pöschl and Otis give far more subtle solutions to this problem, but even their solutions differ in quality rather than in kind from those of Haecker and Eliot. For Pöschl (n. 3, 18–30) Juno is "the divine symbol of the demonic forces of violence" that are finally subdued and therefore necessary for the "harmonious balance of opposites" (173, 281 f.); this conquest of the demonic is the basic theme of the poem. For Otis, Juno has not even that much importance: her functions in the poem range from that of subfate or counterfate (n. 3, 82, 378) to that of one of the lesser deities (n. 8, 49).

[14]V. Buchheit, *Vergil über die Sendung Roms*, Gymnasium 3 (Heidelberg, 1963), 11, 191.

[15]K. Jaspers, *The Great Philosophers*, trans. R. Mannheim (New York, 1966), 2:265.

[16]My text for Dante is that given by P. Franticelli, *Il Convivio e le Epistole* (Florence, 1893); see the translation and comments by R. S. Haller, *Literary Criticism of Dante Alighieri* (Lincoln, 1973), 99–100, and the excellent discussion of allegory in his introduction, xix–xxi, xli–xliv. For the couplet by Nicholas, see J. P. McCall, "Medieval Exegesis: Some Documents for the Literary Critic," in W. F. Lynch, *Christ and Apollo* (New York, 1960), 227–267; McCall includes an explication of Nicholas by W. J. Burghardt (241–243). There is an excellent discussion of the problems of allegory in modern criticism and of the current debates by S. Manning, "Scriptural Exegesis and the Literary Critic," in *Typology and Early American Literature*, ed. Bercovitch (Amherst, Mass., 1972), 47–68. For ancient concepts of allegory, see F. A. Wolfson, *The Philosophy of the Church Fathers* (Cambridge, Mass., 1956, 1970), 30–31; and A. B. Hersman, *Studies in Greek Allegorical Interpretation* (Ph.D. diss., Chicago, 1906), Heraclitus, 21, Philo, 22; K. Schefold, *La Peinture pompéienne*, trans. Croissille (Brussels, 1972) 86–88. But for our present purposes the seminal essay is L. A. MacKay, "Three Levels of Meaning in *Aeneid* VI," *TAPA* 86 (1955):180–189. Galinsky (n. 6, 193) properly draws attention to Pöschl's rejection of the term "allegorical" in favor of the term "symbolism" with a view to stressing multiplicities of meaning (Pöschl [n. 3], 36–37 = 21 ff.), but Pöschl, like Galinsky, keeps stressing a positive and political signification which is nourished by the other significations in the "hierarchy" (40 = 24); that is why we might do better to talk of aspects of allegory rather than levels of allegory. In any case, symbolism is a term that is closely tied to a particular period and school of poetry that has, deceptively, some characteristics in common with the poetry of the *Aeneid*. Cumbersome as it is, I would prefer the terms "multiple allegories, interdependent allegories."

❖ ❖ ❖

SOME TWENTIETH-CENTURY HEIRS:
POETRY AND POWER

These examples of twentieth-century works that resonate with Vergilian echoes all reflect, more or less explicitly, a variety of cultural, historical or political concerns. The arrangement into the groups labeled Pastoral, Georgic, and Epic reveals the fluidity of these categories as much as their integrity. The influence of Vergil on these works ranges from overt to generic. All the works are highly crafted, and many of them move me greatly.

Pastoral
- ✧ Frost: "Build Soil—A Political Pastoral"
- ✧ Brodsky: "Eclogue IV: Winter"
- ✧ Burgess: Spike Lee's "Do the Right Thing"

Frost recited "Build Soil—A Political Pastoral" in 1932, while Franklin D. Roosevelt was running for the presidency. The poem is a criticism of what was to become New Deal agricultural policy. Its characters, Tityrus and Meliboeus, bear the same names as the shepherds in Vergil's first *Eclogue*, which similarly mixes rural and political themes, as well as ideas on what it means to be a poet: "You live by writing / your poems on a farm and call that farming." Brodsky's evocation of Vergil's pastoral poems is as explicit as Frost's, opening with two lines from Vergil's fourth *Eclogue*, about the birth of a new order of the ages. Brodsky translates Vergil's hopeful Italian landscape into Russian winter, where "time equals cold." Nonetheless, the timelessness of the eclogue is transplanted across an old boundary of and against Europe, where Cyrillic, the alphabet of Russian, is the poet's sibyl. Burgess has discovered similar, paradoxical pastoral echoes in Spike Lee's movie of urban life in "Do the Right Thing." What seems a ghetto is a pastoral retreat from the city across the river, as distant for those who live there as Rome is for Tityrus and Meliboeus. The tension that invades this garden is not the land distributions during the Roman civil wars, as in *Eclogue* 1, but racism. Burgess considers "Lee's ability to balance gently the pastoral and the political," one of the "Vergilian modes" of the movie.

Georgic
- ✧ Lewis: "Dedicatory Stanzas. To Stephen Spender"
- ✧ Tate: "Aeneas in Washington"
- ✧ Frost: "Two Tramps in Mud Time"

Lewis prefaced his translation of Vergil's *Georgics* with a poem dedicating the translation to a fellow poet, Stephen Spender. Lewis made his translation during the days of World War II, as Vergil had written the original during the times of Roman civil war. Both poets record their enjoyment of country themes "while history in sheets of fire is writing." For Tate, Aeneas is in Washington, not Troy or Rome, when war was waged midst "the thickening Blue Grass." The second Frost poem in this collection describes the confrontation between choice and need, the intrusion of economic necessity into the pleasant labor of a country dweller. It also expresses the artist's privilege of living where "work is play" and "love and need are one."

Epic
- ✧ Auden: "The Shield of Achilles"
- ✧ Warren: "Turnus (*Aeneid* XII)"
- ✧ Frost: "For John F. Kennedy His Inauguration"

✧   Walcott: *Omeros*
✧   Broch: *The Death of Virgil*

"The Shield of Achilles" is less Auden's conversation with Vergil than a conversation with Vergil's interlocutor, Homer. All three poets have drawn their world in the engravings of a shield. Homer's shield, described in *Iliad* 18, records the order of the universe, and Vergil's in *Aeneid* 8 the march of history, however ordered or not. For Auden, Homer's universe lies in contrast to the history of our century, of war and poverty, where humankind runs the risk of the greatest loss of all, of the ability even "to weep because another wept." Warren's poem is an apostrophe, a poet's direct address, here to the poet Vergil, about his ending of the *Aeneid*: "Here's where you tear a hole in the poem, / a hole in the mind." Almost thirty years after his poetic policy speech, Frost wrote and recited an inaugural poem for John F. Kennedy. This poem reflects the public hopefulness of those days, as surely as its generic cousin, Vergil's fourth *Eclogue*, did in its time: "It makes the prophet in us all presage / The glory of a next Augustan age...A golden age of poetry and power / Of which this noonday's the beginning hour." Walcott's *Omeros* records history as well, but a different story. Like Auden, Walcott's explicit antecedent is Homer; like Auden as well, his technique of rewriting the past's cultural inheritance for new ways of understanding the present is Vergilian. So too Broch, whose novel, *The Death of Virgil*, links Vergil's death-bed wish to destroy the *Aeneid* and his final decision to spare it to the dilemma of art's role in the tragedies of the twentieth century. (Ed.)

BUILD SOIL—A POLITICAL PASTORAL

Why, Tityrus! But you've forgotten me.
I'm Meliboeus the potato man,
The one you had the talk with, you remember,
Here on this very campus years ago.
Hard times have struck me and I'm on the move.
I've had to give my interval farm up
For interest, and I've bought a mountain farm
For nothing down, all-out-doors of a place,
All woods and pasture only fit for sheep.
But sheep is what I'm going into next.
I'm done forever with potato crops
At thirty cents a bushel. Give me sheep.
I know wool's down to seven cents a pound.
But I don't calculate to sell my wool.
I didn't my potatoes. I consumed them.
I'll dress up in sheep's clothing and eat sheep.
The Muse takes care of you. You live by writing
Your poems on a farm and call that farming.
Oh, I don't blame you. I say take life easy.
I should myself, only I don't know how.
But have some pity on us who have to work.
Why don't you use your talents as a writer
To advertise our farms to city buyers,
Or else write something to improve food prices.
Get in a poem toward the next election.

Oh, Meliboeus, I have half a mind
To take a writing hand in politics.
Before now poetry has taken notice
Of wars, and what are wars but politics
Transformed from chronic to acute and bloody?

I may be wrong, but, Tityrus, to me
The times seem revolutionary bad.
The question is whether they've reached a depth

Of desperation that would warrant poetry's
Leaving love's alternations, joy and grief,
The weather's alternations, summer and winter,
Our age-long theme, for the uncertainty
Of judging who is a contemporary liar —
Who in particular, when all alike
Get called as much in clashes of ambition.
Life may be tragically bad, and I
Make bold to sing it so, but do I dare
Name names and tell you who by name is wicked?
Whittier's luck with Skipper Ireson awes me.
Many men's luck with Greatest Washington
(Who sat for Stuart's portrait, but who sat
Equally for the nation's Constitution).
I prefer to sing safely in the realm
Of types, composite and imagined people:
To affirm there is such a thing as evil
Personified, but ask to be excused
From saying on a jury 'Here's the guilty.'

I doubt if you're convinced the times are bad.

I keep my eye on Congress, Meliboeus.
They're in the best position of us all
To know if anything is very wrong.
I mean they could be trusted to give the alarm
If earth were thought about to change its axis,
Or a star coming to dilate the sun.
As long as lightly all their live-long sessions,
Like a yard full of school boys out at recess
Before their plays and games were organized,
They yelling mix tag, hide-and-seek, hop-scotch,
And leap frog in each other's way, — all's well.
Let newspapers profess to fear the worst!
Nothing's portentous, I am reassured.

Is socialism needed, do you think?

We have it now. For socialism is
An element in any government.
There's no such thing as socialism pure —
Except as an abstraction of the mind.
There's only democratic socialism,
Monarchic socialism — oligarchic,
The last being what they seem to have in Russia.
You often get it most in monarchy,
Least in democracy. In practice, pure,
I don't know what it would be. No one knows.
I have no doubt like all the loves when

Philosophized together into one —
One sickness of the body and the soul.
Thank God our practice holds the loves apart
Beyond embarrassing self-consciousness
Where natural friends are met, where dogs are kept,
Where women pray with priests. There is no love.
There's only love of men and women, love
Of children, love of friends, of men, of God,
Divine love, human love, parental love,
Roughly discriminated for the rough.

Poetry, itself once more, is back in love.

Pardon the analogy, my Meliboeus,
For sweeping me away. Let's see, where was I?

But don't you think more should be socialized
Than is?

      What should you mean by socialized?

Made good for everyone — things like inventions —
Made so we all should get the good of them —
All, not just great exploiting businesses.

We sometimes only get the bad of them.
In your sense of the word ambition has
Been socialized — the first propensity
To be attempted. Greed may well come next.
But the worst one of all to leave uncurbed,
Unsocialized, is ingenuity:
Which for no sordid self-aggrandizement,
For nothing but its own blind satisfaction
(In this it is as much like hate as love)
Works in the dark as much against as for us.
Even while we talk some chemist at Columbia
Is stealthily contriving wool from jute
That when let loose upon the grazing world
Will put ten thousand farmers out of sheep.
Everyone asks for freedom for himself,
The man free love, the business man free trade,
The writer and talker free speech and free press.
Political ambition has been taught,
By being punished back, it is not free:
It must at some point gracefully refrain.
Greed has been taught a little abnegation
And shall be more before we're done with it.
It is just fool enough to think itself
Self-taught. But our brute snarling and lashing taught it.

None shall be as ambitious as he can.
None should be as ingenious as he could,
Not if I had my say. Bounds should be set
To ingenuity for being so cruel
In bringing change unheralded on the unready.

I elect you to put the curb on it.

Were I dictator, I'll tell you what I'd do.

What should you do?

                          I'd let things take their course
And then I'd claim the credit for the outcome.

You'd make a sort of safety-first dictator.

Don't let the things I say against myself
Betray you into taking sides against me,
Or it might get you into trouble with me.
I'm not afraid to prophesy the future,
And be judged by the outcome, Meliboeus.
Listen and I will take my dearest risk.
We're always too much out or too much in.
At present from a cosmical dilation
We're so much out that the odds are against
Our ever getting inside in again.
But inside in is where we've got to get.
My friends all know I'm interpersonal.
But long before I'm interpersonal
Away 'way down inside I'm personal.
Just so before we're international
We're national and act as nationals.
The colors are kept unmixed on the palette,
Or better on dish plates all around the room,
So the effect when they are mixed on canvas
May seem almost exclusively designed.
Some minds are so confounded intermental
They remind me of pictures on a palette:
'Look at what happened. Surely some God pinxit.
Come look at my significant mud pie.'
It's hard to tell which is the worse abhorrence
Whether it's persons pied or nations pied.
Don't let me seem to say the exchange, the encounter,
May not be the important thing at last.
It well may be. We meet — I don't say when —
But must bring to the meeting the maturest,
The longest-saved-up, raciest, localest
We have strength of reserve in us to bring.

Tityrus, sometimes I'm perplexed myself
To find the good of commerce. Why should I
Have to sell you my apples and buy yours?
It can't be just to give the robber a chance
To catch them and take toll of them in transit.
Too mean a thought to get much comfort out of.
I figure that like any bandying
Of words or toys, it ministers to health.
It very likely quickens and refines us.

To market 'tis our destiny to go.
But much as in the end we bring for sale there
There is still more we never bring or should bring;
More that should be kept back — the soil for instance
In my opinion, — though we both know poets
Who fall all over each other to bring soil
And even subsoil and hardpan to market.
To sell the hay off, let alone the soil,
Is an unpardonable sin in farming.
The moral is, make a late start to market.
Let me preach to you, will you, Meliboeus?

Preach on. I thought you were already preaching.
But preach and see if I can tell the difference.

Needless to say to you, my argument
Is not to lure the city to the country.
Let those possess the land and only those,
Who love it with a love so strong and stupid
That they may be abused and taken advantage of
And made fun of by business, law, and art;
They still hang on. That so much of the earth's
Unoccupied need not make us uneasy.
We don't pretend to complete occupancy.
The world's one globe, human society
Another softer globe that slightly flattened
Rests on the world, and clinging slowly rolls.
We have our own round shape to keep unbroken.
The world's size has no more to do with us
Than has the universe's. We are balls,
We are round from the same source of roundness.
We are both round because the mind is round,
Because all reasoning is in a circle.
At least that's why the universe is round.

If what you're preaching is a line of conduct,
Just what am I supposed to do about it?
Reason in circles?

                        No, refuse to be
Seduced back to the land by any claim
The land may seem to have on man to use it.
Let none assume to till the land but farmers.
I only speak to you as one of them.
You shall go to your run-out mountain farm,
Poor castaway of commerce, and so live
That none shall ever see you come to market—
Not for a long long time. Plant, breed, produce,
But what you raise or grow, why feed it out,
Fat it or plow it under where it stands
To build the soil. For what is more accursed
Than an impoverished soil pale and metallic?
What cries more to our kind for sympathy?
I'll make a compact with you, Meliboeus,
To match you deed for deed and plan for plan.
Friends crowd around me with their five-year plans
That Soviet Russia has made fashionable.
You come to me and I'll unfold to you
A five-year plan I call so, not because
It takes ten years or so to carry out,
Rather because it took five years at least
To think it out. Come close, let us conspire—
In self-restraint, if in restraint of trade.
You will go to your run-out mountain farm
And do what I command you. I take care
To command only what you meant to do
Anyway. That is my style of dictator.
Build soil. Turn the farm in upon itself
Until it can contain itself no more,
But sweating-full, drips wine and oil a little.
I will go to my run-out social mind
And be as unsocial with it as I can.
The thought I have, and my first impulse is
To take to market—I will turn it under.
The thought from that thought—I will turn it under.
And so on to the limit of my nature.
We are too much out, and if we won't draw in
We shall be driven in. I was brought up
A state-rights free-trade Democrat. What's that?
An inconsistency. The state shall be
Laws to itself, it seems, and yet have no
Control of what it sells or what it buys.
Suppose someone comes near me who in rate
Of speech and thinking is so much my better
I am imposed on, silenced and discouraged.
Do I submit to being supplied by him
As the more economical producer,
More wonderful, more beautiful producer?

No. I unostentatiously move off
Far enough for my thought-flow to resume.
Thought product and food product are to me
Nothing compared to the producing of them.
I sent you once a song with the refrain:

> Let me be the one
> To do what is done—

My share at least lest I be empty-idle.
Keep off each other and keep each other off.
You see the beauty of my proposal is
It needn't wait on general revolution.
I bid you to a one-man revolution—
The only revolution that is coming.
We're too unseparate out among each other—
With goods to sell and notions to impart.
A youngster comes to me with half a quatrain
To ask me if I think it worth the pains
Of working out the rest, the other half.
I am brought guaranteed young prattle poems
Made publicly in school, above suspicion
Of plagiarism and help of cheating parents.
We congregate embracing from distrust
As much as love, and too close in to strike
And be so very striking. Steal away
The song says. Steal away and stay away.
Don't join too many gangs. Join few if any.
Join the United States and join the family—
But not much in between unless a college.
Is it a bargain, Shepherd Meliboeus?

Probably, but you're far too fast and strong
For my mind to keep working in your presence.
I can tell better after I get home,
Better a month from now when cutting posts
Or mending fence it all comes back to me
What I was thinking when you interrupted
My life-train logic. I agree with you
We're too unseparate. And going home
From company means coming to our senses.

Joseph Brodsky

ECLOGUE IV: WINTER
To Derek Walcott

Ultima Cumaei venit iam carminis aetas;
magnus ab integro saeclorum nascitur ordo.
— VERGIL, _Eclogue IV_

["The last age of the Cumaean song is now arriving;
the great order of the centuries is born anew."]

I

In winter it darkens the moment lunch is over.
It's hard then to tell starving men from sated.
A yawn keeps a phrase from leaving its cozy lair.
The dry, instant version of light, the opal
snow, dooms tall alders — by having freighted
them — to insomnia, to your glare,

well after midnight. Forget-me-nots and roses
crop up less frequently in dialogues. Dogs with languid
fervor pick up the trail, for they, too, leave traces.
Night, having entered the city, pauses
as in a nursery, finds a baby under the blanket.
And the pen creaks like steps that are someone else's.

II

My life has dragged on. In the recitative of a blizzard
a keen ear picks up the tune of the Ice Age.
Every "Down in the Valley" is, for sure,
a chilled boogie-woogie. A bitter, brittle
cold represents, as it were, a message
to the body of its final temperature

or — the earth itself, sighing out of habit
for its galactic past, its sub-zero horrors.
Cheeks burn crimson like radishes even here.
Cosmic space is always shot through with matte agate,
and the beeping Morse, returning homeward,
finds no ham operator's ear.

III

In February, lilac retreats to osiers.
Imperative to a snowman's profile,
carrots get more expensive. Limited by a brow,
a glance at cold, metallic objects
is fiercer than the metal itself. This, while
you peel eyes from objects, still may allow

no shedding of blood. The Lord, some reckon,
was reviewing His world in this very fashion
on the eighth day and after. In winter, we're
not berry pickers: we stuff the cracks with oakum,
praise the common good with a greater passion,
and things grow older by, say, a year.

IV

In great cold, pavements glaze like a sugar candy,
steam from the mouth suggests a dragon,
if you dream of a door, you tend to slam it.
My life has dragged on. The signs are plenty.
They'd make yet another life, just as dragging.
From these signs alone one would compose a climate

or a landscape. Preferably with no people,
with virgin white through a lacework shroud,
— a world where nobody heard of Parises, Londons; where
weekdays are spun by diffusive, feeble
light; where, too, in the end you shudder
potting the ski tracks...Well, just a pair.

V

Time equals cold. Each body, sooner
or later, falls prey to a telescope. With the years,
it moves away from the luminary, grows colder.
Hoarfrost jungles the windowpane with sumac,
ferns, or horsetail, with what appears
to be nursed on this glass and deprived of color

by loneliness. But, as with a marble hero,
one's eye rolls up rather than runs in winter.
Where sight fails, yielding to dreams' swarmed forces,
time, fallen sharply beneath the zero,
burns your brain like the index finger
of a scamp from popular Russian verses.

VI

My life has dragged on. One cold resembles another
cold. Time looks like time. What sets them apart is only
a warm body. Mule-like, stubborn creature,
it stands firmly between them, rather
like a border guard: stiffened, sternly
preventing the wandering of the future

into the past. In winter, to put it bleakly,
Tuesday is Saturday. The daytime is a deceiver:
Are the lights out already? Or not yet on? It's chilly.
Dailies might as well be printed weekly.
Time stares at a looking glass like a diva
who's forgotten what's on tonight: *Tosca*? Oh no, *Lucia*?

VII

Dreams in the frozen season are longer, keener.
The patchwork quilt and the parquet deal,
on their mutual squares, in chessboard warriors.
The hoarser the blizzard rules the chimney,
the hotter the quest for a pure ideal
of naked flesh in a cotton vortex,

and you dream nasturtiums' stubborn odor,
a tuft of cobwebs shading a corner nightly,
in a narrow ravine torrid Terek's splashes,
a feast of fingertips caught in shoulder

straps. And then all goes quiet. Idly
an ember smolders in dawn's gray ashes.

VIII

Cold values space. Baring no rattling sabers,
it takes hill and dale, townships and hamlets
(the populace cedes without trying
tricks), mostly cities, whose great ensembles,
whose arches and colonnades, in hundreds,
stand like prophets of cold's white triumph,

looming wanly. Cold is gliding
from the sky on a parachute. Each and every column
looks like a fifth, desires an overthrow.
Only the crow doesn't take snow gladly.
And you often hear the angry, solemn,
patriotic gutturals speaking crow.

IX

In February, the later it is, the lower
the mercury. More time means more cold. Stars, scattered
like a smashed thermometer, turn remotest
regions of night into a strep marvel.
In daytime, when sky is akin to stucco,
Malevich himself wouldn't have noticed

them, white on white. That's why angels
are invisible. To their legions
cold is of benefit. We would make them
out, the winged ones, had our eyes' angle
been indeed on high, where they are linking
in white camouflage like Finnish marksmen.

X

For me, other latitudes have no usage.
I am skewered by cold like a grilled-goose portion.
Glory to naked birches, to the fir-tree needle,
to the yellow bulb in an empty passage—
glory to everything set by the wind in motion:
at a ripe age, it can replace the cradle.

The North is the honest thing. For it keeps repeating
all your life the same stuff—whispering, in full volume,
in the life dragged on, in all kinds of voices;
and toes freeze numb in your deerskin creepers,
reminding you, as you complete your polar
conquest, of love, of shivering under clock faces.

XI

In great cold, distance won't sing like sirens.
In space, the deepest inhaling hardly
ensures exhaling, nor does departure
a return. Time is the flesh of the silent
cosmos. Where nothing ticks. Even being hurtled
out of the spacecraft, one wouldn't capture

any sounds on the radio—neither fox-trots nor maidens
wailing from a hometown station.
What kills you out there, in orbit, isn't
the lack of oxygen but the abundance
of time in its purest (with no addition
of your life) form. It's hard to breathe it.

XII

Winter! I cherish your bitter flavor
of cranberries, tangerine crescents on faience saucers,
the tea, sugar-frosted almonds (at best, two ounces).
You were opening our small beaks in favor
of names like Marina or Olga—morsels
of tenderness at that age that fancies

cousins. I sing a snowpile's blue contours
at dusk, rustling foil, clicking B-flat somewhere,
as though "Chopsticks" were tried by the Lord's own finger.
And the logs, which rattled in stony courtyards
of the gray, dank city that freezes bare
by the sea, are still warming my every fiber.

XIII

At a certain age, the time of year, the season
coincides with fate. Theirs is a brief affair.
But on days like this you sense you are right. Your worries
about things that haven't come your way are ceasing,
and a simple botanist may take care
of commenting upon daily life and mores.

In this period, eyes lose their green of nettles,
the triangle drops its geometric ardor:
all the angles drawn with cobwebs are fuzzy.
In exchanges on death, place matters
more and more than time. The cold gets harder.
And saliva suddenly burns its cozy

XIV

tongue, like that coin. Still, all the rivers
are ice-locked. You can put on long johns and trousers,
strap steel runners to boots with ropes and a piece of timber.
Teeth, worn out by the tap dance of shivers,
won't rattle because of fear. And the Muse's
voice gains a reticent, private timbre.

That's the birth of an eclogue. Instead of the shepherd's signal,
a lamp's flaring up. Cyrillic, while running witless
on the pad as though to escape the captor,
knows more of the future than the famous sibyl:
of how to darken against the whiteness,
as long as the whiteness lasts. And after.

[*1977 / Translated by the author*]

Dana L. Burgess

VERGILIAN MODES IN SPIKE LEE'S *DO THE RIGHT THING*

The street scenes of Spike Lee's *Do the Right Thing* are as redolent of asphodel as of asphalt. Here is an urban *locus amoenus* ["pleasing, or pastoral place"] where the heat of the day may be overwhelming, but where the life of the street offers a small-town familiarity, and Sal's pizzeria, a cool resting spot. The middle-aged men who sit on the corner have come outside to recline on their folding chairs. The heat is the occasion for an open fire hydrant. It is Saturday. Spike Lee shoots the street as a tidy and enclosed space. His camera never wanders away to the rest of Bedford-Stuyvesant, nor to the New York City which feels so remote. This is not the grimy ghetto so often seen in white cinematic visions of black urban life; it is an urban pastoral. But like the ancient pastoral visions it is haunted by a problem; not the subjective anguish of an expiring Daphnis, but the political and territorial tensions of Sal's white pizzeria in the black neighborhood. Vergil appropriated Theocritus' apolitical pastoral and flavored it with Tityrus' reflections on the great city of Rome (*Ecl.* 1.19). Now Spike Lee has created a remote and private ghetto, but one where the public problem of racism continues to intrude. While the residents of the block are enjoying the fire hydrant's fountain, they spray a white man's convertible Cadillac, and are in turn denied their shower by the white cops. The idyll remains idyllic, but there is pressure from within and without. Tityrus and Meliboeus are both in the summer heat, but only Tityrus can recline in the shade, playing on his pipe. Like Meliboeus, the residents of Spike Lee's Bed-Sty may dwell in a *locus amoenus,* but their economic condition makes them feel the heat of the day more than their neighbors. It is Spike Lee's ability to balance gently the pastoral and the political which is one of the Vergilian modes in *Do the Right Thing.*

Mookie moves through his world with heroic grace. He can deliver a pizza, visit Tina for an erotic break, and converse with the locals on the way back to work. Everybody knows Mookie, and though his sister can remonstrate with him for his "responsibilities," it is Mookie who calls out to his friends on the street to "get a job." Spike Lee, in his acting as well as his writing and directing, has balanced Mookie between devotion to duty and an innate indolence. Here is another delicate Vergilian mode, but one more reminiscent of the *Aeneid* than of the bucolic poetry.

Pater ["Father"] Aeneas acts to regulate the responses of his people to the problems they encounter, even as he has his own troubling reactions to those same events. In his first two pieces of directly reported speech Aeneas reveals the fundamental tension between his public role and his private anxiety. Speaking in soliloquy during the storm of book one, Aeneas wishes for the hero's death which would release him

---

Dana L. Burgess, "Vergilian Modes in Spike Lee's *Do the Right Thing*," *CML* 11 (1991): 313–316. Reprinted by permission of CML, Inc.

from his responsibilities, *(Aen.* 1. 94–101), but when he must speak in public he tells his people that all will one day be well, *(Aen.* 1. 198-207). This is not duplicity; it is the genuine conflict within the man who must lead others, but who must also feel his private pain. Mookie is similarly caught. He seeks to mediate between his black neighborhood and Sal's white pizzeria, so it is only Mookie who can both rebuke Sal's sharply racist son, Pino, and the equally volatile Buggin' Out who initiates a boycott of Sal's. But Mookie too has his private fears, and he cannot endure Sal's affection for his sister. Mookie can take ninety minutes to deliver a pizza, and Jade complains that he doesn't carry his own weight in paying the rent. Delivering his pizzas Mookie mediates between the black and white worlds and accepts his responsibility to regulate the passions of each. His anger at Sal's attentions to his sister shows that he is tormented by the same fundamental racism which infects the other characters. Mookie is held in balance by Spike Lee, and like Vergil's Aeneas he has public responsibilities which are in tension with his private passions, fears, and incapacities.

The balance in the character of Aeneas is only fully explored in the last event of the epic. Only Pallas can make Aeneas plunge his sword into Turnus, and only Radio Raheem can make Mookie toss a garbage can through Sal's window. The contradictions within Radio Raheem are Vergilian in their own right, and they also motivate the crucial moral action of the film. Like Pallas, Radio Raheem is the hero's ally, but one who is fundamentally dependent and incompetent. Pallas is only a child, unable to stand up to Turnus in battle. Radio Raheem's weakness is more obscure, but no less debilitating. He has wholly defined his personality around his radio; even his name is "Radio." At one point Radio Raheem's boom box loses power, and at that instant the giant stumbles. He has an essential separation from society, imposed more by his own spooky silence than his radio's deafening roar. When he interacts with a group of Hispanics, it is only to have a radio duel; he cannot connect with others apart from his machine. When he meets Mookie on the street and displays his rings spelling out "love" and "hate," he speaks in mantic metaphoric monologue. His image is of boxing, but the battle is between the right and left hands of a single boxer. His discourse is about relations within society, but he remains apart. In his isolation and social incapacity, Radio Raheem is exceptionally vulnerable, and we expect the protective Mookie to watch out for him, just as he patronizes the other mantic characters: Da Mayor, Smiley, Love Daddy and Mother Sister. In the climactic scene in Sal's, it is Radio Raheem who cannot understand the violence of his own radio. Mookie asks only that the white men comprehend Radio Raheem's pathological relationship to his radio, that they indulge this fragile creature. Like Pallas in armor, Radio Raheem is apparently capable. He does not appear fragile. Just as Turnus may be technically right in killing Pallas on the battlefield, Sal is technically right in smashing Radio Raheem's radio in the pizzeria. The death of Radio Raheem at the hands of the white cops may then only be an objective completion of the destruction of his character which has occurred with the destruction of his radio. He only plays one tape, Public Enemy's *Fight the Power,* the theme piece for the film. Radio Raheem carries the burden of the significant political consciousness for the neighborhood, even as he lugs the mighty radio. It is only Radio Raheem whom Buggin' Out can finally convince to assist in a confrontation with Sal. This fragile giant, tragically alienated, but carrying the community's values, himself embodies a Vergilian mode of ambiguity and tragic contradiction.

Whatever other Vergilian modes of balance and ambiguity we may be able to find, it is in the ending of *Do the Right Thing* that Spike Lee has fashioned his most subtle and disturbing tension. After playing the role of mediator, Mookie finally acts. We might say of Aeneas that his most typical posture is that of stupefied wonder. Confronted over and over with moral confusion, Aeneas stands agape. When, at the end of the poem, he hears the words of Turnus, Aeneas begins to operate in his typically dilatory mode (*Aen.* 12. 940–941), but when he catches sight of the belt of Pallas he acts without that hesitation (*Aen.* 12. 950). Mookie too has been an observer. He has watched the quarrels of Sal's sons and the quirky personalities of the people of the street. He has sojourned with Tina without seeming to commit himself to any details of a relationship, and he has even passively acquiesced in the Hispanic naming of his son, Hector. Sal's attentions to his sister have stirred him, but even here he is willing to avoid a break with Sal. Only the death of Radio Raheem calls for a response from the Mookie who is public and the Mookie who is private; and the only available response is an assault on Sal's. Even as Mookie walks toward Sal's with the garbage can in his hands he recognizes the moral complexity of the moment. He moves with deliberation. He removes the lid and bag from the garbage can before he throws it. He cries out, "Hate!," but we don't see the passion of anger in his face. Neither the character nor the filmmaker believe that this is a moment of ethical clarity, even though a decisive action has finally been performed.

Spike Lee's film ends with passages from Martin Luther King, Jr. and Malcolm X, on the one hand forbidding the use of violence in black revolution, and on the other arguing for its appropriate utility in "self-defense." This closure is Spike Lee's, not Mookie's, and it is designed to assure that no viewer leave the theater believing that there is a simple moral to this story. *Do the Right Thing* has been so hotly debated because of the ethical ambiguity of its closure. Spike Lee refuses to mark one of the statements at the film's close as the "right thing," and those yearning for a better ending to the *Aeneid* are like those who are dissatisfied with Spike Lee's closure. The *Aeneid* is finished as we have it. Vergil has refused to stand back from Aeneas' final act and tell his reader that it is or is not the "right thing." We are left with Aeneas' sword in Turnus' breast, just as we are left with the contradictory words of Malcolm X and Martin Luther King, Jr. In each case the authorial comment is a non-comment. Vergil and Spike Lee will only tell us what is a problem, they will not be so arrogant as to suggest that the problem admits of solution. The forces calling for the death of Turnus are no less compelling than the forces which burn Sal's pizzeria, and the reasons to refrain from each act of violence are equally compelling.

In the final scenes of *Do the Right Thing* the sidewalk in Brooklyn is littered with burnt junk. Now at last we have arrived at the black ghetto so familiar to us from the white man's cinema. And can the Italy after Turnus ever be a *locus amoenus* ["pleasing place"] again? In the death of Turnus, Vergil foreshadows centuries of foreign and civil wars. But Mookie and Aeneas will go on. These are not characters in any way destroyed by the events in which they participate. Mookie, like Spike Lee, looks forward to the continuation of the strife which the film shows, even as he looks forward to the continuing attempt to address the bases of that strife. Aeneas, of course, will found the Julio-Claudian *gens* ["clan, line"] which will continue to play such an active role in all that is good and bad about Rome. The lack of closure is thus true on several levels; the ambiguities must extend forever if they are to be worthy of their tragic status. Before the burning of Sal's, Da Mayor can stand before the crowd begging for dispersal, but the failures of his generation require that he be ignored. Mother Sister's hysteria amidst the riot doesn't stir Mookie who sits a few feet away. The young are looking forward to a lifetime of struggle while the old look back on the same.

There can be no living film directors more intelligent and daring than Spike Lee, for the Vergilian mode is terrifying in literature or in film. We are rarely sent out of a theater with a closure that is not a closure, with no answer to a tragic and significant problem. In groping for a simple message from *Do the Right Thing*, we might latch on to a trivially true statement such as, "racism is bad." But this hardly does justice to the film. Readers of the *Aeneid* might want to come away from the epic assured that Turnus' death may ensure the future greatness of Rome, but the final scene is structured to deny us that soothing understanding. Mookie and Aeneas live in a world that is murky, and we come to a dark epiphany as we finally see that this landscape of ambiguity is our own.

C. Day Lewis

THE GEORGICS OF VIRGIL

DEDICATORY STANZAS
To Stephen Spender

Poets are not in much demand these days—
We're red, it seems, or cracked, or bribed, or hearty
And, if invited, apt to spoil the party
With the oblique reproach of emigrés:
We cut no ice, although we're fancy skaters:
Aiming at art, we only strike the arty.
Poetry now, the kinder tell us, caters
For an elite: still, it gives us the hump
To think that we're the unacknowledged rump
Of a long parliament of legislators.

Where are the war poets? the fools inquire.
We were prophets of a changeable morning
Who hoped for much but saw the clouds forewarning:
We were at war, while they still played with fire
And rigged the market for the ruin of man:
Spain was a death to us, Munich a mourning.
No wonder then if, like the pelican,
We have turned inward for our iron rations
Tapping the vein and sole reserve of passion,
Drawing from poetry's capital what we can.

Yes, we shall fight, but—let them not mistake it—
Not for the ones who grudged to peace their pence
And gave war a blank cheque in self-defence,
Nor those who take self-interest and fake it
Into a code of honour—the distorting
Mirror those magnates hold to experience.
It's for dear life alone we shall be fighting,
The poet's living-space, the love of men,
And poets must speak for common suffering men
While history in sheets of fire is writing.

Meanwhile, what touches the heart at all, engrosses.
Through the flushed springtime and the fading year
I lived on country matters. Now June was here
Again, and brought the smell of flowering grasses
To me and death to many overseas:
They lie in the flowering sunshine, flesh once dear
To some, now parchment for the heart's release.
Soon enough each is called into the quarrel.
Till then, taking a leaf from Virgil's laurel,
I sang in time of war the arts of peace.

Virgil — a tall man, dark and countrified
In looks, they say: retiring: no rhetorician:
Of humble birth: a Celt, whose first ambition
Was to be a philosopher: Dante's guide.
But chiefly dear for his gift to understand
Earth's intricate, ordered heart, and for a vision
That saw beyond an imperial day the hand
Of man no longer armed against his fellow
But all for vine and cattle, fruit and fallow,
Subduing with love's positive force the land.

Different from his our age and myths, our toil
The same. Our exile and extravagances,
Revolt, retreat, fine faiths, disordered fancies
Are but the poet's search for a right soil
Where words may settle, marry, and conceive an
Imagined truth, for a regimen that enhances
Their natural grace. Now, as to one whom even
Our age's drought and spate have not deterred
From cherishing, like a bud of flame, the word,
I dedicate this book to you, dear Stephen.

Now, when war's long midwinter seems to freeze us
And numb our living sources once for all,
That veteran of Virgil's I recall
Who made a kitchen-garden by the Galaesus
On derelict land, and got the first of spring
From airs and buds, the first fruits in the fall,
And lived at peace there, happy as a king.
Naming him for good luck, I see man's native
Stock is perennial, and our creative
Winged seed can strike a root in anything.

June 1940

Allen Tate

AENEAS AT WASHINGTON

I myself saw furious with blood
Neoptolemus, at his side the black Atridae,
Hecuba and the hundred daughters, Priam
Cut down, his filth drenching the holy fires.
In that extremity I bore me well,
A true gentleman, valorous in arms,
Disinterested and honorable. Then fled:
That was a time when civilization
Run by the few fell to the many, and
Crashed to the shout of men, the clang of arms:
Cold victualing I seized, I hoisted up
The old man my father upon my back,
In the smoke made by sea for a new world
Saving little — a mind imperishable
If time is, a love of past things tenuous
As the hesitation of receding love.

(To the reduction of uncitied littorals
We brought chiefly the vigor of prophecy,
Our hunger breeding calculation
And fixed triumphs)

              I saw the thirsty dove
In the glowing fields of Troy, hemp ripening
And tawny corn, the thickening Blue Grass
All lying rich forever in the green sun.
I see all things apart, the towers that men
Contrive I too contrived long, long ago.
Now I demand little. The singular passion
Abides its object and consumes desire
In the circling shadow of its appetite.
There was a time when the young eyes were slow,
Their flame steady beyond the firstling fire,
I stood in the rain, far from home at nightfall

By the Potomac, the great Dome lit the water,
The city my blood had built I knew no more
While the screech-owl whistled his new delight
Consecutively dark.

                        Stuck in the wet mire
Four thousand leagues from the ninth buried city
I thought of Troy, what we had built her for.

Robert Frost

TWO TRAMPS IN MUD TIME

Out of the mud two strangers came
And caught me splitting wood in the yard.
And one of them put me off my aim
By hailing cheerily 'Hit them hard!'
I knew pretty well why he dropped behind
And let the other go on a way.
I knew pretty well what he had in mind:
He wanted to take my job for pay.

Good blocks of oak it was I split,
As large around as the chopping block;
And every piece I squarely hit
Fell splinterless as a cloven rock.
The blows that a life of self-control
Spares to strike for the common good
That day, giving a loose to my soul,
I spent on the unimportant wood.

The sun was warm but the wind was chill.
You know how it is with an April day
When the sun is out and the wind is still,
You're one month on in the middle of May.
But if you so much as dare to speak,
A cloud comes over the sunlit arch,
A wind comes off a frozen peak,
And you're two months back in the middle of March.

A bluebird comes tenderly up to alight
And turns to the wind to unruffle a plume
His song so pitched as not to excite
A single flower as yet to bloom.
It is snowing a flake: and he half knew
Winter was only playing possum.
Except in color he isn't blue,
But he wouldn't advise a thing to blossom.

From: THE POETRY OF ROBERT FROST, edited by Edward Connery Lathem, Copyright 1936, © 1961,
1962 by Robert Frost, © 1964, 1970 by Lesley Frost Ballantine, © 1969 by Henry Holt and Company, Inc.,
© 1997 by Edward Connery Lathem. Reprinted by permission of Henry Holt and Company, Inc.

The water for which we may have to look
In summertime with a witching-wand,
In every wheelrut's now a brook,
In every print of hoof a pond.
Be glad of water, but don't forget
The lurking frost in the earth beneath
That will steal forth after the sun is set
And show on the water its crystal teeth.

The time when most I loved my task
These two must make me love it more
By coming with what they came to ask.
You'd think I never had felt before
The weight of an ax-head poised aloft,
The grip on earth of outspread feet,
The life of muscles rocking soft
And smooth and moist in vernal heat.

Out of the woods two hulking tramps
(From sleeping God knows where last night,
But not long since in the lumber camps).
They thought all chopping was theirs of right.
Men of the woods and lumberjacks,
They judged me by their appropriate tool.
Except as a fellow handled an ax,
They had no way of knowing a fool.

Nothing on either side was said.
They knew they had but to stay their stay
And all their logic would fill my head:
As that I had no right to play
With what was another man's work for gain.
My right might be love but theirs was need.
And where the two exist in twain
Theirs was the better right—agreed.

But yield who will to their separation,
My object in living is to unite
My avocation and my vocation
As my two eyes make one in sight.
Only where love and need are one,
And the work is play for mortal stakes,
Is the deed ever really done
For Heaven and the future's sakes.

W. H. Auden

THE SHIELD OF ACHILLES

        She looked over his shoulder
            For vines and olive trees,
        Marble well-governed cities
            And ships upon untamed seas,
        But there on the shining metal
            His hands had put instead
        An artificial wilderness
            And a sky like lead.

A plain without a feature, bare and brown,
    No blade of grass, no sign of neighborhood,
Nothing to eat and nowhere to sit down,
    Yet, congregated on its blankness, stood
        An unintelligible multitude
A million eyes, a million boots in line,
Without expression, waiting for a sign.

Out of the air a voice without a face
    Proved by statistics that some cause was just
In tones as dry and level as the place:
    No one was cheered and nothing was discussed;
        Column by column in a cloud of dust
They marched away enduring a belief
Whose logic brought them, somewhere else, to grief.

        She looked over his shoulder
            For ritual pieties,
        White flower-garlanded heifers,
            Libation and sacrifice,
        But there on the shining metal
            Where the altar should have been,
        She saw by his flickering forge-light
            Quite another scene.

Barbed wire enclosed an arbitrary spot
    Where bored officials lounged (one cracked a joke)
And sentries sweated for the day was hot:
    A crowd of ordinary decent folk
    Watched from without and neither moved nor spoke
As three pale figures were led forth and bound
To three posts driven upright in the ground.

The mass and majesty of this world, all
    That carries weight and always weighs the same
Lay in the hands of others; they were small
    And could not hope for help and no help came:
    What their foes liked to do was done, their shame
Was all the worst could wish; they lost their pride
And died as men before their bodies died.

    She looked over his shoulder
        For athletes at their games,
    Men and women in a dance
        Moving their sweet limbs
    Quick, quick, to music,
        But there on the shining shield
    His hands had set no dancing-floor
        But a weed-choked field.

A ragged urchin, aimless and alone,
    Loitered about that vacancy; a bird
Flew up to safety from his well-aimed stone:
    That girls are raped, that two boys knife a third,
    Were axioms to him, who'd never heard
Of any world where promises were kept,
Or one could weep because another wept.

    The thin-lipped armorer,
        Hephaestos, howled away,
    Thetis of the shining breasts
        Cried out in dismay
    At what the god had wrought
        To please her son, the strong
    Iron-hearted man-slaying Achilles
        Who would not live long.

1952

Rosanna Warren

TURNUS (AENEID XII)

for Michael Putnam

Not lion, not wind, not fire, not sacrificial
bull, not in strength and sinew godlike, nor even as stag, Silvia's gentle
one, tame, tower-antlered, awash in the sweet blood

of his groin where the Trojan arrow struck—
no beast, no simile, Turnus, but a man alone
when your knees buckle and you look back
at the ashen city, the girl with her eyes cast down,

away. You've crashed to your side, the spear
has whispered its only message through the air.
And when you speak, and He seems inclined to hear,
it's the woods that reply, the shadowed hilltops near

and farther, and what they speak is a groan
for a lost world, for leaflight, the childhood grove
where the small stream stammered its rhymes in amber and green.
And if He pauses? If His sword hovers above

Your chest? Here's where you tear a hole in the poem,
a hole in the mind, here's where the russet glare
of ships aflame and the pyre and the amethyst gleam
from the boy's swordbelt rise and roil in a blur.

We are trapped in meanings that circulate like blood.
The sword descends. And He who kills you is not
a myth, nor a city. His eyes searching yours could
be a lover's eyes. It was love He fought.

Rosanna Warren, "Turnus (*Aeneid* XII)," *Arion*, Third Series 3.2 & 3 (1995/1996) 174. Reprinted by permission of Rosanna Warren.

Robert Frost

FOR JOHN F. KENNEDY HIS INAUGURATION

Gift Outright of "The Gift Outright"

With Some Preliminary History in Rhyme

Summoning artists to participate
In the august occasions of the state
Seems something artists ought to celebrate.
Today is for my cause a day of days.
And his be poetry's old-fashioned praise
Who was the first to think of such a thing.
This verse that in acknowledgment I bring
Goes back to the beginning of the end
Of what had been for centuries the trend;
A turning point in modern history.
Colonial had been the thing to be
As long as the great issue was to see
What country'd be the one to dominate
By character, by tongue, by native trait,
The new world Christopher Columbus found.
The French, the Spanish, and the Dutch were downed
And counted out. Heroic deeds were done.
Elizabeth the First and England won.
Now came on a new order of the ages
That in the Latin of our founding sages
(Is it not written on the dollar bill
We carry in our purse and pocket still?)
God nodded his approval of as good.
So much those heroes knew and understood,
I mean the great four, Washington,
John Adams, Jefferson, and Madison, —
So much they knew as consecrated seers
They must have seen ahead what now appears,
They would bring empires down about our ears
And by the example of our Declaration
Make everybody want to be a nation.

From: THE POETRY OF ROBERT FROST, edited by Edward Connery Lathem, Copyright 1936, © 1961, 1962 by Robert Frost, © 1964, 1970 by Lesley Frost Ballantine, © 1969 by Henry Holt and Company, Inc., © 1997 by Edward Connery Lathem. Reprinted by permission of Henry Holt and Company, Inc.

And this is no aristocratic joke
At the expense of negligible folk.
We see how seriously the races swarm
In their attempts at sovereignty and form.
They are our wards we think to some extent
For the time being and with their consent,
To teach them how Democracy is meant.
"New order of the ages" did we say?
If it looks none too orderly today,
'Tis a confusion it was ours to start
So in it have to take courageous part.
No one of honest feeling would approve
A ruler who pretended not to love
A turbulence he had the better of.
Everyone knows the glory of the twain
Who gave America the aeroplane
To ride the whirlwind and the hurricane.
Some poor fool has been saying in his heart
Glory is out of date in life and art.
Our venture in revolution and outlawry
Has justified itself in freedom's story
Right down to now in glory upon glory.
Come fresh from an election like the last,
The greatest vote a people ever cast,
So close yet sure to be abided by,
It is no miracle our mood is high.
Courage is in the air in bracing whiffs
Better than all the stalemate an's and ifs.
There was the book of profile tales declaring
For the emboldened politicians daring
To break with followers when in the wrong,
A healthy independence of the throng,
A democratic form of right divine
To rule first answerable to high design.
There is a call to life a little sterner,
And braver for the earner, learner, yearner.
Less criticism of the field and court
And more preoccupation with the sport.
It makes the prophet in us all presage
The glory of a next Augustan age
Of a power leading from its strength and pride,
Of young ambition eager to be tried,
Firm in our free beliefs without dismay,
In any game the nations want to play.
A golden age of poetry and power
Of which this noonday's the beginning hour.

OMEROS

BOOK ONE, Chapter XIII

I

"I grew up where alleys ended in a harbour
and Infinity wasn't the name of our street;
where the town anarchist was the corner barber

with his own flagpole and revolving Speaker's seat.
There were rusted mirrors in which we would look back
on the world's events. There, toga'd in a pinned sheet,

the curled hairs fell like commas. On their varnished rack,
The World's Great Classics read backwards in his mirrors
where he doubled as my chamberlain. I was known

for quoting from them as he was for his scissors.
I bequeath you that clean sheet and an empty throne."
We'd arrived at that corner where the barber-pole

angled from the sidewalk, and the photographer,
who'd taken his portrait, and, as some think, his soul,
leant from a small window and scissored his own hair

in a mime, suggesting a trim was overdue
to my father, who laughed and said "Wait" with one hand.
Then the barber mimed a shave with his mouth askew,

and left the window to wait by his wooden door
framed with dead portraits, and he seemed to understand
something in the life opposite not seen before.

"The rock he lived on was nothing. Not a nation
or a people," my father said, and, in his eyes,
this was a curse. When he raged, his indignation

jabbed the air with his scissors, a swift catching flies,
as he pumped the throne serenely round to his view.
He gestured like Shylock: "Hath not a Jew eyes?"

making his man a negative. An Adventist,
he's stuck on one glass that photograph of Garvey's
with the braided tricorne and gold-fringed epaulettes,

and that is his other Messiah. His paradise
is a phantom Africa. Elephants. Trumpets.
And when I quote Shylock silver brims in his eyes.

✧ ✧ ✧

BOOK THREE, Chapter XXVIII

I

Now he heard the griot muttering his prophetic song
of sorrow that would be the past. It was a note, long-drawn
and endless in its winding like the brown river's tongue:

"We were the colour of shadows when we came down
with tinkling leg-irons to join the chains of the sea,
for the silver coins multiplying on the sold horizon,

and these shadows are reprinted now on the white sand
of antipodal coasts, your ashen ancestors
from the Bight of Benin, from the margin of Guinea.

There were seeds in our stomachs, in the cracking pods
of our skulls on the scorching decks, the tubers
withered in no time. We watched as the river-gods

changed from snakes into currents. When inspected,
our eyes showed dried fronds in their brown irises,
and from our curved spines, the rib-cages radiated

like fronds from a palm-branch. Then, when the dead
palms were heaved overside, the ribbed corpses
floated, riding, to the white sand they remembered,

to the Bight of Benin, to the margin of Guinea.
So, when you see burnt branches riding the swell,
trying to reclaim the surf through crooked fingers,

after a night of rough wind by some stone-white hotel,
past the bright triangular passage of the windsurfers,
remember us to the black waiter bringing the bill."

But they crossed, they survived. There is the epical splendour.
Multiply the rain's lances, multiply their ruin,
the grace born from subtraction as the hold's iron door

rolled over their eyes like pots left out in the rain,
and the bolt rammed home its echo, the way that thunder-
claps perpetuate their reverberation.

So there went the Ashanti one way, the Mandingo another,
the Ibo another, the Guinea. Now each man was a nation
in himself, without mother, father, brother.

II

The worst crime is to leave a man's hands empty.
Men are born makers, with that primal simplicity
in every maker since Adam. This is pre-history,

that itching instinct in the criss-crossed net
of their palms, its wickerwork. They could not
stay idle too long. The chained wrists couldn't forget

the carver for whom antelopes leapt, or
the bow-maker the shaft, or the armourer
his nail-studs, the shield held up to Hector

that was the hammerer's art. So the wet air
revolved in the potter's palms, in the painter's eye
the arcs of a frantic springbok bucked soundlessly,

baboons kept signing their mimetic alphabet
in case men forgot it, so out of habit
their fingers grew leaves in the foetid ground of the boat.

So now they were coals, firewood, dismembered
branches, not men. They had left their remembered
shadows to the firelight. Scratching a board

they made the signs for their fading names on the wood,
and their former shapes returned absently; each carried
the nameless freight of himself to the other world.

Then, after wreaths of seaweed, after the bitter nouns
of strange berries, coral sores, after the familiar irons
singing round their ankles, after the circling suns,

dry sand their soles knew. Sand they could recognize.
Men they knew by their hearts. They came up from the darkness
past the disinterested captains, shielding their eyes.

III

Not where russet lions snarl on leaf-blown terraces,
or where ocelots carry their freckled shadows, or wind erases
Assyria, or where drizzling arrows hit the unflinching faces

of some Thracian phalanx winding down mountain passes,
but on a palm shore, with its vines and river grasses,
and stone barracoons, on brown earth, bare as their asses.

Yet they felt the sea-wind tying them into one nation
of eyes and shadows and groans, in the one pain
that is inconsolable, the loss of one's shore

with its crooked footpath. They had wept, not for
their wives only, their fading children, but for strange,
ordinary things. This one, who was a hunter,

wept for a sapling lance whose absent heft sang
in his palm's hollow. One, a fisherman, for an ochre
river encircling his calves; one a weaver, for the straw

fishpot he had meant to repair, wilting in water.
They cried for the little thing after the big thing.
They cried for a broken gourd. It was only later

that they talked to the gods who had not been there
when they needed them. Their whole world was moving,
or a large part of the world, and what began dissolving

was the fading sound of their tribal name for the rain,
the bright sound for the sun, a hissing noun for the river,
and always the word "never," and never the word "again."

✧ ✧ ✧

BOOK SEVEN, Chapter LVI

I

One sunrise I walked out onto the balcony
of my white hotel. The beach was already swept,
and in the clear grooves of the January sea

there was only one coconut shell, but it kept
nodding in my direction as a swimmer might
with sun in his irises, or a driftwood log,

or a plaster head, foaming. It changed shapes in light
according to each clouding thought. A khaki dog
came racing its faster shadow on the clean sand,

then stopped, yapping at the shell, not wetting its paws,
backing off from the claws of surf that made the sound
of a cat hissing; then it faked an interest

in a crab-hole and worried it. If that thing was
a coconut, why didn't it drift with the crest
of the slow-breathing swell? Then, as if from a vase,

or a girl's throat, I heard a moan from the village
of a blowing conch, and I saw the first canoe
on the horizon's glittering scales. The old age

of the wrinkled sea was in that moan, and I knew
that the floating head had drifted here. The mirrors
of the sky were clouded, and I heard my own voice

correcting his name, as the surf hissed: "Omeros."
The moment I named it, the marble head arose,
fringed with its surf curls and beard, the hollow shoulders

of a man waist-high in water with an old leather
goatskin or a plastic bag, pricking the dog's ears,
making it whine with joy. Then, suddenly, the weather

darkened, and it darkened the forked, slow-wading wood
until it was black, and the shallows in that second
changed to another dialect as Seven Seas stood

in the white foam manacling his heels. He beckoned,
that is, the arm of that log brought in by the tide,
then the cloud passed, and the white head glared, almond-eyed

in her white studio with its foam-scalloped beard
a winter ago, then it called to the khaki dog
that still backed off from the surf, yet now what appeared

changed again to its shadow, then a driftwood log
that halted and beckoned, moving to the foam's swell,
one elbow lifted, calling me from the hotel.

They kept shifting shapes, or the shapes metamorphosed
in the worried water; no sooner was the head
of the blind plaster-bust clear than its brow was crossed

by a mantling cloud and its visage reappeared
with ebony hardness, skull and beard like cotton,
its nose like a wedge; no sooner I saw the one

than the other changed and the first was forgotten
as the sand forgets a shadow in widening sun,
their bleached almond seeds their only thing in common.

So one changed from marble with a dripping chiton
in the early morning on that harp-wired sand
to a foam-headed fisherman in his white, torn

undershirt, but both of them had the look of men
whose skins are preserved in salt, whose accents were born
from guttural shoal, whose vision was wide as rain

sweeping over the sand, clouding the hills in gauze.
I came down to the beach. In its pointed direction,
the dog raced, passing the daisy-prints of its paws.

II

Up a steep path where even goats are careful,
the path that Philoctete took past the foaming cove,
the blind stone led me, my heart thudding and fearful

that it would burst like the sea in a drumming cave.
It was a cape that I knew, tree-bent and breezy,
no wanderer could have chosen a better grave.

If this was where it ended, the end was easy —
to give back the borrowed breath the joy that it gave,
with the sea exulting, the wind so wild with love.

His stubble chin jerked seaward, and the empty eyes
were filled with them, with the colour of the blue day;
so a swift will dart its beak just before it flies

towards its horizon, hazed Greece or Africa.
I could hear the crumpling parchment of the sea in
the wind's hand, a silence without emphasis,

but I saw no shadow underline my being;
I could see through my own palm with every crease
and every line transparent since I was seeing

the light of St. Lucia at last through her own eyes,
her blindness, her inward vision as revealing
as his, because a closing darkness brightens love,

and I felt every wound pass. I saw the healing
thorns of dry cactus drop to the dirt, and the grove
where the sibyl swayed. I thought of all my travelling.

III

"I saw you in London," I said, "sunning on the steps
of St. Martin-in-the-Fields, your dog-eared manuscript
clutched to your heaving chest. The queues at the bus-stops

smiled at your seaman's shuffle, and a curate kicked
you until you waddled down to the summery Thames."
"That's because I'm a heathen. They don't know my age.

Even the nightingales have forgotten their names.
The goat declines, head down, with these rocks for a stage
bare of tragedy. The Aegean's chimera

is a camera, you get my drift, a drifter
is the hero of my book."
                                    "I never read it,"
I said. "Not all the way through."
                                                  The lift of the

arching eyebrows paralyzed me like Medusa's
shield, and I turned cold the moment I had said it.
"Those gods with hyphens, like Hollywood producers,"

I heard my mouth babbling as ice glazed over my chest.
"The gods and the demi-gods aren't much use to us."
"Forget the gods," Omeros growled, "and read the rest."

Then there was the silence any injured author
knows, broken by the outcry of a frigate-bird,
as we both stared at the blue dividing water,

and in that gulf, I muttered, "I have always heard
your voice in that sea, master, it was the same song
of the desert shaman, and when I was a boy

your name was as wide as a bay, as I walked along
the curled brow of the surf; the word 'Homer' meant joy,
joy in battle, in work, in death, then the numbered peace

of the surf's benedictions, it rose in the cedars,
in the *laurier-cannelles*, pages of rustling trees.
Master, I was the freshest of all your readers."

✧   ✧   ✧

Chapter LXIV

I

I sang of quiet Achille, Afolabe's son,
who never ascended in an elevator,
who had no passport, since the horizon needs none,

never begged nor borrowed, was nobody's waiter,
whose end, when it comes, will be a death by water
(which is not for this book, which will remain unknown

and unread by him). I sang the only slaughter
that brought him delight, and that from necessity —
of fish, sang the channels of his back in the sun.

I sang our wide country, the Caribbean Sea.
Who hated shoes, whose soles were as cracked as a stone,
who was gentle with ropes, who had one suit alone,

whom no man dared insult and who insulted no one,
whose grin was a white breaker cresting, but whose frown
was a growing thunderhead, whose fist of iron

would do me a greater honour if it held on
to my casket's oarlocks than mine lifting his own
when both anchors are lowered in the one island,

but now the idyll dies, the goblet is broken,
and rainwater trickles down the brown cheek of a jar
from the clay of Choiseul. So much left unspoken

by my chirping nib! And my earth-door lies ajar.
I lie wrapped in a flour-sack sail. The clods thud
on my rope-lowered canoe. Rasping shovels scrape

a dry rain of dirt on its hold, but turn your head
when the sea-almond rattles or the rust-leaved grape
from the shells of my unpharaonic pyramid

towards paper shredded by the wind and scattered
like white gulls that separate their names from the foam
and nod to a fisherman with his khaki dog

that skitters from the wave-crash, then frown at his form
for one swift second. In its earth-trough, my pirogue
with its brass-handled oarlocks is sailing. Not from

but with them, with Hector, with Maud in the rhythm
of her beds trowelled over, with a swirling log
lifting its mossed head from the swell; let the deep hymn

of the Caribbean continue my epilogue;
may waves remove their shawls as my mourners walk home
to their rusted villages, good shoes in one hand,

passing a boy who walked through the ignorant foam,
and saw a sail going out or else coming in,
and watched asterisks of rain puckering the sand.

Hermann Broch

THE DEATH OF VIRGIL

✧ ✧ ✧

...and it was as if all brooks and ponds of yore poured themselves into this stream of memory, drizzling between the fragrant willows, drizzling between banks verdant with trembling reeds, lovely images without end, themselves a cluster picked by the hands of a child, a cluster of lilies, gilly-flowers, poppies, narcissus and buttercups, the image of childhood in a landscape revealed by wandering and wandering, by song after song, the image of the paternal pastures, the image he had been forced to seek wherever he had been driven, the image of the one and unforgettable landscape of his life, ineffable-inexpressible image, despite that it was so very luminous, so sharp of contour, sun-drenched, transparent, despite this unfailing clarity with which it had accompanied him, so inexpressible that however often he had depicted it it only resounded in the unutterable, always only there where language is insufficient, where it strikes beyond its own earthly-mortal boundaries and penetrates into the unutterable, abandoning an expression through words and — only singing itself into the structure of the verses — opening up between the very words a swooning, breathless, momentary abyss so that life could be comprehended and death be apprehended in these silent depths, which have become silent to disclose the completeness of the whole, the simultaneous stream of creation in which the eternal rests: oh, goal of poetry, oh, these moments in which speech sublimated itself beyond all description and all communication, oh, these moments in which it plunged into simultaneousness so that it could not be determined whether memory was gushing from speech or speech from memory, these were the moments in which the landscape of childhood had begun to blossom, leaving itself behind, growing beyond itself and every memory, beyond every beginning and every end, transmuted to a simple, rustic, shepherd's order in some golden age, transmuted to the scene of the Latin emergence, transmuted to the reality of the on-marching, commanding and serving gods, not the primordial beginning, surely not the original order, surely not the initial reality but still a symbol of it, not, to be sure, to the voice which was expected to call out from the furthest unknown, out of the inexpressible and extraordinary, out of the unchangeably and utterly divine, but still a token of it, but surely the echo-like symbol of its being and almost an affirmation of it —, the symbol that was reality, reality that would become the symbol in the face of death. These were the moments of resounding deathlessness, the moments of essential life emerged from its twilight, and it was in these moments that the true form of death revealed itself most clearly: rare moments of grace, rare moments of perfect freedom, unknown to most, striven for by many, achieved by few —, but among those who were permitted to retain such moments, to grasp the fugitive evanescence of death's shape, he who succeeded in giving shape to death by incessant listening and searching would find together with its genuine form his own real shape as well, he was shaping his own death and with it his own shape, and he was immune from the reversion into the humus of shapelessness. Seven-colored and divinely mild the rainbow of childhood arched for him over all his existence, daily seen anew, the shared creation of man and the gods, the creation proceeding from the strength of the word with the knowledge of death: had not this been the hope for which he had been obliged to bear the agony of a hunted life devoid of every peaceful joy? He looked back on this life of abnegation, of an actually still continuing renunciation, on this life that had been without resistance to death though full of resistance to participation and love, he looked back on this life of farewell that lay back of him in the dusk of rivers, in the dusk of poetry, and today he knew more clearly than ever before that he had taken on all this for the sake of that very hope; perhaps he was not to be mocked and execrated because life's great travail had as yet not led to the fulfillment of hope, because the task he had wanted to discharge had been over-great for his weak forces, because the medium of the poet's art was perhaps not intended for this after all, however he also realized that this was not the case, that the justification of a task or the lack of its justification was not to be reckoned by its earthly accomplishment, that it was negligible whether his own strength sufficed or not, whether any other man with greater strength were to be born or whether a better solution than the one put forth by poetry were to be found, all this was irrelevant, for the choice had not been his: certainly day after day and countless times during every day he had decided and acted in accord with his free choice, or at least he had thought that the choice was free, but the great line of his life was not of his own choosing nor in accord with his free will, it had been a compulsion, a compulsion on a level with the redemption and the evil of existence, a fate-enjoined yet fate-surpassing compulsion, commanding him to search for his own shape in that of death and thus to win the freedom of his soul; for freedom is a compulsion of the soul whose redemption or damnation is always at stake, and he had heeded the injunction, obedient to the task of his fate.[1]

✧ ✧ ✧

but he who is destined by the double will of fate and the god to be an artist, damned but to know and surmise, damned but to write down and speak out, he is denied the purification in life and in death as well, and even his tomb means no more to him than a beautiful structure, an earthly abode for his body, providing him with neither entrance nor exit, neither entrance for the illimitable descent nor exit for the illimitable return; destiny denies him the golden bough of leadership, the bough of perception, and in consequence he is condemned by Jupiter. Hence he too had been condemned to perjury and to the abandonment of the perjured, and his glance, forced earthward, had been allowed to encounter only the three perjuring accomplices staggering over the pavement, bringing him the sentence of guilt; his glance had not been permitted to pierce deeper, not beneath the surface of the stones, not beneath the surface of the world, neither beneath that of language nor of art; the descent was forbidden him, most forbidden the titanic return from the depths, the return by which the humanity of man is proven; the ascent was forbidden him, the ascent toward the renewal of the creative pledge, and he knew now more clearly what he had always known, that once and for all he was excluded from those to whom was pledged the help of the savior, because the help of the pledge and human help implemented each other, and only through their conjunction could the Titan fulfill his task of establishing community and, beyond that, humanity, which, though born of the earth aimed toward heaven, because only in humanity and true community which reflected the whole of man's humanness and humanity as a whole did the perception-borne and perception-bearing cycle of question and answer become perfected, excluding those unfit for helpfulness, for duty, and the pledge, excluding them because they had excluded themselves from the titanic task of mastering, realizing, and deifying human life; verily this he knew,

and he also knew that the same thing held true in the realm of art, that art existed — oh, did it still exist, was it allowed to exist? — only insofar as it contained pledge and perception, only insofar as it represented the fate of man and his mastery of existence, insofar as it renewed itself by fresh and hitherto unaccomplished tasks, only insofar as, in achieving them, it summoned the soul to continuous self-mastery, compelling the soul to reveal level after level of her reality as, descending step by step, penetrating deeper and deeper through the inner thickets of her being, she gradually approached the unattainable darkness which she had always surmised and been conscious of, the darkness from which the ego emerged and to which it returned, the dark regions where the ego developed and became extinguished, the entrance and exit of the soul, but likewise the entrance and exit of that which was the soul's truth, pointed out to her by the path-finding, the goldly-gleaming bough of truth which was neither to be found nor plucked by means of force, since the grace of finding it and the grace of the descent were one and the same, the grace of self-knowledge, which belonged as much to the soul as to art, their common truth; verily, this he knew,

and he knew also that the duty of all art lay in this sort of truth, lay in the self-perceptive finding and proclaiming of truth, the duty which has been laid on the artist, so that the soul, realizing the great equilibrium between the ego and the universe, might recover herself in the universe, perceiving in this self-recognition that the deepening of the ego was an increase of substance in the universe, in the world, especially in humanity, and even though this doubled growth was only a symbolic one, bound from the beginning to the symbolization of the beautiful, to that of the beautiful boundary, even though it were but a symbolic perception, it was precisely by this means that it was enabled to widen the inner and outer boundaries of existence to new reality, even though these boundaries might not be crossed, widening them not merely to a new form but to the new content of reality which they enclosed, in which the deepest secret of reality, the secret of correlation was revealed, the mutual relation existing between the realities of the self and the world, which lent the symbol the precision of rightness and exalted it to be the symbol of truth, the truth-bearing correlation from which arose every creation of reality, pressing on through level after level, penetrating toward, groping toward the unattainable dark realms of beginning and ending, pushing on toward the inscrutable divinity in the universe, in the world, in the soul of one's fellow-man, pushing on toward that ultimate spark of the divine, that secret, which, ready to be disclosed and to be awakened, could be found everywhere, even in the soul of the most degraded —, this, the disclosure of the divine through the self-perceptive knowledge of the individual soul, this was the task of art, its human duty, its perceptive duty and therefore its reason for being, the proof of which was art's nearness to death, and its duty, since only in this nearness might art become real, only thus unfolding into a symbol of the human soul; verily this he knew,

but he knew also that the beauty of the symbol, were it ever so precise in its reality, was never its own excuse for being, that whenever such was the case, whenever beauty existed for its own sake, there art was attacked at its very roots, because the created deed then came to be its own opposite, because the thing created was then suddenly substituted for that which creates, the empty form for the true content of reality, the merely beautiful for the perceptive truth, in a constant confusion, in a constant cycle of change and reversion, an inbound cycle in which renewal was no longer possible, in which nothing more could be enlarged, in which there was nothing more to be discovered, neither the divine in the abandoned, nor the abandoned in human divinity, but in which there was only intoxication with empty forms and empty words, whereby art through this lack of discrimination and even of fidelity, was reduced to un-art, and poetry to mere literariness; verily, this he knew, knew it painfully,

and by the same token he knew of the innermost danger of all artists, he knew the utter loneliness of the man destined to be an artist, he knew the inherent loneliness which drove such a one into the still deeper loneliness of art and into the beauty that cannot be articulated, and he knew that for the most part such men were shattered by this immolation, that it made them blind, blind to the world, blind to the divine quality in the world and in the fellow-man, that — intoxicated by their loneliness — they were able to see only their own god-likeness, which they imagined to be unique, and consequently this self-idolatry and its greed for recognition came more and more to be the sole content of their work —, a betrayal of the divine as well as of art, because in this fashion the work of art became a work of un-art, an unchaste covering for artistic vanity, so spurious that even the artist's self-complacent nakedness which it exposed became a mask; and even though such unchaste self-gratification, such dalliance with beauty, such concern with effects, even though such an un-art might, despite its brief unrenewable grant, its inextensible boundaries, find an easier way to the populace than real art ever found, it was only a specious way, a way out of the loneliness, but not, however, an affiliation with the human community, which was the aim of real art in its aspiration toward humanity, no, it was the affiliation with the mob, it was a participation in its treacherous non-community, which was incapable of the pledge, which neither created nor mastered any reality, and which was unwilling to do so, preferring only to drowse on, forgetting reality, having forfeited it as had un-art and literariness, this was the most profound danger for every artist; oh how painfully, how very painfully he knew this,

and by this token he knew also that the danger of un-art and literariness had always encompassed him, and still encompassed him, and that therefore — although he had never dared face this truth — his poetry could no longer be called art, since, devoid of all renewal and development, it had been nothing but an unchaste production of beauty without real creativity, and from beginning to end, from the Aetna Song to the Aeneid, it had been a mere indulgence of beauty, self-sufficiently limited to the embellishment of things long since conceived, formed, and known, without any real progress in itself, aside from an increasing extravagance and sumptuousness, an un-art which was never able of itself to master existence and exalt it to a veritable symbol.[2]

✧ ✧ ✧

"Who are you?" he asked again, after he had put down the beaker, and the persistent questioning going on within and coming out of him astonished him anew. "Who are you? I have already met you…was it a long time ago?" — "Give me a name that you know," was the response….

"I do not know of any name." — "You, my Father, you know them all, you gave a name to everything; they are all in your poem." Names and names — the names of people, the names of fields, the names of landscapes, of cities and of all creation, home names, consoling names in times of trouble, the name of the things created along with the things, created before the gods, the always resurrected name containing the holiness of the word, always to be found by the true watcher, by the arouser, by the divine founder! nevermore might the poet lay claim to this dignity, nay, not even were the sole and final task of poetry to be that of exalting the name of things, ah, even when its greatest moment sounds, were it to succeed in casting a glance into the creative fountain of speech, beneath the profound light of which the word for the thing is floating, the word untouched and chaste at the source of the world of matter, the poem though well able to duplicate the creation in words was never able to fuse the duplication into a unity, unable to do so because the seeming-reversion, the divination, the beauty, because all these things which determined, which became poetry, took place solely in the duplicated world; the world of speech and the world of matter remained apart, twofold the home of the word, twofold the home of the human being, twofold the abyss of the creaturely, but twofold also the purity of being, thus duplicated to unchastity which, like a resurrection without birth, penetrated all divination as well as all beauty, and carried the seed of world-destruction in itself, the basic unchastity of existence which came to be feared by the mother; unchaste the mantle of poetry, and nevermore would poetry come to be fundamental, nevermore would it awake from its game of divination, never-more would poetry turn into prayer, into the sacrificially-valid prayer of truth so surely inherent in the genuine name of things that the supplicant, included in the supplication, closes off the duplicated word so that for him and him alone word and thing shall succeed in becoming one — oh, purity of prayer, unattainable by poetry and yet, oh yet attainable for it, insofar as it offered itself, as it overcame and annihilated its very self. And again as though wrenched out of him, a moan, a cry: "The Aeneid to be burnt!" — "My Father!" He took the great fright ringing through the outcry as rejection of this project, as well he might; displeased he answered, "Do not call me father; Augustus keeps watch, he is guarding Rome, call him father, not me…not me…guarding is not the poet's office." — "You stand for Rome." — "That dream of every boy was perhaps once mine also…but I have only made use of Roman names."[3]

✧ ✧ ✧

Notes

[1] pages 84–6.
[2] pages 138–42.
[3] pages 186–8.

ART AND THE HERO: PARTICIPATION, DETACHMENT, AND NARRATIVE POINT OF VIEW IN *AENEID* 1

This collection ends as the *Aeneid* does, by returning to the beginning. The last image, of Turnus at Aeneas' sword at 12.951, returns us to the first image of Aeneas at 1.92 (*solvuntur frigore membra*, "His limbs are loosed in the chilling cold"). Segal observes that Aeneas, alone among the *Aeneid*'s characters, participates in the story in two ways. The first is as a "detached," authorial voice, a posture Aeneas sometimes shares with the gods and the poet. Aeneas is also a "participant" at times, lacking access to divine knowledge about the meaning of his own story. In dual perspective, with its "mirror-within-mirror effect," the characters can be "spectators of their own acts." That perspective also enables Vergil to reflect within his poetry on himself as its author, to be self-conscious "of the *Aeneid* as an art-world, a realm of aesthetic artifice." These issues guide Segal's close reading of *Aeneid* 1 and reveal the violence of creativity as the tragedy of art. (Ed.)

For all its hero's "adult" seriousness of political responsibility (C. S. Lewis, 1942.37), the *Aeneid* is in its own way no less concerned with art and the artist than the *Eclogues* and the *Georgics*. In the broad sweep of the epic the faces of poetry and poets are many. Against the figured continuo of Homer there are the Hellenistic didacticism of Iopas in 1; Daedalus' sculpted doors at Cumae; Misenus' maddened trumpet-blast in 6, martial song's hybristic challenge to the natural order; Anchises' presentation of Rome's future in the Underworld, with its self-consciously dreamlike quality; and of course in 2 and 3 Aeneas' own bardlike recounting of the fall of Troy and his subsequent wanderings, a narrative which, intentionally or not, exercises song's erotic power to fascinate and seduce (cf. 4.14 ff.). The second half of the poem begins with that seduction of song on Circe's forbidden island (7.11-24) and contains figures like Umbro, warrior-poet, enchanter, and healer, around whose death the lyrical beauty of the Italian landscape echoes in Orpheus-like lamentation (7.752-60), or Cretheus, "friend to the Muses," singer of arms and battles and himself a victim of the martial deeds he celebrates (9.774-8).

At a slight remove from these literal singers or artists stands the epic journey itself. This is not, to be sure, an allegory of the poet's journey of the soul, as Dante saw it. Yet by self-consciously reviewing and recasting the epic tradition, and indeed much of the poetic tradition generally, it forms a poet's (and reader's) journey into the art of the past. It is a journey also into the poet's own creative past. In the *sphragis* ["seal"] of the *Georgics* (4.565 f.) Virgil simultaneously looks back to his earlier pastoral poetry and in the figure of *Augustus triumphans* ["Augustus triumphing"] looks

Charles Segal, "Art and the Hero: Participation, Detachment, and Narrative Point of View in *Aeneid* 1," *Arethusa* 14 (1981) 1, 67-83. Reprinted by permission of The Johns Hopkins University Press.

forward to his new martial epic. In *Aeneid* 8 the hero's up-river voyage is, in some sense, a movement back to the Arcadian purity at the heart of the Roman land and a journey to the Arcadian vision and aspiration of the poet's own youth, a return to origins, in Eliade's sense, where both epic hero and epic poet make contact with the source of vital energies. In this remote "Arcadian" realm the Golden Age of Saturnian peace had its last fabled abode on this earth before war, greed, and passion displaced it. Here the hero receives the injunction, applicable to both poet and reader also, to find an underlying heroic simplicity and clarity beneath the superficies of luxury and excess, and to "shape" (*fingere*) himself into an image worthy of the mythic paradigm who made the same passage from Greece to Rome (8.364 f.).

In the single figure of Aeneas Virgil unites the two facets of the poet which in the Fourth *Georgic* he had separated into two: the distanced manipulator who uses external reality for his own ends, Aristaeus, and the involved, deeply feeling singer, Orpheus, who identifies the natural world with his own passions and makes his art almost entirely from his own emotional, interior life.[1] These two figures symbolize the two sides of a tension probably inherent in all poetry: a pull between analytical directiveness and the flooding of feeling in the timeless moment of high emotion, between structure and sensitivity. Michael Putnam has recently given us some eloquent pages on this important theme in *Georgics* 4.[2] It is also relevant to the *Aeneid* and underlies the narrative technique and the pulls within Aeneas with which this essay is concerned.

Aeneas, of course, is a "poet" only in a very temporary and figurative way; yet the tension between the "Orphic" and the "Aristaean" visions of life and art surrounds him too. One of its forms is an alternating movement in the narrative between what we may call the "authorial" and the "participatory" voice. By the first I mean the voice of the omniscient narrator who controls the action; by the second I mean the voice of characters, including Aeneas, who are wholly immersed in their roles as actors and participants in the narrative events. Often the "authorial voice" is the voice of the gods, especially of Jupiter, the voice of prophecy, of fate, of the destiny of Rome. The "participatory voice" is the voice of emotion, passion, feeling involvement in the striving and suffering of human beings. It is often in direct conflict with the "authorial" voice.

This alternation is inherent within any third-person narrative told from the perspective of an omniscient author. Virgil, however, exploits it with a peculiar effectiveness which I hope to define more precisely by studying the fluctuation between distance and involvement in *Aeneid* 1. Otis' perceptions of Virgil's shift between an "empathetic" or "subjective" style on the one hand and an "editorialized symbol structure" on the other are helpful here, but Otis did not treat the dialectical interplay of the two styles in any detail or relate them to the ambiguity of Aeneas' role in the poem.[3] One aim of this essay is to relate this two-fold narrative perspective to Virgil's self-consciousness of the *Aeneid* as an art-world, a realm of aesthetic artifice. This aspect of the epic runs parallel to and stands in intimate conjunction with its interpretation of the tragedy of history and human suffering. This alternating pattern of narrative voices and the clashes which it creates are also essential to what W. R. Johnson has recently labeled a "dialectic of ...polysematic configurations."[4] I would lay stress on both the dialectical and the polysemous quality of Virgil's epic.

Most characters in the epic speak only the "participatory" voice. They have no access to the privileged voice of the divine perspective. Aeneas occupies a unique position in that he partakes of both voices. Virgil thereby not only depicts the emotional complexity and conflicts of his chief character, but also shapes a richer narrative texture, for the reader is drawn into the alternating rhythm of the two voices, identifying now with one, now with the other.

Although this shifting perspective has some precedent in Homeric epic, with its movement between earth and Olympus, it has a special distinctiveness in Virgil, for his vision, unlike Homer's, is teleological. The action of his epic results in an end predetermined by destiny. Virgil s *fatum* ["divine decree, fate"] is very different from Homeric *moira* ["one's lot, portion"], an individual affair with no such cosmic implications.[5] Virgil's authorial *persona* not only takes in the whole course of narrated events, but also comprehends the divinely destined course of history, from Rome's small beginnings to its domination of the world. Authorial prescience is, literally, divine prescience; it implies some measure of identification with Jupiter's grand sweep of knowledge and power over human affairs.

When human characters speak that voice, they take on something of the divine foreknowledge. Detached momentarily from their participatory role, they step into the ambiguous situation of being spectators of their own acts. A few of Homer's characters occasionally approach this role—Achilles, Helen, Odysseus, but the resultant tension is less because only the individual life is involved, at least directly; for Aeneas it is a question of the entire course of history.

Aeneas in particular serves as a mediator between the purely "participatory" voices of the other characters (particularly Dido in the first half of the poem) and the "authorial" voice of the gods and the omniscient poet-narrator. This mediatory role is one cause of his ambiguity in the epic. His problematical final gesture is the climax to this continual crossing over between authorial distance and audience / reader participation inherent in the dialectics of the "subjective" style. It crystalizes into action the stylistic tension between the transcendent and the immanentist vision of events. As that tension is inherent in Virgil's basic conception of both Rome and poetry, Aeneas' final "participatory" violence is no more resolvable on the level of action than on the level of style.

In a world-order of predetermined outcome, conflict, in both the divine and the human realm, forms the major point of interest. Division and its delaying effects pervade the poem from its very first episode: the hostility of Juno, the disruptive effects of her wrath, and its physical manifestation, disorder in the face of nature, the storm and shipwreck of the Trojans. To that division among the divine powers corresponds a division in the "authorial" voice of the omniscient poet-narrator. Virgil's proem does not merely invoke the Muses and assert the importance of his theme; the poet also asks a question, a question which cuts to the heart of the meaning of the world order: *tantaene animis caelestibus irae,* "Such ire in breasts celestial?" (1.11).[6]

The questioning voice is unexpected, untraditional. There is no precedent in Homer. Homer's gods, of course, have frequent head-on collisions, but Homer's omniscient bardic voice never questions the world-order in this way. The closest parallels are the hard demands for justice and meaning by the choruses of Greek tragedy. One might compare *Oedipus Tyrannus* 895–910 or *Hippolytus* 1103–10. Whatever its origins, this division, as we shall see, carries over into the ambiguous role of the hero between actor and spectator, between imperfect human being and bearer of Rome's future.

Aeneas' mediatory role between authorial and participatory voices is depicted at once in the striking contrast, often noted by commentators, between his first and second speeches in the poem.[7] His first utterance, *O terque quaterque beati,* "O three times blessed and four, you whose lot it was to fall before the eyes of your fathers beneath Troy's lofty walls" (1.94-101), is as fully immersed in the participatory voice as it is in the violence of the storm which sweeps him helplessly now to the heavens, now to the depths of ocean (1.102-7), lacking even the pilot to steer his ship (1.115). In his second speech, addressed to his present companions (*O socii* ["O comrades"]) and not to the remote dead at Troy (1.198-207), he enunciates the divine purposes, takes a broad view of time, and commands the wider perspective of memory (*forsan et haec olim meminisse iuuabit*, "Perhaps at some time you will have joy in remembering even this" 1.203). Memory is also the perspective of the poet who keeps past achievements alive in song. Aeneas' concluding lines on the peaceful abode shown by the fates and the resurgence of Troy in fact anticipate Jupiter's prophetic divine voice some sixty lines later (cf. 205 and 262, 206 and 270-2).

This difference in Aeneas' opening speeches parallels the difference in the visualization of the setting. The storm spins men, ship, and possessions in a dizzying swirl which destroys all centrality of focus (1.103-17). The victims and objects merely "appear." There is no one observer, no single superior point of view, only the random flotsam and jetsam of disparate things in the whirlpool of turbulent waters (1.118-22):

> apparent rari nantes in gurgite uasto,
> arma uirum tabulaeque et Troia gaza per undas.
> iam ualidam Ilionei nauem, iam fortis Achatae,
> et qua uectus Abas, et qua grandaeuus Aletes,
> uicit hiems....

> There appear scattered in the vast flood men swimming, arms of heroes, and tablets and the Trojan treasure through the waves. Now the storm overwhelmed Ilioneus' strong ship, now brave Achates', now that in which Abas was carried and that in which aged Aletes was....

The confused, floating status of *arma uirum* (1.119) is also the momentary confusion or suspension of that authorial voice which takes *arma uirum* as its triumphant theme (1.1).

Divine, authorially omniscient intervention restores order. With that order Aeneas is rescued from the "devouring vortex" (*rapidus uorat aequore vertex* 1.117) which had deprived him of directional guidance, the lost, unnamed steersman of 1.115 f. He now has a wide overview as he climbs to a vantage-point high above the waves (*Aeneas scopulum interea conscendit, et omnem / prospectum late pelago petit*, "Aeneas meanwhile climbs up the crag and seeks an entire view out over the sea far and wide" 1.180 f.). We are reminded of the philosopher's godlike removal and distanced prospect in the proem to Lucretius' second book (*DRN* 2.1-9); but closer at hand is Jupiter's majestic vision fifty lines later (1.223 ff.). "Looking down from the summit of the aether" (1.223 f.), Jupiter sees both sea and land, both the natural features and the "broadly scattered peoples" (*latos populos*) who lie beyond those shores (1.224 f.). The *vertex* where he stands (1.225) is no longer the disorienting whirlpool sucking mortals down to the waters' abysmal depths (1.113), but the removed height of the Olympian dwellings.[8]

Aeneas' godlike vista in 180 f. prepares for the different tone of his second speech, with its purview of Rome's destiny (1.204-7). The enlarged horizons of this authorial voice are all the more striking by contrast to the enclosed setting of his fleet, the *secessus longus* ["long recess"] of the Libyan harbor (1.159 ff.). The overhanging wood, "dark with threatening shades" (*horrentique atrum nemus imminet umbra* 1.165), expresses the human participants' continuing uncertainty of shelter and their vulnerability to a still unknown future (cf. *minantur*, "threaten" 1.162 and 165 above).[9]

Aeneas soon makes his way out of these shadows (1.305–9), in sharp distinction to his companions, who remain enfolded in the darkness of the forest (cf. 1.162 ff.). Through the active verb *occulit* he himself seems to make his ships "concealed" (1.309–11):

> classem in conuexo nemorum sub rupe cauata
> arboribus clausam circum atque horrentibus umbris
> occulit; ipse uno graditur comitatus Achate....

> The fleet he conceals in the hollow of the groves beneath the caverned rock, enclosed all around by the trees and the bristling shades. He himself sets forth accompanied by Achates alone....

The meeting with Venus dramatizes this vacillation of Aeneas between favored hero of destiny and victim of that destiny. The ironies are multiple: a *virgo* ["virgin"] who is not only a *mater* ["mother"] but the very goddess of love is disguised as a maiden-devotee of chaste Diana (cf. 314, 326, 336). The echoes of comedy throughout the scene suggest an element of playfulness, the gods' ambiguous play with mortals.[10] Though the machinations of the Olympians are for Aeneas' benefit, he is as much trapped as Dido in the games of the love-goddess.

Venus' description of Dido subtly insinuates that queen's availability and susceptibility to a passion as great as the one with which she once loved her husband, *magno miserae dilectus amore*, "cherished by the great love of the unhappy (queen)" (1.344; cf. 352). The gods make use of unsuspecting Dido, *fati nescia Dido* ["Dido ignorant of fate"] (1.299). But Aeneas too, unable to recognize his own mother as he wanders in the ignorance of his first *selva oscura* ["dark forest"], is equally unknowing (cf. *ignarus* ["ignorant"] 1.332; *errans* ["wandering astray"] 333). Venus shows him, finally, her true supernatural radiance, but she also covers him with dark mists (1.402 f., 411; cf. also 379, 387). To be the bearer of an historical mission is to be both the favorite and the victim of the gods.

As Venus takes leave, Aeneas inveighs against her deception (1.405–10)

> ille ubi matrem
> agnouit tali fugientem est uoce secutus:
> 'quid natum totiens, crudelis tu quoque, falsis
> ludis imaginibus? cur dextrae iungere dextram
> non datur ac ueras audire et reddere uoces?'
> talibus incusat gressumque ad moenia tendit.

> When he recognized his mother he pursued her with these words: 'Why do you deceive your son so often with false images, cruel you as well? Why is it not granted to join right hand with right hand and hear and return true speeches?' With such words he accuses her and directs his steps toward the walls.

The short, embittered speech is devoid of filial affection or even basic gratitude. The suggestively enjambed, *crudelis tu quoque falsis...imaginibus*, "Cruel you as well with false / images," joins to the authorial questioning of the gods in the proem (1.11) the emotional affect of the participatory voice. Aeneas casts Venus into the form of those fleeting, evanescent ghosts of his human ties—Creusa, Palinurus, Anchises—after whom he so often grasps in vain.[11] Delusion by Venus' "false images" counterbalances help by Venus' supernatural intervention. "Deluded," he is, as much her victim as Dido had been and will be again (cf. 1.352–5, 689 f., 715–22).[12]

When Aeneas meets Dido in the next scene, he seems to enjoy the controlling advantage of divine invisibility. Yet that advantage, we cannot forget, consists in his own enclosure in the delusive mists of the love-goddess (1.411 f., 439 f.).[13] After the manner of love-goddesses, Venus plays with him even as she aids him toward his success, erotic as well as political. Dido, ignorant of the fate which makes of her a doomed instrument of Rome's triumph, has the lovely walk of the goddess Diana (1.496–502); but that attractive feature is only one more advantage for Diana's opposite to exploit. Venus herself took the form of Diana's votary; and to her son, as unsuspecting as Dido here, she even resembled Diana herself (*an Phoebi soror*, "Or are you Phoebus' sister?" 1.329). For an instant Aeneas can glimpse the love-goddess in her proper form (1.402–4), but that momentary *anagnorisis* ["recognition"] (*matrem agnouit* ["he recognized his mother"] 1.405 f.) makes him no less subject to the amorous power of her spell, symbolized in the mists which she casts about him. In his complaint about her "false images" (1.507 f.) glimmers the recognition that protection by Venus also means delusion by Venus.

In the next book Venus, in Aeneas' narrative of Troy's fall, appears in a radiant flash to check his murderous anger against the inspirer of love, Helen (2.588–93):

> talia iactabam et furiata mente ferebar,
> cum mihi se, non ante oculis tam clara, uidendam
> obtulit et pura per noctem in luce refulsit
> alma parens, confessa deam qualisque uideri
> caelicolis et quanta solet, dextraque prehensum
> continuit roseoque haec insuper addidit ore.

> Such words I tossed about and was carried forth with enraged mind when my fostering parent, never before so clear to my eyes, offered herself to my view and shone forth through the night in clear light, declaring herself a goddess and such in form and size as she is wont to appear to the heaven-dwellers. With her right hand she grasped me and held me back and added these things besides with rosy countenance....

Venus' restraining grip (*dextraque prehensum / continuit* ["with her right hand she grasped me and held me back"]) is as solid here as her image, eluding the grasp of right hands (1.408), was evasive in Book 1. Rather than beclouding with the mists of delusive love, she now dispels the mists of war that conceal Troy's ineluctable destruction by hostile gods (2.604–6). Given Aeneas' place between participatory and authorial voices, however, even the aid of an undeceiving Venus carries ambiguity and irony. This very description stands within a speech whose final effect will be Dido's subjection to that mind-clouding goddess. Even while protecting Aeneas from his own dangerous anger, Venus is, incidentally, interfering in behalf of an erotically seductive woman, Helen, who is not only Venus' virtual mortal counterpart (see note 12 *infra*), but also, spared by Venus' agency, lives on in Dido's *inceptos hymenaeos* ["begun marriage-rites," 4.316]. These, like Helen's own *inconcessos hymenaeos* of 1.651 ["illicit marriage-rites"], become the cause of another disastrous war between great civilizations (cf. also 4.99, 127, 3.327–32). Here too then, as in Book 1, Venus' moment of illumination has an immediate pendant in the mists of darkness which she leaves behind: *dixerat et spissis noctis se condidit umbris*, "She had spoken, and hid herself in night's thick shadows" (2.621; cf. 1.411 f.).

The ambiguities of Aeneas between involvement and detachment implicit in Venus' clouds are fully present in the important scene which marks his entrance into Dido's world: his inspection of the doors of Juno's temple at Carthage (1.446 ff.). Seeing but unseen, deciphering his and his people's painful effort, *labor* (1.460), in the *labor* which is also the work of art (*operum labor* ["effort of the work"] 1.455), he takes his place in an emblematic situation where he is both participant and observer. He views the events of his own past, enframed in the artistic design of his enemy-goddess' temple while his very presence at that temple in the distancing invisibility which insures his removed observer-status is part of the design of Juno's foe, Venus.

This mirror-within-mirror effect is doubled as the scene shifts from Aeneas' perception of the Trojan past as aesthetic object to his increasing response to it as lived reality. Verbal repetition frames the Trojan episodes on the doors as art-works, just as the building itself frames them as works of sculpture. Aeneas' initial "wonder (*miratur*) at the craftsmanship of the artists and the effort of the work" (1.455 f.) is echoed at the end as "these things seem wondrous (*miranda*) to Dardanian Aeneas, and he stands in silence (*stupet*) and is stuck fast in single contemplation" (*obtutuque haeret defixus in uno*...1.494 f.). Within the description, however, the intricate movement from narrated event to lived actuality is also expressed in the change of tenses from pluperfect to imperfect to present. The words of temporal involvement like *interea* (479) also contribute to this effect. There is a shift from indirect statement (466–73) to direct description (474–84, 490–93) or participial constructions (485–89).[14]

Aeneas' reactions and ambiguous status as both observer and actor also enact the audience / reader's response of increasing involvement, identification, and vicarious living of the episodes. The reader too moves, like Aeneas, from aesthetic appreciation of the frame and workmanship (455) to the intellectual grasp of the ordered disposition of the whole (456 f.):

> ...uidet Iliacas *ex ordine* pugnas
> bellaque iam fama *totum* uulgata per *orbem*....

He views Ilion's battles *in order* and wars now made familiar by fame over the *whole world.*

Like Aeneas, the reader is then pulled onward to the scenes' overall meaning for the present context (463), with the emotional response of groans and tears (465, 470). The self-consciousness of the spectator, marked by the narrative framing ("he saw how...; he recognizes...," *uidebat* 466; *agnoscit* 470), blends into actual identification with the recounted events as Achilles' horses "carry" Troilus, as the Trojan women approach Pallas' temple, as Achilles drags and ransoms Hector's body, and Penthesilea leads her Amazons. All of these scenes are free of the distancing intervention of observer's eye or artist's hand.

Even as he creates the effect of participating in the "unmediated vision" of "real" experience, however, Virgil retains his pull back to the consciousness of artistry and aesthetic framing. He obtains his continual tension between the different planes of his narrative by reminding us of the spellbinding effect of "wonder" on the viewer at both beginning and end (*miratur, miranda* 456, 494) and by carefully modulating the emotional responses of Aeneas. After noting his initial "many groans" (*multa gemens* 465), Virgil editorially calls attention to Aeneas' next stage of feeling, an even deeper grief, just when the rhythm of the narrative has reached a headlong, forward-moving intensity of involving scenes (485–87):

> tum uero ingentem gemitum dat pectore ab imo,
> ut spolia, ut currus, utque ipsum corpus amici
> tendentemque manus Priamum conspexit inermis.

> Then truly he gives forth a great groan from his heart's depths as he be-
> holds the spoils, the chariot, and the very body of his companion and Priam
> stretching forth his unarmed hands.

The emblematic scene of the doors, then, is a reflection on the narrative's paradoxes of aesthetic distance and emotional involvement. It also prefigures Aeneas' relation to the surrounding events in the very next scene. As he stood in dumb amazement reading those past sufferings (*stupet* 1.495), so he stands in amazement (*obstipuit simul ipse* 513) as he looks upon the arrival of his shipwrecked companions, himself distanced by Venus' mists (cf. 516, *nube caua speculantur amicti,* "cloaked by the hollow cloud they look on..."). The verbal and thematic repetitions reinforce this similarity in Aeneas' paradoxical observer-participant relationship to both the past and the present sufferings.

That enclosure in mist which distances Aeneas as observer, however, also marks his role as an actor on the stage which has been so carefully set up by Venus for the next crucial event in Aeneas' and Troy's fortunes. His frustrated eagerness "to join right hands" here (*coniungere dextras* 514) recalls his delusion and disappointment in his meeting with Venus, where he regards himself as played upon by false images, cruelly prevented from "joining right hands" (*cur dextrae iungere dextram / non datur?* ["why is it not granted to join right hand to hand"] 408 f.).

Aeneas looks at the "toilsome effort" (*operum labor* 455) of artful representation of past suffering which, as he had half-prophetically seen, will end in success and peace (1.205–7); Dido is actually engaged in the administration of "toilsome effort" (*operum labor* 507) which she will not live to complete or enjoy.[15] His hope of "safety" (*salus* 450, 463) will mean Dido's doom. Yet the echoes of his frustration in the inter-view with Venus also remind us that he remains enfolded in the love-goddess' mists at least partly against his immediate wishes in 513 ff., that he too, therefore, is also a victim, in part, of those very games which the gods are playing to insure his success.[16]

A character in a script written by the gods, whose dénouement he does not himself know, he also reflects the situation of reader or listener (whose responses Virgil perhaps anticipates in 1.461 f., *sunt lacrimae rerum....,* "There are tears for the way things are..."). The reader too has, on the one hand, a privileged view of the action and a general grasp of its direction and outcome; but, on the other hand, he participates in the flow of emotion, his sympathy and passions manipulated by the controlling power of the poet. The reader too fluctuates between distance and partici-pation; and, as his attention shifts between the participatory and the authorial voice, he too must continually adjust his stance from the clear judgment and foreknowledge of godlike authorial omniscience to the willingness to share in and identify with the passion, suffering, and error, the *labor* in every sense (cf. 1.330–4), of the mortal actors.

When Aeneas leaves the darkness of Venus' mist, he moves back to the authorial perspective. He is once more the privileged beneficiary of the divine *fata* ["fates"]. As the cloud dissolves into bright aether, Aeneas glows with the supernatural radiance that had characterized Venus herself in her leavetaking:

> uix ea fatus erat cum circumfusa repente
> scindit se nubes et in aethera purgat apertum.
> restitit Aeneas *claraque in luce refulsit*
> os umerosque *deo similis;* namque ipsa decoram
> caesariem nato genetrix lumenque iuuentae
> purpureum et laetos oculis adflarat honores.

Scarcely had Achates spoken these words when the cloud poured over him is suddenly sundered and purified into the open aether. Aeneas stood there and *shone forth in the bright light,* in face and physique *like a god,* for his mother herself blew the breath of grace upon her son's hair, the flushed glow of youth over him, and the joy of handsome dignity upon his eyes (1. 586–91).

> Dixit et auertens *rosea ceruice refulsit,*
> ambrosiaeque comae diuinum uertice odorem
> spirauere; pedes uestis defluxit ad imos,
> et *uera* incessu patuit *dea.*

She spoke, and turning away *shone forth with her rosy neck,* and from her head the ambrosial hair breathed forth the divine perfume; her robe in flowing motion reached all the way to her feet, and in her walk she was revealed *in truth a very goddess* (1.402–5).

Aeneas' prompt identification of himself to Dido, though less boastful than the words addressed to his disguised mother, also recalls that earlier scene (cf. 1.378 f. and 595 f.). But, *mutatis mutandis* ["with necessary changes having been made"], Aeneas is now in the role of godlike controller, while his interlocutor occupies his earlier role, deceived or at least heavily influenced by the divine manipulation of appearances and free play with clouds and disguises.

In the ensuing exchange Aeneas casts Dido into the role of sympathetic spectator-reader of his past (*O sola infandos Troiae miserata labores,* "O you who alone pitied Troy's unspeakable sufferings" 1.597; cf. 460). He uses here the adjective with which he himself will begin the full narration of those "sufferings" in the next book (*infandum, regina...*2.3, "Unspeakable, O Queen, the grief that you order me to renew"). He also uses the authorial words of the poet himself in the proem (*reliquias Danaum* ["remnants of the Greeks"] 1.598 and 1.30), and he promises eternal fame in the authorial rhetoric of vatic-poetic prophecy: *semper honos nomenque tuum laudesque manebunt...*("Always will your glory and your name and praises remain..." 1.609). Now Dido has the role of astonished onlooker that Aeneas occupied before (*obstipuit,* "she stood in dumb amazement" 1.613; cf. 495, 513). Whereas he was spellbound by the artistic representation of Trojan suffering on the temple, she is spellbound by him (614 f.). She soon establishes the bond between them in terms of participatory sympathy (628–30):

> me quoque per multos similis fortuna labores
> iactatam hac demum uoluit consistere terra;
> non ignara mali miseris succurrere disco.

> Me also, tossed through many sufferings like to yours, fortune finally wished to settle in this land; not unknowing of woe do I learn how to come to the aid of sufferers.

At this point the two figures are brought together as co-participants in the controlling divine-authorial scheme, caught up together in Venus and Jupiter's game. Once more works of art play a significant role in the narrative. Those, however, are no longer the self-reflective figural artworks of the doors, but active elements that further the plan of the gods. Both sides bring forth rich tapestries or carvings to adorn the fatal banquet (cf. 1.639 ff., 648, 708, 711). In all of these four cases there is reference to painting or figural representation. Aeneas' gift, a tapestry which Leda gave Helen and Helen brought from Mycenae to Troy (650–2), is certainly of ominous symbolic significance. But in none of these instances is the design described in any detail. No longer points of authorial removal and self-reflective overview of the poem *qua* ["as"] poem, these artifacts are instruments within a fiction which wholly immerses audience and actors as plot and setting work together to precipitate the love between the two protagonists.[17]

In like manner the inset song at this banquet, the song of Iopas, is totally imbedded in the atmosphere of growing passion and its quasi-magical fascination as Venus accomplishes her design. Iopas' song itself remains part of the flawed world-order of Dido's fatal infatuation (1.740–6). He sings of wandering and effort in the heavenly bodies (note *labores* ["labors"], 742), significantly paired sexually; of constellations that bode stormy weather, and of the changing length of night between winter and summer, with a foreshadowing of those long nights of love that will delay Aeneas (746, "what delay stands in the way of slow nights"). His is not the distanced voice of authorial omniscience which can reach beyond the turbulence and confusion of the present to comprehend the total world-order *sub specie aeternitatis* ["under the aspect of eternity"], like Anchises in 6.724–51. This poet is himself a participant and a collaborator in the passion-clouded setting.[18]

One crucial difference still separates Aeneas and Dido. She, "ignorant," "unknowing," and "unhappy" (*ignara* 1.299; *nescia* 718; *infelix* 712, 749; cf. 713), never really emerges from the participatory voice and the gods' manipulative design, whereas Aeneas, as we have argued, mediates the two roles and the two narrative functions. In the last scene of Book 1 she is hanging on his words while he prepares to take stage-center as narrator and participant at the same time. The scenes of Troy's suffering depicted on the doors of Juno's temple are no longer kept at aesthetic remove as subjects of a work of art, but are refocussed through Aeneas' eyes as part of his lived experience soon narrated by him in his participatory voice in Book 2. Instead of being a decorative element on a building that embodies the rising hopes of Carthage, the same scenes become the instruments of Carthage's doom in the design of Juno's enemy and the plan of Jupiter's *fata*. Thus they too shift ambiguously between detachment and involvement, between self-reflection and instrumentality in the plot. That very compassion which led Dido to have those scenes represented on her city's temple becomes a crucial element in leading her to the passion which causes her suffering and death (cf. 1.459–63 and 628–30).

The ambiguity of Aeneas between narrator and participant is nowhere keener and more complex than in Books 2 and 3. The scene on the temple doors and his invisible presence at Dido's first appearance crystalize this ambiguity and prepare for its more elaborate role in the ensuing two books. Aeneas is a bard who, like Virgil himself, "recounted the fates from the gods" (*fata renarrabat diuum*...3.717; cf. *canebat*, "sang" 4.14). Yet this long night of his spellbinding tale blends with the sleepless night of passionate emotion in which Dido drinks in with his words the desperate, destructive love (1.748 f.) that has heavy consequences for him too.[19]

As Dido drinks in the long draughts of love that will eventually cause her death (1.749), she asks Aeneas for details of the war that must be already familiar to her from the engraved doors of the temple which she herself has founded (cf. 1.446 f.). Only then does she go on, in the last lines of the book, to ask questions about the Greek attack and Aeneas' wanderings that she does not yet know (1.753–56).[20] In her fatal immersion in the narrative, knowledge and ignorance become strangely mingled and confused. The willingness to suspend or block out the known under the influence of Venus' magic subtly intimates the self-blinding that love creates. That willing suspension of knowledge also characterizes the reader who, for all his familiarity with an old and familiar tale, is drawn on into a long first-person narrative, thanks to a magical fascination of another kind. Like Dido, but in a different way, he too is *captus amore* ["captured by love"] (*Ecl.* 6.10). Aeneas and Dido's danger now, to take the longer authorial view, is also the reader's danger: entrapment in the passions of the moment at the expense of the meaning of the whole.

The dangers of Aeneas' first encounters at Carthage can also be extrapolated to the end of the work. Beneath the clouded envelope of Aeneas' violent *furiae* ["rages"] and *irae* ["angers"] (12.946) lies, somehow, the ultimate meaning of his civilizing task in the detached perspective of the gods and the fates. Yet Virgil's own interweaving of authorial and participatory voices and stances within Aeneas also shows this affective, emotive envelope as an inextricable part of the meaning: the "message" is inseparable from its "medium." That the transcendent purpose of the gods' ultimate plan is, for good or ill, irremovably imbedded in its immanent matter of mortal imperfection, human suffering, and the emotions which that suffering stirs is an essential part of Virgil's tragic conception of history and possibly of art. The ultimate task for mortals may be, as Anchises suggests in his great eschatological speech of Book 6, to cleanse the soul of its earthy, animal dross and leave only the pure, fiery divine essence. Yet the poetic truth of the *Aeneid* is not abstract or ideal. It is inseparably bound up with the work's sensitivity to the emotional fabric and undertones of all our acts, the human substance of flawed passions, uncontrollable feelings, irrational impulses. It embraces the awareness of both the connotative power of language and the imperfections of language which conveys and contains these passions.

For these reasons too neither the hero's tragic success nor the poem itself in its ambiguous closure is allowed fully to transcend its beginning. The last image, Turnus beneath Aeneas' sword, takes us back to our first view of Aeneas himself, helpless in the divinely sent storm (*soluuntur frigore membra*, "His limbs are loosed in the chilling cold" 1.92 and 12.951), with the connotations of disorientation and loss of an overview.[21]

In this last scene Aeneas is unable to retain the detachment of transcendent purpose in the face of the "reminders of savage grief" which detonate his fury (*saeui monimenta doloris* 12.944). This is the tragic aspect of that crossing between distance and involvement which characterizes his difficult and contradictory role from the beginning. Like the reader or listener, he stands between sympathetic iden-tification and intellectual recognition, between knowledge of past and future on the one hand and immersion in the moment of present passion of act and feeling on the other. This ambiguity is summed up for the entire poem in the scene which surrounds his viewing of the temple doors at Carthage. That artwork is proof that the compassionate *lacrimae rerum* ["tears for the way things are"] exist, but it is also *pictura inanis,* "empty painting" (1.462, 464).[22]

The last phrase suggests Virgil's own consciousness that the aesthetic fiction which humanizes with pity for remote suffering and with the acknowledgment of human weakness and error in the face of violent passions and insoluble moral con-flicts is nevertheless an "artificial," arbitrary, possibly futile construct. We may well ponder whether the hero's last gesture in the poem betrays the poet's understanding of the tragic dimension of his own art, that neither the supreme artistry of the fiction nor the aesthetic experience of those compassionate emotions will ever be enough to prevent the recurrence of violence in history's cycles of vengefulness and hatred. In the *Aeneid,* as in the *Eclogues,* Virgil raises but does not answer the question whether poetry can change anything in the "real" world of politics and history. Of course we may question whether the prevention of violence and suffering is the poet's concern at all. But the ending of the *Aeneid,* transposed from politics to art, may reflect Virgil's acceptance of the necessity of violence, pain, and sacrifice for every creative act, be it the foundation of a city or the writing of an epic poem.

Notes

[1]See Segal 1978.124 ff., with further bibliography in note 40, p. 140; Putnam 1979.308 ff. For the importance of the figure of Orpheus and the theme of art in the *Georgics* and in Virgil generally see Desport 1952.155–65; Parry 1972.35–52, especially 45 ff., 50 ff.

[2]Putnam 1979.315 f.

[3]Otis 1963.95 and 227. Attention to point of view in Virgilian narration has received some attention from critics: see Quinn 1968.77–84, on the alternation between "dramatic" and "descriptive" narration; Sanderlin 1969/70.81–5; Johnson 1976.67 f. on Dido's death. Book 1, however, has not received detailed attention; nor have critics developed the implica-tions of this technique for the problem of interpreting the epic as a whole.

[4]Johnson 1976.20. For the "dualistic" outlook of the *Aeneid* see also Parry 1963.66–80 reprinted in Commager 1966.107–23; Vance 1973.116–25. I use the term "voice" here in a more specific and limited sense than Parry.

[5]See Dietrich 1965. chaps. 6, 10, 13.

[6]Cf. also *Aen.* 12.50 f.; in general Johnson 1976.14 f.

[7]Otis 1963.231–3; Pöschl 1962.34–43; Hunt 1973.4.

[8]Note too that Jupiter will speak of the *fata* in 1.262, *uoluens fatorum arcana movebo,* as did Aeneas in 1.205; but *uoluens* recurs soon after of Aeneas' more troubled state in 305, *per noctem plurima uoluens.* Aeneas' expectation of *sedes quietas* in 1.205, however (*tendimus in Latium sedes ubi fata quietas / ostendunt.* "Our goal is Latium, where the fates show a peaceful abode"), contrasts with the reality of what the *fata* hold in store for him in Latium. Aeneas' breadth of vision thus remains in contrast with his ignorant immersion in events. This ironic contrast is also implicit in the repetition of *quietas* for the gods' preparation of Dido for Aeneas' appearance, 1.303 f.: *in primis regina / quietum accipit in Teucros animum mentemque benignam* ("Especially does the queen receive a calm spirit and kindly mind toward the Trojans").

[9]For the harbor and its symbolism see Pöschl 1962.141–3; Andersson 1976.59 f.; Reeker 1971.12–22, 28–30.

[10]For the language of comedy see Austin 1971 *ad* 314, 369, 370. Austin appreciates the mixture of lightness and "deeper purpose" (see *ad* 314), but does not give the dark and bitter side of this scene its full due. See also Otis 1963.236.

[11]See *Aen.* 2.790–5, 5.738–40; 6.700–2; in general Segal 1973/4.97–101 and 1974.34–52.

[12]It is part of the ambiguity of Venus' role here that she not only recalls the naive freshness of Nausicaa in *Odyssey* 6, but also, in her reading of the omens in 1.393 ff., the more complex erotically colored figure of Helen in *Odyssey* 15.

[13]Otis 1963.65 notes the function of the mist as a symbol of Aeneas' "spiritual removal from the scene," but does not deal with that symbol's ambiguity nor its relation to point of view in narration.

[14]For some good observations on the arrangement of the scenes on the doors and the shifting of tenses see Williams 1960a.145–51. For the thematic relations of the scene see Johnson 1976.99 ff.; Otis 1963.65 ff.; Boyle 1972.74. For some interesting reflections on this kind of ecphrasis see Pöschl 1975.119–23, especially 121: the doors at Cumae are the first description of a work in which an artist explicitly represents his own fate; "Damit ist das Problem des Künstlers angerührt, der sein eigenes Schicksal im Kunstwerk bewältigt...Aber dort, wo das Persönlichste, Schmerzlichste zur Sprache kommt, stösst der Künstler—so will Virgil hier sagen—an eine Grenze. Auch er verstummt. Die Erlösung durch das Kunstwerk ist nicht mehr möglich." The relation between the two scenes of artistic representation deserves a fuller examination in this light.

[15]Note too the use of *laetus*, "joyful," in connection with Dido's grove and its shade in 1.441, *lucus...laetissimus umbrae*, "a grove most joyful—fertile—with shadow." The word recurs in connection with Dido's view of the Trojans in 1.605 f., "What so fortunate age bore you?" (*laeta...saecula*) and her entertainment of them at the banquet (1.636, 685, 732 734), in contrast to her status as *misera* or *infelix* both before and after (1.344, 4.67, etc.). *Laetus Romulus* in Jupiter's prophecy, 1.275 f., contrasts not only with Dido and with 1.605 f., but also with the *aspera saecula* (1.291) that the Aeneadae will have to endure before reaching the *aurea saecula* of Augustan Rome (6.792).

[16]Thus Aeneas' confident and secure narrative to Dido at the end of the book recalls the helplessness and uncertainty of his narrative to the disguised Venus in the forest earlier (1.372 and 753).

[17]For the symbolism of the gifts at the banquet see Pöschl 1962.148 f.; Otis 1963.66 f. and 239; Hunt 1973.18.

[18]For Iopas see Pöschl 1962.150 ff., 166; Segal 1971.336–49, with the further literature there cited, Kinsey 1979.77–86; Segal, "Iopas Revisited (*Aeneid* I, 740ff.)," *Emerita* 49 (1981) 17–25.

[19]For the dangerous atmosphere of Dido's banquet see Pöschl 1962.166 f.; Otis 1963.240 f.

[20]Priam (1.750): cf. 461 and 487; Hector (750): cf. 483–84; Memnon (751): cf. 489; Diomedes' horses (752): cf. 471–72; Achilles (752): cf. 468, 475, 483–84.

[21]The vast literature on the closing scene of the *Aeneid* gives little indication of abating. For a recent survey see McKay 1974/5.39; Johnson 1976.114–34; Boyle 1972.69–74, 84 f.; Putnam 1965.190 ff. and 1972.61 ff.; Segal 1974.49 ff. with the bibliography in notes 17 and 20.

[22]On the importance of *inanis* here see Boyle 1972.75; Parry 1963 = Commager 1966.122 f.

Bibliography

Andersson, T. M. 1976. *Early Epic Scenery. Homer, Virgil, and the Medieval Legacy.* Ithaca, N.Y.

Austin, R. G. 1971. *P. Vergili Maronis Aeneidos Liber Primus.* Oxford.

Boyle, A. J. 1972. "The Meaning of the *Aeneid*: A Critical Inquiry, part I," *Ramus* 1.63–90.

Commager, Steele (ed.). 1966. *Virgil. A Collection of Critical Essays.* Englewood Cliffs.

Desport, M. 1952. *L'incantation virgilienne*. Bordeaux.

Dietrich, B. C. 1965. *Death, Fate and the Gods*. London.

Hunt, J. W. 1973. *Forms of Glory: Structure and Sense in Virgil's Aeneid*. Carbondale, Illinois.

Johnson, W. R. 1976. *Darkness Visible: A Study of Vergil's Aeneid*. Berkeley and Los Angeles.

Kinsey, T. E. 1979. "The Song of Iopas," *Emerita* 44.77–86.

McKay, A. G. 1974/5. "Recent Work on Virgil. A Bibliographical Survey, 1964–73," *CW* 68.1–92.

Otis, B. 1963. *Virgil. A Study in Civilized Poetry*. Oxford.

Parry, A. 1963. "The Two Voices of Virgil's *Aeneid*," *Arion* 2.66–80. (repr. in Commager 1966).

———. 1972. "The Idea of Art in Virgil's *Georgics*," *Arethusa* 5.35–52.

Pöschl, V. 1950. (= 1962) *Die Dichtkunst Virgils: Bild und Symbol in der Aeneis*. Innsbruck. = *The Art of Virgil: Image and Symbol in the Aeneid*. tr. Seligson, G. Ann Arbor.

———. 1975. "Die Tempeltüren des Dädalus in der Aeneis (VI 14–33)," *Würzburger Jahrbücher* 1.119–23.

Putnam, M. C. J. 1965. *The Poetry of the Aeneid*. Cambridge, Mass.

———. 1972. "The Virgilian Achievement," *Arethusa* 5.53–70.

———. 1979. *Virgil's Poem of the Earth*. Princeton.

Quinn, K. 1968. *Virgil's Aeneid: A Critical Description*. London.

Reeker, H. -D. 1971. *Die Landschaft in der Aeneis, Spudasmata* 27. Hildesheim.

Sanderlin, G. 1969/70. "Point of View in Virgil's Fourth *Aeneid*," *CW* 63.81–5.

Segal, C. P. 1971. "The Song of Iopas in the *Aeneid*," *Hermes* 99.336–49.

———. 1973/4. "'Like Winds and Winged Dream,' A Note on Virgil's Development," *CJ* 69.97–101.

———. 1974. "Vanishing Shades: Virgil and Homeric Repetitions," *Eranos* 72.34–52.

———. 1978. "The Magic of Orpheus and the Ambiguities of Language," *Ramus* 7.106–42.

———. 1981. "Iopas Revisited (*Aeneid* 1.740 ff.)," *Emerita* 49.17–25.

Vance, E. 1973. "Warfare and the Structure of Thought in Virgil's *Aeneid*," *QUCC* 15.111–162.

Williams, R. D. 1960a. "The Pictures on Dido's Temple (*Aeneid* 1.450–93)," *CQ* n.s. 10.145–51.

Conclusion

Stephanie Quinn

CONCLUSION: WHY VERGIL?

To those who ask why we should read Vergil's works — Why Vergil — I submit that the answer lies in the rich fabric of our history and culture, which has brought us to this moment at the end of the twentieth century. Does Vergil's golden bough, a symbol of hope and promise (pictured on the book's cover), lead us to some promised land? Or do we follow it to a terrifying world of madness and disaster (evoked by the frontispiece)? Vergil's works can help us live within these two visions of human life and history.

We look back on a past we thought we understood — but find we do not — and forward to a future that will be so different as to be beyond imagination. For such a moment, we need Vergil's particular sensibility, his capacity for ambiguity, his warning, and his version of hope.

In this Conclusion, I seek to put in context a response to the question of the book's title, "Why Vergil," and thus urge the continued, creative conversation such a question invites. I advocate reading Vergil's works on two grounds — a general argument about the role of literature and art, and a particular argument about Vergil's works, especially the *Aeneid*.

First, with reference to the role of literature and art in general, I explore the social role of learning, using the term *scholé*, ancient Greek for both school and play. In that context, I consider the views of several scholars on the importance of literature and the liberal arts generally for a democratic society. I move back and forth between conditions in ancient Athens and Rome and world conditions in the late twentieth century. The role of art in ancient Athens, especially tragedy, and the history of the first century B.C.E., when Vergil lived and wrote in Rome, suggest questions about the social use of art and about the connection between art, politics, and history.

Second, an answer to the title question must arise from Vergil's works themselves. In content and form, themes and methods, his poetry addresses questions that are immediate and urgent today, questions about the relationship of art and society, art and truth. Vergil's poetry and Vergilian scholarship and criticism are relevant to contemporary theoretical and political debates about culture.

Not only, however, do Vergil's works confront these questions, they also suggest an answer, or more accurately, a mode of answering. Vergil's mingling of "voices" and his exploration of aesthetic truth through the revelation of multiple sensibilities about single situations speak to us with special force today. At the same time, his poetic methods return us to a set of fundamental questions in Western culture, which can be captured by the phrase "the quarrel between poetry and philosophy."

The project of creating this anthology touchs on issues that concern me deeply. I end this essay and the volume with thoughts on why Vergil's works are important to me.

Literature, Society, and History

Source of individual enrichment, fixed elements of elite education, banners for electoral or social causes, window dressing of class and power—literature, art in general, seems to partake of many roles, to serve many functions. Among the most difficult to grasp is the value of literature and art for the public good, if indeed such a case can be made. I believe it can, as do many others.

Scholé and Democracy

In the Introduction, I listed several audiences for this book, distinguishing decision makers, general readers, educators, and students. In fact, I hope this project helps bridge the gap between these groups and in so doing answers the title's question more fully.

A text such as the *Aeneid* is currently available and meaningful only to segments of our society; access to its pleasures and especially its benefits are thus limited as well. The inaccessibility of the *Aeneid* and other such works is one of the fault lines in modern Western culture, seismic in its implications. I believe, however, that the *Aeneid* can and should be available to anyone. The social and pedagogical work of bridging the gap between traditionally aristocratic culture and the needs of Western democracy as it extends its embrace to those excluded from it for over two thousand years is the social responsibility of humanists, classicists, and those who love the works of Vergil.

I hope to help adult general readers return to or discover the pleasure of engagement with a challenging text, which they may have fleetingly or uncomprehendingly "gotten through" as students. I hope as well to help students foresee a continuing relationship, past school, with this and other works that stimulate their minds, hearts, and spirits and generously repay a sustained, lifelong relationship. These are ambitious expectations. This book is an invitation to share in a special kind of enjoyment and participate in an expanding community of conversation.[1]

My hopes are based on an old idea and cultural phenomenon, known from fifth-century B.C.E. Athens, the idea of *scholé* as both learning and leisure, school and play. These two sets of terms seem to us in the twentieth century to be diametrically opposed: school is work and leisure a vegetative state. To make *scholé* meaningful today, almost 2,500 years after the golden age of Athens, we must no longer reserve *scholé* for a segment of the community but should instead offer it to a fuller but still imperfect democracy that needs *scholé* in the fullness of its meaning.[2]

These hopes are pedagogically and socially complicated. I want to adapt a social phenomenon of the limited but deep ancient Athenian democracy to the broad but perhaps—considering the small number of citizens who vote—shallow democracy as practiced in the United States. Such an agenda is certainly difficult, perhaps even a little "mad."[3] One could say that that hope is contradicted by the history of the 2,500 years between Periclean Athens and us: we are so different, in important ways for the better but in others for the worse.[4] This expanded hope, certainly unrealizable in a limited project such as this one, is perhaps unrealizable altogether, as was Anchises' vision for his son Aeneas and for Rome.

My interest in *scholé* may be, I hope it is, a small part of the "convergences" of several, seemingly disparate trends in twentieth-century culture.[5] What I am advocating here is a return, in modern dress, to a public arena of social usefulness for the realm of human creativity and interaction we call the arts and humanities, to *scholé*. In that arena, the "nonspecialist is enfranchised," "a commonality at the level of social infrastructures" is created, "the fatal line separating 'school' from 'extracurricular activities' needs wholesale destruction, and the line separating 'school' from 'life' no less."[6] These phrases aptly describe what I am calling *scholé*. What is more, I believe that Vergil is an ideal teacher for this new school.

Even if this hope is not completely or immediately attainable, it speaks nonetheless to the contemporary context within which the readings in this volume have been chosen and to the question the title poses. In the last several decades in the United States, the reading and teaching of a text like Vergil's *Aeneid* have become matters of controversy in at least two ways. On the one hand, the general public, through the explosion of both access to and the expense of elite higher education, and also through political campaigning, legislative decision making, and journalistic opinion making, has become skeptical of higher education as a whole. And subjects like literature, which seem to lack immediate utility in terms of students' postgraduate employment, have become embroiled in theoretical debates that to the public can seem nonsensical or even destructive.

On the other hand, in these very debates, the academic world has called into question the value and even legitimacy of its own perennial bread and butter, the texts such as the *Aeneid* that form the basis of the liberal arts tradition. The debates center on these texts' near exclusive production and reception among elite groups consisting mostly of white men, holders of political and economic power. From without and within, the title's question has become highly complex and contested. Thus, although a single volume of collected scholarship and creative work cannot resolve the issues its title raises, it cannot, with intellectual integrity, ignore them.[7]

We lack automatic and simple answers to the question, Why Vergil, or to many similar questions for that matter: Why art, Why literature, especially Why old literature, and very old literature in a dead language at that. Many answers that are given fail to persuade, seem weak, even tainted.[8] The worth of a work like the *Aeneid* is not now simply taken for granted. It is not the purpose of this volume to lament that lost simplicity. Rather, the case needs to be rediscovered, redemonstrated, reconstructed.

I had an experience seeing a movie with friends a while ago, an experience shared by them and apparently by others too, an experience with the words of another icon of European letters and an experience that I wish for readers of Vergil. The movie was Kenneth Branagh's "Hamlet," by William Shakespeare; it is over four hours long and I expected to fidget. Instead, and despite the movie's faults, hour by hour I became more engrossed, drawn deeper into concentration, led into intimacy with the words. For me, Branagh succeeded in challenging the distinction between regular movies and the style of Shakespeare movies that has become familiar to us through the great actor Laurence Olivier, a particular style of speech and production that distinguished such films from popular entertainment. I found my experience exactly described as follows, although in reference to other Branagh work.

> [Branagh] undertook to make a genuinely popular movie, against odds stiffer than those Olivier faced, at a moment when more than ever before Shakespearean language had to fight for a hearing. *Henry V* played at the local multiplex alongside *Honey, I Shrunk the Kids* and *Indiana Jones and the*

Last Crusade, and it was obvious that Branagh was prepared to meet that competition on its own ground....The continued power of *Henry V* was not to be taken for granted; what for Olivier had been a universally recognized (if far from universally enjoyed) cultural monument now had to defend itself.

The review goes on to name what it was about Branagh's movie that worked so well.

The chief point of Branagh's direction was to keep the language in front of the audience at all times....[T]he job of the actor was to clarify, line by line and word by word, not just the general purport of what the character was feeling, but the exact function of every remark....The result was...a tendency to deflate sonority in favor of exact meaning, while at the same time giving the meter of the verse a musician's respect, and the rhetorical substructure a lawyer's questioning eye. As I first listened, in that same multiplex,...in Dolby Stereo, an unanticipated excitement took hold. It didn't matter that I could read those words any time....The thrill was to hear them in a multiplex, in that public space from which the possibility of such language had been essentially barred.[9]

The cultural critics who sanctify canonical works and those who vilify them both seem to me to rob them of their vitality and to rob us of the chance to determine for ourselves if those texts are indeed vital still.[10] This anthology is offered in hope that the continuing vitality of Vergil's ancient poetry, which the contributors know so well, will be communicated to new readers.

Canonical works themselves are caught in a paradox. Alternately accused and praised, they become the property not of ordinary readers and citizens but of warring camps. The result is that my students come to a text like the *Aeneid,* or the Homeric epics or the Athenian tragedies, either already angry at them before they have read them or — and this is by far more common — frightened, intimidated, and sure that these works are simply too difficult and esoteric for them. The culture wars, no matter which side one takes, make even more difficult for students the demanding job of learning how to encounter the "other" without unexamined fear or unwarranted acceptance, and thus both to know oneself and to learn how to make one's own skilled judgments on important and difficult topics in a changing world. The "wars" increase the alienation of the public from any books, literature, and art that demand effort.

Branagh's work defies the wars' limiting polarities. Instead what he offers us is *scholé,* a way to engage in leisure activity that quickens, not deadens, just as amateur sports enliven bodies stiffened behind immobile desks. In our task of engagement with the *Aeneid,* as we read, or better read aloud,[11] Vergil's lines, let us try to hear the words, "line by line and word by word," so that we can begin to consider with fresh ears if these particular words deserve to be barred from a larger public or whether they can excite us still. Each piece in this collection was chosen because it can help us "keep the language in front" of us and thus "deflate sonority," getting past the way that language has come to be received through centuries of cultural uses and habits. I hope readers find that the collection meets this severe test.

My own academic career reflects the changing times. In my very first Latin class, in seventh grade, our teacher asked us students why we were there. Our answers dealt with law, medicine, religion, and, typically, the lack of our first choices or of other choices that fit our schedules. He rejected them all. His answer was that we were learning Latin in order to read in their original language the works written in it. I was skeptical. It turned out that the fun of learning the language kept me going until the poetry appeared later in high school, and then he turned out to be right.

Many years after seventh grade, in a discussion with faculty members and administrators about establishing a center for the humanities at my university, no one offered the reading of texts as the first rationale for such a center. Instead, we talked about the need to de-center the humanities, to build an eccentric center where new voices would be welcomed in conversation with the old, where the cultural conversation that the humanities represent could be reconstructed after decades of effective deconstruction.[12] And we were right too.

In light of that huge and swift change in cultural understanding and value, the question Why Vergil? is all the more urgent. "Arms and the man I sing," "*arma virumque cano,*" are the first words of the *Aeneid*. Can the story of one man's arms in a war of long ago, a story whose first words are military and male, be relevant to our nearly twentieth-first-century, politically corrected, deconstructed, multicultured, for-profit, wired world? Yes, it can, and especially now — not because Vergil's works are an emblem of culture, but because their content and form, most readily in the *Aeneid*, speak directly to the intellectual, cultural, and moral issues of today and of us all. To the extent that that assertion can be demonstrated, the answer to the question Why Vergil will be clear.

After some years of assault, several scholars are now offering cogent and fresh responses to the generic question of which the query Why Vergil? is but one version. Wendy Steiner, in *The Scandal of Pleasure: Art in the Age of Fundamentalism*, reviews several recent cultural clashes. Of the value of art generally Steiner says, "Experiencing the variety of meanings available in a work of art helps make us tolerant and mentally lithe. Art is a realm of thought experiments that quicken, sharpen, and sweeten our being in the world." Thomas Bender in his essay, "Locality and Worldliness," extends the mind-expanding capacity of art, noting that the "special contribution of scholarship to...public conversation is its access to a refined and severe method of thought."[13]

The issue of teaching thinking and of training students to develop a set of habits of mind is taken up by Martha Nussbaum in *Poetic Justice: The Literary Imagination and Public Life*. Using Charles Dickens's novel *Hard Times* as an example, Nussbaum argues "that the literary imagination is an essential part of both the theory and practice of citizenship." She goes on to explain, "Most social hatred involves the refusal to enter into the life of another in thought, to recognize the other as an individual human being with a distinctive story to tell, someone who one might oneself be. In that sense, the novel cultivates a moral ability that is opposed to hatred in its very structure."[14]

Nussbaum's point is supported by Eli Sagan, regarding the psychological foundations for successful democratic society. In analyzing fifth-century B.C.E. Athens and the twentieth-century C.E. United States, Sagan asserts that the primary psychological enemy of democracy is paranoia, that is, "heated aggression, suspiciousness, and conspiratorial fantasy." Such a state of mind, in an individual or in groups within a society, makes impossible the idea of a loyal opposition, since any difference is a threat. In agreement with Nussbaum but arguing in different terms, Sagan cites the ability to assume the "independence and integrity of other people" as necessary in a democracy: "No democracy is possible unless a large group of people in society have the capacity to live without the defenses of authoritarianism, militarism, and dogmatic ideology," but instead have the skills to live in a heterogeneous world.[15] The traits Sagan explores in psychological terms are the habits of mind Steiner, Bender, and Nussbaum claim are associated with the experience of art, a certain kind of scholarship, and, I would add, education in the liberal arts. They are traits that have a public benefit, especially in a democracy.

The argument for the value of the liberal arts to democracy is also compellingly made by two other humanists, Richard Lanham and James O'Donnell.[16] In separate and stunning challenges to fellow humanists, they argue that electronic technology's transition from static print and book to interactive screen is effecting a transition in the fundamental nature of discourse. Further, they both view this technology as only one part of developments throughout our century—in art, philosophy, and society. The current technology of electronic communication, they argue, is but the latest of trends that taken together are returning to center stage the debate at the core of Western humanistic discourse. That debate is the one between philosophy and rhetoric, between Socrates / Plato and the sophists / rhetoricians. Within that debate, I suggest, lie the core questions of which ours, Why Vergil, is but one instance.

Lanham sees in today's electronic media a return to the patterns of interaction he associates with classical rhetoric and thus also with classical democracy: a rhetorical education "trained people in…the skills needed to create and sustain a public, as against a private, reality. It did not simply train, it created, the public person. It is the perfect training ground for the pattern of government Plato hated most, the genuine, open-ended democracy."[17] O'Donnell argues for an education in which students "actuate their intellects," which provides a "frame of reference, in some ways recognizable and in others alien and defamiliarizing," a "discipline of *seeing*, seeing past resemblances to differences, recognizing the otherness of even the familiar."[18] Both these scholars locate the possibility for such an education in the liberal arts.[19]

Despite their intellectually and emotionally liberating power for a democratic society, the liberal arts alone cannot make us free. They cannot reduce the anxiety, envy, and hatred engendered by economic insecurity, inequality, and deprivation, nor the fear, suspicion, and anger born of systemic injustice and prejudice.[20] What they can do is strengthen citizens in the mental and emotional practice of openness to ways other than their own of seeing the world, which is the opposite of paranoia and which may be a precondition for democratic society. The study of the liberal arts seems to make us smarter in a particular way, according to the writers I have been discussing. They seem to encourage a healthy society, one that develops people who can deal both rigorously and empathically with issues of public life. These authors are not saying that the training of such citizens enhances personal wealth, or that it can by itself guarantee right judgment or domestic tranquility, nor do they assert that such training is easy, only that it is a civic necessity. I agree; reading Vergil is good for the country!

In fact, Steiner claims that the difficulty of understanding a work of art is essential to its nature, value, and pleasure, for art is "inherently paradoxical." This she calls the "ungovernability of ambiguity."[21] Further, the capacity to deal with the messiness of ambiguity, its ungovernability, is precisely the key to good government. And the teachers of that capacity are the liberal and creative arts.[22]

Life is not neat, in private or in public. Our ability to deal with ambiguity in art, literature, or the liberal arts mirrors our capacity to deal with this lack of neatness in public life and policy: "Compared to tyranny, democracy is a messy, inefficient, unpredictable, uncontrolled society."[23] If we can bear another paradox, it would seem that the fields that are the most subjective — the arts and humanities — are the training ground for objectivity, which is necessary to, not an elite adornment of, democracy.

> Now, uncertainty — the sense that not only you don't know the truth but that many complex issues are irresolvably ambiguous — is sometimes the most productive way of allowing you to *act* while at the same time respecting that others are not going to accept your view, approve your action or follow your example. It produces a tentativeness that permits you to see many things from many points of view. Which is, I believe, the best definition of objectivity.[24]

Training in such "objectivity" is the business of the liberal arts, which are, literally from their Latin etymological and Roman historical roots, the skills needed in order to be free citizens.[25]

These difficult intellectual and personal skills can be developed through the study of most of the demanding texts that comprise the liberal arts corpus old and new, including Vergil's work. As we have seen throughout this volume, however, Vergil's technique of creating multiple perspectives on single situations, which Brooks Otis named his "subjective style," demonstrates most particularly just such use of uncertainty, ambiguity, and "objectivity" to create the habit of empathic understanding that Steiner finds in the experience of art, Nussbaum in many nineteenth-century novels, Bender in engaged scholarship, that Sagan claims is essential to a democratic society, and that Lanham and O'Donnell characterize as the rhetorical skills that support a democracy.

Athens and Rome, Vergil and Today

In U.S. society, training in the liberal arts as service to democracy is relegated almost exclusively to schooling. This was not always so and thus we can infer that that social arrangement is not an unavoidable condition in human society. Among the differences between ancient Athens and us are not just the kind and degree of our democracies, in which the West has made great though still incomplete progress. A major difference is the role of art in our societies, and about that issue, we may still have something to learn from Athens.

The dramatic festivals of fifth-century Athens, at which the plays of Aeschylus, Sophocles, Euripides, and Aristophanes were performed (along with works called satyr plays), were public events, rooted in religious ritual, attended by perhaps as many as seventeen thousand people at a time. They were public competitions for excellence and were supported by a combination of private wealth donated to Athens as a civic duty (the same funding system used to pay for Athenian warships and in comparable amounts) and by the public purse.[26] They were popular entertainment.

What the dramatic festivals did was sharpen and quicken with critical discipline the capacities of Athenians to perform the work of citizenship in the *pólis*, the city-state.

> Greek tragedies were meant for the citizens of Athens, not just for a theatre-going minority, but for the whole citizenry of the most powerful city in the

Greek world....Did the Athenians *need* tragedy? Indeed, did they perhaps need it almost as much as they did the Assembly, the Council of the Five Hundred and all the other institutions of their democracy?

It seems possible that we have here a rather special example of a social body carrying out quite publicly the maintenance and development of its mental infrastructure.

It seems most likely that it was essentially as citizens that the citizens saw and heard tragedies....

Athenian tragedy was..."political" in several...senses. At its widest outreach, the Athenian democratic way of life could be represented as 'an education for all Hellas' (the famous phrase of Thucydides' Pericles in the Funeral Speech). But in the first instance participation in the democratic process, including being present to hear such a public civic oration, was conceived primarily as an education for Athenian citizens, most of whom had received no formal schooling during childhood beyond the inculcation (perhaps) of basic literacy, numeracy and musical appreciation. For such average citizens, tragic theatre was an important part of their learning to be active participants in the self-government by mass meeting and open debate between peers.[27]

The work of self-government was accomplished by means of civic decision-making processes in which virtually all citizens participated, and in which virtually all the decisions of the *pólis*, from military strategy, to civic finances, to judicial matters, were made. Tragedy was *scholé,* leisure and school, and the tragic poets were not only the entertainers but also the severe teachers of the community of Athenian citizens, of the body politic.[28]

The tragedies were useful to the Athenians, just as the arts and the liberal arts have been of practical value to educated and ruling classes for hundreds of years. The social function of the liberal arts is complex. They impart power to citizens to control their society, and at the same time they make it harder for those citizens to be controlled.

Five hundred years after Pericles' Funeral Speech, in the ashes of the Roman Republic and birth of the Roman Empire toward the end of the first century B.C.E., Vergil faced in the *Aeneid* the social and historical need, and also danger, of using arts and letters to shape the way a society thinks and the way it thinks about itself.[29] How he did that is instructive to us as we face similar needs and dangers in what may be similar times of fundamental change. Vergil's *Aeneid* became a school text, like the epics of Homer, almost immediately on its creation. What kind of text is it for today?

The feasibility of the claim for Vergil's relevance to the twentieth century rests on, among other things, historical similarities between Vergil's time and ours. Like those of us in the countries that border the North Atlantic, the Romans of Vergil's time lived through an epoch of deep turmoil marked by an extended period of warfare and bloodshed that co-existed with a transformation of their culture and society at its roots, in political structures and social values. The hundred years from about 130 to 30 B.C.E. witnessed the end of the Roman Republic, an institution five hundred years old and the foundation of Rome's success in the ancient Mediterranean world. In the half-century of his lifetime, Vergil experienced half of that grim history. The Republic's foundation, however, proved inadequate to its ultimate edifice, the burgeoning scope of Roman hegemony and influence throughout the Mediterranean world, the future Roman Empire. The twentieth century has seen no less bloodshed and no less destruction of a worldview in the creation of some new way of seeing and living that we cannot yet know. Vergil's project, a great work for his complex and troubled time, could be a poem for our time as well.

Erich Gruen, in his essay in this volume, juxtaposes Roman historical self-creation to our present's reshaping of old ideas for new circumstances. In that light, Vergil's works comprise a case study, as it were, of a shift in historical consciousness, the transition from the Roman Republic to the Roman Empire,[30] a shift comparable to the one happening now in, for example, our growing consciousness of a global set of economic and social interactions and also through the presence and influence of manifold and diverse cultural groups. Such a shift is a grave and exhilarating historical moment. Vergil lived in such a moment, and so do we.

Gruen charts briefly the Romans' creation of their history as an extended series of cultural choices, made more or less consciously. He demonstrates as well that historical identity can be fluid and malleable, not a fixed reality. We can see an analogy for us, through today's voices that bring new perspectives and questions to assumptions about the past and therefore the present that we may have thought were incontrovertible. Vergil's work was part of the construction of Roman self-understanding for his time, which can guide us as we reconsider our own sense of past and present.

We learn from the contemporary writers and artists whose works are included in this volume, as we do from the writers who lived between Vergil's time and ours, that art can creatively and honorably converse on issues of politics, history, and cultural change. This means neither that all good or great art is political nor that only political art can be good or great. It means instead that political interest alone does not define art as bad; bad art can be about anything.

Robert Gurval's essay in this volume raises the question of the *Aeneid* as a political poem, particularly as a work of Augustan propaganda. Gurval concludes that Vergil was not a shallow propandist instructed by his ruler/patron to glorify Rome and himself but was the one who shaped Rome's self-understanding. That conclusion prompts another and perhaps more difficult question, however. Why would a poet use the political events and issues of the day (which are destined to become history) as the subject of his art? If propaganda, whether in support of or opposition to something, does not forge the connection between poet and emperor, between art and history, what does?

In *Promised Verse: Poets in the Society of Augustan Rome*, Peter White offers a suggestion. In an intriguing phrase, he proposes that for Vergil and his circle of poets, "Augustus was a poetically exciting idea."[31] How could that be? How could a politician excite a poet? What connects poetry and history, history and art, poetry and power? Such connections are so difficult for us to imagine, steeped as we are in skepticism and cynicism about institutions and leaders.

Yet, it is possible for the world of history making to have creative appeal. A historical actor can imagine herself as a creator, engaged in *poíesis*, a maker of peace and prosperity, of a vision of the future, of the future itself. For Vergil, what must it have been like to be a great talent in the circle of Augustus, himself also a great talent?[32] Both were makers, but they plied different crafts with different tools, one poetry, the other history. A writer of Vergil's artistic power could have seen in his own capacity to create reality through the art of words an analogue to the emperor's power to create reality through the arts of state. This is *maior rerum ordo, maius opus* indeed ("the greater part of the story, the greater task," *Aeneid* 7.44–5). In this light, poet and emperor become kindred natures, each grasping at a vision within his power to realize, each re-imagining and re-creating the world, in a fullness of each one's personal power, sharing in hopes of glory and risks of failure on a world-historical scale.[33]

Claims for Vergil's contemporary relevance such as I have been discussing have not always been advanced.[34] Although each was celebrated for a different reason, the twentieth-century anniversaries of Vergil's birth and death were fully observed. The nineteenth century hosted no such celebrations. Why? And what do the stark differences in the reception of Vergil's works across merely one hundred years tell us about the works themselves and also about our recent history?

As W. R. Johnson explains in his essay included here, the key to Matthew Arnold's critique of Vergil's work in the nineteenth century is Arnold's notion of "adequacy." The artists of the Athenian fifth century B.C.E., in Arnold's view in 1857, were adequate to the high achievements of that age, whereas melancholy Vergil was inadequate to the Roman age of gold.[35]

> I pass to Virgil....Does he present the epoch in which he lived, the mighty Roman world of his time, as the great poets of the great epoch of Greek life represented theirs, in all its fulness, in all its significance?...Over the whole of the great poem of Virgil, over the whole Aeneid, there rests an ineffable melancholy: not a rigid, a moody gloom, like the melancholy of Lucretius; no, a sweet, a touching sadness, but still a sadness; a melancholy which is at once a source of charm in the poem, and a testimony to its incompleteness....This suffering, this graceful-minded, this finely-gifted man is the most beautiful, the most attractive figure in literary history; but he is not the adequate interpeter of the great period of Rome.[36]

Then, in 1944, as Europe was exploding in its second world war in twenty-five years, T. S. Eliot restored Vergil's reputation, finding in his "maturity" and "manners" the distinction of a universal classic. Because of this maturity, Eliot placed Vergil at "the centre of European civilization."

> The Roman Empire and the Latin language were not any empire and any language, but an empire and a language with a unique destiny in relation to ourselves;...Our classic, the classic of all Europe, is Virgil....It is suffi-cient that this standard should have been established once for all; the task does not have to be done again. But the maintenance of the standard is the price of our freedom, the defence of freedom against chaos.[37]

Many readers in the late twentieth century look with less confidence than Arnold did on the epochs of mighty empire, those of the Mediterranean as well as those of the Atlantic. And they look with less confidence than Eliot to cultural icons, of whatever epoch, as a line of defense in times of turmoil.

Johnson calls Eliot's praise, which reads to me as a desperate plea for security in a world falling apart, a "myth" of the *Aeneid*, a projection of unchanging values and purposes onto the poem. Johnson contrasts this myth with the poem's fictions, its vital stories in service of contemporary understanding. Johnson claims that the myth of the *Aeneid* persists, "obscuring the quality of the poetry and limiting, disastrously, the range and depths of the poem."

The "myths," in Johnson's sense, which readers have foisted upon works like the *Aeneid*, as well as the myths that the works themselves foster, are the subjects of today's cultural criticism.[38] Many recent critics find the *Aeneid*'s supreme contribution in what the nineteenth century rejected as its inadequacy; for them, the *Aeneid* becomes a great work because of its sadness. If, on the other hand, the *Aeneid* is a hopeful song, then it is a problematical one for many readers, witnesses to our century's grim annals. At best, in alerting us to these "mythical" uses that works in the Western tradition have served, the current critical enterprise clarifies our focus on the enlightening and enlarging "fictions" of art and the continuing need for their creativity and vitality.[39]

From the perspective of Johnson's crucial distinction between the myths and fictions of art, one reads afresh a report of the 1930 celebration in Italy of the two-thousandth anniversary of Vergil's birth, attended by Prime Minister Benito Mussolini seated directly under a statue of Julius Caesar, at which Vergil's praises were sung.[40] From this perspective, the great danger is not the politicization of art, but the aestheticization of politics, in which cultural myths become state policy. Such use of art by politics, as Martindale states, can "replace public contestation and argument by a kind of totalizing political theatre, or spectacle."[41] Herein lies the danger that pessimistic critics of the *Aeneid* attach to its optimistic interpretations, readings that assert the poet's confidence in empire and the role of art in it. In light of our century's history, it is no surprise that we hear more loudly than many before us did that other, warning voice. So far from irrelevance, the *Aeneid*'s contemporary resonance all but deafens us to its music.

Recently, barely fifty years after two world wars and many "local" ones, fifty years after Eliot's naming of Vergil as the classic of Europe, Vergil is named again as a defining guide, but of a European enterprise now deeply changed. How different is the timbre of the claim by Theodore Ziolkowski in 1993 from Eliot's:

> Generations of writers and thinkers between Freud and Toynbee who witnessed the passing of the seemingly stable pre-1914 world now sought Virgil's guidance in their own descent into the spiritual and historical underworld exposed by the war's ravages. What they learned to value in the course of that ordeal was a *vates* ["prophet"] whose poems, long considered so perfect as to be morally irrelevant, provided a golden bough for the journey through the extremes of human behavior—our impulse to nobility combined with our capacity for evil, the desire for order set against the terror of history. They came to understand that the *magnus saeclorum ordo* ["the great cycle of the ages"] envisioned by the young artist of the *Eclogues* is always qualified by an awareness of the *lacrimae rerum* ["the tears of the world"] keenly felt by the poet of the *Aeneid*. It was this recognition that impelled many writers, despite the skepticism of detractors and in the face of a growing public indifference to the past, to reaffirm the cultural continuity linking classical antiquity and the twentieth century, binding Virgil and the moderns in a conspiracy of understanding. This reaffirmation, attained at the cost of great spiritual engagement by our intellectual predecessors, we neglect today at our peril.[42]

Vergil's modernity, his relevance to contemporary life becomes no "academic" issue but a matter of life and death.

But interpretations of Vergil's optimism or pessimism, in Arnold, Eliot, and manifold recent readers, in the risk of reductiveness and over-simplification, are not worthy of our text. Neither view alone comprehends the *Aeneid*, neither alone captures the totalizing experience of the work, especially its ending. Neither view evokes the complex workings of art on history and history on art.

Italo Calvino's short 1976 essay, "Right and Wrong Political Uses of Literature," helps us understand. Calvino does not worry in this essay that art is too political. Rather he worries that both art and politics may be "inadequate" to deal with the enormous changes in historical consciousness that our world is experiencing, changes even in what had "seemed to be stable anthropological categories — reason and myth, work and existence, male and female — and even the polarity of the most elementary combinations of words — affirmation and negation, above and below, subject and object."[43] Calvino worries when politicians pay too much attention to literature (the problem of aestheticization) and when they pay too little (usually in fear of questioning certitudes). Literature is important to society because, says Calvino, it is one of society's "instruments of self-awareness." In terms of my discussion in this essay, literature for Calvino is *scholé*.

Calvino describes what he calls two wrong and two right political uses of literature, and finally a third right use. All of Calvino's right uses and none of the wrong resonate with Vergil's work in the *Aeneid*: (1) wrong reasons — that literature should voice a truth already held by politics; that literature should be seen as an assortment of eternal human sentiments; (2) right reasons — to give a voice to whatever is without a voice; to create through its "arduous attainment of literary stringency" a model of values that is aesthetic and ethical and thus essential to any plan of action; and finally, to help politics know itself and to distrust itself, as literature too has learned to distrust itself. If these uses can be assumed to comprise Calvino's view of a standard of literature adequate to our age, then Vergil answers the standard.

The *Aeneid* composes the story of Rome and as such it is art in creation or revision of history and cultural identity; it is, among other things, political art. Walcott's *Omeros* is too, as are other of the twentieth-century works in this anthology. So little, however, does Vergil aestheticize politics or create propaganda that he takes the risk of de-aestheticizing art itself. He takes us to the point at the end of the epic where beauty and ugliness are an identity, and emotional pain risks overwhelming aesthetic pleasure and thus utterly destroying the fiction on which art depends.[44] To understand why and how he did that and what it means for us today, we must return to the starting point of this volume, to Vergil's words.

Vergil's Words

The words of Vergil that we read with pleasure and analyze with precision build a story whose themes and questions, across two thousand years, are as much of our time as they have been for Vergil's millennia of readership. In addition, Vergil's words build, along with themes and questions, a way to address them, and the technique is as modern as the content. Indeed, the poem's technique may be the poem's answer to the poem's questions, and to that of our title. Vergil's objective subjectivity may be our best historical hope and most stringent moral school.

Philology: Love of Words, Power of Words

In reading Vergil, we learn not only the pleasure and play of words, but also their power, to entertain and delight and to move and inspire, to challenge, sadden and provoke.

> ...ever since the time of Christ the Mayans had known it [the power of words] too, and with so much clarity they even had a special god of words. That power has never been as great as it is today. Humankind will enter the third millennium under the sway of words.[45]

Our technical world, far from diminishing the need to know words, vastly increases it. The enormous access to raw information, unvetted by prior acts of selection, verification, or organization, foists back on all of us web surfers the tasks of critical judgment that have been performed for us by the mostly invisible processes that create libraries, curricula, publications, and art. It is becoming ever more imperative that not just some but all of us learn how to make choices among all those cyber-words, to organize them into precise, useful, and valid meaning. Thus, as we play[46] at our computers, making order out of seemingly unlimited combinations of information, we are all makers of meaning, all of us at some level, poets.[47]

If words are toys, as I said in the Introduction, played within poems or on computers, then the work of combining and arranging them is a game played according to a set of rules. We have to know how the game of words is played or we lose control of the board. The better grasp we have of the rules, the more interesting the game is. Alternatively, the important project is to learn and understand so well the rules that govern words that we do more than merely obey them, we control them, even perhaps gain control of the game and thus make the rules ourselves. With these inversions of the metaphor of words as toys, we leave the world of grammars and vocabularies as rules set for us, and we enter the world of power and history. The issues I had posed playfully are the issues at stake in today's debates on culture: whose words by whose rules? The play of words turns serious.

The idea that words affect history and that wars, cultural or otherwise, are fought over them may seem far-fetched. The words in the Bible or the U.S. Constitution, however, are examples of words that move people's hearts or change people's minds, and with only these examples I think we can see the capacity of words to affect many hearts and minds in subtle but important ways over time.[48] Studying the role of words in relation to broad historical issues is part of humankind's continuing search to understand the human condition, even its search for truth. The search is important; it is neither easy nor peaceful, now or ever. Ask Socrates.

The search to understand words, like the search for knowledge in the natural sciences, has adopted professionalized methods and systems that require years of training to master. Many areas of specialized skill have vocabularies of their own to describe their work: to mulch or to hydrate (gardening), to birdie or to bogie (golf). In literary studies, there are fields called, for example, semiotics (the study of signs and symbols) and hermeneutics (the science of interpretation). All these arenas have languages that can be impenetrable to those who do not know them but which help people expert in those areas to say precisely what they mean.

Philology is the name of the academic discipline born out of the love of words over two thousand years ago in the Hellenistic world: *phílos* in ancient Greek means a feeling of attachment, and *lógos* means discourse or word. Classical philologists are experts in the Greek and Latin languages and cultures, and they use their expertise as the primary tool for penetrating the meaning of the literatures and cultures distant from them by thousands of years and deep layers of historical difference.[49]

These two ways of understanding literature, by studying how words make meaning (various interpretative methods and theories) and the way words work (the techniques of philology) are being augmented and challenged by some newer interpretive approaches. Feminism, for example, challenges traditional techniques for reading literature, since interpreters find embedded in those techniques sets of assumptions about people and culture,[50] assumptions that are so traditional and age-old that they seem, in Martha Nussbaum's phrase, "neutral, natural and necessary."[51]

The culture wars are being played out not only between the challengers and supporters of the European canon, but within the discipline that studies the Greek and Roman foundations of the canon itself — within philology.

> In both Classics and medieval studies I sensed a sharp divide. At one extreme stand the self-proclaimed defenders of philology, who fear that extremely refined techniques acquired through centuries of learned enterprise run the danger of being spurned and lost. At the other are positioned those who worry that philologists have lost the ability or desire to test their own presuppositions and to ask new questions, and that consequently their areas of study have become stale and irrelevant.[52]

This seemingly arcane debate emphasizes the importance of our question, Why Vergil, because philology as a discipline is the caretaker of the tradition to which Vergil belongs. The way the profession sees its role and does its work affects the way the texts in its care are read and used and by whom.

Although philology rests on over two thousand years of scholarship, its current style is the product of the nineteenth century, the century of European imperialism and Romanticism, Matthew Arnold's century. It is particularly the product of Germany, vortex of the wars in our century that have brought an end to that European hegemony and worldview. The nineteenth-century origins of philology were criticized amid great controversy by Martin Bernal in *Black Athena*. In that book Bernal claims that nineteenth-century prejudices, especially racism and anti-Semitism, have been projected back onto the Greek and Roman past. Such prejudices have precluded investigation of otherwise seemingly important questions of origin and influence from the Semitic East and from Africa.[53]

At this point, academic criticism of the assumptions long embedded in the philological study of ancient Greek and Roman words and texts coincides with historical study of the profession of philology as conditioned by its modern history. It is not surprising to me that the formative literature of Europe, a society that put women and ethnic or racial minorities on its margins, should be suspect among these groups. This is especially the case since the literature itself, "high culture" in general, was an instrument of the disrespect, perhaps by its intrinsic nature or perhaps not, but surely in the cultural uses to which it was put (for example, regarding who was allowed to become educated, in what types of institutions, and for what purposes; recall Phillis Wheatley).[54] On the other hand, I will not forsake my compelling emotional relationship with the European tradition of arts and letters. The challenge, a moral imperative, is to use the tools taught us by that tradition to reread it with fresh eyes and open minds and for new uses.[55]

The *Aeneid* is not about race, class, and gender as we use those terms today. It is about the march of history, from the points of view of both those leading the march and of those marched over. In that light, it is fascinating to contemplate the meaning of Vergil's Arnoldian "inadequacy," an idea that arose at the same time that philology was being reconstituted as a scientific discipline; to contemplate the newly minted myth of Europe, built on a conception of ancient Greece invented at about the same time; and to think about T. S. Eliot, for whom Vergil became the mythical, classic past of Europe's mythical present. If this is the project that contemporary literary theory and historical study seek to disentangle, or "deconstruct," I say, go for it.

The contents of this collection were chosen because they are examples of accumulated philological knowledge and technique that have been honed by centuries of practice. They also illustrate how new techniques are introduced and new questions asked. Several essays apply particular theories of literary criticism and engage contemporary cultural or social issues, to greater or lesser degree. The collection as a whole advocates not theory for itself but rather scholarly openness to new ideas and rigorous scrutiny of them.[56] The profession of classical scholarship can model in its practice a core value of education in the liberal arts. In the process, we all surely will learn. And possibly in the process we may also extend the reach of the texts in our charge to new audiences in educational circumstances vastly changed from those of their composition and transmission, becoming a profession not just for ourselves or in the name of the past, but for the common good and for our time and the future—a modern philology for a modern democracy.[57]

Although it was not always so, twentieth-century critical opinion has given Vergil not only a secure place in the literary culture of Europe but has also named him one of its definers. Joseph Farrell, speaking to a scholarly organization called the Vergilian Society, goes so far as to criticize Vergil scholars for not taking seriously enough the role the *Aeneid* has played in European letters.[58] So European is Vergil that his very name has been appropriated by Europe's history. In giving Vergil the role of religious seer, the Middle Ages, through its logic of meaning making, converted Vergil's Latin name, *Publius Vergilius Maro*, to an etymological version of the role he played for them: a pre-Christian seer and wielder of a wand, a *virga*, as token of his magical powers. From *virga* comes the spelling "Virgil," which has become standard in Europe and common in the United States.

The question of the role or status of Vergil's work within the European literary tradition connects us with contemporary debates on culture. Does the argument, even the existence, of this collection of essays and poetry align those who read and advocate the reading of Vergil's works—dead white male member of the European canon that he is—automatically and simply on one side of those debates? Is the very claim for the power of Vergil's influence on European culture also an indictment?

At first as a student, it was out of respect for his native language that I spelled our poet's name with an *e*. I do so now as a conscious critical act. Vergil's canonical status is assured, but in light of recent controversy about and analysis of the European canon, the very act of assuming status calls status into question. To affirm the seriousness of current questions about culture, I use the spelling, "Vergil." Out of respect for their views, I have kept the spelling of Vergil's name as the authors anthologized here have written it. That little confusion may itself reflect the nature of the times.[59]

At the same time that classicists and others proclaim Vergil's traditional status, twentieth-century readers are discovering that Vergil's is a particularly important, specifically "modern" voice:

> ...No doubt every national literature can identify writers best left to the solicitude of specialists — but Virgil is not one of them. For Virgil has permeated modern culture and society in ways that would be unimaginable in the case of most other icons of Western civilization.[60]

We will see that Vergil's treatment of the cultural traditions he inherited in the precise historical moment in which he lived reveals an approach to inherited norms and historical change flexible enough to embrace even today's fervid debates. It is also an approach designed to speak directly and constructively to those debates, as Ziolkowski claims. We will see that Vergil's "permeation" of modern letters has functioned in highly complex ways that transcend simplistic notions of canonical texts as pack animals for a static version of some high culture.

As we know from his chapter included here, Brooks Otis in *Virgil: A Study in Civilized Poetry*, asked in what exactly Vergil's modernity consisted. He formulated Vergil's poetic challenge in a way that anticipates, but without today's theoretical and political context, the problem of reworking and revaluing a hallowed cultural inheritance. In literary and historical times vastly different from those of his model, Vergil recast the Homeric tradition, which had been a cultural icon for the seven hundred years between Homer's and Vergil's time. This cultural and artistic problem resembles our own late twentieth-century cultural "crisis."[61]

Otis' book recounts the problems Vergil faced as he attempted to recreate, in a complex world of empire, a style of poetry from the long-past heroic age, to reinvigorate a poetic tradition that, for Vergil's contemporaries, had become genuinely obsolete, no longer artistically viable, especially in light of the many flawed imitations of Homeric tradition that had preceded the *Aeneid*. In a chapter on what he calls the "obsolescence of epic," Otis explains the artistic context in which Vergil worked. He reminds us that the mythic content of Homeric epic had lost much of its symbolic force between the eighth and first centuries B.C.E. Much poetry after Homer written in his style was considered so unsatisfactory that the very idea of long, epic works yielded to ancient literary theories and styles of poetry that were explicitly and intentionally different from Homer, for example, shorter works, often based on esoteric scholarship, that were composed in what was called a light style (in contrast to the grandiose style of heroic poetry).

This anti-heroic style had evolved in Greece in the third century B.C.E. and is known as Callimachean, after one of its most important practitioners, Callimachus. It was taken up, with Roman modifications, in the first century B.C.E. by a loose group of poets known generally as the New Poets, or Neoterics, notably Catullus and Gallus, who in turn influenced Horace, Ovid, Pollio, Propertius, Tibullus, Varius, and Vergil, among others. All these writers achieved a high degree of poetic expertise and aesthetic force in their work, which became a standard for poetic quality. In addition, much of this poetry carries emotional content not present in the Homeric tradition, particularly lyric content, as Michael C. J. Putnam's article on Vergil's lyric voice, included here, explains.

In this artistic climate, Vergil attempted to do what had been regarded as impossible, to recreate the eighth-century heroic style on first-century artistic principles. Otis says that Vergil "conceived of his epic as both Homeric and Augustan,"[62] a melding of two artistic styles and with them, most significantly, two sets of historical experience, two ways of understanding the world, separated by a deep divide of history and culture.[63] In helping us understand the enormity of Vergil's task, Otis reminds us that Vergil fully understood his challenge. According to his biographical tradition, Vergil wondered if it were "a weakness of mind to enter upon such a task," which Otis called "madness."[64] If this is not the routine hyperbole of creative self-doubt, Vergil's doubt deserves our attention. Perhaps it is his very madness that is modern, his perception of the need, and invention of the means, for a thorough yet faithful revision of a hallowed but moribund tradition.

Thus it seems we face still another paradox. Did Vergil relate to tradition as both continuum and discontinuity? Can Vergil's work be both canonical and iconoclastic? Such complexity of contradiction occupying a single soul could indeed cause madness — in a small soul. Along with Vergil's artistic, spiritual, and humane amplitude, however, his profundity may be such that our interpretive skills are just beginning to be able to grasp it. Rather than something foisted on literature to destroy it, in Vergil's case critical thinking may just now be catching up with the artist.[65]

Vergil and the Quarrel Between Poetry and Philosophy

Whatever its successes or sins, I believe that contemporary thinking about culture and literature helps us understand Vergil's methods and questions. To turn that thought around, Vergil's questions and methods have again become contemporary, not just inert objects of former vitality and dead beauty, but active issues in our literature and politics.

The very debate within Vergilian studies between pessimistic and optimistic interpretations of the *Aeneid* signals a connection to contemporary quarrels, both academic and public, and between sets of dualities that had seemed for a long time to be settled in their imperviously separate spheres. Examples of such dualities are subjectivity and objectivity, the feminine and the masculine, art and science, poetry and truth. The duality that contrasts poetry and truth comes to us from Plato as the "quarrel between poetry and philosophy." That question may again have become modern.

The great Greek dramatists, Pericles, the sophists, Socrates, all lived in the Athenian empire of the fifth-century B.C.E. Plato was their near or younger contemporary, writing chiefly in the first half of the fourth century, having witnessed the greatness and the failure of that empire and having known many of its famous men of action, art, and thought.

At the time that ancient Athens was participating in its dramatic festivals, in the mid-fifth and fourth centuries B.C.E., Greek thought was engaging with such fundamental ideas as the meaning of truth or justice. The debates developed and clarified into a distinction we speak of between *nómos* and *phýsis*, between human-made conventions about ideas and practices and a concept of law and truth as embedded in the very nature of the universe. The debates were expressed among thinkers who came to be known as either sophists or philosophers. The sophists were associated with a worldview that made "man the measure," whereas philosophers, especially Plato, were associated with the search for transcendent verities.

The sophists were teachers of rhetoric, and the realm of rhetoric reflects the debate between the sophistic and philosophic worldviews. Thus the teachings of the sophists and the practices of rhetoric were both aligned with one way of seeing the world, and philosophy with a worldview alternative to them both. For example, is the world whole, unitary and idealizable (which is a Platonic answer), or is it mutable, most real and true when its parts are in dynamic relationship and even creative opposition (a rhetorical response)? The debate between philosophy and "sophistry" or rhetoric, or between *phýsis* and *nómos* has remained a (perhaps the) primary issue in all of Western thinking and culture. Far from being an esoteric or "academic" issue, that debate addresses truly basic questions about human nature, society, and the cosmos.

Among the formative philosophical issues Plato explored was the crucial question of the reliability of art, its truth. In Book 2 of the *Republic*, Plato advocates the careful selection of materials in the education of the young, criticizing especially the then common practice of using the epics of Homer as "school" texts. Plato's grounds for caution are that poetry, and art in general, like rhetoric and unlike philosophy, say untrue things through imagery and fantastic fables.

Similarly in Book 10, which is the source of the phrase, the "quarrel between poetry and philosophy," Plato develops the view that art, specifically tragedy, presents imitations of imitations, not the truth, and as such is injurious to the soul, certainly the part of the soul that reasons. For tragedy excites our feelings, offering contradictory versions of its stories as well as multiple perceptions among several characters on a single issue or situation. In that capacity for self-contradiction Plato saw the opposite of truth, indeed lies: "didn't we judge it impossible that one could simultaneously hold contradictory opinions about the same thing?"[66] Tragedy, poetry, in common with the arts of rhetoric, reflect a concept of truth different from the standard for truth explored in the *Republic*. There Plato seeks a truth that is ideal, original, fixed, and stable, a standard that has occupied and inspired the West for almost 2,400 years.[67] Thus for Plato neither the teachings of the sophists, the practices of the rhetoricians, or the works of poets could partake of truth. Only philosophy could venture there.

All this could still seem highly abstract, perhaps even irrelevant, except for one thing—Plato was not a democrat. The solution in the *Republic* to the problem of justice was most certainly not democracy. The democracy of ancient Athens was supported by the teaching and training of the sophists and rhetoricians to strengthen the city's practice of debate in public on civic matters; the goal was not absolute truth but workable solutions. The two views of the world characterized broadly as *nómos* versus *phýsis,* rhetoric and poetry versus philosophy,[68] had immediate and practical consequences for public life in fifth-century Athens.

In the distinction between the world as various and conditioned or as fixed and ideal, and in the question of the education necessary for each view, lies the ancient quarrel between poetry and philosophy. That distinction also informs the current wars about culture. Similar questions are being raised today when groups on both the right and left advocate controlling the contents of curricula, libraries, and public speech. Does it matter what movies and music young people see and hear? How do we decide what speech is a public good and what an individual right? On one thing almost everyone seems to agree: words, the arts, have power.[69] The analysis of art's role and its strange and subtle power is the focus of much contemporary thought.

Proponents of a fixed vision of a common Western culture may be taking essentially a "Platonic" view. Those who would open the canon and set it in conversation with previously excluded voices could be said to be taking a rhetorical one. Whatever society the conservative cultural critics posit as the golden age of a settled and secure common culture, it was not fifth- and fourth-century Athens. In ancient Athens, art was deeply political, and the decisions about the fundamental nature of human-kind and the universe were still wide open and being strenuously argued, in the yet-to-be-settled quarrel between rhetoric and philosophy.

For all our vast dissimilarities, Western society at the end of the twentieth century may be returning to Athens' questions of 2,500 years ago. Our contemporary debates on culture may mean that we have an opportunity today to rethink, to reactivate the quarrel between poetry or rhetoric and philosophy, to put it "*back into time*," back into lived, common experience.[70] It is an opportunity for discourse that must be publicly accessible as well as professionally stringent; it is an opportunity for *scholé*.

Vergil can be a superb guide in this discourse, a teacher in this school. Some of Vergil's readers find that questions about the role of art are asked in his works. Does Vergil's art, in telling the story of Rome, tell the truth or tell lies? To investigate what Vergil himself says about the role of art in telling the truth, some scholars turn to his descriptions of art within his own work of art, which are called *ekphrases*. Examples are his accounts of the pictures carved on the temple of Juno in Carthage in Book 1, the Daedalus scene in Book 6, and the description of the shield in Book 8.[71] Further, analyses of the role of art in the *Aeneid* significantly inform interpretations of the work as a whole.

Adam Parry and Brooks Otis sparked Vergilian studies in the direction of these questions, in speaking of dual authorial voices telling a modern story, by introducing the question of Vergil's self-awareness of his method and intentions. Two decades later, Gian Biagio Conte, in *The Rhetoric of Imitation: Genre and Poetic Memory in Virgil and Other Latin Poets*, restates and updates their insight about the effect of Vergil's vision: "From now on, the world will be seen through more than one pair of eyes."[72]

In his chapter, "Virgil's *Aeneid*: Toward an Interpretation," Conte analyzes what he calls cultural "codes," sets of meanings and values particularly as they are embedded in literary genre, such as Lewalski analyzes regarding Milton. By rearranging the content and uses of genre, Conte claims, artists rearrange the "codes" of their cultures. No wonder Plato thought art was dangerous and that today "wars" are being waged over it.

The norm that was available to Vergil if he wished to compose a grand epic was Homeric. As an encoding genre, Homeric epic is described by Conte as follows:

In the ideology of the epic poem, History appears as a flat, static, monistic surface. This is the vision of a reality that has emerged into its final, definitive, order, a reality that we see as having achieved its uppermost layer by overcoming all other possible perspectives.[73]

In Homer there is basically a single point of view. The relationship that the structure of the text maintains with what [it] represents is of a univocal nature, too. The fixed focus transcends the subjective limits of the author's personality and thus lays claim to represent the truth, on whose behalf the text is speaking. The text unfolds on a single plane, which goes unnoticed just because it is invariable, leaving *no room for contrasts born of comparisons*.[74]

Conte's description of Homeric epic resonates with Plato's question several centuries later, cited above: "didn't we judge it impossible that one could simultaneously hold contradictory opinions about the same thing?" Some similarity seems to exist between what we could call a Homeric and a Platonic sense of truth (despite of course Plato's criticism of Homer). For them both, it seems, truth has one voice.

Vergil broke through the univocal nature of Homeric epic. His means was his subjective style, his two voices or many pairs of eyes, which gave him the technique of contrast born of comparison. Many phrases that have been used to describe Vergil's poetry reflect this difference between Homeric and Vergilian epic: Vergil's modernity and subjectivity; the *Aeneid's* "uncommitted" ending and "open dialectic"; Vergil as a "grave and constant opponent of all positivism, empiricism, dogmatism, and systematization"; Vergil's "further voices" that "insinuate ramifying meanings"; his "simultaneous plurality of points of view." [75]

Instead of a single voice, Vergil's poetry contains room for many voices. That multiplicity, it seems to me, is akin to the give and take of the rhetorical habit. Indeed, Vergil's use of comparison and contradiction is similar to Lanham's description of rhetoric: "we can see one version of ourselves only while inhabiting the other"; rhetoric operates with a "vital oscillation" that opposes polarization. [76]

Conte's description of Vergil's epic style and Lanham's description of rhetoric accord with each other; Vergil's style and the methods of rhetoric have characteristics in common. [77] The heart of the *Aeneid's* mysterious transformation of Homer seems to lie in the properties it shares with rhetoric. The *Aeneid's* rhetorical method, its use of contrast and comparison, enabled Vergil to ask questions within epic that had been alien to the genre and to expand the medium and its range of significance. [78]

One notes in addition, of course, that these characteristics resemble Plato's criticism of poetry's lies. Indeed, the doubleness that Plato criticizes in art in general is what readers see as Vergil's intentional achievement. Vergil's reworking of Homer engages Plato's questions about art and about truth.

Through the association of Vergil's multiple voices with rhetoric, one can place Vergil's reworking of the Homeric epic within a Platonic context. Vergil was concerned throughout his works with the nature of self and history and with the role of art, and his engagement with these issues can also be situated within a tradition of philosophical thought. Vergil's works engage poetically the philosophical question of the quarrel between poetry and philosophy. What is more, Vergil's style and his questions involve philosophical issues that are fundamental to the West, and the West is revisiting those issues in the late twentieth century.

In Vergil's century, the Roman Republic was dissolving. It seems that for us now, too, some things are coming apart. Literary critics, historians, and philosophers are studying the knot of accomplishments, scholarship, and prejudice entangled in the story of Vergil's reception from Arnold to Eliot and beyond to us, and with that knot, a revision of the story of European culture. On history's stage, our century's world wars have undone the hegemony of Western Europe. Along with those unravelings, something else, something basic, is also coming apart. Our century's questioning of issues hitherto felt to be so settled as to be "neutral, natural and necessary" is explosive because it touches matters that are ancient and deeply embedded in us. Centuries ago, philosophy won its quarrel with rhetoric and poetry, and won so successfully that its worldview now seems neutral, natural, and necessary. "Laws" of nature, both physical and moral, science as truth, in the laboratory and the humanities, have been the perceived standard for knowledge.

Vergil's works seem to have been replaying in first-century B.C.E. Rome the fifth- and fourth-century Greek debate between rhetoric and philosophy. We are once more replaying it in the twentieth century.

> How, then, to choose between…a Plato who turns away from the Homeric world in order to efface the turning, and a Plato who inscribes this world in turning away from it? How to choose between a discourse that would seem to tell itself in its own voice and one that would always require two — at least two — voices to be told? Perhaps it is not, in the end, a matter of choosing between two discourses, since it is not yet — and perhaps never will be — absolutely certain whether we ourselves are the masters of our choices, whether we ourselves ever speak with just one voice.

> Well beyond Homer and perhaps right up to Plato, perhaps right up to us, the spindle of necessity still turns by the law of persuasion. Perhaps even for us, then, the turning is still at work, though we are now turning from philosophy (back) to persuasion.[79]

Our century's preoccupation with these profound and difficult questions helps explain our sympathy with Vergil's poetry and our ability to engage its weight of meaning, perhaps also to sustain its answers. Whatever specific answer each reader gives to the interpretive questions that surround Vergil's works, a reply to our editorial question, "Why Vergil," is offered. Vergil's works serve modern questions, provoke responses that resonate with modern issues, and respond to modern concerns in astonishingly modern ways.

The shift that Otis analyzed on the level of Vergil's language and Conte deepened regarding Vergil's use of epic is a shift in worldview. Through the "oscillating" dynamic of Vergil's complex art, he brought into relation to each other forms of expression and modes of thought that had been posited as antithetical and mutually exclusive. Vergil's poetry destroys the separation between these two ways of understanding the world. Instead he engages these opposing theories with each other, not choosing one worldview over the other, nor irresolution for its own sake, but an endless dialogue between the two worldviews as itself a new worldview. In that dialogue, we lose the imagination of perfection as sufficient morality in itself, and we lose hope for human perfectability in history and in art. We gain instead a realistic because hard-tested hope and the grave duty to pursue it.

Our frustration with and disagreements about Vergil's ending of the *Aeneid* and about today's discourse on culture reflect our thwarted wish to settle the quarrel between poetry and philosophy. But Vergil will not let us settle it. He insists that the question remain active and open and that we live within that destabilizing, enraging, exhilarating vision of truth. It is essential to both democracy and morality that neither side of the quarrel "win," but that we sustain the debate between them as fully as possible, embedding in our schooling and our polity the form and meaning of Vergil's textbook, in a public *scholé* for all members of society.[80]

Why Vergil?

The question of this book's title, "Why Vergil," is a valid and valuable one, and the people who may ask it deserve an answer. The question assumes many others, about Vergil and generally about other members of the European literary inheritance, notably those from ancient Greece and Rome: why the liberal arts, the humanities, why literature, poetry, why any individual work in the so-called canon, and especially, why now?[81]

Vergil and the Liberal Arts

Questions such as these are the real core curriculum for the liberal arts. Why should we read difficult texts that take so much time and effort? Why should we concern ourselves with what others have said about them? How can books about experiences so different from ours be meaningful to us? Why bother, especially since it is hard to do?

We who read the works of Vergil have choices about our reactions to these questions: to ignore or deplore them, to fear them or condescend to them, to resent or rage at them. Another response is to engage them.

In fact why, in the late 1990s in the United States, in a world where information explodes and the globe contracts, should we readers of Vergil impose on others our fancy for this ancient art? Why bother, so what, especially when it is hard to do? If we want others to bother, however, so must we. The answers to questions we assume our students should come to us already knowing or understanding are in fact what they need us to help them learn. The reasons that we assume should be apparent to voters and lawmakers are instead our civic responsibility to explain.

Classicists are particularly stung by contemporary cultural criticism; if the sins of the West seem to have originated among the ancients, we respond that the achievements of the West started way back there too. So we play tug-of-war with the past, befouling ourselves in muddied debates while opportunists take advantage of the turmoil for personal or political advantage, and others simply leave the field in uncomprehending dismay.

If the paradigms of Western culture are being taken apart and scrutinized bit by bit, how do we reorganize the pieces? If the cultural world as we know it is falling apart, which indeed it may be, how do we put it back together? Indeed, what pieces should we choose, from what newly proposed sources, for what new design?

What a moment of opportunity! Imagine the artist. Despite continuing skirmishes, the cultural civil war seems at the level of theory largely to have been fought. The agenda now is social, political, and artistic. It is one of re-creation, of realignment among fresh choices and with new hope for better answers than those whose flaws over time are cracking the edifice of Western society at its foundation. This is the excitement and terror of creativity in our time.[82] As it was, I believe, in Vergil's.

Some public voices today would persuade us to believe a vision of a neat and good past, one that is unambiguous, unparadoxical, and static. In the name of that vision, they would persuade us against the need to deal with the complexities and challenges of contemporary art, thought, and society. Such voices make easy, so-called common sense (whereas the *Aeneid* or any of the "great books" of these errant champions do not; they make sense only through our hard work). The result of this polemic is a public discourse that is un-sweet, un-lithe, un-quick, un-sharp, un-severe, and thus unfit for dealing with the complexities and challenges of our time, which also need our hard work. An implicit assumption seems to be operating: if only ideas about social issues would go away, so would the issues. But our social problems remain intractable in the face of political rhetoric that perennially asserts how easy they are to solve; hence the political process, and with it the common good, is weakened.

In recent decades, responses to literature, the arts, and educational or cultural issues in general have been politicized, on the right and left, because those arenas are political.[83] Their politics are not, however, just the scruffy partisan struggles between Democrats and Republicans. The politics of culture are about how effective and how democratic a society we are and will be. Many public voices, however, misunderstand the role of our cultural inheritance in a democratic society. Its role is not to restrict a society's self-understanding to a fixed, stable core of ideas and values but to train citizens for democracy's, not to mention life's, instability, as in ancient Athens.[84]

Today's culture critics, for all their shortcomings, are not altogether wrong, however. The attacks on higher education and current intellectual fashion, although self-advancing, are not without foundation. Higher education must shoulder some blame. The professionalization of knowledge, which over at least the last one hundred years has brought U.S. higher education to its position of world leadership,[85] has come at the cost of direct service to the general public of students, employers, and citizens, who, through their taxes and tuition, just happen to be paying most of the bills.

Charles Segal, a leading proponent and practitioner of theoretical approaches to ancient Greek and Latin literature, two of whose essays are included here, nonetheless observed the following problem:

> It is an insufficiently noted irony in the contemporary critical scene that the professional study of literature is becoming more and more arcane just as students' basic reading skills and interests in literature are diminishing. Some of the contemporary modes of criticism not only run the risk of alienating young readers who might otherwise become emotionally and personally engaged in the ideas and life-issues raised by great literary works, but can also confirm them in the suspicion that reading is painful, laborious, impersonal, purely cerebral, and 'academic,' and that here is a hopelessly impassable divide between any concerns of theirs and literary texts.[86]

Our situation contains another paradox: penetrating and profound analysis of the divisions and differences among us seems lately to deepen those divisions still further, not repair them. To this degree, critics of theory are correct to worry that these approaches limit access to literature and learning.

We have two choices: attack the critics or try to answer them. Many scholars and academic leaders are seeking to reorient higher education to fulfill better its public responsibility. That reorientation often means to teach both more and differently, in different settings and for new audiences, inside and outside the classroom.[87]

Classical philologists have long known the beauty and importance of the texts in our professional scholarly charge, Vergil's among them. Collectively, though, we have not succeeded in sharing our treasure and pleasure. We know answers to the Why Vergil question, but that is no longer, if it ever was, enough. Vergil's works speak to world-weighty concerns that extend beyond the academic departments and professional associations whose members study them. Hence this volume and others like it seek to serve more diverse audiences than they might have a generation ago.[88]

Popularization through teaching and public activities was once an honorable part of a scholar's career, but the same professionalization that led U.S. higher education to a position of world leadership had little room for conversation between scholars and the public. Bernard Knox, a dean of classical scholarship and lifelong popularizer of classical culture, asserts that "it is easier for a philologist to explain to a Latin class the subtleties of the word order of [a line of poetry] than…to tell a class of young people in fifty minutes what the *Aeneid* is really about and why it has been, ever since it was written, one of the basic texts on which Western civilization has been built."[89] Happily, the academy is changing, in no small part due to the attacks on it.[90]

The case for public responsibility with respect to higher learning and especially the liberal arts is forcefully made by Bender: "To the extent that we follow a pattern of withdrawal from the public culture, we become vulnerable to those simple questions that often enrage us: *What do you do? What good is it?* We err if we respond that 'it's none of your business' or that 'you wouldn't understand,' which amounts to the same thing. These are fair questions, and if we cannot answer them for our neighbors in everyday language, we should be concerned."[91] This volume is part of a larger response being made by the academy in the last several years to a barrage of criticism, some fair, some not.

"Why Vergil?" is one of those simple questions than can enrage. The question is particular to Vergil's works—the importance of their concerns and the quality of their execution, but it is also historical and theoretical, social and political. The response needs to be thoroughly explored and fully exposed. No part of the response can be assumed and all of it must be open to wide debate at primary levels of significance. The very act of answering such a question can itself be an exercise in *scholé*.

Why Vergil?

This essay's address to the question of the book's title, Why Vergil, has ranged widely, from the public role of literature and literary scholarship and to the ways Vergil's poetry from the origin has communicated among ancient, classical, and contemporary cultural and historical questions. But finally, the question is a personal one. Each reader takes up a book for his or her own reasons. Why do I read Vergil's works?

I read them because I love the way Vergil makes his words work. His poems hold my interest. They move me. They are worth my time. I take pleasure in a job so well done.

Even more, the way Vergil thinks and feels has moral validity for me; it teaches me—*scholé*. I read and think about his work because he has helped me in my work, as administrator in a government funding agency and at a university. The *Aeneid* teaches reflection on the meaning and value of action.[92] It is useful reading for those who, to any degree, hold power, that is, who in any way perform acts or make decisions that affect other people's lives, and that means most of us.

My question to this poet whose words I have taken into my life is not about the violence Aeneas inflicts on Turnus, important as that question is. My question is why Vergil has inflicted such pain on me. Why has he taken me, his devoted reader, and his myriad readers through that arduous tripartite journey of despair, hope, and devastation, only to leave us morally and emotionally raw? He need not have hurt us, this *princeps* ["first citizen"] of words. He had choices, as did Aeneas, and Augustus; as do we all. What could he have valued so much that he judged it worth the cost of his readers' millennial turmoil and uncertainty as we wrestle with his meaning? What, what could have been so vital to you, Publius Vergilius Maro, that you subjected your own sweet soul to the torment, surely greater than ours, of this creation, to find within your tender capacity to weep for others' tears the capacity equally to cause them? Why, Vergil?

Vergil forces us to relive, not just reread or rethink, the epics of Homer, the foundation of his and our culture in the West, in order, by singing the wrath again, to experience, to feel, with the empathy and subjectivity he has taught us, what it is like to *be* Achilles.[93] To create that reliving, he creates the moment when his hero, his reader, and he the poet-creator recommit Achilles' ancient murder but feel in our act a grief new to the world. He creates violence in order to teach us to feel violence as he feels it, but in so doing he knows his most achieved act of creativity is one of violent destruction, destruction of an old cherished heroism and of easy hopes for new heroes. He knows that art can teach the desire for salvation, but, yearn as he does for things to be different than they are, he knows that art cannot save us from ourselves. He also knows that the worst failure of the artist would be to delude us that it could. Art does not save, it teaches, and no learning that is valuable, however beautiful art makes it, is easy. This is *scholé*.

For that moment of painful instruction, *furor* ["fury, rage"] is a necessary presence so that we may abhor it, just as Vergil has demonstrated our capability for it—in Aeneas, in Vergil himself as Aeneas' creator, and by implication in us his readers as well. The hero may be bound for divine election, as Bacon argues in her article herein, but it is our poet who sacrifices himself by nearly destroying art's fiction to save us from art's lies. Poetry, art itself, is tragically limited, and the tragic hero of our poem is our poet.[94] But that limitation is also the truth that art can tell. Vergil has taught us how to live in the imaginative and moral world between dualities such as subjectivity and objectivity, rhetoric and philosophy. And we have Vergil's poetry itself to guide us in this world of serious play, this *scholé*.

It is this meaning and use of learning that Robert F. Kennedy demonstrated on the night that Martin Luther King, Jr. was killed, when, undeniably risking his own life, Kennedy spoke as scheduled to the crowd in a black Indianapolis neighborhood and gave them, not his campaign speech, but the news of the assassination, quoting from a play of Aeschylus.

> For those of you who are black and are tempted to be filled with hatred and distrust at the injustice of such an act, against all white people, I can only say that I feel in my own heart the same kind of feeling. I had a member of my family killed, but he was killed by a white man. But we have to make an effort in the United States, we have to make an effort to understand, to go beyond these rather difficult times.

> My favorite poet was Aeschylus. He wrote: "In our sleep pain which cannot forget falls drop by drop upon the heart until, in our own despair, against our will, comes wisdom through the awful grace of God."[95]

Almost uniquely in the United States, Indianapolis went to bed in grief but not in riot that night. That politician's wisdom and courage are extraordinary, but so are the words he used, and the power he and they exercised to sustain the democratic social fabric in a moment of most dire peril. I doubt whether Athens can boast a more tragic or a finer moment.

The frontispiece by photographer Alan Cohen, "<u>NOW</u> (Dachau) 26-2, 1992," of the ground in Dachau, site of one of Hitler's concentration camps, with the trace remaining of the wall that separated the death camp's barracks from the life outside, makes me feel the way the end of the *Aeneid* and the story of that murderous spring in 1968 make me feel, when Robert Kennedy was also assassinated a few weeks after King. The photograph captures the *res* of history, its material reality, the matter of Vergil's tears. We have been surfeited for half a century now with horrific images of concentration camp dehumanization, stories of children, survivors, thefts, of rationalizations convincing or wan. Cohen's photograph evokes for me, however, a human horror even greater than the carnage — the knowledge that the events it recalls were a choice. In this knowledge lie the tears of our times, of Vergil's, of all history.

The difference between inside and outside those camp buildings, between human life and manmade hell, was a wisp of human will, a turning of mind, as slight as the shadow of the imprint of an old wall, now gone except for its plinth amid smooth small stones. The difference between human horror and human grace is that slender. It is in such moments, as slight as a few traces of something built fifty years ago or a few lines of poetry after ten thousand, accumulated in a single life or all the ages, that each of us decides, individually and collectively, what kind of person to be and what kind of world to make. Vergil's poem is exercise for making those decisions. And as we make them, we are all heroes of our work, artists of our lives.[96]

So too I made a decision in creating this book, cognizant of my responsibility for its contents — in scholarly judgment of course but also in social value, however limited in scope. Among my many selection criteria in assembling this collection, along with philological expertise and interpretive subtlety, was the writers' display of caring, even passion, for their work of playing with words. I was interested in essays that partake, to some measure, of the art of their object of study. I sought work that displays in its objective (or scientific, or philosophic) scholarship also an authorial subjectivity (or self-awareness, or rhetorical self), work that braces therefore the radical Western conflict between those two postures. That conflict is thoroughly and perennially engaged by most artists, especially Vergil, and therefore it is a conflict interpreters of art need to comprehend.

Various of us philologists will excel at one or the other skill; the great ones at both. Collectively we need to cherish their combining, for the sake of the cultural heritage in our charge and for the readers whom we must invite into that heritage, even if they reshape it with new needs and loves, for their own and all our futures' sakes.[97] Insisting on that criterion because with it rests wholeness, integrity, I am comforted by Vergil as our guide to aesthetic and moral honesty and courage.

At the end of the twentieth century, our historical consciousness seems to be on the verge of accepting that the old center has not held.[98] Yet we have survived, and the *Aeneid* becomes a new text, for penetrating and precise analysis of emotions, motivations, and valuation in making a new world out of chaos, such as Augustus and the first-century Romans made. At such a moment, with all the risks that attend on advocacy and action — the risks in art's beautiful lies — are we left only to conclude that in history no right action, no beauty is possible? Is any hope absolutist, is despair the only legitimate politics, despair the only lesson of the histories of Martin Luther King, Jr. and Robert F. Kennedy? Or is there some kind of hope in these stories as well?

Vergil rewrites all of his world's history, and in the last moment, tears a hole in it.[99] It is in that moment that the *Aeneid* may most justify Otis' claim for its modernity. Our modern world lives with a physics of black holes, visual abstraction that captures all art in a single line or patch of color, electronic means of communication that obliterate distance and difference, logically adduced theories of knowing that doubt logic and knowledge. We are tearing holes in our truths at every turn, as Vergil did. Vergil's gift to our times, as to others, is to teach us a way to see a world in turmoil, to hold many visions of it simultaneously, excruciatingly, all in absolute conflict with each other, and all of them true. Thus does Vergil's art avoid committing the crime of Plato's lie.

We learn from the *Aeneid* what it means to be an agent in such times, to make choices among competing valid claims.

> Accepting the tragedies of the 20th century and the toll they took on all the world's people is the beginning of wisdom. Paradise on this earth, we have learned, is beyond our capacity. But we can, if we are modest and hopeful, possibly establish a reasonably livable purgatory and escape the inferno.[100]

Vergil is modern because, after two thousand years, he remains a guide for us as he was for Dante at a similar turning of the world's tide.[101] The pain Vergil has inflicted on us his readers resonates with the pain of living in the twentieth century — *horrida bella*, horrible wars (*Aeneid* 7.41), like the Roman Republic's hundred years of madness from 130–30 B.C.E.[102] Then as now, an old world ended, a new world not yet born, and we are left to live in a time when "sorrow itself becomes a thing to be desired,"[103] because absent that desire we could no longer even imagine a "world where promises are kept and one can weep because another wept."[104] The hope Vergil teaches is a hard one to love, but once embraced it is a lifetime friend.[105]

In uniting Venus and Juno in Aeneas' final act of love-born rage, Vergil killed one kind of hope, both his and ours, hope for a nostalgic or utopian purity of purpose and result by revealing it as not just illusory but as the greatest of dangers. Aeneas' sword slaughters sentimentality and in so doing makes possible a moral realism. Aeneas is a hero for reality, where there is no divorce between reason and passion, and where, to survive, hope must contend with their combination. Before crusades and inquisitions, before reason was king, before white man's imperial burden, and before the improvements of industrial progress, Vergil knew that in history sentimentally innocent confidence in the goodness, justice, or fated necessity of past achievements and destined futures claims as many (more?) victims as the calculated destruction of a proven danger.[106] History offers Vergil no guaranteed path to progress that justifies its victimizations.

The tensions and ambiguities that beset readers of the *Aeneid* may finally be the essence of Vergil's guidance for us. He teaches us to hold them in continuous alternation and to embrace with empathetic love the furor of their intermingling. That embrace is the artist's control over the uncontrollable, and it is terrifying in its power — the *Aeneid* "is a terrifying poem."[107] Aeneas' last act forces us to face that terror; Vergil's life's work gives us the means to do it.

As Aeneas is brutal with his suppliant Turnus, so Vergil is brutal with us his captive readers. But his artistic brutality is justified if ever it spares the world an instant of suffering because those with the power to harm have learned to hesitate, or spares the world magnitudes of suffering because those with the power to prevent suffering accept that burden with conviction and loathing in equal and simultaneous degree.

Vergil created for us something that perhaps had not existed in quite this way before: the imaginative possibility of moral choices located between tragic recognition and idealized hope.[108] Vergil insists that we strengthen ourselves to navigate conflicting uncertainties, opposing moral certitudes, and infuriating complexity, subtlety, and ambiguity as the surest, yet not sure, route in our paradoxical mortality to create right outcomes. Vergil's popularity in this century and this country[109] may mean that more citizens now share Vergil's artful knowledge. The knowledge is a glimmer, a warning: be prepared, like Aeneas, to believe in something, to act for it, in action to compromise your ideal of it and then, and this is the hard part, to survive with grieving memory to act in hope again, with no promise of success and no choice but to go on.[110]

Vergil anticipated the emotive and moral catastrophes of our century through the comparable experience of his own. With the *Aeneid*, he exercises our comprehension of the moral and emotional incomprehensibility of those histories. Our century's brutality is not news on the world's stage; our understanding of it may be.[111] Maybe. A surety abides. When we have the creative, loving strength for it,[112] when love and need are one,[113] Vergil will be our guide as we work to make the world we want in the world the way it is.

Notes

[1]Bernard M. W. Knox, "On Two Fronts," in *Backing Into the Future: The Classical Tradition and Its Renewal* (New York and London: W. W. Norton and Co., 1994) 300–317: "What I am suggesting is that whenever we write on a subject which might conceivably interest the uninitiated, we should take pains not to bar them at the threshold," 308–9.

[2]See Gregory Nagy, "Death of a Schoolboy: The Early Greek Beginning of a Crisis in Philology,"in *On Philology*, ed. Jan Ziolkowski (University Park: Pennsylvania State University Press, 1990) 37–48. Also Richard A. Lanham, "Conversation with a Curmudgeon," a non-Platonic dialogue between the author and his alter-ego, Curmudgeon, a.k.a. "Mudge": "Hey, Lanham, give me a break! You're proposing that the Renaissance *aristocratic* idea of education be reinstated in the great age of egalitarianism?" in *The Electronic Word: Democracy, Technology and the Arts* (Chicago: University of Chicago Press, 1993) 272.

[3]We will see that a special kind of "madness" may be endemic to a discussion of Vergil's work, as it was to Vergil's times and is also to ours; see Brooks Otis' discussion, "The Mystery of the Aeneid," in *Virgil: A Study in Civilized Poetry* (Oxford: Clarendon Press, 1964) 1–4, 1, and herein. On the other hand, Christian Meier (*The Political Art of Greek Tragedy* [Baltimore: Johns Hopkins University Press, 1988] 7) does not think such an adaptation is possible.

[4]See Eli Sagan (*The Honey and the Hemlock: Democracy and Paranoia in Ancient Athens and Modern America* [New York: BasicBooks 1991]) on the ways American democracy has advanced over Athenian, specifically regarding he says the repudiation of slavery, the inclusion of women, and, conjecturally, the increased psychic health of children that results from the end of a culture of infanticide and the denigration of women-mothers, 244–47; on ways in which democracy in the United States compares less favorably to ancient Athens, since Athens was "probably the most participatory democracy that ever existed in a large, complex state" and had a "deep commitment to community," which the modern "enthronement of individualism"

and with it great accumulations of wealth in the presence of great poverty, has rendered problematic, see 97, 289. Sagan does not mention scientific differences, regarding industrial and medical advances for example and, on the other hand, our recent ability literally to destroy the earth.

⁵Lanham, *Electronic Word*, 84, 195.

⁶James J. O'Donnell, *Avatars of the Word: From Papyrus to Cyberspace* (Cambridge, MA: Harvard University Press, 1998) 136, 160, 188. O'Donnell's point of view would be appreciated by at least two national educational organizations, the National Society for Experiential Education and Campus Compact. The importance of linking traditional and co-curricular education in ways meaningful for students' learning is becoming widely recognized in higher education.

⁷For a recent discussion of the current state of the wars see "An End to the Culture Wars? Commentary by Todd Gitlin, Annette Kolodny, Lawrence W. Levine, Gertrude Himmelfarb, Nell Irvin Painter, Evelyn Hu-Dehart, and Ray Suarez," *The Chronicle of Higher Education*, March 6, 1998, B4–B8 ; see also Wendy Steiner, *The Scandal of Pleasure: Art in an Age of Fundamentalism* (Chicago: University of Chicago Press, 1995) 7.

⁸Barnaby C. Keeney, Chairman (*Report of the Commission on the Humanities* [1964]), lists five needs for the arts and the humanities in the United States: (1) the need of the country for a vision and "whatever understanding can be attained by fallible humanity of such enduring values as justice, freedom, virtue, beauty, and truth"; (2) the need in a democracy for wisdom, a path to which is knowing "the best that has been thought and said in former times"; (3) "to understand other cultures than our own," especially through the arts, and as evidence that the United States "is not a nation of materialists"; (4) world leadership, since "[o]nly the elevation of its goals and the excellence of its conduct entitle one nation to ask others to follow its lead....If we appear to discourage creativity..., if we ignore the humanities—then both our goals and our efforts to attain them will be measured with suspicion"; and (5) the "novel and serious challenge to Americans...posed by the remarkable increase in their leisure time," 4–5. The Commission on the Humanities issued the *Report*, which became the founding document of the National Endowment for the Arts and the National Endowment for the Humanities. These needs seem not only less persuasive now than they did in 1964 but even open to question. Are enduring values so clear as this? Is it the role of the arts and humanities to dress up a world power? How will leisure be filled indeed? What is the role of dissent, criticism, academic and artistic freedom in this list? Of discovery, creativity, play?

⁹Gregory O'Brien, "The Ghost at the Feast, " *New York Review of Books*, February 6, 1997, 12–13. Lanham (*Electronic Word*) argues that interactivity with electronic text "deflates solemnity," 38.

¹⁰O'Donnell (*Avatars*) contends that universities should be places where one takes risks: "School often presents itself to the imagination as [a] kind of sanitized theme park, but as school becomes university, risks need to be taken. Failure to see this is one of the root causes of our so-called culture wars, where both left and right argue over how best to manage the Disney World University and which exhibits to put on display," 144.

¹¹Consider the recordings of Stephen G. Daitz, *The Pronunciation and Reading of Classical Literature: A Practical Guide* (Guilford, CT: Jeffrey Norton Publishers, Inc., 1984); and Robert P. Sonkowsky, *Vergil: Selections* (Guilford, CT: Jeffrey Norton Publishers, Inc., 1984).

¹²The word "deconstruction" evokes, of course, the philosophy of Jacques Derrida and also the uses and abuses of his philosophy in public discourse. I use the term here to invoke those philosophic and public issues broadly but especially to signal more generally the mental habit of analyzing previously unexamined, even unseen, assumptions.

¹³Steiner, *Scandal of Pleasure*, 8. Thomas Bender, "Locality and Worldliness," *The Transformation of Humanitistic Studies in the Twenty-First Century: Opportunities and Perils*, American Council of Learned Societies, Occasional Paper, no. 40, 1997, 4; see also Steiner, 59.

¹⁴Martha C. Nussbaum, *Poetic Justice: The Literary Imagination and Public Life* (Boston: Beacon Press, 1995) 52, 130–131, n. 45. Also O'Donnell (*Avatars*) regarding not literature but history: "...the usefulness of history lies in the sharpening of sight, the heightened awareness of difference, the respect for nuance, and the sense of the possibilities of change," 7.

¹⁵Sagan, *Honey and Hemlock*, 16 (quoting Richard Hofstader); 20, 22. See also Steiner, 212, 19–20, 22, 24.

[16]Lanham, *Electronic Word*; O'Donnell, *Avatars*.

[17]Lanham, *Electronic Word*: "I came to think that the most interesting thing about digital 'text' was how directly it fulfilled the expressive agenda of the strand of artistic thinking and practice we nowadays call postmodern. So here I was committed to argue that electronic text expressed both the postmodern spirit and the classical rhetorical one better than print!" 30; also 189, 161, 203.

[18]O'Donnell, *Avatars*, 123.

[19]Although Lanham (*Electronic Word*) and O'Donnell (*Avatars*) advocate the liberal arts, they see the possibility of, indeed the need for, change in the traditional social and pedagogical patterns of today's colleges and universities. These patterns reflect what Lanham broadly names the "philosophic" mode of Western discourse, in after all, *universities*, where the entire construction is built on the notion that knowledge is unitary and universal. The alternative, rhetorical mode, they claim, relies on the same foundations but in open discourse capable of destabilizing even its own assumptions. These are claims that humanists and university administrators should ponder deeply. Although these issues are addressed throughout both works, see especially in *Electronic Word*, "The 'Q' Question" (for Quintilian) and in *Avatars*, "What Becomes of Universities?"

[20]Steiner (*Scandal of Pleasure*) cites criticism of the academy, not for engaging in politically involved research, but for substituting academic rhetoric on politically charged topics for real political engagement, 153. See also Thomas Bender and Carl E. Schorske (*American Academic Culture in Transformation* [Princeton, NJ: Princeton University Press, 1997]) on the academy's turning away from politics in the 1970s, 39.

[21]Steiner, 75, 80.

[22]Lanham, *Electronic Word*: "What literary experience, if we take that in the widest sense (starting from childhood with nursery rhymes and fairy stories), supplies for us may be the complicated set of neural pathways that sustain higher-level thought. It may not be moral choice, as such, but the neural framework this choice requires, that humanistic education constructs," 261. Nussbaum, *Poetic Justice*: "The reader's emotions and imagination are highly active as a result [of engagement with literature], and it is the nature of this activity, and its relevance for public thinking, that interests me," 5.

[23]Sagan, *Honey and Hemlock*, 155; also 281–82, on Plato and Aristotle, who although not democrats, recognized the importance of an institution for education for a liberal society; further, on the purpose of democratic education, especially in relation to justice: "The *end* of education in a free society is the creation of an environment in which the democratic spirit may thrive. Any morally valid changes in curriculum must serve that end," 330–32. It would be an interesting public conversation to consider how this statement of purpose relates to the list above (n. 8) as reasons for the value of the arts and humanities in civic life.

[24]Alexander Nehamas, Princeton University, quoted in the *New York Times* of Saturday, January 10, 1998, page B9, emphasis added. For what I perceive as the opposite of uncertainty in Nehamas' sense, see Sagan, *Honey and Hemlock*: "The greatest threat [to democratic society] is ideology; the idea that *The Truth* is knowable and ownable and must be imposed on others, by force if necessary, in the interest of a perverted conception of righteousness and justice," 138; also, on the importance to a democracy of the idea of a loyal opposition, 23. For the paradoxical connection between subjectivity and objectivity in Vergil's works, see Gian Biagio Conte, *The Rhetoric of Imitation: Genre and Poetic Memory in Virgil and Other Latin Poets* (Ithaca, NY: Cornell University Press, 1986) 169ff., esp. 171.

[25]See Francis Oakley, *Community of Learning: The American College and the Liberal Arts Education* (Oxford: Oxford University Press, 1992), for the early history of liberal arts education.

[26]"Tragedy's importance in sustaining the quality of public life is indicated by the fact that it was a liturgy ["expected private donation"] equal to the maintenance of a trireme ["warship"], as if to suggest that the cultural survival of the Athenians depended on the courage of its people in confronting the risks of tragedy in the same way as its physical survival depended on its sailors' courageously meeting the risks of battle," J. Peter Euben, ed., *Greek Tragedy and Political Theory* (Berkeley: University of California Press, 1986) 22–23. On the financing of the dramatic festivals see, e.g., J. Michael Walton, *Greek Theatre Practice: Contributions in Drama and Theatre Studies*, no. 3 (Westport, CT: Greenwood Press, 1980) esp. 64–77; and J. R. Green, *Theatre in Ancient Greek Society* (New York: Routledge, 1994) 6–15.

[27]Meier, *Political Art*, 1, 4, 5; Paul Cartledge, "'Deep Plays': Theatre as Process in Greek Civic Life," *The Cambridge Companion to Greek Tragedy*, ed. P. E. Easterling (Cambridge: Cambridge University Press, 1997) 3–35, 19.

[28]See in addition Simon Goldhill, "The Audience of Athenian Tragedy," in *Cambridge Companion to Greek Tragedy*, 54–68; Justina Gregory, *Euripides and the Instruction of the Athenians* (Ann Arbor, MI: University of Michigan Press, 1991) esp. "Introduction"; David Konstan, *Greek Comedy and Ideology* (Oxford: Oxford University Press, 1995); Jean-Pierre Vernant and Pierre Vidal-Naquet, *Myth and Tragedy in Ancient Greece* (New York: Zone Books, 1988); Joseph P. Wilson, *The Hero and the City: An Interpretation of Sophocles' Oedipus at Colonus* (Ann Arbor, MI: University of Michigan Press, 1997) esp. 187–199; Bernard M. W. Knox, "Poet and Polis," *Backing Into the Future*, 191–219. I have some evidence that such an event, so different from the modern circumstances of theater, is nonetheless feasible today, at least partially. In Chicago in early November 1998 we enjoyed our ninth annual Chicago Humanities Festival. During a three-day weekend, about 15,000 people attend many of the approximately one hundred events in the arts and humanities focused on an annual broad theme, this year "He/She." The timing of the Festival near to election day is accidental but not insignificant. The Festival accustoms people in the Chicago area to spend time together, thinking and enjoying themselves, being challenged together, in a nascent form of *scholé*.

[29]C. S. Lewis, *Preface to Paradise Lost* (Oxford: Oxford University Press, 1942) 34–35: "Our life has bends as well as extension: moments at which we realize that we have just turned some great corner, and that everything, for better or worse, will always henceforth be different. In a sense,…the whole *Aeneid* is the story of just such a transition in the world-order, the shift of civilization from the East to the West, the transformation of the little *reliquias*, of the old, into the germ of the new." The shift that the *Aeneid* records may be even greater than the one Lewis notices.

[30]See Thomas Habinek and Alessandro Schiesaro, eds., *The Roman Cultural Revolution* (Cambridge: Cambridge University Press, 1997); also Sagan, *Honey and Hemlock*, on the fall of the Republic as purveying "the essence of tragedy," 350. For Putnam ("The Virgilian Achievement," in *Virgil's Aeneid. Interpretation and Influence* [Chapel Hill, NC: University of North Carolina Press, 1995]), "the killing of Turnus announces the end of the Roman Republic, of two orders balancing each other, of two consuls, of a popular tribune with veto power over aristocratic measures," 24.

[31]Pcter White, *Promised Verse: Poets in the Society of Augustan Rome* (Cambridge, MA: Harvard University Press, 1993) 207.

[32]Richard Jenkyns, "Pathos, Tragedy and Hope in the *Aeneid*," *JRS* 60–77 (1985): "…[I]t is a superficial judgement to suppose that he was unimpressed by Augustus because he recognized that parts of the programme were bogus or unimportant. It is both subtler and more plausible to see Virgil as a man with the sympathetic understanding to discover where Augustus' genius lay (for he was a genius, as hostile historians have acknowledged from Tacitus to Syme)," 62.

[33]Eleanor Leach's comments on the ending of the *Georgics* ("*Sedes Apibus*: From the *Georgics* to the *Aeneid*," *Vergilius* 23 [1977] 2–16) are helpful about the intermingling tasks of artist and emperor: "But even though [Vergil] can prescribe in his poem the steps to make the agricultural world prosper and can conceive an Italy reborn in its ancient Saturnian tradition, he still cannot, by his independent labor of words bring the new order to fulfillment, cannot, as it were, restore a Eurydice to the land of the living. Meanwhile Octavian rushes headlong after immortality. Poet and leader stand far apart in these lines [*Georgics* 4.559–64]; yet the *Georgics* has urged they *merge their separate designs into one* [emphasis added]. To Octavian's practical quest belongs the task of giving substance to the poet's golden age of imagination," 8.

Sigmund Freud ("The Moses of Michelangelo," in *Writings on Art and Literature*, [Stanford, CA: Stanford University Press, 1997] 122–50) sees a similar relationship between another pair of geniuses, Michelangelo and Pope Julius II: "…it can still be asked what motives prompted the sculptor to select the figure of Moses…as an adornment for the tomb of Julius II. In the opinion of many these motives are to be found in the character of the Pope and in Michelangelo's relations with him. Julius II was akin to Michelangelo in this, that he attempted to realize great and mighty ends, and especially designs on a grand scale. He was a man of action and he had a definite plan, which was to unite Italy under the Papal supremacy. He desired to bring about single-handed what was not to happen for several centuries, and then through the conjunction of many alien forces; and he worked alone, with impatience, in the short span of sovereignty allowed him, and used violent means. He could appreciate Michelangelo as a man of his own kind....The artist felt the same violent force of will in himself, and, as the more introspective thinker, may have had a premonition of the failure to which they were both doomed. And so he carved his Moses on the Pope's tomb, not without a reproach against the dead pontiff, as a warning to himself, thus, in self-criticism, rising superior to his own nature," 146.

[34]For a review of the reception of Vergil's works esp. in England from the late seventeenth to the late nineteenth century, see R. D. Williams, "Changing Attitudes to Virgil. A study in the history of taste from Dryden to Tennyson," in *Virgil*, ed. D. R. Dudley (London: Routledge & Kegan Paul, 1969) 119–38.

[35]See Conte's use (*Rhetoric of Imitation*) of a similar word, "competence," regarding literary "codes," 150.

[36]Matthew Arnold, "On the Modern Element in Literature," in *On the Classical Tradition*, ed. R. H. Super (Ann Arbor, MI: University of Michigan Press, 1960) 18–37, 34–36.

[37]T. S. Eliot, "What Is a Classic," in *On Poetry and Poets* (New York: Farrar, Straus & Giroux, Noonday Press) 70–71, 73, 73–74.

[38]See Oakley (*Community of Learning*) more broadly on Arnold and Eliot, 46–47; also on the same pattern in general education, chap. 4, and esp. 131–32.

[39]See also Lanham (*Electronic Word*), who argues that the *lógos* of the Greek rhetoricians, which he sees returning now to the sciences and to cyberspace, "*creates* new meanings, as does poetry, rather than simply communicating preexisting knowledge in a transparent capsule," 254. Hermann Broch (The *Death of Virgil*, Jean Starr Untermeyer, trans. [New York: Pantheon Books, 1945; Universal Library edition, 1965]) 139 and herein, also believes that art creates new meaning, new substance in the universe: "...and he knew also that the duty of all art lay in this sort of truth,...so that the soul, realizing the great equilibrium between the ego and the universe, might recover herself in the universe, perceiving in the self-recognition that the deepening of the ego was an increase of substance in the universe, in the world...."

[40]George McCracken, "The Celebration of the *Bimillennium Vergilianum* by the Royal Academy of Italy, October 15, 1930," *Vergilius* 3 (May 1939) 21–23.

[41]Charles Martindale, "Descent into Hell, *PVS* 21 (1993) 111–50, 117.

[42]Theodore Ziolkowski, *Virgil and the Moderns* (Princeton, NJ: Princeton University Press, 1993) 238–9. Also Bender (in Bender and Schorske, *American Academic Culture*) on a general turn of American scholars to a darker view of the world: "Even as Americans embraced a bright and shiny world of consumer products, American intellectuals became more sensitive to the problem of evil than at any time since the seventeenth century," 26.

[43]Italo Calvino, "Right and Wrong Uses of Political Literature," in *The Uses of Literature*, trans. Patrick Creagh (San Diego: Harcourt Brace, Harvest Book, 1986) 91.

[44]See Steiner, *Scandal of Pleasure*: "Artists glory in this knife-edge between the artificial and the existential, finding ever new ways to narrow the divide," 77. Did Vergil narrow the divide between the artificial and the existential at the end of *Aeneid* almost too much? Is the ending almost too real? Is this the source of its power and why we are obsessed with it?

[45]Gabriel García Márquez, excerpt from a speech to the First International Congress of the Spanish Language, *New York Times*, Sunday, August 3, 1997, page E14.

[46]O'Donnell, *Avatars*: "...the advance of science will be overtaken by the advance of play," 142

[47]"If we think we [academics] are in the information business, we make the...mistake of confusing a tool with a goal. The real strength of the professor has always been as an organizer, an evaluator, and a processor," O'Donnell, *ibid.*, 175, 43; see also Lanham, *Electronic Word*: "In a technological age all men should have an art of creativity, of judgment, of disposition, and of organization,"168, quoting Richard McKeon.

[48]"First and foremost: the history and the essence of politics are a matter of words." John Lukacs, *The End of the Twentieth Century and the End of the Modern Age* (New York: Tichnor & Fields, New York, 1993) 119. In a similar vein, see O'Donnell, *Avatars*: "In the long run, the most important achievements of ancient imperialism had nothing to do with politics and

everything to do with language." See also Thomas N. Habinek (*The Politics of Latin Literature: Writing, Identity, and Empire in Ancient Rome* [Princeton, NJ: Princeton University Press, 1998]) quoting Duncan Kennedy: "[w]ords are the principal medium through which meaning acts to develop, enact, and sustain relationships of power," 6.

[49]See Knox, "On Two Fronts," for a discussion of philology and the American Philological Assocation.

[50]See, e.g., Jonathan Culler, "Anti-Foundational Philology," in *On Philology*, ed. Jan Ziolkowski (University Park: Pennsylvania State University Press, 1990) 49–52: "My point, then, would be simply that the notion of philology as a basis which is somehow prior to literary and cultural interpretation is an idea that one should seriously question, and an idea, moreover, that philology itself, in principle as well as in practice, provides us with the tools for questioning. For if there is one thing that runs through the various accounts of philology and the various accounts in which philology figures it is the linking of philology with close attention to language," 52.

[51]*Poetic Justice*, 32; Oakley, *Community of Learning*, 9 and 147.

[52]Jan Ziolkowski, ed., "Introduction," in *On Philology*, 3. For other discussions of the role of literary theory in classical studies, see Joseph Farrell, "Which *Aeneid* in Whose Nineties?" *Vergilius* 36 (1990) 74–81; and also Daniel L. Seldon, "Classics and Contemporary Criticism," *Arion*, 3rd ser., 1.1 (Winter 1990) 155–178. See also Phyllis Culham and Lowell Edmunds, eds., *Classics: A Discipline and Profession in Crisis?* (Lanham, MD: University Press of America, Inc., 1989). For a general but quite useful summary of various strands of postmodern theory, see Harland G. Bloland, "Postmodernism and Higher Education," *Journal of Higher Education*, 66.5 (September/October 1995) 521–59.

[53]Martin Bernal, *Black Athena: The Afroasiatic Roots of Classical Civilzation, vol. 1, The Fabrication of Ancient Greece 1785–1985* (New Brunswick, NJ: Rutgers University Press, 1987). See also *The Challenge of Black Athena, Arethusa*, special issue (Fall 1989); and the rebuttal volume, *Black Athena Revisited*, eds. Mary R. Lefkowitz and Guy MacLean Rogers (Chapel Hill, NC: University of North Carolina Press, 1996). Suzanne L. Marchand (*Down from Olympus: Archaeology and Philhellenism in Germany, 1750–1970* [Princeton, NJ: Princeton University Press, 1996]) has studied the history of nineteenth-century archaeology especially in Germany and concludes as follows: "The Greek gods, it seems, have come down from Olympus, and philhellenic neohumanism has lost its privileged place in German culture. And though the nostalgic may yet mourn the losses entailed by this process of double demystification, it is certain that the way has been cleared for the creation of more inclusive—if ever imperfect—forms of individual cultivation and varied—if less 'pure'—ideals of beauty," 375. Also Culler ("anti-Foundational Philology"): "...how far [was] the construction of philology as a scientific discipline in the late eighteenth and early nineteenth century...complicitous with or...based on the invention of an Aryan Greece that would serve as origin for modern cultures in northern Europe[?] The invention of that Greece involves the rejection or elimination of the idea of Greece's dependence on Semitic cultures and on Egypt in particular. This is another case in which the supposedly foundational enterprise of philology is in fact dependent on cultural and aesthetic constructions. Clearly it seemed much more satisfying to European cultures to have Greek rather than Egyptian origins," 51. Habinek (*The Politics of Latin Literature*) also discusses the issue in his "Introduction" and chapter, "Latin Literature and the Problem of Rome": "...[T]he invention of modern notions of classical history and culture by late eighteenth- and early nineteenth-century German Romanticism was a process of exclusion and suppression as much as it was one of discovery and articulation," 15. See also O'Donnell, *Avatars*, chapter, "The Ancients and the Moderns: The Classics and Western Civilization," 99–123.

[54]Nagy, "Death of a Schoolboy.": "but the key to the actual evolution of canons must be sought in the social context of performance itself," 42; similarly, Habinek, *Politics of Latin Literature*: "For it is not the tradition itself that defines our politics or our morality, but the use we make of it," 5.

[55]Charles Segal, "Presidential Address 1994. Classics, Ecumenicism, and Greek Tragedy," *TAPA* 125 (1995) 1–26: "We have to remain open to the variety, difficulty, complexity, and even contradictoriness of the ancient texts. For all their beauty, they are not 'the most noble food in the most noble form: golden apples in silver bowls,' as the enthusiastic young Hegel wrote in his essay 'On Classical Studies,' but rather Proteus-like giants that we have to hold

on to and make yield the truths that they have for us in our time and place as they go through their shifting, sometimes terrifying forms," 7. Also, Culler, "Anti-Foundational Philology," 52, "The play of the term *philology*, it seems to me, is valuable insofar as it captures the crucial tension between the reconstructive project and that critique of construction which philology ought to have as its goal." With these thoughts, we are back to the idea of play, albeit very serious play indeed.

[56] See Daniel L. Selden, "Textual Criticism," *Helios*, 14.1 (1987) 33–50: "Ultimately, then, scholarship on Latin does not divide between a philological and a hermeneutic criticism. A more legitimate basis for distinction would be the relative rigor with which a scholar masters the methodological and epistemological problems specific to his or her work," 37.

[57]Some philologist critics of philology offer with their diagnoses of malady also remedy and hope. See e.g., Gregory Nagy, "Death of a Schoolboy," in *On Philology*: "The symptom of a narrowed education is the terminal prestige of arrested development, where schoolboys grow up to be the old boys of a confraternity that they call philology, *their* philology. The hope lies in the capacity of true philology, as also of schools, to reverse such narrowing, to recover a more integrated, integral, *paideiâ*. The humanism of philology depends, and will always depend, on its inclusiveness," 47; Nancy Sorkin Rabinowitz, "Introduction," in *Feminist Theory and the Classics*, eds. Nancy Sorkin Rabinowtiz and Amy Richlin (New York: Routledge, 1993): "One way to counteract the charge of elitism is to take the classics away from the elite and contribute to the cultural literacy of the larger population...," 7; Jan Ziolkowski, "Introduction," in *On Philology*: "But is there a middle ground between the deconstructive aims of some theory and the reconstructive project of all philology?" 11; Margaret Alexiou, "Greek Philology: Diversity and Difference," in *On Philology*: 60: "...Philology must broaden its horizons by going back to its most ancient sense, 'love of argument and reasoning,' 'love of learning and literature,' to include oral as well as written texts, to re-unite the practitioners and theorists of literature, to re-impose the integrity of poetry and music (never lost in Greece, or in many other non-Western cultures), and to admit the beauty and diversity of human cultural interaction," 60.

[58]Farrell, "Which *Aeneid*?": "No member of the Vergilian Society, I imagine, will challenge the idea that the *Aeneid* belongs to that small group of texts that by virtue of their artistic excellence and historical importance, define the canon of European literature. And yet, as compared with those who study other canonical texts, we Vergilians seldom behave as if the *Aeneid* really did belong. Indeed, there is a strong tendency for Vergilians to approach the *Aeneid* in a rather provincial way," 76; see also Theodore Ziolkowski, *Virgil and the Moderns*: "Virgil is too important to be left to the classicists," 1.

[59]K. W. Gransden, ed., *Virgil in English* (London: Penguin Books, 1996) discusses the spelling of Publius Vergilius Maro's name, concluding that the spelling "Vergil" has no real authority in English, xxxv. Charles Martindale, ed., *The Cambridge Companion to Virgil* (Cambridge: Cambridge University Press, 1997) makes a deliberate decision to keep the *i* spelling because his volume "devotes an unusual degree of emphasis to Virgil's reception within European culture." Martindale chooses this spelling not to enshrine that tradition but instead to avoid the inclination among some readers to assume that we can uncover the "reified text-in-itself," 7. I share with Martindale that disinclination. On the other hand, the *Ve* Vergil I use here invites us to be self-conscious about the *Vi* Vergil, and to make fresh decisions about both.

[60]Ziokowski, *Virgil and the Moderns*, ix.

[61]See Habinek, "Culture Wars: First Century B.C.E.," in *The Politics of Latin Literature*, 88–102.

[62]Otis, "Mystery of the *Aeneid*," in *Virgil: A Study in Civilized Poetry*, 39.

[63]What for us may seem a single ancient Greco-Roman world was for the ancient Mediterraneans a mixture of cultural traditions across centuries and of highly diverse cultural norms, often in cultural conflict. See e.g., Jerome J. Pollitt, "The Impact of Greek Art on Rome," *TAPA* 108 (1978) 155–74. Pollitt describes two Roman attitudes to the Greek art that was flooding into Rome by the second century B.C.E., the Catonian and the Connoisseur's: the "essence of the 'Catonian attitude' was that the arrival of Greek art in Rome marked the beginning of a slow decay in the moral standards of Roman society," 158. For a full discussion of Roman cultural self-understanding see Erich S. Gruen, *Culture and National Identity in Republican Rome* (Ithaca, NY: Cornell University Press, 1992). Gruen's essay in this anthology includes some of the argument he makes in that volume.

[64]Otis cites Macrobius (*Sat.* 1.24.11, ed. Jacob Willis [Leipzig: Teubner, 1970]): "sed tanta inchoata res est, ut paene vitio mentis tantum opus ingressus mihi videar,..." 129–130. The Sibyl characterizes Aeneas' wish to enter the Underworld in similar terms: "quod si tantus amor menti, si tanta cupido / bis Stygios innare lacus, bis nigra videre / Tartara, et insano iuvat indulgere labori, / ..." (6.133–35).

[65]Readers see a number of analogies to Vergil in modern thinkers. Regarding dialectic, see e.g., David Konstan, "Venus's Enigmatic Smile," *Vergilius* 32 (1986) 18–25, esp. 25; see also David Quint, *Epic and Empire: Politics and Generic Form from Virgil to Milton* (Princeton, NJ: Princeton University Press, 1993) on Vergil's depiction of "imperial victory as the victory of the *principle of history*," 30. Quint also makes a connection, 50–52 and 65–83, between the design of the two halves of the *Aeneid* and Freud's theory in *Beyond the Pleasure Principle* of the "repetition compulsion," with implications for *Aeneid* 12.

[66]Plato, *The Republic*, trans. Richard W. Sterling and William C. Scott (New York: W. W. Norton & Co., 1985) X.602.e, 293.

[67]Although Plato's questions are central to contemporary culture debates, this is not the place to explore these issues thoroughly. See Thomas Gould, *The Ancient Quarrel Between Poetry and Philosophy* (Princeton, NJ: Princeton University Press, 1990) and Martha C. Nussbaum, *The Fragility of Goodness. Luck and Ethics in Greek Tragedy and Philosophy* (Cambridge: Cambridge University Press, 1986) esp. 122–135 and 223–227. I am making general connections here that in development would distinguish the interplay among poetry, tragedy, and rhetoric in their common distinction from what Lanham is calling philosophy, which in turn is a strand in Plato and the Western philosophical tradition, but not of course the totality. See also J. Peter Euben, ed., "Introduction," *Greek Tragedy and Political Theory* (Berkeley, CA: University of California Press, 1986) 1 (n. 8)–42.

[68]Lanham, *Electronic Word*, uses the terms "philosophy" and "rhetoric" broadly; see for example pp.xi–xii, 15, 25, 61, 63, 84–85, 146–47, 162, 202–3. In reactivating the quarrel between poetry and philosophy and reclaiming value for "poetry" or "tragedy" as it was opposed in the *Republic*, we should not sentimentalize the role of art, rhetoric, and the sophists in ancient Athens, or today. Jacqueline de Romilly (*The Great Sophists in Periclean Athens*, trans. Janet Lloyd [Oxford: Clarendon Press, 1998], e.g., 94, 114) reminds us of the dangers, along with the possibility of reconstruction, that sophistic thinking unleashed in effecting a *tabula rasa*, a clean slate of the assumptions about justice, morality, religion, and their role in the *pólis*. See also Romilly 113–14 briefly on *nómos* and *phýsis*.

[69]Here I differ with Steiner (*Scandal of Pleasure*): "But whatever effect art has, it never has literal control. However much we may give ourselves up to art or be moved by it, we can always withdraw ourselves from it, too, because it is only a virtual experience of power," 76–77. Steiner is arguing against those who would censor a work of art because it might *cause* someone to imitate it, for example, in movies of violence. I believe Steiner underestimates the power of art by concentrating on its influence on the individual, not on a society over time. See Gould on pathos and violence, especially the distinction between "violence told or shown in such a way as to elicit sympathy only for the victims, true *pathé*, and violence that is depicted with sympathy only for the perpetrators, the staple of popular films and television," which may "justify brutality," xxvi–xxvii.

[70]Lanham, *Electronic Word*, 264; also 1976, 33, quoting C. S. Lewis: "Rhetoric is the greatest barrier between us and our ancestors....Nearly all our older poetry was written and read by men to whom the distinction between poetry and rhetoric, in its modern form, would have been meaningless....This change of taste makes an invisible wall between us and them." See Stephen G. Salkever, "Tragedy and the Education of the Dêmos: Aristotle's Response to Plato," in *Greek Tragedy and Political Theory*, J. Peter Euben, ed., 274–303.

[71]See for example Michael C. J. Putnam, "Daedalus, Virgil, and the End of Art," *AJP* 108 (1987) 173–98 and herein; Charles Segal, "Art and the Hero: Participation, Detachment, and Narrative Point of View in *Aeneid* 1," *Arethusa* 14.1 (1981) 67–83 and herein; and Robert Gurval, "Chapter Five. 'No, Virgil, No': the Battle of Actium on the Shield of Aeneas," in *Actium and Augustus: The Politics and Emotions of the Civil War* (Ann Arbor, MI: The University of Michigan Press, 1995) 209–247, selection herein. See as well Michael C. J. Putnam, *Virgil's Epic Designs: Ekphrasis in the Aeneid* (New Haven: Yale University Press, 1998).

[72]Conte, *Rhetoric of Imitation*, 152

[73]*Ibid.,*154. Habinek, *The Politics of Latin Literature,* criticizes Conte's approach as an "essentially formalist and idealist approach to literature," because he does not attend "to the strategic positioning of the phrase or text" and lacks "a sociology rigorous enough to relate the ideology of the text to the material circumstances of ancient society," 9. While Conte does not attempt what Habinek proposes, his analysis nonetheless has sociological or historical implications.

[74]Conte, *Rhetoric,* 152, emphasis added.

[75]Adam Parry, "The Two Voices of Virgil's *Aeneid,*" *Arion* 2.4 (1963) 66–80; Otis, *A Study in Civilized Poetry*; Johnson, *Darkness Visible: A Study in Vergil's Aeneid* (Berkeley: University of California Press, 1976) 22, all herein; M. Owen Lee, *The Olive-Tree Bed and Other Quests* (Toronto, Canada: University of Toronto Press, 1997) 69; R. O. A. M. Lyne, *Further Voices in Vergil's Aeneid* (Oxford: Clarendon Press, 1987) 2; Conte, *Rhetoric,* 154.

[76]See Lanham, *Electronic Word,* 149: "That we can see one version of ourselves only while inhabiting the other violates deep-seated feelings about the wholeness of human vision." In *Motives of Eloquence: Literary Rhetoric in the Renaissance,* (New Haven, CT: Yale University Press, 1976), Lanham cites a series of "parallel dichotomies" that inform his interpretation of epic generally: narrative/speech; serious discourse/rhetorical; serious or purposive discourse/dramatic or playful. Epic is not immutable for Lanham; for him the works of both Vergil and Ovid qualify as epic within this map of dichotomies. He does, however, associate a certain type of epic with the serious, anti-rhetorical side of the equation of dichotomies, and I believe mistakenly, identifies the *Aeneid* with only one of the epic styles, the serious one. In fact, his description of the rhetorical nature of Ovid's epic could refer to Vergil's poem as well: "*The Metamorphoses* denies the possibility of any easy, fundamental legitimations, any one-time beginnings or endings. The violence of man's nature will not permit it. You cannot leave Dido behind. She will not oblige by sacrificing the private life, the life of the feelings, to the greater glory of Rome. She will curse, you, come after you," 63.

[77]The role of rhetoric in Vergil's works has received some but not extensive scholarly attention. Gilbert Highet, *The Speeches in Vergil's Aeneid* (Princeton, NJ: Princeton University Press, 1972), focuses, as the title indicates, specifically and narrowly on the speeches in the poem. Conte's *Rhetoric of Imitation* uses rhetoric in quite a broad sense. The study of rhetoric in Vergil that is closest to my use of the term here is that of Sarah Spence in *Rhetorics of Reason and Desire: Vergil, Augustine, and the Troubedours* (Ithaca, NY: Cornell University Press, 1988).

Highet's "Introduction" on ancient readings of the speeches in the *Aeneid* reminds us of the ancient importance of oratory, to the extent that writers after Quintilian "came to regard the *Aeneid* as a work of oratory and Vergil himself as an orator," 3. Highet eschews claims for an overarching role for rhetoric in the *Aeneid,* instead analyzing the speeches in the epic as examples of formal or informal oratory. Even in his concluding chapter, "Vergilius Orator an Poeta," his concern is more with Vergil's use of the "techniques and ideals of oratory," 278, than with a worldview that rhetoric represents. Highet notes that Vergil had rhetorical training, the standard education for the time, but that unlike Homeric heroes, "he has little praise for it," 282, and that like Plato he "distrusted oratory; although, like Aristotle, he accepted the fact that it is sometimes necessary, or at least useful," 283. Highet notes that "almost all [Vergil's] speakers distort the truth," 285. He concludes (289–90) as follows:

> Vergil, it seems, held that powerful oratory was incompatible with pure truth, and that every speaker presented his or her own case by misrepresenting the facts. He might have agreed with Plato that rhetoric was a part of flattery (*Gorg.* 463a6–466a6)…although he would certainly not have accepted the further Platonic deduction that high poetry also was no more than flattering rhetoric (*Gorg.* 502b1–d8). Truth, for Vergil as for Plato, resided in the other world, the world of immortal souls freed from the body and of immutable incorruptible ideals. Oratory, with all its energy and charm and suppleness, was part of this world, the world of disorder and conflict and pain, inhabited by false dreams.

One could think that Conte takes the opposite view of rhetoric in the *Aeneid.* The definition of rhetoric he uses is as broad as Highet's is focussed — "rhetoric [is] the ability to motivate the linguistic sign" (23), and Conte identifies poetic allusion itself as a rhetorical technique, 26, 39, 52ff. Segal's "Introduction" describes (11) Conte's understanding of rhetoric well:

> To Conte the poet's incorporation of the older work into a new creation by means of allusion has the status of a rhetorical figure and carries with it the knowledge of distorting, transforming, playing with the surface of the text. Instead of being a transparent vehicle to a signified, the text becomes a web of intermeshed overlays of meaning, a complex space where signifiers call not merely to signifieds but also to a series of other signifiers and other signifying systems.

On the other hand, Highet and Conte both refer to rhetoric as a realm of "falsity" (Conte 45, n. 13) or as "incompatible with pure truth (Highet 289). They would differ, however, in the value they place on the role of conflict and disorder and hence of rhetoric in Vergil's poetry.

Spence could seem to mediate Highet's and Conte's approaches. She names rhetoric as "a guide to culture," xiii, a role akin to that played by genre for Conte, and like Highet she is interested in the role of oratory in the *Aeneid* through the hero as orator: "Vergil offers us the Isocratean model for his hero Aeneas," xiii. Through the parallel she observes between Vergil and Isocrates, Spence says that Vergil "questions the priorities expressed in the humanist rhetorical tradition, such as the value of speaker over audience and reason over desire," xiv. Spence and Conte would agree that Vergil is questioning a value system.

Spence however distinguishes two rhetorical traditions, and that distinction clarifies the connections among these three scholars. One is Isocratean rhetoric, on which she says Aeneas is modeled and in which Aeneas is "the hero of a political epic," 6. Spence characterizes Vergil as "disgruntled" with this Isocratean (also Ciceronian) model in his hero Aeneas, and with this kind of rhetoric as a "process of ordering" and as a "rational process" that omits desire, 14. The other tradition, Spence says, is "organic, not intellectual" and "requires the audience to participate," 6. This second rhetorical tradition is close to the meaning of the term as Highet and Conte are using it, as well as Richard Lanham, but it is a value system that Lanham and Conte observe the Plato of the *Republic* to disapprove. Spence further identifies the rhetorical tradition of "eloquence devoid of reason" with Juno, 19.

Spence claims that Vergil is setting up the Isocratean Aeneas in order to attack the values of that system, 20, and that the "*Aeneid* as a whole can thus be seen as at least a partial attempt...[to rethink] the assumptions of the rhetorical tradition," 21. More specifically, in the Dido and Aeneas episode, Spence claims that Vergil is informing us that the pious necessity for Aeneas to leave Dido is itself a "lie," 36. In other words, the absolute system of truth is by definition untruthful, and by inference, the system of rhetorical lies may be more truthful. Spence also connects this supposedly negative role for rhetoric with the female element in the *Aeneid*, along with the role of pastoral, 43–5. The epic's conclusion with Turnus, the oppressed figure in the story, says Spence, "points forward to a new, non-Ciceronian, non-Roman system that emphasizes balance and mediation," 49.

From the perspectives of Conte's and Spence's arguments, Highet's claim seems only partially correct. What he names correctly as the attributes of a type of rhetoric but says that Vergil values negatively, Conte and Spence find to be valued positively in the *Aeneid*. It will be clear that I agree with the later writers. I am especially interested in the role of pastoral and rhetoric in these analyses, in their connection to Greek and Roman philosophical systems broadly, in the importance of rhetoric for Vergil's analysis, and in the importance of both rhetoric and Vergil for contemporary thinking on cultural issues.

[78]Conte describes how radical this shift was: "When Virgil thus remodels the field of signification of the epic norm, he disturbs its inflexible absoluteness and introduces relativity. This "dialectic of contamination" sets in at a moment when the text finds room for a point of view that shifts its axis from the center imposed by the dogmatism of the norm. In this way Virgil allows the potentialities of the epic code that had been denied expression to reemerge from the depths of History. These silent possibilities now claim the right to speak and unfold their own semantic perspectives within the text," 152.

[79]Michael Naas, *Turning: From Persuasion to Philosophy: A Reading of Homer's Iliad* (Atlantic Highlands, NJ: Humanities Press, 1995) 226–27. See also Lanham, *Motives of Eloquence*, 34–35: "The history of Western literature must be rewritten as precisely the symbiotic relationship

of the two theories of knowledge, theories of style, ways to construct reality—rewritten as the quarrel between the central self and the social self, between society as drama and society as highly serious, one-time sublimity. We must, that is, rehearse again the quarrel between philosophy and rhetoric." In addition, for Lanham, post-modernism has affinities with a rhetorical view of the world: "For rhetorical man, there is no such thing as an act, or a text, as it actually happened," 20. And for him this view is essentially anti-Platonic: "'Man is not double,' Plato insists in the *Republic*...(397E). My attempt to explain our continuing taste for formal rhetoric has led to the opposite conclusion....At least half the time his living is play, his motive dramatic and self-contrived, his self a role. It is to sustain this second man and second reality that rhetoric exists," 210.

[80]My work as a university administrator enters here. In an e-mail conversation between two faculty members at DePaul University regarding our process of academic program review, which I direct, the issue of educational research on student learning styles emerged regarding indicators of quality in curriculum, pedagogy, and advising. A professor of sociology and a professor of education, in two separate colleges of the university, exchanged views on the application of generalized, scientific research regarding learning styles in demographic groups (women and minorities) and the application of that research to individual programs and students. One of my colleagues summed up the problem as follows: "Theory does not tell us what to do, and practice does not tell us what is true," (Peter Pereira, Professor of Education, DePaul University, October 16, 1998). As a student of Vergil, I have hope that my university's administrative process of internal faculty review of academic quality will negotiate continually the dynamic exchange between theory and practice and thus partake of a Vergilian vision of "uncommitted," creative truth.

[81]Lord Dacre of Glanton posed the question of this volume in his 1990 presidential address to the Virgil Society, "Why Virgil": "So what is Virgil's secret power? The answer is, I suppose, that most indefinite an[d] elusive of qualities, pure poetry." *Proceedings of the Virgil Society* 20 (1991) 60–75, 65. Annabel Patterson (*John Milton* [London: Longman,1992]) begins her collection of essays on John Milton with a similar question, Why Milton?, but she poses it as an issue "[c]aught in the cross-fire between the market appeal of a 'great' author and the strictures of postmodernism against a 'humanist' or author-centered literary theory....," 1. To address the title's question we will have to navigate those different responses to it, responses that straddle a great divide in current thinking. O'Donnell ("Augustine Today," in *Avatars*) has made a compelling attempt at responding to this generic question: "I want to see more clearly what Augustine has become today, and then to think a bit about where he might be going. While the value of this exercise to Augustinian scholars is obvious, those few of us with those skills and interests must recognize that our (and his) value to the societies of today cannot be taken for granted and must not be assumed to be fixed, stable, and unchanging. Such value is relative, and depends on the recipient as well as the source," 124–25.

[82]O'Donnell, *Avatars*: "Western civilization...is not something to be cherished. Western civilization is us and making it, as well as remaking it, is our job. The thought that we come here in a generation surrounded by opportunities to botch the job might be frightening—or it might better be exhilarating," 91.

[83]See e.g. Garry Wills, "Whatever Happened to Politics? Washington Is Not Where It's At," *New York Times Magazine* (January 25, 1998) 26ff., on "[t]he absurdity of trying to separate our current politics from culture...," 54; and Frank Rich, "Monicagate Year Two," *New York Times* (December 16, 1998) A31, who sees the antagonists Kenneth Starr and Bill Clinton as "merely footnotes to the bitter culture war they've helped re-ignite," a culture war that began in the 1960s and the Vietnam era. As if to confirm Rich's observation, Rep. Tom DeLay said the following during the December 1998 impeachment proceedings in the U.S. House of Representatives, regarding the resignation of Speaker-designate Robert L. Livingston: "Because he understood what this debate was all about. It was about honor and decency and integrity and the truth; everything that we honor in this country. It was also a debate about relativism versus absolute truth," *New York Times*, Sunday, December 20, 1998, 28, in a sidebar headed "On the Floor of the House, Culture War Explodes."

That "war," however, deflects onto culture and especially education issues larger even than the American political scene in which they are being played. See Oakley, *Community of Learning*, "From time to time, one cannot help wondering if part at least of our current educational discontent does not stem from the displacement onto the academy of widespread anxieties and fears spawned by the historic changes sweeping across the world at large," 167. Steiner, *Scandal of Pleasure*, too says that "[e]ducation has been a convenient diversion from…political problems," citing statistics about the occurrence in newspaper coverage of the PC, "political correctness," controversy in relation to electoral politics: "101 PC entries in 1988, 306 in 1989, 638 in 1990, but 3,877 by November 15, 1991," the presidential election year, 139.

[84]Regarding the case for a stable cultural canon, Lanham, *Electronic Word*, discusses the "powerful constraint" of a canon, in that the "timeless perfection [it] represents condemns us to passivity," 38, also 50–51. Lanham identifies, correctly in my opinion, the fundamental error of the defenders of the canon as a fixed and pure tradition: "such teaching…radically disempowers humanistic study, fundamentally misapprehends its nonnegotiable core, cuts us off from the wisdom of Western literature we so vitally need," 190. The disempowerment of humanistic study and the cultural and civic passivity thereby engendered are dangerous to a democracy. Furthermore, arguments for a fixed canon also fudge a factor in the history of the humanities that is little discussed by humanists; again Lanham: "… no one has ever been able to prove that [Western humanism] does conduce to virtue more than to vice," 155. There, someone has said it; the emperor may have no clothes. Or perhaps we have long wrapped the Western humanistic tradition in the wrong clothes, or in clothes many people no longer want to wear. To redress centuries of political, economic, and social wrongs in which the cultural tradition was at least in part complicitous, we must return to the most fundamental questions of that tradition. The power of the tradition remains its ability for even that radical a rethinking of itself. Extending access to that power is, in my view, the role of the liberal arts and the humanities in a democracy.

[85]See for one example, Thomas Bender, *Intellect and Public Life: Essays on the Social History of Academic Intellectuals in the United States* (Baltimore, MD: Johns Hopkins University Press, 1993) ix–xvii. See also Bender and Schorske, *American Academic Culture*, esp. Bender's "Politics, Intellect, and the American University," 17–54.

[86]Charles Segal, "Presidential Address," 4–5.

[87]For example, Ernest Boyer, late president of the Carnegie Foundation for the Advancement of Teaching, "Creating the New American College," *Chronicle of Higher Education* (March 9, 1994) A48, and Derek Bok, former president of Harvard University, "Reclaiming the Public Trust," *Change* (July/August 1992) 13–19. Note the titles of several recent annual meetings of two national higher education organizations: Association of American College and Universities (AAC&U) — Higher Education and American Creativity (1994); Baccalaureate Learning and the Public Interest (1995); Work and Learning: Creating New Connections (1996); The Academy in Transition: Values, Choices and Strategies (1998); American Association for Higher Education (AAHE) — The 21st Century Workplace (1994); The Engaged Campus: Organizing to Serve Society's Needs (1995); Crossing Boundaries: Pathways to Productive Learning and Community Renewal (1996); Taking Learning Seriously (1998). Richard J. Meister's article ("Engagement with Society at DePaul University, *Liberal Education*, [Fall 1998] 56–61) strikes the same note. See also Lanham, *Electronic Word*, regarding the creation of an undergraduate curriculum that realizes the rhetorical implications of technology: "Such an endeavor contravenes what many feel to be the true center of the liberal arts — their 'purity,' their distance in time and place from the ordinary world of human work and pleasure. But the 'humanities crisis' that has been our routine cry for a century and more is one we have manufactured ourselves by distancing ourselves from the world. Claim to be above the struggle, specialize in 'values' that others have to embody, and then wonder why the world sets you aside. Implicit in the revolution in the liberal arts I have tried to describe is a return to a systemic and systematic involvement in the social purposes of our time," 117.

[88]When I visit bookstores, I see considerable evidence of the fact that publishers and classicists are responding to the need for accessible works on ancient and modern authors, for a general public of students and interested readers. Consider e.g., the *Hermes Books*, John Herington general editor, Yale University Press, dedicated to Greek and Roman texts, in which "Virgil" is by David R. Slavitt (New Haven, CT: Yale University Press, 1991); the *Landmarks in World Literature* series, a Cambridge University Press publication, in which the volume on Vergil is by K. W. Gransden: *Virgil: The Aeneid* (Cambridge: Cambridge University Press, 1990). The Oxford series, *Past Masters*, includes Jasper Griffin's *Virgil* (Oxford: Oxford University

Press, 1986). This book itself, *Why Vergil?*, is part of an intended series of *Why [Author]?* volumes (see William S. Anderson, ed., *Why Horace? A Collection of Interpretations* [Wauconda, IL: Bolchazy-Carducci, Publishers, Inc., 1999]). In addition, Harvard University Press apparently has decided to re-issue the famous series of editions of Greek and Latin texts with the original language and a serviceable English translation on facing pages, the Loeb series of the familiar green and red covers, since "sales are running along," *Chronicle of Higher Education*, March 30, 1998, XLIV, no. 28, A21.

There may be some dissonance at the moment between the increasing public interest in the ancient world and the readiness of the classics profession, as an institution within universities, to respond (see Victor David Hanson and John Heath, *Who Killed Homer? The Demise of Classical Education and the Recovery of Greek Wisdom* (New York: Free Press, 1998). Although stressful for those within the profession, the new needs are a good development. That, along with the quantity of excellent, interesting, and important scholarship in classical studies and the willingness to confront new questions (a willingness not universal, but it does not need to be), encourage me greatly about the study of the ancient Greek, Roman, and Mediterranean worlds. Patience and persistence are key, virtues that surely students of the long-ago past know how to exercise.

[89] Knox, "On Two Fronts," 315. See also Josiah Ober, "Responsible Popularization: An Introduction," *CB* 72.2 (1996) 85–91.

[90] An example of a potentially positive change in this direction is the establishment by the American Philological Association of a Division of Outreach, *Newsletter*, December 1998.

[91] Bender, "Locality," 8. See also Steiner, *Scandal of Pleasure*: "For a culture in which professionals feel no responsibility to the public and the public disdains expert opinion is a culture inhospitable not only to art, but to democratic debate, and ultimately to freedom," 8.

[92] Roger A. Hornsby, "The Refracted Past," *Vergilius* 33 (1987) 6–13: "Not one of the enemies of Aeneas perceives that change is inevitable in human existence," 12.

[93] William W. Batstone, "On the Surface of the *Georgics*," *Arethusa* 21 (1988) 227–45: the *Georgics* "make their reader *participate in an experience* of mutability of shifting perspectives," 242 (emphasis added). Lanham, *Motives*, 19: "If we posit a serious reality as referential, then literature is clearly autonomous….But if reality is rhetorical? Is not literature here truly isomorphic, real in exactly the same way as life? Same self and same society? Not mimesis but *enactment*?" 19 (emphasis added).

[94] See Segal, "Art and the Hero," on "the poet's understanding of the tragic dimension of his own art," 82. In general see Philip Hardie, "Virgil and Tragedy," *The Cambridge Companion to Virgil*, 312–326; Lily Panoussi, "Epic Transfigured: Tragic Allusiveness in Vergil's *Aeneid*" (Ph.D. diss., Brown University, 1998).

[95] Arthur M. Schlesinger, Jr., *Robert Kennedy and His Times* (New York: Ballantine Books, 1978) 940. The quotation is from Aeschylus' *Agamemnon*, 176–183, beautifully albeit loosely translated. An affinity may exist between Aeschylus and Vergil; see Philip Hardie, "The *Aeneid* and the *Oresteia*," *PVS* 20 (1991) 29–45, and also Helen H. Bacon, "The *Aeneid* as a Drama of Election," *TAPA* 116 (1986) 305–34, 314–15 and herein. Aeschylus and Vergil may in turn share a connection to our time. See L. A. MacKay, "Hero and Theme in the *Aeneid*," *TAPA* 94 (1963) 157–66: "Vergil is closer to Tolstoy than to Homer, to Thackeray than to Ennius. One is tempted to go even further. To call the Aeneid the Epic of the Absurd would be an exaggeration, but it would be an exaggeration in the right direction….It depicts the triumph of the depersonalized will, the establishment and maintenance of human values by inhuman means….Aeneas is creating the world by which he is to be judged, in a universe at times favorable, at times unfavorable, at times indifferent, and there is no sure way that he can calculate which response to expect. He belongs to the world of Sartre and Camus, more than to the world of Demodocus and Phemius," 163–4. See similarly John Herington, *Aeschylus* (New Haven, CT: Yale University Press, Hermes Books,1986): "Yet the most spectacular recurrence of all [of an Aeschylean worldview] seems to be discernible in our own century. The Theater of the Absurd, for instance, has somewhat similarly opened up the focus of drama to scan not merely the human individual but also the complex of mysterious phenomena that surround and interact with him," 13.

[96] See Mary Catherine Bateson, *Composing a Life* (New York: Penguin U.S.A, Plume, 1990).

[97] Paraphrasing Frost, "Two Tramps in Mud Time," *The Road Not Taken: An Introduction to Robert Frost*, Louis Untermeyer, ed. (New York: Holt, Rinehart and Winston, 1975), 130–32.

[98]Segal, "Presidential Address": "With the gradual disintegration of the hope for a unified European culture, an ever increasing global consciousness, and undiminishing evidence of the human capacity for brutality, cruelty, and destructiveness, we cannot easily return to Eliot's optimistic notion of 'the Classics' as the basis of a Europe defined by civility of manners and maturity of expression. We are increasingly unsure if European civilization has a center, and at the same time our notions of civilization are becoming less narrowly European," 9.

[99]Rosanna Warren, "Turnus (*Aeneid* XII)," *Arion*, 3rd ser., 3.2, 3 (Fall 1995/Winter 1996) 3: "…Here's where you tear a hole in the poem, / a hole in the mind…," 3; herein.

[100]Robert Bellah, *et al.*, *The Good Society*, quoted on the back cover of *Democracy is a Discussion. Civic Engagement in Old and New Democracies: The Handbook*, Sondra Myers, ed. (New London, CT: Connecticut College, 1996).

[101]Joseph Brodsky, "Virgil: Older than Christianity, a Poet for the New Age," *Vogue*, October 1981, 178–180, 180: "Like every human being, a poet has to deal with the questions: how, what for, and in the name of what to live. The *Bucolics*, the *Georgics* and the *Aeneid* answer all three, and these answers apply equally to the Emperor and to his subjects, to antiquity as well as to our times. The modern reader may use Virgil in the same way that Dante used him in his passage through Hell and Purgatory: as a guide."

[102]"The second part of the first century B.C., when Virgil was writing, was a time of terrific civil strife in Rome, accompanied by the ravages of several wars, purges and land confiscations. An individual's existence was, proportionally speaking, endangered about as much as it was in the 'thirties and 'forties of this century," *ibid*, 178.

[103]Parry, "Two Voices," 69 and herein.

[104]W. H. Auden, from "The Shield of Achilles," in *Collected Poems*, ed. Edward Mendelson (New York: Random House, Vintage International, 991) 596–98, 598, herein.

[105]See Jenkyns, "Pathos, Tragedy and Hope": "The *Iliad* ends with ritual and feasting; but deep down nothing has changed. The *Aeneid* ends with an act of violence; but deep down everything has changed. Which of the two endings is, in the larger view, the more hopeful? Which has the more tragic vision of life?…The contrast with the stark tragedy of the *Iliad* combined with the dramatic harshness of the final lines enables [Vergil] to blend ferocity and hope, and through that blend to present a view of life which, whether or not we accept it ourselves, we should recognize as deeply serious and deeply realist, neither complacent nor glibly pessimistic."

[106]On sentimentality, see Wendell Clausen, "An Interpretation of the *Aeneid*," in *Virgil: A Collection of Critical Essays*, ed. Steele Commager (Englewood Cliffs, NJ: Prentice-Hall, 1966): "Virgil's vision of Roman history is not propaganda—though some critics have thought it was; for he does not simply proclaim what Rome achieved; nor is it sentimental: for he does not simply dwell on what the achievement cost.…It is a measure of Virgil's greatness that he withstood the temptation to sentimentality.…at the end of the *Aeneid* there is no clasping of hands, no walking together towards the shining future. The light is hard and clear: Aeneas has killed Turnus, and on Turnus's shoulder gleams the sword-belt of Pallas," 75–88, 86–87 (quote slightly modified from its original appearance [*HSCP* 68 (1964) 139–47]. Regarding sentimentality, see John Frederick Nims, "Sense and Sentimentality," in *Western Wind: An Introduction to Poetry* (New York: Random House, 1983) 103–118: "Sentimentality is the disease to which sentiment is subject," 104; and Gould, *Ancient Quarrel*: "Hard truthfulness, as Aeschylus saw, is one of the requirements for true tragedy. That will save us from sentimentality. Compassion is the other requirement, as Virgil and Yeats and many others saw. That will save us from melodrama. Perhaps the two achievements are linked: a special effort to face those elements in life that must someday defeat us all is rewarded by a new ability to forgive both others and ourselves. This is what some of the very best art can do for us," 296.

[107]W. R. Johnson, *Darkness Visible*, 15; see also Dana L. Burgess, "Vergilian Modes in Spike Lee's *Do the Right Thing*," *CML* 11.4 (Summer 1991) 313–16; "…for the Vergilian mode is terrifying in literature or in film," 316 and herein.

[108]Conte, *Rhetoric of Imitation*: "If a truly dramatic form indeed unfolds along the axis of an 'active' dialectic, and if the epic can be defined by contrast as an absence of dialectic, the deep structure of the *Aeneid* lies somewhere between the two," 163. See also Segal, "Art and the Hero" and herein: Aeneas' final act "crystalizes into action the stylistic tension between the transcendent and the immanentist vision of events," and "Like the reader or listener, [Aeneas]

stands between sympathetic identification and intellectual recognition....," 69, 81. A few years ago, I suggested at a meeting of DePaul's Classical and Medieval Colloquium that the arcadia of Vergil's *Eclogues* seems to have something in common with Plato's idea of *chóra* as used in the *Timaeus*. In reading a draft of this Conclusion, my colleague Susanna Pagliaro, a Ph.D. candidate in DePaul's Philosophy Department, made that suggestion again, in relation to this aesthetic moment or mental space I am describing at the end of the *Aeneid*. Although I would like to develop this issue further, for now, consider the following: "Timaeus is careful to speak of the Receiver as having no character of its own and being, as it were, completely plastic. A little into the exposition Timaeus uses the term *chora* (χώρα) for the Receiver, and it is common to translate it as 'place.' This has, of course, given impetus to treating the Receiver as a receptable. But the term *chora* is associated with a verb that has the sense of 'making room for,' and I think this is the proper clue for Timaeus' use of it," Robert G. Turnbull, *The Parmenides and Plato's Late Philosophy* (Toronto: University of Toronto Press, 1998) 149; and also Anne Freire Ashbaugh, *Plato's Theory of Explanation: A Study of the Cosmological Account in the Timaeus* (Albany, NY: State University of New York Press, 1988): "The cosmologist...wishes to understand phenomena, the possibility of seeing the ideas."

"Images must come to be in a stable medium. Being a good geometer, Timaeus posits space, *chora* as medium. Space becomes the gathering concept, the strange element within being that compels the soul to *unify in thought the two objects it experiences as irremediably separate*," 10–11, emphasis added. The unification of objects, or feelings or thoughts, experienced as irremediably separate, is I believe the core of Vergil's style and meaning. That phenomenon has affinities as well with pastoral of course. I believe Vergil perfected the technique in the *Eclogues*, practiced it in the *Georgics*, and then in the *Aeneid* used it to create a moral and aesthetic experience, or space, culminating in our occupation of something like *chóra* in the last lines of the epic. The connection between Vergilian pastoral and Plato's *chóra* would be an interesting study.

[109]Richard F. Thomas ("Ideology, Influence and Future Studies in the *Georgics*," *Vergilius* 36 [1990] 64–70) suggests that Vergil is at least as American as European: "...I think it is worth pointing out that contemporary America, in its more immediate agricultural roots, in the cultural and racial diversity evident in its foundation and growth (Virgil himself, let us not forget, was an 'immigrant' of sorts [from northern Italy]), in the tensions of how it should deal with the realities of being a world power, and particularly in its struggling to respond to the great cultural burden which is its legacy, would be much more comparable with the Rome of Virgil than is any contemporary European country," 66, n. 4.

[110]Charles T. Plock, C. M., "Community Organizers: Vincent de Paul and Saul Alinsky," St. Vincent de Paul Lecture, April 15, 1997: "The world as it is is a world where the solution of one problem inevitably creates a new problem; a world where there are no permanent happy or sad endings; a world where life is a battle and this planet earth the battlefield; a world where everything is interrelated and interdependent; where for every positive there is a negative; a world where there are no permanent allies and no permanent enemies." Plock is a community organizer.

[111]Lukacs, *End of the Twentieth Century*, 281–82.

[112]Paraphrased from C. Day Lewis, "Dedicatory Stanzas. To Stephen Spender," in *The Georgics of Virgil* (New York: Oxford University Press, 1947) xv–xvii, and herein.

[113] From Robert Frost, "Two Tramps in Mud Time," *The Road Not Taken*, 130–32.

Bibliography

BIBLIOGRAPHY

Bibliographical Resources

Vergilius, the Journal of the Vergilian Society of America, Inc., publishes an annual bibliography edited by Alexander G. McKay, which is without doubt the starting place for further reading. It is carefully organized and partially annotated. Most university libraries will have the journal.

L'Année Philologique, Juliette Ernst, Viktor Poeschl, William C. West (eds.) (Paris) is the international bibliography and essential tool for classical studies. It it published annually, and most university library reference sections will have it.

Cleary, Vincent J., "*Aeneidea*: Important Work on the *Aeneid* (1976–84) for Secondary School Teachers," *CJ* 80 (1985) 3351–56.

———— "*Aeneidea*: Important Work on the *Aeneid* (1984–87) for Secondary School Teachers," Vergilius 33 (1987) 101–110. These lists are especially useful for teachers of beginning Latin and Latin literature.

Hornsby, Roger A. and McKay, Alexander G., *Texts, Commentary & Critical Bibliography for the new Additions to The Advanced Placement Examinations: Vergil*," (Oxford, Ohio: The Campanian Society, Inc., 1998) will be especially useful for secondary school teachers.

Martindale, Charles, ed., *Cambridge Companion to Virgil*, (Cambridge: Cambridge University Press, 1997) contains a nineteen-page "list of works cited," as well as notes for further reading after each of its twenty-one chapters.

Pharr, Clyde, ed., *Vergil's Aeneid: Books I–VI* (Wauconda, IL: Bolchazy-Carducci Publishers, Inc., 1998), includes "A Selective Bibliography" assembled by Alexander G. McKay, 115–150. That bibliography contains current, annotated information on texts, translations, general studies on Vergil and his time, many special topics, and studies organized by each of Vergil's works, including for the *Aeneid* secondary works organized by book of the epic.

Putnam, Michael C. J., *Virgil's Aeneid: Interpretation and Influence* (Chapel Hill, NC: University of North Carolina, 1995) contains a selective eight-page list of works that would be a good starting place for scholarly reading.

Sienkewicz, Thomas J. *The Classical Epic: An Annotated Bibliography* (Pasadena, CA; Englewood Cliffs, NJ: Salem Press, 1991), Vergil, 178–257, contains extensive information, organized by topic, with useful annotations.

Selected List of Individual Books

Anderson, William S., *The Art of the "Aeneid"* (Englewood Cliffs, NJ: Prentice Hall, 1969).

Bernard, John D., ed., *Vergil at 2000: Commemorative Essays on the Poet and His Influence* (New York: AMS Press, 1986).

Bishop, John Huntley, *The Cost of Power: Studies in the Aeneid of Virgil* (Armidale, Australia: University of New England, 1988).

Bloom, Harold, ed., *Virgil* (New York: Chelsea House Publishers, 1986).

———— *Virgil's Aeneid* (New York: Chelsea House Publishers,1987).

Cairns, Francis, *Virgil's Augustan Epic* (Cambridge: Cambridge University Press, 1989).

Camps, William, *An Introduction to Virgil's Aeneid* (London: Oxford University Press, 1969).

Clausen, Wendell, *Virgil's Aeneid and the Tradition of Hellenistic Poetry* (Berkeley, CA: University of California Press, 1987).

Commager, Steele, ed., *Virgil: A Collection of Critical Essays* (Englewood Cliffs, NJ: Prentice Hall, Inc., 1966)

Daitz, Stephen G., *The Pronunciation and Reading of Classical Literature: A Practical Guide* (Guilford, CT: Jeffrey Norton Publishers, Inc., 1984).

Distler, Paul F., *Vergil and Vergiliana* (Chicago, IL: Loyola University Press, 1966).

Dudley, D. R., ed., *Vergil* (London: Routledge Kegan Paul, 1969).

Farron, Steven, *Vergil's Aeneid; A Poem of Grief and Love* (Leiden: E. J. Brill, 1993).

Galinsky, G. K., *Aeneas, Sicily, and Rome* (Princeton, NJ: Princeton University Press, 1969).

———— *Augustan Culture: An Interpretive Essay* (Princeton, NJ: Princeton University Press, 1996).

Gransden, K. W., *Virgil's Iliad: An Essay on Epic Narrative* (Cambridge: Cambridge University Press, 1984).

——— *Virgil: The Aeneid* (Cambridge: Cambridge University Press, 1990).

Griffin, Jasper, *Virgil* (Oxford: Oxford University Press, 1986).

Gurval, R. A., *Actium and Augustus: The Politics and Emotions of Civil War* (Ann Arbor, MI: University of Michigan Press, 1995).

Hardie, Philip R., *Virgil's Aeneid: Cosmos and Imperium* (Oxford: Clarendon Press, 1986).

——— *Virgil* (Oxford: Oxford University Press, 1998).

Harrison, S. J., ed., *Oxford Readings in Vergil's Aeneid* (Oxford: Oxford University Press, 1990).

Heinze, Richard, *Virgil's Epic Technique*, Hazel and David Harvey and Fred Robertson, trans. (Berkeley, CA: University of California Press, 1993).

Hornsby, Roger, *Patterns of Action in the Aeneid: An Interpretation of Vergil's Epic Similes* (Iowa City, IA: University of Iowa Press, 1970).

Horsfall, Nicholas M., ed., *A Companion to the Study of Virgil* (Leiden: E. J. Brill, 1995; *Mnemosyne* Suppl. 151).

Hunt, J. W., *Forms of Glory: Structure and Sense in Virgil's Aeneid* (Carbondale, IL: Southern Illinois University Press, 1973).

Knight, W. F. Jackson, *Roman Vergil* (London: Penguin, 1944; 3rd ed., 1996).

Johnson, W. R., *Darkness Visible: A Study of Vergil's Aeneid* (Berkeley, CA: University of California Press, 1976).

Lee, M. Owen, *Fathers and Sons in. Virgil's Aeneid: Tum Genitor Natum* (Albany, NY: State University of New York Press, 1979).

Lyne, R. O. A. M., *Further Voices in Vergil's Aeneid* (Oxford: Clarendon Press, 1987).

——— *Words and the Poet: Characteristic Techniques of Style in Vergil's Aeneid* (Oxford: Clarendon Press, 1989).

Mack, Sara, *Patterns of Time in Vergil* (Hamden, CT: Archon Books, 1978) .

Martindale, C. A., ed., *Virgil and his Influence* (Bristol: Brostol Classical Bress, 1984)

——— *The Cambridge Companion to Virgil* (Cambridge: Cambridge University Press, 1997).

Moskalew, W alter, *Formular Language and Poetic Design in the Aeneid*, (Leiden: E. J. Brill, 1982; *Mnemosyne* Suppl. 73).

O'Hara, J. J., *Death and the Optimistic Prophecy in Vergil's Aeneid*. (Princeton, NJ: Princeton University Press, 1990).

Otis, B., *Virgil: A Study in Civilized Poetry* (Oxford: Clarendon Press, 1964; rpt. Norman, OK: University of Oklahoma Press, 1995).

Perkell, Christine, ed., *Reading Vergil's Aeneid: An Interpretive Guide* (Norman, OK: University of Oklahoma, 1999).

Pöschl, V., *Virgil's Poetic Art*, trans. M. Seligson (Ann Arbor, MI: University of Michigan Press, 1962).

Putnam, M. C. J., *The Poetry of the Aeneid: Four Studies in Imaginative Unity and Design* (Cambridge, MA: Harvard University Press, 1965; rpt. Ithaca, NY: Cornell University Press, 1988).

———— *Virgil's Aeneid: Interpretation and Influence* (Chapel Hill, NC: University of North Carolina Press, 1995).

———— *Virgil's Epic Designs: Ekphrasis in the Aeneid* (New Haven, CT: Yale University Press, 1998).

Quinn, Kenneth, *Virgil's Aeneid: A Critical Description* (Ann Arbor, MI: University of Michigan Press, 1968).

Quint, D., *Epic and Empire: Politics and Generic Form from Virgil to Milton* (Princeton, NJ: Princeton University Press, 1993).

Slavitt, David R., *Virgil* (New Haven, CT: Yale University Press, 1991).

Warwick, H. H., *A Vergil Concordance* (Minneapolis, MN: University of Minnesota Press, 1975).

Wilhelm, R. M. and Howard Jones, eds., *The Two Worlds of the Poet: New Perspectives on Vergil: Festschrift for Alexander G. McKay.* (Detroit, MI: Wayne State University Press, 1992).

Williams, G., *Technique and Ideas in the Aeneid* (New Haven, CT: Yale University Press, 1983).

Wiltshire, Susan Ford, *Public and Private in Vergil's Aeneid* (Amherst, MA: University of Massachusetts Press, 1989).

Electronic Resources

The web sites listed here, along with the Packard Humanities Institute CD-ROM of Latin Literature, are starting places for electronic searches related to Vergil's works. In addition to this general list, searchers may want to investigate the classics department web sites of colleges and universities, as well as museum web sites. The APA site below has good links to departments; for example, the Rutgers University classics site has good bibliographical aids.

http://classics.rutgers.edu/vergil.html

American Classical League (ACL)
http://www.aclclassics.org

American Philological Association (APA)
http://www.apaclassics.org

Classical Association of the Mid-West and South (CAMWS)
Http://www.rmc.edu/~gdaugher/inter.html

Scholars Press
http://scholar.cc.emory.edu

The Vergil Project
http://vergil.classics.upenn.edu

The Vergilian Society
http://www.vergil.clarku.edu

VROMA
http://vroma.rhodes.edu